Persc

AUSTRALIA
Lawbook Co.
Sydney

CANADA AND USA
Carswell
Toronto

HONG KONG
Sweet & Maxwell Asia

NEW ZEALAND
Brookers
Wellington

SINGAPORE AND MALAYSIA
Sweet & Maxwell Asia
Singapore and Kuala Lumpur

Personal Injury Litigation

Tenth Edition

Nicola Solomon

Solicitor and Deputy District Judge

and

Simon Middleton

Solicitor

and

John Pritchard

Solicitor

Ninth Edition published by FT Law & Tax in 1997.

Tenth Edition
Published in 2002 by
Sweet & Maxwell Limited of
100 Avenue Road, Swiss Cottage, London NW3 3PF
(http://www.sweetandmaxwell.co.uk)
Typeset by Wyvern 21 Ltd.
Printed and bound in Great Britain by MPG Books Ltd, Bodmin, Cornwall

No natural forests were destroyed to make this product;
only farmed timber was used and replanted.

A C.I.P. catalogue record for this book
is available from the British Library

ISBN 0 752 00441 7

Contents

Preface

It has been a busy time for personal injury practitioners. As if the introduction and bedding down of the Civil Procedure Rules was not enough the Motor Insurers' Bureau (Compensation of Victims of Uninsured Drivers) scheme was substantially altered without prior consultation and came into force six weeks later and just when the authors breathed a sigh of relief having completed the manuscript update the Lord Chancellor laid a regulation before Parliament reducing the discount rate to 2.5 per cent. Suffice it to say that there has been a lot to alter and update in this edition.

Despite the changes, we have tried to keep the structure of the 10th edition of the book the same as in previous editions; working from the start of a claim until trial in chronological sequence and then dealing with particular problem areas and compensation schemes not within the usual court claim format. The aim was to produce an accessible text which will provide assistance at all stages of an injury claim.

We felt that there was a danger of updating the text to include the Civil Procedure Rules too early. The limited response by solicitors to the various reports of the inquiry team led by Lord Woolf and subsequent papers from the Lord Chancellor's Department suggested that there would need to be a period of familiarisation with the rules. In addition, we wished to see how the court applied the rules. It is now over two years since the introduction of the rules and practitioners and the court are still on a rapid learning curve. Updates to the rules arrive regularly and authorities filter through. However, that period has enabled us to piece together the practical progress of an injury claim within the new regime of protocol management prior to the issue of proceedings and Civil Procedure Rules governance after the issue of proceedings.

As most of the practical daily management of cases and application of the rules is undertaken by lower courts this edition makes far greater reference to the decisions of those courts. So far, there has been little higher court intervention in the exercise of these broad case management functions.

What is certain is that more change is around the corner. Arguments on conditional fees have some way to run; fixed fees in fast track claims is always on the defendant market agenda; both Motor Insurers' Bureau agreements are under fire; and more revisions of the Civil Procedure Rules are always awaited.

As a result of the changes the tactical hints in this edition are those of the authors. Further court intervention will no doubt show whether the suggestions are as cunning as we would wish. However, they are merely practical suggestions based on the common sense that is the bedrock of the Civil Procedure Rules.

We have done our best to state the law and the relevant procedure as at July 1, 2001.

NS and SM
July 2001

Abbreviations

In addition to the conventional abbreviations, the following are used in this book:

CCR	County Court Rules
CICA	Criminal Injuries Compensation Authority
CPR	Civil Procedure Rules
CRU	Compensation Recovery Unit
DSS	Department of Social Security
DR	District Registry
MIB	Motor Insurers' Bureau
NI	National Insurance
QBD	Queen's Bench Division
RCJ	Royal Courts of Justice
RSC	Rules of the Supreme Court

Table of Cases

Table of Statutes

Table of Statutory Instruments

Civil Procedure Rules

Part I

A SYSTEM OF WORKING

1. Introduction

1.1. General

This is a guide to personal injury procedure and practice.

The guide is in four Parts.

Part I Introduction: This first introductory Part (Chapters 1–3) describes what is involved in the handling of a personal injury claim and emphasises the need for an efficient system of working and client care.

Part II Procedure: This follows the course of a typical personal injury claim (whether in the High Court or county court). Chapters 4–8 deal with investigating the claim and Chapters 9–20 follow the progress of a case once proceedings have been issued. The various procedural points that arise in practice are dealt with in the order in which they usually occur. Each section has a final chapter on settlement.

Part III Special matters: Chapters 21–30 deal with more complicated matters. There is a chapter dealing with limitation periods and other chapters deal with funding, legal aid and conditional fees. There are chapters on fatal cases, claimants under a disability, medical negligence claims, small claims, Criminal Injuries Compensation and Motor Insurers' Bureau claims. Finally there is a chapter on the Personal Injury Panel and Accident Line Scheme.

Part IV Appendices: These comprise the materials that enable the information in Parts II and III to be put to use. Although the procedural steps and devices are discussed in Parts II and III, the detailed procedural rules, precedents, drafts and stock letters are gathered together in the Appendices. By following this format, it is hoped that the main body of the text has remained easily understandable.

The Appendices are set out below.

A Accident questionnaires for completion by the client.
B Stock letters.
C Precedents.
D Procedural tables.
E Specimen pleadings.
F Actuarial tables.
G The MIB agreements.
H Diagrams of bones and muscles in the human body.

I Pre-action protocols for personal injury claims and resolution of clinical disputes.

1.2. Emphasis

Parties

Throughout the text, the emphasis is on the claimant's case, rather than that of the defendant. This is because it is the claimant who takes the initiative at most stages of the action, and who is responsible for ensuring that it is prosecuted without undue delay. However, the defendant's steps in the action will largely be in response to those taken by the claimant and we hope that the book will be as useful to defendants' solicitors as to the claimants.

For simplicity the words 'claimant' and 'defendant' have been used throughout the text to refer also respectively to the claimant's solicitor and the defendant's solicitor, and the terms are only to be taken as referring to the clients, rather than to their solicitors, when the text makes it clear that this is intended.

Courts

As the county court jurisdiction in personal injury cases is unlimited the majority of cases are brought in the county court. Therefore this book concentrates on the county court practice although the High Court will be noted if there are differences. Of course, the Civil Procedure Rules apply to both as the principles involved in the two courts do not differ so the claimant's tactics in the High Court will be the same as those in the county court.

Type of action

No great distinction is made in this book between different types of claim, be they road accident, workplace accident or other claims since the principles applied are usually identical. Where there are differences, these are referred to in the text. Generally, one can say that road accident claims ('runners') tend to be more straightforward than other claims. This is because in road accident claims causation is usually undisputed and liability will often be decided on the basis of applying a common law principle to an agreed police report and plan, whereas other cases are likely to have complex causation, more documents and require the consideration of expert evidence as applied to statutory duties of care. Clinical negligence and group action pose additional problems. An introduction on how to run more complex claims is given in Part III. Although the examples given in the text are usually based on road accident claims, they are just as applicable to other cases unless the contrary is stated.

Further reading

A book of this size cannot attempt to cover all the problems that could possibly arise in a personal injuries claim. The aim has been to provide a guide and summary containing the materials frequently used in personal injuries practice, but without quoting in-depth case references and authorities which can be found in more detailed publications.

Procedure

The Civil Procedure Rules in any volume containing commentary, including the Green Book and White Book, will provide a full guide for the practitioner who requires further advice and authority; and although the Green Book and White Book are formidable publications that the inexperienced litigator may find difficult to follow, they do provide the detailed authority that will be needed from time-to-time.

Relevant law

The practitioner should also be equipped with detailed guides to the law of negligence and to the various statutory duties relating to accident claims, since this book assumes a knowledge of the relevant law.

The traditionally recommended books for personal injury practitioners are: Redgrave's, Fife and Machin's *Health and Safety;* Kemp and Kemp, *The Quantum of Damages* and Bingham's *Motor Claims Cases.* As regards liability, many practitioners will prefer to have less detailed volumes available for easy access. Highly recommended is Tolley's *Health and Safety at Work Handbook.* This provides all the authority that most solicitors are likely to need.

Quantum

'Quantum', the Kemp and Kemp magazine, is very helpful. The Judicial Studies Board's *Guidelines for the Assessment of General Damages in Personal Injury Cases* has quickly become a standard reference work although it contains no authority for the figures quoted which are often on the low side. It is also useful to look at the monthly supplements to *Halsbury's Laws* for up-to-date figures.

Journals

The frequent changes in personal injury law make it essential to keep up to date. While the general practitioner may not need to subscribe to a specialist journal developments should be noted as they are reported in *The Law Society Gazette*, *The Times*, *Solicitors' Journal* or other such publications.

System of working

The solicitor's aim must be efficient litigation, for not only will this be beneficial to the client in ensuring that the case is carefully prepared and progressed quickly; it will also help the practitioner by ensuring that the case is less time consuming than it might otherwise have been. The system of working described in Chapter 3 is neither unique nor original. However, by combining the use of such a system with the drafts and precedents printed in the Appendices, it will be possible to minimise the time spent on drafting, dictation and typing, even if your firm already has a personal injury case management system.

2. A Simple Accident Claim

2.1. Introduction

In this chapter we set out the sequence of a simple personal injuries action so that the details in Parts II and III can be fitted into the overall framework of the action.

2.2. Investigation

The solicitor must investigate the circumstances of the accident to form an initial opinion of the prospects of the defendant being liable to the claimant. If the matter is to proceed, further detailed investigations will start and correspondence will ensue with, in all probability, the defendant's insurers. If no negotiated settlement is achieved quickly it will be necessary to commence proceedings.

2.3. Steps in proceedings

A simple diagram of the steps in a personal injury action is shown overleaf. Note that few personal attendances at court are required (these are shown in circles on the diagram), since most steps take place through the post (in rectangular boxes on the diagram). It can also be seen that the action develops by a series of specified steps being taken within specified time periods.

Pleadings

The first step will be to issue the Claim Form together with the Statement of Case, which is the formal pleading setting out the claimant's version of what happened, why the defendant is liable, and the extent of the claim. This will be accompanied by a medical report and statement of special damage. The solicitor or court then sends these documents to the defendant's solicitor. The defendant should then serve a Defence within 14 days (or 28 days after acknowledgement of service). Each side will then have an outline of the other's case. If the Defence attacks the claimant's case by making allegations of, for instance, contributory negligence, or counterclaiming for damages, it may be necessary for the claimant to serve a Reply and/or Defence to Counterclaim within 14 days of the service of the Defence.

Allocation questionnaires and case management

A major change in the CPR was that automatic directions and timetables were abolished. Now each case is actively managed by the court. After parties have filed their respective Statements of Case, the court will send out allocation questionnaires. On their return, and on the basis of the information contained in them, it will allocate the case to a track and either issue directions and a timetable for the progress of the case or fix a case management conference to consider directions.

Directions will include the following.

Disclosure

The issues in dispute will now be apparent, but neither side will know how the other party intends to prove the case except in respect of the claimant's medical evidence. One of the case management directions that the District Judge will undoubtedly make will concern disclosure of documents. Not all documents have to be disclosed, just those that are relevant to the accident but which were not prepared as a result of the action (for example, the statement made by a witness which is included in the police report is disclosable, but a statement made by the same witness to the defendant's insurers would not be disclosable since it was made for the purposes of litigation).

Exchange of expert evidence

If medical or other expert witnesses are to be called at the trial, then either a joint expert will have to be agreed and instructed or separate experts instructed and their reports disclosed to the other side unless (in very rare circumstances) an order is obtained from the court allowing witnesses to be called without their reports having been disclosed.

Exchange of witness statements

Witness statements must be exchanged.

Interim orders

Various interlocutory orders can be obtained by applying to the District Judge: for instance, that the other side provide a Part 18 further information request of a Statement of Case, that an interim payment be made to the claimant, and so on.

2. A Simple Accident Claim

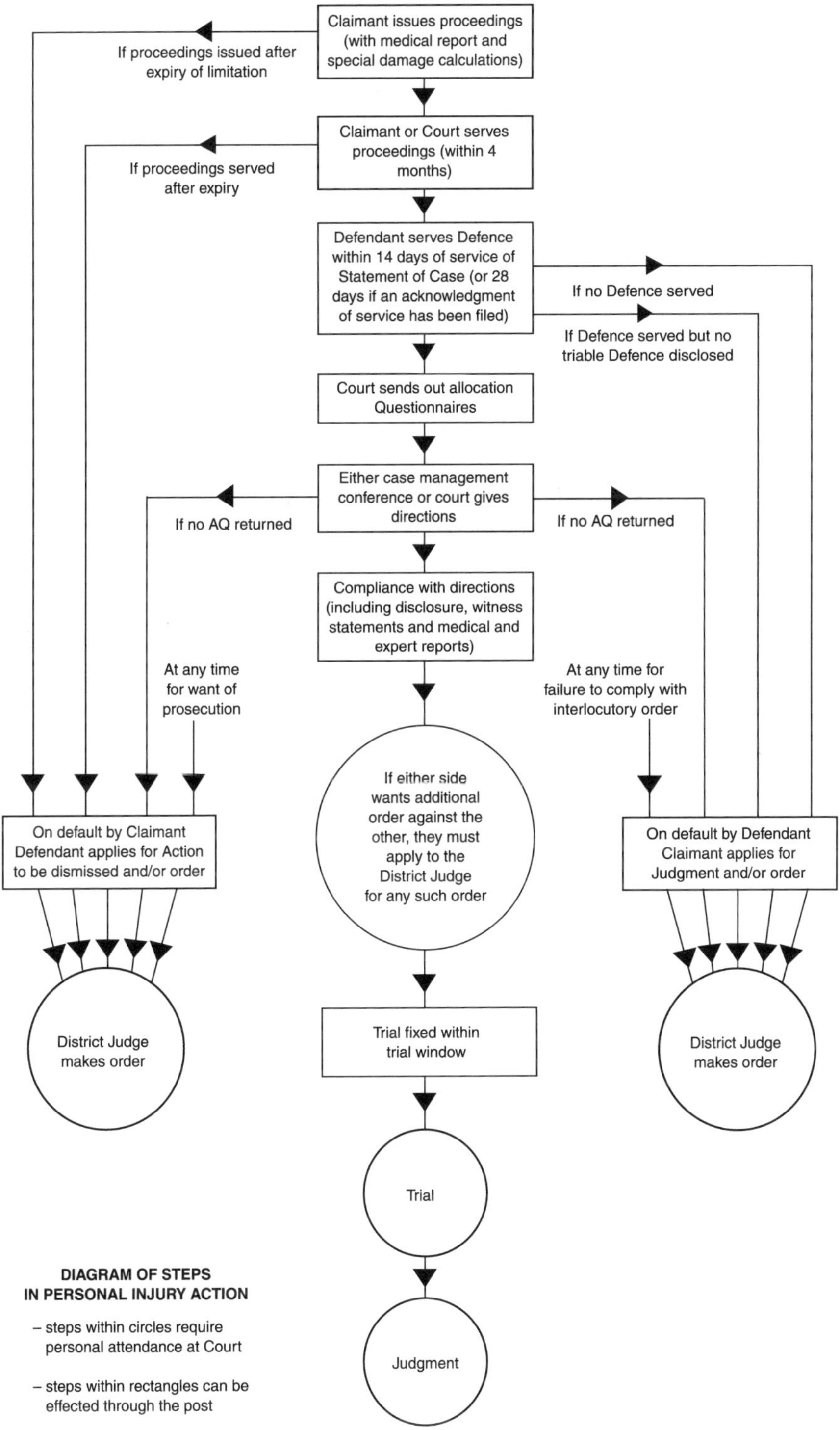

Trial

The next major step will be trial. In a fast track case the date will have been fixed at the allocation stage. In a multi track case it may be fixed at the initial case management conference but it is more usual to see dates to be fixed at a later pre trial review, case management conference or appointment. Counsel will be briefed and the parties will attend court with their witnesses, for trial and judgment.

This may seem a very over-simplified description, but it is true to say that the great majority of personal injury actions (especially road accident claims) involve no steps beyond those set out above.

Possible pitfalls

Many of the problems that arise in the course of litigation are self-made, such as a failure to press on with the action, a failure to diarise time periods, or a failure to prepare the case thoroughly. In order to avoid these pitfalls it is essential to organise a system of working, so that cases are diarised regularly for attention and the various time limits followed.

3. A System of Working

3.1. Introduction

Many firms will have personal injury case management systems which will automatically cover the suggestions made here. However case management systems are only a tool and we set out below a system of working to ensure that claims are processed efficiently, however sophisticated or otherwise your access to information technology.

The system of working described here is neither unique nor original. Like most things that work well, it is both simple and obvious, whilst requiring no real expense or effort to put into operation.

It has three constituent parts:

(1) The diary—to note dates and time periods to ensure that the case does not fall asleep.

(2) The use of draft letters, questionnaires, procedural tables and precedents (as set out in the Appendices) to avoid repetitive dictation and typing.

(3) Easily handled files—which provide information on the state of the case at a glance.

3.2. The diary

This is the one book, whether manual or electronic, that every litigation lawyer must have. The summary in Chapter 2 of a simple accident action shows the importance of time periods in the development of the case. Failure to diarise these time periods can have disastrous consequences. For example, failure to issue proceedings within three years of the accident may well prevent the claimant from pursuing a claim against the defendant, and will probably give the client a professional negligence claim against you. Failure to prosecute the action once it is issued may lead to striking out. Even the more mundane and seemingly less important time periods must be diarised and rigidly adhered to, for it is essential to any system of efficient litigation that files are not allowed to lie dormant and the court will ensure through its case management procedure that the claim is swiftly progressed to trial. If the defendant does not adhere to the time limits laid down in the Rules, then the claimant should not hesitate to apply to the court for an order and, when appropriate, judgment.

Strict adherence to time limits will reduce the amount of unnecessary correspondence and will assist the client by ensuring that the case is heard before his or her memory, and those of the witnesses, fade.

Important dates to diarise

These are the most important of the automatic time limits that should always be diarised—other dates will be fixed by case management and must be carefully diarised and observed:

- from date of accident —three year limitation period for claimant to issue proceedings;
- on issuing proceedings —four months for service of proceedings on defendant;
- on serving claim and Statement of Case —14 days to notify insurers (or Motor Insurers' Bureau) in road accident claim that proceedings have been issued;
- on serving claim and Statement of Case —14 days for defendant to file Defence or Acknowledgment of Service (including Notice of Intention to Defend) with the court;
- on filing Acknowledgment of Service —14 days for defendant to serve Defence;
- on service of Defence —14 days for claimant to serve Reply and/or Defence to Counterclaim (if necessary);
- on a payment into court —21 days for acceptance by claimant after receipt of notice;
- on judgment —three months for detailed assessment of costs.

Remember that time now runs during the vacations.

Diary system

It is usually advisable to make two entries in the diary: one for when the time period expires, and another some time before to act as a reminder. Many firms have computerised diary systems which will automatically note and remind you of these dates. No system is infallible so always keep a personal diary system too. A wall chart can provide a very helpful visual reminder.

Review

Apart from these mandatory dates it is important to review files regularly to ensure that it is being pushed forward and no outstanding matters have been forgotten. It is sensible to diarise a general review of every file no less regularly than every three months. Regular reviews by colleagues can also be extremely helpful. These routine reviews will allow you to consider the case as a whole including tactics and the possibility of settlement rather than specific diary dates which only direct you to the next step necessary to avoid being struck out.

3.3. Use of draft letters, precedents, etc.

Stock letters

Every accident claim will involve the writing of letters to third parties such as doctors, witnesses and the DSS. Often these letters will be in essentially the same form for each case, differing only in the date of the accident and the name and address of the client. Accordingly there is great scope for the use of a system of draft letters whereby letters which frequently recur are not individually dictated, but either kept on computer so that you or your secretary can simply refer to the appropriate draft letter and print it out with the relevant particulars being inserted. Appendix B contains such draft letters, which cover most of the normal letters used in personal injury actions. For example, when commencing a road accident claim, the practitioner would use the standard accident questionnaire and appropriate supplemental questionnaire printed in Appendix A, and then letter 1 (informing the client of the steps in proceedings and essential information) the appropriate costs letter (letters 2–4), letter 5 on being instructed and letter 6 after the first interview, letters 7–9 (to investigate the circumstances of the accident), 16 and 20 (for medical evidence) and 23 (for loss of earnings). Thus the time spent in the routine work of commencing a claim is kept to the minimum, and the use of these letters throughout the action ensures that the solicitor's energies are devoted to the important, decision-making aspects of the file, and not to the routine administration that is an inevitable part of any accident case.

You would normally put the stock letters and precedents on to a word processing or computer system. Alternatively, you could simply print or photocopy the draft letters, leaving blank spaces for the insertion of the particulars relevant to the individual case. Witness letters are an obvious example of how this can save a considerable amount of typing time.

Questionnaires

As mentioned above, the client's initial instructions can be taken using a standard questionnaire. Specimen questionnaires for use in all cases with specific accident questionnaires for workplace cases and road cases, and a supplementary questionnaire for use in fatal accident claims, are printed in Appendix A. The use of these questionnaires as a guide ensures that full details of the accident are taken from the client and that all the details of the case are collected in these easily available documents. Not only will this be helpful to colleagues who may have to refer to the file, but it will also be useful to include in the papers sent to counsel when settling the Statement of Case and will be invaluable when preparing the client's statement.

Precedents

In addition to the use of draft letters and accident questionnaires, it is necessary to have the more commonly used precedents easily to hand, so that, for example, the issuing of a notice of application becomes simple and straightforward, by merely referring to the appropriate precedent and inserting the appropriate details. Appendix C contains the precedents to cover virtually every situation in a personal injury action. In addition, Appendix D contains 16 procedural tables that set out, step by step, the ways in which certain procedural matters are handled. For example, Procedural Table 3 describes how an application is issued which would enable the work to be carried out by support staff.

Forms

The use of pre-printed or computerised forms is clearly another way of saving money and time, and the practitioner should keep a stock of the more commonly used forms. Most of them are found in the appendices to the CPR. There is, of course, no reason (subject to copyright) why the form cannot be typed out instead or put on a computer system. Many systems are now commercially available which contain the forms and update them automatically.

3.4. A standardised filing system

It is vital to keep files in good order so that you or any colleague can see at a glance the stage the case has reached, any important dates and any outstanding matters. Files are more than mere receptacles in which to keep the papers relating to a case. In a well-planned filing system the cover of the file will, alone, provide a summary of the progress made in that claim, *e.g.* the age of the case and whether liability has been admitted.

Correspondence

Most firms will already have standardised filing systems, but in personal injury cases many people like to use at least two correspondence tags: one for party and party correspondence (a separate one for each defendant, if applicable), and one for solicitor/client/miscellaneous. Correspondence can easily become muddled so try using different colour tags for each bundle.

File colour

Each calendar year should have its own colour files. When opening a case it is suggested that the file be of the colour chosen for the year of the accident, and not the colour for the year in which the instructions were taken. This enables the approximate age of the case to be easily seen and thus may provide warning of the impending expiry of a limitation period; at the least, it will enable the older (and, therefore, presumably more urgent) cases to be easily identified as needing attention.

Documents

On issuing the claim (if not earlier) open a second (documents) file, since the papers and copies will soon accumulate and the presence of the second file will be a reminder that proceedings have been commenced. This second file might well be subdivided by paper or plastic folders into sections for Statements of Case, orders, medical reports, other expert reports, legal aid, special damage papers, statements, police reports, discovery, applications, counsel's advices, counsel's papers, copies, etc. (all expert reports and statements should be clearly marked as to whether they have been exchanged). It is vital to subdivide the papers in this way, otherwise you will end up with a morass of unsorted papers, which will mean that you waste time whenever you come to the file. Many people like to keep documents in indexed ring binders or box files.

File record

Devise a system for marking the outside cover of the file as the action progresses. One method is to add strips of coloured tape as certain steps are taken, so that a different colour strip would be added as the conditional fee agreement is signed, the claim issued and served, the allocation questionnaire filed, the case set down for trial, etc.

Important deadlines (*e.g.* for service of issued proceedings) should be written on the cover of the file and crossed out when the necessary action has been taken. These important deadlines should also, of course, be diarised. If there has been a payment into court, or an interim payment, then mark this clearly on the file. It is useful to attach to the file cover copies of orders which are outstanding and tick off each order as it is complied with. This is particularly useful for directions. The same method can be used for counsel's advice on evidence.

Attendance notes

The keeping of full and accurate notes of the work done on a case will be of considerable assistance to the costs draftsperson when compiling the bill of costs, and to the costs judge when looking through the papers on assessment. The file should therefore record all the work done on the case, and not merely the letters written. Thus, full attendance notes should be put in the file of all attendances with the client, witnesses, etc., and also of time spent in considering medical reports or working out special damage. This is important even if you also have a computerised time system as you will have to persuade a costs judge not only that time was spent but that it was spent necessarily and properly.

Filing

Always keep the file up to date and file all correspondence and documents daily. This ensures that important deadlines will not be missed or documents lost, particularly if a colleague unexpectedly has to take over your case. Regular filing is important for all litigation but essential for personal injury where deadlines are short and strictly enforced.

Part II

INVESTIGATING THE CLAIM

4. Initial Interview and Investigation

4.1. Introduction

First the reassurance. For competent lawyers, even those inexperienced in this field, personal injury litigation is fundamentally simple; assess liability, buy in experience that you do not have (such as medics, engineers, care consultants and accountants) quantify the claim and go to trial unless a reasonable settlement can be achieved before then. You will find that experienced injury litigators are often happy to share their secrets, so talk to them if you have queries. There are various lawyer organisations that you can contact for assistance, for example APIL, MASS and FOIL (more information and their addresses appear in Chapter 30), Specialist Panels and Accident Line. It is important to recognise your limitations. Do not be scared of turning away work that you do not feel capable of doing. When a client seeks advice in connection with an accident the first thing is to decide if you feel confident that you can deal with the claim. If so, take full instructions.

4.2. Client care and initial letters

When a client seeks advice in connection with an accident the first task is to take full instructions. This will enable you to form an initial view on liability, deal with funding at the earliest possible stage and advise whether the claim is worth pursuing.

Client care

Remember that while it is essential that you elicit a set of facts, apply the law to them and advise, your client is a human being who has been hurt, is probably confused about the process and may be angry, shocked or depressed. It is important to show that you appreciate the client's concerns and empathise with him or her. Demystify the process as far as possible by communicating with the client in plain language. Clearly explain the information you need and the steps you will take. Be realistic and honest from the outset. Emphasise that you can only obtain money compensation for the client and not punishment or approbation for the wrongdoer. Keep the client informed throughout the process, send the client copies of all important letters in the case and be available to explain every stage. You will find it easier to obtain coherent instructions and prosecute the claim if the client feels that you have his or her best interests at heart. Remember that the source of greatest complaint from clients against solicitors is failure to communicate.

This is your best opportunity to manage your client's expectations. This is an essential part of client care in the modern demanding society. Do not underestimate its importance. If a client understands and anticipates the various stages of the claim process then issues that inevitably arise which might undermine a client's confidence in a lawyer (particularly delays experienced whilst awaiting medical evidence, a final prognosis or even the insurers' initial three month protocol enquiry period) become expected as a necessary part of the compensation process.

Similarly, this is a good time to manage monetary expectation. Whilst some clients have no idea of the likely value of their claim and others appear satisfied with anything they recover there is an increasing number of clients with expectations of levels of compensation much higher than are achievable through our claim process. Whilst it is usually far too early to give any specific indication of the value of any individual claim it is as well to explain the way in which claims are valued and even indicate the broad brackets of award with reference to the JSB guidelines. Be careful how you do this because months or even years later a too specific and now obviously inaccurate and over optimistic figure will come home to haunt you.

Liability

You should explain to the client, in understandable language, that the claimant must prove the defendant's breach of duty or negligence. Many people mistakenly think that they are entitled to damages either simply because they have suffered injury or loss, or, alternatively, because they can show that the accident happened through no fault of their own. It is often helpful to equate negligence with fault as this is something the client will understand.

Steps in proceedings and essential information

Do not expect the client to remember everything that you say at this first meeting. Indeed, reassure the client that you will write to confirm the advice given after the meeting. A well written letter not only explains the pertinent law to the client but also affords you another opportunity to explain terminology and the process the client can expect again assisting in the management of expectations. This letter can be sent with your Rule 15 client care letter confirming the funding arrangement agreed. It is best to keep the two separate otherwise the client may be confronted by one inordinately lengthy letter. The client can then keep this available and refer to it throughout the case. A precedent letter appears in Appendix B (see letter 1).

Initial information and questionnaire

If there is sufficient time before the initial interview, write to the client confirming the time and asking the client to start filling in the appropriate questionnaire(s), particularly as to formal details such as name and address, the circumstances of the accident, injury and special damages. This will concentrate the client's mind on the events that occurred and save time at the initial interview (use stock letter 5 in Appendix B and the questionnaires in Appendix A). Do be flexible. Questionnaires, whilst useful, should not be deemed to be the only form of enquiry. They are a useful aide memoire and starting point.

4.3. Funding

The client will be worried about the cost of a claim so explain about funding at the outset. As with any form of selling put cost in context. In other words, if there is a good claim then say so, give the best cost estimate and indicate if the claim is economically viable. The client can then make an informed decision.

Accident line

If your firm has Personal Injury Panel members and operates the Accident Line Scheme then the first interview (giving a view on liability and costs) may be free (see Chapter 30). In practice, many firms now offer a free first interview for any potential injury client regardless of any scheme membership.

Unions

If the client belongs to a trade union the union may offer free legal advice and assistance. Some trade unions only offer this service to a member whose accident either took place at work or travelling to or from work. However, increasingly unions extend the service to cover all personal injury. If the client is within such a scheme you should advise the client to apply to the union for assistance. If the union agrees to take the case it will normally instruct its own solicitors to act.

Legal insurance

Check if your client has insurance which will cover your legal fees. Legal insurance cover may be provided with motor insurance or travel insurance and is an increasingly common add-on to domestic home insurance. If it is possible that such insurance exists the client should notify the insurers immediately as delay may lead to the claim being refused. The insurers may agree to instruct you to act for the client but often only on their own terms and conditions for solicitors. These conditions are sometimes onerous so check carefully and ensure they are satisfactory before agreeing to act.

It is now particularly important that you do check the legal expense position as many clients are unaware that they have this cover. If you enter in to a conditional fee arrangement without proper enquiry then later you may struggle to recover the premium paid and also possibly any success fee (see Chapter 23).

Legal aid (public funding)

The renaming of legal aid was, for injury practitioners, broadly one of irrelevance. Regrettably, at the same time as the renaming, the public funding of the claims of victims of injury was withdrawn. Whilst there are a few exceptions (most notably in clinical negligence claims) ordinary everyday injury litigation now falls outside the scheme. Legal aid certificates in existence prior to the reforms survive but at the time of writing this book most of those claims will have been resolved one way or another. The argument that personal injury litigation was almost self funding for legal aid purposes, and when credit was given for the treasury income from the Compensation Recovery Unit produced a surplus, curiously seemed only to persuade the reformers that there was therefore no need for public funding of claims.

As a result of the reforms detailed consideration of public funding certificates is unnecessary in this book and only passing references will be made. Further information can always be obtained from the Regional Legal Services Commission if needed.

Conditional fees

You may wish to enter into a conditional fee arrangement with your client (see Chapter 22). If so, explain the scheme to your client, inform him/her of the percentage success fee you intend to charge and explain the conditions of any necessary after-the-event insurance.

Privately paying clients

If the client is paying privately ensure that the client accepts responsibility for legal costs and expenses. Inform your client what costs and disbursements are likely to be incurred at each stage and consider asking your client for money on account. You should certainly obtain the client's signature to a letter setting out your terms of business which clearly incorporates details of how your fees will be charged and when. Note that if you quote an hourly rate you should indicate when that is reviewable and remember to review it then and notify the client of the outcome of that review. It is a good idea to give an estimate of the overall likely costs. This is an estimate only and can be revisited if circumstances change. It does, though, give the client some idea of the funds that will be needed.

Fee letters

Write to your client explaining your fees and method of charging. To ensure that you do deal with financing the claim it is good practice to deal with this as part of your client care letter (see stock letters 1–4 in Appendix B).

4.4. Initial interview

The initial interview will allow you to meet and assess the client, explain your initial opinion of the claim and give information on its progress and costs. It should centre upon the completion of the appropriate accident questionnaires which will provide the information on liability, injury and quantum needed to investigate and pursue the claim. Although we suggest that the questionnaires be sent to the client before the interview so that the client can complete the standard questions and will know what to expect of the initial interview, all answers should be checked carefully and clarified with the client. Many clients find these questionnaires exceptionally daunting and need to complete them with your help in an interview. The amount of information necessary to progress a personal injury claim may mean that the first meeting has to be fairly long. After a while you may find that you no longer use the questionnaires as you have developed your own methods of information gathering. Even then they can be a useful reminder.

4.5. Accident questionnaires

Four accident questionnaires are printed in Appendix A. The first is a general questionnaire outlining details of the client's personal information, employment, benefits received and injuries. Additional questionnaires should then be completed to cover the details of the accident or event causing injury. Two examples are included covering road or workplace injuries. Other questionnaires can be devised for other types of injury such as clinical negligence. The fourth questionnaire is supplementary to be completed in fatal cases.

The questionnaires can provide a very helpful aide-memoire for necessary questions but should not prevent you from asking any other questions which arise. You may wish to print the questionnaire in a booklet or add some information about your firm or an introduction as to the purpose of the questionnaire.

The questionnaires should be self-explanatory. If the reason for information required is not clear it should become clear on reading the following chapters of this book. However, some of the following points may be helpful.

Requirements for all questionnaires

Each questionnaire should:

(a) be headed with the name of the client so that it can be identified if it is sent in with no covering letter or it goes missing from your file;

(b) state the date of accident or injury so that you can see the limitation period at a glance;

(c) have separate sections numbered consecutively to make cross-referencing easier if a client uses a separate piece of paper or when you are making notes in interview.

(d) ask for particular documents to be supplied—you will probably need to remind the client about these at the interview;

(e) be signed at the bottom of every page—this will make the questionnaire admissible as a Civil Evidence Act statement if the client dies before trial; and

(f) be dated so that you know which is the latest material.

General questionnaire (Appendix A Questionnaire 1)

A Personal details

8 A National Insurance Number will be necessary to obtain details from the Compensation Recovery Unit (CRU).

B Employment details

Full employment details will be necessary even if the accident did not happen at work so that you can properly assess present and future losses of earnings. Obviously, further questions will need to be asked depending on the answers to these questions.

11 Exact wage details will be obtainable from the employer or accountant. The figure given by the client provides an approximate check on the employer's figure and will be enable special damage to be stated if there is delay in obtaining the exact figure.

C Welfare benefits

13 *Statutory sick pay.* After April 1, 1994 most employers could not recover sums paid to employees by way of statutory sick pay from the State and such money is therefore not recouped by the CRU. However, statutory sick pay received before April 1, 1994 will still be recouped as is statutory sick pay paid by small employers.

You will need to check the contract of employment, because often this will provide for repayment of any salary (over and above statutory sick pay) if moneys are obtained from any third party. It is therefore possible for a client to tell you that he or she has no loss of earnings whereas in fact the joint operation of statutory sick pay recoupment under the Compensation Recovery Scheme and the employer's right to recoup any contractual or discretionary sick pay means that the whole of pay during time off must be repaid. This is invariably the case in public sector employment.

D Injuries

21 *Continuing injury.* If the client has a continuing injury you should ensure that you take a careful proof of current condition and ask the client to continually update this. It is very helpful for a client to keep a 'pain diary'. Once a client has recovered, memories of injuries and disability will fade and such contemporaneous evidence can be extremely useful to bolster the client's case at trial.

Also, you must obtain hospital details where treatment has taken place as this is now essential information for the CRU so that treatment costs can be recovered from insurers.

24 *Previous Injuries.* It is important to know about previous accidents and injuries to consider whether there is a pre-existing condition which might reduce the level of damages. If so you should consider obtaining past medical records or notes or ensuring that they are provided to any appointed medical expert as this is something upon which they must comment.

Road accident questionnaire (Appendix A Questionnaire 2)

5 *Details of accident.* Make sure you understand exactly how the client alleges the accident happened. It is extremely useful to keep toy cars in your desk so the client can demonstrate at interview what happened. This will often show up any problems or inconsistencies in the client's case. Never be afraid to ask if there is anything you do not understand.

6 *Client insurers.* If the client was driving at the time of the accident, the defendant's insurers will want to know if they have a sharing agreement with the claimant's insurers. In any event you will want the details as you should write to your client's insurers notifying them of your involvement and checking whether they have any outlay they want you to recover or protect if you issue proceedings. You should also ensure that they will take no steps that might prejudice your client's claim (see stock letter 54 in Appendix B).

Client's cover and excess. Even if the client's cover is comprehensive there may well be uninsured losses to be claimed; for example, excess on the policy. If the policy is not comprehensive then the claim will include damage to the vehicle, towage, storage, travel, hire of another vehicle, loss of use, etc.

Seatbelts. It may be up to 25 per cent contributory negligence not to wear a seatbelt, if fitted, unless irrelevant to the injury. Even then though there is likely to be a deduction of at least 15 per cent.

7 *Car driver and car owner.* Details of both are needed as the driver will often be the employee or agent of the owner and the claimant's claim may be directed against both.

Was anyone else hurt in the accident? It is important to find out if anyone else was hurt in the accident or incident either directly or as a witness suffering nervous shock. If there are many claimants, for example in a motorway pile up or product liability case, then you will need to contact witnesses and the Law Society to see if a steering committee has been set up to deal with the aspects of the case common to all parties (the generic aspects). This is one of the few areas where public funding certificates may be available. However, there are restrictions on those deemed experienced to deal with group litigation. Check the position with the Regional Legal Services Commission. The Legal Services Commission may also bring multi-party rules into play and insist that a nominated solicitor carries them out. In any event you should contact other people involved to see if they are prepared to be witnesses or are making claims which may strengthen your client's case: see Chapter 26 on multi-party actions.

9 *Notice of intended prosecution.* If a notice is received it is not conclusive that proceedings will be taken. If a client has been warned to attend as a witness it is likely that the other side is being prosecuted. The police report will not be forwarded until prosecution proceedings have been completed. Increasingly, the police are using written warnings and compulsory attendance on a driver training scheme as an alternative to prosecution. If they do so, your client should receive a letter confirming this course of action has been taken. Most insurers accept this as akin to a prosecution of their insured for liability purposes.

11 *Pre-accident value.* Ensure that any estimates obtained by the client on cost of repairs are from a reputable garage. If there is a statement that a vehicle is beyond economic repair then also obtain an estimate of the vehicle's pre-accident value. This is best done by a local vehicle examiner whom you should instruct as a matter of urgency for your client is under a duty to mitigate loss which includes limiting storage charges and hire charges. The sooner you have a pre-accident valuation the sooner the salvage can be disposed of and the sooner you can seek an interim payment.

The workplace accident questionnaire (Appendix A Questionnaire 3)

The aim must be to elicit as much information as possible about the system of working, previous accidents or complaints, and the amount of experience and training the client had.

10 *Does the client know whether there was a complaints book?* If there was are there any relevant entries that can be used to argue that the employer had been warned of the danger that led to the client's accident?

14 *Safety checks and audits.* Under the 'six pack' of regulations brought into force in 1992 and in particular the Provision and Use of Work Equipment Regulations 1992 (S.I. 1992 No. 2932), the Workplace (Health, Safety and Welfare) Regulations 1992 (S.I. 1992 No. 3004) and the Management of Health and Safety at Work Regulations 1992 (S.I. 1992 No. 2051) employers are obliged to carry out reviews of the safety of equipment, and to document that they have done so. Absence of such documents can be extremely helpful evidence that the employer was failing in its duty to provide a safe workplace.

19 *Accident book.* It is essential that the client reports the accident to the employer as soon as it happens so that there can be no dispute about its occurrence even if it is an injury rather than an accident.

25 *Disablement benefit.* This is a DSS benefit available to persons with a disability arising out of an industrial accident. Not only is it a valuable benefit but in addition the papers received by the claimant (particularly one who appeals against an award) may contain valuable (free) medical opinions. This is especially useful in claims in which there is a dispute as to whether the claimant's condition

arises from work; for example dermatitis. Ensure that the client claims benefit if there is any residual disability; note that the disablement need not be permanent and the applicant need not be incapable of work. The injury does not have to be particularly serious for the client to be eligible for disablement benefit; all that is required is that there is continuing disability. Further, a client who is in receipt of disablement benefit may be eligible for other benefits such as attendance allowance or disability living allowance. Check that the client has applied for all available benefits—any firm which has a legal aid franchise has a duty to be aware of the need for benefits advice.

26 Does the client know if the Health and Safety Executive is involved and if so what are its conclusions?

Supplementary questionnaire for use in fatal accident cases (Appendix A Questionnaire 4)

Fatal accident cases will require additional information; not least, information on the dependants as well as the deceased (see Chapter 25). This questionnaire is intended to obtain the factual details regarding the death, inquest, administration of the estate and names of dependants. However, it does not ask for the information necessary to obtain the detailed calculations of the household income and expenditure which may be needed to calculate dependency. This necessarily artificial calculation almost always causes distress to clients and is much better handled by sensitive and relevant questionning in a meeting than by way of a questionnaire. A list of the information you will require is set out in Chapter 25.

5 A Grant of Administration or Probate must be taken out and it is the administrator who has the right to sue on behalf of the dependant, so ensure that your client is also the administrator.

7 *Inquest.* Has the inquest been held? If not it may be useful to attend on behalf of the dependants and so be able to question the proposed defendant and the witnesses, but note that legal aid will not be available and it may prove impossible to recover this cost from the defendant on taxation. In any event it will probably be necessary to obtain a copy of the inquest depositions.

Do be sensitive when dealing with fatal accidents. Invariably, you are dealing with bereaved relatives. There are certain pieces of information you require, such as whether there was any suffering pre death for Law Reform Act 1934 claims, that are fairly grim. It may be better if this questionnaire is completed by questioning at interview rather than sent through the post. Tread carefully.

4.6. Costs and funding

You will have already spoken to the client about costs and funding (see above). Now make a decision about the type of funding, advise the client accordingly, note down the agreed funding and confirm in writing. The more complicated the funding proposal the more likely the client will want some time to think about it. Do not discourage this. Remember the solicitor client relationship must be based on trust.

4.7. Authorities

Obviously to investigate the claim you will need some written authorities from the client so obtain written medical releases (letter 21) an authority from the employer to release wage details (letter 24) and, if appropriate, consent to the Inland Revenue to release tax returns (letter 26).

4.8. Advising the client

Once you have obtained the necessary details you should advise the client in the meeting and should follow up this advice in writing to the client. A draft letter is set out in Appendix B, letter 7. You can cross-refer to stock letter 1 setting out the steps and proceedings which you will already have sent to your client or you many prefer to incorporate it all in one letter. Your advice should cover the following matters.

Limitation

Tell the client of the limitation period for the claim and explain the importance of answering your letters promptly.

Liability

Set out the name of the party the client can claim against, the basis of the claim explaining what will have to be shown to prove the claim and an indication of any areas of doubt in proving the claim and when and how they might be overcome. You should give the client an indication of the merits of the claim but make it clear that you are relying on the information given by the client in making this assessment and that your assessment may vary if evidence given to you differs. Indicate to the client the likely outcome of the case on the evidence currently available.

Contributory negligence

If you think that the client's claim is likely to be reduced by contributory negligence you should explain this to the client and explain in simple terms the meaning of primary and contributory negligence. Often an example using figures provides an easy illustration of the point.

Quantum

You should explain what the client should be able to claim for, *i.e.*:

(1) Special damages. Losses and expenses to date and future loss. Tell the client what further information you need to prove that claim and inform the client how you will go about obtaining it.

(2) General damages. Explain that general damages are compensation for the pain and suffering and loss of amenity caused by the accident. Give the client an indication (if possible at this stage) of the general damages he/she is likely to receive. This is likely only to be confirmation of quantum discussed at the first meeting.

(3) Bereavement/loss of dependency.

Defendant's means

You should discuss whether the defendant is likely to be able to meet the claim and, if appropriate, the role of insurers and the Motor Insurers Bureau.

Welfare benefits

If applicable you should explain about the possibility of claiming welfare benefits for the injuries, disabilities or financial predicament and the effect these would have on an award for damages under the Compensation Recovery Scheme. In particular advise on a claim for disablement benefit (see p. 21 above).

Special matters

Do not narrow your advice only to a personal injury claim. You should also consider whether your client may claim any of the following:

(1) Criminal Injuries Compensation. If your client was injured as a result of a criminal act you should consider whether the client should make a Criminal Injuries Compensation claim (see Chapter 28). The tariff-based scheme may mean that in some cases damages are more generous than would be paid in a normal personal injury claim but costs are not available. Also, some defendants, for example in assault cases, may be liable but have no assets. Again, the tariff award may be better than an unenforceable paper judgment.

(2) Criminal Injury Compensation Order. If the claim is small and the defendant is being prosecuted consider applying to the court for a Criminal Compensation Order (see Chapter 28). In practice, criminal courts are sometimes reluctant to award compensation for personal injury. Criminal compensation cannot be ordered as a result of a road accident.

(3) MIB. If your client was involved in a road accident and the other driver is untraced or uninsured then the claim will be against the MIB (see Chapter 29).

(4) Small claims. If your client's claim is worth less than £1,000 then a small claims case in the county court may be appropriate (see Chapter 28).

(5) Unfair/wrongful dismissal. If your client has been dismissed because of the accident or injury there may be a case for unfair or wrongful dismissal. It is very important to consider such a case at this stage because:
   (a) an unfair dismissal case must be taken within three months of the dismissal;
   (b) in a claim for loss of earnings the defendant may claim that the loss is not due to the injury but to the dismissal and you may have to disprove this; and
   (c) reinstatement can sometimes be ordered in unfair dismissal cases.

If you are not an employment specialist advise the client to seek employment advice elsewhere and make a note of this advice.

Procedure

You should explain to the client how the case will progress. Obviously, the procedure is set out in your introductory letter (stock letter 1) and you may refer to this. However, you must explain to the client the steps you are going to take in your client's particular case, the steps the client must undertake, the time in which the steps need to be completed and how long the client can expect to wait for the claim to be concluded. Ensure that the client understands that the client has a choice and that the client exercises the choice. Your function is to advise not to be prescriptive.

In particular it is important to explain to the client when the other side will be contacted and why and what to do if the other side contacts the client.

Once you have given the client the advice you should note the reaction of the client to the decided plan of action and ensure that the client instructs you to act and carry out the steps that you have recommended. If the client wishes you to do anything that is against your advice you should note this in writing.

Obviously the client will have queries and you should ensure that you deal with these as politely, considerately and fully as possible. You should make a point of answering all queries even if they do not seem important to you. It is, after all, your client's claim.

If the case is complex or of high value it is good practice to agree a formal case plan with the client and to keep this at the front of the file for easy reference.

Costs

Explain to your client the rules on payment of the other side's costs. This is an area which causes clients a great deal of confusion, particularly the indemnity rules.

4.9. Considering the claim and urgent action

Before you start firing off standard letters consider the claim as a whole so far. If liability is very difficult or the claim is very small advise the client of this and ensure that the client understands the risks. Also consider if there are any urgent matters which need dealing with immediately. If any of the steps referred to below are necessary carry them out without delay and do not forget in all cases to ensure funding has been agreed and put in place before you start making investigations.

Limitation—protective proceedings?

Is the limitation period about to expire? If so you may need to issue protective proceedings to preserve the position while investigating the claim (see Chapter 9, p. 105).

Pre-action inspection or disclosure

Consider pre-action inspection or disclosure. If there is any evidence:

(a) that the prospective defendant has which may disappear or be destroyed (see Chapter 5); or

(b) without which you cannot progress the claim (for example hospital notes in a medical negligence claim) (see Chapter 5).

However, with the introduction of the Personal Injury and Clinical Negligence Protocols compliance with the protocol may deal with your concerns (see protocols at Appendix I).

Other evidence

Is there any other evidence which may disappear or change before investigation in the normal course? If so take steps to obtain information straight away. Note in particular the following:

(a) witness statements by witnesses who are old or leaving the country or (if fellow employees) they are likely to be nobbled by the defendant.

(b) site photos, particularly in road accident sites or photographs of damages to vehicle or property or the layout of a workplace.

(c) photographs of the client's injuries.

4.10. After the initial interview

Opening the file

If you have not already done so open the file, fill in all necessary file opening details and diarise the expiry of the limitation period. Professional rules also oblige you to do a conflicts search to ensure that the defendant(s) is not a client of your firm.

Preparing the client's initial statement

If the questionnaire is full and the accident is simple it may be possible to use the questionnaire instead of writing up a full statement at this stage. However, it is likely that the questionnaire is now a mass of notes written partly by you and partly by the client and therefore it is sensible to type up a preliminary statement at this stage recording all the information covered in the interview. This should be in the form of a witness statement (see Chapter 5). The questionnaire, attendance note or statement should be sent to the client for reference and approval. It may be helpful to extract all special damages information and put this in one statement that can then easily be updated.

Conditional fee agreement

Complete the agreement and pay any insurance premium necessary (see Chapter 23).

Reporting to the client

You should write to the client confirming matters advised on in your meeting (use stock letter 7) and send the statement for approval or amendment. Tell the client of the steps you have taken and remind the client of the steps that the client now has to take.

Letter before action

If you have advised that the claim is good on liability you should not delay in putting the defendant on notice.

This is when you will encounter the first change to the conduct of injury claims arising from the civil procedure reforms. It is no longer acceptable to write a few lines of general notification and expect the defendant to respond substantively. The Personal Injury Protocol now governs pre-action conduct of injury claims. You should also be familiar with the 'overriding objective' set out in The Civil Procedure Rules (CPR) as that gives you a further insight into how the court would expect a claim to be dealt with both before and after issue (see Appendix I for The Personal Injury Protocol)

The letter before action has been replaced by a letter of claim that must contain certain information. There is some divergence on when the letter should be sent. You should send it as soon as you can identify the correct defendant and have sufficient information to explain the accident circumstances and indicate why those circumstances lead to allegations of negligence. Do not try to be too specific. The protocol is plain that these allegations are not meant to be binding upon your client nor necessarily definitive. In truth the sooner you force the defendant to respond to the letter of claim the sooner you will know whether and if so what liability enquiries will be necessary.

There is a standard draft letter of claim set out in the protocol. It is recommended that you use that adapting it to the specific accident circumstances as appropriate (see stock letters 27–30 in Appendix B).

Clinical negligence claims are usually against a hospital trust. The commencement procedure for them is clearly set out in the pertinent protocol (see Chapter 26).

Identifying the defendant

In a road accident this is usually straightforward as your client will have details. Remember it is the driver of the vehicle against whom the cause of action lies and to whom the letter of claim should be sent. This is true even if the owner was not the driver and the claim falls to be defended by the owner's insurers. If your client does not have details but the police were involved contact the local traffic unit for the information. If the client only has a vehicle registration number you can do a search at DVLA for a small fee to ascertain the last registered keeper which may be a useful starting point. If no details are available from any source consider an MIB untraced driver claim. In a workplace accident obviously your client will have his/her own employer's details. If, though, the accident took place whilst in employment but not at employers' premises obtain the names of occupiers of the premises or land where the accident did occur. You may need to involve both.

Voluntary pre-action disclosure

Refer to the personal injury protocol as this provides useful checklists of the documents to be requested in specific types of case if liability is in dispute (see protocol in Appendix I).

Defendant's response

The protocol provides that the defendant or his or her representatives must acknowledge a letter of claim within 21 days and then respond confirming whether or not liability is in dispute within a further three-month period. You should diarise these dates.

Occasionally, and to be fair this is usually because the insured defendant fails to pass the letter to the insurers, it does take a bit longer. The full response must either admit liability or deny it with an explanation and disclosure of relevant documents. Whilst admissions are explicitly stated to be binding in fast track cases only (see Chapter 13) in practice most admissions are binding for all purposes. Indeed, with the openness required by the Rules it is hard to see when an admission would be allowed to be withdrawn by the court, although pre CPR arguments on where the most prejudice lies on an erroneous admission may still take place in the multi track.

Claimant's response

If liability is admitted acknowledge this to the defendant and indicate you are terminating liability enquiries and moving on to quantum. One reason for telling this to the defendant is that if there is a later attempt to withdraw the admission you can show prejudice as you relied on the admission to terminate liability enquiries whilst the evidential trail was hot.

Tell your client the good news.

If liability is denied you now need to follow up the information received from the client and the defendant and investigate further.

5. Liability and Statements

5.1. Introduction

Preliminary considerations

If you either receive no response to the letter of claim or a denial of liability in full or in part and the client wishes to continue then you must move on to the next stage of the process.

Having taken the initial steps you need now to investigate liability. Obviously it is sensible to ensure that the case is good before spending a great deal of time and money assessing the client's exact injuries and special damages. However, it is worth considering the following:

(1) If there is any evidence which may disappear try to obtain it immediately (see Chapter 4, p. 31). This may have been provided by the defendant in the protocol response.

(2) There is no point investigating liability if damages will be negligible so ascertain that the case is worth enough to warrant legal intervention before carrying out investigations. This should usually be clear from the client's statement. By now the extent and duration of the injuries should also be clearer.

(3) It does take time to obtain expert medical evidence and calculate special damages. As medical reports and a statement of special damages have to be served within four months of issue of the claim form you should consider obtaining them without delay if there is any limitation problem.

(4) There is little point in carrying out detailed investigations into liability if it is not going to be contested by the defendant so ensure that the defendant's liability position is clear. If the response simply admits primary liability ascertain if this really means there is a contributory negligence point and if so what or whether it is simply sloppy wording.

Having considered the points above you can now concentrate on establishing liability.

Injury

As stated above you will normally only instruct a medical expert at this preliminary stage if:

(a) liability is not in dispute; or

(b) limitation is a problem; or

(c) it is a clinical negligence case (see Chapter 26); or

(d) the client's symptoms or evidence of injury may disappear and are not adequately recorded, although of course, a full history can be given to the expert by the client.

Chapter 6 explains how to instruct a medical expert.

Medical records

Although you are not yet instructing an expert you may wish to see the client's medical records at an early stage particularly if it is likely that a pre-existing condition may have aggravated the symptoms or the injury. Send the G.P. or hospital the client's consent (stock letter 21) together with a covering letter asking for the documents and confirming that you will pay all reasonable fees. Your client has a right to see copies of all medical records since 1991 under the Access to Health Records Act 1990 (except in exceptional circumstances) but doctors do have a discretion with notes prior to that date. They are allowed to make a reasonable charge for photocopying. Some hospitals have been asking for excessive fees and in 1997 the NHS Management Executive issued guidance for hospitals on fees for post 1991 records stressing that you do not have to give reasons for access and that the only cost of photocopying should only be the actual charge per page and the cost of staff time in making copies. (APIL suggests that 2p per page and 20p per page including staff time would be reasonable). Doctors and hospitals are not entitled to charge a standard or administrative fee.

If there is any difficulty with the release of the documents try telephoning the doctor concerned to find out why. Often it is a sign that there is a pre-existing condition and they are trying to protect your client but clearly you must know about this at the earliest possible stage as defendants may well ask for medical records on discovery and will usually obtain such an order.

It is also amazing how many clents give details of surgeries at which they are no longer registered.

Pain diary

Even if you are not investigating the injury at this stage it is important to remind your client to keep as much evidence as possible of the progress of his/her injury or condition. The client may wish to take photographs at various stages. Ensure that these are dated. You could also suggest that your client keeps a diary of the severity and frequency of pain and limitations on activities caused by the injury. This will provide a vivid and useful record of the client's disability and the progress of the recovery. However, be sensitive about this as some clients find it very depressing to be asked continually to focus on their disabilities and activities they can no longer undertake. Also, be sure to stress that this should be a summary and not a treatise on injury. You do not need that much detail.

Special damages

Again, there is little point in obtaining full details of special damage until you are reasonably certain on liability unless:

(a) limitation is a problem;

(b) there is any evidence or witnesses that are likely to disappear; or

(c) likely damages are so low that you need to consider whether this should be a small claim or abandoned completely (see Chapter 28).

Chapter 7 explains how to obtain information on special damage.

Remember that under the protocol you are required to quantify loss and damage as soon as possible. Accordingly, at the very least at this stage you should give an indication of the types of loss.

5.2. Stock letters

At this stage send off the initial stock letters to investigate liability.

Witnesses

Write to witnesses (stock letter 7 for a road accident and stock letter 8 for a workplace accident) and remember that in workplace accident cases it is permissible to write to an allegedly negligent fellow employee before writing to the employers to claim damages. There is no property in a witness.

Police and ambulance reports

In a road accident case obtain the police report (stock letter 9). The fee is no longer a standard one set by the Home Office but should be reasonable. Again, some forces have been charging excessive fees and in 1997 The Association of Chief Police Officer's Traffic Committee issued guidelines, with the current fee about £56. Interview costs vary. It is police practice that another officer sits in on the interview. Consider whether the ambulance crew would be able to provide any useful additional information; if so write to the ambulance service for a copy report stating the exact time and location of the accident.

Vehicle inquiry unit

If you know the registration number of the other vehicle involved in the accident but do not know the name of the owner write to the vehicle inquiry unit at DVLC (stock letter 11). You will probably have done this already, if necessary, to enable you to send a letter of claim.

Inquest depositions and accident investigation reports

In a fatal case write for the inquest depositions (stock letter 11). In a workplace accident case write to the Health and Safety Executive and ask whether the circumstances of the accident were investigated and, if so, request a copy of the report (stock letter 13). Usually the HSE will not release copies until court proceedings have actually been issued.

Medical notes

In a clinical negligence claim apply for the medical notes (see Chapter 26). These would be from other note holders, not the alleged negligent treaters, so that any expert instructed has the full treatment history of the client.

Photographs

Consider obtaining independent photographs of the accident site or the vehicles/machinery involved (see Chapter 16).

Accident book, memos, etc.

In a workplace accident claim if there was no response to the letter of claim or you think the disclosure was insufficient then as well as reminding the defendant of the protocol obligations, as you would in any case, consider also whether the client is a member of a union from which you can obtain relevant documents.

HSE documents

The Health and Safety Executive publishes numerous booklets on industrial procedures and recommendations for good practice, which can sometimes be good evidence when arguing that there is an unsafe system of work. The Publications in Series List is available free from the Health and Safety Executive Library, St Hugh's House, Stanley Precinct, Bootle, Merseyside L20 3QY.

5.3. Police reports

In a road accident case there will usually be a police report. This can be a helpful document which may save you considerable time and expense in investigating the circumstances of the accident. The format of the report will vary from constabulary to constabulary but it will always contain the same basic information. Recently, these have been of diminishing assistance as the police seem to take fewer statements and you will see only the actual form 72E in many cases. Interview records are now not released.

Police attendance

Check that the report makes it clear that the police did attend the scene of the accident and that the report is not based upon what the police were subsequently told.

General details

The name, age, address and insurers of the parties will be given together with details of the vehicles involved. In cases where you have had no response to the letter of claim also check to see if the police took the defendant's insurance details. You can then write to them direct to ask them to confirm an interest.

The plan

Study the plan. Usually, it will only be a sketch plan and not drawn to scale. If it marks the position of vehicles note whether the vehicles were moved prior to the police arriving on the scene. Were there any skid marks? Was there any debris or wreckage which might indicate the position in the road where the impact took place?

Damage

Check the statement of the damage to the vehicles to see if the damage and point of impact are compatible with the client's and/or any witness's version of the accident.

Statements

At the rear of the report will be all the statements, including those of witnesses. Check whether there is a statement from each witness. If any witness's statement is missing or incomplete write to that witness using stock letter 8. Read the statements carefully and compare them with any statements you already have. When was the statement taken? If taken shortly after the accident it may be regarded in a better light than if taken several days later. Also check the client's statement and ensure that it agrees with the statement given to you. Did the client mention any injuries at the time? Note as well that there may be a statement by the police vehicle examiner which will record any defects found in the vehicle even if they are not directly responsible for the accident.

Criminal proceedings?

Finally, note whether proceedings were taken by the police. The most usual charge is under s. 3 of the Road Traffic Act 1988 (*i.e.* careless driving or driving without due care and attention). A conviction of the other driver will usually be proof of negligence and in practice will mean that the dispute with the other side will be to the extent (if any) of the claimant's contributory negligence. See earlier comments on written warnings and driver training schemes.

5.4. Interviewing witnesses and preparing statements

Interviewing witnesses

Consider the replies from your stock letters to witnesses. Do you need to meet the witness? In practice it is not always necessary to see witnesses since many accidents can accurately be described in a letter or telephone call but if the facts are complicated or the witnesses are poor correspondents do not hesitate to arrange to take a personal interview. Never be ashamed to admit that you do not understand a version of events and ask the witness to explain until you do understand. Harsh experience shows that some witnesses who seem superb on paper are terrible in the witness box. Therefore, if a witness's evidence is fundamental to your case and is disputed then you ought to meet that witness. Do not delegate this task as you need to make a personal assessment of the witness and ensure you are not simply being told the good news.

Preparing witness statements

Information from the client and witnesses will initially be contained in a number of different places: letters, statements given to the police, questionnaires and documents referred to. It is important to prepare full typewritten proofs at the earliest possible stage for the following reasons:

(1) One of the first things that the court will do under the case management provisions is to order a time for exchange of witness statements.

(2) If the client dies or is unavailable for the trial a signed statement in the proper form may be admissible to stand as evidence under the Civil Evidence Act 1968.

(3) Preparing a statement in a standard format allows you to check that you have asked all relevant questions.

(4) Statements will be sent to counsel when advising. As Part 36 offers (see Chapter 12) can be made on liability at an early stage then you and counsel will need the statements then.

Form of statements

It is sensible to ensure that all statements follow the requirements of CPR from the earliest stage.

Issues of fact

Any witness statement to be exchanged should relate only to issues of fact which the witness is able to prove from the witness's own knowledge. It must not therefore contain any hearsay evidence or any statement of information and belief or expressions of opinion. Obviously, at an early stage you may well wish to note inadmissible evidence since it can be useful in testing one witness statement against another or obtaining further information. However, it is important to remember that this is not evidence and should not appear in the final statement for exchange unless you have served the appropriate notice under the Civil Evidence Act 1995 (see Chapter 17). Such information should perhaps be put in a supplementary statement or simply recorded for your own benefit in an attendance note.

Comments or replies to other evidence

Witness statements should include all the information that a witness would give as evidence in chief but should not anticipate the evidence of a witness of the opposite party or deal with it in any way. However, you obviously will wish to know that witness's response to any allegations by the other party. The best way to obtain this is to send copies of the other party's letters or statements raising issues to your witnesses asking for comments. Supplemental statements can then be drafted if appropriate, although you may simply use your witnesses' responses for cross-examination purposes.

Paper

The CPR require that witness statements should be on A4 paper for exchange. Witness statements should be typed double spaced on one side of the paper only. Each page should be numbered. Do not bind the statement with plastic covers or thick plastic strips or anything which would hamper filing.

Style

Always remember that it is the witness's statement. The statement should be in the first person and, as far as possible, in the client's own style and words. It is all too easy to put words into a witness's mouth or slightly alter the emphasis of what a client said and so distort the version of events. Wherever possible use the words and phraseology given in the client's or witness's letters or previous statements. A defendant's counsel will soon pounce if a statement does not seem to fit in with what a witness says in cross-examination or is too sophisticated for the witness to have prepared; you do not wish to be the recipient of allegations of professional misconduct. Courts are also wary of standard statements hot off a word processor. Explain why you are asking the client to set out the details in their own words as sometimes the client seems to regard being asked to do a bit of homework as evidence that you are delegating work that you should be doing. This is all part of managing the client's expectations.

Details and format

The statement should set out the following:

(a) the full name of witness;

(b) an address or place of residence if made in a personal capacity, place of work if made in an official or occupational capacity and in any case it should also include job title;

(c) if the witness is under 18 it is good practice to include date of birth;

(d) if the witness is a party or employee of a party it should be stated; witness's information and belief;

(e) the statement, if it is to be relied upon, must include a statement of truth. See below and CPR Ord. 22.

The format should be as follows:

(a) the statement should follow the chronological sequence of the matters dealt with;

(b) it should be divided into paragraphs numbered consecutively, each containing a distinct portion of evidence;

(c) if the statement contains dates, figures or other numbers they should be expressed in figures not words; and

(d) if any documents are referred to, give a reference in the margin as to where they can be found or better still attach copies of the documents to the statement. This way you ensure that they are not overlooked when you are preparing the trial bundle.

(e) a statement of truth. You do need to explain this to witnesses. One way to do so without causing offence is simply to say that you are obliged to warn anyone whom you ask to sign a document including such a statement of the possible contempt consequences of knowingly providing false information and that this particular witness is not being singled out because of any doubts you have over veracity. At the very least this warning probably serves to ensure that statements are checked thoroughly.

Content of statements

Circumstances of the accident

The statement should record, in full detail, the circumstances of the accident in chronological order. The client's statement should cover all the information contained in the accident questionnaires (see Appendix A) and witness statements should set out as much of that information as is in the witness's knowledge.

Defendant's allegations

If you have now heard from the defendant with details of its defence or allegations of contributory negligence these should be dealt with in the statement so far as you would expect to see in evidence in chief. Do not develop the evidence beyond that actually given by the client or witness. Direct responses to the defendant's allegations should not be included in the statement and are best dealt with by way of a note or supplementary statement for use by counsel when cross-examining.

Injuries

Obviously the client's statement must also deal with the injuries. Include only a brief description of the injuries received since you will be serving a medical report. Specifically, refer to the medical report and confirm that it is accurate. Do set out in full the sort of information which will not be included in the report such as how the injuries affect the plaintiff's social life, hobbies, sports, relationships and ability to carry out everyday tasks such as dressing in the morning. Clients often relish telling you in great detail the effect the accident has had on their sex life—you only need to include a summary of this in the statement!

Special damage

The client's statement need not include a detailed special damage calculation. This will have to be prepared separately and served with the proceedings (see Chapter 7). However, you must show the reason for every item of special damage claimed and how the claimant can prove it, for example if you claim the cost of a car with power steering explain why the client is prevented by injuries from driving an ordinary car. Remember that if later you serve an updated schedule rather than doing another short statement to confirm the figures you can simply ask the client to sign a statement of truth on the document itself.

Employment details

Set out full employment details including the amount of any continuing wage loss and the prospect of the claimant finding employment. It will often be necessary to detail the claimant's employment history for a few years prior to the accident so you can prove that the client had a steady work record and that this would have been likely to continue had the accident not happened. This can be done by reference to the client's Curriculum Vitae which you should then attach to the statement.

Witness approval

Send the proof to the client or witness, ask him or her to read it carefully, check it is full and correct make any alterations or additions that may be necessary and sign the statement of truth. Send witnesses a stamped addressed envelope to return the statement. You should do everything to keep witnesses happy!

On this point remember, once the witness has signed and returned the statement, to send a copy back to the witness. This avoids the acute embarrassment of a witness glaring at you in court saying that the statement has not been seen for years prior to trial!

Time recording

Preparing witness statements is very time consuming. It is vital to keep a note on the file of the time spent in drafting, dictating and amending the statement otherwise the costs draftsperson will be unlikely to include the time on the bill.

5.5. Pre-action inspection and disclosure

Pre-action inspection

Introduction

If evidence may be destroyed or is necessary to prove liability it is important to inspect it at this stage and attend to take photographs and if appropriate, a video. This is particularly important in a workplace accident case or a construction case. If the accident involved a complicated piece of machinery it is advisable to obtain photographs of it so that solicitors and counsel (and eventually the trial judge) are clear as to its appearance and mode of operation. Remember that the accident might lead to the machine being modified (*e.g.* erection of fence or guard) so it is important to obtain photographs before that happens. Consider obtaining an instruction manual for the machine from the manufacturer. Under the protocol some of this information and documentation may already have been provided.

Defendant's consent

You should first ask for the defendant's consent to any inspection (whether with or without an expert). Unfortunately some insurance companies are obstructive on this point. The permission to inspect should not be granted subject to onerous conditions such as the claimant being committed to sending a copy of any expert's report to the defendant. If you do not wish to inspect at this stage you can ask the defendant's solicitors to take photographs and submit them for the claimant's approval.

Application

If the consent is withheld (or unreasonable conditions are imposed) and fortunately with the greater cooperation following the protocol and the CPR this is now rare the proposed claimant can apply to the court for an order that the proposed defendant be obliged to allow facilities for inspection and the taking of photographs and/or video films. Alternatively, you may decide to commence proceedings without further ado, and then issue an application in that action (see Precedent 6 in Appendix C). This is an easier procedure and carries less cost risk, but it is clearly inappropriate if inspection is a prerequisite to being able to decide whether the case is strong enough to issue. You should not hesitate to apply for pre-action inspection in cases where an inspection is vital in deciding whether to take the case further.

Remember that ultimately you will need the permission of the court to rely on any expert evidence. It is prudent to nominate an expert at the time of requesting expert facilities as a joint report is likely to carry greater weight than a unilaterally obtained one. It also makes it harder if, having failed to respond to your nomination, the defendant then seeks permission for its own report.

Experts can be expensive, although good ones are worth their weight in gold. Do agree this expenditure with the client, the Regional Legal Services Commission or any legal expense insurer where appropriate beforehand.

Pre-action disclosure

Disclosure of documents before commencement of proceedings

Just as an inspection of premises may be necessary to advise the client whether there is a case that is worth issuing, so may inspection of documents held by the proposed defendant be essential if the claimant is to know whether to proceed with an action. For example, the proposed defendant in a clinical negligence case may hold case notes and records which will enable the claimant's medical adviser to come to an initial view as to liability. Similarly, the proposed defendant may have records relating to the maintenance and repair of the vehicle involved in an accident.

Requesting documents from the proposed defendant

If all goes smoothly you will have requested and received all the disclosure that you need under the personal injury protocol. As stated earlier documents should be requested with the letter of claim and provided if liability is in dispute (see the protocol and Chapter 4 p. 31).

If, however, there is pertinent documentation not being disclosed you can apply for pre-issue disclosure. This remedy is no longer limited to personal injury claims. To provide your client with adequate cost protection and to satisfy the court that you have been reasonable do ask the defendant to disclose the documentation voluntarily, allowing a realistic time scale for disclosure, before you issue your application.

Making the application

The court will need to be satisfied that:

(a) both parties are likely to be parties in subsequent personal injury proceedings;

(b) the respondent has (or appears to be likely to have) in its possession, custody or power documents which would be relevant in those proceedings.

Note that if the court feels that disclosure is not necessary at this stage but can satisfactorily be postponed until due in the normal course of the action (see Chapter 15) it will not grant the order. In those circumstances the proposed defendant may be awarded the costs. However, if you provided ample opportunity for the defendant to indicate this prior to your application you may not be penalised in costs, and indeed may recover your costs if the defendant only raised the argument at the hearing. If disclosure is given costs should be awarded to your client provided you have adopted the above pre issue approach. Remember also that any hearing of less than a day means you are likely to be dealing with costs summarily assessed. Do not forget to file and serve a schedule of costs 24 hours before the hearing.

Procedure for pre-action disclosure

The application is made using the simple CPR Part 23 procedure. In other words, you simply issue a general form application rather than the old-fashioned originating summons procedure. Use form N244. This must be supported by evidence in the form of a witness statement which confirms that the defendant to the application is likely to be a party to subsequent proceedings as is the applicant and that had those proceedings started then the documents sought should be disclosed under the standard disclosure rules (see Chapter 15 for more detail on standard disclosure). The evidence must also establish that disclosure now is desirable to dispose fairly of the anticipated proceedings, or will assist in resolution and will save costs. In general terms, you need to convey to the court the necessity of seeing these documents and their relevance to early disposal or clarification of issues in dispute (see Appendix C Precedent 6).

It is good practice to draft an order sought. When doing this you do need to identify the document or class of documents sought precisely. That draft order may incorporate, in addition to requirements for disclosure, the time and place for disclosure and/or inspection.

Conclusion

When investigating an accident you should always consider whether you can obtain at this stage what you have traditionally had to wait for until later, namely inspection and disclosure. In a suitable case two applications could be combined into one. These applications should be required less and less frequently as the protocols bed down and courts deal severely with compliance failures.

5.6. Abandoning the claim

Having investigated liability you may decide that the client does not have a case and suggest that proceedings not be issued. If so, make sure you cover your professional position by formally advising your client in writing as to:

(a) your advice; and

(b) the three-year limitation period so the client knows the position should s/he subsequently decide to sue. Use stock letter 14.

Remember the purpose of investigating claims is precisely that. If investigation reveals the client has no reasonable prospect of success the sooner the client is advised the better. The days of a client only being told by counsel at the door of the court that the claim is hopeless always reflected badly on the legal profession. Proper investigation at an early stage should, save in the exceptional cases of late and unexpected fresh evidence, enable you to take a definitive view of liability at this stage. The longer a claim continues the greater the client's expectations will be.

6. Expert and Medical Reports

6.1. Before instructing an expert

Purpose of an expert report

You may need an expert report to prove every aspect of your client's claim; liability (*e.g.* engineer's report) injury (*e.g.* medical report) and special damage (*e.g.* accountant's report). A report may have more than one purpose (*e.g.* a consultant's report on liability and injury in a clinical negligence case). Before instructing an expert you must be clear as to what you want from the report and what it should cover. Not only will this ensure that you apply to the correct expert at the correct time in proceedings it will also allow you to explain to the expert exactly what is needed and thus get a better report. Consider whether a report is really needed; judges are very scathing of supposed 'experts' giving evidence on what is really common sense or general knowledge. In one case the judge asked 'Do I really need an expert to tell me that falling off a ladder is dangerous?' Under the CPR you will need court permission to use any expert. If permission is refused you will not be able to recover the costs involved in instructing that expert.

Obtaining evidence

Before instructing an expert consider whether you have made or can make available all evidence necessary for the expert to prepare the report. An expert is only commenting on facts in the light of specialist knowledge so ensure that the expert has all the information available. This includes

(1) for medical experts: either all medical notes or an appropriate form of authority releasing the notes to the expert a clear letter of instruction in compliance with the personal injury protocol requirements.
(2) for engineering experts: access to the site of the accident or machinery/workplace causing injury; your client's version of events by witness statement or otherwise; the defendant's version of events usually by means of the formal response to the letter of claim; all relevant documents disclosed

(3) for accountancy experts: tax returns, assessments and any accounts; any relevant statistical data such as average earning figures for professions; any relevant medical evidence if that defines a period of absence or restricted employment.

If preparing the instruction shows that you need further evidence before instructing any expert then delay the instruction. You are unlikely to recover the cost of an expert if the report is incomplete or has to be amended at a later date because the original instruction is premature. If you cannot obtain the information without court intervention then apply for an order for pre-action disclosure/ inspection (see Chapter 5) before instructing the expert.

6.2. Types of expert

Some of the most common types of expert you may consider are set out below. Obviously this is not an exhaustive list and you, together with your colleagues and Counsel will have to consider the appropriate type of expert in any given case.

Liability

Road accident

Engineer or accident reconstruction expert If after receiving the statements, police reports and defendant's response to letter before action it is clear that liability is in issue or there is an issue as to contributory negligence you may need an expert to examine the accident site and damage to vehicles, to indicate whether these are consistent with the statements and give an opinion as to speed, pre-accident position of parties and liability. Increasingly, courts take the view that reconstruction experts trespass on their jurisdiction. Do consider carefully whether such an expert adds evidence of genuine value or will simply add speculation.

Weather conditions report If there is a dispute as to lighting or weather causing the accident it is possible to obtain a report from the Meterological Office at Sutton House, London Road, Bracknell, Berks RG12 2SY.

Workplace accident

You may need:

(a) An engineer if the accident involved the use of complicated machinery; or

(b) An ergonomist if consideration has to be given to the safety of a particular system of working.

(c) A factory inspector—if it is a workplace accident case it may be possible to obtain a factual statement (including a description of any machine involved and how it works) from the factory inspector. The minimum charge is about £75 (to be paid in advance) (see stock letter 14). However, this may be of limited evidential value as the role of the factory inspector is different from an expert addressing civil negligence issues.

When to obtain liability reports

Traditionally, many solicitors did not obtain reports until after the Defence had been filed. This approach had many disadvantages, from the extra cost of late amendments to pleadings to the discontinuance of an issued claim. With the early disclosure of documents under the protocol there is no excuse now for failing to deal with expert evidence pre-issue save in those cases raising limitation concerns. Even then expert evidence should be addressed in the four months available between issue and service of proceedings.

The general rule therefore is to obtain expert evidence on liability as soon as possible after obtaining the necessary information to allow the expert to advise once you are satisfied that liability is likely to be in dispute either because of a formal denial under the protocol or a failure to respond at all.

Injury

Types of report

There are various types of report which can be used to determine injury. These include:

(a) a G.P.'s report. If any injury is trivial and is completely healed then a G.P.'s report may be sufficient but a consultant's report will usually be needed as a G.P.'s views do not carry much weight. Proportionality is relevant and should be considered. Can you justify obtaining a consultant's report?

(b) treating hospital's report. In a straightforward case it may be sufficient to rely on a report from the doctor who treated the claimant in hospital. Write to the hospital where the patient was treated. This is rarely appropriate except in the most straightforward cases. Accident and emergency consultants rarely have the time to assist, but the bigger draw-back is that treatment will have been almost immediately post accident. If there are any ongoing symptoms, however brief, then the treater is not going to be able to help. In such situations consider obtaining a report from your client's G.P's surgery as A&E will have sent details of treatment to the G.P. There can be general difficulties with reports from those who have treated your client:

(1) they may not be deemed to be independent;
(2) they tend to put best case scenarios. Inevitably, treaters like to think that treatment recommended will be successful. The Law Commission's report

"Personal Injury Compensation: How much is enough?" (1994 Law Com. No. 225) suggested that pain tends to continue longer than predicted and in about 10 per cent of cases likely return to work dates were seriously over-optimistic;

(3) they are not always experienced in writing reports.

With the protocol requirement of pre-instruction nomination and CPR issues of proportionality always foremost these reports are really only suitable where you have a client making a full recovery within a week or so of the accident. In such cases you may wish to try to persuade the defendant to deal with the claim without going to the expense of obtaining any medical evidence, simply relying on a brief statement from your client.

(c) Independent consultant's report. Ensure that you are going to the correct type of specialist for your client's injuries. The most common is orthopaedic but if you are in any doubt about the range of injuries talk to colleagues, the treating hospital or the GP about the appropriate specialist. You may need a report from more than one specialist, *e.g.* an ENT consultant and an orthopaedic expert. If in doubt start with the obvious instruction. If that expert feels that you need to obtain a report in another specialisation the expert will usually say so particularly if you raise this in your letter of instruction as a concern. The CPR and the concept of proportionality militate against a proliferation of experts unless justified. If in doubt ask someone who knows. Particular types of report to consider are set out below;

(d) Orthopaedic report. This is the most commonly used medical report dealing with injuries from fractures to soft tissue (whiplash) injuries;

(e) Neurologist report. In head injury cases you should start with a neurological report. This will lead you on to any other specialisms to consider for this type of injury such as psychiatrists or psychologists. Indeed, many psychologists will not produce a head injury report without first seeing the neurologist's comments;

(f) Psychiatrist report. In head injury cases and in more generalised trauma injuries;

(g) Psychologist report. In head injury cases and in more generalised trauma cases.

Recently, in soft tissue injury cases there has been a move towards those who treat such injuries on a daily basis, such as chiropractors, physiotherapists, osteopaths and acupuncturists. It may be that by the time of the next edition you will be using their services more. However, at the moment orthopaedic consultants still seem to be the expected expert in the majority of such cases.

When to obtain medical evidence

You would not normally instruct a doctor until:

(a) you have investigated liability and it is clear the case is not hopeless. In most cases this should mean that there is no difficulty instructing as early as you want.

(b) the injuries have stabilised. There is little point in obtaining a report on a broken leg still in plaster;

However beware of the three-year limitation period for starting proceedings and remember that a medical report setting out all injuries must be served with the particulars of claim. Is it better to delay taking proceedings until the condition has stabilised or to carry on with partial information? If on limitation or if the case is disputed and may be suitable for split trial obtain a preliminary report to enable you to serve proceedings. It may also be possible to enter judgment on liability and then wait for stabilisation of the injuries to assess damages. Doctors are notoriously slow in preparing reports and these often raise further questions which need to be resolved. Always ensure that you have enough time to obtain, consider and serve the report without breaking the three-year limitation period or any court imposed timescale for disclosure.

Nowadays, more and more solicitors are turning to medico/legal agencies who source reports from panels of experts who are contracted to the agency on guaranteed turnaround timescales. These reports cost a bit more but in an era of pressure to expedite claims provide a useful service.

Whenever considering instructing a medical expert do put nominations of experts to the defendant, affording a reasonable time for response. This is a personal injury protocol requirement. Breach may mean that the court does not give you permission to rely upon any report you may subsequently obtain if the content is disputed. This has inevitable cost as well as practical ramifications. The protocol does provide for the use of agencies who act as intermediaries for obtaining medical reports. The best way to nominate is to obtain three experts of the specific discipline you require from the agency and nominate the agency indicating that it will use one of the experts whom you then list. Normally, this presents no difficulties. Indeed many insurers now use agencies themselves (see stock letter 16).

Finally, do remember to ensure that your client is happy to instruct you to obtain medical evidence.

Special damage

Types of report

In relatively simple cases it may be possible to prove and calculate special damages without expert help (see Chapter 7). Always consider whether an expert could help to explain, collate or provide specialist information:

(1) Forensic accountant: An accountant can help to collate and sort information and extrapolate it to show future loss of earnings. You can use the client's own accountant who will have in-depth information on the client's financial affairs but often it is better to use an expert forensic accountant who is:

(a) used to collating evidence and preparing it for court;
(b) independent and can give a fresh eye to the evidence and is not tied to the client's present accounting system;
(c) used to maximising profits for the purpose of showing loss of earnings not, as most accountants do, minimising them to mitigate tax—many self-employed clients will come to you who have had a good lifestyle but, mysteriously, their accounts have always shown a loss for tax purposes;
(d) might also be able to advise on proper investment of any damages or a structured settlement.

(2) Actuarial report: Sometimes a plaintiff will have lost pension rights through early retirement brought on by injuries. In such a case the calculation of the loss in value of those pension rights can be extremely complicated.

(3) Care report: If a client is severely disabled a care report can show the cost of future care, nursing and any equipment needs.

(4) Employment consultant: An employment consultant can use demographic trends to show the likelihood of a client obtaining another job. Judges are not keen on these reports and may disallow them saying they only contain matters in common knowledge and are not truly the subject of expert evidence. Accordingly, since April 1999 there has been a marked decline in the use of employment experts.

When to obtain special damage reports

If the case is clear on liability and likely to settle then obtain expert evidence as soon as possible so that you will have all necessary information when negotiating. Delay in obtaining a special damage report may mean that you are not in an adequate position to try to resolve matters pre issue which may cause cost consequences, or pre or post issue that you are not in a position to advise on a Part 36 payment/offer. Obviously, those special damages consequential on medical evidence should not be obtained until you have a final prognosis unless a preliminary report is required to quantify on issue if limitation issues arise. Again, always consider your protocol and Part 35 joint expert obligations.

Mixed purpose reports

These include a consultant in:

(a) a clinical negligence case who would be advising both on liability and injury, condition and prognosis. Ensure that you have the correct expert to cover both areas or, if necessary, use two separate experts; for example in a case where a G.P. failed to diagnose correctly you may need a hospital consultant to advise on the injury and a G.P. expert to advise on the standard of treatment expected of an ordinary G.P.;

(b) a "creeping injury" case. If the client's injury is caused by work conditions, *e.g.* overuse injury, asbestosis or product liability (smoking or drug cases) you will need an expert report to establish the causative link with the defendant as well as describing the injury.

When to obtain mixed purpose reports

These reports must be obtained as soon as possible on the negligence aspect since they will be the main evidence on liability. Do ensure that the expert has all necessary medical notes, statements and evidence to be able to advise. You may need a further updating report on condition and progress once liability has been established.

6.3. Finding an expert

Once you have decided the type of expert you need how do you find one that is suitable?

Experts already on the case

There may be a temptation to use the treating doctor or the client's own accountant. However, you are often better with independent experts both for the reasons set out above and because you will know them and be able to judge the reports.

Firm's approved experts

Most firms keep lists of experts used regularly and approved. Maintenance of such a list was obligatory for legal aid franchising and is for membership of the Personal Injury Panel. Keeping such a list is easy; either on database or card index system. You should update it regularly. All comments on the expert, flattering or not, should be recorded. If you are using an expert on the list who is not personally known to you do discuss the expert with the fee earner who last instructed him or her to ensure that the expert is right for the case.

The advantages of such a list are that you:

(a) know the expert has provided a good and helpful report for someone in the firm;

(b) can ensure that the expert is from the right discipline;

(c) can pool useful information;

(d) will build up a personal relationship with an expert who is instructed regularly. This will allow you to assess the report in light of other reports prepared for you;

(e) can keep information about the availability of the experts.

Personal recommendation

Do not feel obliged only to use experts on the list if you are not sure there are any who are good for the case. A list is only useful if it is extensive and constantly amended and updated. If there is no suitable expert on your firm's list try asking injury lawyers at other firms, counsel or other people in a similar discipline to the expert you require for recommendation. If you do decide to use an expert who is not on the list you should note on your file why the expert was used and remember to add him or her to the list and approve the expert or otherwise once you have seen the report.

Lawyers' organisations

There are three main organisations:

(1) Action for Victims of Medical Accidents (AVMA) keeps an excellent list of experts prepared to give evidence in clinical negligence cases.

(2) The Association of Personal Injury Lawyers (APIL) has set up a database of personal injury experts.

(3) The Law Society runs a helpline in conjunction with *The Law Society Directory of Expert Witnesses* (1998 edition), providing the names and addresses of experts in various disciplines and will also undertake searches on request to find an appropriate expert.

Case reports

Try reading transcripts of recent similar cases or case reports to find out which experts were used and whether the evidence was approved by the judge. If you are considering using an expert from this source speak to the claimant's solicitor in that case who will normally be prepared to comment on the expert's usefulness and suitability.

Adverts and expert directories

Various journals (*Law Society Gazette*, *Solicitors Journal*) run expert issues and these usually include advertisements by experts as well as articles which can be a useful source. There are also some expert directories including the *Law Society*

Directory of Expert Witnesses (see above) in which all experts who appear have to be endorsed by solicitors. You should also look out for books and articles written by experts or consider those whom you have seen lecturing or indeed who have impressed you when appearing on the other side, either on paper or in the witness box.

Professional organisations

You can try the professional organisation of the type of expert you require who can often provide recommendations of experts used to acting in legal cases. Obviously if any expert who is not on your firm's approved list is used you should note on the file why that expert is being used, what source the expert came from and add the expert to the approved list as appropriate.

6.4. Paying for the report

Expert reports are expensive! Previous editions of this book gave guideline figures but these seem to increase so often and vary so widely from discipline to discipline that they are no longer helpful. Instead we suggest the following.

Estimate

Obtain an estimate of the likely expense from the expert—in particular find out the hourly rate if not a fixed fee estimate.

Money on account

If the client is paying privately inform him/her of the reason for the report and likely cost. Obtain the client's authority to instruct the expert and ask for money on account to cover the expert's fees. Remember that you are responsible for paying the expert's fee even if the money is not received from your client. The protocol now requires medical experts to review notes. This leads to release fees. Ensure you advise your client that these will be incurred.

Special conditions

If payment is to be on any kind of conditional basis or not paid until determination of the case then agree this in writing with the expert. At a time when solicitors seem to be funding a growing amount of disbursement one of the major attractions of the medico/legal agencies is the fee referral scheme that they operate. Whilst many are linked to volume of instructions do not be afraid to ask for deferral.

Public funding

This is now of limited relevance. If pertinent seek prior authority on the fee not only from your client but also from the Regional Legal Services Commission.

6.5. How to instruct an expert

Telephoning

Before sending written instructions it is wise to telephone the expert (particularly if it is an expert that you have not used before) to ascertain the following:

(a) if the expert undertakes this kind of case;

(b) how long you will have to wait for the client to see the expert (if appropriate);

(c) how long you will have to wait for the report;

(d) an estimate of the likely fee and any special arrangements as to the fees;

(e) to discuss any particularly unusual features of the case;

(f) if necessary to ask the expert about experience and qualifications;

(g) find out any special requirements the expert has or any particular way the expert would like to be instructed.

This will help the expert when first receiving the papers, ensure you are not wasting time by sending the case to someone who cannot undertake it and may help to give you a general impression of the expert.

You must be open in joint instructions and in instructing an agreed expert and reveal any communications to the other side.

Writing to the expert

Your letter of instruction is important; it should tell the expert:

(a) what the case is about;

(b) why the expert is needed;

(c) what you want covered in the report;

(d) where to obtain all necessary information for preparing the report; and

(e) when you need the report.

There is an excellent suggested letter of instruction for a medical expert in the protocol. Use it (see Appendix I).

Protocol letter to medical expert

This covers:

(a) The client's name, address, telephone number and, if relevant, hospital record number and date of birth. Enclose all these details so the expert can find any records and contact the client direct to make an appointment if necessary;

(b) Details of who is instructing, *e.g.* joint instruction, unilateral instruction or agreed expert basis;

(c) Details in summary form of the injuries;

(d) A request that the notes are reviewed. Remember (if relevant) to include a signed authority for release of notes (stock letter 22);

(e) A request that the expert considers any relevant pre-accident injuries or illnesses;

(f) A request that the expert considers the reasonableness of any time off work and in the cases of continuing absence comments on work prospects in the future;

(g) Any special needs that your client may have, *e.g.* home visit required or language problems;

(h) For those experts unfamiliar with Civil Procedure Rules relevant extracts and highlighted obligations. There is also a BMA guide for the medical profession to which reference should be made.

You must also impose some time limit if possible and in limitation cases ensure that you remind the expert of any necessary timescale.

Non medical experts

(see stock letter 15)
This covers

(a) Your client's statement. Remember that in joint instruction that means the defendant will see it at this stage;

(b) Relevant documents revealed in disclosure on the question of liability that will help an engineer or ergonomist;

(c) Photos of equipment if the equipment is no longer available for inspection;

(d) Previous accounts and supporting documents for a forensic accountant;

(e) Similar Civil Procedure Rules guidance and where appropriate relevant extracts;

(f) Details of who is instructing, *e.g.* joint instruction, unilateral instruction or agreed expert basis

(g) A request for professional qualifications and relevant experience;

(h) Agreement reached on fees to be charged. You should confirm who is responsible for the fee. If no fee has been agreed you may wish to ask the expert to contact you when he or she has had a chance to examine the papers forwarded to give an estimate then of the likely fee. Always pause to consider proportionality. For example, if forensic accountants quote £500 to do a loss of earnings calculation for someone self employed who has only a few weeks loss of earnings give the defendant the chance to agree losses without such an instruction. If they decline you will be able to justify the fee even if disproportionate.

You must also impose some time limit if possible and in limitation cases ensure that you remind the expert of any necessary timescale.

6.6. How to read an expert report

Chasing the report

Ensure you receive the report in the time requested. Diarise the date carefully, remind the expert on the due date and frequently thereafter until the report is received. Your client will probably understand why there is a delay waiting for an appointment but prolonged periods between examination and receipt of report are hard to justify.

Understanding the report

Read the report carefully and ensure you understand it fully. For a detailed explanation of medical terms consult a medical directory (*e.g. Pears' Medical Encyclopedia*). Diagrams of bones and muscles in the human body are reproduced in Appenedix H at the back of this book. If there is anything you do not understand in the report ask the expert to explain. Ultimately, the report may go before a judge. Under the Civil Procedure Rules the expert is unlikely to be at court as permission is likely to be given to rely on the written report. It is imperative, therefore, that the report is put in simple, understandable terms. Often, your client will ask for an explanation. It cannot be confidence-inspiring if you cannot give it.

Checking the report

Ensure the report is full and correct and fulfils your instructions. If anything is missing or if any information is incomplete or incorrect ask the expert to include it. If the instruction was joint any further correspondence that you have with the expert concerning the report should be disclosed.

Problems in reports

Problems with reports and consequences

The difficulty with an agreed or joint expert is that the defendant can see the report whatever the content. The most common problems are therefore;

(a) that an adverse engineer's report may be the end of a case; and

(b) that an unfavourable medical report, particularly one suggesting compensation neurosis, functional overlay or malingering will have severe consequences on quantum.

Sometimes it is right that such reports do cause such outcomes. On other occasions this can be unfair. Your client may indicate that an examination was only cursory and have concerns that comments made have been misinterpreted, taken out of context or worse still that the comments attributed were not made. It is perhaps in recognition of this that the Court of Appeal in *Daniel v. Walker* [2000] 1 W.L.R. 1381 has recently accepted that a joint report is a starting point and does not preclude a party from seeking court permission for a further expert. Whilst there is guidance given to suggest that fishing expeditions for a favourable report based only on frivolous concerns with the initial report will not be allowed the case seems to allow a greater degree of flexibility than the protocol and rules themselves suggest. This has been followed by the case of *Cosgrove v. Pattison, The Times,* February 13, 2001 in which Neuberger J. set out a list of suggested considerations for determining whether a further report would be allowed. Accordingly whilst there will still be credibility issues to overcome an initial unfavourable report may not be fatal to a claim.

Sometimes the expedient of seeking another expert opinion will be unnecessary because the CPR do envisage parties having the opportunity to ask questions of the expert concerning the report. Sometimes this can resolve perceived problems and clarify misunderstandings.

Whilst the problem is less where the expert has been instructed unilaterally there are still credibility issues because if you originally nominated one expert and sometime later nominate another the defendant is likely to guess that means you have received a report that you do not wish to rely upon. Even in this situation there are clear cost consequences for the client that need to be explained.

(c) the expert may not have addressed all pertinent issues. For example, a medical expert may state that a pre-accident problem may have been brought forward by the accident injuries but does not elaborate. It is essential that the expert puts some time period on the acceleration of injury to enable quantum to be determined. In such a case both parties would want the expert to clarify the point and he or she should be asked to do so.

6.7. Reporting to the client

Send a copy of the report to your client explaining it in language the client will understand. Tell your client the effect it has on the case. Ask for your client's comments on the report—in particular any allegations of malingering or anything that does not accord with your client's instructions. If the report is unfavourable raise with the client the possibility of obtaining another report, explain how that will be paid for and the risk that the client will not recover on assessment the costs of a two reports even if the court given permission for a second report. In legal expense cases, either pre or post accident also consider whether permission is needed from the insurers to proceed when unfavourable reports have been received and what the cost consequences are of obtaining a second opinion.

Where you do not think a second report can be justified or the client does not wish to pursue that possibility and the upshot is that you decide that your client no longer has reasonable prospects of succeeding with the claim then you should advise the client to abandon it (see letter 14).

6.8. Defendant's expert report

For the reasons set out earlier there will be fewer cases now where the claimant and the defendant each have their own expert. Certainly the intention of the civil reforms is clear that the court, and therefore the parties, must consider a jointly instructed expert and in fast track cases that is the norm. This means that each party having one expert of a like discipline is likely to arise only in more serious injury claims on quantum and in clinical negligence cases on liability and causation. You should determine in such cases whether a defendant's request for facilities for its own expert to examine is reasonable against this backdrop. This is likely to be in respect of medical experts as the defendant can usually obtain its own engineer's report without you knowing and seek court permission afterwards. If you decide that the request is reasonable do remember to ensure that the defendant agrees to pay all your client's reasonable expenses in attending. You should usually ask for a payment on account of these in advance. It is also best to ensure that appointments are made through you. This avoids the scenario of your client being sent an appointment at very short notice and attending without having an opportunity to discuss what to expect with you beforehand (see letter 18 to notify the client of the request for facilities and stock letter 19 to write to the defendant to put terms).

You will see in letter 19 reference to disclosure of the defendant's expert evidence. The reason for this is that the personal injury protocol provides that prior to issue of proceedings, assuming limitation considerations do not militate against this, the court will expect you in most cases to afford the defendant an opportunity to settle. To do so you will, of necessity, have to disclose your medical evidence. What you wish to ensure is that if the defendant makes an offer at that stage based in reliance on its own evidence, he or she is obliged to send you a copy. If the offer is put by way of Part 36 offer, the rule requires this anyway under its openness obligations.

Finally under this heading you may find that some insurers obtain their own liability or medical evidence even where there is a joint report. Whilst they cannot rely on such a report and do not have to disclose it many use this tactic to enable them better to put questions to the joint expert or for the cross-examination of the joint expert if they wish to discredit the evidence but either do not want or have been denied by the court a formal second opinion.

These comments simply highlight the crucial nature of expert evidence. To some degree all personal injury cases are reliant upon it. The problems referred to illustrate how important it is to have reliable experts who understand their function and the consequences of their comments. This all leads back to the importance of correct expert selection at the outset.

7. Special Damage and Interest

7.1. Special damage: introduction

What is special damage?

Special damage strictly means the claimant's financial loss between the date of the accident and the date of trial. However, the term is frequently used to include also the claimant's projected future and continuing loss after the trial.

Net loss

The basic rule is that the claimant must be put in the position s/he would have been in had the accident not occurred. Therefore the claimant can only claim net loss, for example a claimant will claim loss of earnings, net of income tax and national insurance, save where the claimant seeks a loss of profit of a business when the loss claimed is gross. In the former instance compensation is tax free. In the latter it is taxable to the business.

Statement of special damage

The pre-action protocol requires a claimant to provide details of special damage as early as possible. In practice it is often impossible to do so until you have received a medical report. In such cases you should give the defendant an indication of the broad heads of loss that are likely to be pursued, *e.g.* care costs, equipment costs, loss of earnings, medicinal costs and travelling expenses. Obviously there may be some losses that you can and will quantify early for the purposes of interim payment, *e.g.* vehicle pre-accident value/repair cost, hire costs/loss of use and short term earning losses.

Accuracy of calculation

As soon as you can quantify the special damages you should do so as accurately as possible. However, it has to be accepted that it is often difficult to produce totally accurate figures, and some assumptions have to be made. The aim is to produce an overall calculation that is reasoned and clear and as accurate as possible. Such a schedule will present your client's best case scenario. Again, as a point of client management in anticipation of a later date when offers are received it is important that this is explained clearly to the client who might otherwise wonder why any sum below this should even be considered. It is a starting point from which, save in small and completely non-controversial cases, you will negotiate. Of course, later, if an offer of settlement or if a payment into court is made then it will be necessary to consider the figures very carefully with the client to decide what is realistically likely to be awarded at trial.

7.2. Working out the specials

The questionnaire

The first step is to take proper instructions from the client. At the initial interview you will have asked the client to complete the General Personal Injury Questionnaire (Appendix A Questionnaire 1) and to continue to keep a full note of all losses and expenses arising from the accident, and to forward the list (with all receipts) when requested.

Expenses other than wage loss

Now is the time for you to ask for that list, together with an estimate of likely future expenses, which should include as well as wage loss:

- travel expenses (to hospital, to G.P. for any other treatment and for expert report);
- medical expenses (prescription fees and also private medical fees are recoverable);
- clothes;
- post;
- telephone;
- extra home help;
- special equipment necessary or purchased, *e.g.* modified bath taps, automatic car. See also below
- sums paid to others for work the client would otherwise have done, *e.g.* DIY, gardening.

Advantages of the questionnaire

Listing such information in a questionnaire as in Appendix A Questionnaire 1 will help concentrate the client's mind and so reduce the chances of omitting particular items; it will also avoid any future dispute should the client later remember other expenses and blame you for not including them in the claim.

The use of a questionnaire will help ensure that all the special damage information is kept in one convenient place. Otherwise, it is easy to overlook individual items, if they are referred to in various letters from the client that have been received over a considerable period of time. So, try to get the client to complete the questionnaire, which can then be placed in a separate special damage sub-folder. If later letters are received with further special damage information you may wish to put the original on the correspondence file, but a copy in the special damage sub-folder.

Additional information

It is helpful if the questionnaire also includes the following information (see Appendix A Questionnaire 1):

- name and address of employers at time of accident;
- name and address of subsequent employers;
- name and address of pre-accident employers (if client had only been in this employment for a short time at the time of the accident);
- did the client receive statutory sick pay?
- in addition, did the client receive extra sick pay (*i.e.* on top of SSP) under a sick pay scheme? If so, does that extra sick pay have to be refunded to the employer? (see below);
- the client's national insurance number;
- the names of the various types of benefits received by the client since the accident (there is no need to know how much the client received);
- the addresses of any DSS offices from which the client claimed benefit;
- the address of any Job Centre from which the client claimed unemployment benefit;
- details of any Disablement Employment Adviser who has assisted the client;
- if the claimant was self-employed:
  - what National Insurance payments have been made historically; name and address of accountant;
  - name, address, and reference of tax office (with client's signed authority for Inland Revenue to supply solicitor with details of client's tax affairs);
  - copy tax returns;
- does the client claim a married person's, or single person's, personal allowance for income tax?

7.3. Losses other than loss of earnings

Losses other than loss of earnings are usually fairly easy to quantify (see p. 66 above and the questionnaire in Appendix A Questionnaire 1 for heads of possible losses and expenses). Obviously the need for each item claimed must be strictly proved, so ensure that the client keeps receipts, mitigates all loss and proves (by way of statement, expert report or other method) the need for the expense. However, some losses can be more problematic and arguments most commonly arise in a number of areas.

Car hire

A client must prove that he or she acted reasonably in hiring a car but this will usually be presumed if the client's car was written off or damaged in the accident and s/he hired a similar car to the previous one (*Sanders v. Templar* [1994] 1 A.C. 142, HL). The traditionally miserly offers made by insurance companies for the inconvenience of loss of use of a vehicle has lead to the rapid expansion of the "credit hire" market, an area beset by legal arguments and lack of certainty. The leading case of *Dimmond v. Lovell* clarified the position somewhat and now many insurers and credit hire companies have come to terms. However, others have not. For the unwary this is a complicated field full of potential pitfalls. Before embarking on a case involving credit hire you should seek a more detailed explanation of the law.

This boom in credit hire has meant that traditional hire rates (to which defendants used to object) are now seen to be reasonable. The ABI has also intervened, setting rates, although these are not universally accepted as some see them as a device to try to rein back charges artificially.

Loss of use of car

A client may be able to claim damages for loss of use of a car (often as much as £100 per week) even if this loss continues because the client has not been able to afford to repair the car (*Mattocks v. Mann, The Times*, June 19, 1992). Again, the sums claimed in credit hire cases have rendered large loss of use claims reasonable by comparison.

Voluntary care

If care is provided voluntarily through love and affection the plaintiff is still entitled to claim the full value of these services from the defendant (unless the person who provided the free services was the defendant; see *Hunt v. Severs* [1994] 2 A.C. 350, HL). In such a case ask the defendant insurers whether they will pay for the defendant to provide the service. If this cheaper than sourcing it elsewhere they may agree and then take no point on this later.

7.4. Loss of earnings

The main special damage item is likely to be the loss of earnings whilst the client was off work.

Pre-accident earnings

Wage details should be obtained from the employer setting out the client's pre-accident earnings (use stock letter 23 and authority 24), unless the employer is the defendant and you are in correspondence with its solicitor in which case ask them to forward figures. Whilst you ask for these in the protocol letter do update regularly in prolonged absence cases as there are likely to have been at least annual wage increases.

Checking figures are adequate

Check that the figures provided are adequate; the pre-accident average should be based on a period of at least 13 weeks but check that the client did not have abnormally low earnings in that period (for example, if the work is seasonal or if there was no overtime in that period due to a temporary illness or work shortage). Have there been any wage increases during the period since the start of the list? Is there now more overtime available? Has the claimant lost the chance of promotion, or missed a periodic bonus (for instance, at Christmas, or during holiday)?

Loss of company car

Has there been the loss of use of a company car? If so, how much is that worth? The going rate seems to be around £5,500 per annum. Generally, calculate the loss on AA cost per mile figures, but then be prepared to compromise!

Obtaining details from the tax office

If the client has changed jobs over the years and full wage details cannot be obtained from the various ex-employers, write to the local tax office for copies of the client's tax returns and assessments during those years. The tax office will also be able to provide the names and addresses of the previous employers if these are not known. Remember that the tax office will require the client's written authority before forwarding any of this information; use stock letter 26 to the client for consent, and write to the Inland Revenue using stock letter 25. Although detailed information going back over many years is rarely relevant You may find that some tax offices only retain records for a limited period such as six years. This is only likely to cause problems in disease cases.

Specific discovery

If the tax office cannot provide the full information it may exceptionally be necessary to obtain an order for specific disclosure against an ex-employer who will not supply the particulars requested (see Chapter 5).

Lost earnings

Apart from knowing the client's earnings at the time of the accident, you will need to know the level of wages the client would have earned between the date of the accident and the date of return to work (assuming the client has returned to work).

Client's estimate

Ask the client to give an estimate of the likely loss of earnings over that period.

Employer's estimate

Ask the employers for their estimate. The shorter the period the more likely that the pre accident wage will be the basis for the figure.

Comparables

If it is a large firm, they may be able to supply wage figures for a comparable employee (make sure the figures are gross, not net, because individual tax circumstances could distort the comparison), and that the employee in question is a true comparable (*i.e.* similar length of service; similar skills; similar amount of overtime, etc. worked).

Defendant's estimate

Similar principles apply if the employer is the defendant in the action; ask the defendant's solicitors to obtain a letter from their client setting out the earnings the claimant would have received, or alternatively ask for earnings of a comparable employee. In longer absence cases ask for details of percentage pay rises that would have arisen and when.

If all else fails as good a starting point as any is to take annual inflation rates and increase the gross pre-accident salary by the same rate. Unless the defendant then produces evidence to the contrary it is hard to challenge such an approach as a court is unlikely to be persuaded that pay rises would be less than inflation.

Finally, you must ensure that however you obtain the figures you check them with the client.

Expert report

It might also be worth considering obtaining comparable earnings from different employers in the same field and in complex cases you might consider obtaining an expert report (see Chapter 6).

Specific disclosure of wage records

If it is necessary to obtain wage records from anyone who is not a party to the action (*e.g.* previous employer) then apply for specific disclosure against that person. Refer to Precedent 7 for the steps to be taken. Do not simply rely upon being able to serve a witness summons for production of the documents at the trial. It is important to have an estimate which is as accurate as possible in the schedule served with the claim because this may well form the basis of settlement negotiations. As a general rule, the claimant will have to bear the costs of specific disclosure against a non-party; however, the claimant may eventually be able to recover them from the defendant, by claiming them as costs of the main action. This of course assumes that the claimant ultimately succeeds in the action. In any event, special consideration and advice must be given to the client prior to such an application as the costs to the non party will have to be paid there and then.

Statutory sick pay and repayment of sick pay

An employee who is off work is likely to receive statutory sick pay (SSP) for the first 28 weeks of absence in any three years. At the end of that time, the employee will no longer be entitled to SSP and so will have to claim DSS benefits (*e.g.* incapacity benefit; income support). Until April 1994 SSP paid by employers was refunded by the State and this still applies for some smaller employers; if there are any SSP payments which come into this category the defendant will have to repay any SSP paid to the client under the Compensation Recovery Scheme (see below).

The stock letter to use when asking employers for details of wage losses (stock letter 23) asks for full details of SSP paid. In addition, it asks if there is a separate sick payment scheme. Often, employers (especially in the public service) will pay an employee full net basic wage whilst off sick, and this will be more than the SSP entitlement. However, this payment may, in theory, be made as a loan by the employers with the employee being under an obligation to refund the loan should damages be recovered for the accident from a third party. Thus, it is possible that the client may innocently state there was no wage loss, since full wages were received whilst off work. Indeed it is amazing how often a client does not appreciate this contractual repayment obligation until you ask to see the contract. If in doubt ask the client to check with the employer's personnel department. If there is a contractual recoupment provision take a copy of the contract and ask the employer to confirm the amount. Then simply incorporate the amount as you would any ordinary loss of earnings giving disclosure of the documents to explain how the loss arises. Most schemes also provide for partial repayment only where the full amount is not recovered, such as a contributory negligence case or where medical evidence leads to only limited special damage recovery. There can be difficulties where a lump sum is accepted for less than the full value of the claim without any agreement on the precise recovery for loss of earnings. In such cases you will have to do the best you can to break down the settlement and agree it with the employer, providing that your client authorises you to do this.

This leads to the final point which is that the contractual requirement is your client's. Some are happy for you to deduct the sum from the settlement monies and send it direct to the employer. Others indicate that they will deal with the employers themselves. Be careful what information you release to an employer after settlement in the latter cases since by releasing confidential information you may find that you are in breach of your professional responsibilities.

Self-employed claimant

Problems can arise with a self-employed claimant who has not kept full (or accurate) accounting records. Considerable work may have to be done by accountants to produce presentable figures; the defendants will, of course, refuse to agree figures which are higher than those on the tax returns submitted by the claimant in previous years. Do remember that if the client's earnings had shown an upwards trend this should be reflected in the estimate of future loss. There is a fatal accident case of *Hunter v. Butler* [1995] T.L.R. 2812, CA that suggests that hidden income pre-accident should be ignored by courts when determining loss of earnings or dependency claims.

7.5. State benefits and the Compensation Recovery Scheme

Previous systems

Pre-1989 Benefits

In principle, the claimant can only claim net wage loss but before 1989 there were extremely complicated rules under which some state benefits were deducted in full when calculating the client's loss and some which were only deducted as to half or not at all. The Social Security Act 1989, s. 22 aimed to rationalise the old law and arrange for repayment to the state of money paid to claimants who later obtained damages. That law only affected compensation (a) paid on or after September 3, 1990 and (b) in respect of (i) an accident or injury occurring on or after January 1, 1989 or (ii) a disease where the first claim for benefit was on or after January 1, 1989. However, this rule and its successor the Social Security Act 1989 have now been superseded.

Under that Act the defendant had to deduct from *any* compensation and pay to the Compensation Recovery Unit an amount equal to all the benefits paid in respect of the injury or disease. There was a small payments limit of £2,500 compensation under which benefits did not have to be deducted. This scheme attracted a great deal of criticism as it meant that welfare benefits could be deducted from general damages. As a result the current law evolved.

The Social Security (Recovery of Benefits) Act 1997

This Act was passed to meet some of the criticisms of the 1989 Act. It has been in force since October 1997.

It aims to transfer the burden of recoupment from the victim to the insurer and to ring fence various heads of damage so they will no longer be subject to recoupment.

The rule

The basic rule now is that the defendant has to pay to the Compensation Recovery Unit ('CRU') an amount equal to all the relevant benefits paid in respect of the injury or disease. However the insurer is only permitted to recoup these benefits against pecuniary loss and then only like for like against three broad heads of damage. The Act applies to *all* cases not settled at the date the Act came into force, including pre-1989 benefits.

Like for Like

Schedule 2 Calculation of compensation payment

	Head of compensation	**Benefit**
(1)	Compensation for earnings lost during the relevant period	Disability working allowance Disablement pension payable under section 103 of the 1992 Act Incapacity benefit Income support Invalidity pension and allowance Jobseeker's allowance Reduced earnings allowance Severe disablement allowance Sickness benefit Statutory sick pay Unemployability supplement Unemployment benefit
(2)	Compensation for cost of care incurred during the relevant period	Attendance allowance Care component of disability living allowance Disablement pension increase payable under section 104 or 105 of the 1992 Act
(3)	Compensation for loss of mobility during the relevant period	Mobility allowance Mobility component of disability, living allowance

Full recovery

Note that benefits paid are recovered by the CRU in full even if:

(a) the agreed compensation makes deductions for contributory negligence;

(b) proceedings have not been issued;

(c) the amount paid is an interim payment or payment into court (see below).

Under (a) there can therefore still be an element of unfairness to a claimant who has received benefit but only recovers a proportion of loss of earnings.

Exemptions

Benefits are *not* recovered from:

(1) General damages for pain, suffering and loss of amenity.

(2) Medical expenses.

(3) Pension loss or loss of services.

(4) *Smith v. Manchester* payments or damages for loss of congenial employment.

(5) Fatal Accident Act 1976 cases: money paid in respect of dependants' losses is exempt. Money paid in respect of losses of the deceased is *not* exempt.

(6) Criminal Injuries Compensation Authority (CICA) payments.

(7) Compensation orders in the Criminal Courts.

(8) Benefits paid or payable *after* the date of settlement.

(9) Five-year rule: benefits are only recoverable for a maximum of five years from the date of accident or injury.

(10) Benefits *not* paid in respect of the injury or disease. If your client was receiving a benefit before the date of the accident or injury and continued claiming it with no changes thereafter it is likely that there will be no recovery. If, however, there is a change, including the client now being certified as unfit for work, this may be considered sufficient for benefits received to become recoverable (see Social Security Case C(CR)/1/92 and C(CR)/2/93).

(11) Anything else not specifically covered in Schedule 2.

Procedure

(1) Notifying the CRU: This is the responsibility of the defendant. You must give the necessary information to the defendant upon request. The information you need to obtain is as follows:

- Date of birth;
- National Insurance number;

- Details of employers;
- Details of any NHS trusts from whom treatment has been received as a result of the accident(this is because insurers now how have to reimburse this sum as well, although this has no impact upon the claimant's damages).

You will find many insurers criticise a letter of claim that omits this information and some even suggest that as a result the letter of claim is invalid. They are wrong. Originally, it was intended that CRU information should be supplied in the letter of claim. However, many such letters seem to go astray. To avoid the risk that confidential individual information might then become public the protocol letter was revised so that CRU information no longer has to be included, and indeed from a client point of view should not be. Do, though, obtain this information from the client at an early stage as it will be required.

Notification must take place even when there is plainly no benefit implication, *e.g.* the client has had no time off work and/or has claimed no benefit.

(2) CRU certificate: On filing notification and upon specific request the CRU will send out a certificate of benefits. This is valid for a set period of time; usually eight or 26 weeks depending upon whether there is an ongoing benefit claim or, where five years has elapsed since the accident it is a final certificate. During the validity of the certificate the parties can rely on the amount stated in the certificate to be the benefit sums to be repaid if settlement is reached. Many settlements have to be delayed pending receipt of such a certificate because the defendant has either forgotten to register the claim with the CRU or failed to update certificates when they have expired. This can be frustrating for your client who will not understand the delay, especially where he or she has not received benefit anyway. It is wise to check that you have provided the necessary information to the defendant when commencing negotiations to enable notification and to check that the defendant has a valid certificate or, at worst, has requested one.

(3) Interim payment or payment into court: Note that benefits are deducted from interim payments or a payment into court. If a defendant offers an interim payment ensure that it agrees, in addition, to pay the benefit due at that time, otherwise your client may be left with nothing. Make sure any agreed interim payment or court ordered sum is expressed as being net of CRU. On payments into court the defendant will be obliged to repay all benefits. The defendant can withhold the relevant benefits and tell the court that the amount withheld together with the amount paid makes up the full payment in. The new CPR forms for payment into court now make it plain what has been withheld and what has physically been paid in. If in doubt ask the defendant. For more details see Part 36 Payments and offers Chapter 12.

(4) Review and Appeal: Both parties have the right to ask the CRU to review the certificate or to appeal against it. The easiest course, if time allows, is to ask for a review as soon as you receive it. Most reviews do lead to clear errors or anomalies being resolved relatively quickly. To seek review simply write to the CRU asking for a review and explain why. Sometimes the review leads to no change or there is not time to seek review. Then an appeal should be undertaken. There are strict time limits so ensure that these are diarised appropriately. In many cases the appeal is by both parties jointly and sometimes is a term of settlement, *e.g.* the claimant agrees to assist the defendant in attempts to reduce the benefit where medical evidence suggests that the claimant's medical difficulties and therefore the cause of receipt of benefit, relate to pre-accident injuries or illness. The mere fact that the medical evidence suggests that the claimant may be exaggerating the injury deliberately or otherwise is usually no reason to reduce CRU because the benefit receipt still arises from the accident injuries; real, imagined or make believe.

Tactics

(1) Calculating full loss: Obviously it is extremely important when calculating your client's losses to work out the full loss, disregarding any relevant benefits which have been paid as these will be deducted from the amount paid to the client and repaid to the CRU in any event.

(2) Speedy settlement: As stated above *future* benefits are not deducted. In some cases there is plainly a benefit in early settlement pre *large benefit.* When calculating your client's future loss you should, strictly, take into account the fact that your client may be entitled to state benefits. However, it can often be argued that payment of the settlement sum will take the client over the level of entitlement for means tested benefits so future losses should continue at the higher rate.

(3) Reviewing and Appealing the assessment: Always check certificates carefully and do not hesitate to review or appeal if the certificate is incorrect or if you can argue that the benefit was not paid in respect of the injury or disease. For example: A was unfit to work for a period as a result of the accident injuries, but subsequently other problems would have precluded working on health grounds in any event. It could be argued that only the benefits received up to the time of the supervening event should be subject to recoupment, but often the CRU will not know of the supervening event and simply see a continuous claim for benefit which it seeks to recoup in full.

(4) Breakdown of offers: Always insist on a breakdown of a defendant's offer to ensure that the claimant is not losing out of damages an amount which

should be paid by the insurer to the CRU. Obviously, it is in your client's interest to negotiate higher general or other 'ring-fenced' damages to maximise your client's net award.

(5) Defendant's responsibility: Always remember that CRU deduction and payment is the responsibility of the defendant, not the claimant. You are therefore entirely at liberty to accept any amount paid without deduction and will not be responsible for repayment. However, before agreeing any settlement clarify whether the amounts offered include, or are net of, repayable benefits. If a settlement offer is silent as to deduction then the deduction must be made; if statutory deduction is not intended express agreement is required (*Rees v. West Glamorgan County Court* [1994] 1 P.I.Q.R. 37, CA).

Further information

For further details about the Compensation Recovery Scheme you should obtain the useful guides provided by the Compensation Recovery Unit whose address is Department of Social Security, Reyrolle Building, Hebburn, Tyne & Wear, NE31 1XB (Tel: 0191 201 0500).

7.6. Private health insurance

The client does not have to give any credit for payments under a private health insurance scheme. Unlike state benefits it is considered that a client need not account for benefits obtained through their own foresight and such payments can be ignored by the solicitor preparing the schedule of special damage.

7.7. Income tax and NI

Income tax

Obviously, full credit has to be given for income tax that would be deducted from the wages. This is because it is the net, not gross, wage loss that is claimed save as mentioned earlier where the claim is in fact one for loss of profit. It is for the claimant's solicitor to work out accurately the income tax involved. It is not good enough simply to assume tax at the current rate and deduct it. Doing this fails to give the claimant any credit for personal allowance and for other reliefs that might be available.

National Insurance

National Insurance contributions are usually also deducted in order to give a true net loss figure. However, you can argue that state pension entitlement is dependent on full National Insurance contributions being paid, if the contributions of either employer or employee are reduced then the plaintiff will suffer loss. If there is likely to be a real loss which you are not claiming under the separate head of a lost pension (see below) then do not deduct National Insurance (see *Dews v. National Coal Board* [1988] A.C. 1).

Calculation

It follows that in all but the most simple cases, it will be necessary for the claimant's solicitor to do an income tax and National Insurance calculation. To do this, you will have to know the personal allowances available for each of the tax years (remember there is a larger allowance for a married person than for a single person), the tax rates, and the National Insurance contribution rate. Most accountants as part of their advertising send out handy annual updates. You should keep these so that you have details of all relevant rates for as many years back as you are ever likely to need.

7.8. Calculating the figures

Before you can work out the special damage, you need to have checked all the items referred to above. In particular you will need:

- earnings details for the appropriate period before the accident;
- wage rates applying since the date of the accident;
- details of any earnings received by the claimant since the accident (if there is a partial loss of wages);
- details of the date the client is likely to return to work (and at what salary, if there is likely to be continuing loss);
- details of DSS benefits or certificate from CRU;
- claimant's list of other expenditure;
- claimant's list of likely future expenses.

Calculate the special damage as follows:

(1) Work out the net earnings prior to the date of the accident. Generally, this will be averaged over a thirteen week period (but check that the figures are not abnormally low for some reason, see above).

(2) Calculate the gross earnings that the claimant would have received during each of the tax years (or part year) since the date of the accident. This will be done using the figures supplied by the employer, or the gross earnings of a comparable employee. It is essential to calculate the gross figure for each tax year, so that income tax and NI can be properly worked out. If there was a wage-rate change during the year, then obviously that must be allowed for when working out the gross annual figure.

(3) Now, work out the income tax. The table on p. 86 sets out the necessary information. Take the gross earnings, and deduct:
   (a) the single, or married person's allowance applying in that tax year;
   (b) any other allowances (*e.g.* age allowances).

Having deducted those items, you will be left with the net taxable income for that year. Now, calculate the amount of tax that would have had to have been paid; the rate of tax is printed in the chart on p. 86.

(4) If NI is to be deducted (see above) work out the NI. National Insurance contributions are based on the full (*i.e.* gross, not net) earnings. The percentage rate of contribution is set out, for the different tax years, on the table on p. 86. So, simply multiply the gross wage figure for that tax year (*i.e.* as in 2 above) by the correct percentage figure or if flat rate contributions are made calculate those over the relevant period.

(5) You can now work out the net wage for that tax year. Deduct the amount of income tax (as in 3) and the amount of NI (as in 4) from the gross wage figure (*i.e.* as in 2). This will give you the net amount that the client would have earned in the pre-accident job.

(6) Deduct any wages that the client did, in fact, receive during that tax year. For instance, it may be that the client was able to obtain less well-paid employment for all or part of the year. If so, full credit will have to be given for the wages earned. Simply deduct the net amount received (*i.e.* net wages, net of tax and NI). You now have the net wage loss that can properly be claimed for that tax year.

(7) You must now repeat this procedure for each successive tax year. Do not forget to allow for wage increases that the client would have received; similarly, do not forget to adjust the personal allowance rates, tax rates, and NI rates, in accordance with the figures in the table on p.00 and p.00.

(8) You will now have the claimant's net claimable wage loss from the date of the accident until the present time. It may in fact be convenient for you to project it through to the end of the current tax year. Now state separately the amount which the client has received from relevant state benefits which must be repaid to the CRU if you have a certificate otherwise or perhaps anyway leave it for the defendant to do.

(9) Add on the client's other losses and expenses (*e.g.* expenses attending medical examinations, prescriptions, telephone calls, clothing, special equipment, etc.). See p. 67 and 68 above.

(10) Although not strictly necessary, it is advisable to work out the interest on the special damages. For how to calculate this, see p. 83 and 84. Enter the amount of interest as a separate figure at the foot of the calculation.

(11) You have now completed the special damage calculations to date. Since there may well be a considerable delay before the case goes to trial (when you will have to update the special damage figures again) it is helpful to keep your notes of how you worked out the figures. Also, do not forget to put the date of the calculation on the final set of figures.

(12) Finally put in a figure for continuing loss ie the net annual loss of wages until the anticipated date of return or with a suitable multiplier if the client will not be able to return (see Chapter 8 for guidance regarding an appropriate multiplier) together with an estimate of likely future expenses.

Having worked out the special damages you should send a copy to your client to check and ensure it is full and correct before sending it to the defendant to negotiate settlement or to counsel to draft in final form to accompany the particulars of claim if this is not something you propose to do yourself (See Part III).

Remind your client to let you know of all new expenses as they arise and keep your special damage file up to date so that you can provide amended calculations whenever necessary (for example on serving further medical reports—which may necessitate a change to the estimate of future loss).

If you are sending the schedule to the defendant to try to negotiate settlement do send disclosure in support as otherwise this will be used as a reason to delay proposals.

7.9. Actuaries and accountants

When to obtain a report

In most cases, the solicitor can do the special damage calculation. Why pay someone to do something you can do and charge for. However, sometimes the figures become so complicated that specialist help is needed particularly if the client is or was self-employed. You will have seen above how in fact self employed loss of earning claims are quite straightforward provided you have access to relevant tax and National Insurance rates. You should be able to do most calculations and earn the fee for doing this rather than farm out the work. Where specialist accountancy assistance can help is in claims where the client had only just established a business and detailed understanding of projections, likely growth and profit margins is required. Under the protocol and anticipating Part 35 compliance you should consider approaching the defendant before making such an instruction to ensure that there are no later arguments on admissibility of evidence, (subject always to ultimate court approval of the use of the expert). When providing a schedule of special damage to the defendant using figures obtained from such a report it is sensible to disclose the report to make sense of the calculation.

Cost of report

Accountants' reports are expensive. Their cost is frequently challenged. Obviously, if agreement to the instruction was obtained from the defendant that confines arguments over the fee to the amount rather than whether any fee at all should be paid. The CPR cost provisions also envisage this two step test for expert fees; was it proportionate to incur a fee at all and if so is the fee proportionate in context? Even if there is a risk of part of the fee being disallowed, it will often be worth the client's while to pay the extra money (in the knowledge that it will be a solicitor/client cost) in the hope that the extra expense will be covered by the increased amount of special damage. In any event, as stated, in some circumstances, it may well be the case that only an accountant can calculate the true level of lost earnings, and the likely level of future profits.

Pension rights

Sometimes, a claimant will have lost pension rights through early retirement brought on as a result of injuries. In such a case, the calculation of the loss in value of those pension rights can be extremely complicated. Sometimes the pension trustees will be able to provide approximate figures, but otherwise the advice of an actuary may be necessary. If an actuary is to be instructed, then send a copy of the pension scheme, trust deed, rules, and booklet; the date of commencement of pensionable service; details of pensionable salary; details of pension benefits awarded as a result of the accident or premature retirement; details of pension increases granted by the scheme; details of pension benefits to be taken into account in mitigation. Normally, you have to obtain this information from the employers or the pension trustees. Again, it is best to try to agree not only the necessity of such evidence but also the person to be instructed with the defendant prior to the instruction.

Actuarial assumptions

When preparing a report, the actuary will be faced with the problem of what assumptions should be made; in particular, the presumed annual rate of discount (ie the presumed rate of investment return that the claimant will be able to get from the capital sum invested). Following *Well v. Wells,* despite continuing clamour from claimants for a lower Return and from defendants for a higher one, 3 per cent return was the court accepted rate of return. The government eventually stepped in under its powers set out in the Damages Act 1996 and the Lord Chancellor reduced the discount rate to 2.5 per cent at an end of July 2001.

Be sure to provide the actuary with full instructions (*i.e.* full personal details of the claimant special damage information; counsel's opinions) and medical evidence as this may have life expectancy implications.

7.10. Interest

Claiming interest

A claimant is not automatically assumed to claim interest on damages. To avoid doubt, the Particulars of Claim, and also the indorsement on the claim form should specifically include a claim for interest. See the specimen statements of case in Appendix E, and the claim form indorsements in Appendix C, Precedent 1, for the correct wording. The courts are required to award interest if claimed 'unless the court is satisfied that there are special reasons to the contrary, and provided that judgment was for at least £200'. Thus, in the normal course of events, the claimant can expect interest.

The rates of interest

Different rates of interest apply for the different types of damages. One must differentiate between special damages (*i.e.* financial loss up to the date of trial), and general damages (*i.e.* compensation for pain, suffering and loss of amenities, and future loss, which strictly is deemed to be a general damage item).

General damages

Interest is at 2 per cent from the date of service of the proceedings. There are two points to note here. Firstly, the interest rate is fairly low (the theory is that the claimant benefits through inflation as general damages are valued at current day amount not as at the time of the accident. Secondly, interest only runs from the date of service of the proceedings: it does not run from the date of the accident, or the date of issue of the proceedings.

Special damages

Interest runs at half the court special account rate, from the date of the accident. Note that interest is only half rate, and that it runs from the date of the accident (not the date of issue, or of service of the proceedings). For how to work out the figures, see below. Incidentally, there is authority for saying that the half-rate rule should be confined to cases in which special damage is incurred on a regular basis before trial (*e.g.* weekly wage loss). If the losses are irregular, or do not continue from the date of accident to the trial, then argue for more than half-rate interest. For example, in a minor road accident claim where all special damages are incurred within two months of the accident but the claim does not come before the court for two years you should try to claim full rate from, at the latest, the expiry of the two month period; in other words, when the last item of loss accrued.

The current rate, after many years at 8 per cent, is and has been from August 1, 1999, 7 per cent.

Future loss

Future loss of earnings (*i.e.* from the date of the trial onwards) does not attract interest.

Fatal cases

These are treated in the same way. The pecuniary loss to date of trial is treated as special damage, whilst future pecuniary loss attracts no interest. Remember also that multipliers for dependency in fatal cases run from the date of death.

These guidelines were upheld by the House of Lords in *Wright v. BRB* [1983] 2 A.C. 773. But the court did make it clear that in exceptional cases (in particular, when one party or the other had been guilty of gross delay) the court could increase or diminish the amount of interest, or alter the period for which it is allowed. So, the court has a discretion, which may be exercised in exceptional cases. Often, it seems to be exercised in favour of defendants! With active court management once allocation questionnaires have been filed cases of delay during proceedings should be few and far between requiring the court to exercise its discretion to reduce interest less often.

Working out the interest

Interest on the general damages is easy to work out. Basically, take 2 per cent of the damages, as from the date the proceedings were served.

It is with special damages that the complications arise. Interest runs at half the court special account (formerly known as short-term investment account) rate as from the date of the accident. Since the special account rate changes periodically, it can mean that it is an extremely complicated calculation. The rates of interest are set out in the following table. Fortunately, there are tables available that make the calculation of this interest a relatively straightforward matter. In particular, Mr R. M. Nelson-Jones (of Field Fisher and Waterhouse, London) has an annual article in *The Gazette* (usually in September) which contains a ready-reckoner table for calculating the interest. The table below appeared in his article in September 2000 and is reproduced with his kind permission.

The table shows the total interest (on special account rate) that will have accrued if a case went to trial on October 1, 2000. For instance, if the accident happened on January 1, 1989 the rate of interest would be 110.90 per cent (so the interest on special damage would be 55.45 per cent).

To stop the table going out of date you should add on the daily rate of interest since October 1, 2000. Table 2 sets out the number of accumulated days that run in the six months following October 1, 2000. For instance if a case was settled on January 31, 2001, there would be an extra 123 days interest to be added on. On the assumption that the special interest rate remains at 7 per cent, then the daily rate of interest will be 0.019 per cent (*i.e.* 7 per cent divided by 365). Thus, with 123 days interest accruing there would be an additional 2.33 per cent interest since October 1, 2000.

So, in the case of an accident that occurred on September 1, 1983 the total interest as at January 31, 2001 would be 175.95 per cent (*i.e.* the figure in table 173.62 plus the interest that has accrued between October 1, 2000 and January 1, 2001 being 2.33 per cent).

It must be appreciated that interest can be sizeable if there is a significant special damage claim, especially if the case is old, which is why interest should always be set out at the foot of a special damage calculation. This will provide a useful reminder to the solicitor, and counsel, as to the interest that has accrued and can be particularly valuable when considering the amount of payment into court. All too often defendants think that payment of interest is in some way negotiable. The starting point must be that it is every bit as integral part of the case as any head of loss.

The rules on calculating special damages and interest are identical in the High and county courts.

Personal injury interest calculation

Rates since 1965

From:	
1 October 1965	5%
1 September 1966	5.5%
1 March 1968	6%
1 March 1969	6.5%
1 March 1970	7%
1 April 1971	7.5%
1 March 1973	8%
1 March 1974	9%
1 February 1977	10%
1 March 1979	12.5%
1 January 1980	15%
1 January 1981	12.5%
1 December 1981	15%
1 March 1982	14%
1 July 1982	13%
1 April 1983	12.5%
1 April 1984	12%
1 August 1986	11.5%
1 January 1987	12.25%
1 April 1987	11.75%
1 November 1987	11.25%
1 December 1987	11%
1 May 1988	9.5%
1 August 1988	11%
1 November 1988	12.25%
1 January 1989	13%
1 November 1989	$14\frac{1}{4}$%
1 April 1991	12%
1 October 1991	10.25%
1 February 1993	8%
August 2000	7%

Table 1

	1981	1982	1983	1984	1985	1986	1987	1988	1989	1990
January	208.44	195.72	182.07	169.44	157.32	145.32	133.53	121.76	110.90	97.69
February	207.38	194.45	180.96	168.38	156.30	144.30	132.49	120.83	109.80	96.48
March	206.42	193.30	179.97	167.39	155.38	143.38	131.55	119.95	108.80	95.39
April	205.35	192.11	178.86	166.34	154.36	142.36	130.51	119.02	107.69	94.18
May	204.33	190.96	177.83	165.35	153.37	141.37	129.54	118.11	106.63	93.01
June	203.27	189.77	176.77	164.34	152.35	140.35	128.54	117.31	105.52	91.80
July	202.24	188.62	175.74	163.35	151.37	139.37	127.58	116.53	104.45	90.62
August	201.18	187.52	174.68	162.34	150.35	138.35	126.58	115.72	103.35	89.41
September	200.11	186.41	173.62	161.32	149.33	137.37	125.58	114.78	102.24	88.20
October	199.09	185.34	172.59	160.34	148.34	136.43	124.62	113.88	101.18	87.03
November	198.03	184.24	171.53	159.32	147.32	135.45	123.62	112.95	100.07	85.82
December	197.00	183.17	170.51	158.34	146.34	134.41	122.69	111.94	98.90	84.65
	1991	**1992**	**1993**	**1994**	**1995**	**1996**	**1997**	**1998**	**1999**	**2000**
January	83.44	71.33	61.05	52.86	44.86	36.86	28.84	20.84	12.84	5.25
February	82.23	70.46	60.18	52.18	44.18	36.18	28.16	20.16	12.16	4.66
March	81.14	69.64	59.56	51.56	43.56	35.54	27.54	19.54	11.54	4.10
April	79.93	68.77	58.88	50.88	42.88	34.86	26.86	18.86	10.86	3.51
May	78.94	67.93	58.23	50.23	42.23	34.21	26.21	18.21	10.21	2.93
June	77.92	67.06	57.55	49.55	41.55	33.53	25.53	17.53	9.53	2.34
July	76.93	66.22	56.89	48.89	40.89	32.87	24.87	16.87	8.87	1.76
August	75.92	65.35	56.21	48.21	40.21	32.19	24.19	16.19	8.19	1.17
September	74.90	64.47	55.53	47.53	39.53	31.51	23.51	15.51	7.59	0.58
October	73.91	63.63	54.87	46.87	38.87	30.85	22.85	14.85	7.02	
November	73.04	62.76	54.19	46.19	38.19	30.17	22.17	14.17	6.42	
December	72.20	61.92	53.54	45.54	37.54	29.52	21.52	13.52	5.85	

Table 2

31 October 2000	31
30 November 2000	61
31 December 2000	92
31 January 2001	123
29 February 2001	151
31 March 2001	182

Special damage: tax and NI rates

Tax year	Personal allowances single	married	tax rate (basic)	NI rates	Class 1	payable on earnings up to upper earnings limit of
1986/87	2,335	3,655	29%	£38–£60	5%	14,820
				£60–£95	7%	
				over £95	9%	
1987/88	2,425	3,795	27%	£39–£65	5%	15,340
				£65–£100	7%	
				over £100	9%	
1988/89	2,605	4,095	25%	£41–£70	5%	15,850
				£70–£105	7%	
				over £105	9%	
1989/90	2,789	4,379	25%	£43–£75	5%	16,900
				£75–£115	7%	
				over £115	9%	
1990/91	3,000	4,720	25%	up to £46	2%	18,200
				£46–£350	9%	
1991/92	3,290	5,010	25%	up to £52	2%	20,280
				£52–£390	9%	
1992/93	3,445	5,165	25%	up to £54	2%	21,060
				£54–£405	9%	
1993/94	3,445	5,165	25%[a]	up to £56	2%	21,840
				£56–£420	9%	
1994/95	3,445	5,165	25%[b]	up to £57	2%	22,360
				£57–£430	10%	
1995/96	3,525	5,245	25%[c]	up to £59	2%	22,880
				£57–£440	10%	
				over £440	£39.28 pw	
1996/97	3,765	5,555	24%[d]	up to £61	2%	23,660
				£62–£455	10%	
				over £455	£40.62 pw	
1997/98	4,045	5,875	23%[e]	up to £62	2%	24,180
				£62–£465	10%	
				over £465	£41.54 pw	
1998/99	4,195	6,095[f]	23%[g]	up to £63.99	2%	
				64–485	10%	
1999/2000	4,335	6,305[h]	23%[i]	up to £66.00	nil	
				£66.01–£500	10%	
2000/2001	4,385	no longer exists	22%[j]	up to 76	nil	
				76–535	10%	
2001/2002	4,535		22%[k]	up to 87	nil	
				£87–£575	10%	

[a] reduced to 20% on first £2,500 of earnings
[b] reduced to 20% on first £3,000 of earnings
[c] reduced to 20% in first £3,200 of earnings
[d] reduced to 20% in first £3,900 of earnings
[e] reduced to 20% in first £4,100 of earnings
[f] relief restricted to 15%
[g] reduced to 20% on first 4,300
[h] relief restricted to 10%
[i] reduced to 10% on first 1,500
[j] reduced to 10% on first 1,520
[k] 10% on the first 1,880

Specimen Special Damage Calculation
(Road accidents, self employed)

A Loss of earning

Calculation of pre-accident average wage during tax year 2000/2001

	£
Gross earnings 13 weeks prior to accident	8,650.00
∴ annual expected wage	34,600.00
Tax calculation	
less personal allowance	4,385.00
amount taxable	30,215.00
at 10% 1,520	
at 22% 26,880	
at 40% 1,815	
total tax deduction	6,787.60
voluntary NI fixed rate per week £6.55 × 52	340.60
total tax and total NI deduction	(7,128.20)
Therefore annual net wage =	£27,471.80
Therefore weekly wage net =	528.30

Calculation of wage loss

	£	
Absent from work 2000—(insert any 14 weeks period in 2000) = 14 weeks should have earnt 14 × £528.30		
Net loss while off work =		7,392

B Other losses and expenses

	£
Expenses attending medical examination	9.75
Prescriptions, telephone calls, etc	12.40
Repairs to spectacles	24.00
Value of clothing	19.00
Husband's loss of earnings (2 days)	75.00

Vehicle—pre-accident value	1,450.00
—towage	25.00
—storage	100.00
—hire of alternative transport	56.00
TOTAL LOSSES AND EXPENSES	1,771.15
TOTAL A + (B LOSS TO DATE)	£9163.15

Interest on special damage to date [ ] days × [ ]% = [ ] continuing at [ ] per day

C Future loss

If there are future losses put them in here either as specific sum or best estimate with explanation as to how you arrived at the cstimate.

8. Valuing Client's Case and Negotiating

8.1. Summing up and considering the evidence

Do not present the case to the defendant for negotiation until you have all the information you require.

Receiving evidence

Every time a new piece of evidence is received it should be considered carefully. Do not just file reports and documents without critical analysis. Consider:

(a) does the evidence support your client's case?

(b) is further evidence required, such as another statement or report?

(c) does the evidence fit in with existing evidence? If not, what is needed to reconcile the evidence?

(d) is the evidence complete? If not what more is needed?

(e) do you fully understand the evidence? If not, ask further questions.

Always acknowledge receipt of evidence and thank the sender or witness; you may need them later! With statements remember to return a copy to the maker of the statement together with a polite request that he or she notifies you of any change of address. This avoids pre trial panic trying to trace a crucial missing witness.

Familiarising oneself with facts and law

Obviously, in order to evaluate evidence you have to understand the law applying to your client's case and the facts needed to prove it. Traditionally many solicitors left the finer legal points to counsel; however you cannot know what evidence is necessary if you do not know what you are required to prove. The solicitor should be in control of the litigation; not led by counsel and experts.

Remember to review the case periodically so that you can see the whole picture, not just the step you are currently undertaking. A lot of injury work is responding to correspondence. Do not be sucked into dealing with the case simply on a 'deal with the last letter' approach. Note where you want to be and how you intend to get there, ensure that each letter progresses the case.

Discussing case with your client

It is easy to become so busy collecting evidence that you forget to keep your client informed. Make sure that you:

(a) tell your client of all steps you are taking;

(b) send copies of all new evidence; explain its significance to the case, and ask the client if anything is not clear;

(c) remind the client to update you regularly on any new evidence the client discovers (likely in a workplace case where a client may be in contact with colleagues or former colleagues);

(d) remind the client to keep you informed of any change in condition or circumstances (*e.g.* a further operation or a new job);

(e) remind the client to continue sending all receipts for special damage;

(f) tell the client of any change in prospects of success or likely damages immediately;

(g) update costs. The Law Society now requires cost updates to be sent to each client at least every six months.

Reviewing the evidence

Once you have carried out all investigations review the case:

(a) what are its prospects of success?

(b) what further evidence is needed?

(c) what procedural steps should now be taken?

(d) what is the costs position?

(e) are you now in a position to value the case and negotiate settlement? If so, how best are you going to ensure maximum compensation?

8.2. Valuing your client's case

Losses can be pecuniary or non-pecuniary. Pecuniary losses can include:

(a) losses and expenses to date, including private medical expenses (see Chapter 7);

(b) estimated future losses and expenses;

(c) loss of earnings (or profits) to date; note that this can include the cost of services rendered by others (except the tortfeasor) to the claimant (*e.g.* the husband who looks after his injured wife; the relative or friend who incurs expense whilst visiting the claimant in hospital). Such expenses are recoverable from the defendant to the extent that they are reasonable; so if the claimant needs someone in attendance it is only fair that the claim should include the cost of such professional assistance, even if, in fact, the expense is not incurred because a partner provides the attendance. If the claimant needs the service then the expense is recoverable, even if the work is done gratuitously by a friend or relative. Thus, in many cases, when the husband takes a few days off work to look after his injured wife, his loss of wages can form part of her claim against the defendant. If the care is more long term and there is no loss of earning consider claiming a proportion of local social service care rates. Whilst there is no hard and fast rule you should aim to recover two thirds that rate for an unqualified family carer;

(d) estimated future loss of earnings (or profits), note that the multiplier to use for future losses and expenses should, in theory, be higher than that for future wage losses since the expenses will continue after retirement (called full life multipliers). Explain to the client how each multiplier is assessed (for example a 35 year old male will not receive a multiplier of 30 but one of approximately 21, or less). Consult a book such as Kemp and Kemp when deciding on the size of the multiplier. The multiplier is worked out on the basis of age at the date of trial because, of course, actual loss of earnings will be calculated to the trial date, not at the time of the accident. Examples of multipliers awarded in recent fatal cases are given in Chapter 25.

The cases of *Wells v. Wells*, *Thomas v. Brighton HA* and *Page v. Sheerness* revolutionised multipliers. After the Court of Appeal had robustly favoured no change in the status quo the House of Lords decided that the traditional 4.5 to 5 per cent discount assumed the claimant would take too big an investment risk and opted for the safer gilts market leading to a 3 per cent return. The Lord Chancellor's interventation to set the rate at 2.5 per cent in July 2001 took matters on a stage further. A simple contrast of before and after multipliers reflects the impact of these reductions showing before *Wells*, after *Wells* and under the 2001 regulation:

Male Multipliers before Wells

Period of years to retirement	Multiplier
5	4.39
10	7.85
15	10.64
20	12.91
25	14.77
30	16.28
35	17.51

Male Multipliers after Wells

Period of years To retirement	Multiplier
5	4.54
10	8.39
15	11.72
20	14.62
25	17.17
30	19.39
35	21.32

Male multipliers under The Damages Act 1996 regulation

The difference can be enormous and certainly has lead to a period of reduced profit for insurers and/or higher premiums to recoup this sum. For example, in a 20-year loss of earnings claim where the lost earnings is £25,000 net per annum the difference caused by the increased multiplier is £43,250.

To retirement	
5	4.60
10	8.58
15	12.12
20	15.27
25	18.10
30	20.63
35	22.88

(e) loss of mobility in the labour market: loss of earning capacity, note that even though the client may have returned to a pre-accident occupation without a wage loss, any continuing disability may well put the client at a disadvantage on the open labour market where prospects of employment may have diminished. This may even be true where a client has completely recovered but a new employer may be reluctant to employ him or her, feeling that the client may now have a predisposition to a similar injury, for example in occupational overuse injury (so-called 'RSI') cases. Even if the employers undertake to keep the client employed there is a disadvantage since the client dare not antagonise them, and will be unprotected if the firm should go bankrupt. This is called a disadvantage (or handicap) on the labour market, or a restriction on employment opportunities. Valuation is difficult, varying with the extent of the disability, the claimant's income, and the length of working life. Usually, the court takes a multiplier of the claimant's annual income to reflect the risk. Even in the highest risk cases this rarely exceeds three times salary. Most cases however are awarded less than £10,000. As with multipliers the courts have given no helpful guidance on the way this figure should be calculated. Generally the award is either notional or given as a top-up of general damages. The case that clearly established that a claimant should be compensated for loss of mobility was *Smith v. Manchester Corporation* (1974) 17 K.I.R. 1. So, you may find such a payment referred to in correspondence as a *Smith v. Manchester* or *Smith* payment. Always consider whether you can claim a *Smith v. Manchester* award.

There is also scope for the court to award partial future loss of earnings recognising that the claimant may be employed but the accident will cause periods of absence from work or lower wages. It is difficult to predict what this loss may amount to over a working career, particularly for the younger claimant. Courts tend again to award a lump sum to reflect this loss calculated in much the same way as a handicap in the labour market claim. The case that you may sometimes hear cited on this point is *Moeliker v. A. Reyrolle & Co. Ltd* [1977] 1 W.L.R. 132

(f) Other pecuniary losses, such as value of free board and lodging, concessionary fares, use of a company car, loss of chance of enhancing reputation in one's profession.

Non-pecuniary losses

(a) pain, suffering and shock; if the claimant is unconscious and unaware of pain, it is held that there cannot be suffering and so no damages will be payable;

(b) loss of the amenities of life (for instance, a deaf person can no longer hear the birds singing); an injured person may no longer be able to pursue previous hobbies and interests;

(c) bereavement or loss of expectation of life: see Chapter 25;

(d) inconvenience, discomfort, mental distress, and/or disappointment;

(e) loss of congenial appointment; this is a relatively new head of damage which can be claimed when a claimant can no longer carry out work that he or she particularly enjoyed even though neither earnings nor earning capacity are affected (for example, a gardener forced to take up clerical work). Damages are usually in the region of £1,000–£10,000. APIL journal publishes very useful periodic updates of cases on loss of congenial employment and likely damages.

See for example APIL (1997) Volume 7, Issue 2, pp. 14–18. It has to be said that the majority of reported cases where claims for loss of congenial employment have been allowed have been in respect of public emergency or medical service employees, such as fire officers and paramedics. In the current doom and gloom climate of the law it seems unlikely that solicitors or barristers will ever benefit from this head of loss!

Frequently these heads of damages will overlap. However, they do provide a useful checklist for ensuring that full damages are being claimed.

A note on valuing general damages

Clearly, the most difficult items to value are pain, suffering, shock and loss of amenities of life. Discussions with colleagues may provide guidance, as may analysis of comparable examples quoted in Kemp and Kemp and *Current Law*. The Judicial Studies Board's '*Guidelines for the Assessment of General Damages in Personal Injury Cases*' is a standard reference work for judges when considering awards, so you should also consider its suggestions. They are neatly set out at the start of each quantum section of Kemp and Kemp. Unfortunately its recommended awards can be rather low—consider them a minimum. In more serious cases, take counsel's advice.

General guideline

A starting point for such a valuation can be to decide what damages would be awarded for total incapacity of the part of the body in question, and then work down from there by deciding how the client's injury compares relatively, and what allowances should be made for that client as an individual; for example, sports and hobbies affected, age, occupation, sex and so on.

There can, of course, be so many variables. For example, if the client has an arm injury one can say that the loss or virtual loss of an arm is worth some £55,000 upwards and loss of use of an arm at least £45,000, but there are so many other possibilities, a bad fracture with arthritis may be worth £22,000, a stiff elbow £12,000, but each case has its own peculiar characteristics. Is it the dominant arm? Does it affect hobbies? Is there an increasing risk of arthritis, or would arthritis have occurred anyway?

This is why it is useful to look at the JSB guidelines to give you a bracket and then look at specific cases to narrow the figure further.

Valuing small cases

It is not difficult to decide the value of a serious case, for these are the cases that are reported and the brackets of award are proportionately smaller. It is the less serious cases that present problems of valuation, as these are the cases that are not usually reported and where one is less justified in sending the papers to counsel. Also, you will see a greater discrepancy proportionately between awards from different courts. For example, there are reported authorities on a one week whiplash from £250–£1,250.

In the small cases, worth under £3,000, experienced practitioners can differ by 100 per cent in their estimated valuations and courts can vary even more. Try looking at the Kemp and Kemp Quantum and current law which are particularly helpful on smaller cases.

8.3. Negotiating with the insurers

At some stage—before the issue of proceedings in most cases—you will have to negotiate with the defendant. This is a change in approach finally codified following the reform process of the Lord Woolf committee. The personal injury protocol is clear;

> "2.13 Parties and their legal representatives are encouraged to enter into discussions and/or negotiations prior to starting proceedings . . . parties should bear in mind that the courts increasingly take the view that litigation should be a last resort and that claims should not be issued prematurely when a settlement is in reasonable prospect."

The cost provisions of the CPR make it plain that when considering costs the court must look at the attempts made by the parties to settle the claim. The protocol sets out a mandatory requirement that proceedings should not be issued until the defendant has had twenty one days to consider a medical report from an agreed expert. Even in multi-track cases in which the protocol is not mandatory the message is clear, try to settle before issue or face possible criticism and cost consequences.

The protocol also specifies that where settlement is not possible the parties should try to agree as many issues as possible and highlight and refine the issues that remain.

What is plain from all this is that at some stage you will need to approach the defendant to try to resolve all or part of your client's claim.

Traditionally, defendants insurers liked to send a claims representative to see you (it is harder to say no to someone pleasant sitting across a table from you than it is over the phone or in a letter). However, the centralisation by insurers means that many parts of the country are now not covered by representatives on the road. Increasingly negotiations are carried out by phone or more commonly by letter, particularly in the smaller claims. Whatever forum the negotiations take place in the key to presenting your client's claim successfully is preparation.

8.4. Meetings

Preparation for meeting

Never attend a meeting unprepared:

(a) Carry out a full review of the case. In particular consider the points set out above. Reread the police report, any accident reports, any medical reports and your client's statement if liability remains in issue. Read all medical reports and have some quantum reports of slightly more serious injuries to hand;

(b) Note any weaknesses in your client's case and decide how you will deal with them if raised by the insurers. In particular consider any defence or allegations already raised by the defendant;

(c) Inform your client that the meeting will be taking place;

(d) Consider whether to ask for any interim payment at this stage (see p. 98 *below*); this is a good tactic if liability is admitted but quantum is in dispute;

(e) If you are in a position to assess damages at this stage and believe it is possible the case will settle then also make a rough estimate of your costs. Ensure the estimate is high enough to cover the time spent in the meeting and all the correspondence, advice and necessary work on settlement or you may find yourself heavily out of pocket. Recently, the insurance market has moved en masse to the instruction of various types of cost negotiators. It is now very rare for an insurer to deal with you direct on costs;

(f) When reading the medical report(s) before meeting the insurers it is useful to make a short summary for use during the negotiations so that the full extent of the injuries will not be overlooked;

(g) Go through the various heads of damage listed above to ensure that all possible claims have been included. Apportioning a specific sum to each head of damages will often produce a considerably higher figure than the global sum insurers try to suggest. Do go through the schedule item by item to achieve this. Resist the temptation to avoid confrontation and time consuming argument by doing a global approach;

(h) Set yourself goals before the meeting. What do you want to achieve? Control the meeting to ensure it deals with matters on your agenda.

The meeting

At the meeting there will be an exchange of views on liability and the insurers will wish to know the approximate amounts involved. Both sides will try to learn the strengths and weaknesses of the other side's case so that further instructions can be taken. Accordingly, at this stage, it is unwise to reveal all the details of the client's case. Whilst it can be difficult try to be a listener and not a talker. Answer difficult questions which highlight your client's weaknesses by questions of your own.

Low offers

One of the major changes under the CPR has been the move by defendants to be more realistic in assessments of quantum. Economic considerations have finally come to the fore and the window of opportunity of early, economic settlement has been opened in many cases. Regrettably, there are still negotiators who believe in making unreasonably low opening offers or negotiating by making grudgingly small increases. Do not be sucked in to delays. If an offer is close to what is acceptable, accept it or pick up the phone to see if a small increase can be obtained. If the offer is outside the bracket of possible awards then unless you have liability concerns that militate towards high risks in court process decline the offer and issue court proceedings. You may wish to couple proceedings with a claimant's Part 36 offer (see Chapter 12).

Interestingly, frequent dealings with those insurers who do regularly waste the opportunity for early pre-action settlement seems to make no difference. Even though they know from bitter experience that you will issue proceedings the first offers remain as low as ever. Sometimes, this is because internal systems or case management technology limits the discretion of individual claims handlers and they are compelled to put forward offers that they know represent a significant reduction on likely court assessed damages. If that is the case do not waste time negotiating as the only way to overcome the system is to inject a healthy dose of court reality.

As stated, you will find fewer meetings now taking place. The most common pre-action settlement attempts by claimants are now by way of disclosing medical report/s and quantifying non general losses in letter form allowing the defendant a time capped period within which to put forward proposals. Whilst this is not strictly required in cases where liability is disputed nothing is lost by so doing; there is a chance that an economic compromise with which both sides can live may be reached and it shows willing if the question of conduct is later considered on the issue of costs. You will sometimes find that in cases where no apportionment of liability can be agreed it may still be possible to reach a financial agreement so that liability never needs to be determined.

In cases where you must afford the defendant this opportunity the protocol indicates no proceedings should be issued for 21 days after this quantification and disclosure. Whilst you may wish to stick to this period experience of claims where liability is contested suggests that the defendant will be unable to respond within that time frame in many cases simply because of pressure of work. In cases where liability is not in dispute and the case should settle at this stage it may be better to allow a slightly longer period.

Negotiating styles

Whether in meetings, by phone or in correspondence, each individual has his or her own style of negotiating, which is developed with practice and experience. However, it should be remembered that the lawyer who has a reputation for being a 'tough negotiator' is likely to secure higher settlement offers than an easy-going colleague, although there will always be the exceptional negotiator who is able to use pure charm to secure high offers! Whilst no negotiator, however experienced, can make a weak case strong, there are general guidelines that may assist the inexperienced negotiator, while you develop a style of your own.

Negotiating tactics

Issuing proceedings If no realistic offer is forthcoming after you have allowed a reasonable amount of time from quantification and disclosure then issue proceedings. Too many solicitors become bogged down in fruitless and extended negotiations then realise six months down the line that the time has been wasted. Remember that you can keep negotiation going at the same time as pressing on with court process. The two are not mutually exclusive.

If you give the impression of being a reluctant litigator you will be easy prey. Even in weaker cases if you issue you give the impression of confidence that can cause a defendant to rethink his or her position and buy off any risk.

Do ensure that before you make any threats to issue within a time scale that you have your client's instructions so to do. Idle threats diminish credibility. If you say you are going to issue then do so. If not you lose the initiative and are left presenting the case on the defendant's timescale and in all probability settling it on the defendant's terms.

Information The most basic and important piece of advice is not to reveal the weaknesses in your case at an early stage. Quantify the claim and let the insurer come back to you with detailed comment. You must balance the benefit to your client of an early settlement against the benefit of a tough stance leading to higher offer later.

Interim payment If the case is strong on liability, ask for an interim payment even before proceedings are commenced and suggest that if one is not forthcoming the case will be issued solely for the purpose of making an interim payment application. This is particularly sensible when you are awaiting final medical evidence.

Client's financial status In the negotiations before the commencement of proceedings, the insurers will seek to discover whether the client is really willing and able to litigate. Even if your client has told you he or she does not wish to go to court now is not the time to say so.

Speedy litigation If the case seems reasonable from the liability viewpoint do not delay but issue it as soon as possible (see below). Resist the temptation to postpone proceedings on the basis that if it 'is good on liability, it will settle'. This is most important; apart from giving an impression of aggressive confidence, interest will start running on the general damages as from the date of service (see Chapter 7). Once you have issued press on with the proceedings as quickly as possible. Use all procedural points to put pressure on the insurers.

Contributory negligence Frequently, the negotiations will revolve around the percentage of contributory negligence on the part of the claimant. It is sometimes helpful to compromise by accepting a higher percentage of contributory negligence but with the insurer's representative agreeing to the more generous valuation proposed by the claimant's solicitor. The result is that the client ends up with the same amount of money and the insurer's representative is able to report that they have negotiated a settlement with a high degree of contributory negligence. This comes back to knowing what your goal is at the outset. Unless you already have instructions all discussion must be subject to instructions.

Interest Remind the other side that if the case goes to trial and judgment, they will have to pay interest on the damages; any settlement negotiated after the commencement of proceedings should reflect the interest due (see Chapter 7).

Keeping offers open If an offer is made that is too good to be rejected but it is felt that the case is worth slightly more, do not reject the offer but write to the insurers that 'I cannot advise my client to accept' the offer, and so keep the offer open. Always remember, though, that the insurers are entitled to withdraw the offer at any time before it is accepted and that a counter-offer, formally, amounts to a rejection of the original offer. If your response, perhaps including a claimant's Part 36, does not result in an increased offer then discuss with your client whether this is the time to cut and run and see if, as is usually the case, the offer can be resurrected (see below, increased offers, on the best way to deal with an offer too good to reject but not quite good enough to accept without some hesitation).

Increasing offers Small increases in settlement offers can often be achieved by telephoning the insurers and explaining the problems raised by a 'difficult client' or counsel's opinion or, alternatively, by agreeing to 'recommend the offer' to the client if it is increased slightly.

Negotiating under pressure In an issued case the time for a claimant to negotiate with the defendant is when the other side is under pressure (for example, when the claimant has recently delivered a Request for Further Information or for the defendant to state a positive case on a difficult issue).

Compensation recovery Always remember the effect that recovery of welfare benefits will have on the case (see Chapter 7) as this may lead you to accepting a lower offer earlier on rather than negotiating for more which will be wiped out by the benefits accrued meanwhile.

Costs

When accepting an offer always state that it is accepted 'subject to the payment of our costs'. If the claim settles pre-issue but no agreement is reached on costs these can now be recovered by seeking detailed assessment under Part 8 procedure (see CPR Part 44). Currently, with various cost negotiators instructed by insurers often on terns that they are not prepared to reveal this is one of the most acrimonious steps in the claim process. At a time when representatives are encouraged to settle without recourse to court the number of cases going to assessment after amicable resolution of the substantive issues has increased dramatically prompting concern from senior costs officers. At the moment no easy solution to the problem seems available (see later commentary on the short form procedure CPR Part 44.12A).

Costs in cases settled for less than £1,000 for pain suffering and loss of amenity

The Civil Procedure Rules increased the small claims jurisdiction to £5,000. One of the exceptions is where the pain, suffering and loss of amenity award exceed £1000. In those cases even if the totality of damages does not exceed £5,000 costs will still be payable. The difficulty lies with claims under £5,000 where the injury element is under £1,000. Whilst there is an argument that it is the allocation to small claims track (see Chapter 13) that triggers the cost prohibition and that therefore cost incurred in cases settled prior to that juncture for less than £1,000 are still recoverable this is an argument unlikely to prove successful. It is therefore important that you do make an assessment of the value of the claim as early as possible as a client is unlikely to be pleased with your service if the damages recovered are promptly absorbed by your fees.

Watch out for the helpful error frequently made by over zealous defendants; that is, the habit of marking every offer as a Part 36 offer. Part 36 carries with it an inherent right to costs. Therefore, if you accept a Part 36 offer argue for your costs even if the sum accepted is under £1,000 (see the case of *Dean v. Griffin* (2000) 9 C.L. 53).

Under the new rules the one exception to the 'no costs' rule seems to be when you are dealing with those under a disability. It was widely accepted that under the old rules that this had no affect on cost provisions. Early authority under the Civil Procedure rules suggests the contrary and that these cases will be viewed as an exception (see the case of *K v. Grocutt* (2001) 2 C.L. 49).

8.5. On settlement

When a case is settled, always:

(a) ensure that it is settled subject to payment of costs: There is now a separate

Part 8 procedure that can be used if the only item incapable of amicable resolution pre issue is cost.

(b) consider whether the client is under 18; if so, the proposed settlement will probably have to be approved by the court. This applies whether the infant is the claimant or a dependant in a fatal accident claim: see Chapter 24;

(c) (if proceedings have been commenced) but not reached the time of a defense consider whether the settlement should be recorded in an order of the court: see Chapter 20.

8.6. Conclusion

Some words of warning, before you issue proceedings, do make sure that you are happy to justify your approach to the court. Conduct of the claim, both before and after issue is something that the court will consider on summary and detailed cost assessments. CPR Part 44.5(3) under the general heading "Factors to be taken into account when deciding the amount of costs" requires the court to consider the conduct of all parties before and during proceedings and efforts made before and after proceedings to try to resolve the dispute. To protect your client in costs as much as possible, it is imperative that you do make a genuine pre-issue attempt to settle claims.

Part III

PROCEEDINGS

9. Commencing Proceedings

9.1. When to commence proceedings

Before embarking on proceedings it is always as well to spend a few moments reminding yourself of the function of the court so that you can ensure you are conducting the claim in the appropriate fashion. Bear in mind your obligations within the overriding objective. No apologies are offered for repeating it. The rules are a new procedural code with the overriding objective of enabling the court to deal with cases justly. To ignore it is to ignore the time weary scout motto 'be prepared'. Under the CPR the court must always seek to give effect to that objective whenever it considers a case. Know your case, know what you want to achieve and how best to achieve it at all times whilst ensuring that you conduct the case openly and within the spirit as well as the letter of the rules.

There are some instances set out later where you may consider delaying issue. Otherwise you are likely to be issuing proceedings in the following situations:

- where reasonable attempts to settle the claim before issue have been fruitless either because there are insurmountable arguments on liability or the parties are poles apart on quantum or both;
- limitation is rapidly approaching and proceedings are a necessity. Sometimes defendants offer to agree a voluntary extension of the primary limitation period. Unless you are confident that settlement is imminent it is wise to reject the offer and issue. Otherwise you have another time limit about which to worry, the urgency goes from the case and if the matter eventually does go to trial you may face adverse judicial comment on the amount of time it has taken to progress the claim;
- a final prognosis is not yet available in a large liability case where the client is in financial need and the defendant declines to make a voluntary interim payment so that you need proceedings to enable you to apply to the court for one;
- a final prognosis is not yet available in a case of contested liability and you believe the case is suitable for split trial to determine the issue of liability now.

Reasons to delay commencing proceedings

Before commencing proceedings always carry out the checks set out below and consider the following:

(1) Review the claim thoroughly. Is it sound on liability? If not and you lose or have to abandon the claim your client is likely to have to meet the defendant's costs or you have a duty now to quantify risk for any pre or part legal expense insurers.

(2) What is likely quantum? If the total value of the general damage are under £1,000 your client is unlikely to recover any costs (see Chapter 8, p. 100 and Chapter 28). It may therefore be uneconomic to take the claim further.

(3) What further evidence do you need? Remember that you must serve a medical report detailing all injuries and a statement of special damage with the proceedings.

(4) Are you in a position to press on with the case once issued? Once a defence has been filed the court will send out allocation questionnaires and once completed the court will timetable the action to trial, if liability is disputed, or disposal, if quantum only is disputed. There will be little or no time to play catch up, except in serious injury cases where the period before final prognosis is prolonged or where you receive instructions late in the primary limitation period there is really no reason nor excuse to issue proceedings unless at the time of so doing you are actually ready for trial.

9.2. Checks before issuing proceedings

In a public funded case, check that the certificate covers the issue (and service) of proceedings. In legal expense cases check whether the insurers approval to issue is necessary and if so obtain it.

In a private case, write to the client, putting on record the uncertainties and risks of litigation, and set out the possible financial liabilities. A further bill and request for money on account of costs will help bring this home.

Client's authority

In all cases write to the client, explaining the steps you are going to take and obtain the client's authority before issuing proceedings. If you are not going to ask the client to sign the statement of truth but propose to do so yourself obtain your client's authority for you to do so.

Defendant's ability to pay

Check that the defendant will be able to meet any judgment debt. Usually this causes no difficulty as the defendant is insured but in some unusual circumstances the defendant may not be able to meet its liabilities and will be uninsured. To ensure you have insurance backing in road accident claims remember you must notify the insurers of your specific intention to issue by 7 days post issue at the latest.

9.3. Which court?

Most practitioners prefer to sue in the High Court where damages are higher and the judges more experienced. However, there is now very little choice as to venue and only one method of entry, namely Part 7 proceedings.

Commencing proceedings in the high court

Proceedings which include a claim for damages in respect of personal injuries may only be commenced in the High Court if the total claim is worth £50,000 or more. Remember the £50,000 includes:

(1) Total aggregate value of claim. If you are acting for two or more claimants against the same defendant consider whether their claims can be taken together rather than separately to exceed £50,000. You may also save an issue fee.

(2) All claims including special damage, future loss and claims not arising from the accident (*e.g.* unpaid wages or holiday pay if you are suing an employer).

If, for example, you are acting for A and B against Z:

A's claim	general damage	£10,000
	special damage	£20,000
B's claim	general damage	£5,000
	special damage	£15,000

You could start proceedings in the High Court.

The High Court and County Courts Jurisdiction Order 1991 (S.I. 1991 No. 724), article 9 provides that if the value of an injury claim is less than £50,000 then the claim must be commenced in the county court. This is subject to a revisit on completion of the allocation questionnaire where you can seek a transfer up to the High Court even if the claim is worth less than £50,000. Prime examples of cases suitable for this consideration in the injury field are claims against the police and Fatal Accident Claims (see Chapter 25).

Far more important now than the allocation between High and county court is the track to which a claim is allocated. Allocation will be made after the Defence has been filed and served and after the filing of the allocation questionnaire. On issue you are asked to give an estimate of value but this is mainly to ensure the correct court fee is paid and so that the court has some assistance on allocation beyond the parties, suggestions upon which to form a view about the most appropriate track (see Chapter 13 for detailed consideration of the allocation questionnaire and tracks).

Remember that if the total claim is worth less than £5,000 but includes an injury claim for over £1,000 you should state this as otherwise on the face of it the claim is likely to be placed in the small claims track with fixed costs the norm. Beware of trying to avoid this by placing an artificially high value on the injury as you may find yourself on the wrong end of a wasted costs order.

9.4. Who to sue?

Make sure you are suing the right person and ensure that the defendant is being sued in the correct name.

Limited company

If the defendant is a limited company, it is usually advisable to do a company search. However, if you are in correspondence with the defendant's insurers, then it is often sufficient simply to ask them to confirm the correct name and address of the proposed defendant. Strictly speaking, that may not be good enough, but in practice it is inconceivable that they would be able to avoid liability through supplying the wrong information. If in doubt, do a search. Sue in the registered name of the company and serve the proceedings by sending them to the company's registered office; or another office of the company if it is linked to the claim. You can do instant registered office searches by telephone. Note that many partnerships call themselves "& Co.", without being registered as a company; a Companies House search will reveal the true position as with a registered office search as no registered office will appear if there is no limited company of that name.

Sole trader

Sue in full name, or in trading name; for example, "John Jones (trading as Jones Haulage)".

Partnership

Sue in the name of the partnership or in the names of the individual partners. However, suing in the names of the partners, rather than in the name of the partnership, makes it more complicated to seize goods to enforce a judgment, although that is rarely necessary in personal injury cases. The proceedings need only be served on one partner, or on the person in charge of the firm's principal place of business.

Government departments

Sue in the name of the department, and serve the proceeding, on the solicitor to that department, or the Treasury Solicitor. The White Book and the Green Book (under "Crown Proceedings") both contain lists showing whether departments have their own solicitors or whether they rely on the Treasury Solicitor. You must check this if uncertain to ensure that there is valid service.

Local authority

Sue in the name of the local authority, and serve the proceedings, on the specific department against whom the claim is made, on the chief executive or on the insurance officer.

State schools

Sue in the name of the education authority (usually the county council outside London).

Hospitals

If the hospital is under the control of the local authority sue the local health authority. If it has contracted out sue the relevant hospital Trust. It is rarely necessary to sue the doctor responsible unless it is a claim arising out of private treatment.

Police

Sue in the name of the chief constable, for example "Sir XYZ (Chief Constable of the ... Police Authority)". In London, sue the Commissioner of Police in London. Serve the proceedings on the Chief Constable.

Vicarious liability

Often, an accident will have been caused by an employee acting in the course of his or her employment. Usually in such circumstances it is only necessary to sue the employer. However, you should ascertain this before issue. If you cannot, then you should issue against both the employee and the employer. If you can show you made enquiries of the defendant/s before issue and they did not respond then even if you have to amend later or discontinue against one defendant you ought to have cost protection for your client. The CPR are all about openness. If defendants fail to answer reasonable requests for information then they can expect little sympathy on additional costs that ensue. To be fair, most insurers confirm readily that there is no need to sue the employee.

More than one defendant

If there is more than one possible defendant you will need to try to ascertain pre-issue which is the correct defendant. If that is impossible, for example if two potential defendants blame each other, or one does not respond then you will need to protect your client and issue against all potential defendants. In these situations you must try to set the position up so that your client has cost protection whatever the outcome. For example, obtain written confirmation from each defendant that it blames the other rather than accepting a bare denial. This way if you win against one but not the other you should be able to pass on the costs of the successful defendant and recover your wasted costs of pursuing that defendant from the losing defendant. If you have written to potential defendants and they have failed to respond then refer to that failure as causative of additional costs being incurred if there is any later dispute as to the amount of your costs. If they had responded and admitted liability then you would have been spared the cost of suing other parties or if they had responded and put up a compelling argument then you would not have needed to sue them.

As an aside, lack of knowledge of the identity of the defendant is a factor to consider when determining date of knowledge for limitation purposes.

9.5. Drafting the claimant's Statement of Case

A sure sign that the court process has changed is the immediate use of new terminology. Pleadings are a thing of the past. Each party must now state its case. Whether you use counsel for this is a matter for you. That decision will no doubt be based on complexity of the issues that remain, your own confidence as a drafter and cost. It will be difficult to justify the cost of counsel in a straightforward road accident claim or in a quantum only case. In a complicated employer liability case involving consideration of health and safety obligations then counsel may be invaluable. Be flexible and view each case separately. Build up your own precedent base if you do use counsel as you can learn from their experience. Whatever you decide do make sure that the Statement of Case explains who the parties are, what happened, why the claimant believes that the defendant has been negligent and that it sets out all losses that flow from that negligence, including reference to interest.

Instructions to counsel

If you do decide that you need counsel's assistance then send off the papers. These should be headed "Instructions to Counsel to Settle". Whilst few people now raise the point you "instruct" if you want some document drafted, you send a "case" if you want advice and a "brief" for any hearing.

Most papers sent to counsel are now on A4 and many are no longer held together with pink tape. This is a matter of personal preference. However, if the documents are voluminous a lever arch file divided into clear sections is certainly a more accessible approach. Do not send everything on file and the kitchen sink.

Send counsel the relevant documents only. It is rare in a personal injury claim that there will be much relevant correspondence. The letter of claim and the substantive response are usually sufficient. Save counsel's time by weeding out the unnecessary documents. The papers usually include any client questionnaires or statements, other witness evidence, expert evidence both medical and relating to liability, the letters already referred to and any relevant disclosure that accompanied the substantive response or has been acquired from other sources whether by court order or voluntarily and all documents in support of the special damage claim. Sometimes you might decide to ask counsel to draft the liability portion of the statement of case only and do the schedule of special damage yourself. If so, omit the special damage documents but do tell counsel expressly of your intentions.

If the correct papers are included the instructions need not be lengthy. One hopes you have instructed a counsel who can read. On that assumption do not reiterate what counsel will glean from reading the papers. Simply set out briefly;

(a) for whom you act and under what fee arrangement;

(b) details of the proposed defendant;

(c) the date of the accident or injury;

(d) brief circumstances of the accident or injury;

(e) brief details of injury including any which are continuing;

(f) brief details of special damage;

(g) any particular difficulties;

(h) any offers which have been made to settle;

This will also allow you to use the instructions as a chance to review the case and an aide-memoire to any outstanding matters. Using a standard format will help you each time you update the instructions. When or if you do so continue numbering from where the last papers reached to avoid having a number of documents before counsel of the same number.

Counsel's fee

Counsel's fee will usually be on a fixed scale (see the Green Book for current figures in the county court) although there is discretion to exceed these figures. If the case is public funded, then no fee is marked on the instructions; instead the words 'public fund' are written on the backsheet.

Choice of counsel

The choice of counsel is important. Strictly, the less specialist in the injury field you are the more specialist should be your counsel. This way the client is best served and you can learn from the experience of counsel. Frequently, one sees generalists instruct generalists. Remember that the defendant will be using its highly experienced injury teams. At worst, you want to level the playing field. Do not be scared by counsel. His or her function is to assist your client. The name of a respected counsel on a statement of case will add credibility to the case and will make the defendant know that you mean business.

There may be other considerations such as whether a particular counsel will deal with a case on a conditional fee arrangement. Ring the clerk and find out. Like all businesses chambers want work. Use your purchasing power to secure the best counsel at proportionate cost for your client. Good counsel can win cases and just as importantly bad counsel can lose them.

How to choose counsel

(1) Personal knowledge: obviously it is best to use counsel that you have used before and know will be suitable for the case.

(2) Firm's approved list: most firms keep lists of counsel who are used regularly and approved. Maintenance of such a list is obligatory for public funding franchising and membership of the Personal Injury Panel. Consider your list for suitable counsel. If you decide to use a barrister on the list who is not personally known to you then discuss the barrister with the fee earner who last instructed him or her to ensure that the barrister is right for your case.

(3) Recommendation: do not feel obliged only to use counsel on the firm's list as a list is only useful if it is a specialist one and constantly expanded and updated. If there is no suitable barrister on your firm's list try asking colleagues at other firms or clerks or counsel from chambers experienced in personal injury law for a recommendation.

(4) Lawyers' directories: some directories such as the Legal 500 or Chambers' Directory contain lists of counsel who have a good reputation in personal injury matters.

(5) Law Reports. If colleagues cannot suggest a suitable name then consult the Law Reports and see which junior counsel, from which chambers, are reported.

Obviously, if you use any barrister who is not on your firm's approved list you should note on the file why that barrister is being used and who recommended that barrister. Add the barrister to your firm's list.

The claimant's Statement of Case

The Particulars or Statement of Claim will summarise all the claimant's allegations, and the contentions to be made at trial, so that the defendant will be able to prepare a case in answer. It must be both comprehensive and accurate. In particular:

(1) The claimant's date of birth (or age) must be stated.

(2) Interest must be specifically claimed.

(3) Any conviction recorded against the defendant, and upon which the claimant intends to rely, must be specifically stated with the date and court particularised. If the defendant pleaded guilty then this should also be pleaded. This is especially important in road accident cases, for a conviction or guilty plea to a careless driving charge will often put the defendant in considerable difficulties.

(4) Any breach of statutory duty must be specifically pleaded. Refer to the relevant section of the statute.

(5) Medical complaints should be comprehensively pleaded, for this will give the judge an initial impression of the claim's value. Apart from the medical description of the injuries, include the ways in which they affect the claimant (*e.g.* embarrassment caused by facial scar; inability to pursue favourite hobbies and sports). This is the loss of amenity element of the claim awards.

(6) An application for provisional damages must be specifically stated (see below).

(7) There is no need to claim costs.

Checking the statement

Since the Particulars or Statement of Claim will be the first document read by the judge, it is essential that it is accurate. Any errors may colour the judge's attitude to the claimant's credibility. In addition, the judge is more likely to be sympathetic to an allegation that has been made by the claimant from the start of the case, rather than one that has been inserted later as an amendment seemingly as an after thought or as plan B after plan A has failed.

When the draft Particulars of Claim is received from counsel, it should be checked, first, for inaccuracies, such as incorrect dates or motor vehicle registration numbers, and, second, to ensure that all the necessary allegations (including statutory ones) have been made.

Do not expect counsel to send an advice or opinion with the draft Particulars or Statement of Claim. It would be most unusual to do so, unless this was specifically requested by the instructing solicitor. If there is a particular point that counsel wants to mention it will usually be put in a covering note.

Once you have received counsel's draft Particulars or Statement of Claim, you should read it through carefully. Having done that, you should send it to the client for checking. While you should have all the information the client may well be reassured by seeing the document and if the case is complicated the client should be asked to check the detailed allegations.

The draft Particulars or Statement of Claim is then ready for typing on A4 paper. These days, typing on one side of the paper only (because of word processors) is acceptable. Otherwise, there should be no unnecessary blank sides, and the typing should be immaculate. If your software is compatible with counsel's you may be able simply to amend counsel's draft on your word processor. Out of respect for the court, make sure that it is neat, easy to read, and unmarked. Often, counsel will send drafts by email to make it easy to transpose ready for court.

Beware of the all too common mistake of overlooking blanks left by counsel for completion. Even more embarrassing is to leave in queries that have been raised by counsel such as "instructing solicitors to ask claimant if this is correct". Not only is your credibility harmed and your likelihood of recovering any cost for perusing counsel's draft nil, but in extreme cases it may hurt your client's case and raise professional issues.

Medical report

A medical report, substantiating all the personal injuries alleged in the Particulars or Statement of Claim which the claimant proposes to adduce in evidence as part of the case at trial, must be served with the Particulars of Claim or the Statement of Claim. See CPR Part 16. It is therefore extremely important to ensure that the medical reports are full and complete and substantiate all the personal injuries alleged. You may need a further medical report from an expert in another discipline, *e.g.* a psychiatrist's report to support allegations of memory loss in addition to an orthopaedic report. If you are not able to substantiate an allegation of injury with a medical report consider whether that allegation should be deleted from the Particulars or Statement of Claim. Although you are entitled later to serve updated medical reports, the reports filed with the Particulars have the status of a quasi-statement of case and you will have to obtain leave of the court to amend them or to adduce further medical reports in respect of an injury not stated originally in the Claim.

Statement of special damage

CPR Part 16 states that, similarly, a Statement of Special Damage must give full particulars of the special damages claimed for expenses and losses already incurred and as accurate an estimate as possible of any future expenses and losses (including loss of earnings and pension rights). See Chapter 7 for how to prepare the statement. This should be widely drafted. Any continuing loss of earnings should be given, and losses and expenses should be summarised. It is better to include doubtful items at this stage as they can always be deleted later. If you are still awaiting further information at the time you wish to serve the Particulars of Claim because of time constraints on validity you may put "To be quantified later". However, this is bad practice, breaches the rules and you may well find that the court strikes out that unquantified item of loss.

Provisional damages

When considering your client's case do not overlook the possibility of an award of provisional damages. The rules are complicated, but basically it must be shown that there is "a *chance* that at some definite or indefinite time in the future the injured person . . . will develop some *serious* disease or suffer some *serious* deterioration in his physical or mental condition" (Supreme Court Act 1981, s. 32A). The key points to note about this definition are:

(a) provisional damages can only be awarded in personal injury cases (but this includes disease cases);

(b) only *serious* cases are covered. Accordingly, it will only be a minority of cases that are suitable for provisional damages;

(c) there need only be a *chance* of deterioration (or disease developing); this is a relatively low burden of proof, especially since the claimant does not have to show that there is a probability of such a complication arising. The chance of the event happening is low. Were it high then the court would regard it as sufficiently likely to enable a conventional value to be placed on the risk within the ordinary general damages awarded.

Potentially, the introduction of provisional damages could have transformed the handling of personal injury claims. In practice it has not done so. The courts were reluctant to lay down guidelines as to which cases are suitable, and the general view has been to reserve the use of provisional damages for the exceptional, complicated case and to limit cases to those where there is a clear and severable risk of a different condition developing, such as eplepsy after a head injury. So, for example, it was held that a person who had broken a joint, leading to a risk of future osteo-arthritis, could not claim provisional damages as this risk was simply an aspect of the progression of the condition and not serious deterioration. Having said that, it would seem that many cases could still come within the definition set out above and such claims should always be considered.

Procedure

The main point to note is that a claim for provisional damages must be specifically stated. Thus, it is for the claimant to decide whether or not to include such a claim in the Statement of Case; there is no way that the defendant can force a claimant to opt for provisional damages. Bear in mind that provisional damages only relate to specific risks, within specified time periods; the provisional damages rules do not cover general unforeseen risks in the future. In fact, defendants would not wish to encourage such claims anyway. If an award is made then the insurance company must carry that risk forward and provide for it. For an industry that wishes to crystallise loss having a further possible outlay hanging around for a number of years creates a continuing risk and need for an unwanted reserve. Often, in cases where a provisional loss is claimed the defendant will offer over the odds for the injury then capable of quantification if the provisional claim is dropped. In other words, the defendant buys off the risk of another payout later.

The order for provisional damages

There must be a court order for the provisional damages rules to apply. If the case goes to trial, then the judge's award of damages will recite the disability, and refer to the relevant documents. On the other hand, if the case is settled then it will be necessary for a consent order to be made. If the case is settled before the commencement of proceedings, then it will be necessary to start proceedings merely for recording the provisional damages award by way of a consent order. For the steps to be taken by the solicitors, and for the contents of the court file, see Procedural Table 14—see draft order from CPR Part 41.

Applying for further damages

The provisional damages order will refer to the specific risks (of disease or deterioration) that are covered by the provisional damages order. In addition, it will set out a specified time period within which application can be made. Note, however, that the claimant can apply for that time period to be extended; and can apply more than once. On the other hand, the defendant cannot apply for the time period to be shortened.

If the claimant wants to apply for time to be extended, the application must be made within the stated period. If the claimant wishes to apply for further damages to be awarded, the procedure is:

(1) give 28 days notice of this to the defendant (and the insurers, if known). The notice must be given within the period specified in the provisional damages order.

(2) within 21 days of expiry of the 28 day period of notice, the claimant must issue an application for direction of the future conduct of the action. At the application for direction of the future conduct of the action, the District Judge will give directions for the conduct of the action (*e.g.* disclosure of medical reports, place and date of trial).

Interest

When further damages are awarded, then interest can be awarded on those further damages. But interest only runs from the date when the claimant gave notice to the defendant of intention to apply for further damages.

High Court and county court procedure in detail

Regardless of which court the claim is made in the procedure is governed by CPR Part 16 and Part 41 and it is essential that you examine these Parts before issuing proceedings including a claim for provisional damage.

Part 16.4(d) states that such a claim must be specifically incorporated into the Particulars of Claim together with an explanation of the ground/s on which such an award is sought. Paragraph 4.4 of the practice direction to accompany Part 16 provides a summary of the information required:

- the claimant must state specifically that a remedy is sought pursuant to section 32a of the Supreme Court Act 1981 or section 51 of The County Court Act 1984; and
- that there is a chance that at some future time the claimant will develop some serious disease or suffer some serious deterioration in his physical or mental condition; and
- the disease or type of deterioration in respect of which an application may be made in the future must be specified.

Looking ahead, it is important to note that a default judgment cannot be entered in a action including a claim for provisional damages. The correct course of action in such cases is to apply to the court for directions under Part 23 *at which appointment* there is likely to be consideration of the directions needed to decide whether the claim is suitable for an award of provisional damages and if so on what terms and the amount of immediate damages.

Generally, see Procedural Table 14.

9.6. Form and layout of Statements of Case

The layout of all Statements of Case is the same whether claim or defence, High Court or county court. The heading and statement of parties will be as on the claim form, and will, of course, include the action number. After the parties' names, the nature of the statement is stated (*e.g.* Statement of Claim), and this will be followed by the statement itself. The statement will be set out in neat numbered paragraphs; there will be separate headings for breaches of statutory duty, particulars of personal injury, and particulars of special damage. In the case of a Particulars or Statement of Claim, it will finish with the phrase "AND the claimant claims DAMAGES" followed by the name of the counsel if settled by counsel. Note that this is an unliquidated claim, and no figure is put on the general damages.

Unless the Particulars of Claim are indorsed on the Claim Form which has its own statement of truth section then there must be a separate statement of truth at the end of the Particulars of Claim. If you sign a statement of truth on behalf of your client you must confirm that you are authorised to sign it by your client. Below the statement of truth should be the date of the document and your firm details for service purposes. Refer to the specimen Particulars of Claim in Appendix E for how the document should look.

The backsheet will summarise the document, stating the court, action number, parties, nature of the pleading, name and address (plus reference and phone number) of the claimant's solicitor.

These rules apply for all Statements of Case. In addition, *any* Statement of Case should include:

(a) year, letter, and number of action;

(b) title of action;

(c) the court and the division of the court;

(d) a description of the pleading;

(e) its date of service (if served by post, the date will be the second working day after posting);

(f) the name and address of the solicitor.

(g) contain the signature of solicitor (or name of counsel);

(h) be on A4 paper,

(i) contain a statement of truth;

(j) be divided into numbered, consecutive paragraphs;

(k) show dates, sums and numbers in figures, not words which is not endorsed on the claim form.

(l) if a Statement or Particulars of Claim, state the date on which the proceedings were issued;

(m) a claim for interest.

Issuing proceedings in the High Court and county court

Under the CPR there is only one method of issue of court proceedings. That is by Claim Form involving the procedure laid out in CPR Part 7 and 8. The term Claim Form replaces both writ and county court summons. Proceedings are started when the court issues the Claim Form (see Appendix E for a precedent Claim Form).

The Claim Form states the names of the parties, gives a brief description of the claim, contains a statement of value, affirms whether or not the case raises

Human Rights issues, may contain the full statement of case and must contain a statement of truth.

Issue of proceedings

Proceedings can be issued in any court which is convenient to you. This will usually be the court nearest your office. If the claim is liquidated (which is unlikely) the case will automatically be transferred to the defendant's home court on receipt of a defence. In an unliquidated claim the defendant is entitled to apply for a transfer to its home court but this may well be refused as courts usually take the view that in personal injury actions it is the claimant's solicitor who does most of the work and makes most applications. The most convenient court will usually be that closest to that solicitor's office although the case may be transferred for trial to a court convenient for witnesses and parties.

Wrongful transfer Some county courts have a habit of wrongly automatically transferring both liquidated and unliquidated claims on receiving a defence. If this happens you should immediately write to both new and old courts, pointing out the error and asking for transfer back.

Documents Which documents you send or take to the court for issue depends if you are issuing a simply indorsed Claim Form, one indorsed with the Statement of Case or one with separate Statement attached and whether you wish the court to serve the proceedings. In the first instance you will simply need the Claim Form together with two copies and the appropriate court fee. In the second and third cases you will need the Claim Form with the statement indorsed or the separate document with it on and the medical evidence in triplicate and the court fee. If the schedule of special damages is not within the Statement of Case you will also need this in triplicate. Although it is unlikely now that you will have public funding, if you do then you must lodge with the court the certificate and a copy of the notice of issue of the certificate with a copy of the latter for service. You can use stock letter 32 if writing to the court.

For limitation purposes, regardless of the date upon which the court ultimately issues the Claim Form, the claim is 'brought' on the date that the documents were received by the court so that delay in dealing with incoming work does not prejudice the claimant (see CPR Part 7 PD 5.1). However, it will be a brave solicitor who is happy to rely on this. If you are close to limitation try to have the Claim Form taken to the court and issued then and there. You know that you will sleep easier if you do. Most courts are incredibly helpful and even if volume of work prevents them issuing over the counter most will allow you to return later that day or the next to collect the issued proceedings.

The general indorsement

This does not need to be detailed as that would defeat the very purpose of this facility. In most injury claims wording such as 'This is a claim for injury and loss and damage together with a claim for interest at common law and pursuant to statute arising out of the alleged negligence of the defendant/s in an accident that occurred on the   day of 2001' will suffice. There will be occasions where this wording needs to be adapted somewhat. Otherwise, a widely drafted indorsement like this leaves the door fully open for the subsequent Statement of Case to raise any matters necessary.

Even if you intend to ask counsel to settle the Statement of Case you should deal with the indorsement as use of counsel for this would plainly be disproportionate.

Amendment

A Statement of Case can be amended at any time prior to service. However, remember that the court still has residual power to disallow any amendments.

Any amended Statement of Case must be reaffirmed in the form of a statement of truth.

9.7. Notifying the other side

There is no requirement that a defendant be told that proceedings have been issued but in road accident cases it is vital that the claimant notifies the other side that the proceedings have been issued within seven days of issue whether in the High Court or the county court (see Road Traffic Act 1988, ss. 151 and 152. See also the recent case of *Wylie v. Wake*, December 21, 2000, CA for problems that arise if this is overlooked).

Insurers

If the defendants are insured, the Road Traffic Act 1988 (RTA 1988) s. 151 requires that the defendant's insurers (or their solicitors) be notified within seven days. Use stock letter 35. In fact notice can be given before proceedings are commenced. So, in practice, the best course of action is to write to the insurers giving notice before the proceedings are issued but, if you forget, ensure you also notify within seven days of issue. If you have progress sheets on your files ensure that a reminder to serve a 151/152 notice appears on them.

MIB

If the defendants are uninsured and the claimant's claim includes a personal injury element, then it is likely the MIB will meet any unpaid judgment. The 1999 MIB Agreement requires that they be notified of the issuing of the proceedings within fourteen days (see Chapter 28, section 1). Use stock letter 36. Unlike notification to insurers the MIB *cannot* be given valid notice before the proceedings are issued. There are other requirements at this stage. See Chapter 29 but also read the 1999 Agreement as that must be the starting point for considering the MIB involvement.

This fourteen-day notification requirement only applies to road accident cases. If notification is not given, the action can still proceed against the defendant. But the MIB can then refuse to meet any judgment. In practice the MIB takes a strict line. It is very easy to overlook the fourteen-day period and it is a mistake that is commonly made. If this happens, and the MIB take the point, the only remedy is to issue new proceedings and then give them notice within the fourteen-day period. Obviously this cannot be done if the three-year limitation period has expired; if it has, then a negligence claim against you is likely. Please read the text of the agreement carefully.

Notifying your client's own insurers

This is only relevant in road accident claims and even then only in those where your client's cover is fully comprehensive. Usually in such cases your instructions will relate only to the uninsured loss claim. However, if your client's insurers have incurred an outlay, such as repair costs or pre-accident value of a vehicle and they have no memorandum of understanding or other arrangement with the defendant's insurers and have not recovered their outlay be careful not to issue proceedings and settle without checking whether they want their outlay incorporated in your claim. If you fail to do so, and subsequently settle the court process and they have an outlay that they then cannot recover you may find that your client is unable to reinstate the no claims bonus and cannot recoup over paid premiums and it is arguable that you may have an obligation to the client's insurers of whose interest you should have been on notice. A simple letter to them prior to issue covers your position by placing the onus upon them to be proactive (see stock letter 55).

9.8. Renewing the proceedings

The claim form is only valid for four months (six months if the defendant is outside the jurisdiction); it must be served within that time together with the Particulars or Statement of Claim.

CPR Part 7.6 does allow for limited extensions to the service period. These can only be obtained if the application for extension is made within the initial service period or within any extended service period granted by the court. The rule is clear that generally an extension will only be granted if the application is outside these time periods if:

- the court has been unable to serve the Claim Form; and
- the claimant has taken all reasonable steps to serve but has been unable to do so; and
- in either case the claimant has acted promptly in making the application.

An application for extension must be supported by evidence and can be made without notice.

9.9. Serving proceedings

A court will issue the proceedings and will send you notice of issue. They will normally serve the proceedings direct by post and will inform you of the date of service on the defendant. You should diary 14 days from the date of presumed service for service of the defence.

However the claimant's solicitor may request that the documents are returned for service, in which case they *must* be served within four months of issue (together of course with a copy of the medical report and the Schedule of Special Damage and any public funding Notice of Issue of Certificate).

If the defendant has nominated solicitors to accept service of proceedings as is increasingly likely given the personal injury protocol you must serve on those solicitors. The case of *Nanglegan v Royal Free Hampstead Trust* [2001] 3 C.L. 61 seems to have set an unhealthy precedent which is fairly harsh if you are close to limitation. In this case solicitors were nominated but that was overlooked by the claimant's solicitors who served on the defendant. This was held to be irregular service with the court holding that as solicitors had been nominated service must be on them.

Interest

Interest on general damages (a mere two per cent) only runs from the date proceedings are served (not issued) so delay in service should be avoided.

Service copy

If you are serving the court will send you a service copy with a response pack attached to it. Make sure you do serve the response pack when you come to serve the proceedings.

Acknowledgement of service form (form N9)

This is the response pack that must be served on the defendant. The defendant can choose not to use it and simply to file a defence. However, if the defendant elects to file an Acknowledgement this is not required until the Particulars of Claim have been served. So if you serve a generally indorsed Claim Form the defendant need take no action.

Otherwise, a defendant may file an acknowledgement if more time is needed for the defence. The Defence or an Acknowledgement must be filed within 14 days of service of the Particulars of Claim. If an acknowledgement is filed then the defence is not required until 28 days after service of the Particulars of Claim. In other words, the defendant can secure an additional 14 days for service of the defence by filing an Acknowledgement.

The other reason to file an Acknowledgement is if the defendant wishes to challenge the jurisdiction of the court (see CPR Part 10.1(3)(b) and below for more detail).

The Acknowledgement is filed with the court who must then notify you that this has taken place. The Acknowledgement must be signed by the defendant or the defendant's legal representative and must include an address for service. If anyone else has signed the Acknowledgement it is irregular and should not have been accepted by the court. The exception is where an Acknowledgement is signed for a company. In that situation a person holding a senior position within the company may sign but must state the position held within the company.

Rules regarding service (CPR Part 6)

Unless a specific request is made to the contrary, service of the Claim Form is undertaken by the court. Accordingly, an address for the defendant must be provided. This can be the defendant's solicitor's address so long as the solicitor is instructed to accept service. Do lodge a letter from that solicitor confirming that to be the case where appropriate.

The court will serve by first class post. The court will then send you a notice of service which includes the deemed date of service.

Where you undertake service you do need to familiarise yourself with CPR Part 6 which provides as follows.

Service on an individual

This can be by the following methods:

(i) by first class post;

(ii) by leaving it at the place of service;

(iii) by document exchange;

(iv) by fax or other electronic communication;

(v) where the claim arises in contract and the contract provides for a method of service then that method may be used provided the claim is solely in respect of that contract;

(vi) by personal service.

If you do serve, bear in mind the provisions of Part 6.14 which require you to file with the court a certificate of service within seven days of service. Failure to do so will ensure that until you rectify the defect you are unable to enter a default judgment.

Service on a company

In addition to the methods of service on an individual which also apply to companies you can serve companies under the provisions of the Companies Act 1985 provisions which broadly cover service overseas, service on a branch in Great Britain and service at an authorised place (see the Companies Act 1985, ss. 694a, 695 and 725).

Service on a partnership

Service is either in person or at the usual or last known residence of each of the individual partners or at the principal or last known place of business of the firm. Note Part 6 Practice Direction 6-PD004 that if service is on a person at the principal or last known business address then the documents served must include a notice stating whether the person being served is being served as a partner, as a person having control or management of the partnership business or as both.

Service by an alternative method

Substituted service has gone in name alone. CPR Part 6.8 replaces it with service by alternative method. This appears to give the court wide discretion to order service to take any fashion that appears reasonable. The application must state the form of service sought and be supported by witness statement evidence. The court order must not only set out the ordered form of service but also the date when the service will be deemed to take place by the authorised method.

Although it is hard to see the provision applying to service of the Claim Form the court also now has a general power to dispense with service of a document altogether (see CPR Part 6.9).

Time periods for service

The deemed dates of service are as follows:

- First class post—the second day after posting;
- Document exchange—the second day after posting;
- Delivery to or leaving document at a specified address—the day after it was delivered to or left at the address;
- Fax—If transmitted on a business day before 4.00 p.m., on that day or in any other case on the next business day after the day on which it was transmitted;
- Other electronic method—the second day after the day on which it was transmitted;
- Personal service—if a business day before 5.00 p.m., on that day in any other case on the next business day after the day on which it was served.

Judgment in default

Assuming that service has taken place in accordance with the rules, if no Acknowledgement or Defence has been filed with the court within 14 days of service, subject to any certificate of service being lodged, you can request a default judgment. As most injury claims are for unspecified sums this is usually for damages to be decided by the court and costs. Simply complete the bottom section of the notice of issue which contains the request and send it to the court. Many injury practitioners do just that. However, if you wish the disposal procedure which will follow to enable the court to decide the amount of damages to proceed quickly it is as well to append to your request a list of proposed directions that will set a timescale for outstanding quantum steps and give any permissions that you need to rely on evidence. In most cases this will obviate the necessity of a case management conference, saving costs and also create a timescale that puts a defendant under such immense time pressure to play catch up that often it is easier for the defendant to buy the claim off.

If an Acknowledgement has been filed but no defence follows within 28 days of service of the Particulars of Claim then the same procedure applies in respect of judgment in default of filing Defence.

9.10. Time

As time is a precious commodity within the CPR, and ought to be anyway within an efficient personal injury practice, it is worth setting out a reminder of how to compute court timescales. The definition is set out in CPR Part 2.8. In brief, all time periods in the rules referring to days means clear days. Accordingly, in computing time you ignore the day on which the period begins and, if the rule specifies an end day or event that day or the day of the event. For example, service of a straightforward interim application requires three days, notice. If the application is to be heard on the March 31 then the last day for service is March 27, assuming the 27th–31st are all working days. Remember, referring back to the time for service provisions considered that means you must put the document in the post or DX, etc. by the 25th at the latest.

Where the period specified is five days or less and includes a Saturday or Sunday or a Bank holiday, Christmas Day or Good Friday that day does not count.

Where the period specified ends on a day on which the court office is shut then the time is extended until the next day on which the court is open.

Part 8 Proceedings

In this section we have concentrated on Part 7 proceedings. There is another way to commence proceedings under the CPR and that is under Part 8. We shall return to this Part when considering those under a disability (Chapter 24) and have already touched on it when considering remedies for recovery of costs in claims settled prior to issue of proceedings.

10. The Defence

10.1. Time for service

The rule

High and County Court

The Defence must be filed and served within 14 days of service of proceedings or 28 days from service of proceedings if an acknowledgement of service has been filed.

Extensions

Under CPR Part 15.5 the parties can agree that the period of time for filing a Defence be extended for up to 28 days without court approval, although the defendant must write to the court notifying it of the extended period. Except where the defendant has been guilty of flagrant breach of the personal injury protocol it is hard to envisage situations where to refuse a voluntary extension would be reasonable conduct. However, before agreeing you should obtain your client's instructions, highlighting to the client the cost risk of compelling a defendant to apply to the court for an extension where the request is reasonable.

Note that the voluntary extension is a maximum of 28 days. After that the matter must come before the court in one guise or another, either on allocation questionnaire or for further extension so that the court can exercise its proactive management skills to ensure that claims do not fall into a lacuna between service and progress.

If a further extension is required, even if in principle the parties agree the period, the defendant must apply to the court for confirmation using a CPR Part 23 application notice. The application should be supported by a witness statement explaining the delay and the reason further time is required. If the application is by consent and for valid reason you will often find that the court grants the application without a hearing.

If time is sought less openly by the filing of a bland holding defence denying everything, but advancing no positive case then apply to the court to strike out the Defence if the court does not do so under its general case management function.

10.2. Judgment in default of defence

The rule

See pp 124 and 125 above.

Tactics

In practice, however, if it is relatively clear that the defendant does intend to defend but has simply missed the time limit you would not normally enter judgment in default as a tactical move since the defendant can apply for judgment to be set aside and if some reasonable excuse can be found and there is an arguable defence then it is almost certain that the application will succeed. Sometimes there is little point in the claimant seeking a default judgment when the previous correspondence shows that the defendant intends to defend as it only leads to further delay. However, the claimant will almost certainly be awarded all costs thrown away and entering judgment will show that the claimant intends to prosecute the case vigorously, so it might be worth considering if the defendant has failed to ask for an extension of time to serve the defence and you feel that it is not taking the claim seriously and/or has been dilatory throughout.

10.3. Form and contents of the defence

Form

In appearance, the Defence will look much like the Particulars of Claim, in that it will be a typewritten document, set out in numbered paragraphs and complying with the Statement of Case requirements set out in Chapter 9. See the specimen defences in Appendix E.

Contents

Bare denials are a thing of the past. The emphasis is on advancing a positive case and/or admission where appropriate. Statements of Case should be designed to resolve or narrow the issues leaving outstanding areas of dispute clearly defined. CPR Part 16.5 codifies this.

Accordingly, where anything is denied in a Defence there must be an explanation given as to why that is so. If it is because the defendant intends to dispute the claimant's version of events then the defendant must set out in the Defence the version upon which he relies. This style extends also to statements of value. If a defendant disputes a claimant's statement of value that should be stated specifically in the defence together with the defendant's valuation.

Some things remain familiar. If a defendant does not deny or deal with an allegation then it is deemed admitted (see generally precedent Defence in Appendix E).

10.4. The allocation questionnaire

Except in a case involving a Reply or Defence to Counterclaim you need to diarise no dates on receipt of the Defence. The timescale will come once the court has exercised its initial management powers following completion of the allocation questionnaires by the parties. These are sent out by the court and so whilst you will need to diarise the return date once you have received it at this stage you simply wait for it (see Chapter 13 for detailed consideration of the allocation questionnaire). Do not be idle in the interim. There is still plenty of preparation to be done.

10.5. Responding to the defence

Reporting to the client

You should read the Defence carefully; see what admissions are made (for example, time, place, parties to accident) and what are the real issues in dispute. Write to the client explaining the Defence and setting out the issues and questions it raises. It is often helpful to set out the Defence in the form of a questionnaire with space for comments. Explain to the client what this means in practical terms, and what needs to be done to address issues raised.

Summary judgment

Whilst the wording has changed the remedy remains. The court can give summary judgment against either the claimant and/or defendant on the whole of the claim or a particular issue if it considers that the claimant or defendant has no real prospect of success on the issue or on the claim. The test of real prospect is new. Guidance can be found in the case of *Swain v. Hillman, The Times,* November 4, 1999. This suggests that an application for summary judgment under Part 24 should not become a summary trial. The court considers the merits only so far as is necessary to determine if there is a real issue to take to trial.

It is rare for this procedure to be used frequently in injury claims. Active case management has resulted in courts entering judgments for damages to be decided of their own volition in cases where the Defence consists of a bare denial or where only causation and quantum is disputed in the Defence. Whilst there will be the odd case, and more likely the odd issue, such as the right to a provisional damage award, that may be suitable for summary disposal most liability disputed cases must run to trial if not compromised.

Interim payment

Whether or not the Defence admits liability, the claimant should consider applying for an interim payment. See Chapter 12.

Checklist

The claimant's solicitor will also have to decide how to respond to the Defence. It may well be that there are essential steps that you should now take, and also other steps, which whilst not essential, are advisable. So, you should check for:

(a) allegations of *contributory negligence* against the claimant (see below);

(b) allegations against a *third person* (see below);

(c) a *counterclaim* against the claimant (see below);

(d) allegations that the case is *statute barred* (see below).

In any event, the Defence may be unsatisfactorily stated, and require you to:

(e) request *Further Information* of the Defence (see Chapter 16);

(f) serve a *Notice to Admit Facts* on the defendant (see Chapter 16).

At this stage, the claimant must consider whether items (a) to (d) are raised; if so, you must deal with them immediately. In that case, the tactical matters (*i.e.* (e) to (f)) can be put aside for the moment. On the other hand, it may be that the Defence raises none of these issues, in which case the next stage in the action will be consideration of timetabling the claim to trial and suggesting standard directions for allocation purposes.

Contributory negligence

What is contributory negligence?

Frequently, a defendant will deny liability for the accident and conclude the Defence by stating that "the claimant's alleged accident was solely caused or alternatively contributed to by his/her own negligence in that s/he . . . ", followed by a list of allegations setting out the various ways in which the claimant could have been to blame for the accident. Remember, contributory negligence is not only concerned with whether the claimant is partly responsible for the *cause* of the damage, but also whether the claimant is partly responsible for the damage.

Negligence contributory to damage

The most common example of this is the failure of a passenger in a vehicle to wear a seat belt. For years, the contributory negligence has been accepted at 25 per cent if it can be shown that the accident injuries would have been less severe if a seat belt had been worn or 15 per cent if it can be shown, either on medical or expert engineering evidence, that the wearing of a seat belt would have made no difference or indeed would have caused more serious injury. This rule has recently come under challenge from the insurance industry and there seemed almost to be an inevitability that change was afoot. However, the matter was considered again recently by the Court of Appeal in the case of *Jones (A Minor) v. Wilkins (Wynn and anor third parties), The Times*, February 6, 2001, *CA* where the established 25 per cent deduction was reaffirmed. This is an issue that will crop up repeatedly and the figures are bound to be attacked again. Indeed, the Motor Accident Solicitors Society (see Chapter 30) had reported just before this case that other cases on the point were being appealed and the likelihood was that the deductions would be much larger. Common sense suggests that there is some merit in the suggestion that if there would have been no injury if a seatbelt had been worn then the deduction should be in full.

Negligence contributory to cause

This is the more commonly stated form of contributory negligence. For example, in a tripping case that the claimant failed to look where he or she was going, in an employer liability case that the claimant was acting in a way he or she had previously been told not to and in a road accident claim that the claimant could have in some way avoided the accident or was driving in a fashion that partly caused the accident, such as too fast.

Aim of contributory negligence allegation

The defendant's objective is to obtain a percentage finding of contributory negligence against the claimant which will proportionately reduce the damages, or at least give the defendant something to argue about when negotiating a settlement with the claimant's solicitor.

Stating contributory negligence

Any such allegation must be specifically stated otherwise it cannot be raised at trial (unlike, for example, a defence of inevitable accident) unless the trial judge gives leave to amend.

Reporting to the client

Always put allegations of contributory negligence to the client. This is best done by incorporating the allegations (in easily understandable language) into a questionnaire for the client to complete. Type out the questionnaire, giving the client ample room in which to write answers. Put a space to sign and date the questionnaire, at the foot of each page (this could be useful if the client were to die before trial, and the document was to be put under the Civil Evidence Act). Having the client complete a questionnaire in this way will simplify the preparation of your instructions to counsel to advise, etc. It is also worth considering whether the allegations of contributory negligence should be put to any witnesses. If so, prepare similar questionnaires for them. This is particularly so in employer liability cases where co-workers may be able to give independent input.

Do not forget to explain to the client how, if at all, a finding of contributory negligence will reduce damages. The easiest way is to take the example of £1,000 and illustrate how certain findings of contributory negligence would affect that.

Reply

There is no need to serve a reply to the allegations of contributory negligence. This is because a claimant is assumed to deny allegations of contributory negligence. Only if the claimant wishes to raise fresh matters, or a point of law, will you need to serve a 'reply'. If you do serve a reply, then it should deny all the allegations. A reply will very rarely be necessary, but if one is served then it must contain a statement of truth. Do not serve a reply unless it is essential; if one is put in just for general denial of the contributory negligence allegations, the cost will not be allowed on assessment. In short, it is extremely unusual for a reply to be necessary in a personal injury claim.

Further Information

Allegations of contributory negligence are often made without justification, and are no more than a bargaining counter for the defendant in the negotiations. Weak allegations should be attacked by a request for Further Information (CPR Part 18); if the allegations of contributory negligence can be exposed as being without foundation, the trial judge may possibly view the rest of the Defence with scepticism. So, if contributory negligence is alleged, then consider sending the papers to counsel at an earlier date than one might otherwise have done, to ask whether a request for Further Information of the defence should be made. (See Chapter 16 for more detail of further information request.)

Allegations against third persons

In the Defence, the defendant may blame someone who is not a party to the proceedings. When this happens, you should immediately put any such suggestion to the client for comments and instructions. You must then decide whether to sue that third party. This may raise urgent limitation issues.

The alternatives open to the claimant are:

(1) Ignore the allegation and proceed to trial against the present defendant, on the assumption that should the trial evidence indicate some liability on the part of the third party, a fresh action can then be commenced against that third person. Do not forget that a claimant can opt to sue either or both of joint-tortfeasors. So if the present defendant were found only a few per cent liable, and the third party liable for the rest, the claimant could recover 100 per cent damages from the present defendant and leave it to

the defendant to sue the third person to try to recover that proportion of the damages (Civil Liability (Contribution) Act 1978). However, this is not a satisfactory course of action since:

(a) You must be completely confident of winning the current proceedings; and,
(b) there is the risk of missing the three-year limitation period. However, if the service of the Defence is the first occasion on which the claimant has had grounds for considering that third person liable it may be possible to argue that the three years run from the date of the Defence and not from the date of the accident (see Limitation Act 1980 and Chapter 21). This is unlikely to be the case if there has been compliance with the protocol as the potential involvement of the third party should have come to light much earlier.

(2) Sue the third person. There are two ways of doing this:

(a) Issue separate proceedings against the third person, so that there will then be two separate actions proceeding in respect of the one accident. The two actions can later be consolidated and then proceed together, as one action, to one trial.
(b) Join the third person as an additional defendant in the present action. To do this the proceedings will have to be amended and re-served on the present defendant. Amendment of pleadings is explained in Chapter 11.

In practice, it is hard to imagine when option (a) would be relevant. The danger to you and your client is one of costs. Ideally, if you are to sue two or more potential tortfeasors you wish to create a situation where they blame each other. Then, if you do not succeed against them all, you can justify joining the successful defendant to the action on the basis that another defendant suggested that that defendant was to blame. In that situation the successful defendant may recover costs from the unsuccessful defendant. It should be feasible to deal with this prior to issue and with the openness now required under the protocol there should be very few occasions where you should need to add or substitute a defendant after issue.

Limitation

Whichever option is adopted, it is vital that the expiry of the three-year limitation period against the third person is diarised. It is important to do this, in case it should expire whilst the client's instructions are being taken. This is not a concern if the defendant has already joined the other tortfeasor in a Part 20 claim for contribution or indemnity as special limitation considerations then assist you.

Tactics

If the third person allegation put forward by the defendant seems to be unfounded, you may well be reluctant to incur the delay and expense of suing this new defendant. However, the claimant's interests must be protected, for the evidence available to the defendant is not known and thus the allegation must be taken seriously. It may help to write to the defendant that, in the light of the defence, the claimant's intends to protect the position by proceeding against the third person unless the defendant withdraws the allegations, and should the third person be held not liable it is the claimant's intention to ask that the costs of those proceedings be borne by the defendant in any event (that is, even if the claimant loses his case). This may encourage the defendant to drop an unfounded allegation.

The risk to your client is if the new defendant admits the claim. It may be hard in such a case to persuade a court that the costs of the successful original defendant should be paid by the new defendant. You must ensure that all cost implications of whatever you advise the client to do are explained in detail together with the implications generally of doing nothing or joining a new defendant.

Public Funding and Conditional fee

Remember that adding another party will need an amendment to any public funding certificate and, more pertinently, will require approval for any legal expense insurer who is funding or indemnifying your client. You will also need to consider the implications on any conditional fee agreement signed as that will usually only refer to a claim against the original defendant. You may wish to amend the original agreement or do a fresh one. You should check what effect this will have on premium with the backing insurers.

Third party proceedings

The defendant can go further than just making such allegations in the defence, by actually commencing Part 20 proceedings, for indemnity or contribution. (see CPR Part 20.2(a)).

Here Part 20 proceedings are a claim for an indemnity or contribution should the defendant be held liable to the claimant. The defendant can make a Part 20 claim for contribution or indemnity against a non party without leave of the court if the Part 20 proceedings are issued before or at the same time as the defendant files the defence otherwise court permission is required. Usually such a claim will be without leave because the drafting of the Defence necessitates consideration of all issues. Indeed a later application for permission may suggest a lack of credibility unless in the intervening period new evidence has come to light.

If made without leave the Part 20 proceedings must be served on the Part 20 defendant within 14 days of filing Defence. Once served the Part 20 defendant becomes a party to the proceedings. To facilitate that involvement the Part 20 defendant must be served with a response pack and copies of all statements of case already filed in the claim.

Where there are Part 20 proceedings the court must consider what directions are necessary. Usually, this will be by case management conference since these may be fairly complicated and the Part 20 defendant is inevitably some way behind the other parties.

Although a defendant may make a Part 20 claim for contribution and/or indemnity from an existing co-defendant this is unlikely because the Civil Liability (Contribution) Act 1978 gives the courts a wide discretion to apportion liability and order contribution. Instead, the defendants may simply write to each other indicating that they will be relying on this inherent power.

10.6. Part 20 counterclaim

What is a Part 20 counterclaim?

The defendant's Statement of Case may be not merely a Defence but a combined "Defence and Part 20 counterclaim". The latter part of this Statement of Case will attack the claimant by setting up a fresh cause of action against the claimant. Thus in respect of this claim the defendant takes over the role of claimant, and the original claimant will have to act as a defendant by serving a "Defence to counterclaim" within 14 days, or otherwise run the risk of judgment in default of defence being obtained (see below).

Aim of a Part 20 counterclaim

The object of allowing the defendant to introduce a claim against the claimant is to avoid multiplicity of proceedings: the claim can be of virtually any nature, and need not arise from the original cause of action. It will survive as a cause of action even if the main claim is settled. In injury claims it is a claim usually seen arising from a road accident where each party blames the other and each has sustained loss.

Effect of a Part 20 counterclaim

As stated in practice, the Part 20 counterclaim will usually arise out of the same cause of action, and is frequently encountered in road accident cases. It causes little inconvenience to the defendant's solicitors to incorporate a Counterclaim in the defence and it may well encourage the claimant to compromise. The effects of a Counterclaim can be dramatic. For instance, take the case of a road accident claim where the defendant is basically to blame and suffered serious injury. The claimant's claim may be worth some £5,000 in personal injury and vehicular damage, whereas the defendant's would be worth, say, £30,000 on full liability. The claimant needs to be only 20 per cent to blame for the accident, for the claimant's damages to be less than the defendant's, the claimant will get £4,000 (*i.e.* 80 per cent of £5,000) and the defendant £6,000 (*i.e.* 20 per cent of £30,000).

Response to a counterclaim

On receiving a counterclaim the claimant's solicitor should:

(1) Report to the client. Inform your client of the counterclaim, explain its significance and obtain full instructions on the allegations.

(2) Notify your clients insurers immediately in a road accident case, otherwise they may be entitled to repudiate liability. They should already have been told of the accident and thus should be liable to indemnify the claimant in respect of costs and for any damages arising from the counterclaim. However, if the claimant is uninsured, then it is best to notify the other side (so they can claim against the MIB). Do not forget that an insurance company may have repudiated liability, and yet be obliged to pay any damages, by virtue of their Road Traffic Act 1988 liability (RTA 1988, ss. 151–153). In a typical case, the claimant's solicitors will simply notify the client's insurers of the counterclaim; the solicitor should set out the facts of the case, the prospects of success and enclose copies of relevant papers (including the Statement of Cases). You should also ask for confirmation that the insurers will indemnify the client, and inquire whether the insurers wish the you also to act on their behalf in relation to the counterclaim. Some insurers are willing to do this; others insist that their own solicitors be instructed. This can be cumbersome as the court then has two solicitors on record for one party. Inevitably, this is likely to lead to some duplication of work and an element of irrecoverable cost. However, at a time when insurers have reduced and centralised the firms of solicitors that they are prepared to instruct it is becoming an increasingly common situation. Of more concern is the rising instances of the insurers indicating that economically if the counterclaim is small that they do not propose to defend it. Whilst this can be explained to the court it does create an adverse impression. Suggestions that this cannot be in the client's best interests frequently fall on deaf ears and a deal is done by the insurer in respect of any Part 20 counterclaim or, if the client wants to defend, the client ends up paying for that privilege in addition to having paid a Road Traffic Act insurance premium. Again, ensure that the client understands the implications, particularly as under the CPR cost provisions a larger element of cost than before may be attributed to the Part 20 counterclaim process.

(3) If your client is uninsured consider applying for legal expense cover to defend the counterclaim.

(4) Diary the 14-day period for service of the Defence to Counterclaim. In practice, this is unlikely to be a sufficiently long time period. Accordingly, you should write to the defendant seeking an extension of time, and stating that the client has every intention of disputing the claim. It is usually advisable to state what steps are being taken in response (*i.e.* instructions are being sought from the insurers, or an application for funding is being

made). If a letter in those terms has been written, it is extremely unlikely that the defendant will apply for judgment in default (and if it did, it would almost certainly be set aside). However, if extensions of time are refused, you will have to apply to the court for an extension.

(5) Decide if you want to instruct counsel to settle a Defence to Counterclaim. In practice, you will rarely need to as this is one of the easiest statements of case to draft as on the question of liability you are simply reaffirming the version of events in the particulars of claim and therefore denying liability. Responding to the quantum items raised depends very much on what information has been provided earlier. If the Counterclaim is for injury and not just special damage, *e.g.* vehicle losses, the defendant should have complied with the personal injury protocol.

After the last Statement of Case

Once the court has the last Statement of Case or in the case of two defendants where only one has filed a Defence after the time for filing has elapsed the court will send out allocation questionnaires and active case management and court intervention begins. It will happen in every case where a Defence is filed so get ready for it. Consider what permissions you require from the court for expert evidence, do you want the experts reports before the court in written form or do you require the expert to give oral evidence at trial, do you have witness statements in final form, are you ready for disclosure, what timescale do you want for the directions? Check the availability of client, witnesses and case counsel. Not only does this save time later but it forces you to take stock at a time where you have a few weeks to resolve any problems that may arise.

10.7. Limitation

The defendant may claim that the Limitation Act 1980 bars the claimant's claim (see Chapter 21). If so:

(1) Consider the law. Decide whether the claim is outside the limitation period. If not, serve a Reply saying so.

(2) Report to the client. This is particularly important if the defendant alleges that an injury occurred or accident took place earlier than instructed by your client. Obtain your client's instructions on the allegation and consider if further witness or medical evidence is necessary to rebut it.

(3) Apply under section 33 of the Limitation Act 1980 if it appears that the case is statute barred. Usually this is an issue that arises prior to commencement of proceedings and you will have expected to see the defence raised

and already have discussed tactics and obtained instructions from your client.

(4) In the unfortunate event that you may in some way have caused or contributed to any limitation issue notify your insurers immediately, if you have not already done so, explain the situation to the client who may wish to transfer instructions elsewhere.

11. Amendment of Statements of Case

11.1. Amendment of Statements of Case

Since Statements of Case set out the allegations and contentions of the parties, they must be both accurate and up to date. If a statement contains an error, or if the allegations and contentions have altered since it was settled, then it will be necessary to amend it and to re-serve it on the other side.

When to amend

Amendments can be made at any stage of the case, for the court will not allow the strict rules of statements to defeat justice, unless the amendment will result in prejudice or an injury that cannot be compensated for by costs. In practice, this is where the court must consider the overriding objective. The most difficult balancing exercise that the court will have to do is where the trial date is imminent and the proposed amendment alters the case fundamentally. A lot depends upon the extent of the amendment. The generally held view is that under the CPR the court is likely to grant fewer late amendments than it did under the previous rules. Although there seem to be conflicting views coming down from the Court of Appeal a useful summary was given by Neuberger J. in *Charlesworth v. Relay Roads Ltd* [1999]4 All E.R. 397 when he indicated that the mere availability of financial redress did not mean that a late amendment would be allowed as other considerations such as the anxieties of parties and their expectations of the process also had to weighed up as did the inconvenience to them of last minute adjournments. It is not uncommon, for example, for a defendant to attend the trial court and to ask the judge for leave to amend the defence to include allegations of contributory negligence by the claimant; unfortunately, such applications are frequently successful, although the judge may well adjourn the hearing and order the defendant to pay the costs of the day. Similarly, it may be necessary to amend the particulars of injuries, or particulars of special damage, in the Statement of Claim if the claimant's condition has deteriorated, or to state the outcome of a criminal proceeding relating to the accident which has been tried since the statement was settled (see Chapter 9).

Procedure to amend

The general rule is that you can amend a Statement of Case at any stage prior to service without court permission and that after service you can amend without permission of the court only where the other party consents and where the amendment is not to add, substitute or remove a party. Do remember, though, that the court does have retrospective power to disallow amendments that did not require permission at the time. This usually arises where the amendment was pre- service and, on service, the other party objects. Here, the other party must apply to the court within 14 days of service of the amended statement.

Where permission is required, make a formal application on form N244 attaching a copy of the proposed amended statement to the application. It is usual to explain why the amendment is necessary. If the reason is an oversight in the original drafting do not try to hide that with transparently thin excuses. Apologise but point out that an oversight should not prejudice the party, particularly if costs are conceded.

If the court grants permission, and you may find this granted without a hearing, either on written representations or on desk consideration, the court may give supplemental directions in respect of any other amended statements that may be consequential on this one. Unless ordered otherwise the amended statement must be filed and served within 14 days of the order.

Colouring the amendments

First amendments are in red. Subsequent amendments will be in green, with further amendments in violet, and then yellow. The one change here is that the superseded text no longer remains in the document unless the court so orders.

11.2. Amendments after the expiry of a limitation period

This is an area where really close examination of the CPR is essential and to attempt to summarise the provisions can only ever be a poor second best. You should review CPR Part 17.4 and the helpful footnotes that appear with this section. Broadly, unless the application to amend is to add or substitute a new claim arising from the same facts as apply in the already issued claim, to correct a genuine mistake in the name of a party which would not have caused reasonable doubt as to the identity of that party, or to alter the capacity in respect of which the party claims then the court's power to amend is limited.

Adding or substituting parties after expiry of primary limitation also raises specific concerns. These are governed by CPR Part 19.5. If you find yourself in this situation the rule must be your first port of call again. In summary the court can only add or substitute a party after limitation has expired if:

- the limitation period had not expired when proceedings were issued; and
- the addition or substitution is necessary.

"Necessary" is defined as being where

(i) the new party is to be substituted for a party named in mistake for the new party;

(ii) the claim cannot properly carry on unless there is addition or substitution;

(iii) the original party has died or become bankrupt and interest or liability has passed to the new party.

In the majority of cases none of this is particularly helpful but fortunately Part 19.5(4) refers *to old friends.* The court can in injury cases add or substitute a party where it directs that section 11 or 12 of the Limitation Act 1980 shall not apply to the claim or the question of whether or not they do shall be deferred to be determined at trial. Whilst that may mean a number of sleepless nights ahead you have one foot in the door.

12. Part 36 Offers to Settle and Payments and Interim Payments

12.1. Part 36 payments

The defendant may pay money into court in satisfaction of the claimant's claim (even if liability is disputed). If the claimant thinks the amount paid in is sufficient you can withdraw it within 21 days of notification, agree or assess your costs, and proceed no further with the action. If the claimant thinks the amount paid in is insufficient you can take the case to trial, but should the claimant not recover more from the judge (who will not know about the payment in) then the claimant will bear all the costs as from the date of payment in.

The rule is very similar prior to issue of proceedings. The rule is found in CPR Part 36 hence the reference to Part 36 offers and payments. An offer put by the defendant prior to issue is called a Part 36 offer and after issue, when it should be paid into court a Part 36 payment.

Prior to issue the position is governed by Part 36.10 which provides that a defendant can make a Part 36 offer before proceedings which the court will take into account when making an order as to costs provided that it complies with this subsection. To do so the offer must be open for acceptance for at least 21 days after it is made and if proceedings are subsequently issued then at least that sum must be paid into court within 14 days of service of the Claim Form. The offer is deemed made when received by you on behalf of the claimant.

Experience has shown that this pre-issue offer is widely used by defendants. Unfortunately, as they do not have to stump up the money when making the offer it is often used solely as a threat rather than as a realistic assessment. The hope is that by making creeping increases in Part 36 offers the claimant will opt out at an undervalue on the grounds of concern about costs. Beware of this. If you issue then a far more realistic Part 36 payment is often made.

Part 36 offers rather than payments are also used when the defendant is not in a position to lodge money with the court because an up-to-date Compensation Recovery Unit certificate is not available. This is set out in Part 36.23. In such a situation a payment into court must be made for not less than the offer within seven days of receipt of the certificate. Sometimes, this approach is adopted by insurers even when no items of claim are subject to recoupment. In such a situation you do not need to await the certificate to advise your client as the implications are already apparent.

Defendant's tactics

The payment in is thus a powerful weapon for the defendant since, even if the defendant is clearly liable, the defendant can put the claimant under considerable pressure as to costs by paying in at an early stage of the action. In fact, the defendant need not wait until service of the Defence. The defendant can pay in as soon as proceedings are served. In practice, this is extremely rare; however, when it does happen and it can have an extremely unsettling effect on the claimant! A payment in can even be made during the trial.

Procedure

Procedural Table 10 sets out the steps to be taken to effect a payment which can either be by post or by personal attendance at the court offices. Note that the payment in form has altered considerably. The form is N242A. It allows for part 36 payments in respect of part only of the claim, requires details of earlier payments and interims and the effect of any counterclaim. The reverse of the form ensures clarity over the benefit deduction position.

Claimant's response

On receipt of a notice of payment in, the claimant should:

(a) write to the defendant acknowledging receipt of notice when received from court and indicate the date received;

(b) diary 21 days from the date you received the notice as the time for acceptance. If the payment in is accepted within that period the claimant can withdraw the money without further ado; unless one of the exceptions below applies (for example, an infant plaintiff or where there are several defendants). After that time the claimant who wishes to accept will have to apply to the court for approval. Where the Part 36 payment is made less than 21 days before trial it cannot be accepted without the permission of the court unless the parties agree the cost consequences of acceptance;

(c) Consider whether the sum should be accepted by the client. Clearly, this depends on the facts of the case, but if in doubt the papers should be sent to counsel to advise. Ensure that counsel has the full information needed to value the case including evidence as to liability, allegations of contributory negligence, up-to-date medical reports for calculating general damage and a special damage calculation as well as up-to-date information on special damage. In short, you should send counsel papers you would send if asking for any other advice (see Chapter 16). If there have been previous payments in, be sure to enclose the earlier notices so that counsel is aware of the total sum in court. If you do use counsel it is always a good idea to do your own liability and quantum assessments but not to reveal those to counsel, so he is not influenced by your views and vice versa. If the same or a similar conclusion is reached by both of you this can increase your confidence that the conclusion is the correct one.

If you have made a good selection of counsel there is no difficulty in ensuring the availability of the advice within the acceptance period. In the unusual event of time difficulty, approach the defendant to see if you can secure an extra seven days for acceptance. Tactically, the danger in doing this is it suggests to the defendant that the Part 36 is a good one as you need the extra time to ponder the offer. Try to keep within the 21-day period if at all possible because a rejection within that period exudes more confidence.

(d) Then notify the client and advise whether the sum paid in should be accepted. Care should be taken when writing to the client, especially if you are advising rejection. The effect of the payment in should be explained so that if a case should go on to trial, and the client then recovers no more than the amount paid in, there can be no complaint of not having been properly advised. Ensure that you advise your client:

   (i) that if the client rejects the payment in and receives less at trial the client is at risk of paying your costs and those of the defendant. Highlight that if the client receives more at trial but only because of interest on claim since payment in that does not mean the payment in has been beaten;
   (ii) an estimate of your costs to date and your and the defendant's costs to trial;
   (iii) that any costs to be paid will be deducted from the client's damages;
   (iv) that the Regional Legal Services must be informed of any unreasonable refusals and the consequences of discharge (if your client is publicly funded) This is also true now of many legal expense insurers and has conditional fee implications (see Chapter 23);
   (v) whether the payment in is reasonable having regard to current upper and lower estimates of damage;
   (vi) whether you advise acceptance or rejection;
   (vii) the time limit in which the client must decide.

However, it is not sufficient merely to explain the effect of the payment in; the client is entitled to advice from a solicitor and should be given a recommendation on whether or not to accept. If necessary make an appointment for the client to come in and discuss it; be sure to write to the client after the meeting, repeating the warnings and advice. Stock letters 38 and 39 can be used as the basis of your letter of recommendation advising the client to accept or reject. If you are advising the client to accept you should explain how long it will be before the client is paid.

Do give advice. It is wholly unsatisfactory to regard your function in such a situation as being only to give an explanation of the implications of failure to beat a payment in without giving the client any opportunity of assessing that risk. Add to this the inevitability of your letter arriving on a Saturday so that the client has to stew for two days before being able to telephone you and the client/solicitor relationship has suddenly evaporated. Ask yourself what information you would want in a similar situation and provide that to the client.

Public funding and conditional fee cases

In the unusual event that the client has public funding remember your duty to the Regional Legal Services Commission if your client instructs you to reject a Part 36 payment that you believe should be accepted.

Even if you think it should be rejected the client should be reminded that the cost protection of public funding does not render the Part 36 payment an ineffective weapon. If a claimant proceeds to trial, and recovers damages which are less than the payment in, then the court is likely to order that the defendant's costs from the expiry of the time within which the claimant could accept the payment are to paid out of the damages. Therefore, there is a risk even to a public funded claimant.

As an aside, you will have seen that the cost sanction applies from the expiry of the time period for acceptance. This is a change to the old rules that has passed many by.

More likely, in the brave new world of conditional fees, you will have to consider what implication there may be on a rejection of a Part 36 payment in the context of your fee agreement, particularly one that you feel ought to be accepted. A lot depends on the agreed terms in such an eventuality. Whilst you will need to refer to the conditional fee agreement the time that you really need to consider this eventuality is when agreeing terms with the client in the first place (see Chapter 23 for detailed consideration).

Compensation recovery

The new forms for payment in should take away any uncertainty over whether or not benefit to be recouped under the Social Security (Recovery of Benefits) Act 1997 have been deducted. A look at the form should tell you what the net receipt to your client would be if the payment were accepted. However, confusion may still arise in the context of Part 36 offers made prior to issue. Part 36 makes it plain that openness is required. If the offer is confusing seek clarification immediately. If the defendant is less that forthcoming refer to CPR Part 36 PD-006. If you are in doubt and the defendant is not co-operating then you can apply to the court for assistance. The cost implications and potential to incur the wrath of the court can persuade the most reluctant defendant to co-operate. If you do not clarify the situation then you may be storing up an enormous problem for the client and an even bigger one for your firm.

In the case of *Houghton v. British Coal, The Times,* February 15, 1997, the defendant made a payment in of £15,800 after deducting £9,200 benefit. The notice of payment in stated £25,000. The claimant thought this meant that £25,000 was in court and the total offer was £34,200 so accepted the payment in When the claimant realised his mistake he appealed but the Court of Appeal held that despite the mistake he must accept the money in court and ruled that claimants should assume that the payments in are made net of relevant benefits. If you obtain a copy CRU certificate (which is likely as the defendant will probably apply for one) check with the client that the amount for deductible benefit is correct.

From October 1, 1997 when the Social Security (Recovery of Benefits) Act came into force the defendant has to repay to the CRU the full benefits paid to the injured person but will only be able to deduct benefits in the relevant categories of loss of earnings, cost of care and loss of mobility. It will therefore be essential to ask defendants to let you know exactly how much is in court and, if possible give you a breakdown of payments in into relevant components of damages so that you can fully advise your client. The rules do not provide for a breakdown but you may persuade a court that with the CRU implications some further information by way of clarity is necessary.

12.2. Acceptance

Acceptance within 21 days

If the claimant decides to accept the payment in before the period of acceptance expires you should notify the other side as well as lodging notice of acceptance with the court (form N243).

The steps to be taken on accepting a payment in within the 21-day period are set out in Procedural Table 11.

The procedure and forms for both payment and acceptance under Part 36 are the same in the High and county court.

Whilst it used to be worth trying to see if agreement over costs could also be reached within the payment in period to resolve all issues this is now virtually impossible. The major reason for this is not that time constraints preclude it but that centralisation of insurers' panel solicitors and the move by the insurance market to use external cost negotiators has taken away the established relationships that built up between claimant and defendant law firms and the good will that this engendered has gone.

Acceptance in particular circumstances

There are two occasions when this procedure will not apply, and when it will be necessary to apply to the court:

(a) Person under a disability If the claimant is a person under a disability, then the court must approve the acceptance and to make directions as to the way the money is to be applied. Thus, an application for approved must be issued (see Chapter 24 and Precedent 21(b));

(b) Fatal In a fatal case, the payment in will not apportion the money between Law Reform (Miscellaneous Provisions) Act 1934, or Fatal Accidents Act 1976 claims, nor between the various dependants. Thus, an application may need to be issued for the court to make the apportionment. See Chapter 24.

Acceptance out of time

If the claimant should decide to accept the payment after the 21-day period has expired, you will need to apply to the court for consent. The normal procedure will be to approach the defendant first. If the acceptance period has only just expired there is rarely any problem in agreeing late acceptance and preparing a *Tomlin* Order to reflect the agreement as you will still need an order to secure the release of funds in court. If the acceptance comes some time after the expiry of the acceptance period when a significant amount of additional costs may have accrued you may wish to start negotiations rather than simply indicate a desire to accept. For example, you may wish to say to the defendant that if there is no cost penalty then your client may be persuaded to accept the payment reluctantly just to see an end to the matter. Do make sure that you have client instructions to do this. If the client instructs you to accept without any negotiation or the insurers refuse to allow acceptance without cost sanction then inevitably there will have to be a split order for costs with the claimant recovering costs up to the last day for acceptance without permission from the court and the defendant having costs from that date. Again, this agreement will have to be reflected in a court order.

For the procedure to be followed, refer to Procedural Table 11. Precedent 22 sets out typical forms of order. The order should say who is to get any interest that has accrued on the money in court. Normally, this will go to the defendant, but it might be worth the claimant's solicitor seeing whether you can negotiate for the interest to go to your client. If so, that should be specifically stated in the order. However, it is hard to see what is in this for the defendant and if you have escaped without cost sanction do not push your luck. It may be the point that upsets the deal.

Rejection of payment in

There is no need to inform the other side if the payment in is not accepted. One simply does not file a Notice of Acceptance. If the money is not accepted, it will remain in court and will automatically be placed on a deposit account (the interest will be the defendant's). The case will then proceed to trial in the usual manner, and the payment in will not be mentioned to the judge nor in the Statements of Case. At the trial, when deciding whether the payment in has been beaten, one takes full account of any deductions for contributory negligence, and also full additions for interest.

If the claimant obtains judgment for more than the amount in court, then the judge will order the money to be paid out to the claimant (or to the claimant's solicitor, if the claimant is publicly funded). In the county court the court office will act on the order and arrange for payment out. In the High Court you will need to lodge a payment schedule with a copy of the order providing for payment out indorsed by the court together with the original Claim Form. This can cause delay so advise the client of this in advance. Because of this delay, it is advisable that the judge's order provides that interest on the payment in (as from the date of judgment) should be paid to the claimant. Otherwise, it will go to the defendant.

More than one defendant

Complications can arise where there is more than one defendant and one defendant pays in. The established case law is clear; if the cause of action against joint tortfeasors is the same and you settle a case with one tortfeasor the whole action is dropped. Whilst there may be cases where it is possible to argue two separate causes of action (for example, injury in a road accident followed by a mistake in the treatment of the resulting injuries at the treating hospital), in most injury cases the cause of action will be the same.

Having reminded yourself of this, if there is a Part 36 payment to be considered then you need to advise the client of the cost implications of acceptance. This is when the time spent earlier obtaining confirmation from the tortfeasors that they all blame each other turns out to be time well spent. Issue an application asking the court to allow discontinuance against the remaining tortfeasor/s with their costs to be paid by the defendant who made the Part 36 payment relying on the fact that all defendants blamed each other so the losing one is responsible for the successful one being a party and should pay the costs.

The other way to approach the matter is to write to the defendant who has paid in making your own offer, whether by way of claimant's Part 36 or not, indicating that your client will accept the sum paid in on the basis that, in addition to payment of the claimant's costs, that defendant will meet the costs of the successful defendant/s. It is plain from this that the action against the defendant who has paid in continues only on the question of the costs of the remaining defendants. If the defendant had blamed the other tortfeasors the prospect of resolving the claim, now balanced against the risk of incurring further costs to argue about a liability that almost certainly falls at its door, is usually sufficient to extract the necessary confirmation.

As stated earlier, your difficulty here lies if the paying defendant has never blamed anyone else. In such a situation your client may have to discontinue against the remaining defendant/s and pay the costs flowing from discontinuance.

Interest

Money paid into court is automatically put on deposit once the 21-day period for acceptance has expired. When the money is paid out (*i.e.* at the end of the case) any interest will accrue to the defendant, unless the order specifically says otherwise (see above).

A payment in should take account of any interest that would have accrued on those damages (*i.e.* if there had been judgment). The CPR do not specifically require the defendant to apportion a payment in between capital and interest; but the rules say that unless the notice states to the contrary the payment in will be treated as including interest as if the last date for acceptance was the date of judgment see CPR Part 36.22. If the case goes to trial, it may be difficult to work out whether the claimant has beaten the payment in. Often, it will be obvious.

But, in a marginal case, the judge might have to work out how much of the payment in was interest. For instance, suppose there is a payment in of £20,000. The case goes to trial, and the claimant is awarded £19,000, plus £3,000 interest. Has the claimant beaten the payment in? The judge calculates that, at the date of payment in, interest amounted to £500. That being so, the value of the payment in is £19,500 (*i.e.* £20,000 less £500). On this basis, the claimant has not beaten the payment in (*i.e.* the claimant has recovered £19,000, and the payment in was for £19,500). In practice, of course, it can be difficult to calculate accurately the amount of interest in a payment in. This is because there are different rates of interest for general damages than for special damages. All one can do is make an approximate guess. In practice, these rules are less trouble than one might expect. Perhaps because so few cases see a Part 36 payment so close to the judgment finding that it is not readily apparent if the Part 36 payment bites or not.

12.3. The claimant's offer

This was billed as one of the key innovations of the reforms of The Woolf Committee. The idea was to encourage a claimant to shed the traditional reluctance to join in the bidding by introducing a formal mechanism to make an offer with potentially large benefits in interest payments as an inducement (see below). This has lived up to its billing.

The procedure is found in CPR Part 36.5. The offer must be in writing, identify what it relates to (*e.g.* a specific item of claim or the whole claim), state whether it takes into account any counterclaim and state if it is not inclusive of interest. Like a Part 36 payment the Part 36 claimant's offer, if made more than 21 days before trial, can be accepted within the 21 days without permission but thereafter can only be accepted if the parties agree the cost consequences or the court so orders. If made less than 21 days before trial it can only be accepted if the parties agree the cost consequences or the court gives permission.

CPR Part 36.21 sets out the consequences to a defendant who rejects a claimant's offer where the claimant then does better than the offer. In summary, the court can order interest on any non interest sum awarded to the claimant at the rate of up to 10 per cent above base rate for some or all of the period after the last day on which the defendant could have accepted the claimant's offer. In other words, the penalty interest is on the sum of the compensation excluding ordinary interest to avoid interest on interest. The court can also order costs on an indemnity basis and order interest on those costs at up to 10 per cent above base rate.

If you make a Part 36 claimant's offer clearly express it be so using wording such as "Without prejudice save as to costs Claimant's Part 36 offer". The offer takes effect when received and so when diarising the acceptance period make sure that you allow for the service period set out in CPR Part 6 which have been considered earlier. Place the emphasis for indicating if those periods should be extended on the defendant, *e.g.* "This offer is open for acceptance by you without court permission for twenty one days from the date of receipt by you of this letter which we shall assume to be two days after the date that appears on the letter to allow for the ordinary time for delivery".

12.4. Provisional damages and non monetary Part 36 offers

Provisional damages

In a claim including a claim for an award of provisional damages the defendant may make a Part 36 payment but must specify in the notice whether he or she agrees to the making of a provisional damage award. Where this agreement is forthcoming the notice should specify the amount of the payment now in respect of all injuries other than those the subject of the provisional claim. In other words, the amount offered on the assumption that the injuries or deterioration specified in the provisional claim will not occur and that any claim for further damages is made within a set period and specify the period. If the claimant accepts the Part 36 payment you must apply within seven days of acceptance for an order for an award of provisional damages. Until you do so the payment out will not take place of the damages due at this stage.

Non monetary Part 36 offer

In the injury field this will usually apply to offers on liability. Apportionments can, and in practice frequently are, offered by way of Part 36. Curiously, Part 36.5(4) refers only to the defendant making offers limited to accepting liability up to a specified proportion. There seems little doubt that the same option is open to a claimant whether by a formal Part 36 offer or not. Indeed, the CPR is also plain that on considering the question of costs the court must have regard to all offers made whether by Part 36 or not. Recent cases, whilst stressing the importance of Part 36 also accept that this Part does not render other offers worthless in terms of cost implications.

12.5. The interim payment

The interim payment is grossly under-used by claimant solicitors. Few seem to appreciate that the rules are drawn in such a way as to make an interim payment more likely than not. Obviously, each case depends upon its facts, but it is always worth looking to see whether it is a case in which the claimant would be entitled to an interim payment and would benefit from one.

Unfortunately, defendants (and their insurers) are reluctant to make interim payments. It is sometimes possible to persuade them to make an interim payment without the need for an application to the court, but, in practice, this will usually only happen when it is obvious that the claimant will recover large damages. But the CPR is not so narrowly drawn. The basic requirement is that, if the case went to trial, the claimant would, and the court must be satisfied of this, obtain judgment with substantial damages against any one of the defendants. So, all that is required is a good probability of recovering "substantial" damages although the court will demand a high standard of proof of the probability that the claim will succeed (*Gibbons v. Wall, The Times,* February 24, 1988). The discretion to make an award seems as wide as before the CPR.

The mere fact that there may be substantial contributory negligence by the claimant is irrelevant. As long as the end result (*i.e.* the damages after deducting contributory negligence) is a substantial award, then the claimant is entitled to an interim payment. Unfortunately, there is no definition of what is "substantial", save that it must be over £500, but in practice this is rarely a difficulty.

Note also that the claimant need not show "need". In other words, the claimant does not have to show that the money is needed due to financial difficulty. Personal finances are, to a large extent, irrelevant but see p. 153 below.

Requirements

The detailed requirements on interim payments are set out in CPR Part 25.7. For the application to succeed, the claimant will have to show that:

(a) liability has been admitted; or

(b) the claimant has already obtained interlocutory judgment (with damages to be decided); or

(c) the claimant would recover substantial damages if the case went to trial.

and

(a) the defendant is insured; or

(b) is a public authority; or

(c) is a person of sufficient means to be able to make the payment.

Note that it is now accepted that an interim payment can be obtained against the MIB (see *Sharp v. Paroita* [1998] 4 All E.R. 145).

In practice, of course, the vast majority of personal injury defendants are insured, and so it is merely a matter of you showing (on a balance of probabilities) that the claimant will recover "substantial" damages. If there is more than one defendant, then you will have to show that the client is likely to get damages against that particular defendant (*i.e.* it is not good enough to say that one of several defendants will be liable). This usually precludes an application where they both blame each other.

Need

'Need' is not mentioned in the rules and you do not have to show that your client is in financial difficulty.

In *Stringman v. McArdle* [1994] P.I.Q.R. 230 Stuart-Smith I.J. said "it should be noted that the plaintiff does not have to demonstrate any particular need over and above the general need that a plaintiff has to be paid his or her damages as soon as may reasonably be done". However if the claimant is a person under a disability it is usual to confine an interim payment to the amount needed by the next friend for the claimant's maintenance and living expenses until trial as any payment at this stage must be into court unless the court is satisfied of a genuine and reasonable need.

Procedure (Part 25.6)

Application is made to the district judge in the county court and master in the High Court by notice of application N244. The application for interim payment cannot be made until the time for acknowledgement of service has expired.

The application must be served at least 14 days before a hearing and be supported by witness statement evidence. That evidence should deal with the matters set out in the practice direction to this Part (Part 25 PBD-001) namely, the sum of money sought, the items in respect of which it is sought, likely eventual damages, confirmation that the formal requirements are satisfied, detail of special damages to include both past and future losses and any other relevant matters. In Fatal Accident cases state the names, ages and relationships to the deceased of the dependants and the nature of the claim (see Chapter 25).

The application

A specimen application, witness statement and order for interim payment are given in Precedent 13. Ensure that the copy statement and copy application are served on the defendant at least 14 days before the hearing. This is an important point to note, because the normal period for serving an application is only two days (excluding weekends and holidays). So, be sure to serve the documents well in advance.

Quantum

Little guidance can be given as to the likely amount of the interim payment. It is entirely at the court's discretion. However, a court is likely to be conservative, not wishing to award a sum that risks over-compensating the claimant. In practice, the court has often based the award on the amount of special damages up to the date of the interim payment hearing. The simple advice must be to tell the client to be realistic.

Hearing

In view of the sums involved, it is obviously wise for the solicitor to attend the application personally, rather than rely upon an inexperienced clerk. It is essential for the solicitor to review the file generally before attending the application. This is because the district judge or master must also treat the application as an opportunity to case manage and may make any of the usual directions. The wise solicitor will consider whether there are any directions wanted; if so, you should give notice to the other side of your intention to raise these points.

Interest

The court is entitled to order that interest be paid on the interim payment as well. Precedent 12 can include an application for interest. In practice, it may well be necessary specifically to ask the court to order interest, once it has stated the amount to be paid. It is likely to award interest if the amount of the interim payment is substantial, or if the trial is unlikely to come on for a long time. If interest is awarded, then the court should clearly state the rate of interest awarded, the period for which it is being awarded, etc. This is important in case the trial judge should eventually award interest on a different basis (*e.g.* at a different rate); if that happens the trial judge will want to be able to adjust the amount of interim payment so as to increase or reduce the interest due. Whether or not this is the case, the trial judge will still have to decide how the interim payment is to be deducted from the damages awarded (ie does it come off general damages, special damages, etc)? In view of the markedly different rates of interest awarded on the different types of damages, it can be very important to decide to which head of damage the interim payment is apportioned and the court can expressly state that the award is to be made in respect of a certain head, *e.g.* special damage and loss of earnings. However the claimant should try to resist any suggestion by the defendant that an interim payment (whether voluntary or not) should cover special damages since this can reduce the interest paid at the time of the final award and can mean that CRU recoupment will apply (see below) when it would not to an award made in respect of pain and suffering. For guidance, see Chapter 7.

Further applications

If the application for the interim payment is unsuccessful or for an insufficient amount, there is no reason why a further application cannot be made. The claimant can go back for repeated applications; and does not have to show as used to be the case, that there has been a change of circumstances. Although in the absence of a change it is hard to see an award being made. Having said that, a claimant who makes repeated applications without good cause is likely to have to pay the defendant's costs of unsuccessful applications.

Effect on payment in

If an interim payment is ordered, the defendant will want it paid out of any money that the defendant has already paid into court. So, the defendant should ask the court to order that the money be paid out of the sum already in court. This has no bearing on the amount of the Part 36 payment for the purposes of determining ultimately whether the claimant has beaten the payment. It simply means that a portion of the Part 36 has been released to the claimant on account. If an interim payment is awarded before the defendant pays money into court, then the defendant will obviously want to ensure that any future payment in takes account of the interim payment already made. The defendant should specifically state in the Notice of Payment In that £X has already been paid by way of interim payment, and this is being taken into account for the amount of the payment. The payment in form N242A provides a tick box format to confirm whether the Part 36 payment takes into account any interim payments made under court order or voluntarily.

Disadvantages

Although interim payments are under-used, there are some practical problems which should be borne in mind:

Compensation recovery

The rules on compensation recovery *do* apply to interim payments so these will first have to go to repay any relevant benefits received to date. A client who has already received substantial benefits may find that there is little point in applying for an interim payment which will simply be paid to the CRU. You should therefore make it quite clear that any interim payment should be paid against general damages or other "ring-fenced" items such as medical expenses, rather than special damages. However, a defendant may resist this because of the interest considerations, (see previous page). For a detailed explanation of the rules see Chapter 7.

Welfare benefits

Many personal injury claimants are of limited means. If the accident has been severe, it may well be that the claimant does not have a job and is living on income support. If that is the case, then an interim payment can back-fire even if the whole amount is not swallowed up by the CRU. A person on income support who has capital of more than the current capital limit will automatically cease to be eligible for benefit and (between figures up to that limit there is a sliding-scale reduction in benefit). This is a vital point to bear in mind. The risks are obvious; if the claimants solicitor rushes out and gets an interim payment for the client, the client will be worse off! There is no point in getting an interim payment if the net effect will be to take the client off income support, or seriously to reduce the amount of benefit being received. Far better for the claimant to wait until trial for the award of damages. That way, the claimant will continue to receive income support in the period prior to trial although any benefit received due to the accident will of course be deducted from damages at that time. On the other hand, it might be wise for the claimant's solicitor to ask for an interim payment of an amount that after recoupment by the CRU will bring the claimant's capital up to the lower limit (but not a penny more!). That way, the client will get some money, but will not lose income support. In practice, the defendant may be only too ready to agree to a voluntary payment of this amount, when told that the alternative is an application before the court which may well result in a substantially higher interim payment.

It is hard to see why so few applications for interim payment are made when a claimant will have done most of the necessary work when preparing the statement of case. One hopes that more applications will be made. Perhaps so few are made because those claims that are capable of resolution are being settled far earlier than used to be the case, the fast track procedure is operating sufficiently swiftly to obviate the need for interim payments or that they are being paid voluntarily on request in CPR spirit.

13. Case Management, Allocation and Tracks

13.1. The allocation questionnaire

Reference at the end of the last chapter to fast track leads naturally to consideration of case management after the parties have filed their respective Statements of Case. This is an area of enormous change introduced by the CPR. Gone are the much reviled automatic directions in the county court, particularly by those who fell foul of the 15-month strike out, and the long standing provisions of RSC Ord. 25(8) in the High Court. One sad conclusion of the Woolf committee was that solicitors and parties could not be relied upon to progress actions. Accordingly, the new regime passes the responsibility to timetable to the court. This responsibility and the powers that go with it are to be found in CPR Part 26.

CPR Part 3 gives the court certain case management powers. The first occasion when the court usually intervenes in a claim is by allocating a case to a particular track, or indicating that the case is not suitable to be placed in a track, or when it considers whether a case needs to be transferred to another court.

The last of these functions is automatic. If the claim is for a specified amount of money, the court is not the defendant's home court, the defendant is an individual and the claim has not already been transferred then the court will, automatically, transfer the claim to the defendant's home court on the filing of a defence. However, most injury claims are for an unspecified amount of money because of the unspecified pain, suffering and loss of amenity general damage claim and so this provision will not apply. It is worth noting in passing that specified and unspecified have replaced liquidated and unliquidated.

Regardless of whether transfer is to take place as set out above on receipt of a defence the court must send out an allocation questionnaire to each party. If there are two or more defendants the form is sent out when the last files a defence or when time expires for the last defence to be filed. This form has been updated this year. A precedent is set out in Appendix E together with a listing questionnaire (see Chapter 17).

The form must be returned to the court no later than the date specified on it. On receipt the first thing that you should do is make adequate diary entry of that date. Failure to comply is not only embarrassing but can have most unfortunate consequences. CPR Part 26.5(5) states that failure to comply gives the court the power to make any direction it considers adequate. Worse still in the practice direction accompanying this Part at 26 PD-002.5 the judge will usually order that unless an allocation questionnaire is filed within three days the claim be struck out. If you missed the first date do not miss this one unless you are happy to rely on your insurance policy.

Assuming that you complete the form (aided by your early attention to some of the points that it raises, as suggested in Chapter 10) and returned it in the given time the court will allocate the claim to the appropriate track or simply list for disposal if there is no issue on liability unless the claim for injury is worth less than £1,000 and the overall claim is for less than £5,000 when there will still be allocation to the small claims track.

13.2. Content of the allocation questionnaire

See the precedent form in Appendix E. In brief, the form requires:

- an indication of the track that you consider most appropriate;
- an indication of whether there has been compliance with the personal injury protocol;
- details of experts for whom permission is sought, whether the expert is a single joint expert; whether that evidence is agreed and in what form it is to be given;
- details of costs to date and anticipated costs to trial;
- whether an application for summary judgment or to add a party is contemplated;
- time estimate for trial;
- details of likely trial advocate;
- unavailable dates for counsel and witnesses. Your unavailability is irrelevant.

There is also scope for suggesting directions. For reasons dealt with below you should always suggest directions. In any event, you should be clear about how you wish to take the case forward in the best way and as expeditiously as possible and so want to have input into the directions and timescale.

13.3. Allocation

On receipt of the parties allocation questionnaire the court will allocate the case to a particular track, save where set out above. If it has enough information to do so it may allocate a case even if not all parties have returned the forms. Usually, it will not, instead making a further order giving the defaulting party time to file the questionnaire with the possible sanctions set out above for non compliance. There are two exceptions to this that you will see regularly in injury claims. These are as follows;

(1) If the parties, or one of them, have asked for a stay to enable settlement to be explored whether by alternative dispute resolution or other means. Usually, if one party only requests this, particularly if it is the defendant, the court will grant a stay even if the other party has not requested it. The stay will be for one month. The order will require the claimant to notify the court at a set date whether the claim continues. At that stage the parties can either request a further period of stay for valid reason or the court must give such directions, including allocation, as are appropriate.

(2) Where the claim is over small claims track limits but the defendant has conceded liability. In such cases a request for the court to enter summary judgment for damages to be decided should be made within the allocation questionnaire. Usually, the court will enter such a judgment and Part 26 PD-005.4(2) suggests that the court will then not allocate to a track. This is taken further in 26 PD-0012 which indicates that if summary judgment is entered before a case is allocated it is not then normally appropriate to allocate unless the financial value is such that it is a small claim in which case the hearing to decide damages will be the small claim hearing date or if the defence raises disputes on quantum which are substantial. Otherwise, you will usually find that judgment is entered, directions are given on quantum issues and the matter is listed for a disposal hearing (formerly an assessment of damages appointment).

13.4. Tracks

There are three tracks to which cases may be allocated. These tracks are small claims, fast and multi. To ensure that you complete the allocation questionnaire properly and that you are familiar with allocation you do need to know how to determine the appropriate track.

Small claims

This is the normal track for any injury claim where the value of the pain, suffering and loss of amenity is under £1,000 and the total value of all items sought is under £5,000. It is easy to forget about total value and assume that if the value of the pain, suffering and loss of amenity claim is less than £1,000 then small claims allocation is inevitable. However, if the claim also includes the pre-accident value of a vehicle and some hire charges the total can easily exceed £5,000.

Fast track

This is the normal track for claims over small claims limits but with a financial value of less than £15,000. There are provisos to this as fast track trials can only last one day and expert evidence is strictly limited. Notwithstanding this, fast track is probably the track that caters for most injury claims.

Multi track

Not surprisingly, this is the normal track for cases that are not small claims or within fast track limits. In simpler terms, if the value of the claim is over £15,000 then the claim will be allocated to the multi track.

Assessment of value for allocation purposes

As you can see, allocation requires the court to assess value. Whilst the parties are obliged to indicate which they believe to be the relevant track in the allocation questionnaire that is not binding on the court, which must make its own assessment. In doing so it disregards any claim for interest, any effect that allegations of contributory negligence may have on an award, costs and any items not in dispute. However, any sum for which the defendant does not admit liability is in dispute. So, for example, if certain items of special damage are agreed subject to liability the value of those items must still be considered for allocation purposes.

13.5. Case management at this stage

By and large, allocation rarely causes controversy. The most frequent problems it raises are where financial value dictates fast track but the time estimate for trial exceeds one day or where permission is requested for too many experts. If the court is struggling to allocate on the strength of the information in the allocation questionnaire it can request further information or in extremely rare cases fix an allocation hearing. In the latter instance it will probably fix this with a case management hearing to save costs and avoid delay.

Where allocation is not a problem then the court must allocate and then decide how best to progress the case. Again, this ought not to be too hard as those parties who are proactive will have lodged proposed directions with their allocation questionnaires. Even though the form simply asks if you have, it is good practice to do so and if you do and the defendant does not you may find that whether or not the defendant agrees with your proposals you have shown willing to the court and prevail. Regrettably, far too few parties do lodge proposed directions. This means that the court either does the best it can from the information on file, requests proposed directions or fixes a case management hearing. Usually, practice depends upon the track to which the court has allocated. If small claims and fast track, the court usually gives directions on paper without any hearing. If multi track, then it is customary to see a hearing fixed. Often, to save cost, this is specified to be by telephone with the claimant's solicitor to arrange but with the cost to be joint.

In quantum only disposal cases a lot depends upon whether you have lodged proposed directions. If you have you increase the chance of directions being given without the necessity of a hearing. If a case management conference is arranged and it is to be by telephone, do plan in advance. If the order does not say so find out which judge will be dealing with the case and, if you do not know it, find out the name behind the reference at the defendant's solicitors. You can then make arrangements with the telephone company for the conference. They will call the booking party first, then the other party and finally the judge. The call will be recorded. Experience, and an unpleasant one at that, has shown that these telephone conferences can be arranged as little as 20 minutes before the hearing time, although this is not recommended!

Do prepare for this hearing. You will be expected to provide the judge with a brief summary of the case, know the issues, be prepared to give a rough estimate of value and know what directions you want. If you did not consider directions when lodging the allocation questionnaire do so before this hearing. Work out how long witness statements and disclosure will take you so that you ensure the order provides adequate time whilst not seeming to delay matters unduly.

If the hearing is in person or by telephone and you cannot do it yourself do make sure whoever does do it is fully briefed by you. The days of "Here is the file do the best you can and get me as long as possible for every stage of the action" have no place in modern claim handling—thank goodness.

13.6. Standard directions

Examples of the type of direction that you should consider as standard in personal injury litigation are as follows:

(a) allocation or entry of judgment for damages to be decided;

(b) allocation of a trial window if allocated to track, or a disposal date if judgment entered. Time estimate;

(c) provisions for filing and service of witness statements of fact;

(d) disclosure;

(e) inspection;

(f) permissions for expert/s;

(g) permissions for questions to be put to an expert and time scale for response;

(h) meetings of experts of like disciplines to narrow issues and file agreed note;

(i) split trial if liability in dispute and can conveniently be disposed of first;

(j) requests for further information of any parties Statement of Case;

(k) amendments required.

There is nothing to fear from case management. In fact, the emphasis on expedition and cost saving in most cases works for the claimant. It encourages the defendant to decide at a much earlier stage than usual whether to fight a claim and if so ensures that the process is strictly time controlled. There is no hiding place to drag out a claim. Within a relatively short time period the claim has either settled or been heard by the court. The only danger in case management by the court is for the unprepared. If you have prepared you know what you want and how to obtain it. In practice, most case management conferences see civilised agreement about the way to take a claim forward. There may be differences of view as to where liability may rest and how much a claim may be worth but injury practitioners should usually be able to agree as to how and when to determine those issues.

14. Making an Application

14.1. Introduction

It is very unlikely in the multi track that you will be able to go through a whole action simply relying on the initial directions without having to make an application. Not only are you likely to have to apply for more time or press the other side to fulfil its obligations, there are also many interim orders available which may help advance your client's case.

The solicitor who is aware of the interim orders that are available can use this stage of the action to build up the foundations of a client's case. Your opponent can be pinned down by being forced to clarify the defence or allegations, by being made to disclose some evidence.

The interim orders mentioned in this and later chapters will not be suitable for every case. However, the solicitor must know which orders can be sought and how (and when) to apply for them. But, before considering the interim stage in more detail, it is necessary to understand the mechanics of interim proceedings, how to issue an application and who draws up the order. That is explained in this chapter.

'The court' in interim matters means either the master (in RCJ cases) or the district judge (in District Registry and county court cases), and thence by way of appeal, the judge. In RCJ cases, a master is assigned to the action when the first application is issued and that master will, thereafter, hear all the applications in that case. In the District Registry and county court that rarely happens, although of course it will, in those courts where there is only one District Judge.

14.2. The application

Preparation

An application can either be issued by post, or by personal attendance at the court office. In practice, it is more convenient to issue by post and this is what most solicitors do. The steps to be taken (both for post and personal attendance) are set out in Procedural Table 2.

A stock of blank notices of application (form N244) should be kept in the office although they are now available on the internet and can be used in that form. Specimen notices of application are printed in Appendix E. If preferred, they can be used as a precedent, and typed out on A4 paper. They are now in a significantly different form.

The blank form of Notice of Application is easy to complete. The only difficulty will lie with inserting the terms of the order that is being sought. Appendix C sets out the precedents needed to run a typical personal injury case. The appropriate wording should be inserted in the blank space on the form. Bear in mind that more than one order can be sought on a single application, and such orders can be in the alternative if wished. You will need to give the wording careful thought as it is preferable to attach a draft order to your application.

Issuing the application

Follow the steps in Procedural Table 3 for issuing the application. Three copies should be prepared. One will be retained by the court, one will be sent to you and the final copy will be served by the court unless you request it to be returned for personal service. Obviously, if there is more than one defendant then extra copies will be needed since each defendant will have to be served. You must give the court an estimate of how long the hearing is likely to last. You will see scope to insert the estimated length of hearing at the top of the application notice. Before reaching this stage you must indicate whether you want an attended hearing, a telephone hearing or whether you think that the application can be dealt with without a hearing either by written representations or without notice. It is as well to familiarise yourself with your local court practice or that of the court in which you are litigating. Some courts deal with the majority of applications without hearing. You also need to consider the nature of the application. If it is to compel a party to do something where there is already breach of a court order then plainly this is something that can and will be dealt with on paper. It speeds up the process and saves costs of a hearing on an unarguable point. If you have alerted the other party to the nature of your application in advance and it is hotly disputed and not clear cut you should seek a hearing since otherwise, if the court makes an order without notice the other party is bound to object and the court will then have to list the application for hearing causing increased delay. Do help the court because that will help it to deal with the case in the most expeditious and cost effective way.

If a hearing is plainly required then unless both parties are close to the court a telephone hearing will be the most convenient form. With insurers centralising instructions you may find that nearly all your court work is done by telephone. When it is served the application will indicate if the appointment is to be by telephone and who is to make the arrangements. The arrangements are likely to be the same as mentioned earlier for case management conferences.

Remember that even if the hearing is to be by telephone if there are documents that the court will need to see you should lodge these in advance with your costs schedule ready for summary assessment (see Chapter 22).

The application notice must be served as soon as is practicable after issue and unless a longer period is provided for in the CPR, (such as for interim payment applications), at least three days before the day on which the court is to deal with the application. Calculation of time periods has been considered earlier.

Evidence

Written evidence in support of any application must be served with the application itself. Therefore, where the court is to effect service, as it will in the majority of cases, the evidence must be filed with the application notice. As the application must set out why the order is sought most applications will require some evidence. The evidence can be by reliance on the Statements of Case, as long as they contain the necessary statement of truth, provided by separate witness statement or simply be given in section C of the application notice in which case the statement of truth that accompanies it must be signed.

Any respondent to an application who wishes to rely on evidence should file it as soon as possible if there is no specific time set out in any relevant Part of the CPR or if no directions for the filing of evidence in the application have been given by the court.

If the applicant then wants to file further evidence in reply the same provisions apply although time runs from the service of the respondent's evidence. In this case, you will also need to serve the evidence.

Applications disposed of without hearing

These are set out in CPR Part 23.8. This includes consent orders, applications which the parties agree should be disposed of without hearing and any other applications where the court does not consider a hearing necessary. The latter category is a clear example of active case management within the overriding objective. If the court exercises this function then the application, any evidence that was filed in support and the order made must be served on the respondent by the court with an indication in the order in the terms of the Part 23.9(3) notice that the parties can apply to set aside or vary the order under Part 23.10. Such an application must be made within seven days of service of the order.

The list of orders that the court can make without first serving the application is long. To some practitioners the procedure is not new as some courts, like Bristol, had adopted this practice of considering which applications could be dealt with without a hearing prior to the CPR. Applications that lend themselves to this procedure include application for:

- extension of time for filing Defence;
- unless orders where there is failure to comply with earlier court order;
- setting aside irregular judgment in default or regular judgment where there is plainly a real prospect of defending the claim successfully;
- service by alternative method;
- extensions of validity period of proceedings;
- permission for Part 20 proceedings;
- appointment of litigation friend;

- removal of a solicitor from the record as acting;
- extension of a stay period.

Consent orders

Sometimes, the other side will consent to the order being sought. Typically, this will be at the conclusion of the case, when the parties want a consent order which sets out the terms of settlement (*e.g.* agreed costs; money to be paid out of court to the claimant; interest on the money to go to the defendant, etc.). In such instances, the order can be made by consent; which means that there is no need for an application to be issued, and there is no need for the parties to attend. A different procedure therefore applies. This procedure is set out in Procedural Table 3.

A consent order can be made for any of the following:

- giving judgment with damages to be assessed;
- settlement of the case by dismissal, discontinuance, withdrawal, withdrawal of the record, stay, *Tomlin* Order, etc.;
- setting aside of judgment in default;
- to have money paid out of court (*i.e.* when the 21-day period for acceptance has expired);
- an order relating to costs;
- for the proceedings to be transferred to the county court from the High Court;

However, with the court being responsible for managing a claim consent applications are now no longer the formality they once were. The court must be satisfied that the order is appropriate and proportionate. An example of this is that whilst the parties may agree an extension of 28 days for service of the Defence any period beyond that, even if agreed, requires court approval. This means an explanation must be given for why the extension is necessary. CPR Part 23 PD-10.4 states that on application for a consent order the parties must provide the court with any material that it needs to satisfy itself that it is appropriate to make the order.

This does not mean that the court will refuse to make sensible and proportionate agreed orders. It simply means that the court must be involved almost as a third party to the action. There are still practitioners who overlook this and suggest that as directions have been agreed they will not be attending a case management conference. Ignoring the clear function given to the court by the CPR is decidedly inadvisable.

Amending an application

If an applicant issues an application and subsequently wishes to amend it, there is no need to re-issue. All you need to do is simply notify the other side of your intention to amend, and then ask the district judge or master for permission at the hearing. The key is to give the respondent and the court advance notice of as long as possible.

Adjourning an application or summons

Once the application has been issued, it can be adjourned. If the application has been served, this can only be done with the written consent of the other side. Again, the court will have an active function and mere agreement to adjourn is not enough; there must be a good reason and one you share with the court. The court will no longer adjourn indefinitely. Therefore, you should either seek a further date or consider whether in fact you want to withdraw the application.

Before service

On the other hand, if the application has not been served then consent will not be needed. This will now be unusual as the court will serve the majority of applications.

14.3 Using counsel and special appointments (High Court)

Most applications are conducted by solicitors, or their clerks. But, if the application is particularly important, a party may well want to instruct counsel. It is important to decide in advance whether counsel is to be instructed, because this may result in the case being put in a different list. If the applicant wants counsel to attend, then you should make sure that this is clear to the court when issuing the application. To avoid any misunderstanding, it is best to tell the other side that counsel will be attending on the application. In the county court no differentiation is usually made in the time when cases with counsel are heard. In the High Court all cases with counsel are put in Counsel's List which is heard at noon. Naturally, whenever you are served with an applications you should check that it is not listed for hearing at noon; if it is, then you will know that it is in Counsel's List and may wish to instruct counsel yourself.

Transfer to counsel's list (High Court)

In the High Court if the summons has not been put in Counsel's List (*i.e.* it is in the Ordinary List) but the other party, the party served with it, wants it to be in Counsel's List, then it should write to the other side straight away. It should ask the party who issued the summons to apply to the practice master to transfer the summons, by consent, to the noon list (or adjourn it for a special appointment). It is for the party who issued the summons to make the application to the practice master. If that party refuses to do so, then the party who wants it transferred should still appear at the hearing of the summons (in the General List) and make an application to the master for the case to be adjourned, and transferred to Counsel's List and should also ask for the other side to pay the costs that have been unnecessarily incurred.

Special appointments (High Court)

Counsel's List, at noon, is for the hearing of summonses that are not expected to last longer than 20 minutes. If a summons is likely to last for more than that time, then one should ask for a special appointment. Special appointments are normally given if a summons is likely to last for 20 minutes or more. If this is likely to be the case, then the party issuing the summons should apply for a special appointment. If the party served with the summons (*i.e.* the party who did not issue it) thinks that a special appointment is necessary, then it should ask the other side to apply to the practice master for the case to be taken out of the Ordinary Lists. If they refuse, then it should make application to the master at the normal hearing (*i.e.* as with counsel, above). Solicitors, and their clerks, can appear at special appointments; there is no need to be represented by counsel.

14.4. The hearing

County court and High Court

The person attending the application (normally a solicitor's clerk) should make contact with the court usher (outside the door). Some courts no longer have ushers which means that you must listen to the tannoy system that will be in operation to call cases. If the matter is by consent you should inform the usher of this since you are then likely to be heard earlier.

More often than not now hearings in personal injury cases are allotted a specific time. It is increasingly rare for them to be block listed. Some days, lists will run to time other days they will not. If, as some practitioners have started to do under the CPR, you take your client to a hearing it is worth pointing out the vagaries of listing in advance.

As with most elements of the case preparation is the key to a successful hearing. It is rare for advocacy to win the day. It is common for poor preparation to lose it. Have a handy crib sheet available with all relevant background information on it such as date of accident, brief accident description, brief injury summary, claimant's date of birth, date of issue and date of defence. This avoids the embarrassment of flicking through papers when asked a simple question.

If it helps you make points to the judge then prepare a chronology, (if relevant), and a skeleton argument or statement of issues and file and serve this in advance. It may shorten the hearing and also ensure that if you forget to raise a point in submissions it is before the court anyway. It also smacks of someone who has taken the trouble to prepare and to think about the matter sometime in advance rather than as they grabbed the file for a last minute sprint to court. It impresses clients.

The Bear Garden used to be full of trainees, paralegals and clerks cutting their teeth on simple applications. Under the CPR there is no such thing as a simple application. Avid followers of a certain 60's adventure series will remember well the warning "Anything can happen in the next half hour". As the court must consider what directions it can give in a claim on every occasion the claim does come before it, regardless of why the claim may be before it, the person who attends ought to be you, but failing that must be someone who understands the case and the types of order that a court may consider making in an injury claim. Do not repent at leisure partly because you will not actually have time to do so but mainly because it is easier to get it right first time. It is worth remembering that the court has power to award wasted costs orders. A classic scenario is where a hearing has to be adjourned because one of the parties is not in a position to deal with something that is raised which could have been dealt with properly if the person who has the conduct of the file had been present. If a case is complicated and there are genuine reasons for your unavailability that are known well in advance you should consider asking the defendant to agree to an adjournment. If they agree then apply by consent to the court taking care to explain why you are unavailable and why the hearing requires your attendance. At best the hearing will be adjourned, at worst your representative can always indicate if in difficulties that this is precisely why you wished the matter to be adjourned until you were available.

Power of the court where there is no attendance

CPR Part 23.11 makes it plain that the court can proceed in the absence of one or sometimes both parties. If you attend and the defendant does not then on your application seek the order requested and on the defendant's application ask for it to be struck out. A dismissal is for when a party attends and loses, a strike out is for when they should attend and do not.

If the court does make an order in these circumstances, and of course the overriding objective applies regardless of whether the parties bother to turn up, then the court can subsequently relist the matter on application or of its own motion. This is expressly in addition to any other powers, such as to vary, set aside or discharge the order, that the court may have.

14.5. The order

Every order of the court, whether High or county, will be drawn by the court unless the court orders a party to draw it, it is a consent order lodged by the parties, a party obtains court permission to draw it or the court decides that no order needs to be drawn. Having said this if, as the standard application notice invites you to do, you have prepared a draft order then that will be used, if appropriate, and be initialled by the Master or District Judge.

It is therefore rare that a party draws an order. One example of a situation where it may be appropriate is where the order provides for disclosure of specific and voluminous documents. However, the more likely practice is that the court will make a decision and then invite the parties to go outside to draft an order reflecting the court findings. The parties then reattend when they have done this and the court will finalise the order.

Most orders now specify time scales by reference to dates and therefore confusion that may have arisen in the past over when an order takes effect should no longer arise. However, if there is any doubt, the situation is governed by CPR Part 40.7 which confirms previous provisions that an order takes effect from the day when it is made, unless the court specifies otherwise. This proviso is quite important because where an order is made in the absence of one or both parties, who then will not know the terms of the order until it is served the court is likely to specify a longer time for compliance to allow for service or specify that the order must be complied with so many days after service.

If you are asked to draw an order or successfully seek permission to do so then the order must be filed with the court no later than seven days after the hearing.

Some examples of standard wording of the order that you may encounter

"liberty to apply"	—may be added to allow the parties to come back to the court for matters arising within the order to be resolved. In practice, this arises most frequently in a *Tomlin* Order to embody settlement;
"liberty to restore"	—if part or all of the application is not dealt with then the applicant can resurrect the application without paying a fresh fee. This will not arise very often as under the CPR the judiciary is discouraged from leaving applications that have not been dealt with on file for any lengthy period. You are likely to find that the order will also state that if the matter has not been restored by a set date the application or that part that has not been dealt with be struck out. You do need to keep a careful check on what remains outstanding;
"no order"	—this does not mean that the application has not been considered it simply means that the court is not prepared to make any order on the application. If you are dissatisfied with this then you can either appeal or issue a fresh application. If there is new evidence relevant to the application that has arisen after the order, for example if no order were made on an application for an interim payment but after the application the defendant admitted liability, you could make a fresh application for interim payment without needing to appeal;
"costs reserved"	—the costs will be decided by the judge at the end of the trial or a later date if the order specific to whom or when they are reserved;
"costs in the case"	—costs will ultimately go to the winner of the case. There is a view that even in these circum-

stances the court should summarily assess these costs where appropriate so that once the outcome of the case is known the time for payment starts running without the need for any further court intervention. However it is rare to find a court assessing in such a situation.

"claimant's or defendant's costs in the case" —if the party in whose favour this order is made ultimately wins the case then these costs are recoverable, if not, the order subsequently has no effect. The point made in the previous paragraph about summary assessment applies equally here.

"costs in any event" —whatever the eventual outcome of the case the recipient of this order recovers the costs of this application under this order. In all applications lasting less than a day you will find that instead of this form of order the court will now summarily assess the costs of the hearing. With limited exceptions these costs will be payable within 14 days (see Chapter 22).

"costs thrown away" —this tends to be used where a party has incurred wasted costs where an order or judgment has been set aside, such as judgment in default. Again, the comments concerning summary assessment apply.

"no order for costs" —means exactly what is says. The CPR is also clear that if an order is silent as to costs then no cost implications arise.

"public funding assessment" —this was a legal aid taxation. You should request this where the client has the benefit of a public funding certificate. Only one such order is needed and therefore in injury work it is only needed in any judgment or order dismissing the case. It ensures that any sums not recoverable from the defendant can be sought from the Legal Services Commission.

"costs not to be enforced without further order" —this is usually only seen where there is a public funding certificate and the party who has that is the paying party under court order. In this situation, subject to any offsetting order that might follow, the costs order can only be enforced and turned into money if the publicly funded persons financial circumstances take a substantial up turn. This used to be called a Football Pools Order but now, perhaps to the chagrin of the Pools companies, is frequently referred to as a Lottery Order. Offsetting can take place. For example, if the defendant secures an interim costs order in a case where the claimant subsequently receives damages then the costs can be ordered to be paid out of those damages. To save the parties coming back to the court the order will specify that if the claimant secures damages then offsetting will take place. This is often referred to as a Lockley order.

Finally, whenever an order is obtained against you, it is important to read it carefully. In particular watch out for an 'unless' order. This is an order that requires strict compliance, failing which the claimant's claim will be struck out (or the defendant's Defence be struck out and judgment entered for the claimant). Such orders should always receive top priority; if you fail to comply in time, and the client therefore loses the case, you may well face an action for professional negligence. The courts are generally reluctant to allow judgments, etc., obtained under such orders to be set aside, even allowing for Human Rights, issues. This is particularly so when a trial date has been given. If the unless order requires action from your client make sure you inform the client of the action required, when it is required by and the sanction for non compliance. Do not allow yourself to be sued for your client's failure to comply.

If the court feels that a legal representative has behaved improperly, unreasonably or negligently then under the Supreme Court Act 1981, s.51(7) it may make a costs order against that representative rather than the client. The meaning of these words was considered in detail in *Ridehalgh Horsefield* [1994] 3 W.L.R. 462. This is embodied in the CPR in Part 48.7 where the procedure to be followed is recited. You should note that the court must give the legal representative a reasonable opportunity to attend a hearing and give reasons why such an order should not be made.

Linked to this is the newly introduced, and one suspects frequently overlooked, provision that if your client is not present at a hearing when an adverse costs order is made the client must be informed of this no later than seven days after you receive notice of it (see CPR Part 44.2). This follows the views of the Woolf enquiry team which felt it important that clients know what a case is costing them.

14.6. Appealing the order

CPR Part 52 applies to all appeals and no attempt to summarise the provisions can ever be sufficient. You must read the rules and have a working knowledge of them because you may have to apply them in a rush, such as when seeking permission to appeal after a long interim hearing that has gone against you, when you may be exhausted. The rules are the same in High and county courts.

In all situations which arise in a standard injury claim permission to appeal must be obtained. This can be obtained from either the lower court whose decision you wish to appeal or the court to whom you are appealing. If the lower court refuses permission you may still apply to the court to whom you wish to appeal. This must be done within seven days of notice that permission has been refused by the lower court, which will invariably be the day of the original order as you should seek permission at the hearing.

Permission will only be given where there is a real prospect of the appeal succeeding, which is why most applications to the lower court fail since otherwise the decision you wish to appeal would not have been made by that court in the first place, or if there is some other compelling reason for the appeal to be heard, for example if it challenges some area of the CPR where there has yet to be definitive ruling on interpretation.

Appeals from county court District Judges go to Circuit Judge and from Masters and High Court District Judges to Judge in Chambers.

Funding arrangements

Do not forget that approval will be needed to appeal in virtually every public funded, legal expense and conditional fee case from the relevant funding authority before embarking on the appeal.

14.7. Judgment with damages decided

Sometimes, a claimant will obtain interlocutory judgment with damages to be decided (*e.g.* if the defendant has failed to comply with an "unless" order). When this happens, the claimant should at the same time as asking the court to enter such a judgment, lodge proposed directions to bring the disposal to fruition and request that the court makes those directions. This saves the cost of a case management hearing and expedites the disposal process.

15. Disclosure of Documents

15.1. Disclosure of documents (general)

Disclosure is when the parties send each other details of all the relevant documents they hold. It is an extremely important part of any personal injury claim as it allows each party to know whether the other has any documents to back its claim. Obtaining all relevant documentation can be critical. This chapter deals with disclosure in outline but cannot cover all the detailed points which may arise in a complex case. For those you are referred to specialist works and the detailed notes in CPR Part 31

15.2. Pre-action disclosure

This has already been considered in detail in Chapter 5. The intention of the personal injury protocol is to ensure that disclosure of relevant documents supporting a claim is given prior to issue of proceedings to ensure that parties can properly evaluate the claim at that stage. The protocol provisions are supported by the availability of pre-action disclosure by application on Part 23 notice. It should be rare for relevant documents to come to light for the first time in disclosure within the court proceedings.

15.3. Types of disclosure

There are four types of disclosure; standard, non standard, specific and pre-action. In fast track cases the usual order will be for standard disclosure. In multi track cases (unless there are complicated issues rather than simply an injury with a high value determining the track) standard disclosure is likely to be ordered. If an order for disclosure is silent as to the type of disclosure then the obligation is to give standard disclosure, CPR Part 31.5(1).

Standard disclosure

This provides for a party to disclose the documents upon which that party relies and documents which adversely affect that party's case or the case of another party or support another party's case. In addition, if any further documents are required under any practice direction then those too must be disclosed, in injury claims the latter extends to the protocol obligations in respect of documents to be provided in response to a letter of claim where liability is disputed (see Chapter 4).

Non standard disclosure

No specific definition is given and it is hard to see what pertinent disclosure beyond standard disclosure would be either relevant or proportionate.

Specific disclosure

The court can make an order for specific disclosure of documents or classes of documents, or order a party to search for such documents and disclose those found. The likelihood is that this disclosure is either standard or non standard disclosure.

Pre-action disclosure

This has already been considered in detail in Chapter 5.

15.4. Method of standard disclosure

Each party has to prepare and serve a list of documents in practice form N265 (see precedent in Appendix E). The list should be in convenient order and as brief as possible. The right to withhold a document for inspection must be stated as must the fact that a document may no longer be in the disclosing party's control.

Every disclosure list must contain a formal disclosure statement. This is set out on the practice form. The statement confirms the extent of search for documents, and states, if the party is not an individual why the person signing the statement is the appropriate person to do so. One of the criticisms made by the Woolf Enquiry team was that parties were spending too much money on disproportionate disclosure. They felt that provided a reasonable and proportionate search is carried out that is sufficient, and if the party is not an individual why the person signing the statement is the appropriate person to do so.

The rules specifically allow the parties to agree to dispense with a formal list. You will find that this frequently happens in injury claims. Where liability has been admitted you should have disclosed quantum documents before issue or, as they come to light, after issue. The defendant in those cases is unlikely to have any documents. In straightforward cases of contested liability you should have seen all relevant defendant documents under the protocol. However, it may still be wise to insist on the list as the signing of a disclosure statement is more onerous than simply asserting compliance with a protocol and can induce further disclosure.

15.5. Solicitor's duty

A matter that is frequently overlooked is the solicitor's duty to ensure that clients appreciate their obligations with regard to disclosure Solicitors are obliged to take positive steps to ensure that clients appreciate at an early stage of litigation particularly now there are protocol not only the breadth of the duty of discovery but also the importance of not destroying documents which may have to be disclosed. This obligation extends to taking steps to ensure that, in any corporate organisation, knowledge of the disclosure obligations is passed on to anyone who may be affected by it. It is not enough simply to give instructions that documents be preserved, steps should be taken to ensure that they *are* preserved; an inference may be made against the client if documents are destroyed, particularly those relating to quantum. For a letter of advice to a client about discovery obligations see Appendix B.

15.6. The disclosure list

As stated, this should be a prescribed form see PF N265.

Completing the list

The front page of the list contains the disclosure statement. It is important that even if you have explained to your client the duty to disclose you also advise specifically on the disclosure statement. This advice must be comprehensive because the disclosure statement requires the signatory to certify that the duty of disclosure is understood. It would be embarrassing if a client found to be in breach of disclosure obligations were able to show that no explanation whatsoever had been given other than a directive to "sign the document where marked with crosses".

Do not send the client the form to sign without first taking specific instructions on the search and what has been revealed so that you can complete where appropriate and make sure that the wording of the statement that you are asking the client to sign is correct.

The following sections of the list itself are very similar to the old schedules to previous form of the list of documents. There are three. The first section is for documents that the client has and is disclosing, the second is for documents that the client has but is withholding (together with reasons for withholding) and the third is for documents that are no longer held by the client.

Your client is likely to complete the first with special damage documents and, depending on the type of claim, perhaps the police accident report book, copies of the health and safety documents provided at work, a personnel or occupational health file and medical notes, if relevant.

The second schedule is likely to refer to without prejudice letters, solicitor/client correspondence and counsel's papers.

The third schedule usually only includes the originals of letters sent although you should always check what the defendant inserts as you may see that files have gone missing or important documents have been destroyed suggesting either a carefree attitude to disclosure or deliberate destruction, either of which will create a bad impression before the court.

Once the list is complete and ready for service send it to the client with advice for the client to sign the disclosure statement.

Checking with client

Once you have prepared your list send your client a copy of Schedule 1, Part 1 to ensure it is correct and complete. In particular make sure that it includes all up-to-date receipts for special damage.

Further and supplemental lists

Remember that disclosure is a continuing obligation. If you, at any stage after service, obtain further disclosable documents then you should immediately disclose these to the other side either by way of letter or in a formal supplemental list. If in a list another disclosure statement will be required.

15.7. Defendant's disclosure

In a non-road accident case in which liability has not been admitted, the defendant's solicitor will also need to serve a list. The last two parts, of the form will usually be completed as in the claimant's list. It is therefore the first Part (*i.e.* material documents disclosed), that will interest the claimant. The claimant will want to make sure that the defendant has disclosed all the documents, that were disclosed under the protocol. Sometimes, you will find that there are documents disclosed that did not feature in the pre-action protocol disclosure. This may be because the emphasis of the claim or the defence has changed, that arguably they were not relevant until this stage, that they were not specifically requested pre-issue or that they were overlooked. Whatever the reason, if as a result of disclosure of these documents you take the view that the claim no longer has reasonable prospects then there must be a good argument that if your client then discontinues the claim the defendant should recover no costs and even that the claimant may recover costs from the time when the defendant realised that it had these documents and they were of relevance. The intention of the protocol and the CPR is plain, no trial by ambush. Parties are required to clarify and support their case as soon as possible. As the protocol states, its purpose is "to promote the early exchange of relevant information to help in clarifying or resolving issues in dispute". Failure to disclose a document until much later that frustrates this intention and causes cost expenditure is likely to be penalised.

The relevance of post issue disclosure

In the majority of claims there should be no documents that have not been made available prior to issue. Disclosure at this stage should become, and to a large extent has already become, no more than confirmation by statement of truth of the documents available. There is a danger, though, that representatives will therefore become lazy in compliance with the disclosure obligation. Always ensure that the client is properly advised of the obligation and that the defendant's list is checked carefully by both you and your client.

Do make reference to the protocol checklist for the likely documents that you should see on disclosure in the different types of injury claim. The lists are exhaustive and reiteration here would be pointless (see Appendix I).

It is relevant at this stage to remember that you are not simply checking what documents the defendant has but also those that the defendant does not have. That may be because they have been overlooked and should have been disclosed, but more often because the defendant does not have documents that should exist because they were not created in the first place despite the fact there may have been a statutory obligation to create them. The classic example is a risk assessment under the 1992 Health and Safety at Work Regulations. The basic point is that omission of documents from a list may be more illuminating than the documents actually disclosed.

This is an area where the client can assist enormously. The client may know whether certain documents ever existed.

If there are new documents disclosed and you already have expert liability evidence which the court has permitted then it is important that you send the disclosure to the expert to see if there is anything in the documents that persuades the expert to alter the opinion already expressed. Again, if there is and it undermines your case to the extent that you have to advise the client to discontinue then you should consider the cost implications had the expert been provided with the documents when he or she was first instructed. Most experts should now be either agreed or appointed jointly and should have been supplied with documents by both parties on first instruction.

Unclear documents and inspection

If the contents of a disclosed document are not clear (*e.g.* the handwriting is illegible, or it contains abbreviations) ask the defendant for an explanation. Sometimes, you will be sent copies which are not cross-referenced to the list. At the very least this is irritating and time consuming to sort out, at worst you may not notice that important documents are incomplete or missing. If this happens ask the other party to produce properly paginated and referenced documents pointing out that it will save time when preparing trial bundles. Obviously, make sure that your own file and any documents you send out are in excellent order!

15.8. Privilege

A defendant will frequently argue that a document is not disclosable since it is privileged as "having been prepared for the purposes of litigation". Often this is not a sustainable contention. If you think that the defendant might have documents that would help, but which you presume the defendant is claiming privilege for, then you should begin by looking in that schedule part of the defendant's list. Often, this will vaguely refer to "other documents dealing solely with the preparation of the defendant's case". If you suspect that there may be disclosable documents, you should ask the defendant specifically to list all these other documents referred to in this Part and for which privilege is claimed. If the defendant refuses to do so then there is little you can do because as a matter of public policy the court will not order a party to give further particulars of classes of documents for which privilege is claimed (*Derby & Co. Ltd v. Weldon (No. 7)* [1990] 3 All E.R. 161). That case decided that where a claim was made for professional privilege that claim itself counted as an adequate description of the documents. This authority remains cited under CPR Part 31.10.3 but, as pre-CPR authority it is no longer binding and since the CPR has as its core openness, it may be that the court will look more kindly upon requests for more information about documents for which privilege is claimed although this may be an area where the court determines that the professional obligations governing legal representatives are such that they can rely on the claim being genuine.

If the document that you seek is not in any part of the list then you should consider requesting specific disclosure (see below).

Documents for which privilege can be claimed

Since the decision of the House of Lords in *Waugh v. BRB* [1979] 2 All E.R. 1169, the scope of the argument that a document was prepared for the purposes of litigation has been considerably reduced. The test to be applied is: "what was the dominant purpose of the author of the document?" If the dominant purpose (not necessarily the sole purpose) was in order to obtain legal advice, or aid the conduct of litigation, then it should be privileged. But, otherwise, it will not be privileged and so it will be disclosable. *Waugh* concerned an internal report on a railway accident; it had to be disclosed, despite the affidavit of the defendant's solicitor stating that one of its principal purposes was to enable him to advise BRB on its legal liability. In practice, therefore, if one can show that an internal inquiry is shown as a matter of routine (*i.e.* even when there can be no question of any legal liability) then the report should be disclosable. The same applies if the report is designed to prevent similar accidents occurring in the future, since then it cannot be said that litigation was its dominant purpose. This is particularly so if this is part of an ongoing risk assessment policy as it is plainly relevant to issues. Another useful case for claimant, to quote is *Melik v. Norwich Union*

[1980] 1 Lloyd's Rep. 523. In this case, Woolf J. held that an assessor's report to insurers was not privileged:

> "It is quite clear ... that one purpose of the insurers in instructing the assessors must have been to have a report which could be used for the purpose of obtaining legal advice if that should prove necessary ... However ... it is not sufficient that a document should come into existence for a series of purposes, one of which is obtaining legal advice ... in this case the dominant purpose of the assessors making their report was to enable the insurers to ascertain the facts in order to come to a decision as to whether or not they should rely upon the clause of the policy in order to repudiate liability."

So, the assessor's report was not privileged. In a similar case concerning the NHS (*Lask v. Gloucester Health Authority* [1991] 2 Med. L.R. 379, CA) it was held that an accident report required by NHS circulars was not privileged even though one of the stated purposes of the report is use by solicitors in litigation. The above cases coupled with the CPR open approach in personal injury litigation means that many documents for which privilege has traditionally and still is claimed should be disclosed. The moral is that claimant's solicitors should not be shy of asking for internal reports, provided it can be shown that these reports are prepared as a matter of routine, and that their dominant purpose is not for litigation. If they are not disclosed on request then apply to the court for them. Such applications are often successful.

If either party disclose a document that is privileged then CPR Part 31.20 applies. Any party who has inspected such a document can use it only with court permission.

15.9. Situations where no list is required

Remember that no list can be served without court permission. Therefore, the obligation has changed from the old rules where, save in a few situations, a list had to be served either under High Court automatic directions or county court Ord. 17 unless the court ordered otherwise. That said, there will be few cases only where no disclosure order is made by the court. When seeking directions in a case where a formal case management hearing is unlikely and disclosure is inappropriate do take the trouble to indicate within your proposed directions why no direction for disclosure and inspection is sought otherwise the court may order it thinking that you have simply overlooked the need for such a direction.

15.10. Enforcing disclosure

Where a list has been ordered and is necessary but you may not have received the disclosure list in the appropriate period issue an application on CPR Part 23 notice seeking an unless order without hearing. If you did not want a disclosure order but omitted to explain why to the court and one was ordered common sense dictates that in such a situation the parties write to the court to explain why there will not be or has not been compliance. To seek to enforce such an order would be a nonsense.

In other situations where there is breach of the order, you want to make progress without delay. This is a classic example of a case where the court should make an unless order on your application without a hearing. Whilst this order must contain the usual proviso about the right to apply to vary or set aside the order so made it is hard to think of any satisfactory reason a party might give for delay. Perhaps the illness of a party or the absence of the person required to sign the disclosure statement. Otherwise, you are likely to obtain an unless order providing very little time for compliance in default of which judgment be entered for damages to be decided. You should draft the order to make it easier for the court to make and attach it to your application. When doing so, express the time for compliance by reference to a set time on a set date to avoid any confusion whatsoever. This rarely results in a judgment but does have the benefit of ensuring rapid service of a disclosure list. Similarly, if you are on the receiving end of such an application comply immediately.

Affidavit verifying the list

The introduction of the disclosure statement has seen the abolition of the affidavit verifying the list which, in any event, was a little known and infrequently used tool of the discovery regime.

15.11. Specific disclosure

This disclosure enforcement method survives, which is perhaps a measure of its success. CPR Part 31.12 retains this procedure. An application must be made, again using the standard Part 23 application procedure. The application must specify with clarity the documents sought and be supported by evidence indicating why the document(s) are believed to be in the other party's possession and why they are relevant to issues before the court. Bearing in mind the overriding objective it is probably as well to explain why disclosure is proportionate to the resolution of those issues; this is because CPR Part 31 PD-005.4 specifically reminds the court when considering such an application to have in mind all the circumstances of the case and, in particular, the overriding objective.

You must pursue disclosure of documents that you and/or your client believe to be missing from the defendant's disclosure list because if you do not the sanction for non-disclosure seems curiously ineffective. CPR Part 31.21 indicates that a party may not rely on any document which that party fails to disclose or in respect of which permission to inspect is refused without permission of the court.

15.12. Orders for disclosure from a person not a party

It is possible to obtain an order for disclosure against a person who is not a party to the action (CPR Part 31.17). You may wish to adopt this procedure if you believe that a non party has documents that would assist your client's case; for example, records held by the DSS in connection with disability and incapacity benefit that confirm the extent of your client's injuries. Any party can apply to the Master or District Judge, by way of Part 23 application, for an order that the third party disclose the specific documents requested. The application, which is made using a Part 23 application notice, can be for disclosure of documents which support the case of the applicant or adversely affect the case of any party to the proceedings. Evidence in support by witness statement is again required to explain why the order is sought and should state that the order is necessary to enable the court to resolve the claim justly or in a fashion that saves costs. The latter requirement would be met where, but for the order, the documents could only be obtained by serving a witness summons and securing attendance and documents at trial. Plainly that approach would necessitate the cost of a trial whereas earlier disclosure might obviate the need for a trial. You should attach a draft order to the application which must specify the document/s which must be disclosed, whether documents are no longer in the control of the non party and if so to specify what happened to the document and to provide a timescale for disclosure and inspection of documents held.

This procedure is mainly used against hospitals that are reluctant to forward the claimant's medical notes and records to the parties advisers, or against the HSE for its investigation and enquiry notes and statements.

16. After Disclosure

16.1. Introduction

This is one of the key stock taking opportunities in any injury claim. Under the CPR there will be a limited amount of time to undertake this review. You cannot afford to put it off.

Some of the considerations set out below will already have been reviewed and dealt with by you earlier. Notwithstanding that some may need to be revisited after disclosure as documents may raise further issues.

This is a checklist of the main points that you will need to consider at this stage:

- Is a Request for Further Information justified?
- Is any amendment to the claimant's claim required?
- Is disclosure complete?
- Is a Notice to Admit Facts appropriate?
- Is a Notice to Admit Documents appropriate?
- Is medical evidence complete and ready for trial and is that evidence to be given in written form or by oral evidence?
- Is any further expert evidence required?
- In any relevant case are there sketch plans and photographs agreed to assist the court?
- Is any other evidence capable of agreement?
- Is any approval required from The Regional Legal Services Commission or other funding provider to go to trial?
- Are up-to-date schedules of loss and counter schedules of loss required?
- Are witness statements ready for disclosure?
- Are dates of availability within the trial window up to date?
- Is counsel's advice necessary or desirable at this stage?

16.2. Request for Further Information

The time to consider if a Request for Further Information under CPR Part 18 is required will be as soon after receipt of the defence as possible.

This Part replaces pre-CPR rules for Requests for Further and better Particulars and interrogatories. However, it is not just the terminology that has altered and the rule should be studied carefully.

The purpose of Part 18 is to enable the court, either of its own volition or on the application of a party, to order that further information is provided by a party to clarify any matter which is in dispute or to provide further information in relation to any matter in dispute whether or not that matter is raised in a statement of case (see precedent in Appendix E). The rule is therefore very broad. The court may well intervene in a case after the defence has been filed. If the court regards a Statement of Case as failing to comply with the rules or failing to deal with specific issues it is likely to order that unless the party in breach files an amended statement of case within a set period the original will be struck out.

If you need further information from the defendant you should ask the defendant to provide it voluntarily first since application to the court may not be necessary. The procedure is clearly set out in Part 18 PD-001. The request should be concise and confined to matters reasonably necessary and proportionate and should not, if at all possible, be made in piecemeal fashion. Provided that the request is clearly set out and is highlighted as being made under Part 18 it can be in letter format. Whatever format is adopted the request must comply with the requirements of Part 18 PD-001.6. These include providing a date for reply.

Any reply should be served within the time specified and should contain a statement of truth since it is deemed to be a Statement of Case. If the request was in letter form then the reply can be in that form.

However, if no reply is forthcoming within the time specified or the party served with the request declines to provide the information then you should make an application to the court using the Part 23 application procedure. A copy of the request must be attached to the application. Both parties must consider whether evidence in support in respect of the application will be required. Remember that at the hearing there will be summary assessment of costs and so relevant schedules should be prepared, filed and served.

16.3 Amendment

See Chapter 11 for the procedures to amend Statements of Case.

16.4. Incomplete disclosure

See Chapter 15 for discussion of how to ensure that there is compliance with disclosure obligations.

16.5. Notice to Admit Facts

This procedure has been retained from the old rules as a useful tool in narrowing issues and saving costs. CPR Part 32, which governs evidence, deals with the procedure at Part 32.18.

In brief, (and the rule is no more detailed) if you want to see whether the defendant will admit a fact to save the time and expense of calling someone to prove a point, then you must serve a notice specifying the fact/s in respect of which admission is sought. Such a notice cannot be served less than 21 days prior to trial. If in response an admission is secured it can only be used in the current proceedings and by the party who served the notice.

One of the best uses of such a notice is where there is a dispute about whether the claimant was or is unable to work but agreement is sought as to the amount of pre-accident wage so that if it is found that there is an entitlement the loss can be calculated without someone from the employers having to attend to vouch for the amount of wage earned.

If an admission is not forthcoming and evidence has to be adduced at trial to prove the fact and the court accepts that fact then there can be cost consequences. These are set out in CPR Part 44.3 and 44.5. The court can take in to account this refusal to admit on the question of costs.

16.6. Notice to Admit or Produce Documents

This procedure is also designed to save costs. Under it the authenticity of a document disclosed in accordance with a party's disclosure obligation is accepted unless a notice is served indicating that a party wants the document proved at trial. This notice must be served by the date for witness statement disclosure or within seven days of disclosure of the document whichever is the later. Whilst the procedure is unlikely to be used frequently the limited timescale should be noted.

16.7 Medical evidence

In all bar the most severe injury cases you will find that the medical evidence is complete at issue of proceedings. In those cases all that you need to check is whether you have the necessary court permission to rely on the evidence, whether the expert has dealt with any questions raised and, where each party has separate evidence, and the court has ordered the experts to produce an agreed note of areas of agreement and disagreement they have done so. Check, if you have not already done so, what effect any further comments made by the expert have on the case.

In more serious cases where medical evidence is still awaited because the injuries are so severe that a final prognosis is impossible in the immediate future, consider whether, in cases where liability is in dispute, the trial window should be used solely to determine the issue of liability. In most such cases the court will be amenable to this as the window is kept and used proportionately in the circumstances. If liability is not in dispute but medical evidence is some way from completion, consider an early, rather than eleventh hour, application to vacate the trial window and reschedule outstanding issues.

16.8. Non medical evidence

Broadly, the same considerations arise. Review what remains outstanding and whether the trial window is still realistic for disposal of all or some issues. Ensure that you have any necessary court permission.

16.9. Sketch plan and photographs

In road accident claims it is customary to have these available before the court to enable the court to see rather than try to visualise the accident scene. Photographs can also be helpful in employer liability claims where a complicated piece of machinery is involved. Sometimes, scale models of such equipment are produced. Do try to agree such evidence as it can be frustrating for a court to find that these items are in dispute.

If a sketch plan is produced it should state whether it is to scale and should not be annotated by the party producing it to show what that party states happened.

16.10. Other agreed evidence

Is there any other evidence that could be agreed with the other side in an effort to reduce costs? For example, the police report will contain much independent evidence which neither side disputes, and even if it is not possible to agree the whole report (including the statements attached) it may well be possible to agree the officer's report on the circumstances, weather conditions, place of accident, and so forth. Similarly, employer's letters as to earnings should be agreed with the other side. If the other side do not agree them, then either serve a Notice to Admit Documents (see above), or serve a Civil Evidence Act Notice (see Chapter 17).

In view of the fact that exchange of witness statements is compulsory, you should always consider carefully whether evidence can be agreed in advance. If so, then this will avoid the delay and expense of calling witnesses to prove agreed facts.

16.11. Funding approvals

If your client is publicly funded do check that the certificate is not limited to prevent you continuing. If it is you need to remove the limitation. That may require counsel to advise on the continuing merit. The certificate may also be limited in financial value. Now is the time to consider how much more funding will be required to enable the claim to be taken to trial. Apply for any extensions now as there may be delays or refusals that need appealing which are better dealt with without the pressure in the immediate build up to trial.

Other funding schemes may also require review. For example, is a legal expense insurer's approval needed to go to trial or is the financial limit on the insurance policy cover sufficient to meet the potential costs of both parties should the claim fail? Do read these pre and post event policies carefully. If you have not done so before then at least do it now.

16.12. Schedules and counter schedules of loss

If the schedule of loss produced on issue was final and the losses are not continuing then no update is required. In any other case you should now update the schedule ready for trial. This can be advantageous in ongoing loss cases involving a multiplier as the multiplier is unlikely to be less than when you issued but the quantifiable loss to trial will have increased.

Beware of adding new heads of loss as the update should be no more than that, and it is not an opportunity to think of additional heads of claim. If you add a new head of claim you may need court permission to amend. This is all about openness. The defendant is entitled to know the types of loss being pursued as early as possible even if the amount may not be finally updated until just prior to trial.

If the defendant has already done a counter schedule in a claim where there are no ongoing losses then no update will be necessary. However, remember that if a judgment in default was entered you will never have had a defence stating a case on quantum. In such a case you should ask for a counterschedule and statement of any issues the defendant has on quantum.

In all other cases an up to date counterschedule will be required.

16.13. Trial availability

In all cases where liability is in dispute a listing questionnaire will have to be filed at least eight weeks before the trial window commences (see Chapter 17). To ensure that you can deal with this swiftly and efficiently ask counsel and witnesses, both lay and expert to give you up to date availability within the trial window. With any luck they will be keeping it clear, having been advised of the trial window by you earlier. However, counsel and experts have many court commitments and their availability may have changed in the intervening period. Whilst you will need to update again when the listing questionnaire is received it should be easier if you are only asking if there are any changes from a recent update.

16.14. Witness statements

General content

There is little new in the requirement that witness statements of the oral evidence which a party intends to rely upon at trial most be served (see CPR Part 32.4).

This relates to any witness evidence on any issue of fact that is to be decided upon at trial. Witness statements have been around for long enough for all practitioners to be familiar with their importance.

In most straightforward small injury claims or claims where liability is admitted the likelihood is that witness statements will have been served with disclosure. The simple reason for this is that with proper preaction protocol compliance there should be nothing in disclosure that has not been seen before and the witnesses' evidence should not need altering to deal with any fresh issues that arise on inspection.

As the time between directions being given on allocation and compliance with an order to serve is likely to be brief statements should be prepared well in advance. Indeed, there is a lot to be said in such cases for having the statements ready at the time of issue. It is a good way of ensuring that you and counsel have the correct information available to enable the statement of case to be prepared properly. Some commentators even suggest that the claimant's witness statement should be used as his/her statement of case suggesting, perhaps with a degree of justification, that at least then the Statement of Case would actually tell the court what the case is about.

If the claim is proceeding only on liability at this stage then obviously the statements need only address that element of the claim. If not, the statement must deal with all aspects of quantum as well. Frequently, solicitors still forget to confirm and vouch all items of special damage in the client's statement. That can be fatal, for if the court refuses to allow any further evidence in chief at trial then the special damage claim, or those items not dealt with in the statement, must fail.

As the statement is to form the evidence in chief it is sensible, if you are not that experienced or the claim is a complicated one on liability, or if quantum is substantial, to have counsel check the witness statements prior to service. Whilst obviously neither you nor counsel can put words in to a witness's mouth it is as well to check that the statement covers all factual areas in sufficient detail and clarity. As evidence in chief is usually counsel's domain and counsel is likely to be presenting the claim at trial it is as well to ensure that counsel is happy at this stage rather than run the risk of an unseemly argument at the court door.

The following is a useful preliminary checklist for statements:

- Does the statement cover all issues fully, concisely and clearly without being repetitious?
- Is the statement up to date? For example, if there are further special damages beyond those in the statement of case make sure that there is reference to all of them and an indication of which continue to accrue.
- Is the statement consistent with your client's other evidence, such as medical reports? This can be difficult where the client has reservations about joint expert evidence.
- Is the statement consistent with the way the claim is put in the statement of case?
- If reference is made in the statement to a document, has that document been disclosed?

- Does the statement contain hearsay? If so consider the need to serve a hearsay notice under CPR Part 33.2 (see below).
- Does the statement contain a statement of truth?

If any amendments have been made to a statement, even if it has been signed and the amendments initialled it is good practice, time permitting of course, to retype the statement incorporating the amendments and have it signed again. Otherwise, the statement looks sloppy which is not the impression you want to convey to the judge reading the trial bundle the day before the hearing.

How to cope with an uncooperative witness

If it is not possible to serve and file a statement from a particular witness, for example because they are not co-operating, it is possible to serve a summary of what that witness is likely to say. CPR Part 32.9 deals with the content of a witness summary. The first thing to note is that permission is required to serve a summary and not a statement. This permission can be obtained by application without notice using a general Part 23 application notice form.

Even if it is not clear what evidence the witness may give, permission to serve a summary can still be sought provided that in such a case the summary deals with the matters upon which it is believed that witness can give evidence.

Format of a statement

CPR Part 32 PD-017-022 provides detailed information as to the correct form for a witness statement:

- The statement must bear the action number, it should be on A4 paper with 3.5cm margins, should be single sided, the pages should be numbered as should the paragraphs and all numbers including dates should be expressed in figures.
- Part 32PD-018 highlights that the statement should be in the words of the maker as much as possible. A cautionary reminder for the over zealous representative.
- The statement must be in the first person, confirm the maker's name and address, place of residence or business (if making the statement in a professional capacity), occupation and indicate if the maker is a party or linked to a party by reason of employment.
- The statement must make it plain which parts are based on the witness's actual knowledge and which on acquired information and from where it was acquired.
- The date of the statement should appear clearly on it.
- A statement of truth must appear if the statement is to be relied upon. In practice, statements are often served unsigned with an assurance that the statement of truth will follow. Whilst it may be reasonable to allow a bit of time in such a situation, do monitor it. A statement that reads well may

force you to rethink a claim. Without a statement of truth how can you be sure that the witness will actually give that evidence?

On this point, if a witness cannot read and/or write specific provision is required. Part 32 PD-021 applies. In such a situation an authorised person must certify the statement. Such a person is someone empowered to administer oaths and take affidavits. That person does not have to be independent and so in most cases you will be able to act as that person. The certificate states that the statement has been read to the witness who appears to understand it and approve the content, that the statement of truth has been read to the witness and that that too appears to be understood as does the consequence of making a false statement and that the witness made some identifying mark in the presence of the authorised person. The authorised person then completes the certificate which appears at Part 32 PD-029 in the following terms:

> "*I certify that I(name and address of authorised person) have read over the contents of this witness statement and the description of truth to the witness who appeared to understand (a) the statement and approved its contents accurate and (b) the declaration of truth and the consequences of making a false witness statement, and made his mark in my presence.*"

Service and filing of witness statements

Usually, the order will be for service and filing to take place by the same date for all parties. In exceptional circumstances the court may order sequential exchange, for example where a Statement of Case is unclear on a particular issue and the court wishes to see how the case is put before ordering a statement from another party.

False statements

The importance of advising a client, and indeed any witness, of the necessity to state only the truth in a witness statement is underlined by Part 32.14. Proceedings for contempt of court may be brought against any person who makes, or causes to be made, a false statement in a document containing a statement of truth without an honest belief in its truth. "Causes to be made" might include a representative if there is also no honest belief in the content of the statement prepared. Do take care when preparing statements and do explain to the client and to any witnesses the importance of reading the statement properly and making any alterations that are necessary. Explain the consequences of false statements but do it in an inoffensive fashion otherwise the witness will think that you believe he or she is lying. Perhaps simply say that you are obliged to give this advice to anyone whom you ask to sign a statement of truth and that you are not singling that person out specifically for this advice.

Use of witness statements

As already stated, witness statements form the evidence in chief of that witness. Cross-examination will take place on the statement and of course re-examination also takes place. Whilst the court can decide how it wants evidence presented and can allow further evidence in chief beyond the statement it is unlikely to do so where that evidence was available when the statement was made and could and should have been in the statement. The court does have wide discretion on this under Part 32.5(4).

A statement can only be used in the proceedings in which it has been served unless the witness agrees or the court gives permission for use in some other context. However, once a statement has been put in evidence at a hearing held in public then it is in the public domain and other use is possible.

Failure to serve witness statement

Part 32.10 states that unless service takes place as ordered or the court grants permission a party will not be entitled to call the maker of the statement to give oral evidence. The warning is plain. If you think you need more time to serve a witness statement do not wait for the primary period to expire. Be proactive and apply to the court within that period for an extension to the time period. If there is good reason then provided that the trial date and the parties preparation for that is not prejudiced it is hard to see why permission should be refused.

Hearsay

Hearsay is a statement made by a person other than by the one giving evidence which is tendered as evidence in the proceedings. For this evidence to be put before the court a Hearsay Notice pursuant to Part 33.2 must be served (see Chapter 17 for more detail).

Now is a good time to ensure that the witnesses whose statements you have disclosed or are about to are still contactable. You do not want to discover a few weeks or days before trial that you have no current address for them, cannot therefore serve a witness summons and are out of time to serve a Hearsay Notice.

Counsel's advice

As mentioned above, under certain funding arrangements you may have to obtain counsel's opinion on the continuing merit of the claim before you can go any further. The opinion should be sought after exchange of witness statements (see above). Do make sure that all relevant documents are sent but that no irrelevant ones are included. Forgetting to include a crucial disclosure document and incorporating all inter party correspondence are at opposing ends of the spectrum.

In any case, though, this is usually a convenient juncture for counsel's involvement, if you feel it is necessary. You may decide that it would be sensible for this involvement to be by way of conference. Evidence can then be reviewed as a whole rather than counsel raising queries that go back and forth in correspondence.

How often do you hear clients complain that they only met the barrister at the door of court or that the barrister failed to understand a point when advising? A conference can remove all these problems. Remember to manage your client's expectation.

If your client is publicly funded then you may need prior authority for the advice to be given in conference rather than on paper. Failure to obtain this authority will leave you paying for the conference.

Do prepare the papers neatly and take the time to ensure all enclosures are present and correct before they leave the office as acute embarrassment can be caused if counsel only looks at the papers on the day of the conference and discovers the enclosures are incomplete. Imagine how a client's confidence is eroded if you cannot even be trusted to photocopy the right documents. These things count and rightly so. If you miss out papers for counsel who is to say you will not miss out documents from the trial bundle?

If you have prepared properly then counsel should simply be confirming the advice that you have given. This enhances your credibility with the client. Many clients still regard counsel as fonts of all wisdom, and some may be. To see that your solicitor is as good as counsel . . . now that is impressive!

The solicitor/counsel relationship should be a team one. Experienced counsel recognise that experienced solicitors have a lot to contribute. It is not one person saying what will happen but two people discussing and suggesting the best way forward for the client. Do prepare properly for the conference as you will not be fulfilling your function if you think that you will take it easy and let counsel do all the work. It follows from this that you should attend the conference. There are bound to be other things pressing on your time but do not opt out and send someone else who knows nothing about the file along. What benefit is that to you and what service is that giving to the client? If you take your car to be repaired and then find out that the repairing garage is going to ask someone else to do the work and that someone is less qualified to do the work than it is how would you feel? Imagine if you are then told the reason is that the repairing garage is too busy to spare you, the customer, the time and has, by implication, other more important customers whose work takes priority.

If time and cost are serious considerations consider a telephone conference or video conference. Most chambers can now cope with both. On assessment, the court is likely to look favourably on such a sensible cost efficient arrangement.

Documents for counsel

At this stage counsel will expect to see:

- Statements of Case;
- any further information given under Part 18;
- expert evidence;
- any relevant disclosure;
- public funding certificate if relevant;

- any Notices to Admit;
- all witness statements. This may be from all parties if already exchanged or otherwise your client's draft and those of any witnesses;
- documentation supporting the claim for special damage and in larger cases a draft updated schedule for counsel to amend or approve;
- any Part 36 payments or claimant's Part 36 offers.

It is rare indeed that correspondence is relevant but should there be some letters that you feel counsel needs to see include those. Obviously, any Part 18 information provided in letter form should be included.

Text of case to counsel

The papers should not usually be lengthy but should draw counsel's attention to any specific points that require consideration. In particular they should include the following:

(a) a short narrative setting out a brief background to the case;

(b) details of any directions and orders not complied with and why not;

(c) any particular problems you see with the case and on which you particularly want counsel to advise;

(d) the next steps as you see them or where you would like counsel's help with this;

(e) ask counsel to advise you generally on evidence, liability and quantum.

Further advice

The low counsel fee allowed for advice on quantum and liability makes this a "best buy" for solicitors, so do not be reluctant to use counsel's services and send the papers back for a further opinion in a complicated case. Remember that a solicitor who acts on counsel's instructions will often have a good defence to professional negligence claims besides which clients are always pleased to be told that "counsel advises" and it is often helpful to have an outside view of a case. Sometimes, if you want a genuinely independent expert opinion do not let counsel have your views on liability and quantum until after counsel has given a view. You will be surprised how reassuring a confirmatory second opinion in difficult cases can be.

On receipt of counsel's advice

Checking

Go through the advice carefully. If it is unclear or ambiguous, telephone counsel to clarify the position; make an attendance note of the phone conversation.

File procedures

If counsel has identified work that needs to be done make a list of this and put it at the top of your correspondence pin taking care to ensure it is replaced at the top after anything else is inserted on the pin. This way a quick glance at the file reveals the steps that need to be taken. It is also a good idea to put a date next to each step to indicate when you put in hand the necessary work and another date being the date by which you need to complete the step. When the step has been completed put a big red tick next to it! Doing this avoids the possibility that you either overlook what counsel has suggested or, more commonly put in hand the work but do not follow it up. A second reminder in an office diary system is extra security.

Drafts

Increasingly, counsel are sending draft documents by e-mail making them far easier to transcribe. If they come in traditional written form type them up and deal with them appropriately. The most common document that counsel is likely to draft at this stage is a Part 18 request for further information of the defendant's claim.

Witness statements

If counsel has settled or amended any witness statements then read them carefully, ensure they are correct and send to the relevant witnesses to check, sign and return for exchange.

Reporting to client

Are there any points that now need to be taken up with the client? Send the advice to the client but ensure that you explain it fully in a covering letter. Certainly, in a difficult case it may help to quote extracts from an advice or opinion. The client may also, of course, be able to answer some of the problems that cause concern to counsel. In particular explain counsel's present view on the value of the case and any difficulties with it. If the advice or estimate of the value has changed explain why. Remind the client that this is counsel's best case scenario and not a figure that the client should see as written in tablets of stone. Certainly not in the post Lord Woolf enquiry atmosphere of compromise. Ask the client to let you know of any comments or observations or if there is anything the client does not understand. Consider whether the client wishes to proceed to trial in view of:

(a) likely quantum and likely benefit to client after the effect of costs, compensation recovery and contributory negligence;

(b) any offers made by defendant or any money in court;

(c) extra costs that will be incurred;

(d) potential distress and inconvenience that could be caused to the client;

(e) the risks of litigation generally.

Finally, consider whether the case is worth what you originally thought it was. If it is worth more, should it be transferred to the High Court for trial? If it is worth less and is in the High Court, should it be transferred to the county court? See Chapter 17 for procedure on transfer. If the value is different should you now consider settlement negotiations or late acceptance of a payment in?

Good file keeping

As stated, time is against you. This is probably the last realistic opportunity to take stock of the claim before the last few weeks of pre-trial preparation. The days of finally understanding the claim and how best to present it only in those last few weeks are gone for good. You must do a stock-take now and ensure that you are ready for trial and in a good position to deal with the inevitable queries that crop up at the last minute. If you do this then you can be bullish about going to trial unless the offer is a good one. If you do not then you are more likely to see any offer as a relief and run the risk of undersettling the claim for your own convenience.

Do ensure that all attendances and the amount of time you have spent on the file have been properly recorded. It is quite right that you should build up cost making sure the claim is in order at this stage. Consider all the points raised in this chapter and do not move on to the next file until you are happy that the file is in order.

Doing a thorough stock-take tends to focus your attention. That may enable you to spot weaknesses or omissions in your client's case with sufficient time to rectify them if possible or to conduct negotiations before the defendant spots them.

You may do this stock-take before instructing counsel as otherwise the instructions may be incomplete. Use of counsel is to build a team of advisors not to have one advisor clearing up the mess of another.

Do learn from counsel. Good counsel and practical experience of the right sort can teach more than any text book-even this one! The more you learn the less often you will feel the need to use counsel in the smaller claims and the more competent you will be to deal with these yourself.

17. Preparing for Trial

17.1. Introduction and checklist

The next stage is for the parties to start preparing for the trial. Once the interim orders have been complied with, the case will be fixed within the trial window and eventually the parties will attend court for the trial and judgment. If you have carried out your stock take as recommended in the last chapter and dealt with any further enquires raised by counsel or by disclosure of documents you may be feeling fairly relaxed about trial preparation. To an extent, the work that you have put in to preparing the claim properly and expeditiously earlier may justify that complacency. However, there are still tasks to do. Some are to be expected but inevitably in the final trial preparation unexpected matters arise. By dealing efficiently and promptly with the expected you should have enough time and a good enough understanding of the issues and evidence in the claim to enable you to cope with the unexpected. You should bear in mind that in many cases time will now be short. Trial windows are often only a few months after the last direction time and if specific orders have had to be sought in addition to the standard directions there may be even less time than that.

This is a checklist of the matters that you should expect to arise at this stage.

- Check once again that all directions have been complied with.
- Check that you have factual witness, expert witness and counsel availability dates within the trial window on file.
- Remember in appropriate cases to complete and file a listing questionnaire.
- Have enquires raised by counsel been dealt with satisfactorily?
- Consider if these enquiries alter the nature of the claim or your advice upon it?
- Check that you have all papers that you need in sensible order to enable you to prepare a trial bundle.
- Consider if any witness summonses necessary?
- Consider if you need to transfer from county court to High Court or vice versa?
- Consider if you need to do a final schedule of loss up to actual trial date?
- If no offers have been made or if they have but the passage of time or fresh evidence has rendered such offers inappropriate should a Part 36 claimant's offer be put now?

- In larger cases, consider a structured settlement.
- If there is a claim for provisional damages, is this sustainable?
- Is any evidence or element of the claim capable of agreement with the defendant?
- Brief counsel.
- Prepare your client and your witnesses for trial.
- Does any funding scheme cover the costs of trial and are any approvals required?
- Has counsel been asked to prepare a skeleton argument or statement of issues?
- Prepare the trial bundle.
- Adjournments.
- Late settlement.

17.2. Directions

The listing questionnaire asks for confirmation of compliance with directions and an indication of any further orders that might be required. Do not wait for this as the questionnaire is usually only lodged eight weeks before the start of the trial window. If you have not complied with any order do so now. If there are any orders that you require, apply now.

17.3. Witness availability

You will already have checked this on filing the allocation questionnaire and updated that in accordance with the recommendation in the last chapter. At this stage have final confirmation ready for use in the listing questionnaire. It is advisable to ask witnesses not to book anything for the days that they now state to be available until the court has fixed the date for trial within the window. This avoids changes of availability whilst the diary manager is fixing the hearing. The court will have little or no sympathy if a date is fixed for a time when witnesses said they were available but the witness slots something else in to that date whilst awaiting formal trial date notification.

17.4. Listing questionnaires

See Form N170 and precedent 16.

This document is required in both fast and multi track cases. In fast track cases the procedure is governed by CPR Part 28.5 and in multi track by CPR Part 29.6. The rules are virtually identical. The court will send parties a listing questionnaire specifying a date for its return unless it considers that the claim can be listed without the need for the questionnaire.

As indicated earlier, those cases where liability has been admitted with judgment for damages to be decided are not caught by this rule as they will not have been put in any particular track (unless they are low value and are allocated to the small claims track). Accordingly, in these cases, and in small claim track cases, unless there is a specific order requiring it no listing questionnaire will be needed.

Where you do need to file a listing questionnaire the most obvious point to make is that you should diarise the return date and make sure that you comply with this. Otherwise you run the risk that the court will fix a trial date without being able to consider the availability of your witnesses and case counsel. That could have disastrous and costly consequences. Alternatively, if as a result of non compliance by a party the court does not feel that it has sufficient information to enable it to list the trial the court may fix a listing hearing. If the failure to file is yours then you will have necessitated the listing hearing and will pay the costs of it as a penance. Explaining that to your client, for as already stated you must report any adverse costs order to the client, will be embarrassing at the very least. In multi track cases the remedy may be more draconian and even costlier. CPR Part 29 PD-008(1) states that where neither party files a listing questionnaire as ordered the court will normally then make an order that if neither party files one within three days the claim and any counterclaim be struck out. Beware the brave and cunning defendant who takes his or her chances on a listing hearing in the hope that by failing to comply the claim will in fact be struck out! Curiously, if only the defendant complies and files a questionnaire then the option to strike out goes and you are back to the fast track remedy of a listing hearing.

In fast track the trial window will be no more than 30 weeks from the date that the directions are given and the listing questionnaire will be filed no more than eight weeks before the trial window. Hence the concern over the limited time to deal with any outstanding matters.

In multi track cases the questionnaires will be ordered to be filed as soon as soon as possible. That date will be no less than eight weeks before the trial window and a party will have at least two weeks, notice of this requirement.

17.5. Outstanding enquiries

This was dealt with in detail in the last chapter. If counsel suggested that you pursue any lines of enquiry make sure that those have been completed. If this results in the need for any further witness statements you will need court permission to serve and rely upon those statements. That and any other outstanding orders should be sought immediately. The closer that you are to trial the less likely that you are to receive orders in respect of fresh evidence.

17.6. Is the case still viable and properly stated?

Does any fresh evidence that you have acquired alter your view on either liability or quantum? If it does to the extent that you feel the case no longer has realistic prospects of success you should consider trying to negotiate some form of compromise, even if it is simply that your client may discontinue without an adverse cost order. You will need to discuss such a situation with your client, give clear written advice and receive unequivocal written instructions to avoid any ambiguity later.

What is more likely is that the progress of the case may have altered the thrust and emphasis of your client's case. If so you need to check that the statement of case allows proper presentation of this case at trial. For example, do the particulars of negligence alleged cover what you now believe to be the actual negligence of the defendant? If not you must amend because you will not succeed on a case that your client has not stated. If this problem is not spotted until trial at best you may be given an adjournment for amendment and any consequential amendment that is required but at a heavy cost penalty. There may be one if you apply for permission to amend before trial but it will be less severe and should not result in an adjournment of the trial date. It is far better to bite the bullet now.

17.7. Document control

How often do you struggle to find a key document that both you and your client know that you have? One of the great introductions under public funding franchising and Lexcel and other similar kite mark accreditation is the absolute necessity of keeping documents off the correspondence pins and storing them in sensible separate sections. Whether you do this by use of a separate documents file for each case or by creating a matching computer file and scanning every document received is a matter for personal preference and may vary depending upon the number of documents in any particular claim. If you use the same file for both documents and correspondence then you must divide the file clearly and neatly in marked categories so that any particular document can be turned up with ease. Each separate category should be identified on the front with the name of the client and your file number in the unlikely event that it becomes detached from the file. If you are dealing with four hundred road accidents and you come across a loose unmarked photograph of a road then you will struggle to replace it on the correct file!

This procedure will make both disclosure and preparation of the trial bundle and brief to counsel so much easier.

It is worth checking the documents at this stage so that there is time to go on a document hunt if any should have gone astray. It also serves to focus your attention, you will find that you are planning the trial bundle in advance.

17.8. Witness summons

Even if you are absolutely sure that your witnesses will not let you down and will be there on the day of the trial you should consider serving witness summonses. At least then if a witness fails to attend you cannot be blamed. You will sleep easier the night before trial if you have done this.

This should include any experts who have been given permission to give oral evidence. There used to be an unwritten rule that a personal injury practitioner should never serve a summons or subpoena on an expert as the expert would take offence. Courts made it plain in the few years prior to the introduction of the CPR that anyone adhering to this adage and then finding that the expert was unable to attend trial could expect no sympathy Indeed, if an expert said that he or she were unavailable when served with a summons or subpoena the court started to expect legitimate reasons. Even holiday was insufficient. Anyone making a commitment and being paid a fee to be an expert witness had to accept that attendance at court was a necessary corollary of writing a report in a matter. Under the CPR, with so much warning of trial windows, you may find that experts have many dates in their diaries. This simply serves to make it all the more important that you serve them with witness summonses. Any expert used to the CPR process, and one hopes that any you have used are, will not be surprised or offended by receipt of a witness summons. It is good polite and politic to write and tell then what you are doing in advance.

The procedure for serving a witness summons can be found in CPR Part 34. It is worth pointing out that the summons has replaced both the old county court summons and the High Court subpoena. The witness summons can require a witness to attend court and to produce any documents to the court. The summons must be in the relevant practice Form N20 and is issued on the date entered on the summons by the court which will effect service unless you elect to. Permission to issue a witness summons is only required when service will be less than seven days before the hearing at which attendance is required.

If you are in a last minute rush remember that you can only issue the summons at the court where the claim is proceeding or, if different, at the court where the trial is to be heard. If permission is required then you need to study CPR Part 34.5 which sets out how to obtain permission. The order that you should ask for is for a declaration that the summons will be binding on the witness notwithstanding that service will be less than seven days before the hearing. When calculating whether permission is required remember the earlier references to how you calculate time periods (see CPR Part 2.8).

Unless you make a specific request when lodging the request for witness summons the court will serve. You must offer or pay the witness sufficient money to cover travelling expenses and such sum by way of compensation for loss of time as is set out in CPR Part 34 PD-001 (namely lost earnings or benefit for time spent) at court at the time of service of the witness summons so you must make sure that you lodge an appropriate sum with the court in addition to the court fee so that the court can serve the money.

17.9. Transfer

It is probably a little late to be considering transfer between county and High Court. Possibly this is something that will have been dealt with on case management after completion of allocation questionnaires if it became apparent that the value or complexity of issue merited a transfer.

However, once all evidence is available it is clear how each party proposes to put its case and final schedules of special damage and final medical evidence enable relatively precise valuation of a claim so the court's jurisdiction and transfer may need to be considered again.

CPR Part 30 is devoted exclusively to transfer procedure and should be your first port of call. The main criteria are conveniently set out in Part 30.3(2). Those that are most commonly relevant to injury cases are:

(i) the value of the claim and

(ii) whether the facts, legal issues, remedies or procedures involved are simple or complex.

The question of the value of the claim is relatively straightforward. You will remember the pertinent statement of value of £50,000 to issue in the High Court under the High Court and County Courts Jurisdiction Order 1999.

The second question arises in injury claims where the claim is under the Fatal Accidents Act, involves false imprisonment or is a claim against the police. In such circumstances even though the value may not merit High Court determination the issues raised do.

If you think an order is required for transfer see if the defendant agrees. If so, you can make the application by consent which may make it easier. Otherwise a contested application will ensue. In either case ultimately the decision will be that of the court as transfer, even if by consent, is not a rubber stamp exercise.

It will be rare that you are considering transfer from one District Registry to another or one county court to another at this stage. This is something likely to have been dealt with on allocation and case management directions because the allocation questionnaire asks the parties to indicate what they believe to be the suitable location for trial.

17.10. Final schedule of loss for trial

As soon as the trial date is known it is possible to work out any continuing losses to that date and project forward beyond that date by use of multiplier and multiplicand. You should do so, otherwise either you or counsel will find yourself doing this outside court in a mad rush just prior to the commencement of the trial. As indicated earlier, it also maximises your client's loss as a few months, extra quantified loss to trial is unlikely to cause any reduction in the multiplier.

The court likes, and indeed expects, the majority of special damages to be agreed or at least for there to be a clearly set out schedule and counterschedule to enable it to see the areas of dispute. If you are seen to be trying to put a new schedule before the court on the morning of the trial that is unlikely to create the impression that you, and more importantly, your client, would wish.

17.11. Offers, Part 36 or otherwise

Now that the medical evidence for trial is complete and the schedule of special damages is ready for trial you should revisit your quantum assessment. Earlier, it was suggested that if quantum was now such that it rendered the claim uneconomic or a previously rejected Part 36 payment pertinent then you should try to negotiate a settlement immediately. However, if the claim now seems bigger than before consider whether any previous claimant's Part 36 offers should be formally withdrawn and fresh ones made. The court must look at conduct generally on the question of costs and in particular what efforts the parties have made to settle. So even if no previous offers have been put there is no reason not to consider an offer at this stage. Remember the special provisions that apply if you leave it less than 21 days before trial to make the offer (see Chapter 12).

Settlement opportunities must be considered at all times. Clear advice must be given and instructions received, but the impetus must come from you as the client is unlikely to know of the encouragement to be proactive and the potential cost consequences of being reactive.

This is a good time to make offers as the defendant is also likely to be taking stock of the situation now that the day of trial looms. This can open the most tightly sewn pockets. It is not a sign of weakness but an indication of prudent case management. You have prepared properly, know what the claim is worth, are confident of achieving that level but recognise that the court will have expected you to explore compromise, do not leave it for counsel on the day.

If you think trial preparations are time consuming and the prospect of the trial causes you a few butterflies think how your client may feel: an alien process, the prospect of being cross examined in the aggressive or cunning fashion depicted on television and the importance of the outcome. These are all designed to cause sleepless weeks let alone nights. If a client reaches the court door then that client will have gone through agonies of nerves and possibly indecision. For this reason it is inexcusable to settle a claim at the court door that could have been settled before. Sometimes, the defendant is wholly to blame and there is little that you can do except make a valid Part 36 offer that means the defendant pays for the right to come to the negotiating table late. In other cases be proactive. It does not equate, as many practitioners erroneously think, to underselling. You have the facts at your fingertips, a trial date looming and costs mounting. Negotiate from strength. If you have a bottom line the worst that can happen is that you do not achieve it and the trial goes ahead, in any event you will have tried. Most practitioners who will not discuss cases will not do so because they are not confident enough of their position, their understanding of the case or of their own negotiating skills. Those people are doing their clients a disservice and one that the courts are now likely to notice, comment upon and sanction in cost recovery. Sometimes, it is the defendant that will not discuss the case. One reason for this may be that the defendant insurance company runs its own quantum database. Usually, only cases favourable to the insurer are put on the system, creating an unrealistically low quantum assessment in future cases. If you think this may be the problem ask the defendant if the insurers are operating such a database. If they are then do not be too concerned that their valuation is significantly below yours.

17.12. Structured settlements

Structured settlements are only available in actions settled by consent. They cannot be imposed by the court. You should, therefore, consider whether a structure would be appropriate for your client.

In essence, a structured settlement allows money to be invested in an annuity fund; the income from the annuity is then treated as tax free by the revenue. For instance, in one of the first structured settlement cases, the case was settled for a total of £410,000. Of that, £110,000 was paid out as a lump sum to the plaintiff; the remaining £300,000 was invested in an annuity (producing £25,500 per annum, index linked, and tax free). They are particularly appropriate:

(1) when the potential damages are high;

(2) if the claimant's life expectancy is disputed (since an annual sum is paid);

(3) if the claimant is a person under a disability or likely to be unduly influenced to spend money unwisely or inappropriately;

(4) it is necessary to replace a lost source of income; *e.g.* for dependants in a fatal accident claim.

Advantages of structured settlements

Certainty: a structured settlement allows a claimant to know that he or she will get an amount every year to cover needs however long he or she lives.

Ease: a claimant does not have to worry about the best investment of a large lump sum; or pay management charges; this is dealt with by the defendants.

Tax-free payments: this is particularly useful for higher rate taxpayers.

Disadvantages of structured settlements

Inflexibility: as there is a fixed annuity structured settlements can be disastrous if the claimant's circumstances change or s/he needs a lump sum to spend; for example, a young claimant with uncertain future needs and earning capacity, or one who wishes to use the damage for a specific purpose such as investing in a new business. For this reason only part of any settlement should be structured; the average in reported cases seems to be about 40 per cent.

Discounts: in return for their participation defendants receive a negotiated discount on the agreed damages; obviously if this is too high it can form a disincentive to a claimant. Up to 1992 the discount figure seemed to be around ten per cent but in 1993 7.5 per cent became the average (see article "No Damage Done" by Rodney Nelson-Jones, *Gazette* 91/12) probably due to the cut in base rates and lower return from annuities that structured settlements can purchase. This should become even lower now that s. 142 of the Finance Act 1995 enables annuities purchased for a claimant to be paid gross of tax by the life office and permits the life office to make payments direct to the claimants. These changes remove some of the financial and administrative burdens of structures for defendants.

You should always consider a structured settlement in any substantial case (say over £150,000). They are particularly appropriate for higher rate taxpayers or claimants with uncertain life expectancy. Always obtain a wide range of expert forensic accountancy opinion before recommending a structure. This is an area where you really must ensure that the expert is wholly independent. There are difficulties if the discussions over structure take place before there is any agreement of how the claim would be resolved on a conventional basis as in such a situation a joint expert might be privy to confidential information which has to be released to both parties representatives to enable them to consider the structure. The most obvious piece of such information is what the parties believe the claim to be worth on a conventional basis. If no structure is then agreed that information is then open and makes Part 36 payments easier to judge at the bottom of potential brackets of award.

A final point that may be deemed a disadvantage arises from the recent case of *Beattie v. Secretary of State for Scotland, The Times*, May 4, CA. This case decided that periodic payments made under a structured settlement award came within the definition of capital treated as income and therefore affected, adversely, a claimant's entitlement to income support.

17.13. Provisional damages

These have already been considered in detail in Chapter 8 and the only purpose of mentioning them here is that following finalisation of the medical evidence you should review this aspect of the claim to ensure that the case is still suitable for a provisional damage award. If not then you should amend to remove this but also to ensure that you then claim for any further loss that arises now rather than may do at some time in the future. As well as medical evidence changing the position so may the passage of time as risks for the future that were suitable for provisional award may now have become realities and therefore capable of being assessed for compensation now.

17.14. Considering if any evidence or issue be agreed

One of the phrases often associated with the Lord Woolf enquiry team was "issue resolution". The CPR enshrine this idea. Even if a claim cannot be resolved you should seek to narrow the dispute or issues, agree any witness statements that you can and agree, even if subject to liability, as much of the quantum as possible. The listing questionnaire specifically asks that you indicate if any witness evidence can be agreed. Do consider narrowing the issues. The cost of calling a witness on a point that could clearly have been agreed between the parties is unlikely to be recoverable. Similarly, save in cases where there is wildly divergent medical evidence, general damage ought to be capable of agreement. After all, the same basic case reports are available to both parties. The defendant insurer's use of its own quantum database may prevent agreement as the defendant solicitors are often bound by the system.

Sometimes, you may find that the court takes the decision out of your hands. CPR Part 32.1 gives the court clear powers to control evidence by the giving of directions. The court can indicate upon which issues it requires evidence and the form of that evidence. This power expressly includes the ability to exclude admissible evidence and to limit cross-examination. Do address the issues that the claim raises and ensure that the evidence you wish to give is necessary and not capable of agreement. Expect a raised eyebrow at best if a witness is not asked anything by way of cross-examination. Why was that witness called when clearly the attendance of that witness could have been avoided?

Procedure for approving structured settlements

See the Practice Note [1992] 1 All E.R. 862 which sets out the procedure and a letter from the claimant's solicitor in the *Gazette,* September 6, 1989. There, the judge suggested guidelines that could be followed when seeking court approval. Firstly, one would need a detailed counsel's opinion assessing the value of the claim and its constituent elements on a conventional basis, together with the appropriate lump sum for settlement. Careful consideration of life expectancy (based on the medical opinions) should be included. Next, one would need a report by accountants or other financial experts as to the fiscal and investment advantages of a structured settlement (in particular, as regards the life expectancy, and likely future costs of care). There would also have to be evidence that there are available sufficient funds outside the structured settlement to meet any foreseeable capital needs of the claimant. In addition, one would want a draft of the agreement to have been submitted to the Inland Revenue and approved in principle by them; also, of course, Court of Protection approval might also be needed. Anyone considering a structured settlement should read the Law Society's guidelines—"Structured settlements; guidelines for solicitors" last updated October 96—and CPR Part 40 CPD-002/3 and 4 which sets out draft orders for the conventional settlement and adjournment and a draft structured settlement order itself.

17.15. The brief to counsel

Do not leave counsel's brief until the last moment. It is often tempting to do so in the hope that the case will settle before the work is done, but it is unfair to both counsel and the client to dictate the brief hurriedly at the last moment. Besides which, the preparation and dictation of the brief will be rewarded on assessment of costs. Under the fast track fixed trial fee regime counsel's maximum recoverable fee is prescribed (see CPR Part 46 which is devoted to fast track trial fees, and Chapter 22 on costs generally).

In a private case, telephone counsel's clerk to agree a brief fee. The amount of the brief fee will obviously vary with the complexity of the case, and the experience of the individual barrister. As a rough guide, one can say that the brief fee for a straightforward road accident case will be at least £750. Legal aid briefs do not, of course, bear a fee.

It is important that the preparation of the brief receives undivided attention and concentration; the instructing solicitor will know the case in far more detail than counsel, and it is essential that the solicitor's full views be communicated. Even if counsel knows the case well and has had several conferences with the client, it is still essential to do a full brief. There can be no way of guaranteeing that a particular counsel will not be part-heard on the day of trial, in which case the brief will go to another barrister who may know nothing about the case. As more and more work will be on conditional fee and your payment is dependent on a favourable outcome there is even greater incentive to ensure that if there is a late change of counsel the brief is sufficiently detailed and well structured to enable a fresh counsel to understand the case quickly.

Do not treat counsel as omnipotent and omniscient; counsel will be only too pleased to read the opinion of a professional colleague and to receive a full and detailed brief. It is surprising how many solicitors will have a file open for several years and put a considerable amount of work into the case, only to waste it all by not dictating a full brief to counsel. This is the culmination of all the labours that have gone into the file; it must be given the attention and time it deserves.

Ensure that the brief is easy to follow and well laid out. This is easier to do if you subdivide the brief into headings, so that counsel can easily find a way around the papers.

Additionally, remember that the brief will be examined on assessment and will be a major influence on the cost officer's assessment of the case's complexity. A thin brief of little substance is likely to colour the cost officer's attitude, as are statements in the brief such as "this is a straightforward road accident case presenting no problems": every case has its problems and its own facts.

Dictating the brief

When dictating the brief to counsel it may be helpful to approach it as follows:

List enclosures

If you do this at the outset of the brief it compels you to think about structuring you instructions straight away. Split the enclosures into convenient categories:

- Statements of Case, including Part 18 further information;
- witness statements;
- disclosed relevant documents; expert liability evidence; expert medical evidence; relevant court orders;

- relevant funding documents, including where appropriate a schedule of costs for summary assessment (see Chapter 22);
- any Part 36 offers or payment notices and;
- any relevant correspondence.

Do not get carried away. Whilst a detailed brief is required allow counsel to focus on the important issues of the case. That will be hard within time constraints if every scrap of paper generated in the claim, including voluminous irrelevant correspondence is included with the brief. When your post arrives which gets your attention first: the smaller letters or the huge bundle of disorganised documents? Precisely. Even if counsel has had the papers before, do not return the old papers and just continue the numbering because some of those documents may have been relevant for interim matters but are not for the trial. Start the numbering again. Do remember though that, if counsel has had the papers before, copies of the actual instructions that you sent and any advice given by counsel should be included. If counsel advised in conference you should include your attendance note of that conference.

If you have already prepared the trial bundle then incorporate that and delete elsewhere in the list to avoid duplication. Counsel would prefer the documents in the trial bundle format as that makes preparation easier since cross referencing by page number will be necessary.

Having taken the time to list the documents, spare a few moments when the brief has been prepared to check that the right documents have been included.

Introductory paragraph

Start the brief by telling counsel some short details about the case and the claimant. State why the action is being brought against the defendant, and give the claimant's age, occupation and marital status and dependants (if relevant). An introductory paragraph of this sort will enable counsel to know what the action is about before reading the detailed instructions, and thus to have the relevant questions and issues in mind. It is best at this stage to confirm whether this is a liability only trial, a disposal hearing or a trial of both liability and quantum.

Claimant's case

Give a summary of the client's version of what happened. Counsel will have the witness statement, so there is no need to go into full detail. Stress major allegations and clarify any points that may not be clear. Highlight any discrepancies between statements.

Statements of Case

Go through these. Summarise the allegations in the claim and set out the defendant's admissions and denials. Do not forget to deal with any Part 18 informations. Draw counsel's attention to any allegations of contributory negligence and to the claimant's (and witnesses', if applicable) comments on these allegations.

Notice to Admit Facts and agreed evidence

Highlight to counsel any agreed facts or issues.

Evidence

Next, tell counsel what evidence is available to prove the case. List the witnesses who will be at court; outline the essential features of each witness' evidence and how it helps the client's case. Do not set out the witness' evidence in full, but refer counsel to the witness statement.

Similarly, tell counsel what any expert witness (for instance, an engineer) will say: refer to the strong and weak parts of the report and mention the points that you think counsel might usefully pursue when cross examining the other side's expert. What evidence has been agreed (for example, police report, photos, plans)? List the witness statements that have been disclosed and deal with the contents of the other side's witness statements. If there is a supplemental witness statement that you have served but to date do not have leave to rely upon make sure that you include this with a request that counsel seeks permission to rely on it. If the supplemental statement has not been served and you are not sure if you should serve it ask counsel to address this point now. You should highlight this in the letter accompanying the brief or it might be overlooked until counsel commences trial preparation.

Disclosed

Mention the Documents disclosed and what relevance they have. If there are any glaring omissions, such as risk assessments that should have been but were not done, do highlight this as missing documents can be more important than ones disclosed.

Strategy

So far, the brief has concentrated on factual matters, that is the hard evidence needed to prove the case. Now it is necessary to discuss how counsel can go about winning the case and to suggest which parts of the defendant's case are weak and should be attacked. Tell counsel if there are doubts as to the reliability of some of the client's witnesses, or if it is thought that the claimant will be easily confused during cross examination. How much (if any) contributory negligence should the client be prepared to concede? Refer back to counsel's advice and the action taken since then.

Law

Deal with the relevant law. Many briefs ignore the law and assume that counsel will come to court equipped to deal with any point that arises. Often this is correct, but do not necessarily assume it! Do not be reluctant to tell counsel what the law is, or how you interpret the recent cases. You should know it because you must have considered it to enable you to advise the client.

Medical evidence

Go through the medical evidence. Have reports been agreed? Will any doctor be attending court? If so what medical issues remain as the agreed note may have narrowed the issues?

Special damage

Set out the special damage position. Tell counsel whether the calculation enclosed has been agreed. If not, list the people who will be called to prove it and how the calculation is worked out. Usually counsel will have a copy of the special damage calculation as served on the defendant. Do not forget to explain how you worked out the details of your calculation if that is not clear from the document itself. It ought to be made clear as otherwise how do you expect a court to understand it?

Explain any doubtful parts of the calculation and how much could reasonably be agreed as a compromise.

Refer to the calculation even if an all-in figure has been agreed with the other side, for the judge may want to know how the figure is made up, and it may be important for compensation recovery. Set out your calculations of interest.

Quantum

What is the case worth? If you have views on this, then tell counsel.

At the same time, tell counsel what offers have been made in correspondence, or payments made into court. Some clients have unreasonable expectations of the value of the claim. You should warn counsel of this in advance.

Conference

Does counsel want a conference, other than at the door of the court? As a general rule, it is worth having a conference. Apart from ensuring that the barrister prepares the case properly, it will reassure the client. After all, it is not encouraging to arrive at court on the day of the trial, and to meet one's barrister for the first time only a few minutes before the case begins. A barrister who has not met a client will not know whether the client will be a good witness or the points that are most important to the client. So if you have not had a conference already or if you have but feel the client and counsel would benefit from another, arrange one. It could even be the evening before trial. This creates a team feeling and spirit.

Special orders

In the concluding paragraph remind counsel of any special order that should be sought from the judge, *e.g.* provisional damages. Set out the dates of the accident and service for the purposes of calculating interest. Are there any costs that were awarded at interim hearings that can be claimed even if the case is lost? Tell counsel what time to attend court; ensure that there will be ample time to meet the client and expert witnesses, especially if there is a possibility of "brief-swopping" which will result in a substitute counsel being used.

Ideally, the brief should be delivered to counsel some two or three weeks before trial. For ease of reference in any discussion you may then have with counsel keep an identical copy of the brief enclosures. It is far easier than trying to turn up documents on your file itself.

17.16. Preparing your client and witnesses for trial

Notify everybody. Write to the client, the witnesses, doctors (50) and experts (stock letters 42–49) notifying them of the trial date. If there is a road accident counterclaim, write to the client's insurers who are financing that part of the action and bring them up-to-date on the position and prospects.

Client

Something that many solicitors overlook is the preparation that the client needs for trial. Great care is taken over preparing the Statement of Case, the client witness statement and ensuring counsel is properly briefed for trial but the client is simply asked to be at the court at a set time on the day of the trial. This is the most important stage of a contested injury claim. It is essential that the client understands what is going to happen, feels as familiar as possible with the process and, most importantly, feels supported by you. If time permits it is a good idea to arrange for a client who has never been to court before to attend a hearing before the trial. Under the original Lord Woolf enquiry team proposals it was intended that clients attended case management hearings. Perhaps in recognition of the cost implications of ensuring this and the lost ability to hold these hearings by telephone this proposal was left on the cutting room floor when the CPR were finally drafted. If you do have a hearing on the case consider taking your client since even though the hearing is different from a trial at least your client will see something of the process.

The other option is to find out what trials are on in your local court a few weeks before your trial. If any are in open court and suitable suggest that your client comes to watch one trial with you for a few hours. Even relatively small things like knowing where the court is, where witnesses stand to give evidence and where they sit when not giving evidence can make the process less frightening on the day.

If a court attendance is not feasible at least describe to your client what to expect in both surroundings and procedure. Your client may be concerned about what to call the judge. By all means explain the different titles depending on the relevant tier of judiciary that may hear the case if you want but the simplest answer is to suggest that no title is used at all. The court will be concerned with the evidence not whether your client knows the correct form of address.

Ensure that your client reads his or her witness statement again just prior to trial. Too often when asked whether the statement has been read recently by counsel in evidence in chief there is an embarrassing no or a lengthy pause while the client reads the statement afresh. You should have sent your client a copy of the final version of the statements in the matter and an explanation of how evidence in chief is given will serve to highlight the importance of reading the statement before trial.

Do make sensible arrangements for the day. How often do you see people wandering aimlessly around a court building looking terrified or lost until eventually a tannoy massage summons them to reception to meet their solicitor and counsel? Arrange to meet at least an hour before hand preferably not at court. It looks good if you arrive at court as a team; solicitor; client; witnesses; and counsel. You look like a team that has prepared well. If your office is near the court that will be the best place—a soothing coffee in a calming and familiar environment. If not find a good local café. If you do have to meet at court ensure that the client knows the layout and that the meeting place is obvious.

Witnesses

Whilst your duty to a witness is less than to your client any witness still has a vital function to play. Visits to court may not be necessary but the same comments about statements, explanation of procedure on the day and arrangements to meet apply. A happy and relaxed witness is a co-operative one. Even if a witness is at court only because you have served a witness summons to compel attendance do what you can in advance to cover the above. At the very least a letter setting out the procedure, suggesting where to meet or telling the witness where the rest of you will be meeting and enclosing a further copy of the witness statement in case the last one went in the bin is a good idea.

Sometimes witnesses complain that they never really appreciated what the case was about before hearing the evidence at the trial. For this reason it is a good idea to send all the witnesses, as well as your client, a clip containing the statements of case and all parties witness statements. This way they can see how their evidence fits in and sometimes even offer helpful comments to negate the evidence of another witness.

17.17. Funding for trial

Make sure that you have appropriate funding to take the claim to trial. With public funding certificates this means checking both the work authorised and the financial scope. It is important that you consider how much the trial is likely to cost because you need to be certain before it starts that you have sufficient funding left to cover the trial costs. Under the current public funding rules if you exceed the financial limit on the certificate then you cannot retrospectively rectify this. Even if you win you may be in difficulties in recovering any costs over the scope set out under the indemnity rules.

If your client has union or legal expense backing check to see if specific permission is needed to go to trial. Legal expense policies often have financial limits on the level of cover. This tends to vary from twenty five to one hundred thousand pounds. However, this is usually to cover both your client's costs and, in the event that you lose, the successful defendant's costs. You do need to try to work out roughly what the overall cost liability for both parties is likely to be after the trial to check that your client has enough cover. If you are in any doubt then you should advise the client to purchase top up cover to meet any shortfall. This can either be purchased through the original legal expense insurer or from one of the many "after the event" insurance packages available. At this late stage though the premium is likely to be quite high.

The same considerations apply to any conditional fee funding as again there are likely to be limits on the funding under the insurance backing.

If you are proceeding under a private funding arrangement then it is as well to bill up to trial so that the client has up to date figures and is not caught by surprise after the trial. This should no longer be the case anyway since the alteration to Rule 15 requiring solicitors to update clients with cost information at least every six months. However, the stage immediately before trial can be expensive, resulting in a sudden surge of costs. You should warn your client of this in advance since it will be a consideration to take into account when the client decides whether to continue to trial or not.

17.18. Skeleton arguments or statements of issues

Many courts now insist on, and all welcome, a skeleton argument being lodged by counsel a few days before the hearing. This should be a concise statement of the issues, the claimant's case on those issues cross referenced to any documents in the trial bundle, relevant law and cited authority in relation to the question of quantum. How long the skeleton will be depends on whether liability is an issue, whether quantum is to be dealt with as well as liability and the type of case. For example, a skeleton will be brief in a road accident claim but longer in an employment case where cross referencing to Health and Safety regulations may be necessary. However, remember it is meant to be a concise summary so it should be as brief as possible. The intention is to give the court a snapshot of the case and direct attention to the salient issues.

Each side prepares a skeleton so that the court can easily see areas of dispute. A draft skeleton for use in appeals can be found in the CPR (Form N163).

17.19. Trial bundles

CPR Part 39.5 sets out one rule for both High and county court. Unless the court orders otherwise it is for the claimant to file a trial bundle. This must be done not more than seven nor less than three days before the commencement of the trial. It is worth noting that responsibility for the trial bundle now is placed exclusively on the claimant. In practice, however, you will find that defendants still indicate what documents they wish to see in the bundle and it is sensible to ask them anyway so that there is no unsightly argument before the court as to the content of the bundle. In fact, in all cases it should be fairly obvious what documents are necessary. Make sure that you do not include backsheets to documents as these are superfluous.

CPR Part 39 PD-003 provides a comprehensive checklist which is much as you would expect:

(1) the Claim Form and all Statements of Case;

(2) a case summary and/or chronology where appropriate;

(3) Part 18 requests and responses;

(4) all witness statements to be relied on as evidence in chief;

(5) any witness summaries;

(6) any civil evidence act notices;

(7) expert evidence including joint notes;

(8) any relevant directions orders;

(9) any relevant documents;

(10) plans and photographs, etc.

It is really only under item nine that there is scope for disagreement. However, the documents revealed on disclosure are a sensible starting point.

Do avoid including inter party correspondence as it is rarely relevant. The exception would be where it incorporates Part 18 information.

In cases with a time estimate of a day or less where there is likely to be a summary assessment of costs and where you think that correspondence may be relevant on costs, perhaps as an indication of poor conduct, then consider putting together a separate bundle to be presented when the court comes to determine the costs under summary assessment at the conclusion of the trial (see Chapter 22).

Prepare enough copies of the bundle to ensure that as well as the one for the court there are copies for the witness box, your counsel, you and your client so that he or she can follow the proceedings when not giving evidence. Many practitioners will only send a copy of the index to the bundle to the defendant. Whilst there is nothing wrong with this since you are running off a number of copies anyway it is better to prepare one for the defendant. At least that way you know the numbering of the bundles will match, confusion may otherwise result if a backsheet to a document is inadvertently included throwing the numbering out. Bundles are important not just to ensure a smooth trial with the witnesses and the court being able to refer to documents easily but also for the impression that they create. A near bundle, properly paginated with an index, presented in a lever arch folder that actually works without papers falling out will look professional and again illustrate the time taken on preparation. A badly prepared bundle will cause irritation and enable the defendant's counsel to score cheap points.

17.20. Adjournments

If ever it was possible to secure last minute adjournments, and in the run up to CPR it was becoming increasingly difficult, it is now nigh on impossible. The trial date is not a movable feast. Whilst the timing for compliance with directions can be altered this is only the case if the alteration/s do not jeopardise the trial date. With witness availability considered on both allocation and listing questionnaires it is unlikely, provided that the proper information as to unavailability has been given by the parties, that the trial will be listed for an inconvenient date.

Occasionally, there will be valid reason, such as a late change in medical condition that necessitates further expert consideration or the ill health of a party or an important witness. You will find that provided there is a prompt application and reasonable explanation the court will be sympathetic. The court is likely to consider, though, whether the trial date can be used for another purpose. For example, if there is a change in medical condition in a case where liability is in dispute the trial is likely to remain in the list but for disposal of liability issues only, or if there is a limitation issue to dispose of that.

If the reason is simply that last minute negotiations have commenced or that one party has been dilatory in preparation you will find that the trial will proceed.

17.21. Settlement

Despite all the encouragement to compromise claims at an early stage a high proportion still settle in the run up to trial. In recognition of the inevitability of this the CPR provides that where a claim is settled or discontinued and this disposes of the entire claim for which a trial window or specific date has been set for trial the parties must notify the court immediately. Accordingly, if you settle a claim and are awaiting a signed consent order do notify the court in the meantime that the claim has settled and an order recording that is to be lodged as soon as possible as the longer the notice the more chance that the listing officer will be able to re-use the trail spot vacated by you.

When you lodge an order recording settlement or file a notice of discontinuance you should send an extra copy to the listing officer (see CPR Part 39 PD-004).

Some settlements still require court intervention for approval purposes. See Chapter 20 for the relevant procedure.

18. The Trial

18.1. The trial

Do make sure that you are where it has been agreed that everyone will meet a bit early. You can then greet everyone and tick them off against your checklist. It is as well, if you do not meet in the office, to come armed with mobile phone in case any witnesses need chasing or in the event that counsel has any last minute requests for further documents or extra copies. Sometimes even witnesses you have asked endless times if they have any documents deliver a bundle beaming "I'm not sure if these will be of any use". Ensure that you know where you can get your hands on a photocopier fast.

Settlement offer

Not withstanding all your pretrial attempts be prepared for a settlement offer to be made at this stage. Frequently, the defendant's solicitor will come to court to be advised by counsel that they should settle on a compromise basis. You should therefore have decided beforehand what is the lowest figure that the client should be advised to accept. Do not be pushed into a hasty settlement at the door of the court. Remember that counsel's brief fee, witnesses' and experts' costs have all been incurred and that a settlement at this stage will not save the day's costs. The client may by now be prepared to have the matter heard in court and may be deeply suspicious of any last-minute settlement negotiated at the door of the court.

Witnesses

Marshal the witnesses together. Explain the layout of the court and who is who. Introduce counsel to the client and all witnesses. Remind the witnesses that they will have to confirm their statements when giving evidence; tell them to stand up straight in the witness box, hands out of pockets, and to speak in a deliberate, loud voice to the judge (not counsel), Reassure them against answering questions that they do not fully understand: if in doubt they should ask for the question to be repeated, or simply state that they do not understand the question. Answers should be short and to the point, especially during cross examination; gratuitous comments and asides should be avoided. If the judge is taking a note of the evidence, the witness should pause frequently so that the judge can note down all that is said. Warn witnesses of the dangers of cross examination; the other side's counsel will question their veracity and try to get them to lose their temper or become confused. The above points apply equally to experts as to lay witnesses. Experts are often nervous about appearing in court and need reassurance and explanation about practice and procedure. You will have done all this pre trial but do it again now. It fills nervous time and seems more pertinent with the court there for all to see.

Checking documents

Check with the usher or court clerk to ensure that the court has all the bundles you have filed, together with copies of any authorities for the judge and skeleton arguments. If there are any last-minute documents ensure that the court, witnesses and all parties have properly paginated copies. Check that there is a trial bundle in the witness box.

Solicitor's role

Once in court the instructing solicitor will sit behind counsel (unless there is a leader in which case the leader will sit in front) and be available to answer counsel's queries, take notes, and provide copy documents as and when they are required.

The solicitor should, so far as is possible, take a verbatim note of the evidence given. This is especially important when counsel is speaking and so unable to note down exactly what a witness says. Note the time when the case starts, who is present, the time when a witness gives evidence, adjournments, and so on.

Whilst doing all this, it is very easy to forget about the client. Make sure you explain what is happening at every stage and give the client a copy of any document referred to so that the client can follow the evidence and make comments. That is why it is best to have a spare copy of the trial bundle for the client.

Order

The conduct of the trial is now very much a matter for the court. CPR Parts 28.6 and 29.8 indicate that the court can give a trial timetable if it so wishes. A specimen fast track trial timetable lasting the maximum five hours is actually set out in the White Book.

Usually the case is opened by the claimant's counsel who then calls the claimant and then the claimant's witnesses, who are examined, cross examined, and then re-examined. Usually witness statements will be ordered to stand as evidence in chief so the case will start with cross examination. This can be very difficult for witnesses as it does not allow them to settle by giving their own evidence. In particular it may be difficult for a client who needs a "day in court" or opportunity to give his or her story. At the close of the claimant's case the defendant's counsel may submit that there is no case to answer, or state that the defendant does not intend to call any witnesses (if so, the claimant's counsel addresses the court, and the defendant then has the last word). But, more usually, the defendant's counsel will open the case for the defence and then call the defendant's witnesses, make a closing speech, and then the claimant's counsel has the last word. Finally, the judge will sum up, give judgment and deal with costs.

Often, in fast track cases, the claimant's opening may be dispensed with because a skeleton argument will have been lodged and read by the judge and time constraints are such that the court will wish to move on to the evidence as quickly as possible.

Witness examination

In order to assist the court make sure of the following in relation to witnesses:

(1) Unless there is a good reason, the current or next proposed witness should be sitting in the witness box whenever a trial resumes. This saves the witness being formally recalled. However, some courts do not follow this practice so check before directing the witness.

(2) Ensure that the witness has all bundles relevant to examination or cross examination and that bundles in the witness box are kept up to date.

(3) If a witness is to be asked to refer to a plan or photograph ensure that the witness is familiar with the item in question before going into the box.

(4) When a witness has completed giving evidence, find out if the witness wishes to leave: if so, instruct counsel to ask the judge if the witness may be released. Thank the witness and ask the witness to send a note of net losses and expenses in attending court. Explain that any conduct money the witness has already received will be set off against this loss, and that an employer's certificate should be sent if the sum claimed is sizeable.

18.2. Judgment

Take a full note of the judgment. After it has been given, counsel should ask the judge for any particular orders that may be necessary. In particular:

Payment out of money in court

Only after judgment should the trial judge be told of any sum in court. The money in court can only be paid out by order of the court, so the judge must be requested formally to order payment out to the successful party or, if the claimant's damages are less than the sum in court, to order that the judgment sum be paid to the claimant, and the balance to the defendant. If the damages awarded by the judge are close to the amount paid into the court, it may be necessary to work out the interest element in the payment in (see Chapter 7 for how this is done). In addition, if the claimant beats the payment in, then counsel should ask for an order that the interest arising from the date of trial (not from the date of payment in) be paid to the claimant. Otherwise the interest will go to the defendant (see Chapter 7).

Costs

The costs order will vary upon the type of trial that has taken place. As a fast track trial is for a maximum of one day then at the end of the trial there should be a summary assessment of costs. You should have filed and served your costs statement at least 24 hours beforehand and now, depending on the outcome, will be hoping that counsel will persuade the court to assess at a satisfactory level.

If the trial has been in the multi track then usually there will be an order for detailed assessment if the costs cannot be agreed.

In both cases there may be complications such as conditional fee success uplifts, earlier interim summary assessments and success on part only of the claim.

Payment of money into court

This will be necessary if the successful claimant is a person under a disability, or if the action is a fatal accident claim and one of the dependants is a person under a disability.

Compensation recovery

You may have to ask the Judge to specifically apportion the judgment to different heads of damages so that the compensation recovery figures can be calculated—see Chapter 7

Interest

A claimant who recovers damage, will be entitled to interest. See Chapter 7 for the rules on interest, and how the calculations are made.

A complication can arise if there has been an interim payment. If the interim payment was specifically stated to be for a particular head of damages (*e.g.* it was clearly for an item of special damages) then there is no difficulty; the interim payment will be deducted from the final award of that category of special damage. Thus, the claimant will not get interest from the date of interim payment in respect of that sum. Often, however, the court does not state that an interim payment is attributable to a specific head of damages, and nor is it apportioned between the respective heads of damages. In this case, the trial judge will have to decide how the interim payment is to be deducted. Generally, it will be deducted on a *pro rata* basis between the various heads of damages. However, the judge may be persuaded to deduct it from one head of damage only. Obviously, the claimant should argue that it comes solely out of general damages, and the defendant will want it to be taken solely out of special damages (respectively minimising/maximising the amount of interest that will be lost).

Stay of execution

This is sometimes sought whilst the question of an appeal is being considered. Remember now that under the common appeal procedure laid out in CPR Part 52 you can, and indeed should, seek permission to appeal from the trial court. If you do not it is unlikely that there will be any stay on judgment or costs order.

18.3. The judgment

Under the CPR as with all orders so are all judgments drawn up by the court and sent to the solicitors for the parties.

18.4. Provisional damages

The same exceptions apply under CPR Part 40.3.

If the court awards provisional damages it is likely to use the form of wording that can be found in CPR Part 40. This will begin with the making of an immediate award and then set out the illnesses or diseases that for the purposes of that award it has been assumed will not occur, with a provision that if they do occur within a specifed period the claimant will be entitled to come back to the court for a further award of damage. The court order must also specify those documents that need to be filed and kept as the case file for any further claim. This file must then be kept until the expiry of the time period specified or any extension granted. The documents will normally include:

- the formal judgment and a transcript of the comments leading to it;
- statements of Case;
- medical reports;
- any witness statement or part of witness statement deemed necessary.

Generally, see CPR Part 40 and Chapter 8 above.

19. After the Trial

Do not consider that the case is finished when you receive the judgment. There are many important steps that you must carry out before you can put away the file:

(1) Report to your client.

(2) Should you appeal? What should you do if the defendant appeals?

(3) Contact all witnesses.

(4) Deal with costs.

(5) Consider enforcement if necessary.

(6) Should you claim interest on damages or costs?

(7) Fillet and put away the file.

19.1. Reporting to your client

You will find that judgments are reserved less than before the CPR. Better time estimates, advance opportunity to consider the case and, one hopes, better presented cases, have made it easier for judgments to be given on conclusion of the case. Whilst some courts will launch into the judgment as soon as counsel for the claimant has closed the case other courts will adjourn for a short period.

However, if a reserved judgment is to be given you need to explain this clearly to the client who will not understand what is going on nor why. If the court you are in has a habit of giving reserved judgments this is something that you should have discussed with your client beforehand.

Whenever judgment is given you should explain it in simplistic terms to the client immediately. What the client really wants to know is whether or not the claim has been successful. If it has you will find that more detailed explanation can wait until later. If the claim has failed a more detailed explanation of the findings of the court will be necessary now. Either way, the first thing that you should do after returning to the office is to write to the client providing a detailed but clear summary of the judgment and enclose a typed up copy of your note of the judgment. The letter should deal with the following:

(1) The result of the trial.

(2) Any key points of the judgment.

(3) If the result was unexpected explain to the client why the judge reached the decision and your comments on the judge's decision.

(4) Explain the likely costs effect of the judgment both in relation to your costs and the costs of the other party. If a summary assessment took place explain the implications of this. Will there be a cost shortfall to come out of damages?

(5) Explain when the client is likely to be paid any damages (in particular if there is likely to be a delay until assessment or agreement of costs explain this to the client and give a time estimate).

(6) Discuss the possibility of an appeal with the client (see below).

(7) Explain how the judgment will be enforced if necessary (see below).

(8) Give your client financial advice on investing the money or tell your client where they can find such financial advice. A study published by The Law Commission in October 1994 showed that almost half of plaintiffs receiving settlements of between £20,000 and £49,000 and almost one-third of those receiving between £50,000 and £99,999 had no financial advice and where advice was received it was often not from an independent source. The Law Society Civil Litigation Committee have warned that it is bad practice not to offer a client advice on how to deploy a settlement. The lump sum payment may seem large to many clients but it can easily be used up very quickly and not remain sufficient for the client's needs. This is highlighted because a principal finding of the report was that the period of disability suffered by an accident victim is often under-assessed and in as many as 14 per cent of cases experts' predictions about the victim's ability to work in the future proved to be inaccurate. It therefore makes good sense to suggest to the client that at least some part of the settlement is placed in income providing investments. You have no obligation to make sure your client takes your advice but you should at least give warning about the need for independent financial advice and point out that the client cannot return to court should the money prove insufficient.

(9) You should explain to the client the effect of any particular orders. If the

client may be entitled to return to court (for example, in the future if there is a provisional damages award) explain this and the procedure for doing so (see Chapter 8 and Chapter 18).

(10) Almost as a bolt on to (8) advise your client to prepare a will as any compensation will be part of the client's estate.

The client will probably have a great many questions and it makes sense not only to write but to see the client (in complicated cases in conference with counsel) so that the client can discuss the trial and its outcome. This is usually more likely where the claim has been unsuccessful. If a specific conference is required check you have appropriate funding before incurring costs.

19.2. Appeal

CPR Part 52 now covers all appeals that you are likely to encounter as a result of an injury trial. It is vital that there is compliance with the rules and therefore if you find yourself considering an appeal Part 52 must be your starting point.

The first point to highlight is that permission is needed to appeal any injury trial decision in either High or county court. This permission can be sought from the court whose decision you wish to appeal or from the relevant appeal court on notice. You can apply to the appeal court even if your application to the court whose decision you wish to appeal has been turned down so you should certainly consider the lower court as that way you can have two bites at the cherry.

Permission will only be given where the court considers that the appeal will have a real prospect of succeeding, which is why the lower court will not give permission to appeal its decision in the majority of cases, or if there is some other compelling reason to allow the appeal.

Form of application

Permission from the lower court should be sought orally immediately after the adverse order/judgment of that court.

If that fails or no application is made to the lower court then the application is in writing to the appeal court in form N161. Unless a different time scale has been provided the application must be made within 14 days of the decision that you wish to appeal being made. Form N161 requires you to set out clearly the grounds of appeal including any procedural or other irregularity alleged. If permission is given then at any hearing you cannot rely on a ground of appeal that was not set out in the notice to appeal.

Initially, this is likely to be considered as a paper exercise unless particularly complicated issues arise. If this application fails on paper then within seven days the applicant may request that the matter be reconsidered at an oral hearing.

Service of appeal notice

Unless ordered to the contrary a notice of appeal must be served by you on the respondent to the appeal not later than seven days after it is filed.

Respondent's notice

Any respondent who wishes to appeal part of the decision or seek to have it upheld but on different grounds from those given by the lower court must file a respondent's notice. This must be filed within 14 days of receipt by the respondent of the notice of appeal. Again, this must be served, this time by the respondent to the appeal, no later than seven days after the date filed.

Stay

As indicated in the previous chapter an appeal does not act as an automatic stay on a judgment and therefore, if you are appealing but there is an adverse costs finding against your client, you must consider the question of a stay separately.

Hearing of appeals

Assuming that permission is given by one or other court, ultimately the claim will be heard by the relevant appeal court. This court will not take oral evidence nor, unless an order is made to the contrary, will fresh evidence not available to the lower court be considered. It is not clear when or if it will so order. The pre-CPR rule which required the court to consider whether or not that evidence could have been put before the lower court seems to have gone but no guidance is given as to its replacement.

An appeal will be allowed where the lower court was wrong in findings of fact or law or there was some serious procedural or other irregularity.

19.3. Contacting witnesses

Don't forget to contact your witnesses after a case. You may need them again! Some of your witnesses will not have attended the trial and many more will not have heard the judgment. It is therefore only courteous to let them know the result and to thank them for their input. If the result was unexpected you should also give a brief explanation. Your letter to witnesses should include the following:

(a) thanks for the witness for their input to the case;

(b) explanation of the outcome;

(c) return of any original documents that belong to the witness, for example medical notes to be returned to the doctor or hospital (or explain when they are likely to be returned);

(d) payment of all witness expenses and monies outstanding to the witness or explaining when it will be paid or asking for quantification of expenses if they have not already done so.

19.4. Costs

Summary assessment

This will already have taken place at the trial if the case was allocated to the fast track or at the disposal hearing if it lasted less than one day. See Chapter 22 for a detailed consideration of summary assessment. If you are considering summary assessment at this stage it is probably in the context of wishing to appeal the assessment. An appeal over a summary assessment falls within CPR Part 52 and so the comments set out above in relation to appeals from judgments apply.

Detailed assessment

There are only two forms of cost determination by the court; summary or detailed assessment. If a summary assessment did not take place at the final hearing but the claim was successful then you should have secured an order for a detailed assessment.

There is no room in this book to give adequate time to the detailed assessment. A brief outline of the procedures follows but practitioners requiring more detail should look at CPR Part 47 which sets out the procedure.

Basis of costs

Costs can be awarded either on a standard or indemnity basis. In most cases the standard basis will apply. This basis allows the recovery of costs which are proportionate to the matters in issue. Where there is any doubt as to whether costs were reasonably incurred and proportionate and reasonable in amount the doubt should favour the paying party.

Procedure

Detailed assessment proceedings are commenced when the receiving party serves on the paying party a notice of commencement of the process and a bill of costs. This must be within three months of the order or judgment or other trigger giving the right to costs. There are sanctions if the process is begun late but they are fairly tame ones. However, the delay in cost recovery is surely sanction enough.

If he or she objects to the bill the paying party must, within 21 days of service, serve points of dispute on the bill. If this time period is overlooked then the receiving party can ask the court for a default costs certificate which operates much like a default judgment and also includes the costs of the detailed assessment proceedings.

The certificate can be set aside where the paying party persuades the court that there is some good reason why the detailed assessment proceedings should continue.

If points of dispute are filed within time or a default certificate is set aside then the matter proceeds to a detailed assessment hearing at the request of the receiving party who must ask for such a hearing within three months of the date of commencement of the detailed assessment proceedings.

Hearing

Do try to attend the hearing yourself even if your costs-draftsperson is going to appear. There are always certain things that only you can explain. Experience shows that you will do better if you attend to justify your fees. You have invested a lot of time and money in the claim, it is a shame to waste it for want of a little bit more time to explain what you did and why.

Practice

Until the recent move by insurers to farm out the majority of their work relating to resolution of claimant solicitors' costs to specially formed companies it was probably true to say that most claimant lawyers produced initial schedules of costs for agreement to save the cost and time of the formal procedure. Regrettably, difficulties with reaching agreement at realistic levels with the specially formed companies and the time wasted arguing has now persuaded most solicitors that the claimant is best served by preparing a formal bill straight away and embarking on the assessment except in cases involving smaller costs. This may seem a retrograde step but it is one that has been engendered by the change in the defendant approach to costs. Whether in years to come this new approach will be seen to cost the insurance industry money and therefore cause a rethink remains to be seen. Partly, no doubt, this depends on the terms of retainer of the outside cost contractors. Certainly, it has already caused an enormous amount of bad feeling at a time where cooperation between claimants and defendants would be beneficial.

Using a costs draftsperson

Drawing up a bill of costs is usually best left to a professional costs draftsperson; they advertise their services in the legal journals or you should use one recommended by your firm or by another colleague. Make sure the costs draftsperson you use is experienced in the rates allowed in your area and in the type of work you are doing. Bills of costs drawn up by costs draftspersons can vary enormously and are critically important in achieving a fair settlement of your costs. Costs draftspersons generally charge a percentage of costs of the bill as assessed or a lower percentage of the bill as drawn. Most solicitors find it more profitable to use a costs draftsperson (either an independent professional or one employed in-house) rather than spend time preparing the bill of costs which is a time consuming and complex affair. Further, costs draftspersons are expert at looking through the file and ensuring that all time and disbursements are properly charged.

Preparing the file

Before sending the file to the costs draftsperson ensure it is neat and tidy. The full value of dictating comprehensive attendance notes and keeping proper time records of work done can now be appreciated as they can give considerable assistance to the costs draftsperson when preparing the bill and also the taxing officer when considering the bill as drawn. Prepare a separate note of disbursements and give it to the costs draftsperson together with all invoices. Make it clear whether these disbursements have been paid. Give a short narrative of the case, the parties and the result. In particular set out any complexities. This will be of great use to the costs draftsperson when assessing a suitable uplift and drafting the narrative so as to convince the costs officer that this is more than a run of the mill case and therefore deserves a higher rate. If you have any special expertise or were able to deal with the case particularly quickly for any reason then stress this—again it will be important.

Do make sure the file is complete. Missing attendance notes or carbons cannot be charged and represent money thrown away.

Time

Inform the costs draftsperson of the time by which the assessment must be commenced (see above). Telephone before sending the bill to find out the time it will take and ensure that you receive the bill in that time. If not, do chase until it is returned. Some costs draftspersons are very slow at preparing bills and this can cause you difficulties with the court when lodging the bill for assessment as well as having an adverse effect on your firm's cash flow.

Checking the bill

On receipt of the bill from the costs draftsperson check it carefully. Ensure that the narrative is correct, has no typing errors, and that all disbursements have been included. Check on the estimates of time given and whether you think they are correct. If they are too low ask the costs draftsperson why—it may be that some attendances have been overlooked. Check the hourly rates given and ensure that they have been applied to the appropriate level of fee earner and that they are, in your opinion, correct for the area. If they are too low ask the costs draftsperson to amend them. Remember that costs officers can only reduce bills, they cannot increase them. So make sure that your bill is at the highest realistic level to ensure that you obtain an appropriate level of costs but that you have not breached the indemnity principle.

Further attempts to agree

On receipt of the bill from the costs draftsperson make a first or further attempt to agree costs with the other side; remember that they may be equally reluctant to be inconvenienced by assessment. It is always best to try to agree a costs figure. This is equally desirable if the case has settled before trial or if it is settled before action. It is impossible to give definite figures as to what are reasonable costs as it depends upon the complexity and value of the case, your relationship with the other side, the stage reached in the action and so on. However, there is no doubt that many solicitors greatly undervalue their negotiated costs. To avoid this start the detailed asssessment proceedings. This does not preclude making an offer but gives a clear message that if the offer is unrealistic you are going to press on with the formal process and not become sucked in to negotiations that will delay you and ultimately persuade you to settle too low. You have worked for that money and provided that you are happy that the work is reasonable and proportionate why should you take anything other than a nominal discount?

If a CPR Part 47 costs offer is put (see below) consider it in the context of your opinion of the reasonableness and proportionate nature of the work you have done. Do not be scared by Part 47 offers—they are used to engender fear. Whatever label is put, if an offer is not enough it is not enough. Remember also that the rules make it plain that any cost draftsperson is present as a representative of the solicitor on record who is responsible for their conduct.

The costs of the detailed assessment process are to be determined by the court which will consider any Part 47 offers, the conduct of the parties generally, the amount by which the bill has been reduced and the reasonablenesss of disputing certain items.

Part 47 offers

The other provision relevant to the costs of the detailed assessment is Part 47.19 which sets out a procedure enabling the parties, whether paying or receiving under the costs order, to make a without prejudice offer to settle. Any offer made in accordance with this procedure is one that the court will take in to account when deciding who pays for the assessment process. Do beware of Part 47 offers creeping up gradually. Do not let such scare tactics bully you into settling for too little. The recent move by defendants to use external costs negotiators seems to have resulted in Part 47 offers being put time and again. Often, the final offer is significantly higher than the first proposal. Arguably, this is conduct that the court should penalise under the general Part 47 power. Do not be scared of raising this conduct with the court after the assessment, if it is relevant. Remember that the CPR requires openness and, in turn, reasonable and realistic conduct.

Payment on account

Where you have an order for costs and assessment will take place at a later date the court does have power to order a payment on account of costs. The courts have been encouraged to use this procedure but not many claimant's solicitors seem to make use of this opportunity. Do read CPR Part 44.3(8) and where there is likely to be a delay before a detailed assessment or where you are likely to receive lots of offers over a period, only reaching a realistic level after time, use the procedure to alleviate the cash flow demands that might otherwise persuade you to accept an offer which is too low for a quick settlement.

Final costs certificate

After any detailed assessment hearing the assessed bill must be lodged at the court within 14 days whereupon the court will issue a final costs certificate which will then be served on the parties. This includes the order to pay the costs.

Appealing an assessment

Any party to a detailed assessment can appeal against the decision. Appeals from a county court District Judge are to a county court Judge and from a Costs Judge or District Judge of the High Court to a High Court Judge. Useful guidance on the function of the costs appeal is given in *Mealing Mcleod v. the Common Professional Examination Board* which unfortunately is unreported but neatly summarised in The White Book. It is worth a read before embarking upon an appeal. Broadly, permission to appeal is unlikely to be given simply to allow a party another crack at each and every item in the bill.

Additional costs under funding agreements

See Chapter 23 on conditional fee funding for the detailed rules relating to determination of any additional costs. The basic rule is that such determination can only take place at the conclusion of the claim and not on any interim orders, even if those include orders for costs.

Public funding assessments

Where there is an order for assessment of costs to be paid by the Community Legal Service Fund under a public funding certificate this will be by detailed assessment. Your request to commence the detailed assessment procedure must be made within three months of the order allowing the assessment. The bill must be served on the public funded client. If that client wishes to attend the assessment then a hearing date is fixed otherwise the bill will be provisionally assessed by a costs officer as deskwork. If you are unhappy with any provisional assessment made by the court you should request a hearing within 14 days of receipt by you of the bill.

Time limits

These have been mentioned above. Diarise item all. The case should be diarised for three months from the date of judgment for the commencement of proceeding. You can be penalised if your bill is not served in that time, even if only in less interest as costs.

Interest

Interest runs on costs at the judgment rate from the date of judgment, not the date the costs are assessed. Because the delays in the assessment process mean interest can often be considerable you should not forget to ask for it when costs are either assessed or agreed. If doing a global settlement work out the interest first for you may be giving away too much.

Two or more defendants

Where there are two or more defendants the claimant will sometimes win against one defendant but lose against the other. In such cases, the order for costs is usually a Bullock Order (ie the successful defendant recovers costs from the claimant who, in turn, recovers those costs, plus own costs, from the unsuccessful defendant). If the claimant is publicly funded, or unlikely to be able to pay the successful defendant's costs, the order will probably be a Sanderson Order (ie the successful defendant recovers costs direct from the unsuccessful defendant who also pays the claimant's costs). Always try for a Sanderson Order. If you have set the defendants up to blame each other (see earlier) you should succeed.

Notifying your client

Always notify your client of the progress of the assessment. In particular if your client has an interest in the assessment, for example that your client is a public funded client to whom the statutory charge may apply or privately paying or in a conditional fee agreement, then your client must be notified of the assessment and given a right to appear. In any event it is good practice to ensure that your client knows of the procedure and has the opportunity to attend if she or he wishes. As the process of assessment is highly technical most clients will only find themselves bemused by attending but it is important that you give the client the opportunity to attend so that the client does not think anything is hidden. The process can also take time. As one of the final features of managing expectations make sure you advise your client of the likely time periods involved otherwise it will seem an awfully long period of apparent inactivity.

19.5. Enforcement

Usually the defendant will be an insurance company and there will be no difficulty in obtaining payment of damages and costs awarded. However, if you do have to take enforcement proceedings refer to the detailed procedures set out in the Green Book and White Book. However, any problems with ability to pay ought to have been addressed earlier and decisions made then as to the economic viability of the claim.

19.6. Interest on damages and interest on costs

Do not forget that you will be awarded interest on any judgment (including interest on costs) from the date of the judgment. If there is any delay in payment do not forget to claim interest as this can quickly become substantial. In particular, interest often arises on costs and is seldom claimed. See above.

19.7. Final checks

Once the costs have been dealt with and all necessary amounts paid, arrange to put your file into storage. Before you do so ensure that you do the following:

(1) Notify your client the case is completely at an end and that you will now be putting your file away. Ask the client if there are any particular documents or copy documents the client wants and tell the client how you can be contacted in the future if the client has any questions. This is a good time for marketing so also tell your client of other services your firm can offer (including wills, etc.) and who should be contacted if your client has any problems in the future. Indeed, on any payment of damages you should advise your client of the need to make a will. On larger payments consider what, if any, advice or guidance should be given on investment. There are very strict professional rules that apply. Ensure any guidance that you give falls within the rules.

(2) Look through the file and check that you have no original documents in it. If there are any original documents which should be returned to the owner now arrange to do so. In particular ensure that all medical notes and x-rays have been returned.

(3) Look through the file for any useful precedents. If the file has raised any new or interesting points then keep those. If it has been a complex case or points of principle have been raised then consider putting together a bible of the case so that you can refer to it in future without referring to the whole file.

(4) Ensure that you have collected counsel's papers and any other relevant documents. Otherwise these tend to come in later once you have filed the papers and get mislaid from the originals. Ensure that you have received all bundles back from the court.

(5) Ensure that all disbursements have been paid and that you have been paid all necessary amounts. Either make or chase payment as necessary. Never put away a file until you have a nil balance on both office and client account.

(6) Go through the file and remove all unnecessary copies. If there is a large

bulk of paper to be removed consider recycling it rather than throwing it away. Remove all unnecessary binding and plastic folders. Storage is expensive and there is no point in putting away expensive plastic folders or lever arch files if papers can just as conveniently be tied or bundled with elastic bands. However, don't take away so many folders and dividers that you can't find anything if you need to look up the case in the future.

(7) Ensure that all the papers are kept together and are clearly and properly marked with the case number and title so that any loose papers can be put back with the file.

(8) It is very useful after the judgment or after particular stages in the case to have a debriefing; discussing the case with your colleagues, raising any points of interest or principle that have arisen or any tactical points which can be useful to you or the firm in the future. This can be extremely helpful in increasing your knowledge and the level of knowledge of other colleagues in your firm.

(9) If any important documents are not to be held with the file put a note on the file as to where they are to be held.

(10) Arrange for the file to be put into storage and given a proper storage number in accordance with your firm's procedures.

(11) Decide how long you should keep the file in storage. Arrange a date for review to determine if the file can then be destroyed. As a basic rule injury files should be kept for at least six years but specific cases may require longer, *e.g.* provisional damages cases or claims involving infants where it is prudent to keep the file for six years from the client's 21st birthday.

20. Settling the Case

20.1. Settling before proceedings are commenced

The majority of personal injury claims are settled through negotiation, and without the claimant commencing proceedings. When this happens, there is normally no need for court approval to be obtained; only if the claimant is an infant or other person under a disability must the court be involved.

Accordingly, the settlement will simply be referred to in the correspondence between the parties. The insurance company might ask the claimant to sign a form of receipt, confirming that the settlement is in full and final satisfaction of all claims arising from the accident. Some insurers do; others do not. In any event, such a document is not necessary. If the claimant's solicitor agrees to settle the claim on a client's behalf, and then accepts the cheque, there is little doubt that such a settlement would be binding on the claimant. If the claim had been under-settled, then the client's claim would be against the negligent solicitor, rather than against the insurers.

Obviously, if the claimant does not have legal advice, then it might be possible to have an under-settlement set aside.

Person under a disability

If the claimant is a person under a disability, then the settlement must normally be approved by the court. It will therefore be necessary to issue proceedings solely for this purpose. See Chapter 24 for more on this. Sometimes, insurers may ask you to dispense with formal infant approval through the court and instead ask the litigation friend to sign an indemnity discharge. This is a form that states that if the infant on majority believes further compensation to be due and pursues the insurance company then that company will have an indemnity from the litigation friend. As that person will usually have settled the claim on your advice then ultimately any later claim is likely to end up at your door. For that reason you should beware of dealing with settlement by indemnity. There is a formal procedure and it is there for a purpose. The defendant cannot compel you to deal by way of indemnity, although to save costs which they will have to pay many may suggest it. If the litigation friend is adamant that that is the preferred option then do make sure you highlight any concerns that you may have about the amount of settlement and explain the possible consequences to the litigation friend in writing. At the very least obtain a counsel's advice on quantum.

20.2. Settlement after proceedings have begun

The claimant may begin proceedings and then reach agreement with the other side. This may be through negotiation, or by the claimant deciding to accept a payment into court. The procedural requirements will depend upon how far the case has got:

(1) *If the case has not been served,* then, formally, the court need not be notified. The parties can simply close their files, and that will be the end of the matter. The proceedings are only valid if served for four months and then cease to be. However, a formal order is better because you then have a recorded right to detailed assessment. In an era where costs are so contentious it is preferable to formalise this so that if agreement on costs is not possible you can move quickly to the Part 47 procedure considered in the last chapter. If the client is public funded then even if there is no award of damage or costs inter-parties you will still need a formal order for public funding assessment unless you have the certificate discharged and proceed under that. It must be quicker to proceed by formal order.

(2) If proceedings have been served then you should always conclude the proceedings formally. Certainly, if allocation to track and the fixing of a trial window has taken place then the claim will need to come out of that trial slot and that will require court order. Remember that there is a specific obligation to notify the listing officer of any settlement as soon as it is reached.

20.3. Is it better to obtain a formal order?

Part of the answer is set out above. Plainly, there is an advantage in cost resolution in having a formal order recording a right to detailed assessment.

Sometimes, there is no formal requirement to record settlement in an order (unless the claimant is a person under a disability; money in court being accepted out of time, etc.) The parties can have an order drawn up if they wish, and this will of course be done by way of a consent application. But, is it advisable to have an order? The obvious argument in favour is that it ensures certainty and finality. Everyone knows where they stand. The court will have been notified and the claimant may feel happier with a formal order.

Whether to draw a formal order is ultimately a matter for the solicitor to decide. If in doubt draw an order. You have taken the trouble to bring the proceedings and filing an order rounds them off completely. Also, if the defendant does not comply with the agreement reached, how long do you wait before you do something about it and what do you do if you have not obtained an order? On the other hand, if you have prepared a *Tomlin* order then you may put the matter back before the court under the liberty to apply to implement the terms of the order provision.

20.4. The alternative ways of ending the case

There are four procedural devices that can be used to end the litigation:

(1) *Notice of Discontinuance.* In CPR Part 38 governs discontinuance. To discontinue part or all of a claim a formal notice of discontinuance must be filed with the court (see Form N279). A copy of this must be served on the defendant. The claim is deemed to be discontinued on the date that the notice is served on the defendant. Court permission to discontinue is not normally required. It is most often needed in injury claims because there has been an interim payment.

Before you discontinue do make sure that your client appreciates the costs implications of a discontinuance. Unless the parties agree or the court orders otherwise the client who discontinues a claim or part of it is liable for the costs of the parts discontinued. If part only of the claim is discontinued the amount due under the discontinuance is not assessed until the conclusion of the balance of the claim unless the court so orders.

(2) *Dismissal:* the defendant can obtain an order for dismissal of the action.

(3) *Judgment:* the claimant can enter judgment.

(4) *Stay:* the court can order a stay of proceedings in Tomlin order fashion.

It is the last of these four procedures, the stay of proceedings, that is normally used when recording a settlement. A stay is, in effect, a freezing of the action, and the freezing can be permanent or temporary, depending on the wording of the order. If the action is simply stayed, then it will be frozen permanently, and the parties will be unable to go back to the court if there is some dispute as to the carrying out of the agreed terms of settlement. Thus, for example, if the defendant refused to pay the claimant's costs, the claimant remedy would be to start a fresh action for the costs rather than re-apply for a further order against the defendant.

Accordingly, the stay sought on the order should be temporary rather than permanent unless all matters as to costs and damages have been agreed, finalised, and carried out. If so that should be recorded in the order. The usual order is for a permanent stay, except as to any problems arising in the working of the settlement. For instance, if there is a dispute as to the costs of the action then the parties will be able to go back to the court. This is called a "*Tomlin* Order" and should normally be used when recording a settlement.

20.5. Drawing up the order

Since the parties will be in agreement as to the terms of the settlement, it will be possible to have a consent application or summons (*i.e.* so no attendance in court is necessary). This assumes, of course, that the claimant is not an infant or other person under a disability. For the steps to be taken, refer to Procedural Table 3.

Also, refer to Precedent 22. This sets out various alternative forms of order that can be sought, and the steps to be taken. Follow those steps carefully. It will be seen that a typical order deals with the following points:

- usually it is the claimant who prepares the draft order and sends it to the defendant. The defendant then endorses consent on the draft order. Because it is by consent, the parties do not usually bother to issue an application or summons;
- the order will refer to the action being stayed, and state how much the claimant is accepting in full and final settlement;
- if any interim payments have been made, then it will be stated that full credit is to be given for those (give a total figure; also refer to each individually, by date and amount);
- if there is money in court then it will be ordered that that money be paid out to the claimant's solicitors and usually that any interest goes to the defendant's solicitors;
- if there is any more money to be paid to the claimant (*e.g.* in addition to the payment in) then the order will say it must be paid to the claimant within, say, 14 days;
- next, the order will deal with costs. If these have been agreed, then the figures should be set out (*i.e.* total figure, apportioned between disbursements, profit cost, and VAT). If the costs have not been agreed, then the order will record that the defendant has to pay standard basis costs, to be assessed in default of agreement;
- if the claimant is publicly funded, then there should be an additional clause allowing the claimant's costs to be assessed;
- for certainty, the order should deal with the CRU position and a copy of the latest certificate attached to the order;
- finally, the order will confirm that the defendant, provided that it pays the various amounts referred to, is discharged from all further liability. The order will also say that there be liberty to apply (ie the parties can go back to the court) if there are any problems in enforcing the terms of the order.

The claimant posts the consent order (*i.e.* the draft order with the defendant's consent written on it) to the court with the appropriate fee—£25. When the sealed order is returned, the claimant should then send a copy to the defendant; the defendant will then forward any money (*i.e.* damages and costs) that has yet to be paid.

Money in court

Remember that if there is money in court any order to settle a claim must include provision for the payment out of that money. In the county court if the money was paid in less than 21 days before the order the money will still be at the local court. If more than that period then the county court will notify the central fund and payment will be arranged. In the High Court you will always need to file the appropriate Court Funds form (CFO 201).

20.6. Provisional damages

If the settlement involves provisional damages, then the parties have no choice but to obtain an order from the court. Normally, this is done by simply issuing an application or summons, for a consent order.

In most respects, the wording of the summons will be similar to that in an ordinary consent order (see above). But, in addition, it has to contain full details of the provisional award. Thus, it must specify the disease or deterioration which it has been assumed will not occur, and which will entitle the claimant to come back for further damages if it should arise in the future. Basically, one can adapt the wording that should be used by the judge when giving judgment in a provisional damages case (set out in Chapter 18). However, in all but the most straightforward cases it may be felt that it is advisable to have counsel draft the relevant part of the summons. This is a question of experience. Initially, you will probably favour the use of counsel but as you do more then you will probably feel sufficiently confident to draft the provision yourself. In addition, the summons should set out the documents that will comprise the case file (usually, copy order, statements of case, agreed statement of facts, agreed medical reports). Refer to Procedural Table 14.

When the consent order is made, it is for the claimant, solicitor to prepare the case file, and forward it to the court.

If proceedings have not been commenced, then clearly it is not possible to issue a consent summons to formalise the provisional damages. In this situation then you should consider making an application using the CPR Part 8 procedure. CPR Part 8 PD 1.4(2) specifically indicates that this procedure ought to be used for provisional damage claims settled prior to commencement of contested proceedings where the only purpose of court process is to obtain court approval. As many provisional damage claims involve infants, for example where the full extent of any injury may not be apparent until full growth has taken place, then the Part 8 procedure can be used to combine the two court approvals that are then required.

20.7. Structured settlement

Where agreement has been reached involving a structured settlement as part of the compromise then court approval will be necessary. The procedure under CPR

Part 23 should be used to apply for court approval. If the claim involves an infant or patient then the applications for approval can be combined. If the application does not involve an infant or patient you may find that the court will make the order without a formal hearing.

If a hearing is required then you should ensure that you are familiar with the requirements of CPR Part 40 CPD s.1.7 which sets out what will be required at the hearing.

If the settlement including the structure is reached prior to the issue of proceedings then consider CPR Part 8 proceedings. Although there is no specific mention of approval of structured settlements in Part 8 that is plainly the appropriate procedure for approval of any infant or patient claim and in other cases it appears to be the correct procedure as the approval involves no dispute of fact, which is the major requirement of Part 8 process.

Part IV

MATTERS REQUIRING SPECIAL CARE

21. The Limitation Period

21.1. General rule and exceptions

The basic rule is that a personal injury claim must be commenced (*i.e.* the claim form issued, High or county court proceedings begun) within three years of the date of the accident. There are, however, exceptions to this:

- *Minors:* time does not run against a minor. Thus, the three-year period begins to run when the minor reaches the age of 18.
- *Aircraft accidents:* here there is a two-year, not three-year, limitation period (Carriage by Air Act 1961).
- *Knowledge:* if the claimant did not know of the injury, or of the defendant's negligence, then the three-year period will not start running until the date the knowledge was acquired (Limitation Act 1980, s. 11).
- *Assault:* where an injury arises out of an assault as opposed to negligence then the time limit is six years. You must be aware that in such a situation the discretion under Limitation Act 1980, s. 33 to extend the limitation period (see below) does not apply.
- *Extending the three-year period:* the court has a general discretion to extend the limitation period, if this would be "equitable" (Limitation Act 1980, s. 33).

21.2. When the three-year period starts to run

In the vast majority of cases, time begins to run from the date of the accident. Quite simply, the claimant knows that there was an accident, and that someone else might be to blame. That being so, the limitation period will be three years.

In calculating the three years, the day of the accident (*i.e.* the date the cause of action accrued) is excluded. So, if a claimant was injured on May 3, 1995, the last day to issue proceeding is May 3, 1998. In addition, if the three years and one day expire on a Saturday, Sunday, or Bank Holiday (*i.e.* when proceedings cannot be issued), then time is extended until the next day on which one can issue proceedings.

Although you will not wish to have to rely upon this provision as it is designed to cause sleepless nights, CPR Part 7 PD-005.1 provides that for the purposes of the Limitation Act 1980 a claim is deemed to be brought on the date it is received by the court if that is earlier than the actual date the court issues the claim form. However, and this is the sleepless night aspect of this provision, this rule only applies if, when the claim is issued it is issued in exactly the form in which it was lodged. Therefore, if there is anything wrong with the documents that you have lodged that requires the court office to return them to you for amendment before issue you may find that you are out of time. Be safe. Ensure that the proceedings are issued before the expiry of the limitation period.

Knowledge

To apply the three-year rule from the date of the cause of action, or injury, could produce hardship in some cases when the injured person does not know all the relevant facts. For instance, the person may not know of the injury until well after three years from the cause of action (as in an asbestosis claim, when the disease may not manifest itself until several years after the worker ceases to be in contact with asbestos). Similarly, the claimant may not be aware of evidence that shows that the proposed defendant was to blame for the accident (*e.g.* in occupational overuse injury cases (RSI) the client may not link the symptoms to the work conditions). To deal with such situations, Limitation Act 1980, s. 11 allows the three-year period to run either from the date of the accident (*i.e.* cause of action accruing) or from the date when the claimant first had "knowledge".

Time starts running once 'knowledge' is acquired. This will be when the claimant first knew that the injury was:

(a) significant; *and*

(b) attributable to an act or omission of the prospective defendant.

Thus, the effect of section 11 is to extend the limitation period where the claimant did not have knowledge. However, you should remember that this will not help the claimant whose delay is his or her own fault, or who has delayed because of:

(a) ignorance of the law;

(b) unreasonable failure to use the known information to make further enquiries to find out what did happen;

(c) unreasonable failure to appreciate the significance of the injuries;

(d) unreasonable failure to take medical or legal advice.

In such circumstances, section 11 cannot apply. The claimant's only hope will be to rely upon the court's general discretion (*i.e.* under Limitation Act 1980, s. 33, see below).

In fact, over recent years, the courts have become much more reluctant to extend time under section 11 except in the most obvious cases, for example where a claimant has obtained expert reports which suggested there was no negligence or that an injury was not attributable to a particular cause

Clinical negligence

The question of "knowledge" is particularly relevant in clinical negligence cases. It may be the case that the claimant will not have the necessary "knowledge" until he or she has received a firm indication (*e.g.* from a medical expert) that there was negligence. Thus, sometimes the three-year period in a clinical negligence claim will not run from the date of the negligent treatment, but from the date when the client is told or suspects that there may have been negligence. This is a point that is often overlooked by the inexperienced practitioner. If the clinical negligence is obvious (*e.g.* the wrong limb is amputated!) or if the claimant always felt that the treatment had been negligent but did nothing about it then knowledge will accrue as from the date of the negligent treatment. In recent years the courts have become stricter about fixing the date of knowledge. For example, in *Nash v. Eli Lilly, The Times,* October 7, 1992, CA claimants were claiming persisting photo-sensitivity after taking the Opren anti-depressant drug which was withdrawn in August 1992. In the cases considered there had been a delay in issuing proceedings of between two and four years. Hidden J. said that knowledge does not mean actual knowledge of negligence, nuisance or breach of duty but just some vague or generalised conduct, something for instance like "the operation at the hospital" and decided that a claimant who had taken legal advice would probably be fixed with knowledge for this purpose. You should *always*, therefore, be very wary of relying on this ground. It does seem to be being interpreted in an increasingly restrictive fashion.

21.3. The court's discretion to extend the three-year period

Under the Limitation Act 1980, s. 33, the court can extend the three-year period if it would be "equitable" to do so, but in reaching this decision it must have regard to any "prejudice" to the defendant.

This discretion to extend the limitation period is completely separate from the "knowledge" provisions in section 11. Under section 11, there is still a three-year period, it is just that the date when the three years begins may be extended to the time when "knowledge" accrued. Under section 33, it is the three-year period itself that can be extended.

Factors to be considered

When deciding whether the section 33 discretion should be exercised, the court will, *inter alia*, consider the following matters:

(1) The length of the delay and the reasons for it. For instance, see *McCafferty v. Metropolitan Police Receiver* [1977] 2 All E.R. 756 in which a claimant suffering from deafness due to noise was allowed to proceed out of time. Lawton L.J. commented "in my judgment the court should be understanding of men who, after taking an overall view of the situation, come to the conclusion that they would prefer to go on working rather than become involved with litigation".

(2) The extent to which the evidence in the case will now be less cogent. For instance, if the defendants have dealt with other claims on the same facts, and have that evidence to hand, they will not be prejudiced by the delay, as in *Buck v. English Electric* [1977] 1 W.L.R. 806.

(3) The conduct of the defendant. For instance, has it contributed to the delay by being obstructive? Has it intentionally misled the claimant as to the question of legal liability or in withholding pertinent evidence or disclosure.

(4) The extent of the claimant disability.

(5) The steps taken by the claimant to obtain advice. It may be relevant that the claimant will have a negligence claim against the advisers if the claim is not allowed to proceed out of time.

(6) The overall strength of the claimant's case. In *Nash v. Eli Lilly* (see above) the court held that "if the claim is a poor case lacking in merit there may be significant prejudice to the defendants if the limitation provisions are disapplied". The merits of the case may need therefore to be strongly argued.

An example of how section 33 can be applied, in practice, is found in *Buck v. English Electric* (see above). This was a pneumoconiosis claim where the disease had first been contracted by the claimant in 1959. By 1963 he had become aware of his right to sue but his disability was only small at that time. By 1970, however, he was 100 per cent disabled and by 1973 he had been forced to give up work. The writ was issued in 1975. It was held that, although the claim was some nine years out of time, the court would allow it to proceed by virtue of its discretion under section 33. Despite the inordinate delay, the defendants had been involved in several similar claims in recent years and so it was unlikely that the delay would prejudice them since they had all the relevant information and evidence to hand.

Prejudice to the claimant

It has to be said that there is some judicial conflict as to how section 33 should be applied. Does the court have a complete discretion, or must it be satisfied that the normal three-year limitation period has "prejudiced" the claimant? The answer seems to be that the court will want to look for prejudice to the claimant. Thus, for instance, if the claimant sues within the three-year period, and then allows the action to lapse (*e.g.* fails to serve the claim in time; and the action is struck out), then the claimant cannot use section 33 to justify the commencement of further proceedings outside the limitation period as it will not have been the three year period that would have prejudiced the claimant, but the claimant's own (or a solicitor's) default and inefficiency. The position seems to be that if the claimant:

(a) has begun proceedings within the three-year limitation period, then the claimant cannot use section 33 to bring a second set of proceedings outside the period against the same defendant

(b) does not bring an action within the three-year period, then the court has a discretion under section 33 to extend the time period, and allow the claim to proceed.

So, the claimant who has not yet sued will be better off than the claimant who has already tried to sue the same defendant.

Some recent good news

Whilst you should try not to need to rely on the section 33 discretion the recent case of *Steeds v. Peverel Management Services Ltd, The Times*, May 16, 2001, CA gives an indication of the latest thinking of the Court of Appeal. In this case there was no dispute that the limitation period had expired almost two months prior to issue and that the failure to issue was that of the claimant's solicitor. Sir Christopher Slade with Tuckey L.J. agreeing held that the mere existence of a cast iron claim for the claimant against his solicitors did not justify a court refusing to extend the period by way of punishment on the solicitors. The faults of the solicitor were not to be visited on the claimant although the existence of a claim against the solicitors was not an altogether irrelevant factor (it should be noted that the Court also held that the delay had caused the defendant no prejudice).

21.4. Adding a new defendant, out of time

The claimant may have begun proceedings within the three-year period and then found, when the defence is served, that allegations are made against another party. At this stage, the claimant may well find that the three-year period has expired, and so is apparently out of time for joining the third person as a defendant to the action. When this happens, the claimant may be in difficulty. However, it should not be forgotten that the three-year period runs from the date of "knowledge"; so, if the claimant did not realise that the third person might be to blame, then it can be argued that the three-year period does not run until date of service of the defence. Alternatively, the claimant can simply proceed against the third person, and rely upon the court's general discretion under section 33. (See Chapter 11 Amendment of Statements of Case, for the relevant procedure.)

21.5. Fatal cases

The Limitation Act 1980 also applies to fatal cases. Thus, the three-year period can run from the date of "knowledge", and there is also a general equitable discretion to extend time.

Knowledge

As regards the acquisition of "knowledge", section 12 sets out the rules. These are basically similar to those in section 11 (for non-fatal cases). The three-year period runs from whichever is later of the date of:

(a) cause of action accruing (*i.e.* date of death); and

(b) the acquisition of the relevant knowledge (as defined above).

In a fatal claim the "knowledge" will be that of the personal representatives (in a Law Reform Claim) or the dependants (in a Fatal Accidents Claim). Note that different dependants may have acquired their knowledge at different times and thus will have different limitation periods for their claims, whereas in the case of personal representatives the date of the acquisition of knowledge will always be the date it was first acquired by any one of the personal representatives.

Statute-barred claims

No claim can be brought if the deceased was statute-barred at the time of death. In deciding whether the deceased could have brought an action, one applies the test of whether the deceased died within three years of the accident or the date when the deceased acquired knowledge. If the death occurred more than three years after both those dates then no claim can be brought, for the court's equitable discretion under section 33 cannot be used to extend the limitation period for the deceased's claim. However, the section 33 discretion can be used to alter the limitation period for the statutory claim. Thus, if the deceased was not statute-barred at the time of death, but no claim was brought within the three years of death (or the necessary knowledge being acquired), then the court could exercise its discretion and allow a claim to proceed; but the contrary would not apply, for if the deceased was statute-barred at the time of death, no action could be brought under the Law Reform (Miscellaneous Provisions) Act 1934 or Fatal Accidents Act 1976, even if it was sought to do so within three years of the death.

21.6. Procedure

There is no set procedure for dealing with a limitation dispute. What happens is that the claimant issues proceedings in the usual way (the court staff should not refuse to deal with it because the three-year period has expired) and the defendant will usually file a Defence stating that the claim is statute barred. The rest of the Defence will then be stated to be without prejudice to that contention as the defendant will not wish to place all the Defence eggs in the one basket of limitation. Equally, the balance of the defence is unlikely to be that detailed because the defendant wants to show the court that the delay has caused prejudice preventing a full Statement of Case. The tactical games we play!

What will usually happen under the CPR is that on allocation and initial case management the court will order that the issue of limitation be determined first and give directions and a trial window for that issue alone. If the claim survives the limitation issue then the court determining that issue will give directions for the balance of the claim. Accordingly, with proactive case management it is rare that a party now needs to issue a specific application for the determination of limitation as a preliminary issue.

Sometimes, it is not practical to resolve limitation issues in isolation as the factors that determine the outcome are inextricably linked to the facts of the case and finding of facts that will need to be made on evidential matters at the heart of the case generally. These situations will be rare but may arise where there is a date of knowledge dispute.

Some claimants take a proactive approach to limitation and in the Statement of Case deal with it in anticipation of a Defence on this basis. Certainly, if the claimant is going to argue date of knowledge then the case on that should be clearly stated. If the argument is solely on section 33 discretion the case may be better saved for the witness statement that is bound to be required in the determination of this issue.

Funding and limitation

Whether there will be as many limitation arguments in the future remains to be seen. With more and more work being done on conditional fee funding or with legal expense backing it will be interesting to see if lawyers will be prepared to take on the risk of limitation to add to the other risks of an injury claim on any scheme that links remuneration with outcome. Even if they are prepared to do so it may prove hard to find an after the event insurer prepared to quote an affordable premium for such a high risk case.

Striking out of Statements of Case and dismissal of proceedings

Striking out

The thrust of the CPR is to give a far greater input into the conduct of a claim to the court. It is hardly surprising that to facilitate this involvement the CPR gives the court case management powers that enable it to strike out a statement of case.

CPR Part 3.4 indicates that the court may strike out any Statement of Case:

(1) that discloses no reasonable grounds for bringing or defending a claim;

(2) that is an abuse of the court process;

(3) if there has been a failure to comply with court order.

Whilst some courts took a proactive approach to pleadings before the CPR and struck out holding Defences many did not. Now it is rare that any such Statement of Case will slip through the net.

Whilst the first two grounds for strike out relate to the content of the Statement of Case the last refers solely to how the parties conduct either the claim or Defence. Recent authority seems to suggest that where no trial date has been fixed the court should be wary of exercising its power to strike out for breach of an earlier order or rule. However, it is a brave practitioner that takes the risk. If you are in difficulties in complying with an order do not wait until you have breached it and then seek relief. Apply before the expiry of the time period for an extension with supporting evidence explaining the reason for the request. Remember that the court must have regard to the overriding objective. If a brief extension of time will enable the matter to be dealt with justly then by being proactive you are likely to obtain your extension.

Although the CPR was drafted in anticipation of the Human Rights Act and was designed to be compliant with it striking out a claim or a Defence is one of the areas where there is concern that too draconian application of the CPR may raise human rights issues. It is for that reason that the imminence of the trial date has become an important consideration. The key consideration seems to be whether any breach has rendered the prospect of a fair trial taking place on the date fixed impossible.

If you wish to make an application to strike out the defendant's Statement of Case you should do so as soon as possible. At the very latest you should intimate that you are considering such an application when completing the allocation questionnaire.

Dismissal

The court still has a residual inherent jurisdiction to strike out or dismiss a claim. This can include situations where the conduct of a party has put the question of a fair trial in jeopardy.

With more court control of timescale and the early fixing of trial windows it should become harder, if not impossible, to be struck out for want of prosecution of a claim, but the remedy still seems to exists. This is under the court's inherent jurisdiction to take any step or make any order for the purpose of managing the case and furthering the overriding objective (see CPR Part 3.1) and that the specific instances for striking out set out above do not limit any other powers to do so that the court may have(see CPR Part 3.4(5)). The most likely use of this power is in older cases started before the introduction of the CPR where there has been delay. How frequently this power will be exercised once those transitional cases have worked their way through the system remains to be seen. It is clear though that when this power is exercised the court must consider the application under the CPR and not old authority such as *Birkett v. James* [1978]

A.C. 297 which is not even cited in the White Book. For a CPR authority on the subject see *Purefuture Ltd v. Simmons & Simmons* [2000] 9 C.L. 71.

Failure to pay a court fee

Virtually every strike out or dismissal involves some unforgivable conduct by a party or a representative. Under the CPR perhaps the least excusable is where the claimant has omitted to pay a court fee.

This applies to failure to pay an allocation or listing fee. In such circumstances the court will serve a notice on the defaulting party requiring payment by a set date. If the fee is then not paid the claim will be struck out and, unless the court specifically orders otherwise the claimant will be liable for the defendant's costs. Even then there is one last chance. An application for reinstatement can be made supported by evidence and the court can reinstate the case provided that the fee is then paid within two days of the order for reinstatement. When preparing the evidence in support, deal with the criteria that the court must consider when deciding whether to reinstate. These are set out at CPR Part 3.9.

The quid pro quo

Whilst the CPR may have imposed higher standards of Statement of Case, have preserved many striking out and dismissal procedures and have added fee default to the list of grounds for strike out there is a brighter side. The little loved and much litigated CCR Ord. 17 has gone. With the court now fixing trial windows or disposal dates there is no longer an onus on the claimant to set a county court action down for trial within fifteen months of close of pleadings. The sanction for failure to do so has inevitably also gone. It will not be missed and indemnity insurers will sleep all the easier for its passing. *Rastin* is gone—long live the CPR!

A[illegible] which is not even cited in the White Book. For a CPR authority on the [illegible] subject see [illegible] [2001] [illegible].

[illegible]

[illegible] unless the [illegible] [illegible] spe[illegible] [illegible] date's [illegible] [illegible] [illegible] [illegible] and the court can refuse [illegible] [illegible] provided that the [illegible] is [illegible] [illegible] [illegible] [illegible] [illegible] with the [illegible] [illegible] [illegible] [illegible] [illegible] CPR [illegible]

The [illegible]

Whilst the CPR may have imposed tougher standards [illegible] [illegible] have [illegible] interest[illegible] many sticking [illegible] and [illegible] [illegible] to the list of grounds to strike [illegible] [illegible] The little [illegible] much-hated CCR Ord. 17 has gone. [illegible] the court [illegible] [illegible] [illegible] dates there is no longer [illegible] [illegible] [illegible] [illegible] [illegible] within [illegible] [illegible] The sanction [illegible] [illegible] also [illegible] and indemnity [illegible] will [illegible] easier for [illegible] [illegible] the CPR

22. Summary Assessment of Costs and Part 8 Procedure for Cost Proceedings Only

For the majority of injury lawyers the most common cost assessment you are likely to encounter is summary assessment. This may be a summary assessment of part or of the whole of a claim or where the claim is settled pre-issue but no agreement on the amount of recoverable costs can be reached in cost only Part 8 proceedings. All these scenarios are considered in detail in this chapter.

22.1. Summary assessment

Background

Throughout the book there has been reference to costs and the two types of court assessment of costs. Detailed assessment has been considered in Chapter 19. Summary assessment was mentioned when considering interim orders and in Chapter 18, the Trial. It may be that chronologically it ought to have been considered in Chapter 18. However, the procedure is a new one and is likely to play an increasingly important part in personal injury litigation. Whilst claimant personal injury lawyers tend to be relatively altruistic the bottom line is that law is a business and costs are the lifeblood of that business. Summary assessment is crucial to the success or otherwise of a personal injury business. The procedure is not that complicated but failure to comply can have disastrous results. For this reason until the procedure becomes common place and second nature it merits this separate consideration.

What is a summary assessment?

A summary assessment is a determination by the court immediately following a hearing of less than a day or a fast track trial of costs that are not fixed by the rules. It is not a determination dealt with by the formal detailed process that has been considered earlier. There is no formal bill to be considered item by item nor formal notices of objection to certain items as you see in the detailed procedure, merely a somewhat rough and ready assessment by the court.

When does it take place?

Usually, you will encounter the procedure after a fast track trial or any hearing that lasts less than a day. This can include an appeal. However, the CPR make it plain that the court can extend the scope of summary assessment. CPR Part 44 PD-007 suggests that whenever the court is considering the question of costs that are not fixed the court should consider whether to deal with the question by summary assessment.

When can it not take place?

When the receiving party is publicly funded then the court cannot undertake a summary assessment of the costs. Whilst the court can make a summary assessment against a publicly funded party remember that that is not in itself an order creating a liability to pay the assessed costs. For that to arise the procedure set out in CPR Part 44 PD-017 must be followed. This effectively preserves the costs protection that a publicly funded claimant enjoys. The old "football pools" order that any costs against a public funded party cannot be enforced without further leave of the court is now referred to as a "lottery order".

When the receiving party is an infant or patient the court cannot undertake a summary assessment unless that party's lawyer has waived the right to costs beyond those assessed. However, the court may make a summary assessment of the costs payable by these categories of parties.

Procedure

Like so much of personal injury work the key to achieving reasonable levels of cost recovery in summary assessment is in the preparation.

In any case where you think that summary assessment will or may take place you should prepare an estimate of costs in advance of the hearing and ensure that you serve and file it at least 24 hours before the relevant hearing when the costs will be considered. The rule is quite clear that the role of the parties and their lawyers in summary assessment is to assist the court to carry out its function. Failure to comply with the time limit is likely to result in some sanction, most probably that the summary assessment will have to be adjourned to a separate hearing and the costs of that hearing will be paid by the party in default, usually the receiving party. In other words, hard earned costs are reduced and payment is delayed.

The estimate should set out:

- The number of hours claimed. It is best to divide this between correspondence, telephone and personal attendance and preparation and perusal of documents and between time spent on the client, the other side, counsel and the court.
- The grade of fee earner. Under the guidelines there are three grades, although this is soon to change to four. These grades depend on experience and legal qualification.

- The hourly rate sought and if this includes different categories of fee earner set out a clear breakdown of what work is charged at what rate.
- Details of any disbursements.
- The costs of the hearing or trial itself. Remember that if the schedule is for a fast track trial those will be fixed in relation to the amount of damages awarded (see Part 46.2: Up to £3,000 awarded—£350, £3,000 to £10,000 awarded—£500, over £10,000 awarded—£750 with a further £250 if you brief counsel but attend yourself and can show that your presence was necessary to assist the advocate).
- The VAT to be added.

The assessment

The amount of recoverable cost must be assessed by the court that awards the cost entitlement. In other words, whether or not the summary assessment can take place on the day of the hearing giving rise to the entitlement to costs or not the summary assessment cannot be done by any costs officer other than the one who conducted the hearing. Therefore, the summary assessment takes place either at the end of the hearing or at a later date before the same costs officer. If it is to be at a later date then the court should give directions for the subsequent hearing.

The factors that the court must consider when carrying out a summary assessment are no different from those applicable to a detailed assessment. As well as the usual considerations that apply to standard basis costs (which is going to be the usual basis) the court should consider the following:

- The conduct of the parties both before and after issue of proceedings. So, for example, if you fail to comply with the personal injury protocol you may find that this is when it comes home to roost.
- The attempts made to settle the proceedings. Likely considerations here are whether the claimant has been open in disclosing information at as early a stage as possible to enable the defendant to value the claim and whether the parties have made any CPR Part 36 proposals.
- The value of the amount in dispute.
- The importance of the matter to the parties.
- The complexity of the matters in dispute. It is trite to point out that the average road accident claim is likely to be less complicated than the average accident at work claim.
- The skill, specialised knowledge and responsibility involved. This is quite a useful counter to suggestions that too senior a grade fee earner dealt with the matter. Any additional hourly rate will be more than offset by expertise that has lead to the claim being dealt with in far less chargeable time.
- The time spent on the claim (see above).
- The place where and the circumstances in which the work was done. This provision is to reflect that with a shift towards the institutional provision of more claimant work as well as culls by insurers of their panels of soli-

citors leading to centralisation, the rate where the work was done may not be the relevant rate applicable to the area where the client lives so that the work could have been sourced locally for lower cost at an adequate level of representation. If you practice in a low cost allowance area you may wish to argue the reverse scenario applies (the writer is based in Cornwall).

More often than not the summary assessment that will concern you the most will be a fast track trial where, save for any interim orders made, all your costs will be up for grabs there are a few important things to note:

(i) As set out above, trial costs are fixed. You should therefore try to ensure that your chosen counsel is of the right seniority to ensure that the brief fee is as close as possible to the allowed fixed fee.

(ii) In any claim there are costs that are inevitably incurred carrying out essential work to enable the claim to be presented properly. Sometimes, simply undertaking that essential work will render the claim disproportionate on a straightforward cost/damage analysis. CPR Part 44 PD-005 recognises this. The good news is that it confirms that no solicitor is expected to conduct necessary litigation at uneconomic rates. The rule specifically envisages situations where the allowed costs will exceed the damages.

(iii) If the claim settles before trial but after a brief has been delivered the fees allowable for counsel in preparation must be assessed with regard to what counsel would have received had s/he had to prepare and appear for the fixed cost.

(iv) When making a costs order in the first place the court must consider whether a party has succeeded in whole or in part. If, for example, you state numerous allegations of negligence which require separate investigation and only succeed on one ground you may find that your cost recovery is limited. This is why it is essential that you take stock at regular stages of the claimand make any amendments to the statement of case that are necessary as the case proceeds.

(v) Beware of tactical estimates of costs. It seems that some defendants, anticipating a loss put in low schedules thinking that the risk of losing is so high and of being responsible for the claimant's costs so high that they will put in a low schedule so that they can then argue that your costs are high in comparison and should be reduced. This can back fire if the defendant then wins as the recoverable costs have been restricted. Do not be tempted to do this if you think you may lose as the court is likely to see through this attempt anyway and you only prejudice your client's position if you win.

The procedure following summary assessment

See Chapter 23 as matters do arise after a summary assessment if there is conditional fee funding and a success fee is sought.

22.2. Part 8 cost only proceedings

One of the uncertainties of the early CPR was how to resolve the question of costs that could not be agreed in cases that were otherwise settled prior to the issue of proceedings. With the introduction of the personal injury protocol increasing the out of court settlement rate significantly this was a problem area that needed to be addressed. It has been. CPR Part 44.12A provides a specific procedure for just this eventuality. Part 44.12A provides a short form procedure to put the question of costs before the court. However, it is important to bear in mind that this procedure can only be invoked where there is a written agreement between the parties on all issues INCLUDING who is to pay costs. If any offer is silent on costs, and some are simply because parties think it so obvious where the responsibility lies that it is not specifically mentioned, then you need to obtain written clarification of the costs position before considering the offer with your client.

Assuming that you have an offer that is acceptable to your client and there is an agreement to pay costs but the amount of those cannot be agreed then to invoke the short form procedure you should make application under Part 8 for a cost determination. Guidance is given on the format of proceedings to adopt in CPR Part 44 PD-011.

Procedure

You should use Part 8 proceedings. These must;

- identify the nature of the claim in which the dispute over costs arises; and
- state the details of the agreement reached upon which reliance is placed; and
- attach a draft of the order sought. This is likely to be a request for detailed assessment; and
- state the amount of costs sought under the agreement; and
- state whether the costs are sought on the standard or indemnity basis. If the application is silent on this then the costs will be on the standard basis.

You should file with the Part 8 proceedings copies of the documents that form the agreement reached giving rise to the cost entitlement; in other words, the documents that you have carefully obtained confirming an agreement to pay costs.

The court will either make an order for costs or dismiss the claim. Curiously, the court must dismiss the claim if the defendant opposes the application. It is hard to see how that sits with the content of the rule generally that where there is clear evidence of agreement to pay costs this is the correct procedure to adopt. It is also hard to see how a claim in this form could be disputed where there is a written agreement confirming that costs will be paid. Again, the practice direction accompanying the rules gives some guidance, although it does not resolve the concerns set out above. The guidance simply states that where the defendant files an acknowledgement of service contesting the proceedings or seeking some other remedy then that is deemed to be an opposed application and an order dismissing the claim must follow. The guidance suggests that you may then issue another Part 8 application or a Part 7 one. It seems inevitable that in such circumstances there is no point in issuing another Part 8 application as the defendant will oppose again. The better course is to issue Part 7 proceedings to enforce the agreement. In those proceedings you should pursue indemnity costs as it would seem that the conduct of the defendant has become relevant in failing to perform the agreement without court intervention.

The rule at the time of writing is relatively new and there is so far no reported authority on the topic. However, it seems unlikely that a defendant having agreed to settle a claim before issue, including an agreement to pay costs that cannot then be agreed, is going to oppose the Part 8 procedure.

An order for costs made under this rule will be for detailed assessment of the costs in dispute. Such an order is likely to be made on paper consideration by the court rather than at a formal hearing. The usual detailed assessment procedure will apply. Experience to date suggests that where agreement on costs prior to issue cannot be reached and Part 8 process is necessary the proceedings are usually by consent as both parties want then to move to detailed assessment and resolve the issues between them as quickly as possible. As the detailed assessment will be under the CPR Part 47 procedure there is a clear pattern amongst those instructed by insurers to try to negotiate costs to make Part 47 offers with consequential cost threats. In such situations you should try to establish the nature of the retainer of the costs negotiators to ascertain whether the Part 47 offer actually carries any risk. The reason for this is that Part 47.14.17 plainly sets out situations where a party (and here it would be the defendant) can be represented by costs draftsmen. Unless you know the terms of the retainer you cannot assess whether the person with whom you are negotiating falls within Part 47.14.17. Where the criteria set out are *not* met then the cost negotiator is not entitled to represent the party so cost threats made by those costs negotiators carry no weight. This is information that you need so that you can properly advise your client and in an era of open litigation is information that should be provided.

The situation becomes more complicated when the cost negotiators instruct their solicitors in any Part 8 process as again the rule is plain that to represent any party the cost negotiator must be instructed *by* the solicitor for that party. You need to ensure that the actual party, namely the defendant has instructed the solicitors who then instruct the cost negotiators rather than the reverse as it may be in the latter scenario the cost negotiators actually have no right of audience on any subsequent detailed assessment (see *Waterson Hicks v. Eliopoulos*, November 14, 1995, CA).

23. Public and Conditional Fee Funding Arrangements

Funding of claims has always been a concern of injury practitioners. Legal aid traditionally provided the most common and secure form of fee arrangement. Not any more. For the past two years or so legal aid funding has been unavailable for nearly all new injury claims. The panacea sold as its successor has been the conditional fee agreement. At the moment, there are a few legal aid certificates still in existence and an increasing number of conditional fee agreements. As arranging and explaining a fee agreement to your client is fundamental it is necessary to consider both these forms of funding.

23.1. Public funding (legal aid)

Introduction

Recent editions of this book have seen the gradual reduction of space devoted to public funding (legal aid as was). If it is not presumptuous to talk at this stage of an 11th edition you may find, assuming also that you buy it, that public funding no longer features at all.

Residual elements of public funding have been touched upon where they arise in the course of an action, including consideration of the detailed assessment process. For clinical negligence and group litigation specific mention has been made of the arangements that apply. The reference has been brief because the application of the rules relevant to those situations is limited by the number of lawyers able to undertake such public funded work. Those lawyers should understand the pertinent provisions that apply.

There are still a few old legal aid certificates around, although the number must be reducing daily. Certainly, the Cornish cabinet is now down to the last few.

In the circumstances an examination of procedures from the application for funding to the discharge of the certificate is no longer merited. Instead, a few key points should be highlighted. Some have been mentioned in the general text. The intention of grouping them together under a general heading is to create a section which operates as an aide memoire.

The certificate

It may seem too obvious to mention that an appreciation of the scope of the work you are entitled to do under a certificate is crucial. However, many solicitors still undertake work that is not covered by a certificate in terms of both the activity and the cost expenditure authorised by the certificate. At best, this means that you will not be paid for the work done that is outside the scope of the certificate. At worst, you expose your client to the risk of losing the cost protection provided by the certificate.

Do check what work you are entitled to do and the amount of the financial limitation on the certificate and record these clearly on the file. You should note any changes to the scope as the action continues. If you keep a regular record of the costs on a file and have a separate disbursement ledger you should be alerted to the need to seek an increased financial limit in sufficient time to enable the claim to proceed without delay.

Even if this close scrutiny is kept there are still traps for the unwary. For example, "limited to counsel's opinion" means that if counsel produces an advice in which he or she says that to enable the opinion to be finalised further information is required you will need to obtain an extension to the certificate to enable the final view to be obtained once you have the information. Otherwise, although only one opinion is expressed it is contained in two written documents it is deemed to be two opinions.

The older the certificate is and the nearer that you are to trial the easier it becomes to forget to obtain extensions, even fundamental ones such as an extension to enable the claim to go to trial. You have become so used to having the certificate that you forget to review it. The other classic time to overlook the limitation of the certificate is when you need to issue proceedings to protect your client on limitation. At that stage the certificate is quite likely to be limited to initial investigation up to but not including issue or to all steps to comply with the personal injury pre-action protocol.

One final point on obtaining any amendments to the certificate is that you should remember to advise your client what you are doing and why as otherwise the client will receive an amended certificate out of the blue. If this includes a cost increase that goes beyond any cost estimate that you have provided to the client previously you should advise your client in advance of the increase you are seeking, the reason why it is necessary and the revised best overall cost estimate.

23.2. Notifying the court and the other parties of a public funded client

Both the court and the other side must be told if the client is public funded. You do this by service of notice of issue of legal aid (see below).

Effect on defendant's costs

A defendant who is being sued by a public funded claimant is at a disadvantage. Quite simply, the defendant is likely to recover costs from a public funded claimant. Thus, it is important to advise the other side of the fact that the claimant is public funded. In some borderline cases where costs may be disproportionate to damages it may be the factor that persuades the defendant to settle.

Notice of issue of certificate

A Notice of Issue must be served on all parties to the proceedings. As soon as the proceedings are commenced (or when the certificate is issued, if proceedings have already been commenced) a Notice must be served on each of the defendants. A precedent Notice of Issue is printed in Precedent 35. Do not forget to keep a copy of the Notice of Issue, since it is one of the documents that has to be included in the bundle of papers when you prepare the trial bundle (see Chapter 17). The Notice of Issue must set out the scope of the client's certificate (*e.g.* "to bring an action for personal injuries against the defendant arising from an accident on . . . "). It is not necessary to and you should not set out any limitation in the certificate. Many claimant's solicitors wrongly set out the limitation. It is wrong for you to disclose the limitations in a client's certificate; by doing so you weaken your client's position. The only time when a limitation must be stated is if the certificate relates to appeal proceedings. Otherwise, never reveal a limitation. What credibility does a claim have if it took three limitation of super extensions to get to issue?

Often solicitors forget to serve a Notice of Issue until the proceedings are well under way. Failure to do this does not invalidate the client's legal aid certificate, or mean that the claimant automatically becomes liable for the other side's costs. However, in an extreme case, the claimant's solicitor could be held responsible for costs if the defendant has suffered serious prejudice. To avoid this difficulty, you should adopt the habit of asking the court to serve the Notice of Issue with the proceedings.

Filing the certificate with the court

In the same way that the other side must be notified of the claimant being public funded, so must the court. To do this, file one of the copy legal aid certificates with the court. You should prepare a backsheet (*i.e.* with title of action; stating it is a legal aid certificate; name and address of your firm, reference, phone number, etc.). Note that there is no need for a copy of the legal aid certificate to be supplied to the other side, they receive a Notice of Issue (see above). You should file a copy of the Notice of Issue as well.

Once again, it you should file the certificate when commencing proceedings. See stock letters 37 and 38.

Remember, it is all too easy to forget to lodge the certificate with the court, and to serve Notice on the other parties. Always double-check that this has been done.

There is a different form to be used if a legal aid certificate is amended, discharged or revoked. See Precedent 35. Note that there is no need to serve office a Notice of Amendment merely because the limitation on the client's certificate has been removed or amended.

23.3. The duty to the Legal Services Commission

Apart from the duty to your client, you also have a duty to the Legal Services Commission.

The general duty

There is a general duty on the solicitor not to take unjustifiable steps in the action; not to incur unjustifiable expenditure, and a duty not to continue litigation unjustifiably. In effect, if you continue with a hopeless case, which should have been brought to the attention of the Legal Services Commission, then you run the risk of losing any entitlement to costs, and, in an exceptional case, being ordered to pay some of the other side's costs.

Recoupment of money

All money obtained from the defendant on behalf of the claimant, except interim payments, must be paid to the claimant's solicitor (not the client direct) and be paid to the Legal Services Commission pending determination of the case and your's costs. This rule is designed to protect the statutory charge but is not particularly convenient as this often causes delay and however many times you have warned the client about this the client will often become impatient particularly where there has already been the delay of a full detailed assessment.

If the costs come to a lot less than the damages and you know this in advance of receiving the settlement moneys then you may consider releasing the difference to the client on an interim basis as there is no risk in respect of costs. If you do not propose to seek any payment from the Legal Services Commission and you are prepared to take a gamble that the defendant insurer will pay your costs then you may decide to release the entirety of the damages whilst you are still trying to resolve the recovery of your costs. If you do so it must be on condition that the client co-operates in the recovery of cost process. For example, on a case settled before issue where costs cannot be agreed the clients permission will be needed to the issue of CPR Part 8 process.

To obtain costs

There is a general duty to obtain standard costs from the other side (whether by agreement or order). This is coupled with a general duty to safeguard the interests of the Fund on any *inter partes* assessment, and to take any steps that may seem necessary for a review of that assessment.

The duty to report to the area office

You must immediately notify the area office if any money is recovered or preserved for the client, and also you must account to the area office, not the claimant, if any money is received on behalf of the client (see above).

In addition, there is a general duty to report to the area office if there is:

(a) abuse by the client of public funding (*e.g.* the client behaving unreasonably, such as telephoning frequently and so increasing the costs liability of the Fund); or, more usually,

(b) when there are no reasonable grounds for continuing with the case. For instance, if there is new evidence that shows the client no longer has a cause of action, or if there has been a change in the prospects of success due to a payment into court, or if the defendant is shown to have no assets, or if there is now a CICB determination that will give the client full compensation, etc. If you are in doubt as to the position, report to the area office and let them decide.

Furthermore:

(1) You must provide the area office with a report of the progress in the proceedings, if requested.

(2) The area office must be told if the client dies, or if a receiving order is made.

In addition, you have a discretion to report to the area office, for example, if you doubt your client's honesty. If you report doubts and fears to the area office this will not be in breach of the professional duty to the client, and the prudent solicitor will therefore, when faced with a difficulty, consult the area office and leave it to them to decide whether the case should continue or not. However, there may be a delay before any decision is made.

Prior authority

The necessity to obtain authority to incur expenditure, or take certain steps, can be either mandatory or discretionary. Authority is sought by way of application on Form CLS App 8 the area office, and you should remember that if the area office authorises the step or the expenditure, then the costs cannot be disallowed by the costs officer on a legal aid assessment (although they may, of course, be disallowed *inter partes*).

Authority is *mandatory* if the intention is to:

(a) add a further party to the proceedings;

(b) defend a counterclaim or enter a cross-appeal;

(c) instruct more than one counsel (see below).

You have a *discretion* to seek the area office's authority (and thus cover the costs position) to:

(a) lodge an interlocutory appeal (not an appeal to the Court of Appeal on judgment, which would require the issue of a new certificate);

(b) obtain a transcript (often the authority will be limited to obtaining only certain relevant parts of the transcript);

(c) take an unusual step, or incur unusually large expenditure;

(d) obtain expert evidence (see below).

If you do not obtain authority before taking any of the above steps, you run the risk that some (or all) of the expenditure, and of your costs, will not be allowed on assessment, in which case you will bear the loss since the money can neither be recovered from the client nor from the Legal Services Commission. Accordingly, it is wise always to seek prior authority if there is any doubt as to the propriety of the step being taken. The authority will be given on the form from the area office, and there is, of course, no need to serve a copy of that letter on the court or on the other parties to the action. If authority is refused there is no right of appeal, although there is no reason why a fresh application cannot be made.

Completing the form

Form CLS App 8 is self-explanatory but note that you will need an estimate of fees or costs to be incurred. The area office will often refuse a fee it considers excessive so explain carefully why the expenditure is necessary or why that particular expert or step in the proceeding, is necessary.

Counsel and counsel's fees

Authority must be obtained before instructing a second junior or before taking in a leader. When deciding whether to authorise a leader, the area office will consider such matters as the sum of money involved, the importance of the case to the client, whether the case involves a specialised field of law, and whether it raises a difficult point of law. However, the Commission will not authorise a leader solely because, for example, the junior originally instructed has been taken ill, or because the other side has brought in a leader, or even if junior counsel is not sufficiently experienced (in such a case the application should be for authority to instruct a second more senior junior). Beware the wording of the authority. For example, it may be limited in relation to the work it covers—if the authority is to "brief counsel" that will cover the hearing itself and any necessary consultation or conference on the brief after it is delivered. Conversely, the authority may be limited in number. For example, is it limited to briefing leading counsel alone or briefing leading and junior counsel?

Opinions

These (written or in conference) will be allowed on:

(a) the merits, where any reasonable doubt exists;

(b) the summons for directions;

(c) quantum or on a proposed settlement.

Conferences

These will not usually be allowed for an interim application, where counsel has already been allowed a fee for settling the application, or advising on it, or for settling the evidence in support of it. Nor will a fee usually be permitted for a conference on the settling of documents where these have already been settled by counsel, or where counsel has already given a written opinion on them. However, you may still deem these steps necessary and take yourchances on winning and recovering inter parties.

Settling

Counsel's fee will normally be allowed for the settling of:

(a) any statement of case;

(b) Part 18 requests;

Counsel's fee will not be allowed for settling a claim form without particulars of claim.

Generally

Fees for opinions, conferences and summonses not mentioned above may be allowed if the costs officer is satisfied that they were "necessary". Fees for views of the locus by counsel will rarely be allowed. If in doubt, one should obtain authority.

Experts' reports

When instructing an expert, be it doctor, engineer, or survevor, there is always the risk that the fee will not be allowed on assessment, if it was "unreasonable". Some solicitors state in the letter of instruction to the expert that the fee cannot exceed the amount that will be allowed on assessment. By doing this, the solicitor seeks to avoid personal liability should the fee not be allowed. Many experts will not accept this. Indeed, many now have there own terms of retainer. This presents no difficulties in some locations as there are many different experts from whom to choose. In other areas this can prove more problematic. The difficulties may be increased if you source experts through an organisation as their terms of retainer will not provide for the possibility that the fee will not be payable at some stage.

Really, you need to take a view. For example, in a whiplash case of more than a few months, duration orthopaedic evidence is necessary. If the fee is within usual brackets there is really no risk if you do not obtain prior authority. Conversely, in a head injury case if instructing a psychologist undertaking seriological tests, where the fee will be substantial, it is obvious that prior authority is necessary.

Any authority will be up to a maximum. You should remind the expert of this in instructions and ask that he or she contact you if this will not be sufficient before undertaking any work over that fee level.

Ensure that the authority is obtained before the expenditure is incurred and remember that there can be delays in obtaining such authority. When applying to the area office for authority, it is often convenient to ask for payment on account of that, and other, disbursements (see below).

Obtaining the client's authority

If the client is public funded, it is all too easy to forget that one must also obtain the client's authority for any unusual expenditure. Few solicitors forget to obtain the area office's prior approval for such expenditure, but it is surprising how many forget to obtain the client's approval. The reason for consulting the client is that the client might, via the statutory charge, eventually have to meet the bill. Thus, the client should also be consulted.

It is not enough simply to advise the client of how the statutory charge works. You must also advise the client if you are going to incur expenditure that may not be recoverable. For instance, suppose you are thinking of obtaining actuarial evidence to support a future loss of earnings claim. In general, such evidence will not be admitted at trial and there is a likelihood that the costs of the actuary's reports would not be recoverable on an *inter partes* assessment. The public funded claimant should therefore be advised that such expenditure may not be recoverable, since the client may well have to pay for it, through operation of the statutory charge. You should, of course, advise your client of the pros and cons of obtaining the evidence and how you expect it to assist your client's case. If you do not advise the public funded client that such expenditure may not be recoverable, then you may find that you are unable to recover the disbursement under your solicitor client costs [See standard letter].

Recovering the cost of disbursements

The Legal Services Commission will reimburse the solicitor for any disbursements incurred. There is no need to wait until conclusion of the case. Accordingly, it should be standard practice always to request reimbursement of any disbursement as soon as you know that it is likely to be incurred. There is a standard form for this purpose CLS Claim 4.

Extending a limitation or condition

A public funding certificate when granted will usually be subject to a limitation *e.g.* "all steps up to close of pleadings" or a costs condition *e.g.* "up to £2,500". Such limitations and conditions should be carefully noted on the file and you should regularly ensure that you are still within any limitation since you will not be paid for any work done outside a limitation. However necessary it may be for your client's case. You will not be paid for any work done which exceeds a costs condition unless specifically authorised on assessment. Apply to extend the certificate as soon as possible by using CLS A008

Payment into court

If the defendant makes a payment into court or part 36 offer pre issue check whether there is a limitation on the claimant's legal aid certificate requiring that the area office be notified of all payments in (or offers of settlements). Such a limitation is now unusual and probably superfluous.

The reason for this is that if you believe that a Part 36 payment or offer is reasonable and the client refuses to accept this then you are obliged in any event to report this to the Legal Services Commission who, in most cases, will then issue a notice to show cause as to why the certificate should not be discharged.

Special advice is needed to public funded claimants on such offers anyway. Many claimants will think that the cost protection under a certificate means that a Part 36 payment or offer cannot hurt them. Wrong. If such a client fails to beat such a payment or offer then the damages actually recovered can be used to discharge the cost liabilities that flow from that failure. In some cases this can erode the entirety of the damages (see consideration of Part 36 above).

Discharge or revocation of the certificate

The certificate *must* be discharged if the assisted person:

(a) no longer has reasonable grounds for taking, defending, or being a party to, proceedings; *or*

(b) has required the case to be conducted unreasonably, or so as to cause an unjustifiable cost to the public Fund;

(c) becomes financially ineligible.

In addition the certificate will be discharged if it is unreasonable in the particular circumstances that the assisted person should continue to be public funded or if the Legal Services Commission is persuaded by representations made by other parties.

Up until discharge the client remains public funded and costs to that date will be met by the Legal Services Commission.

In these circumstance before a certificate is discharged, the assisted person will be given notice and afforded an opportunity to show cause why the certificate should not be discharged.

The area office *may,* in its discretion, discharge the certificate:

(a) on request; *or*

(b) if the contribution is in arrears; *or*

(c) on the death of the assisted person, or on a receiving order being made; *or*

(d) at the conclusion of the case, or of the steps authorised.

Revocation

Discharge is not the same as revocation. If a certificate is revoked, it is as though the certificate had never been issued and so the client is responsible to the Legal And Board for all costs incurred. A certificate can be revoked (or discharged) if the assisted person:

(a) made untrue statements, or if there was material non-disclosure as to resources;

(b) knowingly made an untrue statement, or failed to furnish information, on other matters;

(c) failed to attend an interview or give information, when required.

Before a certificate is revoked, the assisted person will be given notice and afforded an opportunity to show cause why the certificate should not be revoked

Procedure

If a certificate is revoked or discharged, then you must:

(a) serve notice of revocation or discharge on the other party (see section 7);

(b) notify counsel;

(c) file a copy with the court. A backsheet should be prepared. It should be endorsed "we certify that reg. 82(2) of Civil Legal Aid (General) Regulations 1989 has been complied with" (this confirms that notice of discharge/revocation has been served on the other parties, and that counsel has been notified). There is no need for you to apply to go off the record; by filing the certificate, and serving notice on the other parties, the retainer is automatically terminated.

(d) apply for costs within three months of the revocation or discharge to be assessed as appropriate (see below). If the client has an interest in the assessments because the: and Chapter 17
   (i) statutory charge applies because property has been recovered or preserved;
   (ii) certificate was revoked (in which case the client is liable to repay all the costs incurred to the Legal Services Commission and to pay the surplus of your costs charged on your private rates);
   (iii) client was liable to pay a contribution;

then the client must be given notice of the assessment and an opportunity to make representations.

23.4. Costs

Standard fees

In respect of certificates issued from February 25, 1994, standard fees will be paid. However, at present, "standard" refers to the hourly rate granted and not a standard fee for the job, so the file will still have to be assessed to ascertain the appropriate time and disbursements allowed and the appropriate uplift. Uplift (called 'enhancement') will now only be given in exceptional circumstances. Note though that standard rates only apply when the costs are payable by the Legal Services Commission. If the costs are to be paid by the other party then they will be on the normal standard basis (see Chapter 19) even if these are higher than the standard rates (as they normally will be). For further details see the Legal Aid in Civil Proceedings (Remuneration) Regulations 1994 (S.I. 1994 No. 228) and the Practice Directions made in respect of the regulations.

Assessment

See Chapter 19 on detailed assessment procedures.

23.5. The client's liability for costs

The assisted party who loses a case will be liable for the defendant's costs up to the amount which the court thinks to be reasonable in all the circumstances, bearing in mind the means of the parties and their conduct in the action. Most often the assisted party is not ordered to pay anything. If the court decides a contribution is appropriate then, although the courts have stated that the contribution figure assessed on the issue of the public funding certificate is not an appropriate guide when quantifying what is a reasonable amount for the losing assisted party to pay the contribution figure is sometimes the figure decided upon as being reasonable in the circumstances of the case.

It is for this reason that the knowledge that the claimant is public funded may well induce a defendant to settle. For example, suppose that the claimant's claim is unsuccessful and so the defendant is entitled to assess costs at, say, £8,000, although its actual costs will be £12,000. If the claimant's maximum contribution was assessed at £1000 then the defendant will be unlikely to recover more than that amount; thus the defendant will end up some £11,000 out of pocket. Tactically if the client has a certificate with a nil contribution then it may be worth leaking that information.

Note that the other side can apply at any time for the order as to costs to be varied if there is a change in the circumstances of the assisted person. Whether or not the successful non-assisted party will recover the balance of its costs from the Legal Services Fund will depend upon whether it can show that it will suffer financial hardship otherwise, and whether it would be just and equitable in the circumstances. It is for this reason that insurance companies are reluctant to incur heavy costs against a public funded claimant. Do not bank on this. Some companies, rightly, recognise that they must fight some uneconomic cases if they are to avoid a reputation for always paying out public funded claims.

It is an irony of recent reform that defendants, who for years have bemoaned the unfairness caused by public funding of many claimants and roundly welcomed its withdrawal, are now complaining even more vociferously about the cost to them of the conditional fee replacement.

23.6. Settling the case

If costs have been agreed with the other side and you will not be making a claim on the Public Fund then you do not need to pay the costs into the area office or obtain its approval. Simply complete and send in form CLS CLAIM 2 setting out the amount agreed. In addition, it will be necessary to confirm that there is no Green Form payment to be refunded (or to refund Green Form payments and any payments that have been made on account), that the client agrees to discharge the certificate, and that no further claim will be made on the fund. You will also need to provide certain information about the progress of the claim.

23.7. Franchising

What is franchising?

Since October 1, 1993, it has been possible to apply for a legal aid or Public Funding franchise to carry out personal injury work. The first franchises were granted in 1994 However, the withdrawal of public funding from the majority of injury victims has rendered the franchise in this field of increasingly less use.

Perhaps the benefit that remains relates to the frequency and amount of interim payments on account of profit costs that can be claimed. Soon even this will have gone and Legal Services Commission audit of files day will be the challenge of someone else.

For those who read this and practice in other areas of law as well as personal injury and still have franchise audits rest assured that institutional providers of bulk instructions have as rigid service standards and often more frequent audits of files than the Legal Services Commission. As for interim payments of profit costs . . . pigs may fly! So, a fond farewell to Legal Aid, a friend to accident victims over the years and on to the future.

23.8. Conditional fees

Historical background

Traditionally, solicitors were not allowed to have an interest in the outcome of the proceedings. The ability to give objective and impartial advice being thought to override the other considerations. The prospect of a costs regime where a fee would be charged only if the claim were successful was not only remote but one that would require a change of the Solicitors Practice Rules. As recently as 1990 Rule 8 forbade such an arrangement. In addition, there would be a clear breach of the indemnity principle, rendering recovery of costs impossible. This principle states that the costs recoverable by one party from another are an indemnity for the costs actually incurred. They are neither a bonus nor a punishment on the losing party (*Hirold v. Smith* (1860) 5 H&N 381. This means that a solicitor who agreed not to charge a client unless the client won the case was not entitled to recover costs as they would have been a bonus as a result of winning. This was upheld in the 1993 case of *British Waterways Board v. Norman, The Times*, November 11, 1993. In that case, a solicitor acting for a claimant in an injury claim agreed only to take costs if the claim was successful. No costs were therefore payable. However, this case emphasised that the practice of deferring fees to the end, provided that they were then payable win or lose was quite acceptable as was a fee arrangement involving payment by instalments.

The law was then turned upside down by the case of *Thai Trading v. Taylor*, heard in the Court of Appeal; which found that 'no win no fee' arrangements were perfectly proper even if the solicitor would thereby be in breach of practice rules. The case of *Hughes v. Kingston upon Hull County Council* (unreported) decided the opposite in 1998 although in January 1999 the Law Society amended Practice Rule 8 to allow contingency fees in some cases.

These cases came to the fore as a result of concern mounting during the 1980s that those of middle income were becoming ineligible for Legal Aid (legal aid eligibility had not kept pace with inflation) but were not wealthy enough to afford to pay lawyers on a private basis, notwithstanding the high success rate of injury claims and the likely recovery of costs at the conclusion of the claim.

During that period it became clear that despite the indemnity principle many solicitors were sailing close to the wind in the fee deferral services that they offered. Some more formal scheme to fund claims was necessary.

This culminated in the Courts and Legal Services Act 1990, s. 58. This section states that conditional fee agreements made between solicitors and clients would no longer be unlawful if made under regulations to be brought in by order of thhe Lord Chancellor. From January 12, 1993 by virtue of the Solicitors Practice Rules 1990 (Contingency Fees), Rule 8 was amended to state that that it would not apply to a conditional fee agreement made under the requirements of the Courts and Legal Services Act 1990, s. 58.

The next step was to introduce regulations. Initial attempts proved unsuccessful. The first regulations were finally introduced in 1995 by the Conditional Fee Agreements Order 1995 (S.I. 1995 No. 1674). These were introduced in July 1995. They were replaced by an order of the same name in 1998 and these in turn have recently been replaced by the Conditional Fee Agreements Order 2000 (S.I. 2000 No. 823) and the Conditional Fee Agreement Regulations 2000.

23.9. What is a conditional fee?

A conditional fee agreement is one which provides that a client will only pay his or her own solicitors' fees in certain circumstances (normally if the client wins the case).

Uplift

The quid pro quo for the solicitor running the risk of non payment is that if the client is successful, the solicitor can claim a success fee (to be agreed at the beginning of the retainer) on ordinary fees. The maximum uplift specified in the regulations is 100 per cent. However, whether ultimately the uplift agreed will be recovered by the solicitor is, in the absence of agreement with the defendant, a matter for the court (see below on costs). There is a school of thought that the uplift in all cases should be 100 per cent. The evidence in support of that is that a review of the fees of a firm doing a substantial amount of conditional fee work suggested that having done about 60 cases on varying uplifts and lost only one or two the costs written off on those lost cases were greater than the amount recouped under the uplift on all the successful cases. The converse viewpoint is that the success rate of injury claims is frequently put at between 90–95 per cent. Therefore, the risk of failure on a case is between 5–10 per cent and that should therefore be the standard uplift. Initial research on post 1999 results suggests that the vast majority of claims run on conditional fee have been successful (93 per cent) and the success fee as a percentage of damages has averaged only 15 per cent.

Note that there is now no 25 per cent cap on the uplift as there was until 1999. In other words, even if the success fee represents more than 25 per cent of the damages it can still be recovered. Prior to 1999 this was not the case. Many still choose to insert that cap voluntarily. For an example of how it works see the client care conditional fee letter that refers to an agreement with a 25 per cent cap (Appendix B stock letters).

The same research has in fact suggested that the 25 per cent cap should be made compulsory again. In the light of the earlier results it may not make much practical difference. However, watch this space.

Is it a contingency fee?

Conditional fees should be differentiated from the contingency fee system which applies in other jurisdictions (most notably the United States). In a contingency fee arrangement the lawyer's fee is based on a percentage of the damages awarded to the client (commonly 25–33 per cent in the U.S.). It therefore bears no relation to the amount of work actually carried out on the client's behalf. The conditional fee is paid on the lawyer's normal hourly rate. It could be said therefore that in a contingency fee arrangement there is an incentive to settle very quickly in order to do the least possible work for the most possible return while the conditional fee arrangement there is an incentive to continue the case to run up more hours and uplift. Conversely it could be said that in a contingency fee arrangement there is more incentive to try to maximise the client's damages (because the lawyer gets a share) than in a conditional fee arrangement.

23.10. Advising the client

Before advising a client on a conditional fee you must advise them on the following (clauses 2 and 4 of Conditional Fee Agreements Regulations 2000):

(a) the particular proceedings or part of them to which the agreement relates including whether it relates to any counterclaim, appeal or proceedings to enforce a judgment or order;

(b) the circumstances in which your fees and disbursements and any part of them are payable;

(c) what, if any, payment is due:

  (i) on partial failure of the specified circumstances to occur (for example, if your client wins one part of the claim and loses another);
  (ii) irrespective of the specified circumstances occurring (for example, disbursements which have to be paid in any event);
  (iii) on termination of the agreement for whatever reason;

(d) the amounts payable or the formula to be used in calculating them, for example, your hourly rates and the success fee and whether or not there is a cap based on damages awarded (see section 4 below).

The agreement must be in writing and must be signed by both the client and the representative. If you advise orally as you will, then you must confirm that in writing.

Before you enter into an agreement you must advise your client both orally and in writing on the following matters as well:

- the circumstances in which the client may have to pay your fees in accordance with the agreement;
- the circumstances in which your client may seek assessment of the costs and how this is done;
- whether you think that the client already has insurance that would cover the cost of the proceedings being contemplated;
- whether there are other methods of funding available and how they would apply to this client in these proceedings;
- the type of funding that you recommend and whether the client should take out any insurance in connection with that method of funding.

There is also an all encompassing obligation to explain to the client the effect of a conditional fee agreement. This must include advising on the success fee as well as agreeing it and if that is divided between risk and the cash flow implications of fee deferral you should explain to the client the component parts to show how the success fee has been calculated (see below).

23.11. Basis of costs and recovery of costs

Basis of costs

The conditional fee agreement is a normal contentious business agreement and the conditional fee will be paid on your normal hourly rate, not on rates awarded by the court. These will mean that there is often a shortfall between the costs payable by the other party on the standard basis and the costs payable to you under the conditional fee agreement on an indemnity basis even before the success fee is added. This should be clearly explained to the client. Obviously, this is no different from an ordinary private fee retainer or the statutory charge in public funded cases.

23.12. Recovery of costs

General points

CPR Part 44.3A(1) provides that any additional liability, being the success fee and insurance premium, will not be assessed by the court until the conclusion of the proceedings or of the part of the proceedings to which the conditional fee agreement relates.

So much of cost consideration has proportionality as a cornerstone. Additional liabilites for costs are an exception to proportionality. CPR Part 44 PD-005 at 11.9 recognises this and makes it plain that the court will not reduce an uplift just because when it is added to the base costs which are reasonable the total then appears disproportionate.

Summary assessment

Beware of cases where you would normally expect to see summary interim cost assessments. As success is a condition precedent to recovery of costs then no costs can be payable until the conclusion since the case may ultimately be lost and the client will have no liability to you for costs and therefore even interim orders will not be payable. There is no point winning the battles if you do not win the war. Hardly CPR language but the point is well made. In such circumstances the court may make an order but not to be enforced until further order or order the paying party to pay the money into court to await the ultimate outcome of proceedings when it can either be paid to the recipient if the claim is successful or returned to the payer if the claim fails. The order will relate to the inter parties costs only. The additional amount can then be calculated simply at the end of the proceedings by applying the percentage awarded to this figure.

Summary assessment of both base cost and success fee can take place after the final hearing in those cases where the court would normally deal with costs by way of summary assessment. For the factors that the court must consider see below.

Detailed assessment

The general rules already considered concerning detailed assessment apply to the base cost in recovery of ordinary fees inter parties (see Chapter 19). However, the claimant is entitled to try to recover the success uplift and any premium paid for insurance to back the conditional fee agreement. There are certain procedural pre-requisites to this attempted recovery. These are set out in CPR Part 44.3B, they are as follows:

- If the insurance is effectively through a membership organisation and the cost of using the organisation is higher than the likely cost of an insurance premium that would have covered the risk of any cost liability to the defendant then you are unlikely to recover the extra.
- You must have provided the requisite funding information as prescribed by the rules (see Chapter 9). You will remember the provisions relating to service of form N251 Notice of Funding of Case or Claim. If you have not served the relevant notice you will not recover any additional liability on the base costs for the period during which you have breached this requirement.
- You must have complied with any practice direction or court order to disclose in any assessment process the reasons for setting the success fee at the level set (see below). This requirement is to be found in CPR Part 44.15.

Detailed assessment of the ordinary costs and success fee may be carried out at the request of either the defendant, your client, counsel or you.

Recovery of uplift and premium from the defendant

As a starting point you cannot recover that part of your success fee that has been charged to reflect the fact that there is postponement of payment of your fees and expenses. However, this can be recovered from your client. You are required to state this specifically in your agreements so that the court can determine what, if any, amount of the overall fee is attributable to the postponement.

Beyond this, the recovery of your success fee is one for court discretion. That is why it is also a requirement of the regulations that the agreement must specify why the success fee was set at the level that it was. The more detailed and reasoned you can show your original assessment to have been the more likely you are to persuade a court to allow it. Although at the time of writng this there has been no authority on the subject it may be that if, after an admission or other resolution of the liability aspect, you vary the agreement to provide for a lower uplift from that date the court will be more likely to allow the initial higher amount as it shows that you acted reasonably as soon as some of the risk evaporated. However, it is very early days and you should ensure that you examine any decisions that are forthcoming as they will give guidance on the approach the court will take.

CPR Part 44 PD-005 gives some guidance to the court on the factors to consider:

- The risk of non payment
- Who is paying for the disbursements as the action progresses?
- What other means of financing were open to the client? In other words, if a pre-event legal expenses policy would have covered this claim but the client was prevailed upon not to use this then expect a hard time justifying any success fee. If there was good reason make that clear, such as the legal expense insurers insisting on use of their panel solicitors and the nearest were 100 miles away.

The one area which at the time of writing it is safe to say is already steeped in controversy and uncertainty is the recoverability of premium. The week of writing this chapter was the week that the case of *Caffery* was being heard in the Court of Appeal. Despite what seems to have been clear government intention in drafting, defendants are arguing that if a claim is settled before issue no insurance premium is recoverable as the claimant did not need the security of cost protection until issue of proceedings. The initial court approach seems to be to reject this argument that overlooks at least four fundamental points:

(1) That your client wants peace of mind and security on costs from day one. It should be remembered that the client is already coming to terms with one trauma caused by the potential negligence of the defendant and wishes to avoid a second; and

(2) That insurance premiums are based on a broad spread of risk. If only cases that required issue needed to have insurance then the likelihood is that this would represent the high risk cases and the insurance premiums would then be enormous and in many cases unaffordable. Current premiums have been set taking on board the entire risk spectrum to include weighting for the fact that some cases will settle before issue; and

(3) At the time of taking out the insurance the defendant's response to the claim is unknown. Whilst the CPR, and protocols in particular, have seen a change of attitude by defendants there are still cases where despite clear liability an admission is only made late in the day. Why should the claimant not have cost security from day one in those cases?; and

(4) Disbursements must be incurred pre-issue. If subsequently a claim is defended and proceedings are issued which fail the claimant is then left without cover for those.

The Court of Appeal, who invited Senior Costs Judge Hurst to sit with them, have reserved judgment on the reasonableness of success fees and premiums. They have suggested that success uplifts are likely to be much lower than figures currently used and may, if the letter of claim results in an immediate admission of liability, even be nil. The final decision is likely to have huge ramifications for the future of conditional fee funding and therefore the future of injury claims. Given the importance of the decision the Court of Appeal has invited representations from interested parties.

However, the Court of Apeal has already decided that section 29 of the Access to Justice Act 1999 permits recovery of premiums for policies taken out prior to the issue of proceedings, irrespective of whether substantive proceedings are subsequently issued.

By the time this book is published the Court of Appeal decision will be known in full. More than anything else certainty is required. At the moment, the advice you have to give to clients is confusing, illogical and uncertain. All traits that as a profession solicitors are trying to shed in dealings with clients.

Assessment of uplift by the client, counsel or you

The rule is simply put, perhaps belying the difficulty of the task. CPR Part 48.8(3) states that:

> "Where the court is considering a percentage increase, whether on the application of the legal representative under Part 44.16 or on the application of the client, the court will have regard to all the relevant factors as they reasonably appeared to the solicitor or counsel when the conditional fee agreement was entered into or varied."

There are really two situations when the court will be asked to consider its role under CPR Part 48.3(3). The first is where the client wants to challenge the base cost or the success fee or both; the second is where the court has disallowed part of the success fee inter parties and you or counsel still wish to recover that portion from client.

In the first situation the client must be pro-active and apply to the court to reduce the uplift. In the notice so doing the client must set out his or her reasons for stating that there should be a reduction and state what percentage should be substituted for the agreed amount.

In the second situation the court will already have determined what additional cost to allow inter parties and in so doing will have reduced the uplift. If you wish to pursue recovery of the portion not allowed inter parties then you can only do so with court permission because the Conditional Fee Agreements Regulations 2000 state that the agreement must specify that any uplift disallowed against the defendant can only be sought from the client if the court is satisfied that this should be the case. This is regardless of whether the assessment has been summary or detailed.

CPR Part 44.16 provides that in such a situation the court has power to adjourn to enable your client, if he or she is not present, to be notified of your request. Part 44 PD-014 then sets out the procedure for you and any counsel whom you have instructed on a conditional basis to try to recover any disallowed uplift. The procedure is different depending upon whether the assessment leading to the reduction was summary or detailed. The reason for this is that the detailed assessment procedure will have involved the defendant serving notice of objections to your bill which will have put you on notice of any dispute on uplift, whereas arguments on costs are not known nor are they relevant in advance of the hearing leading to the summary assessment. The rules for detailed assessment are complicated and you should study them in detail to ensure that you comply and enable counsel, in appropriate cases, to comply with them. There are time scales for notifying counsel and your client and requirements that you provide various explanations to your client. These are clearly set out in CPR Part 44. For example, within 14 days of receipt of the points of dispute that the dispute exists, you must explain to your client what it means and the effect of the objection being upheld and inform your client that he or she has a right to attend the hearing. Time and experience will make you familiar with the rules, for now know that the rules exist, where to find them and make sure that you read them each time a dispute on uplift seems likely.

CPR Part 48 PD-006 explains how the court will approach any dispute between you and your client over uplift. The court will consider:

- the risk that fees or expenses would not be payable at all;
- the cash flow disadvantages (this is the portion that you can never recover inter parties);
- whether there is a cap on the uplift in the agreement (see above);
- whether there is also a conditional agreement between you and counsel;
- who has paid for the disbursements as the action has progressed.

When considering these factors the court will bear in mind the situation as it would have been for you or counsel at the time of entering into the agreement.

Note also that your best hope probably lies under points 2, 3 and 4 as the other two factors will have been considered when looking at the inter party liability and presumably have failed to attract court sympathy. You may also find particular difficulties if you try to enforce a disallowed percentage against a patient or a minor. It is hard to see a court allowing any significant reduction of damage for uplift irrecoverable inter parties.

23.13. Counsel's fees

You may wish to consider what is the best way to deal with funding of counsel required to assist in a claim. You can either do this on an ordinary private retainer with fees falling due as incurred or agree that counsel will also deal with the claim on a conditional fee basis.

If you opt for the former then you will have to pay these yourself or make it clear to the client what options there are, why you believe that a private instruction is best and that this means the client will have to pay the fees as they arise. As many clients cannot afford counsel's fees the likelihood is that you will be funding those. At first blush, the private retainer of counsel appears unattractive. However, it can be beneficial. One of the major concerns of conditional fee funding is that a solicitor may not be or be seen to be objective. After all, the solicitor has a vested interest in outcome. What of a difficult case on liability that is "all or nothing" with sustantial work in progress where out of the blue a low quantum offer comes in? No sigh of relief? No silent prayer that the client will accept the offer? Of course not, but wouldn't it be beneficial to have the view of someone who has no financial interest at all in the outcome?

If you decide that financial considerations are paramount and a conditional fee agreement with counsel is the best course the first stage must be to explain this and the ramifications to the client. The next is to ascertain that your chosen counsel does do conditional fee work and if so is prepared to take on this specific case. Some counsel will want to charge for a preliminary vetting of the case. Try to avoid this. Many specialist counsel will do this for nothing and some chambers publicise this as a route to getting work. However, the Bar Council still produce a standard "terms of retainer for preliminary work where retainer on a conditional fee basis is contemplated". Rarely do you get paid for deciding whether or not to take a case on this basis. You may decide that counsel should be in the same position.

If counsel does take on the case then it will be on the same basis as you, namely if the case fails then neither of you will be paid for the work done. Most counsel will wish the agreement between you to be on the basis of the Association of Personal Injury Lawyers (see Chapter 30) and Personal Injury Bar Association draft agreement. This is reproduced at 7B-25-34 in volume 2 of the White Book 2001. Even if you or counsel do not wish to use it do study it to see the matters covered. Perhaps most important is to agree counsel's uplift as this will have to come out of your uplift.

23.14. Paying the defendant's costs

A conditional fee agreement has no effect on costs to be paid to the defendant and the client will still be liable for these if the case is lost. This is a large deterrent to many clients who look for risk-free litigation in a conditional fee arrangement. As a result, an insurance policy offering protection against a cost liability is essential. Some solicitors are prepared to take a risk on cases they regard as sure fire winners and effectively self insure. In other words, if the case failed they would pay the defendant's costs. Counsel of caution is that sure fire winners have lost and insurance is a necessary safety net.

23.15. Insurance

As mentioned above, your client can buy insurance to protect against the risk of a cost liability if the claim fails. The choice must be that of the client based on the advice that you must give. There is even specific provision in the Law Society model conditional fee agreement for details of the insurance and the advice given to be inserted. Whilst you are not expected to operate like a broker considering every product there are various on the market.

The first scheme was Accident Line Protect, an insurance scheme arranged by the Law Society on the launch of conditional fees. However, when it became apparent that conditional fees were here to stay others moved into the market. With the changes that have taken place to the Accident Line scheme the continuation of this policy is now only available to a limited number of solicitors on an approved panel. If you are on that panel then beware of writing any insurance through a different insurer as membership of Accident Line requires you to write all free work (work that is not passed to you with insurance already arranged) with Accident Line Protect even if the case is not one referred to you under the scheme. For more detail see Chapter 30. The rationale behind this is that if you use various schemes then you could load all your high risk cases to one insurer and give all the low risk ones to another. The first insurer would suffer as premiums are set on the basis of a spread of good and bad risk cases. Here the weighting of risk would be much higher.

Many other companies now offer after the event insurance. The various providers are too numerous to mention. Not all provide the same type of cover and therefore you should be wary of making a decision solely on the basis of cost. For example, some may cover counsel's fees and some may provide a lower cap on financial cover. Do read the small print to ascertain precisely what it is that you are recommending to your client.

The only certainty about all insurances now on offer is that premiums have moved a long way from the initial Accident Line Protect fee of £85 regardless of the nature of the claim. The practical reality is that it will usually be you and not your client who pays the premium. Indeed, many schemes actually envisage this, advertising the scheme to potential customers on this basis and offering solicitors who use the insurance favourable rates with a specific bank with whom the insurer has reached some kind of agreement. Whilst obviously you would wish to write as many conditional fee agreements as possible do pause for thought in advance and plan for the cash flow problems that may arise intially when you are funding sizeable premiums and accruing work in progress that has yet to be turned into recovered profit costs.

23.16. Risk assessment

Comments made earlier about recovery of success uplift illustrate how important that it is that you carry out a detailed and reasoned risk assessment. However, the need to do so is far more fundamental than mere recoverability of uplift. The major reason for carrying out an exhaustive assessment is that you do not wish to spend your time doing work for which ultimately you are not paid.

There is no guaranteed way to ensure that you only take on successful claims. However, it is imperative that you make the correct assessment nearly every time.

As is apparent from earlier chapters some cases require a great deal of investigation on either liability causation or quantum issues before one can be reasonably certain that the case is viable. Some even go to trial. On the other hand, some are more easy to assess, assuming that your client is telling the truth (a risk factor should be built in for the possibility that this is not the case). A passenger injury claim, where the passenger was wearing a seatbelt and the driver was both qualifed and in a fit state to drive the car is as close to a home banker as claims go.

However reasoned you wish your approach to be a lot will still depend on gut instinct, perhaps more eloquently described as the application of experience to a particular set of facts. Various commentators have suggested a formula or approach to adopt. None are foolproof. A nice rule of thuumb for borderline cases that are causing you to procrastinate is to decline to take them on. If you are in that much doubt before even starting it can only get worse. Better to pass now than to do so many wasted hours later.

The more injury work you do the more you will be able to make the first assessment which is "Do I want to take this case on whatever the success uplift?". If, and only if you answer yes to this, do you need to look at the level of success fee. You may still need to revisit your earlier decision if the uplift that you think you will need is above 100 per cent as you will be able to recover 100 per cent only.

When looking at success fee it may be best to talk a case over with someone else. You may be lucky enough to have someone at your firm to help. Otherwise, provided that you bear in mind client confidentiality it may be something, if you are a member of the Association of Personal Injury Lawyers you could discuss with other local members. Another option is to have a general chat with counsel. If you send a lot of injury work to a certain barrister then he or she may wish to maintain the relationship and may not be averse to a general discussion on a set of facts. This may serve to crystallize your thoughts. The longer the decision takes you and the harder it is the more it suggests that the case is not one to be taken on a conditional fee basis.

The Law Society has produced a survival guide which may be of some assistance and there are specialist texts that suggest ways of undertaking a risk assessment. At the end of the day though the decision is yours. If you do decide to take a case at a set success fee and the client tries to seek a reduction of that stand firm. If you do not then you may as well not have undertaken the assessment in the first place. Do not let desire or need for work persuade you to take on cases where the risks are too high or to take on cases with too low a success fee for fear that the client may go elsewhere. Work in progress is only useful if converted into profit cost.

The cost in both solicitors' time and disbursements in actually doing the work to assess the viability of the case can make the case itself uneconomic. The reason that contingency fees are so successful in America is that although the risks are high the possible rewards (particularly in large cases) are also very high, amounting to tens or hundreds of times what the lawyer would have obtained if charging an hourly rate. For example, if your hourly rate is £200 per hour and you spend 50 hours in preparing a case your normal fee would be £10,000. However, on a contingency fee basis of 25 per cent if your client recovered £750,000 (which is by no means a large personal injury payment in the U.S.) the fee the lawyer would obtain would be £187,500. In the same case taken on a conditional fee basis the most the solicitor would obtain on a 100 per cent contingency would be £20,000. If the case is settled quickly or the damages are higher the differences become even more marked.

Fighting fund

There is no doubt that if you take cases on a conditional fee basis you will occasionally get it wrong and lose. You will need to consider this very carefully to ensure that your firm can afford not to be paid in some cases and the amount of success fee you will need to charge on other cases to compensate for that. It is a good idea to start a 'fighting fund' so that, say, five per cent of the costs on successful cases are paid into a separate account and can be used to cover nominal costs (and disbursements) in cases where you are not successful. This may be feasible in larger firms where the turnover of cases provides the cash flow to pay out profits. You will also need to consider how to deal with the fighting fund in the firm's accounts.

Cash flow

You or the firm will also need carefully to consider the effect on its cash flow of the fact that conditional fee cases are not paid until the end and your firm will have to bear the expenses of paying solicitors (and possibly funding disbursements) for a number of years before seeing any return. Also, the value of fees will be less because some of the work done will be at a rate that when received has been devalued by intervening inflation.

23.17. When can a conditional fee be charged?

For the purposes of the personal injury lawyer conditional fees are applicable to all cases. This includes professional negligence cases where the negligence arises from the original injury claim. In fact, section 58 of the Courts and Legal Services Act 1990 as substituted by section 27 of the Access to Justice Act excludes only a few types of process from the conditional fee regime, mostly being criminal or matrimonial cases.

23.18. Terminating the retainer

Termination can be by either the client or you. The standard Law Society draft agreement provides for both situations.

The client can end the agreement at any stage. Otherwise, the entering of such a form of retainer would fetter the freedom of choice of representation to which the client is entitled. However, termination is not without consequence. At your election the client must either:

(1) pay your basic charges (solicitor/own client), your disbursements and any counsel's fees when you ask for them, inevitably in such a situation that is likely to be straightaway, or

(2) pay your basic charges, your disbursements, counsel's fees and any success fee if the client carries on with the claim and wins.

In other words, even on termination of the agreement you have to carry out further risk assessment. Often, the choice does not exist in reality because you know that the client does not have the means to pay there and then. If you are going to wait to be paid and to have any chance of payment the client must improve his or her financial situation first you may as well opt for the second option.

Your right to terminate is more restricted. It arises in four types of situations.

(1) The first is where the client:

- Fails to give you proper instruction, or
- Asks you to work in an improper or unreasonable way, or
- Deliberately misleads you, or
- Does not co-operate with you, or
- Does not go to a medical or other expert examination that you have arranged and which is necessary to progress the claim.

If you terminate the retainer in this situation then the position over recovery of your costs is exactly the same as if the client terminates the retainer.

(2) The second situation is where you believe that the prospects of success are,

or have become, such that the client is unlikely to win. In that situation the conditional part of the agreement cuts in and fees are not payable save in respect of disbursements if it was agreed that the client would pay these. If counsel was not on a conditional fee agreement then his or her fees count as disbursements for these purposes.

(3) The third situation is where the client rejects your advice about settlement. In such a situation the client must pay the basic charges, disbursements and any counsel's fees now and pay the success fee if the client carries on and wins the claim for damages.

(4) The final situation in which the agreement terminates is upon the death of your client. If this happens you will be entitled to recover basic charges up to death from the client's estate. If the client's personal representatives wish to pursue the claim with you on a conditional fee basis then a fresh agreement will be required.

23.19. A final word

Conditional fees are a rapidly evolving funding option. It is difficult enough trying to make accurate risk assessments but at the moment the relatively new CPR provisions on conditional fee cost recovery add to your burden. There is little or no authority on levels of success fee recovery and so no pattern has emerged as to the court approach. Insurers seem geared up for battle and it seems that any authorities are likely to be hard earned.

Amidst relative uncertainty you must ensure that you continue to offer the correct advice for each client who approaches you. It is therefore very important that you understand the rules both of the Law Society and of the court. Whilst the answers to some of the concerns raised by practitioners may not yet be known it is important that you are in a position to advise the client of any uncertainty and how that might impact on his or her claim. Make sure that any advice given is confirmed in writing.

At the introduction of conditional fees in 1995 there was a view that personal injury litigation would now lay the golden egg. Experience, some of it bitter, has proved that this view was simplistic. The amendments since introduction have further complicated matters. Time will tell if conditional fees represent a panacea or simply a post Legal Aid placebo.

23.20. A first word on collective conditional fee agreements

Introduced by the Collective Conditional Fee Agreements Regulations 2000 which has been in force from November 30, 2000 these are agreements that do not refer to a specific claim but are designed for fees payable on a common basis in relation to a class of proceedings or, if they cover more than one type of proceeding, then on a common basis within class.

In general terms, you are most likely to encounter agreements such as this when acting for a bulk institutional referrer of work, such as a trade union or legal expense insurer. In such cases there will be a collective agreement between funder and panel solicitor which specifies when the panel solicitors fees are payable. The purpose of the introduction of this type of ageement is to facilitate conditional fee work that may be provided in significant numbers by the same referrer to the same solicitors. Instead of having to do an individual conditional fee agreement with the specific client that client will be covered by the collective agreement.

However, if you receive work under such an agreement you must still provide certain advice when accepting instructions in respect of a specific proceeding. In essence, you must advise the individual client of the circumstances when he or she may be liable for your fees and provide any further advice that the client specifically requests. As you may have been instructed from a central source then you must confirm your instructions to the individual client in writing.

Similar provisions to those relating to individual conditional fee agreements apply on detailed or summary assessment when you are seeking an uplift, particularly the requirement that court confirmation of any uplift between client and solicitor that is not allowed inter parties is required.

As the agreement may appear standard there is a danger of setting a standard success uplift. The regulations try to prevent this by indicating that if you receive instructions under such an agreement you must prepare and retain a written statement setting out:

- your assessment of the probability of the chance of the success uplift becoming payable; and
- your assessment of the amount of the success uplift having regard to your risk assessment; and
- your reasons by specific reference to your risk assessment for setting the uplift at the level that you do.

At the time of writing the market place has yet to be flooded with such agreements although word is that many bulk providers are actively drafting such agreements for introduction in the near future. Given the move towards centralisation of instruction, with new referrers emerging in the market almost every day by the time of any subsequent edition of this book a lot more practical experience of the workings and difficulties of collective agreements is likely to exist.

24. Persons under a Disability

If the claimant is a minor or Mental Health Act 1983 patient then he or she will be regarded as being under a disability. As such:

- the person cannot sue in his or her own name, but has to sue through the name of an adult (the "litigation friend");
- the court must approve any settlement of the claimant's claims. This is to ensure that the claimant is not being taken advantage of, and that the claim is being settled for a proper sum;
- the claimant's solicitor must have any costs sought from the claimant approved by the court. Once again, this is to protect the claimant from exploitation (by a solicitor who might otherwise overcharge). However, it is customary for solicitor, to waive any charges over and above those recovered from the defendant.

24.1. Litigation friend

Since a claimant under a disability cannot sue in his or her own name, a willing adult must be named as the "litigation friend" and assume responsibility for the costs of the action. Usually, the litigation friend will be a parent, although any other adult friend is competent to act. The solicitor should write to the litigation friend, pointing out the potential liabilities, and explaining that the litigation friend's role is to act as an officer of the court in conducting the claimant's litigation. The mere presence of the litigation friend gives the defendant some security as to costs. Thus, the litigation friend assumes responsibility for the costs of the action, although there is a right of indemnity against the person under a disability. Because of this costs liability, the litigation friend should not be treated as a mere cipher by the claimant's solicitor; instructions and advice should be sought as though the litigation friend were a claimant. Certainly all usual costs information must be provided.

When you write to the litigation friend, you should ask him or her to confirm:

(a) date of birth (so there is no doubt the litigation friend is over 18) and

(b) that there is no conflict of interest with the claimant (for instance, as would be the case if the person under a disability had been injured whilst a passenger in a car driven by the negligent litigation friend).

The litigation friend will also have to sign a certificate of suitability agreeing to act in this capacity. The form requires the litigation friend to confirm that he or she:

- consents to act as a litigation friend;
- believes the claimant to be a child or a patient. If the latter, then an explanation must be given of the reasons for so believing;
- is competent to act and has no contrary interest;
- undertakes to pay any costs which the claimant may be ordered to pay in the proceedings subject to a right to be repaid from the assets of the claimant.

It is important that you explain the full responsibilities of the litigation friend, particularly the potential cost consequences.

There is now just one form regardless of whether the claim proceeds in the country or High Court. This is Form N235. A precedent is printed at 15.

24.2. Protocol compliance and proceedings

Any claim for a person under a disability must be conducted in the same way that any other personal injury claim would be presented. There must be full compliance with the protocol. It is wise in the letter of claim or when an acknowledgement to that letter is received to indicate that the claimant is pursuing the claim by litigation friend.

If the claim cannot be settled under the pre-action protocol then proceedings will be necessary. The procedure for initiating proceedings will be unchanged save that the certificate of suitability must be filed and served and the title of the action will appear as:

For children
"A.B., a child by C.D. his/her litigation friend"

For patients
"A.B. by C.D. his/her litigation friend"

The certificate of suitability must also be served on the child's parent or guardian, if that is not the litigation friend. In those circumstances a certificate of service of the certificate of suitability must also be filed.

When a child reaches age 18 or a patient ceases to be a patient

As soon as a child reaches age 18 the litigation friend's appointment ceases. There is no requirement that the child obtain a formal order discharging the litigation friend; it happens automatically. However, the claimant must then serve a notice on the other parties to the claim stating that the appointment of the litigation friend has ceased, providing an address for service and indicating whether the claim is to be continued. Failure to do this within 28 days can have draconian sanctions as the court can strike out the claim on the application of a party. The requirement for the matter to come before the court rather than there being any automatic procedure for strike out is so that the court can ascertain whether the claimant wishes to continue by positive rather than negative act. There is no precedent notice in the rules.

If a child does serve the requisite notice and wishes to continue then from the date of the notice the title of the action will be:

"A.B. (formerly a child but now of full age)"

If the child does not serve notice then the litigation friend can do so. If the claimant on reaching age 18 has not served the notice within 28 days this suggests lack of interest in pursuing the claim and the litigation friend may well wish to serve notice because the cost liability of the litigation friend continues until the notice is served (either by the claimant or the litigation friend) confirming the litigation friend has ceased acting. The litigation friend therefore has a vested financial interest in ceasing to act. This may at least save the litigation friend the cost of any application made by the defendant to strike out the claim.

The procedure is different for a patient who during the course of a claim ceases to be a patient. In this situation an order of the court is required to remove the litigation friend and until one is obtained the appointment of the litigation friend continues. The requisite order can be sought by the claimant (former patient) the litigation friend or another party.

As for a child, once the litigation friend has ceased to act (in other words, after an order has been made to terminate that appointment) the patient must serve the same notice of termination with the same possible sanctions for failure to do so.

When a claimant becomes a patient during proceedings

Should a party who was previously capable of acting without a litigation friend become a patient during the course of proceedings then no party may take any step in the claim without the permission of the court until a litigation friend has been appointed. Any step that is taken, whether because the party taking it did not know that the claimant had become a patient or for any other reason, has no effect unless the court orders that it should.

24.3. Settlement of a case involving a child or patient

Any settlement of a claim, whether before or after issue of proceedings, must be approved by the court who will want to approve the amount being paid in settlement of the claim, any amount to be deducted from the settlement for your costs and what should be done with the damages until the person under a disability becomes capable of dealing with their affairs.

The procedure for approval does vary depending upon whether the settlement is reached before contested proceedings under CPR Part 7 have been commenced or after the commencement of such a claim.

If proceedings are already issued then the procedure will be by way of issue of a CPR Part 23 application within those proceedings. If Part 7 proceedings have not been issued then CPR Part 8 process will be required. The procedure is the same whether the claim is within the country or High Court.

Procedure

Pre-issue

A Part 8 claim form is required (N208). Brief details of the nature of the claim should be given. The claim must include a specific request for approval of the settlement reached. This means that the actual terms of settlement must be set out. The most convenient way to do this, although it is not essential, is to append a draft order to the application (see precedent 16). At long last, the convention that the application for approval should not cite the figure so that the court could consider the matter reaching an appropriate figure in splendid isolation has formally gone.

The Practice Direction to Part 21 summarises the information that the court will require. In fact, this does no more than codify the information that the court has always required. That information is:

- Whether the settlement is based on full liability, and if not the extent to which liability is admitted.
- The age and any occupation of the person under the disability.
- Confirmation that the litigation friend approves the settlement.
- A brief description of the accident circumstances. If liability is to some extent in dispute then this will need to be more detailed.
- The relevant medical evidence relied upon.
- Counsel's opinion. This will be necessary in all cases. It is therefore worth obtaining this as soon as you have final approved medical evidence rather than waiting for any offer so that you have it ready when any offer is put. If liability is in dispute then the advice should also deal with any liability apportionment. Curiously, unless the instructions are sufficiently set out in the advice then a copy of the instructions must also be provided.
- A schedule of losses both past and anticipated in the future.
- If liability is in dispute in a road accident then the police accident report

book and details of any convictions arising from the accident should be included.

Although the rule does not specifically say so you also need to lodge evidence of the offer, for example a copy of the defendant's letter making the proposal. If the offer is by telephone you should ask that it be confirmed in writing. This is because in the simplest cases you will find that the court armed with clear agreement between the parties is likely to deal with the approval without a formal hearing as a paper exercise. If there is no evidence of agreement then plainly the court will be unable to do this and either there will be a delay whilst the evidence is submitted or the court will serve the proceedings in the usual way again wasting time until the defendant acknowledges the proceedings and confirms the agreement. A paper consideration is not always possible. For example, in serious injury cases, claims involving a dispute over liability, where the court has concerns over the amount of the settlement proposed, or where the injuries include scarring it is almost inevitable that the court will wish there to be a hearing. Broadly, this seems to be a matter for discretion of the judge before whom the proceedings initially come.

Post issue of proceedings

As stated above, when seeking approval of settlement terms within already issued proceedings then a Part 23 application (N244) should be used. The application should ask for approval of a settlement received the terms of which are set out in a draft order appended to the application. At the same time, you should ensure that all medical evidence and counsel's opinion are lodged with the application. Again, if there is a dispute over liability and the settlement is on apportioned terms then you should ensure that any witness statements disclosed are before the court and the police accident report book and details of convictions arising from the accident are included.

The court will then carry out the same exercise as in the Part 8 procedure and the approval will either be dealt with as a paper exercise or it will consider it at a formal hearing.

The hearing

If a hearing is required do ensure that you prepare properly for it. That includes advising both the litigation friend and the claimant, both of whom should attend in a child approval, of the purpose of the hearing. You must remember that to many people a court will be an intimidating place even for what is an uncontested hearing that will bring the claim to an end with the claimant receiving damages.

It is wise to prepare a brief outline of the accident circumstances, the injuries and the cases pertinent on quantum.

Make sure that you have the medical reports and counsel's opinion handy in case the copies have not reached the court file.

It is rare for the defendant to attend a hearing unless there is an apportionment of liability where the defendant's explanation for its position may be helpful to the court in deciding whether the parties have resolved this issue reasonably when determining the agreed percentage of full damages.

The most usual reason for the court declining to approve a settlement is that either the medical condition is not sufficiently clear form the medical evidence filed or that when the claimant is asked, as inevitably happens, by the court whether the medical evidence correctly sets out the position either the litigation friend or sometimes the claimant answers "Yes, but I still have . . . " and then describes ongoing injuries that the reports before the court assure the court have been resolved. In both situations the approval is likely to be adjourned to enable further medical evidence to be obtained.

However, if the court is unable to approve the settlement because it disagrees with the apportionment of liability and that cannot be resolved then if the approval came before the court under Part 8 it now contains disputed evidence and the court may well decide that the claim is no longer suitable for Part 8 procedure. The claim is then likely to be allocated to track and directions given to progress the matter.

On this point it is worth remembering that usually any Part 8 claim is deemed to be a multi track claim. Applications solely for approval are not caught by this provision and unless the situation above arises will never be allocated to track.

If the application arises within existing proceedings then the court may not have to give directions provided that allocation has already taken place as the claim can continue under the already ordered timescale. The court must consider whether any further directions are needed. If directions have not been given then the court must then give them to progress the action. This may include tracking the claim and allocating a trial window.

Although it is not always the case often if the court refuses to approve a settlement the discussions immediately after the hearing lead to revised proposals that are acceptable. Certain courts leave the parties in no doubt as to what they regard as acceptable terms and even suggest a brief adjournment to enable a few telephone calls to be made. A prime example of robust case management.

General points

Whether the approval takes place by way of court deskwork or hearing the court will always need to see the claimant's birth certificate in a child approval and in any case a Court Funds form (CFO 320) to deal with the investment of the money, any payment out and what happens when capacity is obtained by the person under the disability.

24.4. Settlement

When the case has not been issued

Most personal injury claims are settled without recourse to the issuing of a CPR Part 7 claim. Claims by persons under a disability are no exception to this generalisation. However, when the claimant is a person under a disability then you must bring the claim before the court so that it can approve the terms of settlement. This must be done however small the amount involved.

In practice, if the sums involved are trivial (*e.g.* under £500) it is not uncommon for the insurers to pay the settlement moneys to the claimant's parents, and to accept their discharge as a receipt, alternatively, the insurers may call the offer an *ex gratia* payment. These solutions have the advantage that the funds will be paid immediately and not held in court, however they are risky and should be avoided. Counsel of perfection is that you should always advise the litigation friend to seek court approval.

From the litigation friend's point of view, it is better if the claim is approved by the court; that ensures that the claimant cannot later sue for under-settling the case. The defendant will also be better protected if the court approves the settlement; the person under a disability will be bound by the terms of settlement, and will be unable to reopen the case at a later date. So, you should resist any suggestion of an informal settlement, and instead should insist that an Infant Approval Part 8 claim be issued. This is especially so if there is the slightest possibility of a future deterioration in the person under a disability's medical condition (*e.g.* a risk of epilepsy because of concussion).

As the procedure is one required by the court you should seek to recover costs of the approval process even if the claim is a small claim as approval is a cost you would not incur in an ordinary small claim (see the case of *K v. Grocutt* [2001] 2 C.L. 48).

Procedure

Accepting a payment into court

If a person under a disability wants to accept money paid into court, an application or summons will still have to be issued. The person under a disability cannot simply withdraw the money from court. The usual procedure applies: issue an application asking for the proposed terms of settlement (including payment out of the money in court if any payment out of sums is required now) to be approved. Specimen orders are set out in Precedents 16 and 17. There is no need to serve the usual notice of acceptance of payment in on the other side, because the application or summons will have to be issued to accept the money. However, to ensure that there is no adverse cost sanction it is well to notify the defendant within the Part 36 payment period that, subject to court approval, the Part 36 payment is being accepted.

Court of Protection

If the claimant is a patient and the action is brought with the sanction of the Court of Protection then no compromise can be made without that Court's approval. The damages will also have to be paid to the Court of Protection. Depending on the amount involved, it may well be the case that the damages have to be administered by the Court of Protection not the High or county Court. (See CPR Part 21 21PD-011 and form N 292)

24.5. Costs

In the same way that the settlement figures must be approved by the court, so too must the costs if you wish to erode the settlement figure in respect of costs.

Inter-party costs

The typical Infant Approval Application will state that the defendant pays the claimant's costs, to be assessed if not agreed, on the standard basis.

Until relatively recently, the person under a disability's costs had to be assessed; there was no way that the parties could simply agree their costs, and have that agreement rubber-stamped by the court. That is no longer the position. The parties can agree their costs (*i.e.* as between claimant and defendant, but not between a person under a disability and own solicitor) and have those costs approved by the court. In practice, that is what claimant's solicitors will usually attempt to do. The usual procedure is to state in the Infant Approval Summons the amount agreed as costs so that the court can consider the level of costs, and then agree that assessment can be dispensed with. The claimant's solicitor will also be expected to waive any additional costs (*i.e.* "the claimant solicitor waiving all further costs").

In a legal aid case, there is a further complication. Under reg. 106 (see Chapter 23) of the 1989 Regs, the Legal Aid Board must assess costs that are agreed without taxation. In practice, this is likely a formality, fulfilled by completing and submitting form CLAIM 2

Solicitor and own client costs

What of the costs between the claimant and you? It may well be (and often is the case) that the you will accept the costs being paid by the defendant in full and final settlement. In other words, you will waive the excess that could be recovered. If so, that will be recorded in the order. However, if you are not prepared to accept the amount of costs being paid by the defendant, then you will have to have the costs assessed. The position will depend upon whether the claimant is a private client, or legally aided:

(a) in a legal aid case, the order will simply be that your costs be assessed on a public funded basis

(b) in a non public funded case the court must order a detailed assessment of any claim for costs from a child or patient to his solicitor. If this situation arises then the court should at the same time conduct an assessment of any costs payable by the defendant. This is not a particularly convenient arrangement for you because it puts off the time for payment of the inter party costs as those must then be subject to the delay of assessment. There is also the risk that the defendant will make a good offer and therefore the costs of the inter party assessment may be irrecoverable. Whilst it is plainly arguable that that should not be the case as you are compelled by court rules to use this procedure the position is not ideal. The procedure also compels you to involve a costs draftsperson. Again, this fee may be recoverable as part of the costs of assessment but there remains the same risk.

Taken as a whole, you may well conclude that it is not worth pursuing any costs from the child or patient over and above those recoverable form the defendant. In practical terms, this is why so many solicitors waive the right to any further costs. The other practical reason for reaching the decision is that it creates that valuable commodity called goodwill upon which all injury lawyers should depend (see CPR Part 48.5 for more detail).

24.6. Investment and paying out of the settlement money

The court will have to order what is to happen to the settlement money.

Often, the order will provide for relatively small sums to be paid out to the litigation friend to cover expenses (*e.g.* loss of wages when attending solicitor's offices for appointments, etc.). Normally, that money can be paid out direct to the litigation friend, without difficulty. Obviously, if the money is not yet in court then that sum can be paid to you for the litigation friend and the balance can be paid into court.

It is as regards the rest of the settlement money that the difficulties are likely to arise. The courts take a cautious attitude. Clearly, if the sums are large, then they will have to be invested. But, many solicitors and parents feel that it is not unreasonable to hand modest sums (*e.g.* £2,000 or so) to parents, so they can administer the money for the child's benefit. However, this is not the attitude taken by the courts. Only if the sums are trivial (*e.g.* £150 or so) is the court likely to agree that the money can be paid to the parent or guardian. Even then, the court may prefer that the solicitor buy National Savings Certificates for the child. Perhaps the conservative approach is the preferred one. Increasingly, requests are made for expensive items. Often, there is a good reason, such as a computer to assist with school work. However, closer consideration reveals that this is often something that the parent or guardian would ordinarily purchase with their funds rather than ask the child to pay. Is it then right, simply because the child has a fund, to seek to use that money? It is a matter for court discretion but you should advise the litigation friend of the likely refusal to pay out substantial sums unless there is a genuine need. In such circumstances the child is likely to be a ward of the Court of Protection anyway and the application must be made to that court.

The approach does not seem to vary even when dealing with older children, although again there may be regional variations. Applications for payment out can be made throughout the period of court investment and not just at the time of approval. If you are asked to make an application for a specific need to ensure that to assist the court you collate, or your client does, quotes for whatever expenditure is deemed necessary.

The Court Funds Office Form CFO 320 provides for the approving court to indicate the investment requirements. In most cases this is likely to be capital growth with any interest accruing to be paid back in to the fund. This is administered centrally and not at the local Court approving the settlement. In Court of Protection matters that court will administer the fund.

24.7. The order

Once the court has made the order, it will have to be drawn up in the usual way, by the court. It should be drawn up promptly however, the defendant should not await receipt of the order before paying any money into court.

Refer to Precedent 16 and 17 for specimen orders in typical cases.

Some courts like to see a majority direction, that is an order for automatic payment out to the child on his or her 18th birthday without the need for a further order, within the body of the order itself. You will see this in precedent 16. However, this is not strictly necessary as there is space for the court to give such a direction within the body of Court funds form CFO 320. Find out what practice your local court adopts.

24.8. After the approval

It may be many years before payment out is to take place. A lot can take place. Your client may move. So may you. It is therefore important that as well as ensuring that your file is stored properly and until at least six years post the child becoming 18 you also take steps now to ensure that the payment out oes without a problem.

To achieve this it is wise to send a copy of the approval order to the litigation friend suggesting that it is kept safe and that if there is ever need to contact the court the case number is given. Suggest also that either the child or someone on his or her behalf contacts the court a month or so before the 18th birthday to check that everything is geared up ready for payment out. The final, and most important piece of advice must be that if the child or litigation friend move then the court is notified of the new address as otherwise any payment out will be to the wrong address.

25. Fatal Accidents

25.1. The two causes of action

There are two different causes of action that arise on a death. The first is on behalf of the estate of the deceased (the Law Reform claim), and the other is on behalf of the dependants (the Fatal Accidents claim). The two are distinct: the former is on behalf of the estate, the latter on behalf of the dependants.

25.2. The Law Reform claim

This claim is brought on behalf of the deceased, under the Law Reform (Miscellaneous Provisions) Act 1934. It will cover:

(a) financial loss incurred by the deceased prior to death (*e.g.* lost wages and expenses whilst in hospital);

(b) compensation for the pain and suffering arising prior to the death. Obviously, if death was instantaneous then there would be no compensation under this head;

(c) funeral expenses (if paid by the estate).

25.3. The Fatal Accidents claim

This gives the relatives of the deceased a separate claim for the losses they have suffered. This has three heads:

(a) "bereavement" (£7,500) for certain dependants;

(b) the dependency claim for the financial losses suffered by the relatives;

(c) the funeral expenses (if paid by the dependants).

Bereavement

The fixed sum for bereavement is £7,500. This seems to be the subject of many Law Commission papers and much campaigning but has remained at this level for many years. But, the bereavement payment can only be claimed by:

(a) the spouse; or

(b) the parents, if the deceased was unmarried and under 18.

If the deceased was over 18, and not married, then no bereavement payment can be made. Note in particular that parents of adults cannot claim bereavement nor can children and nor can a common law spouse (or an ex-spouse). This is particularly hard to explain to the relatives of a deceased who was unmarried but only just 18. Quite often you will find that they do not believe you. In such circumstances it may be tactful to suggest they take a second opinion.

Who is a dependant?

A dependency claim can only be brought by certain categories of relatives. In fact, the definition is fairly wide. It can include parents, grandparents, children, spouses, ex-spouses, etc. In addition, it can include a common law spouse but he or she must have been living with the deceased for at least two years before the accident (it is therefore a stricter test than under the Family Provision legislation). Also, any person treated as a parent, or a child of the family, can claim to be a dependant, as can grandparents, step-parents, foster parents, etc. In practice, there are relatively few dependants who cannot bring a Fatal Accidents claim (except a partner of the same sex, a platonic friend or a recent co-habitee).

Nervous shock

Note that *Alcock v. Chief Constable of South Yorkshire* [1992] 1 A.C. 310, HL limits the class of people who can claim damages for psychiatric injury (so-called 'nervous shock') following the death of a relative. It also places limits on claimants to those proximate in space and time to the accident.

25.4. Taking instructions

When taking instructions in a fatal claim, use the questionnaires in Appendix A. Use the general personal injury questionnaire, appropriate road or workplace questionnaire, and in addition use the supplementary questionnaire. Be sure to obtain the birth and marriage certificates of the dependants, and the birth, marriage and death certificates of the deceased. Arrange for personal representatives to be appointed so that they can bring the claim; however, if they fail to commence the proceedings within six months of the death, then any one of the dependants can sue for the Fatal Accidents claim.

In addition, consider whether any of the dependants could be in any way to blame for the accident (for example, road accident claim in which deceased was passenger in car driven by spouse). If so, ensure that the dependant in question is not appointed as a personal representative.

The proceedings will bear the name of the claimant, for example:

"ABC (Widow and Administratrix of the Estate of DEF Deceased)".

Precedent claim form indorsements for use in Law Reform and Fatal Accidents claims are printed in Precedent 1(3).

Particulars of claim

Ensure that the particulars of claim includes the following information required by CPR Part 16PD-005;

(a) date of birth of each dependant;

(b) a statement that the claim is brought under The Fatal Accidents Act 76;

(c) details of dependants who are claiming;

(d) details of the nature of the dependency claim.

CPR Part 16 PD-005 makes it plain that you may bring a Law Reform claim within the same proceedings that you bring a Fatal Accident claim. If so then further information will be required; this will be details of the accident and of the deceased, including date of birth and details of the pre-death suffering and include quantifiable losses.

Schedule of special damage

This should cover all the matters set out in Chapter 7 but remember it should set out both the deceased's pre-death losses (see above) and the losses suffered by dependants.

Conflicts

Difficulties can arise if there are disputes between the dependants. If one set of dependants brings the Fatal Accidents claim, and another claims to be joined as dependants, you will be in a difficult position. Quite simply, there will be a conflict between clients and those who claim to be dependants. The correct procedure is for you to continue to handle the case, and the application will have to be heard by the trial judge. The courts have decided that it is not possible to have more than one firm of solicitors conducting the litigation on behalf of the claimant and only one Fatal Accident Act claim can be brought.

The inquest and inquest notes

Explain to the family that legal aid will not cover the cost of attending the inquest. Do they want to pay privately for you to attend? Bear in mind that the inquest notes can be obtained from the coroner, after the inquest, for a modest fee. However, those inquest notes will not be admissible at trial, unless the coroner is called strictly to prove them. To avoid this inconvenience, it is usual for the parties to agree an interlocutory order that the notes be admissible in evidence. Whether you attend depends very much on the liability position. If liability has been admitted it may prove hard to recover the cost of attending even though the family may wish you to help them find out as much about the accident as possible.

Limitation period

The limitation period in a fatal claim will usually be three years from the date of the death, although no claim can be brought if the deceased was statute-barred at the time of death. However, it is possible under the Limitation Act 1980 for the limitation period to be extended, although those provisions will not apply if the deceased was statute-barred at death. Generally, see Chapter 21.

When the claimant dies

If the death does not occur until some time after the accident, it is likely that the deceased will have commenced proceedings prior to death. If so, that action can be taken over by the deceased's personal representatives as the Law Reform claim, and they should apply for permission to the court, *ex parte*. Evidence in support should be filed, setting out the nature of the action, the stage reached, the change that has occurred (ie death), their interest, the fact that the cause of action survives, and the order sought. The personal representatives' written consent to act should also be produced. The order will be noted in the court records, and should be served on all the other parties to the action.

If there is also a Fatal Accidents claim arising on behalf of any dependants, the personal representatives should simultaneously seek the court's leave to amend the pleadings to include the new cause of action (the application could, of course, no longer be made *ex parte*), or alternatively, issue separate proceedings and consolidate the two actions at a later date. As CPR Part 16 PD-005 specifically contemplates claims under both statutes being made together amendment may be better than separate proceedings.

Which court?

Although the proceedings will have to be started in the county court if the case is worth less than £50,000 (see Chapter 9) fatal cases are in the category of those considered suitable for trial in the High Court if they are worth over £25,000 and in these circumstances you should always consider transferring the matter up to the High Court.

25.5. Assessment of damages: the multiplicand

The Law Reform claim should be relatively simple. It is a straightforward injury claim. The only difference is that the pain and suffering claim is capped in time terms not by recovery but rather by death. However, the period of suffering is certain and therefore readily quantifiable.

The real difficulty lies in working out the size of the dependency claim (under the Fatal Accidents claim).

The first stage of the calculation is to work out the net annual financial loss (that is the "multiplicand"), which will then be multiplied to cover future loss. The calculation of the dependency is a purely financial calculation.

Client care

It can be a distressing and difficult task for the dependants since they often feel that it suggests that they, not the defendants, are on trial and resent the suggestion that they are only interested in the financial worth of the deceased, not their distress and anger at the unnecessary loss of a loved one. You should therefore be very sensitive when asking the questions. It is best that you complete the questionnaires in interview with the dependants rather than sending them out for completion so that you can explain the process of personal injury litigation and the need for accurate completion of the questionnaires. It is vital that you manage to convey to them that the process is not one of retribution but is, and can only ever be, a financial exercise.

Preparing the calculation (Method A)

The calculation must be accurate and comprehensive. Add up all the financial benefits received by the dependants from the deceased, including the following:

(a) housekeeping;

(b) rent;

(c) mortgage;

(d) council tax;

(e) gas;

(f) electricity;

(g) water;

(h) fuel;

(i) insurance;

(j) television hire and licence fee;

(k) hire purchase payments;

(l) telephone bills;

(m) school fees;

(n) clothes;

(o) holidays;

(p) gifts of a regular nature (such as Christmas or birthdays);

(q) the value of a car provided by the deceased or employers;

(r) any other items provided by the deceased.

Deduct that proportion of the expenditure which is attributable to the deceased (for example, that part of the total food bill that will now be saved). Also, calculate the value of services rendered to the dependants by the deceased which will now have to be paid for, such as house repairs and maintenance, or garden produce if the deceased was a keen gardener.

The starting point for calculating the children's dependency is now accepted by the courts as the net wages that would be payable to a professional carer for looking after the children (*Hay v. Hughes* [1975] 1 All E.R. 257) but if a relative has reasonably given up work to care for the children you can use the net loss of earnings of the new carer (*Mehmet v. Perry* [1977] 2 All E.R. 529). Do not forget to take into account things like holidays, gifts, and clothes. This may well increase the dependency by a considerable amount.

Similarly do not forget to include the work that the deceased did towards maintaining and improving the home. The loss of a DIY enthusiast can result in a significantly increased dependency. When the deceased was a homemaker, then one must take care when calculating the loss of those services. It is not good enough to simply take the cost of hiring a housekeeper. Bear in mind that the homemaker will have worked for much more than eight hours a day, and those additional lost services can be included in the dependency claim.

Wherever possible, support the dependency figures with documentary evidence. Obtain bills and receipts of household expenses for the year prior to the death. If these cannot be obtained, try writing to the deceased's bank for the return of all cheques and details of standing orders. Obtain copy tax returns from the Inland Revenue, and compare the total dependency with the net income. In cases where no documentary evidence can be produced, it may be necessary to calculate the dependency by taking a sum that can reasonably be attributed to the deceased's own expenses and benefit: the balance will be the dependency. Additionally, be sure to take a detailed proof describing how the household was run and how expenses were met.

Do not deduct the value of benefits (*e.g.* death benefit; insurance benefit) when calculating the dependency. It is arguable whether you should deduct assets which passed on death to the dependants and from which they derive an income. Generally you should not. See *Wood v. Bentall Simplex Ltd, The Times,* March 3, 1992.

Preparing the calculation (Method B)

It has to be accepted that Method A can often be an artificial calculation. Further, it can often be extremely difficult to apportion expenditure between various members of the family in any sort of realistic fashion. There is also the practical difficulty of collating the necessary information from the distressed dependants.

An alternative, and much more straightforward, approach is to simply take the deceased's net income, and deduct from that a figure to cover the money that the deceased spent on himself or herself. The balance will presumably be the dependency for the rest of the family. Obviously, any other sums that would have been received by way of fringe benefits, etc. (*e.g.* cheap mortgage; company car) will have to be added to the net earnings figures. In practical terms, this is a much easier approach. Even so, it may still be difficult to apportion items of expenditure between the deceased and the other dependants. When this is the case, the courts are generally prepared to accept a fairly rough and ready approach. As a generalisation, you will find that if there is a husband and wife and the wife did not work, and the husband is killed, then the wife's dependency will probably be in the region of 66 per cent of the husband's net income. If there is joint income then the dependency is 66 per cent of the total joint net income and you deduct from that the continuing earnings to calculate the loss of dependency. If there are children, then you should be thinking in terms of a dependency of 75 per cent. If a working mother is killed then the children's dependency may crudely be seen as 50/50 (one child), 33/33/33 (two children) or 25/25/25/25 (three children).

Authority for this comes from the judgment of O'Connor L.J. in *Harris v. Empress Motors* (1983) 127 Sol. Jo. 647, CA. The judgment is not reported in full, but quotes from the transcript are useful: "In the course of time the courts have worked out a simple solution to the . . . problem of calculating the net dependency under the Fatal Accidents Act 1976, in cases where the dependants are wife and children . . . The modern practice is to deduct a percentage from the income figure to represent what the deceased would have spent exclusively on himself. The percentages have become conventional in the sense that they are used unless there is striking evidence to make the conventional figure inappropriate . . . Where the family unit was husband and wife the conventional figure is 33 per cent and the rationale of this is that broadly speaking net income was spent as to one-third for the benefit of each and one-third for their joint benefit . . . No deduction is made in respect of the joint portion because one cannot buy or drive half a motor car . . . Where there are children the deduction falls to 25 per cent . . ." (*i.e.* 75 per cent dependency).

So, you should normally adopt O'Connor's approach, unless you think that a detailed calculation of the dependency in the Method A (as outlined above, going through all the items of expenditure, one by one) would be more advantageous or more appropriate.

However, there is an authority that if the deceased was moonlighting, not declaring income, then the court may ignore that income when calculating the multiplicand (see *Hunter v. Butler*).

Adjustments from the multiplier on death of a mother

The services figure must be adjusted upwards to reflect the special qualitative factor of a mother's care (see *e.g. Cresswell v. Eaton* [1991] 1 All E.R. 484). The courts have not given definitive guidance as to an appropriate uplift but in *Spittle v. Bunney* [1988] 3 All E.R. 1031 the court raised the children's award by ten per cent to take account of this factor.

The services multiplicand must then be reduced to take into account a child's decreasing reliance on a mother's services as he or she gets older. Courts in recent cases have all accepted this principle but differ on what deduction should be made.

There is a futher reduction in the multiplicand where a mother was working to reflect the supposedly part time nature of the care given. Again this is a question of fact and no real guidance has been given by the courts.

In *Stanley v. Saddique* [1991] 1 All E.R. 529, the court said that the multiplicand should be reduced if the mother's quality of care was poor or if she might have been likely to leave the children. Clearly such a line of questioning would be deeply distressing to relatives and it is best ignored unless the mother was evidentially neglectful. That care after the death is better is a benefit which must be disregarded.

25.6. The multiplier

Having calculated the dependency, it is necessary to multiply that multiplicand by the appropriate multiplier, so as to cover losses in future years. Remember that unlike a conventional loss of earnings multiplier in an injury claim in a Fatal Accidents Act dependency claim the multiplier runs from the date of death.

This gives rise to the current clamour for reform as it is felt that taking just one multiplier cannot create a just result. Support for this view comes from the comments of Lord Lloyd of Berwick in *Wells v. Wells* [1998] 3 W.L.R. 329 who expressed disquiet with the generally adopted practice of looking at past cases to find comparables. The decision in *Wells* on discount rate now makes that difficult as the cases are based on different percentage anticipated returns. Inevitably, to take account of the lower returns, there is a suggestion that actuarial evidence is now imperative.

Lord Lloyd was in no doubt that the correct approach was to adopt the Government Actuary's tables and make a discount for the risk of death up to trial date. There is detailed consideration of this in both *Kemp & Kemp* and an abridged version for a readily accessible read in [2000] J.P.I.L. 142.

Factors which affect the multiplier

The multiplier will vary with the age and health of the dependants, the age and pre-accident health of the deceased.

If the deceased was a person whose earnings could reasonably have expected to have increased over the years (for example, a professional person, or an apprentice), then it is fair to add a year or two to the multiplier. Similarly, if the deceased could reasonably have expected to continue working after the normal retirement age (for example, if self-employed) then the multiplier should be increased to reflect the fact.

Conventional multipliers

Beware of looking at previous cases given the comments earlier about the effect on these of the decision in *Wells v. Wells*. You will need to use the Ogden tables to obtain appropriate multipliers.

Multipliers for spouses

When assessing the multiplier you must ignore a widow's prospects of remarriage, and even ignore a remarriage that occurs prior to settlement or trial. But, you do not ignore the remarriage prospects of a widower, and nor do you ignore the mother's prospects of remarriage when considering the children's dependency. The court must take into account the benefit which the child is likely to receive from a stepfather but, even so, the court may well apportion more than is usual to the children, on the basis that if the mother remarries she will have a new husband with a duty to maintain her; also, of course, the court will be conscious of the fact that the children funds will be under the control of the court, whereas those of the widow will not.

Divorce

The court can, however, take into consideration the likelihood that the parties may have divorced and in doing so must have regard to the fact that an increasing percentage of marriages end in divorce. *Martin v. Owen, The Times,* May 21, 1992, CA.

Cohabitees

As regards cohabitees, the court has to take into account the fact that there was no legal obligation on the deceased to maintain the cohabitee. The net effect is that a cohabitee can expect a lower multiplier than if he or she had been a spouse.

Multipliers for children

Multipliers for children will usually only cover the child's presumed period of dependency (*i.e.* up to age 18). If a child is likely to go on to continuing education then you can argue that the multiplier should be increased to reflect this (see *Corbett v. Barking, Havering and Brentwood Health Authority* [1991] 1 All E.R. 498, CA). Although financial support often continues after provision of services ends usually only one multiplier is used.

On the topic of dependency claims of children a recent court decision suggests that the court will now recognise the dependency status of children unrelated to the deceased, for example where the child is a dependent of her mother's deceased boyfriend.

Medical evidence

The defendants may request facilities for a medical examination of the dependants in the hope that a finding of poor health will enable them to argue for a lower multiplier; facilities should be refused and the defendants left to apply for an order.

Actuarial evidence

The use of actuarial tables is likely to lead to a higher multiplier than under the conventional approach. See Appendix F for the difference that the use of an actuarial table (such as that published by The Stationery Office) can make.

25.7. Funeral expenses

Funeral expenses should be recoverable (under the Law Reform claim, if paid by the estate; under the Fatal Accidents claim, if paid by the dependants). However, funeral expenses must be reasonable. Generally insurers will try to save a few pounds by querying the funeral charges. You might find it useful to bear three cases in mind.

(a) In *Gammell v. Wilson* [1982] A.C. 27, the burial was in Ireland.

(b) In *Quainoo v. Brent and Harrow AHA* [1982] N.L.J. 1100 the funeral expenses were those of a member of the Ghanaian royal family, with the body being returned to Ghana. The cost of air fares for the relatives to return to Ghana, together with air freight for the coffin, London funeral director's expenses, and of the cars for the Ghanaian funeral procession, were allowed. But, the costs of printing funeral cards, wreaths, photographer, hire of hall and, party after funeral, and the funeral clothes, were disallowed.

(c) In *Smith v. Marchioness/Bowbelle* January 27, 1993 (QBD) the claimant was allowed funeral expenses including £400 spent on a reception with wine and canapes for 300 people after the funeral. The Master held that the claimant could not ignore the social obligation attendant on a funeral to serve and provide refreshment to guests on a warm day, the social decencies had to be observed and he allowed the claim in full.

The majority of funeral expenses that you are likely to encounter should be recoverable in full.

25.8. Apportioning the settlement moneys

If there is a Law Reform claim, and also a Fatal Accidents claim, then the defendant can make one payment into court in respect of both claims. If this global payment in is accepted, then the court will have to apportion the damages between the respective claims. Similarly, if there is a Fatal Accidents claim, and several dependants, then the court may have to apportion the payment in between the various dependants. Certainly, if any of the dependants are persons under a disability, then the court's approval (and apportionment of the moneys) will be mandatory. Any settlement involving persons under a disability must be approved by the court (see Chapter 24).

Procedure

Procedurally, the position is the same as with an infant approval. If proceedings have been begun, then you issue a CPR Part 23 application. If proceedings have not been begun, then you commence proceedings by way of CPR Part 8 proceedings. Specimen summonses and orders are printed in Precedent 17. Refer to Chapter 24 for general guidance on infant approval settlements applications, since the principles are the same.

Court's practice

If children are involved, and the court has to apportion between a parent and those children, then the court should begin by estimating the costs of maintaining that child from the date of the order (not the date of death) until the child reaches 18. The court should then apportion a sufficient sum to cover those maintenance costs, and also, if possible, allow the child a small capital sum with which to start life on attaining the age of 18. This exercise will be repeated for each child. Any balance will then go to the surviving spouse. In practice, of course, there is usually not enough money to go around; when that is the case, it would be necessary to reduce everyone's entitlement (including the children's), proportionately. However, in practice, the approach of the court where there is more than one child is usually simply to divide the multiplicand between the number of children and work out each child's dependency from that. This rough and ready approach is easier but disregards the fact that the award is supposed to be on the basis of the value to the child of the lost services. Certainly, the courts do not approve of simply paying all the money to the surviving spouse, in the hope that he or she will utilise it properly towards maintenance, etc of the children.

The courts take the view that this is too risky; they would prefer to have the children's money invested, under control of the court. The point to appreciate is that children's funds are controlled by the court, but surviving spouses' funds are not (until the mid-70s, widows' funds were also controlled by the court, but since that rule has been changed the courts have been less generous with their apportionments to widows).

Exceptionally, if there is a dispute between the dependants, or if there is a dispute between the surviving spouse and children, the court may allow other dependants to be joined as parties to the action. The court may also decide that the Official Solicitor should represent the children. The most likely scenario is where an illegitimate child comes forward after the death and wishes to present a claim for dependency.

26. Clinical Negligence Claims

26.1. Introduction

You can spot a serious clinical negligence lawyer because he or she will refer to him or herself as precisely that. Medical negligence is a thing of the past. There is a serious point to this and that is that is has long been accepted that clinical negligence cases are difficult. Indeed those who specalise in this field may well feel that clinical negligence is now no longer suitable for consideration within a book on personal injury litigation. There are many reasons for this:

- There is a separate public funding franchise category with very few firms accepted by the Regional Legal Services Commission as qualified to do this work.
- There is a separate pre-action protocol that governs conduct prior to issue of any proceedings.
- There is a need, either in house or with clear external relationships, to have suitably medically qualified staff to enable sensible early risk assessments of a case to be made.
- The establishment of the Clinical Disputes Forum in 1997 was a recognition of the individual problems and issues that clinical negligence raises.
- Medical experts are needed on negligence and causation as well as on condition and prognosis and consequently the outcome of any claim hinges far more on an expert than in other injury work.
- The necessity of front loading costs to make preliminary enquiries.

This is not meant to be an exhaustive list but one merely to highlight basic points that set clinical negligence work apart from other injury work.

Does this negate the need for this chapter? This comes back to a point made earlier that good lawyers are good lawyers. Good personal injury lawyers, with suitable experience can, and do, become good clinical negligence lawyers. The difficulty is gaining the experience. With increasing accumulation of clinical negligence claims in far fewer firms it is difficult, particularly in the provinces, to acquire the experience deemed necessary to satisfy panel requirements to enable a greater volume of work to be done. Whilst this may be a good thing for those firms that do have the work sometimes it does leave holes in client choice and it does mean that perfectly competent lawyers cannot offer a service to clients, who at a difficult time would wish to turn to them for help. This is not meant to be an encouragement to anyone to take on clinical negligence work, but for those who do feel competent to do it, and knowing your limitations must be a prerequisite, then there is still a place in this book for a brief consideration of clinical negligence claims. The chapter was never intended to be exhaustive and for those without sufficient experience a specialist text is a necessity.

Claims generally

In theory, there can be as many as four different types of action that can be brought by a complaining patient: trespass to the person (assault and/or battery); misrepresentation (if a patient is given misleading information); breach of contract; and negligence. In practice, of course, it is in negligence that most claims lie.

Test of negligence

To win a case, the claimant in a negligence action must show that the doctor followed a course of action that is not supported by any responsible body of medical opinion. The classic test was laid down in *Bolam* [1957] 2 All E.R. 118, in which it was said that a doctor "is not guilty of negligence if he has acted in accordance with a practice accepted as proper". Similarly, it has been said that "the true test for establishing liability in diagnosis or treatment on the part of a doctor is whether he has been proved to be guilty of such failure as no doctor of ordinary skill would be guilty of" (*Hunter* 1955 S.L.T. 101). In practice, this is likely to mean that if the defendant can produce a reasonably qualified doctor to support the treatment that was given, or can refer to a leading textbook, then the doctor is likely to be able successfully to defend the claim. The vital point to appreciate is that it is not sufficient for the claimant merely to be able to show that many other doctors would have behaved in a different manner.

Similarly, it is now established that there is no general duty to advise a patient of all the risks involved in a course of treatment unless the patient specifically asks (*Sidaway* [1985] A.C. 871).

Anyone handling claimant medical negligence claims should join AVMA (Action for Victims of Medical Accidents) Bank Chambers, 1 London Road, Forest Hill, London, SE23 3TP. Tel 0208 291 2793.

In chapters 23 and 30 there is reference to the AVMA panel. This, like the Law Society Clinical Negligence panel, is a passport to a public funding franchise. However, membership is closely controlled for AVMA is not an organisation set up for lawyers, but one for the assistance of victims. It does not wish to refer those victims who approach it to firms unless satisfied that by so referring it is helping the victims.

Even if you do not qualify for the panel you might consider joining AVMA because it does provide a useful recommendation system for experts. The correct choice of an expert is crucial so if you envisage needing even a few experts a year and do not already have your own favourites who are tried and tested then access to the expert database will more than justify the membership fee.

Taking instructions

The first step will be to take the client's statement. Use the general questionnaire in Appendix A. In addition, make sure that you have:

(a) a full chronological record of all the treatment given;

(b) the names of the doctors (if known);

(c) the addresses of the hospitals concerned;

(d) the patient or hospital record numbers;

(e) the name and address of the client's G.P.;

(f) full details of any advice or information allegedly given by doctors or staff;

(g) details of the client's pre-injury condition and current condition.

Ensure that you understand exactly what the client alleges. You cannot confirm the claim without medical evidence but you cannot even get that far unless you understand the fundamental complaint. Patience is necessary as establishing this can be more difficult than you might imagine.

Indications of negligence

In many cases, this preliminary statement will be used to support an application for funding. Any conditional fee funder will want as much information as possible to determine risk. Concentrate on trying to get some indication of this. For instance, has the client's G.P. made off-the-cuff remarks that indicate that all is not well; why does the client think that the treatment was not satisfactory? Bear in mind that you are not required to prove your case at this stage. You are trying to find some pointers that will enable you in this context a lay person, to determine if this is a case that carries sufficient prospects of success for you to take a preliminary favourable view that necessitates a consideration of funding options and to put in place a suitable arrangement with a third party, if appropriate (see below on funding).

Advising the client

Consider the allegations carefully, in particular:

Will the client be able to show negligence?

For example, if your client admits that the treatment received was standard and only alleges that a better method is practised elsewhere then the claim has no chance of success (see above), or: if your client accepts that a known complication which was explained prior to the operation occurred not through any particular error.

Will the client be able to show damage?

There may be negligence but if a client has not suffered damage or if likely damages are very low then you may wish to suggest that there is no point in taking a claim and the client may be better advised simply to complain to the hospital. This can be difficult to explain to a client who may see fault as leading inevitably to compensation. See *Bolitho* for examples on difficulties of causation.

Limitation

Is the case within the primary limitation period? (see Chapter 21). If not, is there a case for extending the period? Knowledge in a clinical negligence case usually runs from the date of the negligent procedure or operation although this is the main area of dispute over limitation periods in clinical negligence cases. Point out to the client that clinical negligence cases present difficulties. Explain the standard of proof that will be needed to win the case. Emphasise the likely costs, especially if the case is to be privately funded. It is worth breaking those costs down into various stages. Certainly, you should provide the client with an estimate of the initial investigative costs that will arise before you are able to offer a more definitive view of the prospects of a claim.

26.2. Funding

Public funding

As already mentioned, public funding is now strictly for those with a clinical negligence franchise. There is no point considering the complicated arrangements that accompany that as those with the franchise will understand them only too well. The only other points to make about public funding are that:

(i) there is an inevitable question mark about the long term prospects of this source of funding; and

(ii) if a client plainly qualifies financially for public funding and you do not have a franchise then you must advise the client of the availability of this funding source elsewhere.

You will have to accept that where a client can obtain representation under the public funded scheme elsewhere then their financial circumstances are such that it will be rare for you realistically to expect to retain the instruction. One way would be to fund any conditional fee premium yourself. This, though, may raise issues as to its recoverability.

Conditional fee funding

Whilst there are insurance companies and intermediaries that are prepared to offer underwriting of a clinical negligence conditional fee agreement many expect first to be satisfied of your experience and track record in dealing with such claims. That may raise similar difficulties to those which arise with the Law Society and AVMA panel selection. In other cases the conditional fee premium may be substantial.

You need to inform the client in a suitable case that you will obtain a quotation. Once you have this you have to decide who is to pay the premium, identify what the insurance actually covers and determine who will pay the disbursements as they arise. The last point is of more importance than in an other injury conditional fee considerations because of the heavy reliance on experts in clinical negligence and the simple fact that liability and causation reports are on average anything up to four or five times more expensive than a condition and prognosis report.

Finally, you will need to consider what success fee to suggest to the client. As you may have only a very preliminary view of prospects, often no more than an instinct that this is certainly a case that requires preliminary investigation, agreeing on the success fee may prove difficult. However, this really should be non negotiable. If you have formed a view of the risk and set the success fee accordingly then any reduction will be undermining that assessment.

Private clients

If your client is paying privately most of the same considerations apply as for a conditional fee arrangement.

In particular:

(1) Ask for a realistic amount on account of your fees and disbursements at the outset.

(2) Bill your client regularly so that he or she is aware of the costs position.

(3) Warn your client as to the risks of losing, particularly in respect of defendant's costs.

(4) Regularly review prospects of success and likely damages so that your client can make an informed decision on the costs/benefits of continuing.

(5) Explain that initial record collation and expert advice is a necessity, except in the most obvious of negligence cases where liability has already been admitted to the client or is admitted as soon as the protocol form is sent, and that that will cost in the region of £2,500 or so, depending on the type of case and the number of experts who may be required. Complete this advice by stressing that the investment of that money may simply lead to evidence being obtained that in fact does not support any claim. Again, this is all about client management and explaining the process and the risks.

26.3. The pre-action protocol for the resolution of clinical disputes

Why was it introduced?

As a result of the inquiry by the Lord Woolf team it was accepted that change was required to try to make clinical negligence claims less adversarial and so move away from the culture of claim that was seeing spiralling cost to both the NHS and the Legal Aid Board.

The first step was the creation in 1997 of the Clinical Disputes Forum. One of the first things that the forum undertook was the creation of this protocol. The preamble to the protocol should be read as it provides a summary of reasons for a protocol and its aims—bear those in mind when using the protocol—it may alter the approach you adopt.

How will it change the traditional approach?

In simple terms, the reasons for and intentions of the protocol mirror the CPR reforms generally are to try to ensure that claims are dealt with openly, cost effectively, with litigation as a last resort and as expeditiously as possible. It should sound familiar by now. To try to achieve these laudable goals the protocol encourages:

- early communication of perceived problems between health provider and patient;
- patients to raise concerns with any treatment as soon as practicable;
- health providers to develop systems of early reporting and investigation of serious adverse outcomes from any treatment and to provide prompt and full explanations;
- disclosure by all parties of sufficient information to enable the other to take an informed view in the hope of early resolution.

A simple explanation of the steps set out in the protocol

It is assumed by the protocol that before instructing you your client will have discussed the outcome with the medical provider and either remain dissatisfied or have been told that the outcome was caused by negligence and so the next step must be taken.

On that assumption then once you have obtained full instructions, have been appointed to act and have in place a funding agreement of one sort or another you should obtain your client's health records. The procedure for so doing is set out in annex B to the protocol. This suggests the use of an agreed form and it is suggested that you use this. Prior to sending it you should send a copy to your client for approval of the information given in it and to request that the client signs it as that is necessary.

Within 40 days the records should be sent to you. Use this time to obtain all health records other than those held by the health provider against whom you have been instructed to act using the ordinary forms for applying for disclosure. The reason for this is that the expert you instruct will need to see all records to put the treatment and the outcome in context. For example, he or she needs to see if there is anything in the G.P. notes to suggest that some symptom had been flagged up to a treating consultant which was overlooked and was relevant to the outcome.

Once you have the notes put them into usable order if they are not already. Many firms have in-house medical staff who do this. If you have not then there are outside agencies who, for a fee, will do this for you. They may also flag up any poor copies or records that are not present that they would expect to have sorted. You must do this as any expert instructed is not going to be at all impressed to have to sort the notes into logical sections him or herself before being able to embark on the task instructed. This may result in substantial delay or even the return of the papers.

Depending on the outcome of the expert instruction you then prepare a letter of claim, have it approved by the client and send it to the health care provider. You wait for the formal letter of response. Again, a template is set out in the protocol.

If the letter of claim does not lead to resolution of the dispute then issue proceedings

Potential problems

The failure of the health care provider to disclose the notes within a realistic timescale is a potential problem.

Although 40 days is the expected period set out in the protocol there will be occasions when, for valid reason, that is insufficient time. If a problem with compliance is notified to you, an indication given as to what is being done to overcome the problem and a revised timescale provided, be reasonable.

If there is simply delay and no, or no justifiable, explanation then you should issue a CPR Part 23 application for pre-issue disclosure. As long as you can show that you have been reasonable you should seek your costs of this process.

The failure of another holder of records to provide copies is another potential problem. Again, the CPR Part 23 procedure is available for non party disclosure (on these applications see Chapter 5 for more detailed consideration).

Guidance generally

The form for requesting disclosure and a template letter of claim are set out at annexes B and C of the protocol itself. The intention of the protocol is very similar to the personal injury protocol requirement for the claimant to set out the claim at as early a stage as possible. The letter of claim in clinical negligence cases must set out clearly the alleged negligence, the current condition and the prognosis for the client's injuries and must quantify special damages. Note that you cannot issue proceedings, unless there are limitation issues, for three months from the date of the letter of claim to enable the defendant to make full inquiry and, if appropriate, put forward settlement proposals.

26.4. The expert

By now you will appreciate the importance of selecting the correct expert. As so much turns on this some would say that the real skill in a clinical negligence claim is the choice of expert. In practice, there are very few experts in each field of specialism who are sufficiently well qualified (which includes their experience of relevant claims) from initial report to trial and who are prepared to take on this type of work. As stated earlier, this is where the membership fee to AVMA may be justified. AVMA tries to monitor feedback on experts, although not all solicitors provide the necessary information, to ensure that the database at any given time only includes experts whom it can currently recommend.

The other advantage of a service such as this is that it can point you to the right type of specialism. This may sound ridiculous but there are many cases when it is not clear what type of expert you need or indeed if you need more than one to consider various aspects of the complaint.

Instructing the expert

So far, every time there has been reference to an expert being instructed there has followed fairly quickly the words joint instruction. Not necessarily so here. The clinical disputes protocol recognises that a joint expert may not be suitable, certainly not on the questions of liability and causation. Accordingly, whilst the parties are still asked to consider joint instruction the protocol accepts that greater flexibility and freedom should be given to the parties in this area. The "protocol does not attempt to be prescriptive on issues in relation to expert evidence".

Once you have selected your expert you need to ensure that the expert is prepared to take on the case and ascertain the likely timescale for and cost of the preparation of the report. The latter is necessary so that you can obtain approval to the fee from your client or from the Legal Services Commission, etc.

If the expert is prepared to assist you should then instruct him or her properly. The report will be expensive and fundamental to the claim. At best it would be embarrassing if the expert had to be asked to reconsider the matter because the original instruction had been inadequate. It does take time to do it properly but it is essential that you find that time. General considerations of expert instruction have been discussed in Chapter 6. In addition, in clinical negligence cases make sure that you send the expert the following:

- A legible copy of all notes and records properly sorted and paginated. It is so much easier to follow a report if it refers to page numbers which you can happily cross refer with your copy of the notes.
- Your client's statement. There are different views on this and it may be wise to ask the expert first if he or she wants a copy of the statement. The difference arises because there is a danger that if the expert reads the statement the matter is then judged with the benefit of hindsight whereas the expert really needs to consider the position of the health care provider at the time of the alleged negligence based only on the information that was available at that time.
- Any relevant comments that may already have been received from the proposed defendant.
- Any expert reports that are pertinent that you already hold. It is unlikely that you will have any but conceivable that you may have a condition and prognosis report.
- A complete letter of instruction explaining (at the risk of teaching your expert to suck eggs) the standard of care that a court would expect, reference to any useful leading texts on any issue, the importance of speed of report if limitation looms, the function of the report itself and the CPR Part 35 obligations of the expert.

If you wish the expert to deal with condition and prognosis as well as liability and causation you should specifically ask for that and request two separate reports so that you can serve the former as required with any subsequent particulars of claim but then seek simultaneous service and filing of the latter. Stock letter 20 can be used as a starting point for the expert instruction.

Reading the report

When you receive the report read it carefully. Ensure it is full and correct. Raise any queries with the expert. If you do not understand terminology in the report then you should ask the expert for a brief lay explanation as you cannot indicate to the client the effect of a report on a claim if you do not understand it. In addition, you really should have, as a bare minimum, an encyclopaedia of medical terms. Send a copy to the client with a covering summary briefly setting out its content and opinion. Ask the client for comments and consider them carefully. Advise the client of the effect of the report on the client's case and prospects of success. This is one of those occasions where the telephone will not do. Arrange for the client to come in to see you.

Supplementary reports

Sometimes, one report leads to another. For example, the expert recommends a more specific examination of the treatment provided or the treatment overlaps medical fields. Remember, before rushing off to obtain another report, that many funding schemes limit the number of experts or insist that prior approval is obtained before any expert is instructed. Usually, sight of one expert report recommending another is persuasive enough.

This situation is, of course, completely different from the situation where you have received an unfavourable report and attempt to obtain a second opinion from the same type of expert.

Unfavourable reports

If the expert's report is not favourable to the client, then the client may wish to go to a different expert. That is the client's right. You should explain the difficulties that may arise on funding, such as the likelihood of the Legal Services Commission giving notice to show cause, the question of who funds the report under any conditional fee scheme and the inevitable problems that will arise as to recovery of one or other fee even at the end of a successful claim. The other point that you must highlight is the fact that this could be throwing good money after bad. In other words, that there is no guarantee that a second report will be any more favourable that the first.

The other course to consider is asking further questions of your expert, or if you think certain areas have been overlooked highlighting those to the expert and asking for comment. For many clients this first report is the only chance that they realistically have to progress the claim. Someone will have paid a lot of money for the report. Do not be scared of raising matters with the expert. It may be that an explanation is all the client wants and will then be satisfied with the report even if no claim for compensation is feasible. Many clients probably do not come to you for money anyway but simply to find out what happened to them.

26.5. Commencing proceedings

If the clinical dispute protocol does not lead to satisfactory resolution then proceedings will be necessary. They may be necessary in any event if you have limitation concerns. Date of knowledge may be an argument but there is nothing better than issuing within three years of the treatment or incident of which complaint is made. For a general consideration of limitation see Chapter 21.

Drafting

As with the choice of expert, so it is vital to select the correct counsel to draft the claim. Relatively few counsel specialise in clinical negligence cases, but it is well worth your while making enquiry to find one. Not only will this help your client and make your life easier, but this is a superb way of ensuring that you learn from good experience and add to your skills in the field. AVMA will also help here or you can look out reports of clinical claims in various journals such as Kemp and Kemp casewatch or the Journal of Personal injury Law which reveal the same names cropping up frequently. Annual guides recommending specialists also contain details of counsel. Do not be put off by your real or perceived inexperience. That is all the more reason to use expert counsel. If specialist counsel takes on the case the worst that will happen is that he or she will put the case back on track if it has come off the rails.

Issue and post issue

The claim will be issued using the same CPR Part 7 process considered in Chapter 9. The requirements for service of medical evidence and a schedule of special damage are the same as those for all injury claims and the High Court and County Courts Jurisdiction Order 1991 is applicable to determination of the correct court within which to commence the claim.

Once issued, the claim will be subject to the same rules of allocation and case management that apply to all injury claims and will eventually proceed to trial on a date fixed within the trial window allocated if the claim does not settle. There are a few points particular to clinical negligence claims that do arise within the proceedings which merit specific comment. These are:

Medical evidence on issue

This has been touched upon earlier. As in an injury claim, you need a condition and prognosis report to serve with the particulars of claim. Some inexperienced practitioners disclose their liability and causation report at this stage. You should have separate reports even if they are from the same expert.

Disclosure

Whilst records may have been released before-issue under the protocol you should still insist on a formal disclosure list. This will involve the defendant signing the disclosure statement, which will be reassuring if you thought that there might be any missing records as it should serve to focus the attention of the person signing it. Sometimes further documents come to light, perhaps not records but internal memos, investigations, incident reports, etc.

Expert evidence

Occasionally, issues of sequential or simultaneous exchange of such evidence still arise. As a general rule, try to ensure that there is simultaneous exchange. There may be occasions where this is neither practical nor realistic so do look at each case with some flexibility. Do remember, if there is any suggestion by the defendant that it has been waiting for you to clarify your case and has therefore had little time to obtain evidence, that the protocol specifically envisages that investigations are commenced by the health care provider if a patient raises concerns over the outcome of treatment and that in other cases the form for request of notes highlights a potential claim. The illustrative flowchart in the protocol indicates that at this stage as well as providing notes the health care provider should be continuing investigations. Indeed, the suggested content of the letter of response from the health care provider to the letter of claim even considers the provision of expert evidence by the defendant a possible enclosure to accompany the response.

Consideration of a conference with counsel at which the expert is present

Although this happens in larger injury claims, particularly where there are many experts, it is far more common and fundamental in clinical negligence work. The first draft of the expert's report may have been general views only. The final version for service may need to be discussed in conference. Often, you will find at such a conference that what you thought an expert was saying robustly is not quite as firm a view as you believed. Conversely, when experts meet counsel and talk through their findings with the benefit of direct guidance on what the court function will be experts can become firmer simply by equating their terminology to legal expression.

26.6. A final word

Anecdotal evidence suggests that attitudes to the conduct of clinical negligence claims may be hardening again after an initial thawing of approach immediately after the introduction of the CPR. Problems with funding and the initial expense of investigation ensure that this type of claim still presents unique difficulties. However, the major problem still seems to be the emotions and mistrust that these claims often create between health care providers and patients and their representatives.

This is an area where there is likely to be further change. The audit office has produced some damning figures concerning the cost of clinical negligence claims. Whilst claimant representatives argue that the data upon which the conclusions are based dates from before franchise specialism, given the current interest in the public health regime, it is inevitable that further attempts to reduce expenditure on claims or the cost of claims will follow.

In the meantime, do remember your limitations—personal rather than time. If you do not feel capable of dealing with a clinical negligence claim in the new climate then refer your client to someone whom you know to specialise and do it as soon as possible. You may not appreciate it, but you have just completed the wisest risk assessment that you could on that particular case.

27. Group Actions

27.1. Introduction

For the first time group litigation merits its own section in the CPR accompanied by significant commentary and supported by practice direction. This can all be found in Part 19. Although the practice direction is aimed at claimant group actions, there is comment on situations where the multiple parties are defendants in Section III of CPR Part 19. For this text consideration will be given only to the claimant provisions.

Extracting from the wording of CPR Part 19.10, a group action is one made subject to a group litigation order (GLO) where there are or are likely to be claims giving rise to common or related issues.

Examples of situations giving rise to personal injury group actions include:

(a) consumer claims for defective goods (including drugs) or services, *e.g.* Benzodiazepine litigation;

(b) contract claims for defective goods falling outside the Consumer Protection Act 1987;

(c) instant disaster claims arising out of a common cause such as an aircraft, shipping or train disaster, *e.g.* the King's Cross fire disaster;

(d) claims arising out of environmental pollution either by disease (such as legionnaire's disease) or by the diffusion of gas, chemicals or radiation, *e.g.* the Sellafield litigation.

Obviously there are also other non-personal injury group action claims, for example the Lloyd's litigation. However this book is not concerned with those.

27.2. How could you find yourself involved?

(1) You may find that you are approached by a client who has been involved

in a disaster (such as a rail disaster) or has taken a drug which has caused damage. If you believe that this is a matter in which other victims may have consulted other solicitors then you should contact the Law Society Multi Party Action information service to see if there is already a group action, whether by formal GLO or not. If there is then this service will put you in touch with the group. You may find that one firm of solicitors has already been appointed to head the group and that there is a steering committee to assist. Ultimately, any such arrangements will be subject to court approval.

(2) Some solicitors advertise for claimants in particular areas now the restrictions on solicitors' advertising have been removed. Your client may have seen such an advert but come to you for advice. In that case you should contact the Law Society or the solicitors dealing with the case for details of any steering committee and the progress of the action.

(3) You may be approached by a group of claimants with similar claims. In such a case, if you think there are more possible claimants you may wish to advertise for claimants and inform the Law Society so that inquirers can be directed to you.

You may find that your case is not now to continue under the normal procedures set out in this book but that you will be severely limited in the way you run the case and the work you do and in particular you may find that the limitation period is effectively reduced.

If there is a steering group or a lead solicitor has been appointed then your first step should be to make contact so that you can establish the statge which other claims and any court proceedings have reached. This is vital as you may find, for example, that a batch of cases has already been made the subject of a court order to proceed as a series of test cases and that any other claims subsequently notified should be issued and then stayed. It would be embarrassing if you started to fire off letters of claim and endeavoured to seek further clients if you then found out that the litigation had been ongoing for some time and your actions were out of line with court order for late presented claims. A few years after the benzodiazepine litigation collapsed as there were not deemed enough viable claims there was an advertisement in the Help section of one legal journal which read "Has anyone been instructed in a claim involving use of benzodiazepines. If so please contact us to share information". No doubt the advert drummed up quite a response.

27.3. Court procedures

In 1988 the National Consumer Council produced a report entitled "Group Actions—learning from Opren". This report set out in some detail the pros and cons of group or class actions and recommended a new court procedure. The Legal Aid Advisory Committee of the Lord Chancellor's Department considered the question of class actions but no steps were taken to set up such a scheme, save for the inclusion in the Legal Aid Act 1988 of the powers under which the Board's multi-party actions arrangements were made (see below). In May 1991 the Supreme Court Procedures Committee produced a Guide for Use in Group Actions. This guide did not deal with the merits of reform but the present state of the law. Lord Woolf's report recommended wholesale reform of the procedures for dealing with multi-party action. In June 1997 the Legal Aid Board published a report called "When The Price is High" recommending reforms to their procedure for dealing with group actions. Both Lord Woolf's report and the Legal Aid Board suggstions have lead to significant reform which will become apparent from thje comments below.

27.4. Ways of dealing with group actions

As stated above, group action now merits its own mention and procedurs in the CPR. However, there are differnt ways in which such actions can be brought before the court. Indeed, CPR Part 19 BPD-007 highlights the options.

A representative action

This is where one or more claimants can begin or carry on a claim as representatives of others who have the same interests. The disadvantage is that all claimants must be named. The outcome of the representative claim is then binding on all claimants so represented.

Joint claimants in one action

In a claim where there are unlikely to be many claimants this may be a sensible course. However, it is rarely feasible and causes difficulties where further claimants then emerge.

Separate actions by individual claimants

Often, particularly where limitation is approaching or may have expired, you will find many individual claims have been issued. However, it is likely that at early court case management stages consideration will be given to a more convenient and proportionate fashion in which the claims should continue. Most likely by the making of a GLO.

Group actions and test cases

As already indicated, the court can make a GLO where a number of claims raise common or related issues of fact or law. These rules embody suggestions made over the years by those with experience of trying to deal with multi party claims without specific rules to assist and the field evolved by way of lawyer ingenuity. As such, the new rules merit close consideration.

27.5. Group litgation orders and subsequent claim progress

Who can apply and how?

An application for a GLO must be made by general application under CPR Part 23. This application can be made either before or after any proceedings have actually been commenced. More often than not the application is likely to be made by the lead claimant solicitor/s. In public funding cases the identity of such lawyers has probably already been determined under the tender process. This is the process where the Legal Services Commission invites tenders from lawyers to conduct the generic or the generic and specific work for those with a group action who are in recepit of public funding. However, there is provision for the application to be made by a defendant or for the court to consider making a GLO of its own motion.

The application must state what order is sought and why. The information is best supported by evidence in witness statement form that provides the information required under CPR Part 19 BPD-011 namely:

- a summary of the nature of the litigation;
- the number and nature of claims already issued;
- the number of parties likely to be involved;
- the common issues of law and/or fact;
- whether there are sub groups within the main group and if so, why.

The order

You should note at the outset of this section that a GLO can only be made in the Queen's Bench Division of the High Court with the consent of the Vice-Chancellor and within the county court with the consent of the Head of Civil justice. The applications must be heard by certain tiers of judiciary which should save an over eager Deputy District Judge wading in without jurisdiction or knowledge of the pre-condition to making an inappropriate order. In practical terms, this means that if the court thinks that a GLO ought to be made it must send to either the Vice Chancellor or the Head of Civil Justice, as appropriate, a copy of the Part 23 application and evidence in support and confirm in writing why it believes that a GLO is desirable. This can be done in advance of or after hearing the application. The CPR specifically states that the relevant judge should consider the application on paper as soon as possible to decide whether to seek consent before or after hearing the application.

Once consent has been obtained and an order is made it must deal with certain matters, it must

- provide for the establishment of a register of claims which are to be managed under the GLO (the group register);

- specify the GLO issues which then make it possible to determine if a claim raises those issues and falls within the GLO;
- specify the court that will manage the claims on the group register (the management court).

Other points may be dealt with within the order such as the transfer of all cases raising GLO issues to the management court, directions for their entry on the group register, directions that future issued claims raising GLO issues be issued out of the management court and be put on the group register, and that the GLO be publicised to ensure that claimants have an opportunity to join the GLO group register. The court can also then decide how to progress the claims.

The effect of the order

Once a claim is on the group register then any judgment or order made on any of the issues raised in the GLO is binding on the claim. The court can consider separately the effect of a judgment or order on any claims that are entered on to the group register after the judgment or order. Those on the group register have no right of appeal, nor can they apply to have the order on the issue be varied. Their only remedy is to apply for an order that the ruling is not binding on them. You must remember this as it may be your client's only remedy.

Progress of the GLO

The GLO will be subject to case management by the management court just as individual claims in ordinary injury cases are subject to court intervention. However, the management court has additional issues that it must consider. These include the formal appointment or ratification of lead solicitors, specifying a date after which no more claims can be added to the group register without court permission, the addition of claims to the register and, crucially, provision for one or more claims on the group register to proceed as test cases.

You should note that unless the management court orders to the contrary all cases on a group register shall be allocated to the multi track. If any individual cases have already been allocated to other tracks then they should be reallocated.

Cut off dates

On giving case management directions the court can order a cut off date for claims to be added to the group register. The timing of this will vary from case to case. Ininstant disaster cases where the identity of victims is ascertainable relatively quickly then the cut off date is likely to be earlier than in creeping disaster claims where the victims may present overa much longer period. Do be careful of these dates. Permission can be sought for late addition to the register, but there is no guarantee of a successful outcome to any such application.

Test cases

The management court can provide for certain cases to be taken as test cases. If these cases settle the court can order a further claim from the group register to be substituted as a test case. Unless the court provides to the contrary any order already made in the original test case shall stand as against the substituted claim.

The practice direction provides that common issues and test cases will usually be tried at the management court, althought issues raised in individual claims may be directed to be tried at a court more conveniently located to the parties.

This highlights the two broad areas of investigation required for the presentation of group actions: generic and client specific issues.

27.6. What are generic and specific issues?

Generic issues are those common to all cases. Usually these are dealt with by lead solicitors whereas the other solicitors simply investigate the issues specific to their client.

Generic issues are most likely to be the issues on liability which are common to all cases; for example, was the defendant negligent in producing the product? Specific issues are likely to be those on quantum such as the exact injury your client has suffered or the financial loss it has caused. However matters are not always so simple; there may also be generic issues on quantum; for example, the lead solicitors may negotiate a standard amount for pre-death terror in the cases of people killed in a boat sinking incident or some other conventional figures of damages. A solicitor dealing with specific cases may be involved in deciding issues of liability particularly in finding out facts about your client's case such as what date the client took particular drugs and the warnings that were given about them. You will be finding out those issues which are specific to your client. You will have to apply them to the generic findings regarding the general liability of the defendant in specific circumstances. In order to do so you will have to familiarise yourself with all the important elements of the action and how they affect your client; however, you will normally do this with the assistance of information provided by the lead solicitors rather than carrying out your own independent investigation. It is because of these complications and the likelihood that there will be duplication of work that the Legal Service Commission has recommended that generally it will give "all-work" contracts to the lead firms. You may find, therefore, that if your client wants public funding he or she will be obliged to transfer to another firm.

27.7. Cost provisions and funding in brief

Consideration of costs in a group action raises problems that have for years vexed parties, representatives and courts. Again for the first time the CPR provides specific guidance on this and a read of CPR Part 48.6A is essential.

In brief, this refers to two areas of costs, to match the two areas of work considered above:

(1) Individual cost. This is the cost that relates solely to issues specific to a claimant.

(2) Common cost. This is cost incurred in GLO issues, costs incurred in a specific case for the time that it was a test case and the lead solicitors costs in administering the group litigation.

The general rule, again subject to court determination otherwise, is that common costs are shared equally between the claimants in the group on a several basis, whilst individual costs are payable by the specific claimant to whose claim they relate.

The court, when dealing with generic and specific issues should direct which proportion of costs incurred relates to common or individual liabilities. If it does not do so then this is a matter with which, ultimately the costs judge will have to deal.

Do watch out for provisions in situations where your client joins or leaves the group after work has already been done on generic issues. In the former situation the court may order your client to become liable for already incurred costs. In the latter situation your client may still be liable for a share of the common costs up until the date of departure from the group. It is important that you advise your client of these provisions. What remains clear from the cost provisions is that the court, whether through the management of the claim, or by costs judge still retains a large degree of discretion over cost liabilities within group actions.

27.8. Case plan and liaison with lead solicitors

If you are acting for an individual claimant in a case where other solicitors are carrying out the generic work then it is likely that the solicitors dealing with the generic aspect of the action will prepare a case plan and will inform all solicitors dealing with individual issues of the work which they have to carry out and the timetable for doing so. You should follow carefully whatever case plan has been prepared and liaise with the lead solicitors to ensure that the work is correct, otherwise you may find your client's claim struck out and yourself facing a negligence action.

27.9. Problems with present group actions

If there are a large number of cases there is a danger of both generic and individual cost of actions escalating in an uncontrollable way without sufficient resulting benefit to any party in the action.

The costs of these actions, particularly pharmaceutical actions or environmental actions where there is a large amount of disclosure against the defendant, mean that it would be uneconomic to take one case because the costs would so far outweigh the likely benefit. It is therefore important to take a number of cases. However, each individual case may be very small and they may differ as to the damage suffered and when and how caused. In particular the issues involved in liability are likely to be complex. It is for this reason that test cases are selected carefully to ensure that in hearing them the court is able to deal with all general and common issues that arise.

The numbers of claimants and the complex generic issues can cause delay of many years even before lead cases are brought to trial. The Court of Appeal considered these difficulties in the Benzodiazepine cases and has set out criteria to Judges to assess whether group actions are economically viable. They will consider the proportionality of irrecoverable costs as against likely damages and take the view that cases where costs are likely to outweigh individual damages should not proceed.

Many of the orders which have been made historically in group actions such as costs sharing and cut-off dates have little or no formal statutory basis and there are still many areas of great uncertainty, for example how can claimants who miss a cut-off date pursue their claims? Cost sharing orders are complex and regularly bring up legal and practical difficulties of interpretation and application.

Progress of the action can become swamped by the progress of investigating individual claims. It may only be at a late stage that a true picture of the action merges. Meanwhile defendants may be unable to assess risk and early settlement of an action may be impossible. Defendants sometimes object to generic issues being tried first and try to insist on all cases being proved early on. This is often considered by claimants simply to be a tactic to make the litigation so expensive that claimants are forced to abandon claims.

Accordingly, whilst the new rules for group actions are welcome some of the old uncertainties still remain. This is not necessarily a criticism. How does one cater for those potential claimants who present a case significantly after the bulk of claims have either been disposed of or after a GLO cut off date has passed? One of the difficulties of global settlement can be that apportionments between claimants may be impossible until the full extent of those entitled to compensation is known. The reverse is how long should a defendant have to wait before being in a position to assess total exposure on a group claim?

27.10. Cases not suitable for special rules

Some actions will, although there are common factors, not be considered suitable for special rules; particularly if there are a small number of claimants (say under 50) or if there are no sufficient common issues to have the cases decided together. Other circumstances where the lead solicitors will play little role is, for example, in a case where the defendants admit liability early on or agree to pay damages without proof of liability. In such a case those negotiations and letters will normally be done through the steering committee and thereafter you will be involved on behalf of your client to negotiate a settlement on normal principles.

27.11. Settling the action

Obviously, if you are an individual solicitor you may hear of the settlement offer from the lead solicitors. It is for you to advise your client on this offer with the guidance of the lead solicitors. If your client's action is not one of the lead actions then you may be in some difficulty because insufficient investigation may have taken place, if your client's action was stayed at an early stage, to allow your client properly to be advised on damages. If you advise a client who rejects the offer then there is the risk that the client would not obtain more if they continued but, much more problematic is the fact that your client is unlikely to be able to take on the generic costs of the action alone. You must therefore speak to the lead solicitors about the offer and the advisability of settlement. If necessary, you must ask for a stay to get the information for you to advise your client properly; for example, further medical and expert reports. In the end you may just have to advise your client as to the pros and cons and the costs of continuing and allow your client to make the decision.

27.12. Overseas claims

You should always be aware in group cases, particularly in pharmaceutical ones, that there may be a possibility of claims continuing in other jurisdictions, particularly the U.S. In recent years it has become much harder to litigate in the U.S. but it is always worth considering forum shopping to obtain the best deal for your client. The silicon implant litigation was a classic example of such a group action.

27.13. Conclusion

If you are acting in a group case where legal aid is involved and you are not the lead solicitor you need to read carefully the relevant Legal Services rules. You should be aware that defendants may take all sorts of tactical steps to try and stop the litigation including making representations to the Legal Services on the application for public funding. This is very difficult for the claimants because at the time of the application for public funding claimants will seldom have enough information to counter allegations made by the defendants to state that cases have little prospect of success. Group actions in the country have, in recent years, been very difficult and many of them have been unsuccessful. Probably this was not because the cases were not good but because they got bogged down in procedural and logistical problems which became impossible to solve without the costs being astronomic. If you are involved in a group action it is very important that you liaise with other solicitors dealing with the action to ensure that there is no unnecessary duplication of costs. However, it is important to ensure that your client's interests are properly addressed. Do not assume that other solicitors know better than you. If your client has come up with a completely different set of symptoms or does not seem to fit into the generic statements of claim then you must make this point quickly in order to ensure that something has not been overlooked.

If you and your client do not like the way the lead firms are dealing with the generic issues, do not assume that you can simply opt out and take the case alone. The effect of the court orders and public funding make it likely that you will be subject to the lead firm's decisions and that you will only have the freedom to act in obtaining reports and dealing with the individual aspects of your client's claim. Increasingly, your client will not be able to choose which solicitor acts. Therefore it is very important to make sure that you do not run up unnecessary generic costs which will be irrecoverable on behalf of your client. Remember also that unless the court indicates otherwise on your application once on the group register your client will be bound by orders and judgments made within the GLO.

A few final words of caution: Before you embark on any involvement in this type of litigation do consider whether it is economic for you to do so. This is not necessarily the same as deciding if it is economic for your client to pursue the claim. Different considerations arise. If you have only one of many claimants, are not doing the generic work but may be expected, at fairly short notice, to advise on quantum or to present the claim within a fairly tight timescale, the risks to you may completely outweigh what costs you may make. This is particularly so if this is your first involvement in a group claim and you are having to research the rules, for which you will certainly not be paid. Managing a client's expectations may, in such situations, best be achieved by referring the client to the lead solicitor. Rarely will you lose other business of a client by so doing as most clients accept this form of claim is unique and that you can still service their other needs. Indeed, your stock with the client may even increase as a result of your honesty.

If you do undertake generic work do pause to consider your insurance situation. Check with your insurers what their policy is if you are negligent in dealing with generic issues to the extent that all claims fail. Some will treat that as one claim, as there will be one act of negligence. With many potential disgruntled claimants the limit on your insurance for one claim may not be high enough to meet the liability to them.

28. Small Claims, Criminal Injuries Compensation and Compensation Orders

This chapter covers some less formal means of obtaining compensation which you may have to consider with your client. They all have limited, or non existent cost recovery provisions.

28.1. Small claims

What is the small claims procedure?

The Small Claims Scheme (Formerly known as Court Based Automatic Arbitration Procedure) was an American idea which started in Philadelphia in the early 1950s and came to England in 1973. It provides that in defended small claims which are currently those claims with a value under £5,000 (save for a few exceptions) on allocation the claim will be allocated to the small claims track which means that there will be a small claim hearing. One of the exceptions arises where the total value of all losses is under £5,000 but the "pain suffering and loss of amenity" damages will exceed £1,000. In this situation the claim will not be allocated to the small claims track.

The difficulty in advising your client in such a claim is that there is only limited provision for recovery of cost. If the claim settles before issue then you can only recover disbursements from the other side and if the claim settles after issue of proceedings or by order on small claim hearing then fixed fees only are recoverable. However, when you first see the client it may be difficult to assess what the likely damages will be. For example, if you are consulted within a few weeks of an accident by a client suffering from a whiplash injury that might resolve within days, weeks, months, years or not at all. In such situations you must be careful what advice you give about cost recovery and about incurring any substantial fees without first seeing whether there is a sufficiently speedy recovery to make advice on the small claims procedure a necessity.

The situation is not ideal. Even if you correctly identify the cost problem and advise that in fact from a financial point of view your client must be better off pursuing the claim him or herself is it right then to leave a claimant to deal personally with experienced claims negotiators from an insurance company who are likely to instruct solicitors or a junior counsel to attend any small claim hearing on their behalf? This concern is a trite one aired many times before. It has perhaps ensured that the small claim limit is significantly less in injury claims than the normal financial cut off. However, it still leaves claimants in person to try to deal with the personal injury protocol, evidence gathering, the obtaining of medical evidence and the presentation and valuation of a claim. The hearing may be informal but the client still needs to have appropriate evidence before the court to vouch the losses.

Proposals for reform

In December 1993 the Lord Chancellor's Department put out a consultation paper on costs in small personal injury actions suggesting that limited costs could be awarded in these cases. The Lord Chancellor's Department agreed that the then current no costs regime in cases under £1,000 was particularly unfair to PI claimants because when the final judgment is in their favour they cannot recover the cost of obtaining the advice they needed in order to prosecute the claim. The proposals met with a storm of protest as being insufficient to protect the interests of personal injury claimants. However, in June 1994 *Afzal v. Ford Motor Company Ltd, The Independent,* June 16, 1994 was decided (see below) in which the Court of Appeal decided that personal injury cases, including Employers' Liability cases, were suitable for the normal arbitration procedure and that no costs should be awarded. In light of this decision, the Lord Chancellor's Department announced in August 1994 that it would take no further steps on its proposals and consultation paper despite the fact that it admitted in that paper that the small claims procedure was not appropriate for personal injury claims.

Similar concerns were considered by the Lord Woolf enquiry team. The upshot is that the "pain, suffering and loss of amenity" limit was increased to £1,000. Increased is probably correct term as most courts before CPR interpreted the previous "personal injury" limit to mean £1,000 for the pain, suffering and loss of amenity **and** any special damages arising from the injury such as loss of earnings, treatment fees, etc. In other words, the "pain, suffering and loss of amenity" award might be £400 but a loss of earnings caused by the injury of £700 would mean that the claim would not be in small claims. Under the CPR a claim with similar losses would fall well within the small claims track.

The reference to small claims

If the claimant cannot reasonably expect to be awarded more than £1,000 you should state this in the Particulars of Claim.

The Claim Form requires you to complete a statement of value in all claims (see precedent 1 in appendix E). When dealing with lower value injury claims be realistic as over valuation may be a mistake that comes home to roost (see below). If you believe that the "pain, suffering and loss of amenity" claim is worth in excess of £1,000 but in the defence the defendant states to the contrary then this will be a matter for the court to consider on receipt of allocation questionnaire when considering allocation to track. On this point it is worth noting that in cases where liability is admitted and the claim proceeds to disposal only the claim is not usually allocated to a track, as we have seen before. The exception is where the disposal will be for less than the small claims limit. In such situations the court will allocate the claim to the small claims track and fix a small claims hearing that will be the disposal. This will happen even if the claim becomes disputed on quantum only by virtue of a default judgment. Accordingly, the loophole in the County Court Rules that enabled a full cost recovery where judgment was entered in default for a sum to be assessed has now gone.

Inflated claims

You may decide that to try to avoid a referral to the small claims track you will inflate the likely value of the claim for the purposes of the statement of value. This is unlikely to succeed under the CPR. The defendant will no doubt state in the defence that the value is less and the court will have to address this on considering the allocation questionnaires that will then follow. The chance of a claim plainly not worth £1,000 for "pain, suffering and loss of amenity" slipping through the net is slight. All that may happen is that the court may have to fix an allocation hearing for which if you lose you may find a wasted cost order being made against you as valuation is a solicitor rather than a client point.

There is, though, a difference between deliberate over statement of the claim and a genuinely held view, even if it is ultimately one that the court does not share. With the wide disparity of awards reported on smaller injuries it can be very difficult to be definitive about whether a claim is going to be small or fast track. Take, for example, reported cases on minor neck injuries (whiplash). There are some cases where a full recovery was made in a week where awards now worth over £1,000 have been made. Equally, there are cases where the full recovery may have taken between four and six months where similar awards have been made. In such cases surely in advising a client properly you must explain the broad band of possible awards but ought to conclude by advising that you may be artificially limiting the claim if you limit it to £1,000. As awards at this level are rarely, if ever, suitable for appeal a lot depends on where within the band your local court fits. Of course, that raises questions of whether you should 'court shop' for a more generous court than your local. Whilst the final hearing is likely to be transferred back to your local court your concern is with the value that the allocating court places on the claim.

Sometimes, you are helped in solving this dilemma by the defendant using the Part 36 procedure to your advantage. Often, defendants will erroneously make a formal Part 36 offer for a sum below small claim level. However, it is the allocation to the small claims track that is relevant. If the offer is made before that then an acceptance should give rise to ordinary cost recovery. This buys off the risk factor for you and your client as for the client the difference between damages of £900 and £1,000 is not worth an argument save for the cost implications. Defendants do try to argue that in such situations there is no cost liability as the offer was for less than £1,000. Both the rules and current decisions seem against them (see *Dean v. Griffin* (2000) 9 C.L. 53).

The defence

If the defendant thinks that there is no reasonable prospect that the claim for "pain, suffering and loss of amenity" will exceed £1,000 then the defendant should not apply for the action to be struck out for misuse of process or stay the action but should state in the defence that the claim cannot reasonably exceed £1,000 for "pain, suffering and loss of amenity" of the claim and ask for the action to be allocated to the small claims track. This request will be repeated in the allocation questionnaire and the court will then decide.

Factors relevant to allocation to small claims track

When considering the track to which a particular claim should be allocated the court must consider the following:

(i) the financial value of the claim;

(ii) the complexity of the claim;

(iii) the nature of the remedies sought;

(iv) the number of parties (although the value of the claim against more than one defendant is not aggregated as the claim against each defendant is viewed separately);

(v) the value of any Part 20 counterclaim;

(vi) the amount of oral evidence (presumably on the basis that a fast track trial should be a maximum of one day and it would be odd to allow a small claim hearing for longer);

(vii) the importance of the matters raised in the claim to the parties;

(viii) the views of the parties;

(ix) the general circumstances,

and it must ignore:

(i) any amount not in dispute;

(ii) any interest claimed;

(iii) costs claimed;

(iv) contributory negligence alleged.

If you wish to challenge any reference to the small claims track then you will need to satisfy the court under the above criteria that the wrong track has been used. Realistically, it is hard to see that you will succeed on this given previous court views, culminating in *Afzal,* about the complexity of injury litigation unless you can succeed on the value point. If you are successful, remember that the small claim costs rules apply only whilst the claim is in that track.

The small claim track procedure

Before the hearing

On allocation to the small claims track the court will fix a small claims hearing date, usually for the first open date, will give a time estimate and give any directions that it deems necessary. There are some standard directions for suitable cases. Sometimes the standard holiday claim or road accident claim directions set out in the practice direction accompanying CPR Part 27 assist. In other cases directions are likely to include permission to rely on the written report of a medical expert and the lodging and service of any other relevant documents to support the claim of a party at least 14 days prior to the hearing.

At the hearing

The whole idea of the small claims process is that it should be as informal as possible. Therefore, whilst one party may be represented and another not that should make no difference as the District or Deputy District judge that hears the claim is likely to ask most of the questions or at least ensure that appropriate examination of the represented party's evidence takes place so that the court has the evidence of both parties put properly to enable a decision to be reached. Most judges are now fairly interventionist believing that the process was not designed for representation and preferring to ask the questions of all witnesses themselves avoiding lengthy and unnecessary examination in chief and cross-examination.

The process is not rough and ready justice but it is designed to be a cheap and speedy dispute resolution forum using the court imposed decision where the parties have failed to resolve matters themselves.

Part 36 Payments

Part 27, which governs the small claims track, specifically precludes Part 36 payments once a claim is allocated to this track.

Costs

As previously stated, costs are limited in the small claims track. Usually, only the following are recoverable if you act for the successful claimant:

- The fixed costs stated on the claim form on issue. These fixed costs are set out in CPR Part 45.

- Court fees. This will be the issue fee and, if the claim is worth over £1,000, the allocation fee of £80.
- Expenses of witnesses limited to £50.
- Expert fees for attendance of a maximum of £200. You will find that it is hard to recover the full £200 if the hearing is relatively brief as this is the maximum fee that can be awarded if for a whole day hearing. However expert attendance should be rare and requires specific court permission.

Note that there is no discretion to increase the fees set out above.

The final possible fee recovery through the small claims track arises if the defendant has conducted the defence unreasonably. The mere fact that the defendant loses at the hearing is not in itself evidence of unreasonable conduct however poor the defence may have been. What is more likely to result in an order for costs is if the defendant waits until the 11th hour to admit liability where no new evidence arises that causes the late change of heart or perhaps where the defendant makes numerous miserly offers and fails to settle or only settles just prior to the hearing. At the moment, this is clearly an area where court practice has not yet become apparent. However, courts have historically been reluctant to make such orders, no doubt on the basis that the small claims process should not really involve lawyers and their fees anyway and the court should not discourage use of the informal no costs procedure by being seen frequently to make costs orders that undermine the purpose of the process.

Appeals

An appeal from a small claim track decision can only be made where there has either been a mistake of law or a serious irregularity in the proceedings. As the whole thrust of the small claim hearing is informality, for example with no evidence being given on oath, it is difficult to envisage a situation where a serious irregularity in proceedings will arise. It would require a situation that it is impossible to see a District or Deputy District Judge allowing to arise such as using the power to control evidence to prevent one party putting forward a case.

From the October 2, 2000 appeals from a small claim track hearing are dealt with under the common CPR Part 52 procedure. Permission will be necessary to appeal (see Chapter 19 for detailed consideration).

Tactical points

The main tactical point is to avoid the small claim track if at all possible and reasonable. Do be careful though. Inflation of the value of the claim leads to the threat of wasted costs, a disgruntled client who has been advised that all the costs will be recovered from the defendant and worse still if it happens a lot the acquisition of an unhelpful local reputation that will damage your own credibility in the court.

A final thought: There are some clients who prefer the no or limited cost security of the small claim court. Do not rail road them into trying to have the claim heard in a different track in pursuit of your own cost agenda. If you have clients such as this then it may still be viable to agree a fixed cost for them. This no doubt depends on how busy you are and whether you have suitable level fee earners for whom this work if done in sufficient volume might even be profitable.

28.2. Criminal injuries compensation

Criminal injuries compensation is an *ex gratia* government scheme to compensate victims of violent crime. It is distinct and separate from compensation orders or civil awards. You are entitled to apply for more than one but if either a criminal compensation award or civil award has been made then these will be offset against any criminal injuries compensation to be awarded. If your client is eligible for both civil damages and criminal injuries compensation you should consider carefully which scheme is likely to give your client more damages. Because of the new tariff provisions (see below) clients who have suffered no loss of earnings may well be better off under the criminal injuries compensation scheme. An equally important question is whether any civil claim is worth pursuing. Whilst your client may have a clear cut case there may be a very real prospect that the defendant will be worth nothing. The final consideration is whether it is wise for your client to start an adversarial and, in these cases, often confrontational process against someone who may have already assaulted them.

The old scheme and the tariff scheme

Up to March 31, 1994, criminal injuries compensation was assessed on a similar basis to common law compensation (although there were different rules as to contributory negligence); that is there was a detailed investigation of the degree of a client's suffering and financial loss. However, in 1993, the government published a White Paper entitled "*Compensating Victims of Violent Crime: Changes to the Criminal Injury Compensation Scheme*" (Cm. 2434) December 15, 1993. This paper suggested that the criminal injuries compensation scheme should not be intended to give full compensation for losses but should be an expression of public sympathy to victims of violent crime. In order to obtain prompt and consistent decisions they stated that instead of the compensation based scheme, victims would be paid on a tariff according to the severity of their injuries.

The new scheme was brought in by the Secretary of State for the Home Office, Michael Howard, without going through Parliament. In *R v. Secretary of State for the Home Department, ex p. Fire Brigades Union* [1995] 2 All E.R. 244, HL(E) the House of Lords held that the introduction of the scheme on this basis was unlawful. This meant that applications between April 1, 1994 and April 5, 1995 were reviewed and decided on interim arrangements (see practice set out in Law Society's Gazette 92/17, May 3, 1995). Applications from April 6, 1995 to March 31, 1994 were made on the old scheme. The Government then enacted the Criminal Injuries Compensation Act 1995 which came into force on April 1, 1996. This also introduced a tariff scheme that applies to all applications that have been received after April 1, 1996. It is now very rare to see old cases being decided under the old scheme. Those that are left tend to be serious injuries where the final medical prognosis has taken a long time and where there have been various appeals in the process slowing it down.

The tariff

There are 25 tariff levels (currently from £1,000 to £250,000) and some 360 odd injury groupings. The tariff awards are meant to include something for the degree of shock which an applicant in normal circumstances will suffer. If, though, the shock is so serious that it would in fact qualify in its own right for a higher award than the physical injury then it is only the shock that is compensated. For multiple injuries the compensation is calculated as the tariff amount for the higher rated injury plus 10 per cent of the tariff amount for the second-highest rated injury plus 5 per cent of the tariff amount for the third-highest rated description of injury. This may obviously mean that some victims of multiple injury go under-compensated.

Loss of earnings

No loss of earnings or other expenses are payable for the first 28 weeks of injury. If the applicant has lost earnings or earning capacity for longer than 28 weeks as a direct consequence of the injury then they can apply for loss of earnings and special expenses.

(i) Loss of earnings. This is the net loss after taking into account deductions. Social Security benefits, payments under insurance arrangements and pension receipts. There is a maximum net loss of one and a half times gross average industrial earnings (around £30,000 per year). If the loss is continuing it will be calculated on a multiplier/multiplicand basis.

(ii) Special expenses; these include certain loss of property, NHS and private health treatment and costs of long-term care.

Financial limits

The lower limit for making a claim for criminal injury compensation is £1,000 which is the tariff, for example, for a loss of one tooth, other than the front tooth, or a fractured rib. The upper limit is £500,000 which would cover, for example, £250,000 for quadriplegia plus loss of earnings (*see above*) (note that before the tariff it was not uncommon for cases of the upmost severity to attract CICB awards of over £1 m).

How to apply

The application form

Applications are made on an application form issued by the Criminal Injuries Compensation Authority. The form is simple, in plain English and has full guidance notes. The address is CICA, Tay House, 300 Bath Street, Glasgow G2 4JR tel: 0141 331 2726. The form is accompanied by guides to the scheme.

Medical evidence

In particular, note that your client does not have to send medical evidence with the claim; you simply set out details of the treating doctor and the Police and Criminal Injuries Compensation Authority carries out the investigations and contacts the doctor direct and at its own cost for a report. Sometimes, your client may be asked to attend for a medical. This will be as near to where your client lives as possible.

Conditions for applying

Crime of violence

The injury for which your client seeks to claim must arise from:

- a crime of violence or threat of violence, or
- employment by a railway company leading to presence and sight of another person being injured or killed as a result of trespassing on the railway or discovering a body on or beside a track, or
- an attempt to catch an offender, a suspected offender or an attempt to assist the police catch an offender, or
- a crime of arson, or
- poisoning, or
- animal attack that constitutes a crime of violence, or
- deliberate use of a car as a weapon. In this case you will find that more often than not the Motor Insurers Bureau deals with the claim if the driver was uninsured or unidentified given how hard it is to determine whether in fact a vehicle has been used as a weapon. Do check in each case but there is an apparent unwritten rule that in such cases the MIB rather than the CICA should be the first port of call. Be particularly careful if you are approaching the two year limitation within the CICA scheme. You may not then be able to await an MIB decision and may have to apply to both to protect your client's position until a decision as to who is to deal is made) See Chapter 29 for how to apply to the MIB.

A conviction is unnecessary but it would obviously make the claim harder if there has been no conviction. It is possible to obtain criminal injuries compensation if the perpetrator of the violent acts has never been found. It is also possible to obtain compensation in cases where the perpetrator cannot be convicted, for example in the case of a child assailant. However, see the guidance that raises particular difficulties where the assailant and victim are both children. Whilst a conviction may not be necessary what is necessary is that your client informs the police of the circumstances and co-operates with enquiries and any subsequent prosecution.

Limitation

An application must be made within two years of the date of the incident *not* the date of the conviction. The Authority will waive this requirement in exceptional circumstances when it is just and reasonable to do so. One classic example of this is in sexual abuse cases where it takes the applicant some time to pluck up courage to report the matter.

Refusing or reducing the award

This is one of the most contentious areas of the scheme. The Board is entitled to withhold or reduce the award if:

(a) your client did not take all reasonable steps to inform the police and to do so promptly

(b) your client failed to co-operate with the police;

(c) your client failed to co-operate with the Criminal Injuries Compensation Authority;

(d) your client's conduct before, during or after the event makes it inappropriate that full award or any award be granted;

(e) your client's character shown by a criminal conviction (not spent conviction) or any other evidence available to the claims officer makes it inappropriate that a full award or any award at all should be granted (see paragraph 13e of the scheme for how the deduction is calculated)

The Authority often initially refuses to give an award under grounds (d) and (e) and there need be no causal connection between the conduct or character and the criminal incident complained of. For example, awards have been refused under (d) because an applicant who was threatened with violence stood up; the authority held that this was threatening behaviour which made an award inappropriate. Under (e) awards have been refused because the applicant who had been the subject of an unprovoked attack in the street had, ten years previously, been convicted of possessing cannabis. Such decisions should always be appealed and often are successful on appeal.

Another ground on which awards can be withheld is that the Authority will not pay if there is any likelihood that the person who caused injury were to benefit (paragraph 15) and, in particular, under paragraph 16 it will not make an award to a husband and wife still living together or to members of the same household unless there has been a prosecution.

Interim awards

The normal award is by way of a lump sum. Interim awards can be given if the final award cannot be assessed because injuries have not stabilised.

Fatal cases

A simple point to start. If you are acting for a client who is applying for compensation following the death of a victim of violent crime then you should ensure that you do so on a Fatal Injury application form as opposed to the normal Personal Injury application form. In fatal cases (which include cases where the applicant dies before the date of the award) the compensation is calculated very differently than in civil cases (see Chapter 25 for Fatal Awards in civil cases). The rules are complex and if you are assisting with a fatal case you should read the Authority's Guide to Applicants for Compensation in Fatal Cases. Your client must be from the category of those entitled to apply, being either a relative or dependant of the deceased. These categories are refined by specific reference to the applicant being someone who was at the time of the deceased's death their:

- husband or wife; or
- unmarried but long term partner of the opposite sex; or
- parent; or
- child of any age; or
- former husband or wife who was financially supported by the deceased.

There is a distinction to be made between cases where the violence caused the death and cases where the deceased subsequently died of another cause. In the latter, the same losses as arise in a personal injury CICA claim can be claimed if appropriate. In the former, there are an increased number of heads of claim. These include:

(a) Funeral expenses.

(b) A "standard amount" payable to spouses, persons who lived with the deceased as husband and wife for two years immediately preceding the death or a parent or child of the deceased (whatever the age of the deceased). If only one person qualifies under this head they will be paid £10,000. Two or more will be paid £5,000 each. It should be noted that this category is wider than for a statutory bereavement payment and the amount payable is higher. This is called a fatal injury award.

(c) Dependency award, payable to the categories mentioned above. This is calculated on a similar basis to a loss of dependency in civil claims.

(d) Loss of parental services. This is a new head for children under 18 who will be paid £2,000 pa until they reach 18. It is additional to any dependency award received under (c) above.

The total award paid under all these heads is subject to the maximum of £500,000 and the award can be refused or rejected on the same basis as any other claim.

Reviews and appeals

If you consider that your client's application has been dealt with wrongly then you can ask for that to be reviewed. You must do this within 90 days of the date of the letter giving you the decision. This should be diarised and notified to the client who must appreciate the need for urgency. When asking for review you must set out your reasons. In other words, explain why you think that the decision is wrong. The decision, whether on eligibility or amount or both, will then be reviewed and a fresh decision with reasons will be provided. The review can lead to the same outcome, an increase *or decrease* in award or a determination that no award is due when previously something had been offered. This is something else that you need to consider carefully with your client before embarking on a review. Like unit trusts awards can go down as well as up! Your function is to ensure that is not in the small print of the information given to the client. If the review is unfavourable and you believe that the client has good grounds for contesting that then there is an appeal process. This must be commenced within 30 days of the letter giving you or your client the outcome of the review process. The appeal is to the CICA panel the members of whom are wholly independent of the CICA. The appeal can be an oral or a paper exercise and like the review can lead to the same, a better or a worse outcome than that being appealed. The same warnings should be given to the client as were prior to the review process.

Costs

Solicitors' costs are not paid in the criminal injuries compensation scheme either for the original application or for any appeal. The applicant can bring a friend or legal adviser to assist any oral appeal and the panel has a discretion to pay the reasonable expenses of an applicant and witnesses. If the panel decides that the request for a hearing is frivolous then they may withhold expenses and/or reduce any award previously offered.

Legal aid

Regardless of recent cut backs in public funding this has made little difference. The CICA procedure is that of a tribunal and public funding has never been available under a full certificate.

Tactical points

You should always advise your client of the possibility of taking a criminal injuries compensation claim particularly because damages may in certain circumstances be higher than in a civil claim; it is a fairly inexpensive and simple procedure which can be undertaken by the client personally or with limited lawyer involvement and is a non confrontational remedy that does not exacerbate a situation that may already exist.

28.3. Criminal compensation orders

A compensation order can be made in respect of personal injury, loss or damage resulting from an offence for which an offender is convicted or any offence taken into consideration. This includes injury, loss or damage which would not be actionable in the civil courts (see below). You should particularly consider applying for a compensation order if your client's claim is easily quantifiable and if the quantum is low so it would be in the small claims jurisdiction or would be below the threshold for criminal injuries compensation (see above). Criminal courts are meant always to consider compensation orders. If the court has power to make a compensation order but does not do so it must give a reason for not doing so on passing sentence. Legal aid is not available for an application for a compensation order. The maximum compensation order that can be awarded in the magistrates' court is £5,000 (Magistrates' Court Act 1980, s. 40). In the crown court there is no upper limit.

The compensation order is payable by the offender so there is no point making an application if the offender has no means. However, if the offender is under 18, the order can be made against the parent(s) or guardian. The court can order that the payment be made by direct debit instalments to the victim or that the offender be given time to pay.

Exemptions

Motor vehicle accidents

Compensation orders cannot be made for incidents arising out of an accident caused by the presence of a motor vehicle on the road. Such claims should be compensated for by insurance companies or the MIB. However, orders can be made if:

(a) the claim is in respect of damage to property stolen under the Theft Act; or

(b) it is an area where there is no MIB Agreement and the driver was not insured.

Fatal accidents

Criminal compensation orders can be made on death (except by motor vehicles) to cover funeral expenses and bereavement payments. The maximum bereavement payment is limited to the persons and the amount set out under the Fatal Accidents Act 1976 (see Chapter 25). The current financial limit is £7,500.

Scale of awards

The court can award such amount "as the court considers appropriate, having regard to any evidence any representations" made by the prosecutor and the accused. The court must have regard to the means of the offender and must not make and order which the offender would be unable to pay. In personal injury cases the court should use the current CICA

Guidelines on quantum (see above) and have reference to the Judicial Studies Board Guidelines. Home Office Circular 53 of 1993 suggested the following figures:

- graze up to £50;
- bruise up to £75;
- black eye up to £100;
- cut with no permanent scarring £75–£500;
- sprain £100–£1,000;
- loss of tooth £250–£500 (front tooth £1,000);
- facial scar (however small but leaves permanent disfigurement) £750 as a starting point plus;
- vicious slash wound (ear to corner of mouth or under chin) £6,000–£9,000 plus;
- simple broken wrist £1,750–£2,250;
- minor injury leading to reasonable absence from work of about two to three weeks £550 to £850.

Figures are also given for more serious injuries.

How to apply

The procedure is very informal which is one of its advantages. It must be made "on application or otherwise" and the normal method is to ask the prosecutor to ask for a payment on your behalf. Most police officers and the Crown Prosecution Service are willing to do this. However you should provide them with the necessary evidence.

An order must not be made unless the injury can fairly be said to arise from the event and it should not be made unless the fact that the loss was incurred or the extent of the loss is either proved or admitted. The court can make assessments and approximations but these must be based on real evidence and the Court of Appeal discourages criminal courts from embarking on complicated investigations of quantum or liability. A criminal injuries compensation order is therefore only appropriate in a fairly straightforward case. However, there is no problem with claiming damages for personal injury as long as you give details of evidence of the precise injuries. For example, in the case of *R v. Welch* [1982] 4 Cr.App.R.(S) 213 the appellant battered the victim in the face following a driving incident. It was shown that the appellant had cuts to his nose and the tip of his nose was broken. The Court of Appeal upheld the compensation order of £400 since it was a small amount and details of the precise injuries had been given. Interest can be granted on an award.

An award can be given for emotional distress but the court will only uphold the modest amount for this and there must be evidence of it.

Appeal and review

The offender is entitled to appeal and under the Powers of Criminal Courts Act 1973, s. 37 the court may review the case at any time before the whole amount has been paid if it thinks that:

(a) civil procedures have assessed damage at less than the court ordered;

(b) property has been restored; or

(c) the offender's means have changed and the offender has insufficient means to pay.

If a subsequent award is made in civil proceedings then the amount of the criminal injuries compensation order is taken into account. You cannot recover twice for the same injury.

Enforcement

If there is default it is heard by the magistrates' court even if the crown court imposed the original order. The magistrates have various penalties at their disposal including imprisoning the offender for a term shown under the table of the Magistrates' Court Act 1980, Sched. 4. The crown court can direct a longer maximum if the table is inadequate and the compensation order was for more than £20,000.

Tactical points

It will be seen that a criminal compensation order can be useful in cases where the injury is easily discernible or where there is a large amount of property loss. It is much cheaper and quicker than using the civil courts and will not result in solicitors' costs. However, it is not appropriate if the damage does not flow clearly from the injury or if there is complicated evidence to be given on liability or quantum. Obviously, it is of no use in cases where the offender has little or no means which is why it is a remedy that you will encounter infrequently. It may be something to offer clients whose cases fall within small claim track jurisdiction and for whom it would be uneconomic for you to represent in a civil claim.

29. The Motor Insurers' Bureau

The Motor Insurer's Bureau (MIB) will deal with two types of claim: those in which the defendant motorist is uninsured, and those in which the defendant cannot be traced (*i.e.* "hit and run" cases). If the motorist's identity was never known (because, for example, he gave a false name) then it is treated as a hit and run case, with the motorist being untraced, rather than uninsured. Sometimes, the MIB will try to suggest that because an address at which the potential defendant cannot be traced was given at the accident scene then the claim is under the untraced driver scheme. Do investigate this properly as you may find that a successful criminal prosecution for driving without insurance, etc. took place with that address being used for service purposes. As the amount of financial recovery possible is significantly greater under the uninsured scheme that must be the preferred scheme for your client.

The liability of the MIB to deal with these claims is set out in two separate agreements; the texts of both agreements, and the explanatory notes that accompany them, are set out in Appendix G.

29.1. The uninsured defendant

Without prior consultation and to the consternation of many claimant lawyers organisations a new MIB (Compensation of the Victims of Uninsured Drivers) Agreement came into force on October 1, 1999 which applies to accidents occurring on or after that date. For accidents occurring before that date the 1988 agreement continues.

The new agreement contains many changes and many potential pitfalls for the unwary. The agreement will be considered in this chapter but it should be stressed at the outset that this chapter just constitutes a broad outline and if you have a claim that falls within the agreement then there is absolutely no substitute for reading the agreement in full.

Broadly speaking, if the claimant has complied with the various obligations imposed under the agreement, then, if the claimant obtains a judgment against a person following a road accident in a court in Great Britain which is unsatisfied the MIB will pay the relevant sum to the claimant.

There are a number of exclusions set out in clause 6 of the agreement the one most frequently encountered being that the claim arises out of use by the claimant of a vehicle that is not covered by a contract of insurance in force at the time of the accident covering the use to which the vehicle was being put at the time of the accident, and the claimant knew or ought to have known that this was the case.

This exclusion has caused an enormous amount of controversy because the corresponding provision in the Road Traffic Act refers only to actual knowledge. The Motor Accident Solicitors Society obtained leave for judicial review of this provision but a decision was then deferred because another case was already en route to the House Of Lords on this point.

Judgment in that case (*White v. White, The Times*, March 6, 2001) was delivered in March 2001. The House of Lords (Lord Scott dissenting) decided that a claimant was not debarred from making a claim under the agreement by mere carelessness or even negligence in ascertaining whether the driver of the car in which he or she was a passenger was insured. This was despite the fact that Judge Potter at first instance had concluded that whilst the claimant may not have actual knowledge that the driver was uninsured the fact that he was stood out a mile. In other words, the House of Lords decided that the exception should be construed restrictively. Good news for passengers claiming under the scheme although the old arguments on whether or not there was actual notice will remain.

Essential requirements

Under the 1999 agreement the MIB incurs no liability unless you comply with various conditions precedent. There were important notice provisions in the previous scheme but those seem few in the light of the new requirements. Again, there can be no substitute for reading clauses 7–15 of the agreement itself. In summary the conditions are as follows:

(1) Notice of issue of proceedings must be given to the MIB not later than 14 days after the commencement of those proceedings.

This notice requirement includes:

- notice in writing that proceedings have been issued together with a copy of the sealed claim form providing evidence of commencement of proceedings and, in Scotland alone a statement of the means of service;
- a copy of any insurance policy, or details of it, that provides any benefit in the case of death or injury or damage to property to which these proceedings relate where the claimant is the insured under such a policy and benefits are available;
- copies of all correspondence that you or the claimant have had with the defendant, any representative of the defendant or any potential insurers of the defendant which is relevant to the claim being pre-

sented or any other policy of insurance that might cover the defendant;

- a copy of the Particulars of Claim. If this is not indorsed on the claim form then the Particulars of Claim need to be served on the MIB within seven days of service on the defendant (remember the deemed time periods for service in Chapter 9);
- copies of all documents required to be served with the claim form or Particulars of Claim (for example medical evidence, schedule of loss, public funding notices, certificates of suitability and notices of funding). Again if the Particulars of Claim have not been served then these documents have to be served within seven days of service of the particulars of claim on the defendant.

(2) Notice of the date of service of the claim form must be given to the MIB no later that seven days after the the date on which the claimant receives notification from the court that service has occurred, the date of actual personal service or the date when the claimant receives notification from the defendant that service has occurred OR within 14 days after the date on which service is deemed to take place under the CPR (see Chapter 9) **whichever is the earlier.**

(3) Notice of receipt of a defence in the claim, of any amendment to the Particulars of Claim, any schedule or other document to be served with the Particulars of Claim, the setting down of the case for trial or when the court gives notice of the trial date the date when that notice is received (the question arises-is this the date on which the court gives a trial window or the date on which the actual date is fixed within the window? Caution suggests that you give appropriate notice of both just to make sure) must be given to the MIB not later than seven days after which any of the above occurs. If the occurrence is one involving an amended document then a copy of the amended document must also be served within this period.

(4) You must, within a reasonable time after request from the MIB, provide it with such further information or copies of any further documents as the MIB may reasonably require. Notice of any intention to apply for judgment must be given to the MIB at least 35 days before applying for judgment

(5) You must have demanded the information and particulars set out in section 154 of the Road Traffic Act 1988 from the defendant and if the defendant has not complied with the section 154 request made a formal complaint to the police (note that some police forces insist that the section 154 notice is served by recorded post) and used all reasonable endeavours to obtain the name and address of the registered keeper of the vehicle the defendant was driving (you can make an application to DVLA for this information on payment of a fee).

(6) If required to do so by the MIB and on provision of a full cost indemnity

from the MIB, the claimant must take all reasonable steps to obtain judgment against any person who may be liable in respect of the claim or, on request from the MIB, consent to it being joined as a party to the proceedings. The claimant must assign to the MIB the unsatisfied judgment and any order for costs even if the judgment includes a sum not covered by the agreement (for example the MIB excess) and undertake to repay to the MIB any sum paid by the MIB in respect of any judgment that is either set aside in whole or in part or any sum paid by any other person by way of compensation for the same losses.

As timescales play such a large part in the agreement you should be familiar with clause 2 which defines how to calculate periods. In essence, a timescale expressed to be within a specified period of an event means a period beginning on the day after the happening of the event and where a time is expressed to be within or not less than a specified period before an event the period ends on the day immediately before the happening of the event. If the period is seven days or less then you exclude Saturdays, Sundays, Bank holidays, Christmas Day and Good Friday.

Notice to insurance company

Often, though, the notice will be given to an insurance company and not to the MIB. This happens when the defendant had a policy of insurance but the insurers have been able to repudiate it, thus leaving the defendant uninsured (*e.g.* if there has been the unauthorised use of a vehicle for business purposes; false statements made on the proposal form, etc.). In these circumstances the insurer concerned will have to deal with the claim, and therefore you should give notice to the insurance company, not the MIB. This is because the insurers are liable to deal with the claim, for the Road Traffic Act 1988, ss. 151 and 152 make them responsible for claims made against their insured, even if the policy has been repudiated; this is called the "RTA liability" and is completely separate from the MIB scheme. This notice can be given either before proceedings were started *or* within seven days of proceedings being commenced. To be safe do both. Make sure that the notice is absolutely clear and is not a mere hint or unspecific vague threat of proceedings.

Some further exclusions

Note also that the scheme does not cover:

(a) crown vehicles (but, in practice, the government department concerned will deal with the claim in the usual way);

(b) a claim arising out of the use of a vehicle which is not required to be insured under the Road Traffic Act 1988;

(c) a vehicle that he or she knew or ought to have known to be stolen and the applicant could have been reasonably expected to have removed him or herself from the vehicle as soon as he or she became armed with this knowledge or assumed knowledge.

There are further exceptions and these can be found with more detail on those mentioned above at clause 6 of the agreement.

Proceedings

In practice, unless the MIB is joined to the claim an MIB uninsured motorist claim proceeds like any other claim. As soon as the MIB are notified of the claim they will usually nominate an insurance company to deal with it on their behalf. Thereafter the claimant will correspond with the insurance company, and the case will proceed in the usual way, often being settled without judgment being obtained. Legal costs will form part of the claim to be met by the MIB.

Finally, if the name and address of the driver are known but the driver later becomes untraceable, the correct procedure is to apply under CPR Part 6.8 for service by an alternative procedure on either the MIB or any insurer that it has appointed. The procedure for applying for alternative service has been considered in Chapter 9.

The text of the Uninsured Motorists' Agreement is set out in Appendix G; the notes at the end of the text provide a useful summary of the main provisions.

29.2. The untraced motorist (the hit and run cases)

A separate MIB agreement, the Untraced Motorists' Agreement, deals with liability for untraced motorists. Broadly speaking, the MIB must deal with a claim arising out of the negligence of an untraced motorist if the:

(a) applicant cannot trace the person responsible for the accident;

(b) accident happened in circumstances that would make the untraced person liable to pay damages for negligence;

(c) liability should have been covered by insurance (*i.e.* the agreement only relates to "death or bodily injury"—see Road Traffic Act 1988, s. 145).

This agreement does not cover property damage.

The claim to the MIB must be made within three years of the accident. There are no provisions for the three-year limitation period to be extended; as would be the case with a civil claim (*i.e.* under the Limitation Act 1980).

Progress of proceedings

Note that this is a compensatory scheme, requiring the MIB to embark on an inquisitorial process and does not involve the usual adversarial process of claims handling. You should not therefore do your own investigatory work as this will simply duplicate the MIB's work and the costs will be irrecoverable. However you should check the MIB's offer to ensure it is correct.

On being notified, the MIB will investigate the claim, which will usually involve interviewing your client by way of local enquiry agent and obtain medical reports, etc. Eventually, the MIB will give its written decision which can be appealed against (on either liability or quantum) within six weeks. The grounds of appeal are set out in clause 11 (see Appendix G). The appeal lies to an arbitrator (who will be a Q.C.) who looks through the papers, and who can, if considered necessary, call for further information before giving a decision. The arbitrator's fees will be paid by the MIB unless the arbitrator states that they should be borne by the applicant because there was no reasonable ground for the appeal. There is no appeal from the decision of the arbitrator. Experience reveals that many untraced claims are turned down and unless the claim is really speculative you should consider the appeal process.

You should note that the MIB will only pay £150 profit costs (plus VAT and reasonable disbursements) to the successful applicant's solicitors. Therefore, to protect your client's interests ensure that the MIB does as much of the work as is possible.

If the solicitor acted for more than one applicant in claims arising out of the same accident, then an additional fee of £75 will be paid for each extra claimant. An applicant should always be told that the MIB will not pay:

(a) vehicular damage, damage to property, towage charges and the like, since these items are not compulsorily insurable;

(b) legal costs (other than as set out above);

(c) the sick pay loaned by an employer whilst the claimant was off work (with a civil claim, this would be recoverable).

Frankly, it is often better for the client to be directed to the MIB direct and for you to become involved only at the decision stage on liability and quantum.

One final general and frightening point. The increase in those driving uninsured and those leaving the scene of an accident is such that a significant proportion of the insurance premium paid by the average driver now goes to fund the victims under the two schemes considered. In the ten years from 1990 to 2000 the call on insurers from the MIB for contributions grew from an estimated £39m to an incredible £265m.

Text

The text of the Untraced Motorists' Agreement is set out in Appendix G; the notes at the end of the text provide a useful summary of the main provisions. The procedure for making a claim on the MIB is by letter addressed to "the Secretary", setting out the claim and enclosing any supporting documents. You should ask for a form from the MIB at 152 Silbury Boulevard, Central Milton Keynes, MK9 1NB. They have an extremely helpful telephone advice service. The general telephone number is 01908 830001.

30. Specialist Panels and Accident Line

If you find yourself regularly doing personal injury work (and needing to refer to this book only on more complex points!) you may wish to consider joining the Personal Injury Panel and/or the Clinical Negligence Panel.

30.1 What are specialist panels?

In its Green Paper the *"Works and Organisation of the Legal Profession"* the government stated:

> "the main advantage of Specialist Panels to the public is to give them easier and more informed access to practitioners who they can be assured are skilled in a particular field of law. At the same time, not every area of law requires specialist expertise. Care must be taken to ensure that only those areas of law which need to be specialisms are designated as such, and that the criteria for recognition of a specialist are high enough to ensure competence for maintaining standards but no higher. The criteria must not become unnecessary obstacles which discourage practitioners from becoming specialists, or which artificially limit the supply of legal services to the public in a particular field."

While the Law Society recognise that specialist panels impose a significant burden both on practitioners and on the Law Society, they felt that it would be desirable to establish separate non-exclusive panels covering medical negligence and general personal injuries work since these are complex areas and research evidence shows that the outcome of claims for claimants depends very substantially upon the skill of the solicitor that they instruct. The Law Society put out consultation papers on proposals for the establishment of a Personal Injury Panel and Medical Negligence Panel members in March 1991. After much discussion in the profession the final criteria were established. The first admissions to the Personal Injury Panel were made in November 1993 and by mid-1997 there were about 2,300 registered panel members. Applications for membership of the Medical Negligence Panel were accepted from August 31, 1993 and the first admissions were made in early January 1994. By mid-1997 there were still only about 120 medical negligence panel members. The Personal Injury Panel membership was for a period of five years with renewal then necessary. In fact, renewal was deferred and many of the first batch of members have only just had to renew.

30.2 Criteria for membership of the Law Society Personal Injury and Clinical Negligence Panels

Personal Injury Panel

Despite some concern amongst specialists that the criteria for membership of the Personal Injury Panel had been set too low these remain unaltered.

Applicants must be solicitors or fellows of the Institute of Legal Executives, who have passed the Institute's civil litigation and tort papers. Solicitors must hold practising certificates and have been admitted for three years. Fellows must have at least three years, experience after achieving fellowship of the Institute and must be current fellows.

Applicants must have carried out or directly and actively supervised at least 60 injury cases in the five years prior to application or renewal or at least 36 injury cases in the three years prior to application. As many as half of either number may be clinical negligence cases. Note that this is not reversed and personal injury cases do not count for membership of the Clinical Negligence Panel.

Applicants must have dealt with at least one case where the claimant was under a disability and court approval was necessary and have had ten cases fixed for trial of which two must have involved issues of liability.

There is a general discretion for admittance where the strict criteria are not met if the applicant can illustrate a suitable level of expertise.

Training is a core requirement of membership of the panel. Compulsory attendance on specific courses can be used as a condition precedent of acceptance onto the panel. All applicants must have attended or undertake to attend within 12 months of acceptance a specific one day course on risk assessment.

Clinical Negligence Panel

As with the Personal Injury Panel so the clinical negligence one is open to solicitors and current fellows of the Institute of Legal Executives who have passed the Institute's tort and civil litigation papers. No three year qualification period is specified as the remainder of the criteria require such experience in any event.

The necessary experience requires a good grounding in general personal injury work, although no non clinical negligence cases count in the numbers exercise.

Numbers of cases is again the basic requirement. Applicants need to have conducted 36 clinical negligence cases over the three years prior to application, including at least three cases set down for trial, which one assumes now means fixed for trial. At least one case must involve an award approved by the court where the claimant was under a disability and there must be at least two cases of maximum severity or four involving damages over £1,00,000. If all the criteria cannot be met there is a general discretion to allow panel membership based on successful demonstration of a suitable level of competence or experience.

Certain training requirements are also necessary including at least one major conference on clinical negligence, and AVMA, of course, have an annual conference, and one medical course for lawyers devoted specifically to enhancing lawyers understanding of medicine generally. Both course attendances must have been within the three years immediately prior to the application for panel membership.

The number of panel members and anecdotal evidence confirm that it has proved far harder to achieve membership of the clinical negligence panel than it has the personal injury panel. Whether that is because the criteria for the former are too hard to achieve or the latter too easy is a moot point.

30.3 How to apply

The easiest way is to contact the Law Society by telephone (020 7242 1222), you will be put through to the relevant department. Forms will then be despatched to you.

The application is initially by form rather than interview or examination. However, applicants who are borderline are called for interview to deal with any specific areas of concern or to enable a more detailed exploration of experience to take place.

The form is divided into two sections. The first covers the general systems that your firm has in place. The second covers your own experience, systems and approach. In this section you are required to complete a number of case forms providing clear dates for the progress of claims which highlight how expeditiously you progressed matters and how you dealt with problems. Do remember your client confidentiality obligations, particularly if you are called for interview when you are asked to bring the files that you have used for the case report forms with you for possible scrutiny.

If there is already someone in your firm on the panel then you will not need to complete the first section as information about the firm only needs to be provided once.

An appropriate partner should sign the part of the form relevant to the firm and the second part should be signed by you. The application should be returned with a cheque for the application fee. The application then goes before one of the appointed assessors who determines the application either by approval, rejection or request for interview.

30.4 Other panels

As well as the Law Society Panel there are other panels for specialists that may actually be of more practical use. For example Headway, the organisation for the victims of head injuries and The Spinal Injuries Association both operate panels for acknowledged specialists in these fields. The criteria for membership of these panels are very specific. However, for those qualified to be on the panels then, in addition to the potential for referral work, there is the opportunity to extend expertise as the organisations run training courses, produce magazines and introduce a network of colleagues with whom ideas can be exchanged. One of the major benefits of membership of these panels is that it acts as an eye opener to problems experienced by those with head or spinal injuries that sometimes do not crop up when considering injury claims in the strict parameters of the compensation process. This can assist in producing a better understanding of the needs of a client with such an injury.

In the clinical negligence field AVMA (Action for the Victims of Medical Accidents) still remains preeminent. Membership of this panel like that of the Law Society Clinical Negligence Panel is a necessary passport to a clinical negligence franchise (see Chapter 26).

30.5 Office and personal procedures

In addition to the above, candidates for either panel must show that they:

(a) have a knowledge of the relevant law and access to relevant books;

(b) have a knowledge of procedure and in particular procedures detailed in the Law Society's Civil Litigation Committee's Guide to Good Practice;

(c) understand the ethical issues arising in respect of use of expert witnesses, disclosure of medical reports and conflict;

(d) have professional skills such as negotiating, drafting pleadings, assessing injuries, case management and representation of persons under a disability and that they have advocacy skills.

30.6 Why apply to a specialist panel?

As all panels charge a fee for membership it is worth pausing before applying. For example, the Law Society Personal Injury Panel application fee is £300 + VAT of £52.50 for a single application. You need to evaluate the overall benefit to your practice of injury law. As indicated, some panel membership leads to educational bonus that will have direct application and therefore benefit to you. Some panel membership acts as a passport to potential sources of work. For example, Law Society panel membership can act as an introduction to Accident Line (although this is no longer an automatic entitlement and Accident Line subscriptions are now substantial) and for a public funding clinical negligence franchise.

Membership can also look good in any advertising that you do. However, with potential clients increasingly being pursued by institutional providers of work the benefit to you in terms of off the street work may be slight.

It is possible that membership evidences a sufficient level of expertise so that you will find it cheaper to purchase "after the event" funding for your clients because the funders will accept that specialism means less risk to them However, track record is often more important to an insurer and you may have to prove your expertise to them first rather than rely on an acquired reputation being taken on trust.

The arguments for panel membership are perhaps not as strong as they once were. With increasing pressure on profitability of work it may be that you decide that the cost of the application for membership is an expense that you can now save from your budget.

30.7 Accident Line

When the Law Society Personal Injury Panel was first established one of the major benefits was the automatic membership of Accident Line that this provided. At the time conditional fees were the latest thing and the premium sought to back a conditional fee agreement by Accident Line was the best on the block. Things have moved on. Other insurers entered the conditional fee market, legal aid was withdrawn from virtually all injury work and institutional collectors and providers of injury work came on the scene. The amount of work that Accident Line could provide has dropped, not surprisingly when a comparison is made between the amount spent by various referral sources on advertising.

Something had to change and it was the Accident Line scheme itself. A relaunch in a substantially altered fashion took place in the summer of 2000. With very little warning existing members of the scheme were invited to reapply for membership on the basis that not every one would be successful, that there would be a substantial initial fee for membership (£3,231.25 including VAT for early application) which would then be payable on an annual basis and that a charge would be made for every referral at £58.75 including VAT.

The upshot is that Accident Line now has a much smaller membership and a larger advertising budget. Initial literature suggested that there would be 100 representatives trying to generate referrals. The revamped scheme is still in its infancy and the jury is out on its success.

The scheme may also be a bit too restrictive for many. All conditional fee agreements written by the member firm, or office of the firm with the membership, must use the Accident Line package unless the client arrives with compulsory use of another product as an integral part of the instruction. Otherwise even if the client is not referred by Accident Line there is no discretion and the Accident Line product for insurance must be used. It should be said that linked to this, Accident Line offers its members use of a funding scheme through the Bank Of Ireland.

Unlike the old scheme the insurance premium backing the conditional fee insurance is not set at one level. The premium depends now upon whether the claim is a fast track or multi track case and on the type of accident (road accident, occupational disease or any other type). Current premiums are:

	Fast track	*Multi track*
Road accident	£315	£693
Occupational disease	£892.50	£3,045
Other	£682.50	£2,520

You will notice the enormous increase in price from the previous scheme premiums.

Other specialist organisations

The acceptance that injury work is a specialised area and that there is much that injury lawyers can do not only to improve the services that lawyers provide to the public but much evidence that they hold that can be of use in trying to shape legislation or procedural reform to assist victims of accidents has lead to the establishment of a few collective organisations. The three most prominent are:

APIL—the Association of Personal Injury Lawyers. This organisation has worked on various issues pertinent to injury law since its formation over 10 years ago. The organisation is keen to improve the quality of representation of victims. Any practising lawyer can join, provided that their injury work is predominantly claimant. There are regular, inexpensive and useful training courses aimed at all levels of experience.

MASS—the Motor Accident Solicitors Society. This is an organisation of specialist firms, where each member office of any firm must conduct over 500 road accident claims per year and be predominantly claimant instructed. The organisation is aimed at enhancing the rights of road accident victims and at endeavouring to make the roads safer. Campaigns have included opposition to small claim increases and attempts to persuade insurers and government of the sense of all vehicles having to display an insurance disk.

FOIL—the Forum of Insurance Lawyers. This is effectively APIL's opposite number being an organisation aimed at defendant lawyers. Recent CPR spirit seemed to have seeped into relations between FOIL and the claimant organisations but that now seems to have gone in the light of the dispute as to the recoverability of conditional fee premiums on cases settled before issue.

Appendix A

Client's Accident Questionnaires

Contents

* * *

1 General personal injury questionnaire

Name of client:
Date of accident or injury:

A Personal details

1 Full name
2 Address
3 Telephone number
Work:
Home:
4 Date of birth
5 Do you live alone or with a partner?
Partner's name and relationship
6 Children:
Name(s)
Sex
Date(s) of birth and age
7 Next friend if child
8 National insurance number

B Employment details

9 Professional qualifications and job history

10A (If employed at time of accident) Present or most recent employer

(a) employer's name

(b) employer's address

(c) place of employment

(d) date commenced (i) this employment (ii) this particular job

(e) occupation (job title)

(If self-employed at time of accident)

(a) occupation

(b) name of business

(c) address of business

(d) date commenced business

(If unemployed at time of accident)

(a) were you employed immediately prior to the accident?

(b) date of termination of your last job

(c) occupation/profession when employed

(d) name and address of last employer

10B (If employed now)

(a) employer's name

(b) employer's address

(c) place of employment

(d) date commenced (i) this employment (ii) this particular job

(e) occupation (job title)

(If self-employed now)

(a) occupation

(b) name of business

(c) address of business

(d) date commenced business

(If unemployed now)

(a) have you been employed at all since the accident?

(b) date of termination of last job

(c) occupation/profession when employed

(d) name and address of last employer

11 (If employed or previously employed)

Normal earnings per week prior to accident or in last employment/now

(a) Gross salary

(i) basic
(ii) overtime

(b) Average net take home

(If self-employed)

(a) average drawings/profit

(b) name and address of accountant

(c) name address and reference of tax office

Please attach copies of your most recent accounts

12 Time lost

(a) date(s) of time lost from work due to accident

(b) date of return to work

(c) has your job been terminated due to the accident? If so date of termination

(d) have you received any sick pay or health insurance due to your accident? If so please set out details

Please enclose the following documents if possible
Contract of employment, accounts if self-employed. Wage slips for the last six months prior to the accident and since the accident if employed.

C Welfare benefits

13 Please complete this section if you have received any welfare benefits since the date of the accident (including statutory sick pay)

(a) address of local DSS office

(b) amount and description of welfare benefits received (*e.g.* income support, incapacity benefit, disability living allowance, statutory sick pay, disability working allowance, mobility allowance, attendance allowance)

(c) address of any job centre from which you claimed unemployment benefit

14 Are you still receiving benefits? Which and how much?

D Injuries

15 Name and address of general practitioner
16 Name and address of hospital(s) where treated
17 Hospital record number
18 Name and address of any specialist doctor seen
19 Name and address of any counsellor or social worker
20 Injuries:

(a) nature and extent of injuries (please attach any doctors' reports)

(b) when did the injuries become apparent?

(c) did you lose conciousness during the accident? If so when was this and for how long were you unconscious?

(d) did you receive any treatment for your injuries? Where was the treatment received, what was the treatment exactly, for how long were you treated? Are you still receiving treatment?

21 Duration and prognosis. Are your injuries continuing—if so please describe pain you are now suffering, the treatment you are receiving and the disablement you suffer.
22 If your injuries involve continuing treatment do you know how long this is likely to last either your own opinion or a doctor's opinion?

23 Effect of the injuries on you.

(a) Are you now able to work? When do you think you can return to work? If you do not think that you can carry out your previous job is there any other job that you would be suitable for?

(b) Are there domestic activities you are unable to undertake due to the accident (*e.g.* housework gardening or DIY)? If so have you had to pay another person to do that work or has someone voluntarily taken over that work on your behalf?

(c) Leisure activities you were or are unable to undertake due to accident.

24 Have you had any injuries or disabilities in the past which may have had an effect on your present condition?

25 Name and address of any disablement resettlement officer who has assisted you.

E Losses and expenses

26(a) loss of earnings if not set out above

(b) clothing or belongings lost or damaged in accident. Please set out details plus replacement cost

(c) repair costs of vehicle if appropriate/hire costs

(d) costs of taxis and other travel expenses

(e) prescription charges or medical costs

(f) cost of home help or other help

(g) special equipment necessary or purchased, *e.g.* modified bath taps, automatic car

(h) postage and extra telephone bills

(i) any other losses and expenses

Please enclose copies of all receipts for the above and do not forget to keep receipts for any expense you incur. Also, keep a note of all mileage for treatment as we can claim a mileage allowance for you.

Thank you for completing this questionnaire. Please now complete the details of the accident on the separate questionnaire which has been sent to you. Please sign every page of this questionnaire and return it to us as soon as possible.

2 Road accident questionnaire

Name of client
Date of accident or injury

Please complete this questionnaire and the general questionnaire which has been sent to you.

Sign every page and return them to us as soon as possible.

The accident

1 Date of accident
2 Time of accident
3 Place of accident
4 Traffic conditions, weather and lighting
5 Please give a full description of how the accident occurred including all events leading up to the accident and the accident itself. It will be helpful to include a sketch showing position of cars, witnesses, etc. and photographs of the accident site if you have any.

6 You and your passengers

Where were you sitting in the vehicle? Were you wearing a seat belt? If not, why not? Names and position in car of any passengers? Were you driving? If so:

(a) have you got any current motoring insurance—if so please give details:

(i) name of company insuring you
(ii) certificate number
(iii) extent of cover
(iv) any excess

(b) do you have any previous convictions or endorsements? Please give details

7 Other parties

(a) name and address of driver responsible for the accident

(b) name and address of driver's insurers and policy number if known

(c) name and address of owner of vehicle responsible for accident (if different)

(d) registration number, make and insurers of vehicle responsible for the accident

Name and address of any passengers in the other party's vehicle. Please put in details (a) to (d) above for any other persons involved in the accident or hurt in the accident

8 Witnesses

Please give the names and addresses of any witnesses to the accident and any means of contacting them. Do you know if they are going to be in your favour?

9 Police

Were the police called? If so please give the names, numbers and police station of the police called
Have you received any notice of intended prosecution either of yourself or the other driver?

10 How did you and any other parties react after the accident? In particular did you or they make any admissions to each other or to the police?

11 Your vehicle details

(a) registration number of the vehicle

(b) make of vehicle

(c) insurers

(d) extent of damage

(e) estimated cost of repair, etc.

(f) hire charges

(g) where your vehicle is stored and where it can be examined

(h) storage charges

Please enclose the following documents: receipts in respect of any damage caused, rough sketch, any correspondence you have received or had with the other party, insurers or the police or witnesses regarding the accident

3 Workplace accident questionnaire

Name of client
Date of accident or injury

Please complete this questionnaire together with general accident questionnaire, sign every page and return them to your solicitor with all relevant documents as soon as possible.

The accident

A If your injuries were caused by an *accident* at work:
1 Date of accident
2 Time of accident
3 Place of accident
4 The parties involved in the accident; names and addresses of people involved or hurt
5 What were you supposed to be doing there?
6 Please give a full description of how the accident occurred. It will be helpful to put in a sketch showing position of all parties and of the witnesses etc. Please enclose photographs of the accident site or machinery involved if you have any

B If your injuries were the result of a *condition* caused by work:
1 Please set out a full description of how your injuries occurred
2 Please send a sketch showing workplace if relevant together with photographs of workplace if any
3 Date first noticed condition or injury
4 Any other relevant details

C Please answer the following questions in all cases
1 Your job title and a brief description of the work you undertook
2 Your work conditions—hours of work, type of work, etc.
3 What is your status regarding other employees?
4 What is the name and address of the person in immediate authority over you? Was your work supervised? By whom? What was the nature of that supervision? Was your supervisor present when the accident occurred?
5 Who was responsible for health and safety at your workplace?
6 Were you given any training or information which could have prevented the injury?
7 Were there any other safety precautions taken by the employer, for example the presence of warning notices? Were they visible?
8 Were you given any verbal warnings regarding safety?
9 Had you made earlier relevant complaints to the employers regarding the safety of your workplace? If any were in writing please let us have copies
10 Do you know of any previous similar accidents or history of safety complaints regarding the matter which caused your injury? If so please let us have copies
11 Has any union memoranda been sent regarding the injury or any similar incident?
12 If the injury was caused by faulty equipment please give full details (*i.e.* make and type of the equipment that caused the injury and exact fault
13 If appropriate was any protective clothing or equipment available and offered to you?
14 Was your workplace regularly checked and written reports made of those checks?

15 How long had you been employed at this particular job?
16 What was your experience of the job you were currently doing?
17 Were you obeying instructions?
18 Who in your view was responsible for the injury? Why?
19 Was the injury reported in an accident book? If possible please let us have a copy of the entry in the accident book if you have one.
20 Were there any witnesses? If so please put in their names, addresses or other means of contacting them
21 Has there been a factory inspection following the injury?
22 Has the matter lead to the involvement of Health and Safety?
23 Has to your knowledge anything been changed by your employers as a result of the injury?
24 Did the company doctor see you? If so please send any report
25 Have you received disablement benefit? What percentage disablement was assessed? Please send copies of all assessment documents

Please enclose copies of the following relevant documents:
1 Contract of employment
2 Accident book or other report if you have them
3 Any memos regarding health and safety
4 Details of any training relevant to the injury
5 Any other relevant information
6 Any company doctor's report
7 Any disablement assessment or appeal documents

4 Fatal accident questionnaire

Name of client
Date of accident or injury
Date of death

Please complete this questionnaire, the general questionnaire and the questionnaire regarding the accident causing death. The general questionnaire should be filled out both for the deceased and, so far as relevant, for the deceased's dependants.

Please sign the questionnaire on each page and return it to your solicitor as soon as possible

1 Date of birth of deceased
2 Date of death
3 Date of accident leading to death or date of onset leading to condition leading to death
4 Legal relationship of deceased to client
5 Will you be administering the deceased's estate? Please give the name and address of any executor or administrator. Do you wish us to take out a Grant of Administration? In what capacity?

6 Details of any dependants of the deceased; name, address, age, sex and relationship
7 Date of inquest. If already held—what was the verdict? Address of coroner's court. Please attach any statements
8 Was death instantaneous? If not please give details (although necessary to determine if there is a Law Reform claim you may elect to delete this question and raise it less starkly in discussions with the client)

Thank you for completing this document. Please enclose copies of the following:
1 Death certificate of the deceased
2 Copy of Grant of Administration if any
3 Receipt for any expenses
4 Any other relevant documents

Appendix B

Stock Letters

Contents

* * *

1 Client care letters

Steps in proceedings and essential information

Re: Personal injury claims—the legal process

This letter is important. It sets out the main steps in a personal injury claim. Keep it safely—you can then refer to it as the action progresses.

Terms

PARTIES
You will be called "the claimant". The person you are taking the claim against will be called "the defendant".

A Your claim

To succeed in a claim for damages for personal injury you will have to prove that you have suffered injury, that someone else was negligent (*i.e.* to blame) and that this negligence caused your injury. It is not sufficient only to prove that you have been injured. If the claim is about the defendant's negligence and/or breach of statutory duties, you will have to show, on a balance of probabilities (*i.e.* that it is more likely 51%+ than not) that the defendants were negligent or in breach of their statutory duties. In order to do this you will need to give full details of the facts alleged against the defendants.

1 Documentary evidence

Because you must prove your claim it is *very important*:

(a) that you keep all documents including:

(i) any expenses and receipts relating to your injuries, *e.g.* taxi fares to hospital or special equipment purchased;
(ii) all correspondence you have had regarding the claim;
(iii) all documents relating to your treatment;

[If your claim is against your employer

(iv) your contract of employment;
(v) your job description;
(vi) correspondence with your employer;
(vii) copies of the accident book or any other relevant documents;]
(viii) any other documents which you think may be relevant.

IMPORTANT—you must keep *all* documents relevant to the claim, not only those that will help your case.

2 Expert evidence

I shall need to obtain:

(a) a medical report setting out the nature of your injuries and how they were caused;

Under the Civil Procedure Rules that will govern the conduct of your claim I shall try to agree an expert with the defendant so that you only need to be seen by one expert per medical discipline that is required. The effect of a joint expert is that, save in certain circumstances, the report produced will be binding. If the expert's findings are not favourable the court may allow a further expert but there is no guarantee of this.

(b) *For relevant cases* An engineering experts report to comment on (work place/machinery being used/etc depending on type of claim); an accountant/employment consultant's report on your loss of earnings.

The defendant may, in certain circumstances, be entitled to have you examined by its own medical expert; may be entitled to have its own engineering and/or accountant and/or employment consultant.

3 Witnesses

(a) *You* You must give a detailed statement which I shall draft in accordance with your instructions. Your statement is one of the most important documents in the legal proceedings. It will be used by me or any barrister whom I may instruct for you to draft your claim for court purposes. It will be shown:

(i) to the defendant before the trial to set out your case;
(ii) to your barrister so she/he knows what you will say if your claim proceeds to trial;
(iii) to the experts to assist them in preparing their reports.
(iv) to the court to explain your case to the judge.

In court you may also be required to give oral evidence before the judge and the defendant will cross-examine you on your statement and anything relevant to your claim;

(b) *Other witnesses* I shall also need to obtain detailed statements from other witnesses who can support your claim. It will be very helpful if you could give me names and addresses of such witnesses as soon as possible.

B Legal proceedings

1 Once I have completed the intial inquires, to include obtaining the necessary expert evidence, then prior to issue of any court proceedings I shall quantify your claim to the defendant to see if the claim is capable of settlement at that stage. If by then the defendant has admitted liability(fault) then I would hope to be able to resolve the claim at that stage provided the defendant values the claim realistically.

If liability is disputed, or if the offer put forward is insufficient, and not one that can be increased to realistic level by a prompt negotiation then I shall arrange for court proceedings to be prepared. These will be drafted for your approval by either me or a barrister whom I would instruct for you.

As a rule of thumb if your claim is worth in excess of £50,000 then any proceedings will be in the High Court. If the value is less than that they will be in the county court. In practical terms, this will make very little difference as the Civil Procedure Rules apply in both courts.

2 Issuing and serving the claim

Once I have prepared the documents I shall issue the claim in the appropriate court and, within four months, I shall serve on the defendant the initiating document, the Statement or Particulars of Claim, the schedule of special damages and medical reports. Normally, service will take place immediately following issue to keep the momentum going, but there are some cases where the four month period can be necessary, for example if your medical condiition has not stabilised sufficiently for a final medical prognosis until this stage.

3 Defence and request for further information

The defendant has about four weeks from service of the proceedings within which to file a defence. This can be extended by a further four week period but after that the court has to consider whether to allow further time as the court does not wish to see claims drag indefinitely.

Once a defence has been filed then within a few weeks the court will impose a timescale to ensure that the claim is progressed to trial if not settled in the meantime.

If the defence raises issue upon which I require further information then I can make a request for this from the defendant.

4 Disclosure

Once of the stages that the court will timescale is known as disclosure. This is when I must send the defendant a list of all documents that you have that are relevant to your claim, whether or not they support the case. The purpose is to enable an evaluation of the strength of a case. I would like those documents now to assist in my investigations. Some, such as ongoing treatment cost receipts, etc. will continue to arise. Please ensure that you keep those documents and send them to me.

If you do not keep documents that are vital to your case that may prejudice the claim or part of it. Similarly, if you do not keep any documents that may adversely affect your claim then you will be criticised by the court and this may raise credibility issues for the claim as a whole.

It is therefore essential that you give me all relevant documents not only those which you are holding but also those which you can obtain from another person or organisation.

The disclosure obligation is a mutual one. The defendant must comply as well. In fact, under the Civil Procedure Rules I am likely to see what documents the defendant has far earlier than your obligation to disclose. However, it will be useful to me to see what you have as by cross referring I may find that the defendant is being economic with disclosure.

5 Exchange of witness statements

Either at the same time as disclosure or very soon after it I must disclose your statement. This will, in effect, be a swap. I disclose the statements upon which you base your claim and the defendant discloses any statements to support the defence.

6 Usually, when the court first considers the claim after the defence the court will give a period some months in the future when the case will be heard. This is called a trial window. Nearer the time the court will indicate which date/s within the window will actually be allocated for your claim. You will have a chance to indicate when you are unavailable. If the trial is fixed for a date that you have indicated is available the court is unlikely to be sympathetic if later it becomes inconvenient to you. Give dates in the claim priority.

7 Trial and judgment

I shall warn you in good time before the trial of the action. At that time you and the defendant will present your case before a judge and the decision will be given by the judge. There is no jury. It is possible that the judgment will not be given at the end of the trial but will be delayed for some days or weeks. I stress that you will be represented at trial by me or a barrister.

C Damages

1 The amount of compensation ("damages") you receive is divided into:

(a) "General damages" which compensate you for pain and suffering and loss of enjoyment of life; and

(b) "Special damages" which consist of your quantifiable financial damages to the date of the trial and any claim for ongoing loss of earnings. Special damages are set out in the schedule of special damages which is served when legal proceedings are commenced and updated throughout the process. They include medical expenses, transport costs, nursing or childcare costs (in some cases) and your claim for loss of earnings if appropriate.

2 Mitigation

You are under a duty to mitigate your loss. You must therefore ensure that you return to work or obtain alternative employment as soon as you are able to do so. If you are looking for other jobs you should keep copies of all applications and responses to show that you have taken steps to mitigate your loss.

3 Welfare benefits—the Compensation Recovery Unit

The Compensation Recovery Scheme operates to "clawback" DSS benefits you have received as a result of your injuries from any relevant compensation you recover. The Compensation Recovery Unit will tell the defendants how much benefit has been paid to you. The defendants must withhold this amount from any relevant damages they agree to pay to you and forward it to the DSS. This can have a large effect on your damages. However, in most cases the effect is neutral as you still recover the amount of the loss. Only part is paid on account by the State and the balance is paid later by the defendant.

4 Costs

(a) The general rule is that if you are successful in legal proceedings the defendants will be ordered to pay your costs. If the defendants do not agree the amount of costs you claim from them, the court will determine whether the costs you claim are reasonable in nature and amount by what is called an assessment procedure. This takes place after the ruling. In some cases the court will determine the amount of costs there and then. In other cases, usually those that last for over a day or raise complicated issues the court will determine costs at a later date. This may be some months later.

There are exceptions to the "winner takes all" rule. I shall notify you if I think an apportionment of costs is likely. However, provided the claim is conducted reasonably and is successful on the basis presented the order should be for costs in your favour.

This does not mean that all costs as between you and my firm are necessarily recoverable from the defendant even if the claim is wholly successful (see my costs letter to you.)

(b) If you are unsuccessful in your claim the defendants will seek to recover their costs from you. In some circumstances it is possible to take out insurance to guard against these costs (see my cost, letter to you).

(c) If you have the benefit of a public funding it is very unlikely that you will be ordered to pay the defendants' costs even if you lose. However if you succeed the statutory charge may be applied to any damages you recover. I have sent you a letter setting out the application of the statutory charge but if you have any queries please do not hesitate to contact us.

D Information and advice

1 You will be provided with information about the progress of your claim at each stage. You can expect to receive copies of all medical reports and all important letters and documents received from the defendants so that you are fully aware of what is going on in your case. I shall advise you of the effect of each important stage. If you do not understand anything at any stage or if you need any further information do not hesitate to contact us. If I am unavailable my secretary can always arrange a convenient time for me to telephone you so that you do not sit by a phone waiting for it to ring.

2 Client care/inhouse complaints system

The principal person with the conduct of this file is   who is a partner/solicitor/legal executive etc under the supervision of   who is a partner/solicitor/legal executive, etc. If   is unavailable messages can be left with his/her secretary or my telephonist can put you through to someone else to try to assist. By the nature of litigation I am likely to be in court on occasions or out on meetings. Your call will be returned as soon as I am able.

It is my intention to deal with your claim in a prompt and efficient manner. I am confident that this is the service that you will receive. However, if you feel unhappy or concerned by any aspect of the handling of your claim or have suggestions to help us improve our service please raise these with
the partner in charge of the department/office/firm (*as appropriate*).

2 Costs: private—contentious business agreement

Fees in personal injury matters

This letter sets out the basis on which I shall act in your case. As explained to you at our meeting my fees are calculated principally by reference to the amount of time spent in dealing with your case. This may be by me or by others whom. I ask to assist with various tasks to ensure that the claim is presented quickly, efficiently and economically. A list of the charging levels of all staff is as follows:

Clerks	£	to £
Legal executives and junior solicitors	£	to £
Senior solicitors	£	to £
Partners	£	to £

These fee levels are reviewed annually as, common to all businesses, my firm needs to increase fees in line with inflation.

It is my firm's practice to ask for money on account. Accordingly, I await your payment of £ .

In addition, so that you know the fee liability as matters progress, I shall interim bill every three months. If an interim bill is not paid then I am afraid that at that stage I would have to cease acting for you.

In addition, it may be necessary for the proper presentation of your claim for us to incur the fees of others (disbursements) such as medical experts, barristers and the courts. These are additional costs for which you are responsible.

I have set out in a separate letter the best estmiate of costs that I can give at this stage. That is £ . Obviously, the ultimate fee liability will depend very much on the extent and speed of your recovery and on the approach adopted by the defendant, if in the light of these factors it becomes apparent that the estimate is unrealistic I shall notify you. I shall in any event send you an update on costs incurred in total every six months.

So far as time scale is concerned again a lot depends on the factors that I have mentioned above. At this stage though I believe that your claim is likely to take months to conclude.

I attach a copy of this letter for you to sign and return to confirm my instruction. I cannot undertake any further work for you until I have the letter signed by you.

If you have any queries on the above please contact me.

3 Costs: Public Funding

Whilst you are unlikely to start any public funding matters unless within a group litigation or clinical negligence franchise you may take over some cases begun under legal aid. In those situations it is still best to send a formal reminder of the cost implications of a public funding certificate.

Re: Terms of business in public funding

We have agreed to represent you under your public funding certificate in connection with your claim for compensation following your accident on .

We refer to our discussion and separate letter confirming the advice given to you. That letter also contains our best cost and time estimates for your case. You should read it carefully.

Certain matters arise as a result of the nature of the public funding of the case.

Statutory charge

The statutory charge arises where proceedings are successful or are settled with payment of compensation in either scenario. It does not apply if you lose the case.

Where you win then in most cases you will recover costs over and above your compensation from the losing defendant. In some cases these costs recovered are sufficient to meet the actual costs of your case. However; the statutory charge arises where:

(a) an order is made against the defendant for payment of costs but those costs cannot be recovered [this should rarely arise in an injury claim as most claims involve insurers];

(b) no order for costs is made on all or part of the claim. For example; this might arise if your claim only succeeds on some of the grounds that you have claimed. The costs of investigating the other grounds may not be recovered. In an extreme case the court may award no costs. For example; if it thinks that your conduct in the claim does not merit any costs. In these situations although you have won you will be responsible for part/all of your costs;

(c) the costs recovered are not sufficient to meet the costs that you have actually incurred;

(d) the claim is settled with no provision in the settlement for payment of your costs by the defendant.

If any of these situations arises then the Legal Services Commission is entitled to recover from your compensation before you receive it such amount as is necessary to cover any costs falling due. Obviously, the amount is capped by the amount of compensation recovered for example if the costs were twice the damages then the Commission could only recover the amount of the compensation. It would be responsible for the costs over and above that amount. Some examples may assist:

(a) You recover £1,000 compensation without any costs and your costs are £500. The Commission deducts £500 to cover the costs and you are paid the balance of £500.

(b) You recover £1,000 compensation with costs in addition. The costs to be paid by the defendant are £250 but your actual costs are £500. The Commission receives £250 and you receive the balance of £750.

(c) You recover £1,000 compensation with costs in addition. The costs to be paid by the defendant are £500 and your actual costs are £500. You will receive all your compensation as the amount from the defendant discharges the cost liability.

Examples (b) and (c) assume that the defendant pays the costs due.

Orders not to be enforced

If you lose the case usually you will find that an order is made against you for you to pay the defendant's costs of defending the claim. This arises either by court order or as an almost inevitable consequence of any withdrawal of the case.

As you are in receipt of public funding you have some protection from these costs. The law provides that the order cannot be enforced against you unless and until the court has determined that, taking into account your financial circumstances, it is reasonable to enforce the award. As your financial circumstances are such that you qualify for public funding then unless they alter dramatically the court is unlikely to allow enforcement of any costs order against you.

Contributions

If you are required to make a contribution to your public funding by way of monthly payment it is important that you pay each and every instalment when required. Failure to do so will result in your certificate being discharged. Should this occur we would be instructed by the Commission not to undertake any more work for you on the claim. You will remain liable for the contributions you have and should have paid. You may then lose those.

Failure to co-operate

Should you fail to co-operate with the Commission in any assessment of your means they can revoke your certificate. This may happen in other circumstances. If your certificate is revoked then even if you have no contributions the Commission can pursue you for any sums that it has to pay in costs. This is because the effect of revocation is that you are deemed never to have had a certificate in the first place.

Do make sure that you respond to any correspondence that you receive from the Commission. If in doubt contact us.

[Then set out the standard comments about fee level fee earner responsible for the file and complaints procedure that appear in the precedent above].

4 Conditional fee agreement

This letter is to confirm the advice that I gave to you on the operation of the conditional fee arrangement that I have proposed. It should be read in conjunction with the draft agreement that I have given to you.

In an injury claim such as yours there are a number of ways in which legal fees can be met. For example, through pre-existing insurance cover in limited circumstances, public funding through the state and on a private pay as you go scheme. I have explored the methods of payment with you and we have agreed that the conditional fee scheme is the best option available to you. I have suggested that you take the time to review your options before coming to a final decision. A little time taken at this stage is well spent.

If you do decide to go ahead on a conditional fee basis here are a few points you may want to consider:

The initial cost

Sometimes it is necessary for me to undertake preliminary enquiries before confirming that a case is one that I think justifies a conditional fee agreement. Yours is one of those cases. I have suggested that we agree that those costs, for which you will be responsible, will be limited to £ .

Assuming that the claim is viable and a conditional fee arrangement is agreed between us I would recommend that you buy insurance cover. This will operate if your claim is unsuccessful. In such a situation you are likely to face a claim for costs from the defendant. You are also likely to have incurred substantial disbursements yourself. The policy that we discussed would cover any liability that you incur for these costs. The policy costs £ .

Obviously, the policy would not operate retrospectively. In the meantime I have suggested that you/my firm meets these disbursements as they arise.

What happens at the end of the claim if it is successful?

If you are successful (and this is defined in the agreement) then your opponent will usually be ordered to pay your normal costs. However, under the agreement we are entitled to charge you a success uplift of up to 100 per cent of our normal charges. You should read the definition and explanation in the agreement and accompanying notes.

This success uplift may be partially or fully recoverable from the defendant in addition to our normal costs as may the insurance premium that you have paid.

What happens if the claim is unsuccessful?

We shall not be paid and nor will any barrister who is instructed on your behalf on a similar conditional fee arrangement.

You will claim on the insurance which we have recommended above that you take out. This will cover the defendant's costs and your disbursements.

As you have claimed on the policy then the premium will not be refunded.

The success fee

As there is a risk that my firm may not be paid I am entitled to agree with you that in addition to our ordinary costs which will be charged at the following rates:

Clerks	£	to £
Legal executives and junior solicitors	£	to £
Senior solicitors	£	to £
Partners	£	to £

we may charge a success fee of up to 100 per cent of the normal costs If your claim is successful this success fee should be recoverable from the defendant as should the normal fee. If not all the success fee is recovered then the balance can only be recovered from you by me with court approval.

I have also indicated that whatever the strict sum due under the conditional fee arrangement may be at the end of the claim it will be capped at 25 per cent of the total value of your compensation.

Example

Success fee 100%
Normal costs £1,000
Damages £2,000
Strictly speaking, the uplift is £1,000. However, with the operation of the 25 per cent cap the success fee will be £500.

The success fee will obviously be set taking account of the risks that I perceive to be inherent in your case. A portion, which I shall identify, is allocated to cover the cash flow implications of delayed payment (and payment of disbursements on account for you).

To try to assist you I estimate that the total costs in your claim will be in the region of £ . I believe that the claim is likely to take approximately months. This is a delay that will be relevant to success fee for cash flow implications.

(then set out standard information about complaints, etc.)

I look forward to hearing from you when you have decided whether you wish to pursue the claim under a conditional fee agreement. If you have any questions not covered in our meeting or this letter please contact me.

2 Investigating the accident

5 To client on being instructed

Re: Your claim for personal injury

I look forward to meeting you to discuss your proposed claim for personal injury at [these offices] at o'clock on [date].

To succeed in a claim for damages for personal injury you will have to prove that you have suffered injury, that someone else was negligent [at fault] and that this negligence caused your injury. It is not sufficient only to prove that you have been injured. We shall discuss this further in our meeting.

I enclose the following for you to consider before our meeting:

1 A questionnaire on your accident and injuries;

2 A questionnaire on your losses.

Please complete these questionnaires as far as possible. If for any reason you are unable to complete them fully do not worry as we shall discuss them further in our meeting. It would be helpful if you would return the questionnaires completed as far as possible together with copies of the documents requested before the meeting as this will save time at the meeting;

3 A letter which explains how we progress personal injury claims and the firm's complaints procedure;

[4 A standard letter which sets out the basis on which this firm charges in private matters; or

[5 A standard letter providing information you will need in legal aid matters including the operation of the Legal Aid Board's statutory charge];

[6 Our conditional fee agreement and letter confirming the cost operation of this agreement and letter confirming the cost operative of the agreement]

Please read these documents carefully as they contain much information which will be important throughout your claim. If there is anything in them that you do not understand please raise it with me as soon as possible.

I look forward to receiving the completed questionnaires and meeting you on [date]. Please make sure that you mark all letters to me with the reference which appears at the top of this letter otherwise delay may occur. I enclose a stamped addressed envelope for your use.

6 To client following interview

Re: Your claim for personal injury

Statement

It was a pleasure to meet you on [date]. I now enclose a statement/note/completed questionnaire setting out the information you gave me in our meeting. Please read this carefully and ensure that it is full and correct. Please make any amendments necessary, sign each page and return it to me as soon as possible.

Advice

I am writing to confirm the advice I gave you in our meeting. This is based on the information you have given me; obviously if any of this information is different on investigation or cannot be proved of if further facts arise then my advice will change accordingly. I shall advise you immediately if this occurs.

Limitation

You must take your claim by [date] otherwise you will not be able to claim.

Your claim

1 You may be able to bring a claim against [name].
2 In order to succeed in that claim you have to show that the defendant was negligent or in breach of statutory duty. In particular the facts you will have to prove are as follows [ ]. The difficulties I see in proving your claim are as follows [ ]. [You may be found contributorily negligent] because [explain].
3 On present information I consider that you have realistic prospects of success but are likely to see a deduction of about per cent from your compensation to reflect your share of blame [contributory negligence].

Damages

If you are successful in your case you will be able to claim for the following:
1 Losses and expenses to date [set out details and estimate together with further information necessary to prove these].
2 Future losses [set out how these will be proved and calculated]. You are under a duty to mitigate your loss. You must therefore ensure that you return to work or obtain alternative employment as soon as you are able to do so and that any expenses you incur are necessary and reasonable.
3 Damage in respect of your injuries suffered.
4 [If applicable]. Bereavement payment and/or claim for dependency.

Recommended action

Either I advise that we send a Letter of Claim to the defendant. I enclose a copy for you to approve/amend. Please return it to me

or In the light of my views I cannot recommend that you pursue the claim. If you do decide to you must bear in mind the limitation period set out above [in this case do not take the letter any further].

Other remedies

You may have other remedies including the following:

(a) Welfare benefits [set out details—and explain CRU];

(b) MIB (if appropriate) [set out details];

(c) CICA (if appropriate) [set out details];

(d) Criminal Compensation Order [set out details];

(e) Small claim in the county court [set out details].

Funding

[Set out details of the way the case is going to be funded and any disbursements, etc you require or any agreements you need to be signed]. [Include other sources of funding/representation if we will not be representing on any aspect, *e.g.* inquest/FRU].

The progress of the case [Set out any urgent action to be taken]

I shall now proceed to investigate the case on your behalf as discussed. I shall be contacting your witnesses, obtaining your medical notes and a medical statement and obtaining details of your losses from your employer as well as obtaining an expert report regarding the causes and liability of the accident [explain in detail]. I shall of course let you know the results of these investigations.

As discussed I need the following information from you [ ]. I look forward to receiving this as soon as possible.

If the defendant contacts you directly you should not answer any queries but should let me know as soon as possible.

Obviously investigations can take time. However, I would hope, if there are no major difficulties, your claim will be dealt with within approximately [ ] months.

I hope that this information is clear and helpful. Please do not hesitate to contact me if you have any queries. I look forward to receiving the signed statement and other information I have requested from you as soon as possible.

7 To witness of street accident

Re (*name and address of client*)

I am acting for in connection with the accident which took place on the (*date*) at (*place*).

I believe you witnessed this accident. Please would you send me a short statement describing what happened, who was to blame, and how you think the accident could have been avoided. A sketch plan would be most helpful. To assist I enclose a questionnaire for you to complete.

Your assistance in this matter would be greatly appreciated; I look forward to hearing from you can enclose a stamped, addressed envelope. If you wish to telephone me to discuss the matter please do not hesitate to do so. If necessary I can then arrange for us to meet.

8 To witness of workplace accident

Re (*name and address of client*)

I am acting on behalf of (*name*) in connection with the accident which took place on the (*date*) at (*place*).

I believe you witnessed the accident. If that is correct, please would you send me a short statement describing what happened, who was to blame, and how the accident could have been avoided.

Even if you did not witness the accident it may be that you will still be able to help; if you know the background to the accident or know of anyone who has had a similar accident perhaps you would let me know.

Your assistance in this matter would be greatly appreciated; I look forward to hearing from you can then enclose a stamped, addressed envelop. If you wish to telephone me to discuss the matter please do not hesitate to do so. If necessary I can arrange for us to meet.

9 For police report

To road traffic unit

Re: Road Traffic Accident on (*date*) at (*place*) at o' clock

We act on behalf of (*name*) of (*address*) in connection with the above street accident.

Please will you forward us a copy of the police report and statements. If proceedings are pending please will you let us know the name and address of the accused, the charge, and details of insurers. We enclose our cheque for £ being the report fee

10 To trace vehicle's registered owner

To Record Section, Vehicle Enquiry Unit, DVLA, Swansea, SA99 1AJ [Tel 01792 772134]

We act on behalf of (*name*) of (*address*) in connection with an accident on [date] involving vehicle registration No [Make], [Model].

I should be grateful if you would let me know the name and address of the vehicle's registered owner at the date of the accident. I enclose a remittance of £*

[*Fee is £2.50 per vehicle made payable to Department of Transport. You may prefer to use the standard DVLA information request form.]

11 For inquest depositions

To: The Coroner's Office

Re: (*name*) Deceased

We act for the dependants of the above named deceased. Please will you note our interest and inform us of the date of the inquest

[If the inquest has already been held please may we have a copy of the evidence and depositions, for which we undertake to pay the appropriate fee.]

12 To union representatives requesting works records

We act for [name] in his/her claim for damages arising from injuries caused on [date]. We understand that you are [name]'s union representative and responsible for health and safety issues at [name]'s workplace.

We believe that the injury may have been caused by the negligence or breach of statutory duty of the employer. In order to prove this it will be extremely helpful if you would let us have copies or any of the following documents or any information you have as to whether any such documents were completed:

1 Any entry in the accident book regarding [name]'s injuries;
2 Any entry in the accident book in respect of previous similar accidents;
3 Any relevant entries in the complaints book;
4 Any minutes of the works safety committee or inter office memoranda or complaints regarding the circumstances which led to the incident in particular [ ];
5 Any memorandum or notice issued by the employer before or after the accident giving guidance on (or amending) the system of work;
6 Any training records setting out training given to the employee and others in use of the equipment involved in the accident or union correspondence regarding appropriate training;
7 Does the employer keep and do you have copies of the following?:

(a) Health and safety records for the workplace;

(b) Health and safety records for the piece of equipment involved in the accident or injury;

(c) Written warnings on the equipment;

(d) Operation manual for the equipment involved in the injury

(e) Risk assessments for the task being undertaken.

8 Any other information you feel would be helpful.

If you wish to telephone us to discuss the accident please do no hesitate to do so.

13 To Health and Safety Executive

We act for (*name*) of (*address*) in connection with an accident at work on (*date*) at (*place*) whilst in the employ of (*name of employers*).

Would you please let us know if the accident was investigated and, if so, please forward us a copy of the report, with any accompanying statements, photographs, etc. We enclose a cheque for the fee of *(plus VAT of £).

*As the fees vary, phone HSE to find the appropriate fee before requesting a report.

14 Advising client to abandon claim

Set out reasons for abandoning claim, enclose bill of costs, and include the paragraph below. You may choose to incorporate this into an adapted version of letter 6.

It is my professional duty to remind you of the three-year limitation period which arises in a case such as yours; accordingly, if you wish to pursue the claim further you should ensure that proceedings are commenced within three years of the date of the accident, *i.e.* by [date] otherwise you will probably be barred from bringing a claim.

15 Letter of instruction to an expert witness (pre issue joint expert)

Re: Client's name, address and telephone number.

We act on behalf of of in connection with an accident that happened at , her place of work on December 31, 2001. We are instructed to investigate the possibility of bringing a claim against her employers.

The employers are insured with May Pay Insurers Ltd. We have agreed with them that this instruction be on a joint basis.

We attach the following documents:

(a) The claimant's statement.

(b) The defendant's pre-issue disclosure under the personal injury protocol.

(c) A copy letter from the defendant's insurers confirming joint instructions and providing details of their insured's representative through whom an appointment to examine the accident scene is to be arranged.

(d) A copy of the Letter of Claim and the defendant's response to that.

(e) A copy of the joint medical evidence.

Please could you liaise with the employer's representative to arrange a convenient date for inspection. Our client has indicated that she will fit into any arrangements made. A representative of this firm will also be in attendance.

We do not propose to reiterate the claimant's statement which sets out the accident circumstances. The parties positions are set out in the Letter of Claim and the response to that. In brief, the accident circumstances were [insert]

You will note that liability is in dispute for the reasons set out by the defendant. Proceedings have not been issued.

Please prepare a report commenting on, amongst other things:

(a) The accident circumstances.

(b) Why you think the accident occurred.

(c) Whether the machinery being used was functioning properly and if not whether that may have caused the accident.

(d) The standard and appropriateness of any training given.

(e) Whether the task was being carried out in accordance with training.

(f) The relevance of any risk assessments conducted by the defendant before and after the accident.

(g) Whether the injuries are compatible with the mechanism of the accident.

This list is not meant to be exhaustive. We would remind you of your function as an expert as set out in CPR Part 35 (a copy of which is attached for ease of reference). Obviously, you should consider all factors that you consider relevant to enable you to fulfil these requirements. If you believe that further documentation or information is necessary to enable you to do this please contact us immediately.

The report should include a brief CV and contain a statement as per Part 35.

As stated, this is a joint report. The parties confirm that they will meet your agreed fee of £   . We await confirmation of the appointment date.

3 Medical Matters

16 Medical expert instruction

Use the draft letter set out in the protocol amended as is appropriate for each individual claim.

17 To client notifiying of the medical examination

I have today written to   *(name hospital or doctor)* requesting a report on your injuries. The doctor will send you an appointment and it is important that you attend when requested.

Please co-operate fully with the expert and let me have a note of your losses and expenses in attending the appointment so that they may be included in your claim.

Please contact me a few days before the appointment so I can discuss with you what to expect.

18 To client notifying of the examination by other side [if no joint report]

The defendant's insurers have requested permission to have you medically examined by doctor *(name)* of *(address)*.

This is a reasonable request and you should therefore attend any convenient appointment the doctor may give you. The doctor will wish to have details of your medical condition but you should not discuss the facts of the accident or liability for it; you should not sign any documents without first sending them to me for approval.

Please let me have a note of your losses and expenses in attending the examination and I shall arrange for these to be refunded.

Please contact me as soon as an appointment has been arranged so I may discuss with you what to expect.

19 To other side agreeing to examination

You may have our client examined by Doctor *(name)*.

Please ensure that a convenient appointment is made through us.

Facilities for this examination are granted on the basis that Doctor *(name)* has not previously treated our client; in addition you will be required to reimburse our client for any losses and expenses in attending the examination. Facilities are also granted on the basis that you will disclose any report on which you intend to rely or the making of any offer by you or in accordance with court imposed time scale, whichever is the earlier.

20 To consultant in clinical negligence case

Re: (client name, address and date of birth)

Thank you for confirming that you are able to assist in this matter.

Fees

The fee that you estimated has been agreed. If it becomes apparent that this fee is going to be exceeded please let me know as soon as possible so that I may seek legal services/legal expense and client approval to the increased fee.

Documents

You will see from the enclosed documentation that my client wishes to investigate a possible claim for clinical negligence arising out of treatment received a [*insect*].

To assist you I enclose the following documents:

(a) My client's statement.

(b) Paginated G.P. records.

(c) Paginated health trust records.

(d) A copy of the protocol form for release of notes that sets out my client's basic concerns.

You will see that the notes have been collated and paginated. I have an identical copy. If you refer to the notes in your report then it would assist if you refer to page numbers for easy reference.

Legal background

As you are no doubt aware the approach of the courts to clinical negligence claims was summarised in the leading and much cited case of *Bolam*. This stated that [*set out the standard of care test*].

Your report

Please could you study the enclosed documentation to prepare your report. This should set out the problems with which my client presented, the treatment received and his/her progress since then. If you feel able please also provide a prognosis.

Please comment on the standard of treatment received. If you have any criticisms of the treatment please identify those and indicate what treatment you would have expected to see and/or how the treatment provided was substandard.

If you conclude that there was negligence as set out in the test above in the provision of treatment and care please particularise each and every criticism. If you are able to support the criticism by reference to at least one contemporary authority that would be extremely helpful. Ideally, I would prefer to see text book citations as well as those from more specialist periodicals and journals.

Assistance and guidance

If you want guidance on the legal aspects of the matter please telephone me. If you feel that the matter raises particularly complex issues which you wish to discuss before preparing the report or after it then it may be possible to arrange a conference with the case barrister and with my client, if that would assist.

Status of your report

At this stage the report you prepare will be for initial consideration by me, my client and the case barrister. It will not necessarily be the final version for disclosure purposes. The function of the report at this stage is to determine whether or not the claim should be investigated further. It is meant to be an indication of the evidence that you would give if it were necessary to call you as a witness at court.

Sometimes the initial report will be used in the court process and will be disclosed to the defendant. I shall notify you if that is the case. A lot will depend upon whether you believe that you are in a position to produce a final report at this stage or whether you suggest any further lines of enquiry.

If you have any questions please contact me.

I look forward to receiving your report within the [*try to agree a set timescale*] weeks agreed.

21 Client's consent to release of notes to joint expert

To [*name and address of G.P. and treating hospital/s*]

I of hereby authorise you to release to Mr/Dr of all my medical notes, to include X-rays and any scans that he or she may request.

I confirm that these notes are not sought in connection with any claim for clinical negligence.

....
Signed Dated

22 Client's consent to release of notes in clinical negligence claim

Use the standard notification form which provides for release of notes that appears in the clinical negligence protocol when requesting the notes from the treaters against whom negligence is alleged. For the collation of other records;

To [*insert name*]

I of hereby authorise you to release to my solicitors Messrs of copies of my medical notes held by you [*to include those set out in the attached schedule*] (if you wish to specify documents).

....
Signed Dated

4 Special damage

23 To employer (not defendant) for wage details

Re (*client's name and address*)

Payroll No:

We are instructed by (*name*), an employee of yours, in connection with an accident on (*date*).

One aspect of our client's claim relates to loss of earnings.

In order that we can calculate our client's wage losses arising out of the accident please forward to us:

(a) details of our client's net and gross earnings for the 13 weeks prior to the accident differentiating between basic pay and overtime;

(b) details of our client's net and gross earnings since returning to work differentiating between basic pay and overtime;

(c) the amount of Statutory Sick Pay received during absence

(d) details of any other sick pay, if any, which you have forwarded to our client and which is refundable to you, should damages be recovered from a third party [if these is any please send us a copy of the contractual recoupment clause.]

(e) any other employment losses (for example, lost bonus or promotion) arising from the accident.

(f) confirmation of our client's dates of absence;

(g) [*if the employment has been terminated on sickness grounds*] Confirmation of the date of and reason for termination of our client's employment with you;

(h) [*on the same assumption or if still employed where the period of absence has been lengthy*] Details of all pay rises to which our client would have been entitled had he remained working with you;

(i) [*if employment has been terminated on sickness grounds and the client was entitled to an occupational pension*] Details of your pension scheme and specific information as to what our client would have been entitled to by way of lump sum and annuity if he had remained in your employment together with details of his current residual entitlement.

Your assistance in providing this information would be greatly appreciated by our client and by us. We look forward to hearing from you. We enclose a stamped addressed reply envelope for your use.

24 Client's consent to employer to release wage details

Client's name and address

Payroll number

I, [Name and address of client] authorise you to provide Messrs [name and address of solicitors] with such information as they may require in connection with my wages, bonus, sick pay pension or any other information they require about my employment prospects or record.

Signed

Date

25 To Inland Revenue for client's tax returns

Re (*name and address of client*) National Insurance No:
Ref No:

We are instructed by (*name*) in connection with an accident on the (*date*).

Please will let us know:

(a) names and addresses of our client's employers during the (*time period*) prior to the accident and also since that time;

(b) the dates of these periods of employment and the net and gross earnings during each period;

(c) our client's code number throughout this time.

Please provide copies of our clients assessment and returns for the previous [ ] years.

26 Client's consent for Inland Revenue

I (*name and address of client*) authorise you to provide Messrs (*name and address of solicitors*) with such information as they may require in connection with my financial affairs.

Signed Date

6 The action

27 Initial letter of claim—road accident: (a) to driver

Use the protocol letter of claim duly amended to deal with the specifics of each individual claim. For example in;

A road accident claim

"The accident happened when our client's vehicle was stationary at traffic lights at . You drove your vehicle into the rear of our client's vehicle."

The reason that you are held responsible is that you failed to brake, failed to leave adequate or any braking distance, drove too fast and drove your car into collision with our client's stationary vehicle."

An accident at work

"The accident happened when our client suffered a traumatic amputation of his left index finger in the circular saw.

The reason that you are held responsible is that you have failed to comply with your statutory and common law duty to our client. In particular you failed to provide our client with any or any adequate training, required him to work on a machine on which he was not sufficiently qualified and failed to provide any or any adequate supervision."

A public liability claim (highways)

"The accident happened in   opposite No. 48. Our client tripped over a paving slab that was raised over two inches above surrounding slabs.

The reason that you are held responsible is that you have breached your statutory and common law duty to our client. In particular you failed to maintain the highway properly, failed to inspect it regularly or with sufficient care and failed to heed concerns as to the condition of the pavement which we understand were expressed to you by others prior to this accident".

28 Initial letter of claim—road accident: (c) to insurers

We act on behalf of   in connection with an accident that occurred on December 31, 2001.

We understand that you may be the insurers of   . We attach a copy of our letter of claim to your insured. Please confirm whether you have an interest in this matter. If so please may we hear from you or your insured in compliance with the protocol obligations.

29 Initial letter in clinical negligence claim

We represent   of   who has consulted us to investigate treatment received from your trust/surgery.

We enclose appropriate protocol form for release of notes.

We await the notes.

30 Letter of claim in clinical negligence claim

Use the template set out in the clinical negligence protocol.

In brief you need to identify your client, the date of and type of treatment received. You must set out the allegations of negligence and how those have caused the problems that you allege.

If you wish you can put forward an offer of settlement at this stage, suggest a meeting to try to resolve issues or even suggest some form of mediation although reaction to this amongst practitioners seems mixed.

31 To insurers accepting negotiated offer pre issue

We are instructed to accept your proposal of £   (net of/subject to deduction of £   CRU) provided that:

(a) you also meet our client's reasonable costs to be subject to detailed assessment through the Part 8 process if not capable of amicable pre-issue agreement. We attach a schedule of costs; and

(b) your cheque in the agreed sum due to our client is received by us within 14 days of receipt by you of this letter.

32 Requesting Court to issue proceedings

We enclose(as appropriate in particular cases):

(i) Claim Form and Particulars of Claim in triplicate;

(ii) schedule of special damage in triplicate;

(iii) medical evidence in triplicate;

(iv) public funding certificate;

(v) notice of issue of public funding in triplicate;

(vi) certificate of suitability;

(vii) cheque for the court fee;

Please could you issue and serve proceedings on our behalf (or Please could you issue proceedings for us and return them to us for service purposes.
[*enclose an extra copy of (i) (ii) (iii) (v) and (vi) for every additional defendant.*]

33 To solicitor nominated to accept service for insurers

We note that you have been instructed to accept service of proceedings in this action by *May Pay Insurance Co.*
We enclose by way of service the following documents:

(a) sealed Claim Form and sealed Particulars of Claim and schedule of special damage (if separate);

(b) copy medical evidence;

(c) response pack;

(d) notice of public funding (if relevant);

(e) copy certificate of suitability (if relevant).

Please acknowledge safe receipt.

34 Service on defendant

We enclose sealed copy writ, Acknowledgment of Service form, Statement of Claim with medical report* and statement of special damage*, and Notice of Issue of Legal Aid Certificate. *Please acknowledge receipt.

We suggest you forward these documents to your insurers or solicitors and confirm to us that you have done so.

[*If applicable.]

35 Advising insurers of issue against their insured

Please accept this letter as notice pursuant to sections 151 and 152 of the Road Traffic Act 1988 that proceedings are being commenced against your insured/a driver under your insured's policy.

36 Advising Motor Insurers' Bureau of issue against uninsured defendants

Write to the MIB at 152 Silbury Boulevard Milton Keynes MK9 1NB:

"Please accept this letter as notice under The Compensation of Uninsured Drivers Agreement 1999 that proceedings have been commenced against (name of uninsured driver). We attach the following documents (see the agreement clause 9(2) for the list of relevant enclosures to be served at this stage)."

37 Duty of disclosure—advice to clients

I have recently agreed that I will act on your behalf in the above claim.

As I have explained it is very important that you send me all documents which are relevant to your claim. This includes not only documents which are helpful to you but also those which may be helpful to the other party. Please let me have any such documents as soon as possible. The reason for this is twofold:

1 I can only properly advise you on the strengths and weaknesses of your case if I am able to consider all the documents.

2 All relevant documents in the case have to be disclosed to the other party at a stage of the action which is known as "disclosure". At that point we will have to give a defendant a list of all relevant documents which are or have been in control. This means not only documents which you actually own but documents over which you have control such as any documents held by a third party on your behalf. "Documents" does not only mean documents written on paper but includes anything upon which evidence or information is recorded including tape recordings or videos.

Continuing duties

The duty of disclosure is a continuing one. It does not stop at the date on which I ask for the documents or even the date at which we send the Disclosure list to the other side but continues right up to trial and judgment. Therefore if any documents come into your possession or are created before the judgment you must let me know and send me copies so that I can disclose their existence to the defendant if I deem them relevant. If in doubt send the document to me so I may determine the relevance.

Destruction of documents

The duty of disclosure is extremely important and you must not destroy any relevant documents. If you do destroy or fail to produce any relevant documents you could be held in contempt of court or the court may make an inference against you particularly if those are documents which affect the amount of damages you might obtain (*e.g.* receipts).

Documents held by other people

It is important to ensure that not only you but anyone else who may have your relevant documents is informed of this duty. Please will you circulate copies of the letter to them.

I suggest you keep a copy of this letter in a safe place as I will refer to it again in later stages during the litigation.

38 Offer of settlement—advice to client

The defendants have now offered the sum £ to settle your claim. In addition they will pay your reasonable costs.

Your case

Describe client's case and Counsel's advice. In particular set out current upper and lower estimates of damages and any particular difficulties with the case. Set out the general damages and the special damages and Compensation Recovery as well as specific difficulties with any evidence and any other factors. Set out the likely amount you believe the client will win at trial, the likely time the case will take to get to trial and the further costs of going to trial.

Consequence of rejection

If you decide to reject this offer (including making a counter offer) then the offer will be deemed withdrawn by the defendants and cannot later be accepted unless they agree to reinstate the offer.

Cost Consequences of rejection

You should be aware that the court has the power to take into account any offers put, regardless of the fashion in which they are put to determine the reasonableness of the parties and who should pay whom what by way of costs. Therefore, no offer is one to be dismissed lightly without consideration.

1 *Advising Acceptance* In view of what I have written above my opinion is that you should accept the offer of settlement.

2 *Advising Counter Offer* The offer is not far from the mark. On the wrong day in the wrong court you may be awarded damages at this level Certainly, I think that if you wish to reject the offer you should at the same time make a counter offer. This can either be done informally of by way of what is called a claimant's Part 36 proposal (so named because the provisions governing such an offer are contained within Part 36 of The Civil Procedure Rules).

This is a procedure where you offer to accept a set amount. The defendant then has 21 days from receipt of your proposal to decide whether to accept it and conclude the claim or whether to reject and press on. If accepted the sum offered would be your compensation with the defendant in addition paying your reasonable costs. If rejected and either later the defendant wished to accept the proposal or a court awarded a higher sum to you then there would be interest and cost complicatios for the defendant.

An offer in Part 36 format can act as a cudgel to persuade settlement if the offer is within the bracket within which the defendant put proposals as the cost risk outweighs the difference in view over the worth of the claim.

I look forward to discussing this with you when we can also discuss the amount of any offer to put to the defendant.

3 *Advising Rejection* Litigation is uncertain and I can give no guarantee that you will recover more than has been offered if the matter progresses. My own opinion and that of Counsel is that there are reasonable prospects of your recovering a greater sum together with legal costs Accordingly I would advise you not to accept the payment. However, the decision must be yours alone.

Please consider the matter carefully and let me have your instructions. Please do not hesitate to telephone me to discuss anything in this letter.

39 Part 36 offer or payment

The defendant has now made an offer under Part 36 of the Civil Procedure Rules to settle all your claim. The sum offered is £ .

Under the rules you now have 21 days to decide whether or not to accept the offer. If you do then I notify the defendant(and the court if the offer is by way of Part 36 payment). The money is then paid to me and I shall forward it to you. This represents final settlement of your claim.

If you do not accept the offer then the claim proceeds either until trial when the court will determine the compensation due or until a further offer is put. If no further increased offer is put to you and accepted and at the trial of the action you receive £ or less or only more by virtue of the interest that has been earned on your claim since the date of this offer then the court will determine that you have rejected a reasonable proposal. The likely sanction then is that the court will order you to pay all my costs and all the defendant's costs of the claim from the expiry of the period when you could have accepted this offer. These costs would be deducted from any compensation that was awarded. If the costs exceeded the compensation then you would have to make up the shortfall.

You will appreciate that a Part 36 offer is a very effective weapon in the armoury of the defendant. The key is whether the offer puts you at cost risk. Clearly, you need to give this careful consideration.

On the evidence available I recommend that (*here advise on the offer*).

[You should adapt the letter as necessary if the Part 36 is for part only of the claim or if the client is public funded or under a conditional fee agreement.]

40 Further Part 36 offer or payment

The defendant has made a further Part 36 offer. The total sum now offered is £ .

I refer you to my letter of the day of 2001 setting out the implications of an offer in the form of Part 36. The only difference is that the sum involved is now £ and not £ .

On the evidence available (*here advise on the offer*).

Please consider the matter carefully and let me have your instructions within 14 days. Obviously you are welcome to discuss the matter with me.

41 To court accepting payment in within twenty-one days

We enclose, Notice of Acceptance of payment into court and await your cheque for the sum held by you.

42 Advising client of trial window

The court has now allocated a trial window from the to 2001. This is the period during which your claim will be heard. A specific date within the window will be given nearer the time. In the meantime please could you ensure that you keep these dates free as the trial could be on any day within the entire window.

43 Advising client of forthcoming trial fixed date

You will remember that I advised you of the trial window allocated for the hearing of your claim.

I have now heard form the court that the trial has now been allocated a specific date within that period. Your claim will be heard on the of 2001. Please confirm availability by return.

I shall contact you within the next few weeks to discuss the procedure at trial.

44 Advising witness of trial window

You will recall providing me with a statement in this matter and more recently a list of dates when you would be unable to attend court over the next few months.

The court has now considered the claim and decided that the trial will take place in a time window between the   and the   2001. A specific date within that period will be allocated nearer the time. I shall notify you of that straight away. If you know now that any dates within that period are inconvient please tell me now and let me know why as the court will want to know the reason.

45 Advising witness of forthcoming trial (fixed date)

You will recall that you kindly provided a statement in connection with our client's accident on   (*date*). I wrote to you recently regarding available dates when you could attend the trial and the period of dates allocated by the court.

A time has now been fixed for the trial and it will be heard at (*address*) on   (*date*).

I am sorry to inconvenience you by requiring your attendance at the hearing but I can assure you that your evidence is necessary. You will be reimbursed your losses and expenses.

I am arranging for a Witness Summons to be served on you. This is a formal step in respect of your attendance and may also avoid any problems with your employer.

Please use the attached pre-paid envelope to acknowledge receipt of this letter. It is important that you notify me of any change of address between now and the trial, however temporary.

Finally I enclose copy of the evidence which you provided. [*If witness statements have been exchanged*—a copy of this has now been sent to the other side and you will not be able to raise any matters of fact which are not in the statement. It is therefore important that you re-read the statement shortly before trial since you will be asked questions covering the points raised in the statement].

You will be asked to confirm at trial that the content of the statement is true.

For the sake of completeness so that you can put your evidence in perspective I attach a copy of the statements that I have served for my client and a copy of the statements that the defendant relies upon. If you have any comments on these please contact me as soon as possible.

I shall contact you nearer the trial date to discuss the trial procedures with you and to arrange when and where to meet on the day. If you have any questions please contact me.

46 To court requesting witness summons

We attach request for issue of witness summons in connection with the forthcoming trial of this claim. We also enclose appropriate fee and £   conduct money to be served on the witness. Please issue and serve a witness summons.

47 Letter to expert asking for unavailablity dates for listing

You will recall preparing a report/reports on my client in connection with this claim.

Unfortunately the claim has not been settled and your evidence has not been agreed.

either (for allocation questionnaire completion). I must now give the court a list of dates over say the next 9 months when you will be unavailable for trial. Please could you forward those by the day of 2001 as I must lodge the dates with the court the next day.

or (for listing questionnaire purposes) I must now let the court know on which days between the day of and the day of 2001 my client and his/her witnesses are available for trial. Please confirm convenient dates within that period by the day of 2001 as I must lodge the dates with the court the next day.

48 Advising expert of date of trial (fixed date)

Re (*client's name and address and date of birth*)
—Your ref

I refer to the report(s) which you kindly prepared on my above named client and our recent correspondence regarding the trial date.

I regret that it has not been possible to agree the medical evidence with the defendant's solicitor and it will therefore be necessary for you to attend the court at (*address*) on (*date*) to give evidence.

I apologise for any inconvenience this may cause you. It will be helpful if you would let me have an estimate of your fee for attending at the trial.

I shall arrange for a witness summons to be served on you. I shall contact you nearer the time to arrange where and when to meet and to arrange any pre trial conference with counsel.

49 Advising counsel's clerk of trial window

The court has now allocated this claim to the claims track and fixed a trial window between the day of 2001 and the day of 2001. Please could you note this in counsel's diary. We shall contact you for up to date availability within the window prior to lodging our listing questionnaire.

49(a) Letter to counsel's clerk prior to lodging listing questionnaire

We refer to the above claim in which we notified you of the trial window.

We must lodge the listing questionnaire by the day of 2001. To enable us to complete counsel's unavailability please forward a list of unavailable dates within the trial window annotated with the reason for unavailability so that we may lodge this with the court.

We shall notify you as soon as a date is fixed.

49(b) Letter to counsel's clerk confirming booking of counsel

We refer to our conversation advising you of the date fixed for trial in this matter.

Thank you for confirming counsel's availability. We shall deliver a brief nearer the date. In the meantime if the claim settles or the claim is taken out of the list for any other reason we shall notify you immediately.

50 To witness after case heard and judgment given

Many thanks for attending court. I am grateful to you for your co-operation and trust that you were not unduly inconvenienced.

If the witness did not stay until the end of the case include a brief indication of the outcome.

Please could you let me have details of your expenses in attending court. Obviously the money served on you prior to the trial will offset part of this expense. I

If you have any questions please contact me.

51 Following judgment to client if client was successful

As you know the court found in your favour at trial. This means that the court determined that the defendant was responsible for your accident.

As a result of finding the defendant negligent the court awarded damages to you. These were in the sum of £ . This figure is calculated as follows:

General damages for pain and suffering	£
Loss of earnings	£
Other items of loss	£
Interest on sums awarded to you	£
Total	£

Out of this sum will be deducted £ in respect of sums to be repaid to the state through the Compensation Recovery Unit leaving you with the net amount of £ .

The court also awarded you the costs of the claim *These were assessed by the court in the sum of £ OR these will be assessed by the court at a later date. I shall provide you with more information on this process at a later date.*

The court ordered the damages to be paid within 14 days I have made a note of this time period and if payment is not made by then I shall advise you on what remedies are then open to us. However, the meantime I have written to the defendant by way of reminder of the time scale involved As soonn as I have the money I shall notify you.

Whilst the defendant has a limited right of appeal no application for permission to appeal was made to the court at the end of the hearing. The facts of the case and the findings of the court are such that I do not envisage that there will be any appeal.

I trust that you are satisfied with the outcome.

52 To client following judgment if the client been found to be partially to blame

As you know at the hearing of this matter the court found that whilst the defendant had been negligent you were also partially the author of your own misfortune. In those circumstances the court found you % to blame and the defendant % to blame.

The court then determined that the full financial value of your claim was £ calculated as follows:

[*see letter above*]

The effect of the liability apportionment is that you will only receive % of that sum, namely £ .

Out of this sum will be deducted £ in respect of the sums to be repaid to the state through the Compensation Recovery unit. Unfortunately as I had previously explained to you the amount to be repaid is not reduced by a similar percentage as your damages. The whole amount remains repayable.

The court decided that costs would [insert as appropriate. Either defendant to pay all, defendant to pay sum or both parties to pay sum. Indicate if summary or detailed assessment. If the claimant has conditional fee insurance explain how that now operates. This will depend on definition of success and policy terms].

Both parties have a limited right of appeal. No permission was sought to appeal on your behalf for the following reasons or permission was sought but refused or was sought and was granted [*advise accordingly*]

OR

53 To client following judgment for the defendant and dismissal of the claim

As you know the court decided that the defendant had not been negligent and accordingly your claim for compensation was dismissed. The major reasons for this seemed to be[insert]

[Set out as in above letter provisions for appeal] *either* The court also decided that you must pay the costs of the defendant. These were set at £

or The court also decided that you must pay the costs of the defendant. These will be determined at a later date. I shall advise you on that as the need arises.

[Advise as appropriate if the client has conditional fee/legal expense or public funding as to the operation of such schemes at this stage where a costs order against has been made].

54 Letter to client's comprehensive insurers at the outset of the claim

We are instructed on behalf of your insured to recover uninsured losses incurred as a result of the above accident. Please note our interest.

Should you be involved in any claim by the other driver or in respect of our client's insured losses please liaise with us on the question of liability.

We reserve the right to commence court proceedings for the recovery of our client's uninsured losses as and when we deem it appropriate. Should you wish us to incorporate a claim in respect of the insured losses please confirm your instructions and provide us with documentary evidence in support of these. We also require your confirmation that you will meet any unrecovered costs on a pro rata basis.

55 Letter to client's comprehensive insurers immediately prior to issue of proceedings

You will recall that we wrote to you on the   day of advising you of our involvement on behalf of your insured in respect of uninsured loss recovery arising from the above accident. Unfortunately it has proved impossible to settle the claim for uninsured losses amicably. Court proceedings are now required. Unless we hear from you within seven days from the date that appears on this letter indicating that you have losses to recover we shall assume that there are no insured losses that you wish to incorporate in the court proceedings. You will appreciate that it will not be possible to issue subsequent proceedings solely for the insured loss.

If there are losses you wish incorporated we await your response within the timescale set out above, Confirming the loss, providing evidence in support and confirming that you will meet our costs of recovering this loss.

56 Letter to client's insurers after successful resolution of the uninsured (and insured) losses

We are pleased to report that we have recovered our mutual client's uninsured (and insured) losses in full from the defendant. In those circumstances please confirm that you will reimburse any over paid premium and/or reinstate any lost no claims discount as appropriate.

Appendix C

Precedents

Contents

* * *

1 Claim Form indorsement

The Claim Form provides for a brief description of the claim. If you plan to use the Claim Form in isolation of Particulars of Claim, for example where you are up on limitation and simply wish to protect your client's position, then make sure the brief statement is more like an old fashioned generally indorsed writ.

(A) Indorsement of Value—all cases commenced in the High Court

This claim includes for personal injury but may be commenced in the High Court because the value of the action for the purposes of Art 5 of the High Court and County Courts Jurisdiction Order 1991 exceeds £50,000.

(B)(1) Road accidents

(a) When defendant is the driver and not servant or employeee of someone else

The claim is for compensation for injury and other loss and damage arising out of the negligence of the defendant in a road traffic accident on the day of 2001 to include a claim for interest pursuant to statute (either section 35 of the Supreme Court Act 1981 or section 69 of the County Court Act 1984) and at common law.
(b) As above except the negligence of the *1st defendant driving a vehicle as servant agent or employee of the 2nd defendant.*

(2) Workplace accident (against employer)

As above except the negligence of the defendant *in causing an accident that occurred in the course of the claimant's employment with the defendant* on the day of 2001.

(3) Fatal cases

(a) Road accident

The claimant is the Administrator and Testator of the estate of [*name*] deceasewd ('the deceased') and claims:

(1) Damages under the Law Reform (Miscellanous Provisions) Act 1934, on behalf of the estate opf the deceased

—and—

(2) Damages under the Fatal Accidents Act 1976 on behalf of the dependants of the deceased

To include a claim for interest pursuant to statute (either section 35 of the

Supreme Court Act 1981 or section 69 of the County Court Act 1984) arising out of the negligence of the defendant in a road accident on the day of 2001 which caused the death of the deceased.

(b) Workplace accident

As above except " arising out of the negligence and/or breach of contract and/or statutory duty of the defendants, their servants or agents in causing an accident that occurred in the course of the deceased's employment with the defendant."

(4) **Minor cases**

As for other cases but remember the correct claimant details are "A B, a child by C D his litigation friend."

2 Renewing the claim form

To renew the claim form if the validity is about to expire you will need to make a CPR Part 23 application with supporting evidence and pay a court fee of £25. The application is *ex parte*.

3 Defendant failing to file Acknowledgment of Service, Notice of Intention to Defend, or a Defence

Use the section at the bottom of the notice of issue of proceedings that will have been returned to you on issue. Complete that and either post this to the court or hand deliver it. Remember that in cases where you have served the proceedings you cannot enter a judgment until you have filed a certificate of service. The wording of the application is already on the form. In injury cases for an unspecifed amount then the judgment will be for *damages to be decided and costs.*

Provisional damages

If you have claimed provisional damages then you cannot simply enter judgment in default. You must issue an application under CPR Part 23 for directions.

4 When there is no Defence save as to quantum CPR Part 24

There are two ways to apply for summary judgment for damages to be decided.
The first is if the defence filed admits liability indicate on your allocation ques-

tionnaire that you will be applying for summary judgment unless the court enters a judgment of its own volition. As part of active case management most courts then will enter judgment.

The second is to apply under CPR Part 24. You will need to issue a Part 23 application notice, pay a fee of £50 and serve evidence relied on with the notice. The defendant can serve evidence in opposition at least seven days before the hearing date and you can reply at least three days before the hearing date (see procedural table 3 for the steps to be taken).

In either case if you are successful the order will be for *judgment for the claimant for damages to be decided and costs.* In both cases you should also ensure that you provide the court with proposed directions to progress the claim to a subsequent disposal hearing.

5 Extension of time

The party seeking the extension of time issues a Part 23 application setting out the further time required and giving reasons why this is the case. Consent applications require a £25 fee and disputed ones a £50 fee.

You will find that these applications, unless patently unreasonable, often now result in an order without a hearing.

Bear in mind, also, that the claimant can agree an extension of time for filing and serving a defence for up to 28 days but beyond that period, even if by consent, the court must make an order.

6 Disclosure

(1) Prior to issue of proceedings

The proposed claimant to an action for injuries should issue a Part 23 notice (see procedural table 16) against the proposed defendant. The application must be supported by evidence. The court fee of £50 will also be payable.

Simply fill in the application notice as though proceedings had already been issued. The only thing that you normally complete that you will leave blank will be the case number. Indicate the order sought Usually, if a number of documents are required you should state that you wish to have disclosure by disclosure list of the documents set out in the schedule annexed to the application. This makes the application look tidier. The application should also seek a time scale for inspection of any documents disclosed within the disclosure list.

As the personal injury protocol provides for most disclosure if there has been a breach of this you should seek your costs. Ensure that you have filed and served a cost estimate for summary assessment purposes. If the documents are more unusual provided that you can show your request to be reasonable and that you have given sufficient time for voluntary disclosure then again you should recover your costs.

The evidence is likely to be by witness statement either on the application notice or separately. It must state:

(a) that the defendant is likely to be a party to subsequent proceedings;

(b) that the applicant is likely to be a party to those proceedings;

(c) if proceedings had started then the defendant would have to disclose the documents sought in standard disclosure;

(d) that disclosure now is desirable to dispose fairly of anticipated proceedings, will assist the dispute resolution without proceedings and will save costs.

For example, where a training records have not been disclosed the witness statement may say:

"I of solicitor state that:

(1) I am informed by the claimant that on June 1, 2001 he was operating a circular saw at the defendant's premises as part of his employment with them. This was the first time during his employment with the defendant that he had been required to use this saw. Whilst using the saw the middle finger of his right, dominant hand, became caught in the saw causing the traumatic amputation of the last phalanx.

(2) The defendant in response to the letter of claim has stated that the claimant was given specific training on how to operate the type of saw being used at the time of accident. Specific request has been made for documentary records to vouch any training but these requests have gone unanswered.

(3) It is my belief that the claimant has a claim against the defendant. It is also my belief that any traing records are relevant, would form part of any ordinary standard disclosure and early disclosure of them will result in a cost saving and are likely to lead to a prompt and fair determination of the claim as without them the strength of the defendant's case cannot be ascertained leading inevitably to the issue of contested Part 7 proceedings."

How much you care to expand on the basic information is a matter for you. The key is to ensure that the essential information is provided.

(2) When defendant fails to serve a list of documents

The claimant issues an application (see Procedural Table 2) completed as follows:

"The claimant seeks an order that: unless the defendant do file and serve its disclosure list pursuant to the earlier order of day of 2001 by 4.00p.m. 31st December 2001 the defence be struck out and judgment be entered for the claimant for damages to be decided and costs and the defendant do pay the costs of this application to be summarily assessed".

Note that as the standard disclosure list requires a disclosure statement there is no longer provision to request that a list is verified by affidavit as that is now superfluous.

(3) Disclosure of specific documents

This procedure is used to obtain disclosure of specific documents which have not been disclosed in the other side's disclosure list. You should issue a part 23 application (see Procedural Table 2), supported by evidence which should explain why you or your client believes the further documentation exists, that it is relevant to the issues and that disclosure is proportionate to those issues.

The application is likely to read: "The claimant seeks an order that: the defendant do by 4.00 p.m. December 31, 2001 file and serve a supplemental disclosure list disclosing any of the documents set out in the schedule annexed to this application that are held by the defendant and/or carry out a search for these documents disclosing any documents revealed by that search.

The defendant do give inspection of any further documents disclosed under Paragraph one of this application by 4.00 p.m., January 7, 2002.

The defendant do pay the claiamnt's costs of this application to be summarily assessed".

For the witness statement in support adapt the precedent set out above for pre-action disclosure as is necessary. You must add in something on the point of proportionality and that the overriding objective anyway demands that the documents are disclosed.

See Procedural Table 9 for the form and layout of a witness statement.

If the application is successful court will draw the order. The order might read as follows:

(*set out classes of documents*)

"That the defendant do by 4.00 p.m. December 31, 2001 serve a supplemental disclosure list limited to the following documents(or classes of documents)

(*sets out the documents or classes of documents*)

and that the defendant do give inspection of any such documents by 4.00 p.m., January 7, 2002".

(4) Disclosure against a person who is not a party to the action

The applicant should issue apart 23 application in the usual way (see Procedural Table 2) completed as follows:

"FOR AN ORDER pursuant to (Section 53 of the County Courts Act 1984 and or Section 34(2) of the Supreme Court Act 1981 and CPR Part 31 17 that (*name and address of non-party*) do give disclosure of the following classes of documents

(*set out classes of documents*)

Stating whether they have at any time been in the control of the said and if not in its control at present, when it parted with them and what has become of them AND that the COSTS of and occasioned by this Application may be provided for."

The application should be served on the parties to the action in the usual way, and on the non party. Evidence in support should also be served with the application this evidence must comply with the following requirements:

(1) specify or describe the documents,

(2) show, if practicable, by reference to a statement of case, that the documents are relevant to an issue arising or likely to arise in the personal injuries action, and that the non-party has them in its control and that disclosure is necessary to dispose fairly of the claim.

If the application is successful the order will be drawn by the court and might read as follows:

"UPON HEARING for the parties and for (*name and address of non-party*) AND upon reading the witness statement of IT IS ORDERED that the said do by 4.00 p.m. 14th January 2002 give disclosure of any documents of the following classes:

(*set out classes of documents*)

that are in its control, and if not in its control at present, state when it parted with them and to whom AND that the do pay the costs of the said occasioned by this Application, assessed in the sum of AND that the costs of this Application including the costs paid to the said be in the case. (or as is appropriate)"

7 Inspection of property prior to the commencement of proceedings

The proposed claimant should issue Part 23 Application notice against the proposed defendant (see Procedural Table 12). This application should be typed out so as to comply with the requirements of a statement of case (see Chapter 9), using the specimen printed in Appendix E as a precedent, with the wording below inserted into the main body of the form.

Refer to the specimen wording in Precedent 6 which can be amended as follows:

"IN THE MATTER of an application under (Section 52(1) of the County Courts Act 1984 or Section 34(2) of the Supreme Court Act 1981)

BETWEEN: (*etc*)

. . . an Application by the claimant for an Order that the defendant do upon seven days' notice give inspection to the claimant, his/her solicitor, and Jo Bloggs engineering expert of (*property in respect of which the Order is sought*) and do allow the making of any drawing and the taking of any photograph or video film of the same by the claimant, his/her solicitor, and engineering expert.

AND that the costs of this Application be the claimant's in any event. (to be summerly assessed)."

The witness statement in support of the application must comply with the following requirements:

(1) describe or specify the property,

(2) show, if practicable by reference to any statement of case which it is intended to serve, that the property may become the subject matter of proceedings and is relevant to issue that will arise in proceedings Such witness statement might commence by setting out, in the usual way, who the makes is and how s/he is authorised to make the statement, who the client is, and how and when the accident occurred.

This is an extract from an statement that was used in a workplace accident case (the claimant said that a shelf had fallen on him):

"2 I received the claimant's instructions to act on his behalf on and on the I wrote to the defendants claiming damages. Since then I have been in correspondence with the defendants' insurers and solicitors and have informed the former that the claimant alleges that the shelf which fell on him was inadequately secured to the adjoining wall."

(3) I am of the opinion that the defendants were in breach of their common law duty to provide a safe place of work and a safe system of working for the plaintiff, their employee, and that they were also in breach of their statutory duty to the claimant, including that under s 28(2) of the Factories Act 1961.

(4) Although the defendants' insurers and solicitors have denied these allegations I am of the opinion that the defendants are likely to be made party to an action for damages for personal injuries. They state that the have been refixed in the same fashion

(5) On the I wrote to the defendants' insurers and asked for facilities for an inspection by myself and/or a qualified engineer of the scene of the accident. Subsequently, I made further requests for permission to inspect but such permission has not been forthcoming. I nominated a joint engineering expert, Jo Bloggs of High Tech Experts Ltd but that suggestion has been ignored by the defendants.

(6) There is now shown to me and produced as exhibit No, a bundle of correspondence which has passed between the defendants' insurers and/or solicitors and me on the point

(7) I am informed by the claimant and believe that the shelf and the method by which it was attached to the adjoining wall will be the subject matter of the intended proceedings referred to in paragraph 4, above. Accordingly, I request that the claimant, his solicitor and engineering expert be granted permission to inspect and photograph the site of the accident, and the shelf which fell on the plaintiff.

Statement of truth, etc.

If the application is successful, the court will draw up the order; the wording of the order would be similar to the wording used in the Part 23 application seeking the order.

8 Inspection of property after the commencement of proceedings

(1) Against the defendant

The claimant should issue Part 23 application notice (see Procedural Table 3) completed as follows:

> "That the claimant, his/her solicitor and engineering expert Jo Blogg, of High Tech Export Ltd may upon giving seven days' previous notice to the defendant be at liberty to enter upon the defendant's premises at to inspect machinery the subject matter of this action, namely,
> and to make any drawings, to take photographs or video films of the same and that the defendant be ordered to permit the plaintiff, his/her solicitors, and engineering expert, to enter and be upon the said premises for these purposes, AND that the costs of this Application be the claimant's in any event, to be summarily assessed." Refer to Procedural Table 2 for the steps to be taken.

If the application is successful the court will draw up the order.

(2) Against a person who is not a party to the action

The applicant should issue a Part 23 application notice (see Procedural Table 2), completed as follows:

> "FOR AN ORDER pursuant to CPR Part 25.5 that (*name and address of non-party*) do upon seven days' notice give inspection of to the claimant, his/her solicitor, and engineering expert and do allow the making of any drawings and the taking of any photographs or video films of the same by the claimant, his/her solicitor, and engineering expert AND that the costs of and occasioned by this Application may be provided for."

The application should be served on the parties to the action in the usual way, and should be served on the non-party. A statement in support should also be served with the application; this statement must comply with the following requirements:

(1) describe or specify the property;

(2) show, if practicable by a reference to a statement of case in the action, that the property is the subject matter of the personal injuries action, or is property as to which any question arises in the action.

If the application is successful the court will draw up the order which might read as follows:

> "UPON HEARING for the parties and for (*name and address of non-party*) AND upon reading the statement of IT IS ORDERED that the do upon seven days' notice give inspection of to the claimant, his/her

solicitor, and engineering expert, and do allow the making of any drawings and the taking of any photographs of the same by the claimant, his/her solicitor, and engineering expert AND that the claimant do pay the costs of the (non party) occasioned by this Application assessed at £150 AND that the costs of this Application including the costs paid to the non party be in the case."

9 Notice to Admit Facts

Prepare the layout, heading and style of the notice as though it were a statement of case. The notice should read as follows:

'We give you notice that you are required to admit the following facts or part of the case in this claim: (set out the relevant facts or part of the case)

We confirm that any admission of fact/s or part of case will be used only in this claim'

Signed Position or office held
Dated

....

Admission of facts

We admit the fact/s or part of the case set out above for the purposes of this claim only and on the basis that the admission will not be used on any other occasion or by any other person

Signed Position or office held
Dated

10 Part 18 requests for further information

Part 18 is plain that a request under its provisions, that have basically replaced requests for further and better particulars and interrogatories, does not need to be made in a formal document but can be made in letter form provided that the letter only deals with the request. You can use a court headed document if you prefer the formality. The key factors are to make sure that the request is plainly headed as made under Part 18 giving the title of the claim and that a reasonable time period for response is allowed. Where possible requests should be made in one document and not on a piecemeal basis.

The response can similarly be in a letter or on a separate document provided that it states that it is a Part 18 response and provides the claim details.

If no response to a Part 18 request is received then issue a Part 23 application notice seeking a formal court order. Adapt precedent 6(2) as appropriate. On the first application you ought not to seek an unless order but simply that the response is provided by a set date. The unless sanctions should only be sought if the first order is then breached.

11 Amendment to statements of case

Check Chapter 11 first to see whether you do need permission to amend a Statement of case. If you do then adapt the following precedent to refer to the appropriate document being amended. The application is again made on a Part 23 application notice with the now familiar heading information to be completed. The specific request is then that:

"The claimant seeks an order that s/he have permission to amend the particulars of claim in this matter in the fashion set out in the attached draft document and that reservice be dispensed with (unless you are looking to add a party).

The costs of this application be provided for (in practice you will usually have to pay for the right to amend including any costs consequential to your amendment as well as the costs of the application."

Again, the court will draw the order.

You should then put across the top of the document amended the words:

"Amended particulars of claim by order of District Judge
Dated day of 2001."

If no permission was necessary insert "pursuant to CPR Part 17" in place of reciting the order of court details.

12 Amendment of proceedings to join a new party to the action

Any amendment to include addition or substitution of parties requires court permission. Again, apply on a Part 23 application notice. The order that you seek is as follows:

"The claimant seeks an order that s/he have permission to amend the proceedings in this claim by adding/substituting . . . . .. as a/the 2nd defendant in this claim in accordance with the draft attached to this application.

The costs of the application be provided for."

As with all CPR general applications you must then set out your reasons for making the application.

If permission is given then you will need to add the amendment details as set out in precedent 11 above. Obviously, service will then be necessary on the new party.

13 Obtaining an interim payment

The claimant's, solicitor should issue a Part 23 application in the usual way completed as follows:

"The claimant seeks an order pursuant to CPR Part 25.7 that the defendant do make to him or her an interim payment on account of damages in the sum of £ (this is not strictly necessary in the application notice but must be put in the evidence in support if not).

The defendant do pay the claimant's cost of the application to be summarily assessed."

The application must be supported by evidence that:

(a) sets out the sum of money sought;

(b) identifies the items or matters in respect of which the interim payment is sought;

(c) gives the sum of money for which judgment is likely to be given;

(d) gives the reasons for believing the criteria in Part 25.7 are met;

(e) details the past and future special damages.

The wording of this evidence will vary from case to case but will begin with the standard details of the parrty making it, identify the accident details, when the claim was issued and any time scale for trial. It may well then include something along the lines of:

"The defence in this claim admits liability and a judgment for damages to be decided has been entered. Accordingly, on the basis of this judgment the claimant will reover damages against the defendant.

The defendant is insured with May Pay Insurance Company Ltd.

There is attached to this statement marked SNM1 an up to date schedule of loss and copies of all the medical evidence relied upon by the claimant.

I ask that the court do make an inteim payment in the sum of £3,000 net of any CRU recoupment on account of this claim by way of interim payment.
Statement of truth, etc."

Do make sure that any order is clear as to the involvement of the CRU as otherwise you may find that an entire interim payment goes to discharge CRU to date.

If there is money in court you may wish to have the order provide for payment out to discharge the interim payment.

14 To obtain a split trial

The applicant should issue a Part 23 application notice in the usual way completed as follows:

"The claimant seek AN ORDER that the question of liability of the defendant to the claimant in this claim be tried as a preliminary issue before the question or issue of any damages, and that subject to the defendant being found liable to the claimant, the issue of damages be tried subsequently as may be directed by the trial judge AND that the costs of this Application be costs in the case."

In fact, a specific application may not well be necessary if it is apparent at the time of completion of allocation questionnaires that liability is in dispute and quantum issues are some way from final presentation. The court may well make its own order for split trial and utilise any trial window fixed or available for that giving directions to bring on the liability issue.

15 Litigation friend

Certificate of suitability

The heading needs to be completed as per normal. Then the body of the form is as follows:

I consent to act as the litigation friend of .... (claimant/defendant)

I believe that the above named person is a child   patient

I am able to conduct proceedings on behalf of the above named person competently and Fairly and I have no interests adverse to those of the above named person.

I undertake to pay any costs which the above named claimant may be ordered to pay in these proceedings subject to any right I may have to be repaid from the assets of the claimant.

Mr Miss Surname ....
Ms Other Forenames ....

Address for service

I certify that the information given in this form is correct
Signed ....
Dated ....

16 Infant approval

Pre issue of CPR Part 8 proceedings

You will need to complete a CPR Part 8 claim form and attach Particulars of Claim that should provide the accident details, the allegations of negligence and particulars of injury in the usual way and then seek court approval of an agreed compromise. The prayer should seek damages in a sum to be approved and costs.

With the Part 8 claim form lodge medical evidence, CFO 320, birth certificate and counsel's advice together with something from the defendant to confirm what agreement has been reached subject to court approval. The court then has all necessary paperwork and the opportunity to dispense with service and a hearing if it deems this appropriate.

Post issue of Part 7 process

You will need to apply on a Part 23 application notice. You will need to set out the usual claim information on the Part 23 notice. The application then simply states that:

'The claimant seeks approval of the terms agreed between the parties as set out in the draft order attached to this application.'

Draft order

[Insert the claim heading]

(either) upon reading the papers filed(or) upon hearing the representatives of the parties

the following terms of compromise are approved and made an order of the court and it is further ordered by consent that all further proceedings in this action be stayed save for the purpose of carrying the agreed terms into effect and that there be liberty to apply for that purpose:

The claimant may accept the sum of £ in satisfacion of the claim

The said sum be satisfied as follows:

(set out the means for payment.

If there is nothing to come out of the settlement sum at this stage the money is paid into court. If there is then the order should provide for that to go to the litigation friend within a set period and the balance to be paid into court within a set period).

There be a majority direction that the accumulated fund be paid out to the claimant on his/her 18th birthday, namely the day of 200 .

The defendant do pay the claimant's cost on the standard basis to be subject to detailed assessment if not agreed and to be paid within 14 days of the costs officer's certificate or agreement whichever is the earlier, with the claiamant's solicitors waiving any right to further costs (or as appropriate if no waiver including a public funding assessment).

Upon payment by the defendant of the damages and costs set out in this order the defendant be discharged from all or any further liability to the claimant arising out of the accident forming the subject matter of these proceedings.

If there has already been a payment in and the money has been in court pending approval the order will need to deal with the interest. A suitable clause may be:

"Any interest that has accumulated on the sums in court until the date of this order *either* (a) be added to the sum to be retained in court for the claimant *or* (b) be paid out to the defendant's solicitors forthwith."

Form giving directions over infant's moneys

On seeking approval Court funds Form 320 is required. This gives the court an opportunity to give directions for the investment of the fund in court. You will also need to state the full name of the infant whether tax is paid by the infant and whether any money is sought by way of payment out at this stage. The form should be signed by the litigation friend.

The balance of the form is to be completed by the court on approval and is set out as follows:

1 Fund to be invested in Court £
2 Legal Aid First Charge: Yes/No
3 Majority Directions: Yes/No
4 *Investment requirements*
    Capital growth Yes/No
    Capital growth and income Yes/No
    Maximum income Yes/No
5 Payment directions:

(i) Pay income during minority (*or* until) to
    or

(ii) Pay £ monthly to commencing on until

(iii) (Insert any other payment ordered)

6 Income directions, subject to above payments directions:
    Accumulate and reinvest Yes/No
    Invest in a special account Yes/No
7 Tax directions. Recovered tax to be:
    (i) retained by next friend for the benefit of the minor
        or
    (ii) paid by next friend into minor's fund in Court
8 Dates of birth confirmed Yes
    Dated the day of 19 . (*signature*)
    Master District Judge

17 Infant approval: in a fatal claim

If a fatal case involves apportionment of money to a infant or patient then the settlement will have to be approved by the court. Similar principles apply as in an ordinary infant approval.

The order may look slightly different as it needs to divide damages between the various claims and to allocate monies between various dependants. Draft clauses to consider as appropriate are as follows:

"The settlement sum be apportioned as follows:

to the claim under the Law Reform (miscellaneous provisions) Act 1934 £ .

to the personal claim of the claimant under The Fatal Accident Act 1976 £ .

to the personal claim of (the infant) under The Fatal Accident Act 1976 £ ."

If the money for all damages claims is already in court you will need to make provision in the order for part of the money to come out and the balance for the infant to remain in court and be invested for the infant. For example:

"That in satisfaction of the sum apportioned to the infant there be allocated £ from the sum currently standing to the credit of this claim in court."

18 Notice of appeal to judge in chambers/circuit judge

The appeal notice must be in set form. This is Form N161 and can be found in the forms section of the White Book. You can also apply on this notice for permission to appeal. Details about the parties, the order being appealed, the parts being appealed and the grounds for appeal must be set out as must the remedy that you seek, *e.g.* a new trial, the original order be set aside, the matter be remitted to the original court for rehearing.

19 Hearsay evidence (*i.e.* Civil Evidence Act notices)

(1) Evidence such as a proof or statement

Where hearsay evidence is to be relied upon but it will be in the form of either part of the oral evidence of a witness at trial or is within a witness statement of a person who is not to be called at trial no formal notice is required provided that in the latter case:

(a) when serving the witness statement confirm that the maker is not to be called to give evidence; and

(b) you specify why the witness is not to be called.

In all other cases a hearsay notice must be served on all other parties which:

(a) identifies the hearsay evidence; and

(b) states that youg propose to rely on the hearsay evidence at trial; and

(c) indicates why the witness will not be called.

This notice must be served no later than the date for service of witness statement evidence and must, if the hearsay is in a document, be accompanied by a copy of that document. The notice should be given the claim heading.

20 Witness summons

A witness summons will be issued if you file the appropriate request. This should specify the name of the witness, the trial venue and time and indicate if any documents are to be brought to the trial.

The court will then issue a witness summons in form N20. Remember to give the court conduct money for the witness.

Usually, the court will serve the summons. If time is short, and you might even have had to have it abridged, then you may wish to request that the summons when issued be passed to you for service.

The form has a specific section for production of documents. Ensure that you list those that you want on the request.

21 Notice of discontinuance

Notice of discontinuance must be in Form N279. This form should be completed with the claim heading. It is addressed to both the court and the defendant. You must indicate whether you discontinue all or part of the claim. If the latter, you must specify which part and confirm that the notice has been served on all parties to the claim. The form must then be signed and dated.

22 Compromise or settlement of the action

The parties should apply for an order, by consent, which embodies the agreed terms of settlement; rather than issuing an application or summons in the usual way, it is normal to draw up the actual form of order required and have this signed by solicitors for all parties. This can then be sent to the court with a request that it be initialled by the district judge or master, or dealt with by an appropriate court office be drawn and returned to the parties. The normal form is for an order to stay the action, but with a "Tomlin Order" attached, which allows the court to enforce the terms of settlement. A consent court fee of £25 is payable. You may wish to draft the order and send it to the defendant to sign and return. This means that you can keep track of when the order has been lodged for if you sign it and send it off you have no idea when, or if, the draft has been lodged.

A typical form of *Tomlin* order is as follows:

"By consent

It is ordered that:

The parties having reached the terms of settlement set out in the schedule annexed hereto this claim be stayed save for the purposes of enforcing the said terms.

The sum of £3,000 currently standing to the credit of this action in court be paid out to the claimant's solicitors forthwith with any interest that has accrued thereon being paid out to the defendant's solicitors forthwith.

The defendant do pay the claimant's costs of the claim on the standard basis such costs to be subject to detailed assessment if not agreed and to be paid within 14 days of costs officer's certificate or agreement whichever is the earlier.

The schedule

The defendant do within 14 days pay to the claimant the sum of £2,500 which together with the payment out as set out in paragraph 2 of this order be in full settlement of the claim there being no recoupment pursuant to The Social Security (recovery of benefits) Act 1997 and related regulations.

Upon payment of the aforementioned sums, payment out and payment of costs the defendant be discharged from all or any further liability to the claimant arising out of the accident forming the subject matter of these proceedings.

Dated the .... day of .... 2001"

23 To change solicitors

The newly instructed solicitor should complete Form N434.

The notice should indicate that you have been instructed in place of the previous solicitors and give an address for service. You must also confirm that the notice has been served on all parties to the claim. The original notice should be lodged with the court.

24 Transfer from High Court to county court

The rules remain the same as before. The relevant provisions are in sections 40, 41 and 42 of the County Courts Act 1984. Where such an order is made notice is given to all parties and the file is then transferred to the new court. As the CPR requires a court file with copies of all statements of case and orders the transfer proces is now far simpler than before. The transferring court sends notice to the receiving court which includes the name and number of the case. Note that any orders made before transfer remain valid.

To apply for transfer apply on a Part 23 application notice in the usual way identifying the appropriate county court to which you request transfer and explain why Often, this will be because the value of the claim turns out to be significantly less than originally expected.

25 Public funding: Notice of Issue and Revocation/ Discharge

The Notice should be typed out in the form of a statement of case (see Chapter 9, section 6) with the heading of the action, and the names of the parties, etc.

A Notice of Issue will read:

"TAKE NOTICE that a Public Funding Certificate No dated the day of 2001 has been issued in Area No to in connection with the following proceedings:

TAKE further notice that, in consequence thereof, the claimant in these proceedings is and has been from that date an assisted person.

(*Signed and dated*) ."

With a Notice of Amendment, Discharge, or Revocation, the certificate will be similar. Set out the heading in the usual way and then the main body of the form will be:

"TAKE NOTICE that a Public Funding Certificate dated the day of 199 issued to the above named claimant has, on the been [amended] [discharged] [revoked].

[The amendment provides:

that the certificate shall [not] extend to the following proceedings:

(*Signed and dated*) ."

Appendix D

Procedural Tables

Contents

* * *

1 Issuing proceedings

Prepare the claim form and Particulars of claim. The claim form (see Chapter 9) is largely self-explanatory. The first page requires name and address of both claimant and defendant; also name and address of next friend if claimant is a person under a disability. You must complete the brief details of the claim and the certificate of value. Since October 2000 you will need to indicate if the claim raises Human Rights issues. Most injury claims will not.

The Particulars of Claim can either be indorsed on the claim form or be in a separate document.

Take or send the claim form in triplicate (assuming that there is one defendant. If more add an extra copy for each one) and the court fee to the court requesting that the court issues proceedings (see stock letter 32) If the client is public funded then the appropriate notices and certificate must also be filed. If you want the court to serve the Particulars of Claim at the same time and they are on a separate document then you will need to lodge that in triplicate together with copy medical evidence in triplicate. If the Particulars of Claim are indorsed then you simply need the medical evidence in triplicate.

The court will then issue the claim and either serve it or return it to you if you have asked for them to do so. In both cases the court will also give you a notice of issue which will give either the date of deemed service, if the court serve, or indicate that service is to be by you. Remember that service time is now set out in CPR Part 6.

As indicated, you can issue by post or by attendance at court. If approaching limitation then it is sensible to attend court so that you have time to deal with any queries that may arise.

2 Obtaining an order: by application

This procedural table explains how to issue an application and how to obtain an order after an interim hearing. There are, however, two other alternatives:

(a) *Consent order:* if the other side will consent to the order being made, then the procedure is simplified. Use Procedural Table 3, not this procedural table.

(b) *Ex parte application:* a few orders can be obtained *ex parte*. A simplified procedure applies; use Procedural Table 4 not this procedural table.

County court and High Court

Prepare CPR Part 23 application notice with an original for the court and a copy for you and one for every other party. You must endorse the application with an indication as to whether you wish the application to be dealt with at a hearing and if so insert a time estimate.

If there is any need for evidence in support of the application you should prepare that.

Send or take the application and supporting evidence to the court with the appropriate fee, which on contested applications is currently £50.

The application will be put before the District Judge who will either list for hearing, ask for written representations from the parties by a set date with the intention of dealing with the matter on paper or deal with the matter on paper there and then.

If a hearing is listed then the court will serve the notice of hearing on all parties. This will indicate if the hearing is in person or by telephone. If the latter, the notice should specify who is to make the telephone arrangements.

An order will be made. If made without serving the application then the usual notice providing for a party to apply to vary or set aside will be indorsed on the order.

The court draws and serves the order.

3 Obtaining an order: by consent application

If the other side will consent to the order being sought, then it may be possible to issue a consent application. If the other side will not consent, then follow the steps set out in Procedural Table 2. Remember that a few orders can be obtained by *ex parte* application—in which case, use Procedural Table 4. The fee for a consent application/order is £25.

Is court approval needed for the consent summons?

Most consent orders can be obtained without the need to go before a master or district judge. But this is not always the case. In certain instances (eg infant approval, and amendment to change a party) the court's approval must be obtained. This does not necessarily mean that you have to attend court simply that court permission is a requirement.

There is no need to obtain the court's approval if the consent application:

- involves settlement of the case (*e.g.* consent *Tomlin* Order)
- pays money out of court
- Time Summons
- transfers case to county court (but permission is needed for a transfer from county court to High Court)
- gives judgment with damages to be decided
- sets aside judgment in default
- relates to costs.

If the order is in the list, follow the procedure in (b) below. But if the order does not come within any of these categories (for instance if it is infant approval or amendment to party to claim) then the order must be approved by the court—follow the procedure in (a) below.

(a) **When the court must approve the consent application**

Prepare the Part 23 application notice in the usual way and append to the application, as you are encouraged to do a copy of the proposed draft order headed *By consent* indorsed with the consent of the other party. The best way to do this is at the bottom of the order to insert:

"We hereby consent to an order in the above terms

Signed	....
Solicitors for the claimant	Solicitors for the defendant"

In fact many solicitors when seeking a consent order dispense with the formal Part 23 application altogether and simply lodge the draft, indorsed order. Even if it is appropriate in a specific instance to do this the £25 fee remains payable.

Again, you can send or take the application to the court. It will be put before the Master or District Judge as desk work and he or she will decide how best to deal with it.

Once an order has been made then the court will serve that order on the parties.

(b) When the court need not approve the consent order

In The High Court and the county court

The procedure will be very similar to (a) above. It will even rarer that you need to make a formal application, instead simply lodging the indorsed order and the appropriate fee either in person or by post. Once the order has been made the court will serve this.

4 Obtaining an order: ex parte application

The standard form Part 23 application requires you to indicate at the top whether you wish there to be a hearing, a determination without hearing or for the court to deal with the application *ex parte*.

You may wish to adopt this procedure, for example, when seeking to extend the validity of a Claim Form.

Apply to the court on the Part 23 application notice with any evidence in support of the application. You should tick the *ex parte* box on the notice. The fee is £25 Send or take these to the court where the application will be put before the Master or the District Judge as desk work.

Again, if the order is made then the court will serve the order.

5 Appealing district judge or master's interim order

High Court and county court

(1) Prepare Notice of Appeal.

(2) The notice must be filed with the court within 14 days of the date of decision to be appealed unless the court making the original decision has provided for any other time period to apply.

(3) No later than seven days after the notice has been filed it must be served on the other party.

(4) The court office will insert return date for the hearing of the appeal before the judge and will serve it on all of the parties.

(5) The parties attend before the judge in chambers. The judge will determine the case in accordance with CPR Part 52 powers.

(6) The decision of the judge will be served in order form upon the parties.

6 Entering judgment pursuant to an unless order

High Court and county court

If there is breach of an unless order where the sanction is the striking out of the defence then you should write to the court with a formal request stating that the right to a judgment has arisen under the order with which there has not been compliance. In an injury claim the judgment will be for damages to be decided.

This has the effect of negating the threat of unless orders where there is an admission of judgment and a pre-existing judgment for damages to be decided. In such cases when applying for an unless order try to think of a more appropriate sanction. For example if the defendant is in breach of time to serve medical evidence perhaps the sanction should be that "*unless the defendant do by 4.00p.m., December 31, 2001 file and serve the medical evidence upon which he or she intends to rely then the defendant be debarred from relying upon her or his medical evidence a the disposal hearing*".

Relief can be obtained from judgment for non compliance with an unless order. There must be an application to set aside the judgment within 14 days of its service upon the party in default.

7 Entering judgment when no defence

High Court and county court

If no defence is filed then apply for judgment in default of defence using the bottom portion of the notice of issue. If you have served proceedings then you can only do so if you have already filed a certificate of service. When doing so it is best to append a list of your proposed directions to deal with disposal issues. If you do so then the court can enter a judgment for damages to be decided and then timescale the claim to a disposal hearing. This expedites progress of the claim.

The court will enter and serve the judgment.

8 Disposal hearing (after liability judgment)

High Court and county court

However you obtain your judgment for damages to be decided you must then look to progress the claim to a final disposal hearing as soon as possible, save in those more serious injury cases where the prognosis is still uncertain.

The way in which to do so is to send to the court a set of proposed directions to bring the quantum issue on for disposal. On the allocation questionnaire you can reqúest the court to enter judgment of its own motion. The questionnaire also invites you to lodge directions. On any application for summary judgment you can address the court on directions if the application is successful. If you obtain default judgment of any sort when you request the judgment from the court append a list of directions for approval to the request.

Likely directions will be for witness statements disclosure lists, permissions for experts and disposal listing including time estimate.

9 Preparing a witness statement

There are two types of witness statements. These are:

(1) a statement that deals with the facts of the accident and quantum issues; and

(2) a statement made in support of an interim application which can either be indorsed on the back of a Part 23 application notice or in a separate document. You should ensure that whichever type is produced it should:
 (a) start in the same way with confirmation of the name, address and occupation of the maker of the statement; and
 (b) have the pages numbered chronologically; and
 (c) be bound in a manner that does not hamper filing; and
 (d) be divided into numbered paragraphs; and
 (e) have all numbers and dates in figures; and
 (f) give in the margin the reference to any documents mentioned.

10 Part 36 payment into court

Payment in can be either by post or by personal attendance at court.

Whichever method is adopted the court must be given the appropriate notice in Form N242A and the cheque for the amount being paid in.

On receipt the court will send out a standard form notice to the other party and enter the 21-day acceptance period.

If the money is not accepted within the 21-day period it will automatically be put on deposit. At that stage the money will cease to be held in the local court but instead be transferred to be held centrally. This is important because if you later accept this amount as part or all of the settlement sums it will have to be retrieved which can mean that there will be a short delay. You should explain this in advance to the client.

Under the new CPR Part 36 payment provisions the payment in may be in settlement of part only of the claim. If accepted the balance of the claim continues. For allocation purposes, if pertinent, the part settled by this procedure would then not be in dispute and would not count to value when assessing appropriate track.

11 Acceptance of money paid into court

(a) **Within 21 days of payment in**

To accept a Part 36 payment you must lodge with the court within the 21-day period, whether by post or in person a notice of acceptance in Form N243. There are various options on this form so check it carefully. There is no fee for lodging this with the court.

It is customary to serve a copy of the notice on the defendant's solicitors at the time of lodging.

(b) **More than 21 days after payment in**

Out of time acceptance pre-supposes that you have reached some kind of agreement with the defendant about any consequences of late acceptance. Sometimes there are none. However, whatever the agreement a court order will be needed to pay out after the 21-day acceptance period has elapsed.

Usually, the order takes the form of a *Tomlin* Order (see Appendix C).

If you are just a few days late then invariably the defendant will allow you to accept without cost sanction. You will still need a court order. There will be some cost sanction as you will not recover inter parties the cost of the consent application (£25) nor your costs of preparing and lodging it.

12 Pre issue applications

Whether applying for pre-action disclosure or inspection facilities the correct procedure is to use a Part 23 application notice. This must set out the order that you want and the reasons that you require it. The application must be supported by evidence that must satisfy the relevant pre-conditions (see Chapter 5 and Appendix C).

The application and supporting evidence is then lodged at court by personal attendance or in the post with the appropriate fee. The court will then deal with the application in the manner considered in procedural table 2.

The court will make an order and it will be sent to the parties.

13 Part 8—infant approvals

High Court and county court

Lodge the following documents with the court:

(a) Part 8 claim form;

(b) certificate of suitability;

(c) birth certificate;

(d) CFO Form 320;

(e) all medical evidence;

(f) counsel's opinion;

(g) evidence of agreement (for example draft order indorsed with the consent of the defendant's nominated solicitors;

(h) draft order.

The court will then decide if the matter can be approved as desk work or whether a formal hearing is required.

If a hearing is required then service of the documents follows and a date is set for approval. However, the court chooses to deal with the matter if the settlement is approved the order will be served by the court.

Any sums to be paid out to the litigation friend will be paid out and the balance will be invested in court.

You will need to resolve the costs issue by agreement or detailed assessment.

14 Provisional damages

(a) Following trial

1 The judgment will have specified the deterioration (or disease) that is to be covered by the provisional damages order, and the time period during which application for further damages can be made.

The order will usually set out wording such as:

"*The defendant pay the claimant the sum of £ by way of immediate award made up as to(specify general, special and future damages and interest) on the assumption that the claimant would not at a future date as a result of the act or omission giving rise to the claim develop the following disease/type of deterioration namely set out specifics and that if he or she does at a future date develop that disease/type of deterioration he or she shall be entitled to apply for further damages provided that the application is made by. . . .*"

2 The judge will also direct what documents are to be lodged and preserved for the case file. Normally, this will include:
   (a) copy judgment;
   (b) statements of case
   (c) transcript of judge's oral judgment;
   (d) all medical reports that were before the court;
   (e) transcript of such parts of the claimant's own evidence as to his/her physical condition, and of the medical evidence, as the judge may think necessary.

3 The associate court clerk ensures that the case file documents are provided by the parties representatives if not already on the court file and then endorses the file as containing the specified documents, the time period for which the file must be retained and arranges for the file then to be preserved in the court office where the proceedings took place.

The parties are under a duty to the court to retain their own files.

4 There are no specific guidelines on what the claimant's solicitor should do to protect a client's position for the future. It is suggested that:
   (a) the claimant be specifically warned of the importance of the specified time period (ie the client must apply for an extension of time within that period, or apply for further damages within that time);
   (b) the client should be told that the you will not write again with a reminder of that time period and therefore the onus is on the claimant to remember it and approval you if there are any problems. There is a risk that you may find that a court takes the view that as solicitors originally on record you still owe a duty to the client and should remind the client of the imminence of expiry of the period. However, the longer the period the harder it is to see this being a reasonable requirement under your original retainer;
   (c) you should extract from the file those parts that seem relevant to the provisional damages award (*e.g.* letters, statements, etc. relating to the medical condition, and possible effect on earning capacity, etc.).
   It would probably be advisable to put those in a separate sub-file which is marked: "Not to be destroyed until [the specified date]" and to send a copy to the client. It is also suggested that a lengthy covering note is put inside the file, which will simplify matters should an application be made for time to be extended, or for further damages to be awarded. You may decide that it is safer to store the file all together with a review date for just before the cut off date for further application.
   (d) consider diarising the case prior to the expiry of the specified time period, so that a reminder letter can be sent to the client. If you do

diarise the cut off that suggests that you think that there is some on going duty of care under the original retainer. In such a situation it would be hard to argue that the purpose of diarising was not because you felt there was a duty on you to remind the client of the cut off.

(b) Provisional damages by way of consent order (not trial)

Similar procedures have to be followed if the provisional damages are agreed, by consent order, without the case going to trial.

Issue a Part 23 application notice and append to it a draft order. You can use the type of wording set out above to assist in the drafting. Include in that order a provision for retention by the court of documents. These will be slightly different as there will have been no evidence given and therefore no record of facts. Accordingly, the documents should be as follows:

(a) a copy of the consent order;

(b) any statements of case;

(c) an agreed statement of facts;

(d) any agreed medical evidence.

If any of the above are not already on the court file then you should lodge copies. The file should then be endorsed and stored as for an award after a trial.

(c) Action settled prior to commencement of proceedings

If proceedings have not been begun, it will be necessary to commence proceedings so that the provisional damage rules can apply. Likewise the Part 8 procedure for the. Once those proceedings have been commenced, a consent order can be sought—following the procedures set out above.

15 Trial windows and fixing trial date

As early as possible and usually on lodging allocation questionnaires or at the first case management conference the court will fix a trial window. This is confirmation that within that period the trial will take place. Windows are some way off but allow for the proper presentation of the claim in themeantime. Within fast track the window should be no more than 30 weeks post allocation and can be less.

The specific date within the window is fixed by the circuit diary manager after the filing of listing questionnaires no later than eighth weeks before the start of the window. There is a fee payable by you on lodging the claimant's listing questionnaire. This is either £200 or £300 depending on the value of the claim.

16 Trial bundles

High Court and county court

Unless there is an order to the contrary you must file with the court not more than seven days and not less than three days before the trial date a bundle for use at the trial. This should include:

(a) the Claim Form and all statements of case;

(b) a case summary and where appropriate a chronology (in practice this will usually be included in the skeleton arguments that will be filed pre-trial by counsel or you, if you are undertaking the advocacy);

(c) part 18 requests and responses;

(d) all witness statements to be relied upon together with any witness summaries;

(e) any hearsay notices or notices of admission of fact;

(f) all medical reports relied upon, including any joint notes;

(g) any other experts reports relied upon, including any joint notes;

(h) Any other necessary documents (for example in an accident at work case training records, accident report health and safety record, etc.).

The bundle should be paginated and indexed. If the bundle exceeds 100 pages then coloured dividers should be put in between groups of documents. You will need to think about this in advance as one of the questions on the listing questionnaire asks for the approximate number of documents that will be in the trial bundle.

Put the bundle in a ring binder or lever arch file.

If possible, the contents of the bundle should be agreed. If this is not possible the bundle should be accompanied by a short note summarising the points on which the parties are unable to agree.

Finally, remember that there must be enough copies of the bundle for the court, the legal representatives, the witness box, your client and for any witnesses whom you wish to have separate copies.

Appendix E

Specimen statements of case and other court documents

Contents

* * *

Claim Form Part 7

Claim Form

In the	
Claim No.	

Claimant

NICOLA BIGCLAIM

SEAL

Defendant(s)

DENY IT LTD
Registered office

Brief details of claim

This is a claim for compensation for injury and loss and damage together with interest pursuant to s.69 County Court Act 1984 and at common law arising out of the negligence of the defendant in an accident at work on the 31st day of December 2001

Value

in excess of £100,000

Defendant's name and address

DENY IT LTD
Registered Office
OLD SHED
TIP LANE
WORST TOWN

	£
Amount claimed	in excess of £100,000
Court fee	
Solicitor's costs	to be assessed
Total amount	n/a
Issue date	

The court office at

is open between 10 am and 4 pm Monday to Friday. When corresponding with the court, please address forms or letters to the Court Manager and quote the claim number.

N1 Claim form (CPR Part 7) (10.00)

Printed on behalf of The Court Service

Claim No.	

Does, or will, your claim include any issues under the Human Rights Act 1998? ☐ Yes ☒ No

Particulars of Claim (~~attached~~)(to follow)

Statement of Truth
*(I believe)(The Claimant believes) that the facts stated in these particulars of claim are true.
* I am duly authorised by the claimant to sign this statement

Full name ______________________________

Name of claimant's solicitor's firm ______________________________

signed ______________________________ position or office held ______________________________
*(Claimant)(Litigation friend)(Claimant's solicitor) (if signing on behalf of firm or company)

**delete as appropriate*

Dogged & Stubborn
of etc.

Claimant's or claimant's solicitor's address to which documents or payments should be sent if different from overleaf including (if appropriate) details of DX, fax or e-mail.

Notes for claimant on completing a claim form

Further information may be obtained from the court in a series of free leaflets.

- Please read all of these guidance notes before you begin completing the claim form. The notes follow the order in which information is required on the form.
- Court staff can help you fill in the claim form and give information about procedure once it has been issued. But they cannot give legal advice. If you need legal advice, for example, about the likely success of your claim or the evidence you need to prove it, you should contact a solicitor or a Citizens Advice Bureau.
- If you are filling in the claim form by hand, please use black ink and write in block capitals.
- Copy the completed claim form and the defendant's notes for guidance so that you have one copy for yourself, one copy for the court and one copy for each defendant. Send or take the forms to the court office with the appropriate fee. The court will tell you how much this is.

Notes on completing the claim form

Heading

You must fill in the heading of the form to indicate whether you want the claim to be issued in a county court or in the High Court (The High Court means either a District Registry (attached to a county court) or the Royal Courts of Justice in London). There are restrictions on claims which may be issued in the High Court (see 'Value' overleaf).

Use whichever of the following is appropriate:

'In the ....County Court'
(inserting the name of the court)

or

'In the High Court of Justice........................Division'
(inserting eg. 'Queen's Bench' or 'Chancery' as appropriate)
'............................District Registry'
(inserting the name of the District Registry)

or

'In the High Court of Justice........................Division,
(inserting eg. 'Queen's Bench' or 'Chancery' as appropriate)
Royal Courts of Justice'

Claimant and defendant details

As the person issuing the claim, you are called the 'claimant'; the person you are suing is called the 'defendant'. Claimants who are under 18 years old (unless otherwise permitted by the court) and patients within the meaning of the Mental Health Act 1983, must have a litigation friend to issue and conduct court proceedings on their behalf. Court staff will tell you more about what you need to do if this applies to you.

You must provide the following information about yourself **and** the defendant according to the capacity in which you are suing and in which the defendant is being sued.
When suing or being sued as:-

an individual:

All known forenames and surname, whether Mr, Mrs, Miss, Ms or Other (e.g. Dr) and residential address (**including** postcode and telephone number) in England and Wales. Where the defendant is a proprietor of a business, a partner in a firm or an individual sued in the name of a club or other unincorporated association, the address for service should be the usual or last known place of residence **or** principal place of business of the company, firm or club or other unincorporated association.

Where the individual is:

under 18 write '(a child by Mr Joe Bloggs his litigation friend)' after the name. If the child is conducting proceedings on their own behalf write '(a child)' after the child's name.

a patient within the meaning of the Mental Health Act 1983 write '(by Mr Joe Bloggs his litigation friend)' after the patient's name.

trading under another name

you must add the words 'trading as' and the trading name e.g. 'Mr John Smith trading as Smith's Groceries'.

suing or being sued in a representative capacity

you must say what that capacity is e.g. 'Mr Joe Bloggs as the representative of Mrs Sharon Bloggs (deceased)'.

suing or being sued in the name of a club or other unincorporated association

add the words 'suing/sued on behalf of' followed by the name of the club or other unincorporated association.

a firm

enter the name of the firm followed by the words 'a firm' e.g. 'Bandbox - a firm' and an address for service which is either a partner's residential address or the principal or last known place of business.

a corporation (other than a company)

enter the full name of the corporation and the address which is either its principal office **or** any other place where the corporation carries on activities and which has a real connection with the claim.

a company registered in England and Wales

enter the name of the company and an address which is either the company's registered office **or** any place of business that has a real, or the most, connection with the claim e.g. the shop where the goods were bought.

an overseas company (defined by s744 of the Companies Act 1985)

enter the name of the company and either the address registered under s691 of the Act **or** the address of the place of business having a real, or the most, connection with the claim.

N1A - w3 Notes for claimant (4.99) *Printed on behalf of The Court Service*

Brief details of claim

Note: The facts and full details about your claim and whether or not you are claiming interest, should be set out in the 'particulars of claim' ***(see note under 'Particulars of Claim').***

You must set out under **this** heading:

- a concise statement of the nature of your claim
- the remedy you are seeking e.g. payment of money; an order for return of goods or their value; an order to prevent a person doing an act; damages for personal injuries.

Value

If you are claiming a **fixed amount of money** (a 'specified amount') write the amount in the box at the bottom right-hand corner of the claim form against 'amount claimed'.

If you are <u>not</u> claiming a fixed amount of money (an 'unspecified amount') under 'Value' write "I expect to recover" followed by whichever of the following applies to your claim:

- "not more than £5,000" **or**
- "more than £5,000 but not more than £15,000"**or**
- "more than £15,000"

If you are **not able** to put a value on your claim, write "I cannot say how much I expect to recover".

Personal injuries

If your claim is for 'not more than £5,000' and includes a claim for personal injuries, you must also write "My claim includes a claim for personal injuries and the amount I expect to recover as damages for pain, suffering and loss of amenity is" followed by either:

- "not more than £1,000" **or**
- "more than £1,000"

Housing disrepair

If your claim is for 'not more than £5,000' and includes a claim for housing disrepair relating to residential premises, you must also write "My claim includes a claim against my landlord for housing disrepair relating to residential premises. The cost of the repairs or other work is estimated to be" followed by either:

- "not more than £1,000" **or**
- "more than £1,000"

If within this claim, you are making a claim for other damages, you must also write:

"I expect to recover as damages" followed by either:

- "not more than £1,000" **or**
- "more than £1,000"

Issuing in the High Court

You may only issue in the High Court if one of the following statements applies to your claim:-

"By law, my claim must be issued in the High Court. The Act which provides this is ....(specify Act)"

or

"I expect to recover more than £15,000"

or

"My claim includes a claim for personal injuries and the value of the claim is £50,000 or more"

or

"My claim needs to be in a specialist High Court list, namely.................................(state which list)".

If one of the statements does apply and you wish to, or must by law, issue your claim in the High Court, write the words "I wish my claim to issue in the High Court because" followed by the relevant statement e.g. "I wish my claim to issue in the High Court because my claim includes a claim for personal injuries and the value of my claim is £50,000 or more."

Defendant's name and address

Enter in this box the full names and address of the defendant receiving the claim form (ie. one claim form for each defendant). If the defendant is to be served outside England and Wales, you may need to obtain the court's permission.

Particulars of claim

You may include your particulars of claim on the claim form in the space provided or in a separate document which you should head 'Particulars of Claim'. It should include the names of the parties, the court, the claim number and your address for service and also contain a statement of truth. You should keep a copy for yourself, provide one for the court and one for each defendant. Separate particulars of claim can either be served

- with the claim form **or**
- within 14 days after the date on which the claim form was served.

If your particulars of claim are served separately from the claim form, they must be served with the forms on which the defendant may reply to your claim.

Your particulars of claim must include

- a concise statement of the facts on which you rely
- a statement (if applicable) to the effect that you are seeking aggravated damages or exemplary damages
- details of any interest which you are claiming
- any other matters required for your type of claim as set out in the relevant practice direction

Address for documents

Insert in this box the address at which you wish to receive documents and/or payments, if different from the address you have already given under the heading 'Claimant'. The address must be in England or Wales. If you are willing to accept service by DX, fax or e-mail, add details.

Statement of truth

This must be signed by you, by your solicitor or your litigation friend, as appropriate.

Where the claimant is a registered company or a corporation the claim must be signed by either the director, treasurer, secretary, chief executive, manager or other officer of the company or (in the case of a corporation) the mayor, chairman, president or town clerk.

Claim Form Part 8

Claim Form
(CPR Part 8)

In the	
Besttown County Court	
Claim No.	BT 007452

Claimant

SEAL

Nicola Passenger
[a child by Mr Nicholas Passenger
her litigation friend]

Defendant(s)

John Speedster

Does your claim include any issues under the Human Rights Act 1998? ☐ Yes ☒ No

Details of claim *(see also overleaf)*

This is a claim for infant approval of an award for pain suffering and loss of amenity and other loss and damage caused by the defendant's negligence in a road accident that occurred on the 31st December 2001

Defendant's name and address

John Speedster
10 The Drive
Fasttown

	£
Court fee	120
Solicitor's costs	to be assessed
Issue date	

The court office at

is open between 10 am and 4 pm Monday to Friday. When corresponding with the court, please address forms or letters to the Court Manager and quote the case number.

N208 Claim form (CPR Part 8) (10.00) *Printed on behalf of The Court Service*

Claim No.	BT007452

Details of claim *(continued)*

1. On the 31st December 2001 the claimant was a passenger in a vehicle being driven by her father and next friend Mr N. Passenger. This vehicle was stationary at the junction of The Drive and The Avenue Fast town when it was struck from behind by a vehicle driven by the defendant.
2. The accident was caused by the negligence of the defendant.

<u>Particulars of negligence</u>

(a) Driving too fast
(b) Failing to brake adequately or at all
(c) Failing to leave any or sufficient braking distance
(d) Driving into the rear of the vehicle in which the claimant was a passenger

3. In the circumstances the claimant suffered loss and damage and injury.

<u>Particulars of injury</u>

The claimant, who was born on the 8th April 1993, suffered a soft tissue injury to the neck from which she fully recovered within 6 months. There is served with this claim a report from Dr Malingerer of 9th September 2002.

<u>Particulars of loss and damage</u>

(a) Travel expenses for treatment	£20
(b) Pain killer costs	£10
(c) Lost deposit on school ski trip	£45

Proposals have been put which the claimant by her litigation friend wishes to accept.

And the claimant claims

1. Damages in a sum to be approved by the court
2. Costs

Statement of Truth
*(I believe)(The Claimant believes) that the facts stated in these particulars of claim are true.
* I am duly authorised by the claimant to sign this statement

Full name ____________________

Name of claimant's solicitor's firm ____________________

signed ____________________ position or office held ____________________
*(Claimant)(Litigation friend)(Claimant's solicitor) (if signing on behalf of firm or company)

**delete as appropriate*

Claimant's or claimant's solicitor's address to which documents should be sent if different from overleaf. If you are prepared to accept service by DX, fax or e-mail, please add details.

Notes for claimant on completing a Part 8 claim form

- Please read all of these guidance notes before you begin completing the claim form. The notes follow the order in which information is required on the form.
- Court staff can help you fill in the claim form and give information about procedure once it has been issued. But they cannot give legal advice. If you need legal advice, for example, about the likely success of your claim or the evidence you need to prove it, you should contact a solicitor or a Citizens Advice Bureau.
- If you are filling in the claim form by hand, please use black ink and write in block capitals.
- You must file any written evidence to support your claim either in or with the claim form. Your written evidence must be verified by a statement of truth.
- Copy the completed claim form, the defendant's notes for guidance and your written evidence so that you have one copy for yourself, one copy for the court and one copy for each defendant. Send or take the forms and evidence to the court office with the appropriate fee. The court will tell you how much this is.

Notes on completing the claim form

Heading

You must fill in the heading of the form to indicate whether you want the claim to be issued in a county court or in the High Court (The High Court means either a District Registry (attached to a county court) or the Royal Courts of Justice in London).

Use whichever of the following is appropriate:

'In the ....County Court'
(inserting the name of the court)

or

'In the High Court of Justice.........................Division'
(inserting eg. 'Queen's Bench' or 'Chancery' as appropriate)
'.............................District Registry'
(inserting the name of the District Registry)

or

'In the High Court of Justice.........................Division,
(inserting eg. 'Queen's Bench' or 'Chancery' as appropriate)
Royal Courts of Justice'

Claimant and defendant details

As the person issuing the claim, you are called the 'claimant'; the person you are suing is called the 'defendant'. Claimants who are under 18 years old (unless otherwise permitted by the court) and patients within the meaning of the Mental Health Act 1983 must have a litigation friend to issue and conduct court proceedings on their behalf. Court staff will tell you more about what you need to do if this applies to you.

You must provide the following information about yourself **and** the defendant according to the capacity in which you are suing and in which the defendant is being sued. When suing or being sued as:-

an individual:
All known forenames and surname, whether Mr, Mrs, Miss, Ms or Other (e.g. Dr) and residential address (**including** postcode and telephone and any fax or e-mail number) in England and Wales. Where the defendant is a proprietor of a business, a partner in a firm or an individual sued in the name of a club or other unincorporated association, the address for service should be the usual or last known place of residence **or** principal place of business of the company, firm or club or other unincorporated association.

Where the individual is:

under 18 write '(a child by Mr Joe Bloggs his litigation friend)' after the child's name.

a patient within the meaning of the Mental Health Act 1983 write '(by Mr Joe Bloggs his litigation friend)' after the patient's name.

trading under another name

you must add the words 'trading as' and the trading name e.g. 'Mr John Smith trading as Smith's Groceries'.

suing or being sued in a representative capacity

you must say what that capacity is e.g. 'Mr Joe Bloggs as the representative of Mrs Sharon Bloggs (deceased)'.

suing or being sued in the name of a club or other unincorporated association

add the words 'suing/sued on behalf of' followed by the name of the club or other unincorporated association.

a firm

enter the name of the firm followed by the words 'a firm' e.g. 'Bandbox - a firm' and an address for service which is either a partner's residential address or the principal or last known place of business.

a corporation (other than a company)

enter the full name of the corporation and the address which is either its principal office **or** any other place where the corporation carries on activities and which has a real connection with the claim.

a company registered in England and Wales

enter the name of the company and an address which is either the company's registered office **or** any place of business that has a real, or the most, connection with the claim e.g. the shop where the goods were bought.

an overseas company (defined by s744 of the Companies Act 1985)

enter the name of the company and either the address registered under s691 of the Act **or** the address of the place of business having a real, or the most, connection with the claim.

N208A - w3 Notes for claimant (CPR Part 8) (4.99) *Printed on behalf of The Court Service*

Details of claim

Under this heading you must set out either
- the question(s) you wish the court to decide; **or**
- the remedy you are seeking and the legal basis for your claim; **and**
- if your claim is being made under a specific CPR Part or practice direction, you must state which.

Defendant's name and address

Enter in this box the full name and address of the defendant to be served with the claim form (i.e. one claim form for each defendant). If the defendant is to be served outside England and Wales, you may need to obtain the court's permission.

Address for documents

Insert in this box the address at which you wish to receive documents, if different from the address you have already given under the heading 'Claimant'. The address you give must be either that of your solicitors or your residential or business address and must be in England or Wales. If you live or carry on business outside of England and Wales, you can give some other address within England and Wales.

Statement of truth

This must be signed by you, by your solicitor or your litigation friend, as appropriate.

Where the claimant is a registered company or a corporation the claim must be signed by either the director, treasurer, secretary, chief executive, manager or other officer of the company or (in the case of a corporation) the mayor, chairman, president or town clerk.

Particulars of Claim

IN THE BESTTOWN
COUNTY COURT
BETWEEN

Case No. BT 9710560

NICOLA BIGCLAIM

<u>Claimant</u>

and

DENYIT LTD

<u>Defendant</u>

PARTICULARS OF CLAIM

---

1 At all material times the claimant was employed by the defendant as a lathe technician at the defendant's premises in Besttown, Illyria.
2 At all material times the defendant was a company engaged in the production of engineering equipment.
3 The Provision and Use of Work Equipment Regulations 1992 applied to the claimant's employment.
4 On the 31st December 2001, in the course of his employment the claimant was operating a lathe. He was wearing a dust coat provided by the defendant to be worn when operating the lathe. The dust coat became entangled in the shaft of the lathe and the defendant's right arm was pulled into the lathe.
5 The claimant was unable to stop the lathe as he was unable to reach the stop controls. He remained trapped in the lathe until a colleague noting his problem turned off the lathe and summoned assistance.
6 As a result the claimant has suffered severe injuries to his right arm and shoulder. These injuries were caused as a result of the defendant's negligence and/or breach of statutory duty.

PARTICULARS OF BREACH OF STATUTORY DUTY

All references in 1 are to the Provision and Use of Work Equipment Regulations 1992

1 (a) Failing contrary to regulation 5(1) to ensure that the lathe was constructed or adapted so as to be suitable for the purpose for which it was used or provided as the stop controls were inadequate Failing contrary to regulation 11(1) to take effective measures:

(i) to prevent access to a dangerous part of the machinery or a rotating stock bar

(ii) to stop any movement of a dangerous part of the machinery . . . before any part of the claimant entered a danger zone.

Failing contrary to regulation 15 to ensure that the lathe was provided with a readily accesible stop control.

Failing contrary to regulation 16 to ensure that the lathe was provided with a readily accessible emergency stop control

2 Providing for the claimant a piece if equipment which was defective and dangerous as a result of the absence of guard. The claimant will rely on the provisions of the Employers Liability (Defective Equipment) Act 1969.

PARTICULARS OF NEGLIGENCE

The particulars of statutory breach are repeated.

1 Failing to carry out any or any adequate risk assessment in respect of the operation of the lathe or failing to take heed of any such risk assessment.
2 Failing to act upon or heed the duties set out in the Management of Health and Safety at work Regulations 1992 in respect of risk assessment.
3 Failing to fit a guard to the lathe.
4 Failing to ensure that the lathe was fitted with a brake or stop control which was accessible from any point alongside the machine.
5 Failing to provide suitable clothing that could not become caught in the lathe.
7 As a result of the accident the claimant has suffered injury, loss and damage.

PARTICULARS OF INJURY

1 The claimant who was born on the 23rd February 1956 suffered a soft tissue injury to his right shoulder and a fracture of the right humerus with associated nerve damage. The injury was fixed with nail and wire. Further surgery to improve function has proved unsuccessful. The claimant is left with permanent and significant residual disability and pain.
2 The claimant has not been able to return to work. In the alternative to a full future loss of earnings the claimant will be left with significant disadvantage in the labour market and/or will suffer partial future loss of earnings.
3 The claimant relies on the medical reports of the joint expert Mr Cure, an orthopaedic surgeon dated 23rd November 2002 and 24th April 2004.
8 The claimant also claims interest at such rate and for such period as to the court seems just at common law and pursuant to [either s. 69 County Courts Act 1984 or s. 35a Supreme Court Act 1981.

AND the claimant claims:

1 Damages
2 Interest as set out

[*insert statement of truth if this document is not indorsed on the claim form. Also indorse counsel's name if the particulars were settled by him or her.*

Dated this day of 2004

[Dogged & Stubborn of, etc.]

Schedule of Special Damage

IN THE BESTTOWN
COUNTY COURT
BETWEEN Case No. BT 9710560

NICOLA BIGCLAIM

Claimant

and

DENGUT LTD

SCHEDULE OF SPECIAL DAMAGE

The claimant was born on the 23rd February 1956. She was 45 at the date of the accident and is now 48. Prior to the accident the claimant's net monthly wage was £1,000. She would have received no pay rises had she remained in this employment She had no occupational pension.

1	*Loss of Earnings* 1st May January 2002 to date 35 months at £1,000.00 per month		£35,000
2	*Value of Clothing*		
	Overalls	£13.00	
	T-shirt	£ 4.00	
	Ring—cut off and repaired	£10.00	
	Total		£27.00
3	*Travelling expenses*		
	Physiotherapist—60 journeys at £2.00 per journey		£120.00
4	Private physiotherapist fees		£250.00
5	The claimant's husband has had to provide care beyond natural love and affection since the accident averaging out at two hours per day, discounting local care rate, say £3.00 perhour		£3,285.00
6	Hospital parking 65 visits at £1.00 each		£65.00
7	Medicinal costs £70 per annum		£210.00
8	Help with the garden two hours per week @£ 7.50 per hour		£2,340.00
9	Equipment needs		£5,000.00
	Total to date		**£46,297.00**

and continuing losses under items 1, 3, 4, 5, 6, 7, 8, and 9 above [if you have final medical prognosis and can quantify the future loss using an appropriate multiplier then you should do so at this stage, if the prognosis is uncertain so that all you know is that the losses continue but you are not yet sure for how long the above approach may be the best simply identifying which losses currently continue].

Dated this day of 2004

[insert statement of truth

SIGNED ....
Messrs. Dogged and Stubborn

Response Pack

Response Pack

You should read the 'notes for defendant' attached to the claim form which will tell you when and where to send the forms

Included in this pack are:

- either **Admission Form N9A** (if the claim is for a specified amount) or **Admission Form N9C** (if the claim is for an unspecified amount or is not a claim for money)
- either **Defence and Counterclaim Form N9B** (if the claim is for a specified amount) or **Defence and Counterclaim Form N9D** (if the claim is for an unspecified amount or is not a claim for money)
- **Acknowledgment of service** (see below)

	Complete
If you admit the claim or the amount claimed and/or you want time to pay	the admission form
If you admit part of the claim	the admission form and the defence form
If you dispute the whole claim or wish to make a claim (a counterclaim) against the claimant	the defence form
If you need 28 days (rather than 14) from the date of service to prepare your defence, or wish to contest the court's jurisdiction	the acknowledgment of service
If you do nothing, judgment may be entered against you	

Acknowledgment of Service

Defendant's full name if different from the name given on the claim form

In the	Besttown County Court
Claim No.	BT 1
Claimant (including ref.)	Nicola Bigclaim
Defendant	Deny it all

Address to which documents about this claim should be sent (including reference if appropriate)

Rebuttal & Co
1 Glasshouse Court
Centraltown
Centraltown

Tel. no. 214 Postcode CT 1

	if applicable
fax no.	008872
DX no.	N/A
e-mail	undervalue.com.uk

Tick the appropriate box

1. I intend to defend all of this claim ☐
2. I intend to defend part of this claim ☐
3. I intend to contest jurisdiction ☐

If you file an acknowledgment of service but do not file a defence within 28 days of the date of service of the claim form, or particulars of claim if served separately, judgment may be entered against you.

If you do not file an application within 28 days of the date of service of the claim form, or particulars of claim if served separately, it will be assumed that you accept the court's jurisdiction and judgment may be entered against you.

Signed Relentless & Co
(~~Defendant~~)(Defendant's solicitor)
(~~Litigation friend~~)

Position or office held (if signing on behalf of firm or company) Partner

Date

The court office at

is open between 10 am and 4 pm Monday to Friday. When corresponding with the court, please address forms or letters to the Court Manager and quote the claim number.

N9 -w3- Response Pack (4.99) *Produced on behalf of The Court Service*

Certificate of Service

Certificate of service

In the	
BEST TOWN COUNTY COURT	
Claim No.	BT 1
Claimant	NICOLA BIGCLAIM
Defendant	DENY IT LTD

On the ....(*insert date*)

the claim form, particulars of claim, response pack, medical evidence of Mr Cure and the schedule of special damages (*insert title or description of documents served*)

a copy of which is attached to this notice was served on (*insert name of person served, including position i.e. partner, director if appropriate*)

Deny it Ltd at their registered office

Tick as appropriate

- [x] by first class post
- [ ] by Document Exchange
- [ ] by delivering to or leaving
- [ ] by handing it to or leaving it with
- [ ] by fax machine (..................time sent) (*you may want to enclose a copy of the transmission sheet*)
- [ ] by e-mail
- [ ] by other means (please specify)

at (*insert address where service effected, include fax or DX number or e-mail address*)

OLD SHED
TIP LANE
WORST TOWN

being the defendant's:

- [ ] residence
- [x] registered office
- [ ] place of business
- [ ] other (*please specify*) ....

The date of service is therefore deemed to be .... (*insert date - see over for guidance*)

I confirm that at the time of signing this Certificate the document has not been returned to me as undelivered.

Signed ....
(Claimant)(~~Defendant~~)('s solicitor)(~~'s litigation friend~~)

Date ....

Position or office held ....
(if signing on behalf of firm or company)

N215 - w3 Certificate of service (4.99) *Printed on behalf on The Court Service*

Notes for guidance
Please note that these notes are only a guide and are not exhaustive
If you are in doubt you should refer to Part 6 of the rules

Where to serve

Nature of party to be served	Place of service
Individual	• Usual or last known residence
Proprietor of business	• Usual or last known residence; or • Place of business or last known place of business
Individual who is suing or being sued in the name of a firm	• Usual or last known residence; or • Principal or last known place of business of the firm
Corporation (incorporated in England and Wales) other than a company	• Principal office of the corporation; or • any place of within the jurisdiction where the corporation carries on its activities and which has a real connection with the claim
Company registered in England and Wales	• Principal office of the company or corporation; or • any place of business of the company within the jurisdiction which has a real connection with the claim

Personal Service - A document is served personally on an individual by leaving it with that individual. A document is served personally on a company or other corporation by leaving it with a person holding a senior position within the company or corporation. In the case of a partnership, you must leave it with either a partner or a person having control or management at the principal place of business. Where a solicitor is authorised to accept service on behalf of a party, service must be effected on the solicitor, unless otherwise ordered.

Deemed Service - Part 6.7(1). A document which is served in accordance with these rules or any relevant practice direction shall be deemed to be served on the day shown in the following table.

Method of service	Deemed day of service
First class post	The second day after it was posted
Document exchange	The second day after it was left at the document exchange
Delivering the document to or leaving it at a permitted address	The day after it was delivered to or left at the permitted address
Fax	If it is transmitted on a business day before 4 p.m., on that day, or otherwise on the business day after the day on which it was transmitted
Other electronic method	The second day after the day on which it was transmitted

• If a document (other than a claim form) is served after 5 p.m. on a business day, or at any time on a Saturday, Sunday or a bank holiday, the document shall, for the purpose of calculating any period of time after service of the document, be treated as having been served on the next business day.

• In this context "business day" means any day except Saturday, Sunday or a bank holiday; and "bank holiday" includes Christmas Day and Good Friday.

Service of documents on children and patients - The rules relating to service on children and patients are contained in Part 6.6 of the rules.

Claim Forms - The general rules about service are subject to the special rules about service of claim forms contained in rules 6.12 to 6.16.

Defence

IN THE BESTTOWN
COUNTY COURT
BETWEEN

Case No. 9710560

NICOLA BIGCLAIM

Claimant

and

DENYIT

Defendant

DEFENCE

---

1 The defendant admits paragraph 1, 2 and 3 of the Particulars of Claim.

2 The defendant denies that the claimant was wearing a dust coat provided by the defendant. It is the defendant's case that the claimant was wearing her own coat, something he had been warned previously not to do as it was too long and had flapping material hanging down.

3 The defendant denies that the accident was caused by its negligence or breach of duty as alleged or at all. The accident occurred because the claimant wore her own coat, contrary to express instruction and the loose material on this coat became caught in the lathe. The defendant also states that the lathe had and has a foot pedal brake that runs its length. The claimant had been given full instruction in the use of this lathe and knew about/or should have known about the brake. Had she used it the lathe could have been stopped without any accident occurring.

4 he accident happened in whole or in part as a result of the claimant's negligence.

PARTICULARS OF CLAIMANT'S NEGLIGENCE

1 Wearing non standard equipment.
2 Failing to heed earlier warnings to change into standard equipment.
3 Failing to operate the lathe as instructed.
4 Failing to use the foot brake on the lathe.
5 Failing to take any care for her own safety by deliberate breach of company procedures with which she was aware.

5 It is admitted that the claimant has suffered the injury set out in the medical reports of Mr Cure.

6 The defendant admits items 2, 3, 4, 6, 7, and 8 of the schedule of special damage. So far as item 1 is concerned it is the defendant's case that the reports of Mr Cure indicate that the claimant could have returned to non manual work

within a year of the accident. The defendant therefore admits loss of earnings of £12,000. The defendant has seen no evidence in support of items 5 and 9 of the schedule and therefore can neither admit nor deny these items.

The claimant's entitlement to interest is admitted.

[Insert statement of truth and counsel's details if defence settled by him or her]

Dated this day of 2004

Rebuttal & Co of, etc.

Allocation Questionnaire

Allocation questionnaire

To be completed by, or on behalf of,

who is ~~[1st][2nd][3rd][ ]~~[Claimant]~~[Defendant]~~
~~[Part 20 claimant]~~ in this claim

In the	BEST TOWN COUNTY COURT
Claim No.	
Last date for filing with court office	

Please read the notes on page five before completing the questionnaire.

You should note the date by which it must be returned and the name of the court it should be returned to since this may be different from the court where the proceedings were issued.

If you have settled this claim (or if you settle it on a future date) and do not need to have it heard or tried, you must let the court know immediately.

Have you sent a copy of this completed form to the other party(ies)? ☑ Yes ☐ No

A Settlement

Do you wish there to be a one month stay to attempt to settle the claim, either by informal discussion or by alternative dispute resolution? ☐ Yes ☑ No

B Location of trial

Is there any reason why your claim needs to be heard at a particular court? ☑ Yes ☐ No

If Yes, say which court and why?

All witnesses for the claimant and the expert Mr Cure are from Besttown

C Pre-action protocols

If an approved pre-action protocol applies to this claim, complete **Part 1** only. If not, complete **Part 2** only. If you answer 'No' to the question in either Part 1 or 2, please explain the reasons why on a separate sheet and attach it to this questionnaire.

Part 1 **please say which protocol*

The* personal injury protocol applies to this claim.

Have you complied with it? ☑ Yes ☐ No

Part 2

No pre-action protocol applies to this claim.

Have you exchanged information and/or documents (evidence) with the other party in order to assist in settling the claim? ☐ Yes ☐ No

N150 Allocation questionnaire (11.00) 1 *Printed on behalf of The Court Service*

D Case management information

What amount of the claim is in dispute? £ all of it

Applications

Have you made any application(s) in this claim? ☐ Yes ☑ No

If Yes, what for? (e.g. summary judgment, add another party) For hearing on

Witnesses

So far as you know at this stage, what witnesses of fact do you intend to call at the trial or final hearing including, if appropriate, yourself?

Witness name	Witness to which facts
The claimant	Liability and quantum
John Sawitall	accident circumstances

Experts

Do you wish to use expert evidence at the trial or final hearing? ☑ Yes ☐ No

Have you already copied any experts' report(s) to the other party(ies)? ☐ None yet obtained ☑ Yes ☐ No

Do you consider the case suitable for a single joint expert in any field? ☑ Yes ☐ No

Please list any single joint experts you propose to use and any other experts you wish to rely on. Identify single joint experts with the initials 'SJ' after their name(s).

Expert's name	Field of expertise (eg. orthopaedic surgeon, surveyor, engineer)
Mr Cure	orthopaedic

Do you want your expert(s) to give evidence orally at the trial or final hearing? ☑ Yes ☐ No

If Yes, give the reasons why you think oral evidence is necessary:

only if defendant does not agree Mr Cure's evidence

2

continue over

Track

Which track do you consider is most suitable for your claim? Tick one box

☐ small claims track ☐ fast track ☑ multi-track

If you have indicated a track which would not be the normal track for the claim, please give brief reasons for your choice

E Trial or final hearing

How long do you estimate the trial or final hearing will take? 1½ days ___ hours ___ minutes

Are there any days when you, an expert or an essential witness will not be able to attend court for the trial or final hearing? ☑ Yes ☐ No

If Yes, please give details

Name	Dates not available
Mr Cure	all August

F Proposed directions *(Parties should agree directions wherever possible)*

Have you attached a list of the directions you think appropriate for the management of the claim? ☑ Yes ☐ No

If Yes, have they been agreed with the other party(ies)? ☐ Yes ☑ No

G Costs

*Do **not** complete this section if you have suggested your case is suitable for the small claims track **or** you have suggested one of the other tracks and you do not have a solicitor acting for you.*

What is your estimate of your costs incurred to date? £15,000

What do you estimate your overall costs are likely to be? £35,000

In substantial cases these questions should be answered in compliance with CPR Part 43

3

H Other information

Have you attached documents to this questionnaire? ☐ Yes ☑ No

Have you sent these documents to the other party(ies)? ☐ Yes ☑ No

If Yes, when did they receive them?

Do you intend to make any applications in the immediate future? ☐ Yes ☑ No

If Yes, what for?

In the space below, set out any other information you consider will help the judge to manage the claim.

Signed   Date

~~[Counsel]~~[Solicitor][for the]~~[1st][2nd][3rd]~~[   ]
[Claimant]~~[Defendant][Part 20 claimant]~~

Please enter your firm's name, reference number and full postal address including (if appropriate) details of DX, fax or e-mail

Dogged & Stubborn of etc.	if applicable	
	fax no.	
	DX no.	
Tel. no. Postcode	e-mail	

Your reference no.

4

Notes for completing an allocation questionnaire

- If the claim is not settled, a judge must allocate it to an appropriate case management track. To help the judge choose the most just and cost-effective track, you must now complete the attached questionnaire.
- If you fail to return the allocation questionnaire by the date given, the judge may make an order which leads to your claim or defence being struck out, or hold an allocation hearing. If there is an allocation hearing the judge may order any party who has not filed their questionnaire to pay, immediately, the costs of that hearing.
- Use a separate sheet if you need more space for your answers marking clearly which section the information refers to. You should write the claim number on it, and on any other documents you send with your allocation questionnaire. Please ensure they are firmly attached to it.
- The letters below refer to the sections of the questionnaire and tell you what information is needed.

A Settlement

If you think that you and the other party may be able to negotiate a settlement you should tick the 'Yes' box. The court may order a stay, whether or not all the other parties to the claim agree. You should still complete the rest of the questionnaire, even if you are requesting a stay. Where a stay is granted it will be for an initial period of one month. You may settle the claim either by informal discussion with the other party or by alternative dispute resolution (ADR). ADR covers a range of different processes which can help settle disputes. More information is available in the booklet 'Resolving Disputes Without Going To Court' available from every county court office.

B Location of trial

High Court cases are usually heard at the Royal Courts of Justice or certain Civil Trial Centres. Fast or multi-track trials may be dealt with at a Civil Trial Centre or at the court where the claim is proceeding. Small claim cases are usually heard at the court in which they are proceeding.

C Pre-action protocols

Before any claim is started, the court expects you to have exchanged information and documents relevant to the claim, to assist in settling it. For some types of claim e.g. personal injury, there are approved protocols that should have been followed.

D Case management information

Applications

It is important for the court to know if you have already made any applications in the claim, what they are for and when they will be heard. The outcome of the applications may affect the case management directions the court gives.

Witnesses

Remember to include yourself as a witness of fact, if you will be giving evidence.

Experts

Oral or written expert evidence will only be allowed at the trial or final hearing with the court's permission. The judge will decide what permission it seems appropriate to give when the claim is allocated to track. Permission in small claims track cases will only be given exceptionally.

Track

The basic guide by which claims are normally allocated to a track is the amount in dispute, although other factors such as the complexity of the case will also be considered. A leaflet available from the court office explains the limits in greater detail.

Small Claims track	Disputes valued at not more than £5,000 except · those including a claim for personal injuries worth over £1,000 and · those for housing disrepair where either the cost of repairs or other work exceeds £1,000 or any other claim for damages exceeds £1,000
Fast track	Disputes valued at more than £5,000 but not more than £15,000
Multi-track	Disputes over £15,000

E Trial or final hearing

You should enter only those dates when you, your expert(s) or essential witness(es) will not be able to attend court because of holiday or other committments.

F Proposed directions

Attach the list of directions, if any, you believe will be appropriate to be given for the management of the claim. Agreed directions on fast and multi-track cases should be based on the forms of standard directions set out in the practice direction to CPR Part 28 and form PF52.

G Costs

Only complete this section if you are a solicitor and have suggested the claim is suitable for allocation to the fast or multi-track.

H Other Information

Answer the questions in this section. Decide if there is any other information you consider will help the judge to manage the claim. Give details in the space provided referring to any documents you have attached to support what you are saying.

5

Part 18 Request

IN THE BETWEEN BESTTOWN COUNTY COURT
BETWEEN Case No. BT1

NICOLA BIGCLAIM

Claimant

and

DENY IT LTD

Defendant

PART 18 REQUEST FOR FURTHER INFORMATION ABOUT THE DEFENCE

This is a request by the claimant for further information about the defence pursuant to CPR Part 18.

The information is requested from the defendant by day of 2004.

Of Paragraph 3 "... wore her own coat contrary to express instruction..."
Please indicate who it is alleged gave this express instruction to the claimant stating where, when and what was said.
If it is the defendant's case that such instruction was given in written form please indicate to which document reference is made and state how the information in any such document was conveyed to the claimant.

Of paragraph 3 "... knew or should have known about the brake..."
Please state how the defendant alleges that this information was provided to the claimant. If in written form please state how the information in any such document was conveyed to the claimant. If orally please state who conveyed the information, where, when and what was said.

Dated this day of 2005
Dogged & Stubborn of etc.

Part 18 Response

IN THE BESTTOWN COUNTY COURT
BETWEEN Case No. BT1

NICOLA BIGCLAIM

Claimant

and

DENYIT LTD

Defendant

PART 18 RESPONSE PROVIDING FURTHER INFORMATION ABOUT THE DEFENCE

(*repeat the question*)
Response: The health and safety handbook provided to the defendant at the commencement of her employment with the defendant on the day of 2001 makes specific reference to the standard issue clothing to be worn. This information was re-iterated by Joe Quartermaster, the defendant's stores officer when giving the defendant her overall and other standard issue clothing. He told her to wear the standard issue clothing at all times whilst in the factory. This information was provided on the day of 2001, being the defendant's first day working for the defendant.

(*repeat the question*)
Response: The claimant was given specific training on the machine in question by Bill Practical, the defendant's senior engineer. This took place on the claimant's first day working for the defendant. This training included a description of the braking mechanism of the machine, including the foot pedal brake. The defendant was then supervised in the use of the machine for the first week of her employment by Bill Practical.

There is also an operational manual for this machine kept in the staff room for consultation by any member of staff. Indeed, copies of the operational manuals for all machines in the factory are kept in the staffroom.

Dated the day of 2005
Rebuttal & Co of, etc.

Application Notice

Application Notice

In the	Besttown County Court
Claim no.	BT 1
Warrant no. (If applicable)	
Claimant (including ref.)	Nicola Bigclaim
Defendant(s) (including ref.)	Deny it all
Date	

You should provide this information for listing the application

1. How do you wish to have your application dealt with
   - a) at a hearing? ☐ } *complete all questions below*
   - b) at a telephone conference? ☐
   - c) without a hearing? ☑ *complete Qs 5 and 6 below*
2. Give a time estimate for the hearing/conference _____(hours)_____(mins)
3. Is this agreed by all parties? ☐ Yes ☑ No
4. Give dates of any trial period or fixed trial date _____
5. Level of judge District Judge
6. Parties to be served defendant's solicitors

Note You must complete Parts A **and** B, **and** Part C if applicable. Send any relevant fee and the completed application to the court with any draft order, witness statement or other evidence; and sufficient copies for service on each respondent.

Part A

1. Enter your full name, or name of solicitor

~~I~~(We)(1) Dogged & Stubborn (on behalf of)(the claimant)~~(the defendant)~~

2. State clearly what order you are seeking and if possible attach a draft

intend to apply for an order (a draft of which is attached) that(2)

3. Briefly set out why you are seeking the order. Include the material facts on which you rely, identifying any rule or statutory provision

because(3) The defendant provides a response to the Part 18 request for further information about the defence by 4.00p.m. the day of 2005. A copy of the information is needed to clarify the defendant's stated case and to enable the claimant properly to investigate the defence.

Part B

~~I~~(We) wish to rely on: *tick one box*

the attached (witness statement)(affidavit) ☐ my statement of case ☑

evidence in Part C in support of my application ☐

4. If you are not already a party to the proceedings, you must provide an address for service of documents

Signed _____ (Applicant)('s Solicitor)('s litigation friend)

Position or office held _____ (if signing on behalf of firm or company)

Address to which documents about this claim should be sent (including reference if appropriate)(4)

Address		if applicable	
Dogged & Stubborn of etc.		fax no.	
		DX no.	
Tel. no.	Postcode	e-mail	

The court office at

is open from 10am to 4pm Monday to Friday. When corresponding with the court please address forms or letters to the Court Manager and quote the claim number.

N244 Application Notice (4.00) *Printed on behalf of The Court Service*

Part C

Claim No.

I (We) wish to rely on the following evidence in support of this application:

[use if necessary]

Statement of Truth

*(I believe) *(The applicant believes) that the facts stated in Part C are true

**delete as appropriate*

Signed (Applicant)('s Solicitor)('s litigation friend)

Position or office held (if signing on behalf of firm or company)

Date

Application Notice Pre-issue

The application notice to be used is as per document 11. However, the wording is altered to seek an order against Deny it Ltd of etc. for the pre-action disclosure of (and list the documents).

Because Deny it Ltd is likely to be a defendant in a subsequent claim, would have to give standard disclosure of the documents sought in such a claim and the documents are necessary to assist in the early resolution of issues and possibly the claim.

In such a case you should rely on witness statement evidence on the back of the form. For example:

I, Verity Dogged, solicitor and partner of Dogged & Stubborn solicitors of etc. will say as follows:

I represent the claimant to this application, Nicola Bigclaim. I have been instructed to investigate a possible claim for compensation arising out of an injury that my client suffered at work with the Defendant to this application, Deny it Ltd on the 31st December 2001.

On that day the claimant, who had been employed by the defendant for two weeks, was operating a lathe. As she did so her dust coat became entangled in the lathe. The claimant was then pulled into the lathe until her right arm was jammed causing traumatic fracture.

The claimant was unable to stop the machine and remained trapped until a colleague turned off the machine, having been alerted by her cries.

I have appended to this statement a copy of; my firm's personal injury protocol letter of claim; the list of documents that I wished to see if liability was disputed and; the defendant's protocol response.

It is clear that liability is disputed. Notwithstanding this the defendant failed to provide any documents with the response letter and has ignored three letters since then repeating the request for documents. My attempts to speak to the defendant's representative have proved equally fruitless as my calls are never taken and no-one returns my calls.

It is the claimant's case that; the defendant is responsible for her injuries as a result of negligence and breach of statutory duty as set out in the letter of claim. As such, the defendant is likely to be a defendant to formal Part 7 proceedings; the documents requested are those that are deemed relevant in order to comply with the protocol and would form part of standard disclosure in any Part 7 proceedings; the provision of these documents now will enable proper investigation of the defence and assist in the resolution or clarification of issues both of which will lead to cost savings in the future.

I ask this court to order pre-action disclosure of the documents listed in the application notice by disclosure list by 4.00 p.m. day of 2004 with copies of any documents being provided by the same time.

This application has been rendered necessary solely as a result of the defendant's failure to comply with the protocol and give reasonable disclosure at this stage. In these circumstances I ask for the costs of this application to be summarily assessed by the court.

I believe that the facts stated in Part C are true.

Etc.

Order

IN THE BEST TOWN
COUNTY COURT
BETWEEN **Case No. BT9710560**

NICOLA BIGCLAIM

Claimant

and

DENYIT

Defendant

Before District Judge Correct

It is ordered that:
The defendant do file and serve responses to the Part 18 requests for further information served by the claimant by 4.00 p.m. the day of 2005.

The defendant do pay the claimant's costs of this application summarily assessed in the sum of £75+VAT. Such costs to be paid by the same date.

Dated the day of 2005

Disclosure List

List of documents: standard disclosure

In the	
Besttown County Court	
Claim No.	
Claimant (including ref)	Nicola Bigclaim
Defendant (including ref)	Deny it all
Date	

Notes:

- The rules relating to standard disclosure are contained in Part 31 of the Civil Procedure Rules.
- Documents to be included under standard disclosure are contained in Rule 31.6
- A document has or will have been in your control if you have or have had possession, or a right of possession, of it **or** a right to inspect or take copies of it.

Disclosure Statement

I state that I have carried out a reasonable and proportionate search to locate all the documents which I am required to disclose under the order made by the court on *(insert date)* the day of 2005

~~(I did not search for documents -~~

~~1. pre-dating~~

~~2. located elsewhere than~~

~~3. in categories other than~~

I certify that I understand the duty of disclosure and to the best of my knowledge I have carried out that duty. I further certify that the list of documents set out in or attached to this form, is a complete list of all documents which are or have been in my control and which I am obliged under the order to disclose.

I understand that I must inform the court and the other parties immediately if any further document required to be disclosed by Rule 31.6 comes into my control at any time before the conclusion of the case.

(I have not permitted inspection of documents within the category or class of documents (as set out below) required to be disclosed under Rule 31(6)(b)or (c) on the grounds that to do so would be disproportionate to the issues in the case.)

Signed Nicola Bigclaim **Date**

(Claimant)~~(Defendant)('s litigation friend)~~

Position or office held *(if signing on behalf of firm or company)*
Please state why you are the appropriate person to make the disclosure statement.

N/A

List of documents: continued overleaf

N265 - w3 standard disclosure (4.99) *Printed on behalf of The Court Service*

List and number here, in a convenient order, the documents (or bundles of documents if of the same nature, e.g. invoices) in your control, which you do not object to being inspected. Give a short description of each document or bundle so that it can be identified, and say if it is kept elsewhere i.e. with a bank or solicitor

I have control of the documents numbered and listed here. I do not object to you inspecting them/producing copies.

1. Copy letter from Dogged & Stubborn to Deny it Ltd	[date]
2. Wage schedules provided by Deny it Ltd	[date]
3. Copy various invoices for gardening work from Cut it down Ltd	dates various
4. Copy various invoices from Help around the House Ltd	dates various
5. Copy schedule Best town social services carer rates	2001/2/3/4/5
6. Copy various prescriptions	dates various
7. Copy and original documentation in respect of incapacity benefit, including copy assessments	dates various

---

List and number here, as above, the documents in your control which you object to being inspected. (Rule 31.19)

I have control of the documents numbered and listed here, but I object to you inspecting them:

letters from my solicitors
advices from counsel
all documents that have come into existence for the purposes of this claim

Say what your objections are

I object to you inspecting these documents because:

they are privileged

List and number here, the documents you once had in your control, but which you no longer have. For each document listed, say when it was last in your control and where it is now.

I have had the documents numbered and listed below, but they are no longer in my control.

The originals of the documents listed as copies overleaf. In respect of letters they were last in my control when despatched to the recipients.
In respect of prescriptions when given to the pharmacist.
In respect of invoices when paid and receipted copy provided.

Witness Statement

IN THE BESTTOWN COUNTY COURT
BETWEEN **Case No. BT1**

NICOLA BIGCLAIM

Claimant

and

DENYIT LTD

Defendant

WITNESS STATEMENT OF NICOLA BIGCLAIM

I Nicola Bigclaim, formerly a factory worker now on incapacity benefit of, etc. will say:

I am the claimant in this claim.

On December 16, 2001 I started work at the defendant's factory in Tip Lane Worsttown. Prior to that I had always been employed in clerical work. However, the firm that I had worked for went bust and I had to find work quickly to support my family. I saw an advertisement by the defendant for workers "no skills required Training to be provided". The wages looked good. I applied, had an interview and started the following week.

When I arrived on the 16th I was one of five people starting. A man who I later found was called Bill Engineer told us that over the next few weeks we would be provided with proper clothing for work but that whilst some was on order they had run out. He asked if we could wear any old overall that we had at home until the new ones arrived.

Bill then introduced us to five other factory workers and said that each of us recruits would be assigned to one of them. That person would show us where to work and what to do. He then left us with the other factory workers with whom we paired off. That was the last time that Bill Engineer spoke to me. Over the time I was at the factory he seemed to be busy mending equipment as there always seemed to be something broken.

The person with whom I had paired off, Ethel, told me that I was to be working on a lathe. I expressed surprise and concern as I had never worked on any machinery before. "Don't worry" she said "We all started like that. I'll show you what buttons to push and you just sit back and watch the machine do the work. Anyway it is quite an easy job as the lathe is really old and is out of use more often than not".

Over the next week I watched Ethel work and then started to work with her. On the last day of the first week she watched whilst I used the lathe. During this entire period Ethel only showed me how to use the controls that I would need for what I was going to be doing. There were other knobs and buttons which we did not touch. Ethel told me that she had no idea what they were for.

At no stage did Ethel show me how to stop the lathe other than by using an on off button that was at one end of the machine. She did not indicate to me that there was a foot pedal brake that ran the length of the lathe. I don't even remember seeing any such pedal.

During that week I wore an old dustcoat that I had at home for housework. This was quite old and the bottom of it was all frayed. At the beginning of the second week, which was just prior to Christmas Ethel told me that she had been told the new coats would be arriving in the new year.

The second week was only three days either side of Christmas. It was much like the first with me assisting Ethel.

When we returned to work after Christmas I was told by Ethel that she had been asked to fill in for someone off sick. I was to continue to operate the lathe as she had shown me. "If you have any problems I'm over by the staff room" she said.

The first few days I was over bothering Ethel every few minutes. Towards the end of New Year's Eve I could see that Ethel was becoming fed up with me bothering her. As a result later on when I needed help to do something I did not feel that I could ask her. I tried to do the best I could on my own but suddenly the machine started to make a funny high pitched noise. I realised that I had to have some help like it or not. I swung around to look over to see if Ethel was busy. The next thing I knew was that I was swept off my feet and dragged towards the lathe. I put my right arm up. I felt pain almost immediately. I think I must have started screaming but I am not sure as I think that I passed out. The next thing I knew was that people were all around me. My dustcoat was being cut by one of them. I noticed that the cut off bit was jammed in the lathe.

I was taken to hospital where I underwent surgery that night. In total I was in hospital for six days. The surgeon told me that I was lucky not to have lost my arm.

I refer to the orthopaedic reports of Mr. Cure served with these proceedings as these set out the injuries that I received and the treatment that I have undertaken. Four years and three further operations on I am left with an arm that I can only move in a swinging motion and that can tolerate no weight. It is functionally useless. The only treatment now is in terms of pain relief but even that sems to make no difference. Unless the arm is supported all the time the pain is like a throbbing headache.

As well as the operations I have had extensive outpatient treatment. Whilst the treatment is free I have incurred travel and parking expenses attending for physiotherapy, to see my G.P. and my consultant.

Prior to the accident I was a keen gardener and runner. I have been unable to return to these activities and have been told that I never shall.

My husband and I have two children. Fortunately they are at an age where they can virtually look after themselves. This was not true initially and so my husband had to do all the household chores as well as work. He also had to help me as I could not dress, wash, go to the loo, etc. without his help. Some of these problems remaain although I have tried as far as possible to recover my independence. Whilst I suspect it is more I have claimed for him undertaking care beyond love and affection demands for me of about two hours per day. In addition he still works and still helps the children. For example I can no longer drive so he has to do all the taxing for their various activities.

Inevitably because of my injuries our social life has suffered. As I find the arm becomes uncomfortable unless supported I struggle if we go out to friends, the pub or a restaurant. Anyway I find it embarrassing that my husband has to cut my food up for me.

The doctors treating me have said that I shall never work again in any job involving manual work. It is hard to see what job that I could do with the constant pain and restriction of movement. So far I have not seen anything suitable.

As stated earlier, I used to love gardening. Now I cannot do it. It makes my heart bleed to have to employ a gardener. My husband simply does not have the time to do the garden. He also no longer has the time to do any DIY because he is so busy running the family on his own. In the past he has always done all our decorating. Now we have to employ someone.

To assist me around the house I have purchased several aides, like a grabber to pick up things I drop. I have also adapted the bathroom to insert a shower as I could not get in or out of a bath. I have purchased a special bed that provides mire support and various cushions for the same purpose. The invoices for this work have been disclosed to the defendant.

It is impossible in a statement to convey the way that my life has been altered. To claim for the injury and other losses in the schedule of special damages cannot begin to redress what I have lost. My whole life, and as a result, that of my family has been altered for ever.

I believe that the facts stated in this witness statement are true

....

Nicola Bigclaim Dated the day of 2005

Listing Questionnaire

Listing questionnaire

In the

BEST TOWN COUNTY COURT

Claim No. BT 1

Last date for filing with court office

To

- The court will use the information which you and the other party(ies) provide to fix a date for trial (or to confirm the date and time if one has already been fixed), to confirm the estimated length of trial and to set a timetable for the trial itself. In multi-track cases the court will also decide whether to hold a pre-trial review.
- If you do not complete and return the questionnaire the procedural judge may
  - make an order which leads to your statement of case (claim or defence) being struck out.
  - decide to hold a listing hearing. You may be ordered to pay (immediately) the other parties' costs of attending.
  - if there is sufficient information, list the case for trial and give any appropriate directions.
- Separate estimates of costs incurred to date and those which will be incurred if the case proceeds to trial, should be given using Form 1 in the Schedule of Costs Forms set out in the Civil Procedure Rules. This form should be attached to and returned with your completed questionnaire. (This relates only to costs incurred by legal representatives.)

A Directions complied with

1. Have you complied with all the previous directions given by the court? ✓ Yes ☐ No

2. If no, please explain which directions are outstanding and why

Directions outstanding	Reasons directions outstanding

3. Are any further directions required to prepare the case for trial? ☐ Yes ✓ No *(If no go to section B)*

4. If yes, please explain directions required and give reasons

Directions required	Reasons required

N170 -w3 Listing questionnaire (6.99) *Printed on behalf of The Court Service*

B Experts

1. Has the court already given permission for you to use written expert evidence? ✓ Yes ☐ No *(If no go to section B6)*

2. If yes, please give name and field of expertise.

Name of expert	Whether joint expert *(please tick, if appropriate)*	Field of expertise
Mr Cure	✓	orthopaedic

3. Have the expert(s') report(s) been agreed with the other parties? ✓ Yes ☐ No

4. Have the experts met to discuss their reports? ☐ Yes ✓ No

5. Has the court already given permission for the expert(s) to give oral evidence at the trial? *(If yes go to Q8)* ☐ Yes ✓ No

6. If no, are you seeking that permission? ☐ Yes *(If yes go to Q7)* ✓ No *(If no go to section C)*

7. Give your reasons for seeking permission.

N/A

8. What are the names, addresses and fields of expertise of your experts?

Expert 1	Expert 2	Expert 3	Expert 4
N/A			

9. Please give details of any dates within the trial period when your expert(s) will not be available.

Name of expert	Dates not available
N/A	

C Other witnesses

(If you are not calling other witnesses go to section D)

1. How many other witnesses (including yourself) will be giving evidence on your behalf at the trial? *(do not include experts - see section B above)* ☐ *(Give number)*

2. What are the names and addresses of your witnesses?

Witness 1	Witness 2	Witness 3	Witness 4
Claimant 80 Credible Street Besttown	John Sawitall Reliable House Besttown		

3. Please give details of any dates within the trial period when you or your witnesses will not be available?

Name of witness	Dates not available
claimant	1st day of window
John Sawitall	1st week of window

4. Are any of the witness statements agreed? ☐ Yes ☑ No *(If no go to Q6)*

5. If yes, give the name of the witness and the date of his or her statement

Name of witness	Date of statement
N/A	

6. Do you or any of your witnesses need any special facilities? ☐ Yes ☑ No *(If no go to Q8)*

7. If yes, what are they?

N/A

8. Will any of your witnesses be provided with an interpreter? ☐ Yes ☑ No *(If no go to section D)*

9. If yes, say what type of interpreter e.g. language (stating which), deaf/blind etc.

N/A

D Legal representation

1. Who will be presenting your case at the hearing or trial? ☐ You ☐ Solicitor ☑ Counsel

2. Please give details of any dates within the trial period when the person presenting your case will not be available.

Name	Dates not available

E Other matters

1. How long do you estimate the trial will take, including cross-examination and closing arguments?

Minutes	Hours	Days
		1½

If your case is allocated to the fast track the maximum time allowed for the whole case will be no more than one day.

2. What is the estimated number of pages of evidence to be included in the trial bundle?

120

(please give number)

Fast track cases only

3. The court will normally give you 3 weeks notice in the fast track of the date fixed for a fast track trial unless, in exceptional circumstances, the court directs that shorter notice will be given. Would you be prepared to accept shorter notice of the date fixed for trial? ☐ Yes ☐ No

Signed of Dogged & Stubborn

~~Claimant/defendant or Coun~~sel/Solicitor for the claimant/~~defendant~~

Date

Appendix F

Actuarial Tables

In 1984 HMSO published 'Actuarial tables with explanatory notes for use in personal injury and fatal accident cases'. These notes were the result of a working party comprised of actuaries and lawyers and were expanded and updated in 1994. The Law Commission suggested that courts should be obliged to have regard to them and section 10 of the Civil Evidence Act 1995 provided that actuarial tables would be admissible in evidence without having to be proved. Until recently there was not the case. However, following the House of Lords in *Wells v. Wells* [1998] 3 W.L.R. 389 the actuarial tables should now be the starting point.

The courts have recently reaffirmed use of a 3 per cent return as set out in *Wells*.[1] What follows is the explanatory notes, together with the tables. In summary, the tables should be used as follows:

1 Choose the right table. There are different tables for men and women, and for:
- losses for the rest of the claimant's life, beyond retirement age (Tables 1 and 2);
- losses to normal retirement age (Tables 3 and 4 to age 60 and 5 and 6 to age 65);
- loss of pension rights from retirement age (Tables 7, 8, 9 and 10).

2 Choose the rate of interest. The tables set out multipliers based on rates of interest ranging from one and a half per cent to five per cent. If some or all of the award will bear interest then reduce the rate of interest accordingly.

3 Use the appropriate table to find the appropriate multiplier (based on age at trial—unless fatal case, in which case it is age at death). Multiply that by the net annual loss.

4 Make any necessary deduction for contingencies (other than early or late death).

[1] The Lord Chancellor has now reduced that to 2.5%.

Section A: General

Purpose of tables

1 The tables have been prepared by the Government Actuary's Department. They provide an aid for those assessing the lump sum appropriate as compensation for a continuing future pecuniary loss or consequential expense or cost of care in personal injury and fatal accident cases.

Application of tables

2 The tables set out multipliers. These multipliers enable the user to assess the present capital value of future annual loss (net of tax) or annual expense calculated on the basis of various assumptions which are explained below. Accordingly, to find the present capital value of a given annual loss or expense, it is necessary to select the appropriate table, find the appropriate multiplier and then multiply the amount of the annual loss or expense by that figure.

3 Tables 1 to 36 deal with annual loss or annual expense extending over three different periods of time. In each case there are separate tables for men and women.

— In Tables 1, 2, 19 and 20 the loss or expense is assumed to begin immediately and to continue for the whole of the rest of the claimant's life, allowing for different potential lifespans, including the possibility of early death or prolonged life. The tables apply to both the deceased and the dependants' lives in fatal accident cases.

— In Tables 3 to 10 and 21 to 28 the loss or expense is assumed to begin immediately but to continue only until the claimant's retirement or earlier death. The age of retirement is assumed to be 55 in Tables 3, 4, 21 and 22, 60 in Tables 5, 6, 23 and 24, 65 in Tables 7, 8, 25 and 26 and 70 in Tables 9, 10, 27 and 28.

— In Tables 11 to 18 and 29 to 36 it is assumed that the annual loss or annual expense will not begin until the claimant reaches retirement but will then continue for the whole of the rest of his or her life.

4 In Tables 13 and 31 (males) and Tables 14 and 32 (females) the age of retirement is assumed to be 60. In Tables 15 and 33 (males) and Tables 16 and 34 (females) the age of retirement is assumed to be 65 (and similarly for retirement ages 55 and 70). These tables all make due allowance for the chance that the claimant may not live to reach the age of retirement.

Mortality assumptions for Tables 1 to 18

5 As in previous editions of these tables, Tables 1 to 18 are based on the mortality rates experienced in England and Wales in a historical three-year

period, in this case the years 1990 to 1992, and published by the Government Actuary's Department as English Life Table No. 15 (ELT 15). Given this assumption about mortality, the accuracy of these tables, which were prepared by the Government Actuary's Department, has been accepted by all the actuaries on the Working Party, which included actuaries nominated by the Institute and the Faculty of Actuaries, and the Association of British Insurers (ABI) and the Family Law Bar Association. Consequently, the courts can have confidence in the accuracy of these tables. Members of the Working Party nominated by the ABI have reservations about the application of the tables and other matters and these are set out in Appendix C.

6 On the basis of some reported cases, it appears that tables for pecuniary loss of life, *e.g.* cost of care, may have been misunderstood. As stated hereafter in Paragraph 25, the tables do not assume that the claimant dies after a period equating to the expectation of life, but take account of the possibilities that the claimant will live for different periods, *e.g.* die soon or live to be very old. The mortality assumptions relate to the general population of England and Wales. Unless there is clear evidence in an individual case to support the view that the individual is atypical and will enjoy longer or shorter expectation of life, no further increase or reduction is required for mortality alone.

Tables adjusted to take account of projected mortality (Tables 19 to 36)

7 The actuaries on the Working Party consider that failure to have regard to current and reasonable projected future improvements in mortality rates will result in awards of damages which are lower than they should be. At Appendix A is an extract for ELT 15 which shows graphs indicating rates of mortality expressed in percentages of 1911 rates on a logarithmic scale. They demonstrate in a stark fashion the improvement in longevity which has taken place since 1911 and, which, according to all the available evidence is continuing. The sole exception to this trend is a small increase recently in the mortality of males in their late twenties and early thirties due to AIDS and increasing numbers of suicides. The same effect is present, albeit to a lesser degree, for females. Even if this slight worsening of mortality at these ages were to continue, the effect on the tables of multipliers would not be significant. (For comments by the ABI see Appendix C.)

8 The graphs, and the figures on which they are based, point to the conclusion that, on the balance of probabilities, the mortality rates which will actually be experience in future by those who are alive today will be lower than in ELT 15 which is already nearly a decade out of date, and will be increasingly so the further into the future one goes. This, implies the need for higher multipliers. For the purposes of preparing the official national population projections, the Government Actuary makes a prudent estimate of the extent of future improvements in mortality. Tables 19 to 36 show the multipliers which result from the application of these projected mortality rates derived from the mid-1998 based population projections for England and Wales. The actuaries on the Working Party (save for the dissenting views expressed at Appendix C) consider that these alternative tables provide a more appropriate estimate of the value of future

income streams than Tables 1 to 18, which are based on historic mortality and almost certainly underestimate future longevity. The Working Party therefore recommends the Courts to use Tables 19 to 36 rather than Tables 1 to 18.

9 Paragraphs 5 to 8 appeared in the Third Edition. So far as the Working Party is aware, all Judges are now using the tables based on projected mortality rates (Tables 19 to 36). Consequently, the majority of the Working Party would have omitted the tables which are based on historic mortality (Tables 1 to 18). However, they have been retained at the request of the ABI in case any of its members wishes to test the point on appeal.

Use of tables

10 To find the appropriate figure for the present value of a particular loss or expense, the user must first choose that table which relates to the period of loss or expense, for which the individual claimant is to be compensated and to the sex of the claimant, or, where appropriate, the claimant's dependants.

11 If, for some reason the facts in a particular case do not correspond with the assumptions on which one of the tables is based, (for example, it is known that the claimant will have a different retiring age from that assumed in the tables) then the tables can only be used if an appropriate allowance is made for this difference; for this purpose the assistance of an actuary should be sought, except for situations where specific guidance is given in these explanatory notes.

Rate of return

12 The basis of the multipliers set out in the tables is that the lump sum will be invested and yield income (but that over the period in question the claimant will gradually reduce the capital sum, so that at the end of the period it is exhausted). Accordingly, an essential factor in arriving at the right figure is to choose the appropriate rate of return. The tables set out multipliers based on annual rates of return ranging from $\frac{1}{2}$ per cent to 5 per cent (previous editions gave multipliers based on annual rates of return between $1\frac{1}{2}$ per cent and 5 per cent). In addition, a 0 per cent column has been included to show the multiplier without any discount for interest (*i.e.* expectations of life, or the equivalent for different periods). These are supplied to assist in the calculation of multipliers in Fatal Accident Act cases (see Section D).

13 Currently, the annual rate of return to be applied is 3 per cent (net of tax), based on the judgment of the House of Lords in *Wells v. Wells*. After a Commencement Order has been made in respect of the Damages Act 1996, section 1, the rate or rates of return are expected to be specified by the Lord Chancellor, after receiving advice from the Government Actuary and the Treasury. Should it become necessary, further tables will be issued.

14 Previous editions of these tables explained how the current yields on index-linked government bonds could be used as an indicator of the appropriate real rate of return for valuing future income streams. Such considerations were endorsed by the House of Lords in *Wells v. Wells* and it is expected that this will continue to be the case when the Lord Chancellor sets the rate on commence-

ment of Section 1 of the Damages Act 1996. A description of how to use market rates of return on index-linked gilts to determine the appropriate rate of return is given in Appendix B. In cases outwith the scope of these tables, the advice of an actuary should be sought.

Tax

15 In order to arrive at a true present capital value of the claimant's future loss or expense it is necessary to consider whether he or she will have to pay a significant amount of tax on the investment return arising from his compensation. If he or she will pay little or no tax, no adjustment of the rate of return will be required. If he or she will have to pay a significant percentage of that income in tax, then the rate of return chosen to determine the present capital value of the loss or expense should be reduced accordingly. Attention is drawn to the decision of the House of Lords in *Hodgson v. Trapp* [1989] A.C. 807 concerning the treatment of the incidence of higher rate tax on the income arising from a compensatory fund. This position was confirmed by Lord Steyn in the House of Lords judgment in *Wells v. Wells*, namely that:

> "the position regarding higher tax rates should remain as Lord Oliver of Aylmerton in *Hodgson v. Trapp* [1989] 1 A.C. 807 at 835B described it, *viz.* that in such exceptional cases claimants would be free to place their arguments for a lower rate before the court."

16 In cases where the impact of personal Income Tax and Capital Gains Tax is likely to be significant, more accurate calculation of the value net of tax of payments to the individual may be desirable. Such calculations may be able to be carried out by using software of the type referred to in paragraph 73 but the advice of an accountant and an actuary should be sought.

Different retirement ages

17 In paragraph 11 above, reference was made to the problem that will arise when the claimant's retiring age is different from that assumed in the tables. Such a problem may arise in valuing a loss or expense beginning immediately but ending at retirement; or in valuing a loss or expense which will not begin until the claimant reaches retirement but will then continue until death. Tables are provided for retirement ages of 55, 60, 65 and 70. Where the claimant's actual retiring age would have been between two of these retirement ages for which tables are provided, the correct multiplier can be obtained by consideration of the tables for retirement age immediately above and below the actual retirement age, keeping the period to retirement age the same. Thus a woman of 42 who would have retired at 58 can be considered as being in between the cases of a woman of 39 with a retirement age of 55 and a woman of 44 with a retirement age of 60. The steps to take are as follows:

(1) Determine between which retirement ages, for which tables are provided, the claimant's actual retirement age *R* lies. Let the lower of these ages be *A* and the higher be *B*.

(2) Determine how many years must be subtracted from the claimant's actual retirement age to get to *A* and subtract that period from the claimant's age. If the claimant's age is *X*, the result of this calculation is $(X + A - R)$.

(3) Look up this new reduced age in the Table corresponding to retirement age *A* at the appropriate rate of return. Let the resulting multiplier be *M*.

(4) Determine how many years must be added to the claimant's actual retirement age to get to *B* and add that period to the claimant's age. The result of this calculation is $(X + B - R)$.

(5) Look up this new increased age in the Table corresponding to retirement age *B* at the appropriate rate of return. Let the resulting multiplier be *N*.

(6) Interpolate between *M* and *N*. In other words, calculate:
$(B - R) \times M + (R - A) \times N$
and divide the result by 5.

18 In the example given in paragraph 17, the steps would be as follows:

(1) *A* is 55 and *B* is 60.

(2) Subtracting 3 years from the claimant's age gives 39.

(3) Looking up age 39 in Table 22 (for retirment age 55) gives 12.61 at a rate of return of 3 per cent.

(4) Adding 2 years to the claimant's age gives 44.

(5) Looking up age 44 in Table 24 (for retirement age 60) gives 12.54 at a rate of return of 3 per cent.

(6) Calculating $2 \times 12.61 + 3 \times 12.54$ and dividing by 5 gives 12.57 as the multiplier.

19 If the claimant's actual retiring age would have been earlier than 55 (but not less than 50), he or she may be treated as correspondingly older than his or her true age, but keeping the same period to retirement age. Thus a woman of 42 who would have retired at 52 is treated as though she were 45 and retiring at 55. The appropriate multiplier is then obtained from Table 4 or 22. A further correction should then in principle be made, because the claimant's chances of survival for ten years are slightly greater at 42 than if she were in fact 45. However, the effect of this would be small for retirement ages down to 50.

20 When the claimant would have expected to retire later than the highest retirement age for which tables are available (age 70), say up to 75, the procedure is reversed. Thus a man of 42 who would have retired at 75 is treated as though he were 37 and retiring at 70. The appropriate multiplier is then obtained from the table (in this case Table 9 or 27) and the further correction required is made by reducing the multiplier for a male by three-quarters of one per cent for each year by which the retiring age of the claimant exceeds the retiring age assumed in the table. So, in this example, the multiplier from Table 27 at 3 per cent rate of return would be 20.21 at age 37. Reducing the multiplier by three-quarters of one per cent for each of 5 years' later retirement means taking off $3\frac{3}{4}$ per cent (or multiplying by 0.9625), which brings the multiplier to 19.45 (= 20.21 × (1 – 5 × 0.0075)). In the case of a woman the reduction would be by one half of one per cent for each year. So, for a woman of 49 who would have retired at 73, the multiplier from Table 28 for a woman aged 46 (three years younger to correspond to the difference between a retirement age of 73 and one of 70) would be 16.57. Reducing the multiplier by one half of one per cent for each year of early retirement means subtracting $1\frac{1}{2}$ per cent for three years' early retirement (or multiplying by 0.985), bringing the multiplier to 16.32 (= 16.57 × (1 – 3 × 0.005)).

21 When the loss or expense to be valued is that from the date of retirement to death, and the claimant's date of retirement differs from that assumed in the tables, a different approach is necessary, involving the following three steps.

(1) Assume that there is a present loss which will continue for the rest of the claimant's life and from Table 1 or 2 (or 19 or 20) establish the value of that loss or expense over the whole period from the date of assessment until the claimant's death.

(2) Establish the value of such loss or expense over the period from the date of assessment until the claimant's expected date of retirement following the procedure explained in paragraphs 16 to 19 above.

(3) Subtract the second figure from the first. The balance remaining represents the present value of the claimant's loss or expense between retirement and death.

22 The adjustments described in paragraphs 19 and 20 for retirement ages below 55 and above 70 cannot reliably be applied for retirement ages of less than 50 or more than 75. In such rare cases the advice of an actuary should be sought.

Younger ages

23 Tables 1, 2, 19 and 20, which concern pecuniary loss for life, and Tables 11 to 18 and 29 to 36, which concern loss of pension from retirement age, have been extended down to age 0. In some circumstances the multiplier at age 0 is

slightly lower than that at age 1; this arises because of the relatively high incidence of deaths immediately after birth.

24 Tables for multipliers for loss of earnings (Tables 3 to 10 and 21 to 28) have not been extended below age 16. In order to determine the multiplier for loss of earnings for someone who has not yet started work, it is first necessary to determine an assumed age at which the claimant would have commenced work and to find the appropriate multiplier for that age from Tables 3 to 10 or 21 to 28, according to the assumed retirement age. This multiplier should then be multiplied by the deferment factor from Table 37 which corresponds to the appropriate rate of return and the period from the date of the trial to the date on which it is assumed that the claimant would have started work. A similar approach can be used for determining a multiplier for pecuniary loss for life where the loss is assumed to commence a fixed period of years from the date of the trial. For simplicity the factors in Table 37 relate purely to the impact of compound interest and ignore mortality. At ages below 30 this is a reasonable approximation (for example, allowance for male mortality in accordance with ELT 15 from age 5 to 25 would only reduce the multiplier by a further 1 per cent, *i.e.* apply a factor of 0.99 to the multiplier) but at higher ages it would normally be appropriate to allow explicitly for mortality and the advice of an actuary should be sought.

Contingencies

25 Tables 1 to 18 have been calculated to take into account the chances that the claimant will live for different periods, including the possibility that they will die young or live to be very old, based on historical levels of population mortality. Tables 19 to 36 make reasonable provision for the levels of mortality which members of the population of England and Wales alive today may expect to experience in future. The tables do not take account of the other risks and vicissitudes of life, such as the possibility that the claimant would for periods have ceased to earn due to ill-health or loss of employment. Nor do they take account of the fact that many people cease work for substantial periods to care for children or other dependants. Section B suggests ways in which allowance may be made to the multipliers for loss of earnings, to allow for certain risks other than mortality.

Impaired lives

26 In some cases, medical evidence may be available which asserts that a claimant's health impairments are equivalent to adding a certain number of years to their current age, or to treating the individual as having a specific age different from their actual age. In such cases, Tables 1, 2, 19 and 20 can be used with respect to the deemed higher age. For the other tables the adjustment is not so straightforward, as adjusting the age will also affect the assumed retirement age, but the procedures described in paragraphs 16 to 20 may be followed, or the advice of an actuary should be sought.

Fixed periods

27 In cases where pecuniary loss is to be valued for a fixed period, the multipliers in Table 38 may be used. These make no allowance for mortality and any other contingency but assume that regular frequent payments (*e.g.* weekly or monthly) will continue throughout the period. These figures should in principle be adjusted if the periodicity of payment is less frequent, especially if the payments in question are annually in advance or in arrears.

Variable loss or expense

28 The tables do not provide an immediate answer when the annual loss or expense to be valued is not assumed to be stable; where, for instance, the claimant's lost earnings were on a sliding scale or promotion was likely to be achieved. It may be possible to use the tables to deal with such situations by increasing the basic figure of annual loss or expenses; or by choosing a lower rate of interest and so a higher multiplier than would otherwise have been chosen. In some cases it may be appropriate to split the overall multiplier into two or more parts and apply different multiplicands to each. More complicated cases may be suited to the use of the software referred to in paragraph 73. In addition to contingent widows' pensions, cases such as *Singapore Bus v. Lim Soon Yong* [1985] 1 W.L.R. 1075 at 1079 D-108A, *Taylor v. O'Connor* [1971] A.C. 115 at 127, 130, *Davies and others v. Whiteways Cyder Co. Ltd and another* [1974] 3 All E.R. 168, etc., may necessitate actuarial advice with regard to other losses.

29 If doubt exists whether the tables are appropriate to a particular case which appears to present significant difficulties of substance, it would be prudent to take actuarial advice. This might be appropriate in relation to the level of spouses' benefits, if these are to be assessed, since these are not readily valued using Tables 1 to 36. The value of these would generally be very small for a female claimant (*i.e.* benefits to the male spouse) but could add 10 to 20 per cent to the pension loss for a male claimant.

Section B: Contingencies other than mortality

30 As stated in paragraph 24, the tables for loss of earnings (Tables 3 to 10 and 21 to 28) take no account of risks other than mortality. This section shows how the multipliers in these tables may be reduced to take account of risks other than mortality. This is based on work commissioned by the Institute of Actuaries and carried out by Professor S. Haberman and Mrs D. S. F. Bloomfield (*Work time lost to sickness, unemployment and stoppages: measurement and application* (1990), Journal of the Institute of Actuaries 117, 533–595). Although there was some debate within the actuarial profession about the details of this work, and in particular about the scope for developing it further, the findings were broadly accepted and were adopted by the Government Actuary and the other actuaries who were members of the Working Party when the Second Edition of the Tables was published.

31 Since the risk of mortality (including the risks of dying early or living longer) has already been taken into account in the tables, the principal contingencies in respect of which a further reduction is to be made, particularly for earnings loss up to retirement age, are illness and unemployment. Even with the effective disappearance of the "job for life" there appears to be no scientific justification in the generality of cases for assuming significantly larger deductions than those given in this section. It should be noted that the authors of the 1990 paper (Professor Haberman and Mrs Bloomfield) wrote "All the results discussed in this paper should be further qualified by the caveat that the underlying models ... assume that economic activity rates and labour force separation and accession rated do not vary in the future from the bases chosen. As mentioned already in the text, it is unlikely to be true that the future would be free from marked secular trends". The paper relied on Labour Force Surveys for 1973, 1977, 1981 and 1985 and English Life Tables No. 14 (1980–82). However, although it is now somewhat out of date, it is the best study presently available. It is hoped that further research into the impact of contingencies other than mortality will be carried out in due course.

32 Specific factors in individual cases may necessitate larger reductions. By contrast, there will also be cases where the standard multipliers should be increased, to take into account positive factors of lifestyle, employment prospects and life expectancy.

33 The extent to which the multiplier needs to be reduced will reflect individual circumstances such as occupation and geographical region. In the short term, levels of economic activity and unemployment, including time lost through industrial action, are relevant. Reductions may be expected to be smaller for clerical workers than for manual workers, for those living in the South rather than the North, and for those in "secure" jobs and in occupations less affected by redundancy or industrial action.

34 The factors described in subsequent paragraphs are for use in calculating loss of earnings up to retirement age. The research work did not investigate the impact of contingencies other than mortality on the value of future pension rights. Some reduction to the multiplier for loss of pension would often be appropriate when a reduction is being applied for loss of earnings. This may be less of a reduction than in the case of loss of earnings because of the ill-health contingency (as opposed to the unemployment contingency), particularly in cases where there are significant ill-health retirement pension rights. A bigger reduction may be necessary in cases where there is significant doubt whether pension rights would have continued to accrue (to the extent not already allowed for in the post-retirement multiplier) or in cases where there may be doubt over the ability of the pension fund to pay promised benefits. In the case of a defined contribution pension scheme, loss of pension rights may be able to be allowed for simply by increasing the future earnings loss (adjusted for contingencies other than mortality) by the percentage which the employer pays to the scheme in contributions.

35 The suggestions which follow are intended only to provide a "ready reckoner", as opposed to precise figures.

The basic deduction for contingencies other than mortality

36 Subject to the adjustments which may be made as described below, the multiplier which has been selected from the tables, *i.e.* in respect of risks of mortality only, should be reduced by *multiplying* it by a figure selected from the table below, under the heading "Medium".

TABLE A
Loss of Earnings to Pension Age 65 (Males)

Age at date of trial	High	Medium	Low
20	0.99	–0.98	0.97
25	0.99	0.98	0.96
30	0.99	0.97	0.95
35	0.98	0.96	0.93
40	0.98	0.96	0.92
45	0.97	0.95	0.90
50	0.96	0.93	0.87
55	0.95	0.90	0.82
60	0.95	0.90	0.81

Levels of economic activity and employment

37 The medium set of reductions is appropriate if it is anticipated that economic activity is likely to correspond to that in the 1970s and 1980s (ignoring periods of high and low unemployment). The high set is appropriate if higher economic activity and lower unemployment rates are anticipated. The low set is appropriate if lower economic activity and higher unemployment rates are anticipated.

Lower pension ages (Males)

38. The figures will be higher for a lower pension age. For example, if pension age is 60, the figures should be as shown in Table B.

TABLE B
Loss of Earnings to Pension Age 60 (Males)

Age at date of trial	High	Medium	Low
20	0.99	0.99	0.98
25	0.99	0.99	0.97
30	0.99	0.98	0.97
35	0.99	0.98	0.96
40	0.98	0.97	0.94
45	0.98	0.96	0.93
50	0.97	0.94	0.92
55	0.96	0.93	0.88

Female lives

39 As a rough guide, for female lives between ages 35 and 55 with a pension age of 60, the figures should be as shown in Table C. As for males, the factors will be lower if the pension age is higher (*e.g.* 65) and higher if the pension age is lower (*e.g.* 55).

TABLE C
Loss of Earnings to Pension Age 60 (Females)

Age at date of trial	High	Medium	Low
35	0.95	0.95	0.94
40	0.93	0.93	0.92
45	0.90	0.90	0.88
50	0.91	0.90	0.88
55	0.95	0.94	0.93

Variations by occupation

40 The risks of illness, injury and disability are less for persons in clerical or similar jobs, *e.g.*, civil servants, the professions and financial services industries, and greater for those in manual jobs, *e.g.* construction, mining, quarrying and ship-building. However, what matters is the precise nature of the work undertaken by the person in question, rather than the industry as such; for example, a secretary in the Headquarters office of a large construction company may be at no greater risk than a secretary in a solicitor's office.

41 In less risky occupations the figures in Tables A to C should be *increased* by a maximum of the order of 0.01 up to age 40, rising to 0.03 at age 55.

42 In more risky occupations the figures in Tables A to C should be *reduced* by a maximum of the order of 0.01 at age 25, 0.02 at age 40 and 0.05 at age 55.

Variations by geographical region

43 For persons resident in the South East, East Anglia, South West and East Midlands, the figures in Tables A to C should be *increased* by a maximum of the order of 0.01 up to age 40, rising to 0.03 at age 55.

44 For persons resident in the North, North West, Wales and Scotland, the figures in Tables A to C should be *reduced* by a maximum of the order of 0.01 at age 25, 0.02 at age 40 and 0.05 at age 55.

Section C: Summary of personal injury applications

45 To use the tables take the following steps:

(1) Choose the tables relating to the appropriate period of loss or expense.

(2) Choose the table, relating to that period, appropriate to the sex of the claimant and according to whether historical mortality is to be used (Tables 1 to 18) or a realistic estimate of actual mortality (Tables 19 to 36).

(3) Choose the appropriate rate of return, before allowing for the effect of tax on the income to be obtained from the lump sum.

(4) Allow for a reduction in the rate of return to reflect the effect of tax on the income from the lump sum.

(5) Find the figure under the column in the table chosen given against the age at trial of the claimant.

(6) Adjust the figure to take account of contingencies other than mortality, as specified in Section B above.

(7) Multiply the annual loss (net of tax) or expense by that figure.

46 In principle an allowance for an expected increase in the annual loss or expense (not due to inflation) can be made by choosing a lower rate of return or by increasing the figure of annual loss or expense. In cases where the claimant's expected age of retirement differs from that assumed in the tables, the more complicated procedure explained in paragraphs 17 to 21 should be followed.

Example 1

47 The following is an example of the use of the tables in a personal injury case.

The claimant is female, aged 35 at the date of the trial. She lives in London and is an established civil servant who was working in an office at a salary of £25,000 net of tax. As a result of her injuries, she has lost her job. Her loss of earnings to retirement age of 60 is assessed as follows:

(1) Look up Table 24 for loss of earnings to pension age 60 for females.

(2) The appropriate rate of return is decided to be 3 per cent (based on the decision of the House of Lords in *Wells v. Wells*).

(3) Table 24 shows that, on the basis of a 3 per cent rate of return, the multiplier for a female aged 35 is 17.41.

(4) Now take account of risks other than mortality. On the assumption of high economic activity for the next few years, Table C would require 17.41 to be multiplied by 0.95.

(5) Based on Section B, further adjustment is necessary because the claimant (a) is in a secure non-manual job, and (b) lives in the South East.

(6) The adjustments should be made as follows:

Basic adjustment to allow for short-term high economic activity (Table C)	0.95
Adjustment to allow for occupation, say	+0.01
	0.96
Adjustment for geographical region, say	+0.01
	0.97

(7) The original multiplier taken from Table 24, namely 17.41, must therefore be multiplied by 0.97, resulting in a revised multiplier of 16.89.

(8) The damages for loss of earnings are assessed as £422,250 (16.89 × 25,000).

This example takes no account of the incidence of tax on investment return (see paragraph 15) above. It is assumed that this was taken into account when determining the 3 per cent rate of return.

Example 2

48 The following is a second example of the use of the tables in a personal injury case:

The claimant is male, aged 48 at the date of the trial. He lives in Manchester and was working in a factory. His retirement age was 65 and his pre-retirement multiplicand has been determined as £20,000 a year net of tax. The multiplicand for costs of care is deemed to be £50,000 a year. As a result of his injuries, he has lost his job. His loss of earnings to retirement age of 65 is assessed as follows:

(1) Look up Table 25 for loss of earnings to retirement age 65 for males.

(2) The appropriate rate of return is decided to be 3 per cent (based on the decision of the House of Lords in *Wells v. Wells*).

(3) Table 25 shows that, on the basis of a 3 per cent rate of return, the multiplier for a male aged 48 is 12.88.

(4) Now take account of risks other than mortality. On the assumption of medium economic activity for the next few years, Table A would require 12.88 to be multiplied by 0.93.

(5) Based on Section B, further adjustment is necessary because the Plaintiff (a) is in a risky manual job, and (b) lives in the North West.

(6) The adjustments should be made as follows:

Basic adjustment to allow for short-term high economic activity (Table A)	0.93
Adjustment to allow for occupation, say	–0.02
	0.91
Adjustment for geographical region, say	–0.03
	0.88

(7) The original multiplier taken from Table 25, namely 12.88, must therefore be multiplied by 0.88, resulting in a revised multiplier of 11.33.

(8) The damages for loss of earnings are assessed as £226,600 (11.33 × 20.000).

49 The damages for cost of care are assessed as follows:

(1) Look up Table 19 for multiplier at age 48.

(2) The appropriate rate of return is 3 per cent.

(3) Table 19 shows that, on the basis of a 3 per cent rate of return, the multiplier at age 48 is 20.22.

(4) No further adjustment is made for risks other than mortality.

(5) The damages for cost of care are assessed at £1,011,000 (20.22 × 50,000).

Section D: Application of tables to fatal accident cases

50. Whereas in personal injury cases the problem to be solved is that of setting a value on an income stream during the potential life of one person (the deceased), the situation is generally more complicated in fatal accident cases. Here the compensation is intended to reflect the value of an income stream during the lifetime of one or more dependants of the deceased (or the expected period for which the dependants would have expected to receive the dependency,

if shorter) but limited according to the expectation of how long the deceased would have been able to provide the financial support, had he or she not been involved in the fatal accident.

51 In principle, therefore, the compensation for post-trial dependency should be based on the present value at the date of the trial of the dependency during the expected future joint lifetime of the deceased and the dependant or claimant (had the deceased survived naturally to the date of the trial), subject to any limitations on the period of dependency and any expected future changes in the level of dependency, for example, on attaining retirement age. In addition there should be compensation for the period between the date of accident and the date of trial.

52 A set of actuarial tables to make such calculations accurately would require tables similar to Tables 1 to 36 but for each combination of ages at the date of the trial of the deceased and the dependant to whom compensation is to be paid. The Working Party concluded that this would not meet the criterion of simplicity of application which was a central objective of these tables and recommends that, in complex cases, or cases where the accuracy of the multiplier is thought by the parties to be of critical importance and material to the resulting amount of compensation (for example in cases potentially involving very large claims where the level of the multiplicand is unambiguously established), the advice of a professionally qualified actuary should be sought. However, for the majority of cases, a certain amount of approximation will be appropriate, bearing in mind the need for a simple and streamlined process, and taking into consideration the other uncertainties in the determination of an appropriate level of compensation. The following paragraphs describe a methodology using Tables 1 to 36 which can be expected to yield satisfactory answers.

Damages for the period from the fatal accident to the date of trial

53 The period of pre-trial dependency will normally be equal to the period between the date of the fatal accident and the date of the trial, substituting where appropriate the lower figure of the expected period for which the deceased would have provided the dependency, had he or she not been killed in the accident, or if the period of dependency would have been limited in some say, for example if the dependant is a child.

54 A deduction may be made for the risk that the deceased might have died anyway, in the period between the date of the fatal accident and the date at which the trial takes place. In many cases this deduction will be small and could usually be regarded as de minimis. The need for a deduction becomes more necessary the longer the period from the date of accident to the date of trial and the older the deceased at the date of death. As an illustration of the order of magnitude of the deduction, Table D shows some examples of factors by which the multiplier should be multiplied for different ages of the deceased and for different periods from the date of accident to the date of the trial.

TABLE D

Factor by which pre-trial damages should be multiplied to allow for the likelihood that the claimant would not in any case have survived to provide the dependency for the full period to the date of trial

Age of claimant at date of accident	Period from date of accident to date of trial or date of cessation of dependency, if earlier (years)%					
	Male deceased			Female deceased		
	3	6	9	3	6	9
10	1.00	1.00	1.00	1.00	1.00	1.00
20	1.00	1.00	1.00	1.00	1.00	1.00
30	1.00	1.00	1.00	1.00	1.00	1.00
40	1.00	0.99	0.99	1.00	1.00	0.99
50	0.99	0.99	0.98	1.00	0.99	0.99
60	0.98	0.96	0.94	0.99	0.98	0.96
70	0.95	0.90	0.85	0.97	0.94	0.90
80	0.88	0.76	0.65	0.92	0.81	0.73

Note: The factor is clearly one for a period of zero years. Factors for other ages and periods not shown in the table may be obtained approximately by interpolation.

55 The resultant multiplier, after application of any discount for the possibility of early death of the deceased before the date of trial, even had the accident not taken place, is to be applied to the multiplicand, which is determined in the usual way. Interest will then be added up to the date of trial on the basis of special damages.

Damages from the date of trial to retirement age

56. The assessment of the multiplier involves the following steps:

(1) Determine the expected period for which the deceased would have been able to provide the dependency (see paragraph 57).

(2) Determine the expected period for which the dependant would have been able to receive the dependency (see paragraph 57).

(3) Take the lesser of the two periods.

(4) Treat the resulting period as a term certain for which the multiplier is to be determined and look up the figure in Table 38 for this period at the appropriate rate of interest.

(5) Apply any adjustment for contingencies other than mortality in accordance with Section B.

(6) If necessary, make an allowance for the risk that the deceased might have died anyway before the date of the trial (see paragraph 59).

57 The expected periods at (1) and (2) of paragraph 56 may be obtained from the 0 per cent column of the appropriate table at the back of this booklet. For (1), if historical mortality is to be used, Tables 3 to 10 will be relevant, according to the sex of the deceased and the expected age of retirement, or Tables 21 to 28 if the Court agrees with the recommendation of the Working Party that projected mortality is more appropriate. The age at which the table should be entered is the age which the deceased would have been at the date of the trial. For (2) Tables 1 and 2 or 19 and 20 can be used, according to the sex of the dependant and looking up the table at the age of the dependant at the date of the trial.

58 If the period for which the dependency would have continued is a short fixed period, as in the case of a child, the figure at (2) would be the outstanding period at the date of the trial.

59 A deduction may be made for the risk that the deceased might have died anyway before the date of trial. The need for such a deduction becomes more necessary the longer the period from the date of accident to the date of trial and the older the deceased at the date of death. As an illustration of the order of magnitude of the deduction, Table E shows some examples of the factor by which the multiplier, determined as above, should be multiplied for different ages of the deceased and for different periods from the date of accident to the date of the trial.

60 The resulting multiplier, after application of any discount for the possibility of early death of the deceased before the date of trial, even had the accident not taken place, is to be applied to the appropriate multiplicand, determined in relation to dependency as assessed for the period up to retirement age.

61 If there are several dependants, to whom damages are to be paid in respect of their own particular lifetime (or for a fixed period of dependency), separate multipliers should be determined for each and multiplied by the appropriate multiplicand using the procedure in paragraphs 55 to 59. The total amount of damages is then obtained by adding the separate components. If a single multiplicand is determined, but the damages are to be shared among two or more dependants so long as they are each alive, or during a period of common dependency, then the multiplier will be calculated using the procedure in paragraphs 56 to 60. However, at step (2) of paragraph 56 the expected period will be the longest of the expected periods for which the dependency might last.

TABLE E

Factor by which post-trial damages should be multiplied to allow for the likelihood that the claimant would not in any case have survived to the date of trial in order to provide any post-trial dependency

Age of claimant at date of accident	Period from date of accident to date of trial or date of cessation of dependency, if earlier (years)%					
	Male deceased			Female deceased		
	3	6	9	3	6	9
10	1.00	1.00	1.00	1.00	1.00	1.00
20	1.00	0.99	0.99	1.00	1.00	1.00
30	1.00	0.99	0.99	1.00	1.00	0.99
40	0.99	0.99	0.98	1.00	0.99	0.99
50	0.99	0.97	0.95	0.99	0.98	0.97
60	0.97	0.92	0.87	0.98	0.95	0.92
70	0.90	0.80	0.68	0.94	0.87	0.78
80	0.75	0.53	0.33	0.83	0.64	0.45

Note: The factor is clearly one for period of zero years. Factors for other ages and periods not shown in the table may be obtained approximately by interpolation.

Damages for the period of dependency after retirement age

62 The method described in paragraphs 56 to 61 for pre-retirement age dependency cannot satisfactorily be applied directly to post-retirement age dependency with a sufficient degree of accuracy. We therefore propose a method which involves determining the multiplier by looking at dependency for the rest of life from the date of trial and then subtracting the multiplier for dependency up to retirement age.

63 The assessment of the multiplier for whole of life dependency involves the following steps:

(1) Determine the expectation of life which the deceased would have had at the date of trial, or such lesser period for which the deceased would have provided the dependency (see paragraph 64).

(2) Determine the expected period for which the dependant would have been able to receive the dependency (see paragraph 64).

(3) Take the lesser of the two periods.

(4) Treat the resulting period as a term certain for which the multiplier is to

be determined and look up the figure in Table 38 for this period at the appropriate rate of interest.

64 The expected periods at (1) and (2) of paragraph 63 may be obtained from the 0 per cent column of the appropriate table at the back of this booklet. For (1), if historical mortality is to be used, Tables 1 or 2 will be relevant, according to the sex of the deceased, or Tables 19 or 20 if the Court agrees with the recommendation of the Working Party that projected mortality is more appropriate. The age at which the table should be entered is the age which the deceased would have attained at the date of the trial. For (2) Tables 1 and 2 or 19 and 20 can be used, according to the sex of the dependant and looking up the table at the age of the dependant at the date of the trial.

65 Deduct the corresponding multiplier for post-trial pre-retirement dependency, as determined in paragraphs 56 to 61, but without any adjustment for contingencies other than mortality, or that the deceased may have died anyway before the date of trial. The result is the multiplier for post-retirement dependency, which must then be applied to the appropriate multiplicand, assessed in relation to dependency after retirement age. The adjustment for contingencies other than mortality in respect of the damages for the period of dependency after retirement age will often be less than that required for pre-retirement age damages (see paragraph 34).

66 A deduction may finally be made for the risk that the deceased might have died anyway before the date of trial. The need for such a deduction becomes more necessary the longer the period from the date of accident to the date of trial and the older the deceased at the date of death. As an illustration of the order of magnitude of the deduction, Table E shows some examples of the factor by which the multiplier, determined as above, should be multiplied for different ages of the deceased and for different periods from the date of accident to the date of the trial. The factors for this purpose are exactly the same deductions as used in the calculation at paragraphs 56 to 61.

Cases where dependency is not related to employment

67 The layout of paragraphs 56 to 66 is based on the assumption that the dependency provided by the deceased would have changed at retirement age. This may not be appropriate in some cases, particularly in the important case of the deceased wife and mother whose contribution has been solely in the home or in the case of an adult child caring for an elderly parent or parents. In cases like this, where the deceased might have provided the dependency throughout their lifetime, paragraphs 62 to 66 should be ignored and paragraphs 56 to 61 used, with the difference that the expected period required at step (1) of paragraph 56 should be a whole of life expectancy, taken from Tables 1 and 2 or 19 and 20. This is also the approach to use when the deceased was already a pensioner.

Example 3

68 The dependant is female, aged 38 at the date of the trial, which is taking place six years after the date of the fatal accident which killed the male deceased,

at that time aged 37, on whom the dependant was financially dependent. The Court has determined a multiplicand, up to the deceased's normal retirement age of 65, of £30,000 and has decided that no post-retirement damages are payable. The damages are to be calculated as follows:

Pre-trial damages:

(1) Period between fatal accident and trial: 6 years

(2) Factor for possible early death (Table D for male aged 37 and 6 years): 0.99

(3) ∴ Pre-trial damages = 6 × 0.99 × £30,000
= £178,200 (plus interest as special damages)

Post-trial damages:

(1) Expected period for which the deceased would have provided the dependency (Table 25 at 0 per cent for male aged 43, the age as at the date of trial): 21.14

(2) Expected period for which the dependant would have been able to receive the dependency (Table 20 at 0 per cent for female aged 38): 46.36

(3) Lesser of two periods at (1) and (2) = 21.14

(4) Multiplier for term certain of 21.14 years at 3 per cent rate of return (interpolating between the values for 21 and 22 years in Table 38).
= (22 – 21.14) × 15.65 + (21.14 – 21) × 16.17
= 15.72

(5) Adjustment factor for contingencies other than mortality (in accordance with Section B). Assume medium economic activity. Factor from Table A: 0.96

(6) Adjustment factor for the risk that the deceased might have died anyway before the date of trial (Table E for male aged 37 and 6 years): 0.99

(7) Post-trial damages = 15.72 × 0.96 × 0.99 £30,000
= £448,209
or £450,000 say.

Example 4

69 The dependant is female, aged 50 at the date of the trial, which is taking place four years after the date of the fatal accident which killed the man, at that time aged 47, on whom she was financially dependent. The Court has determined

a multiplicand, up to the claimant's normal retirement age of 60, of £50,000 and has decided that post-retirement damages should be payable based on a multiplicand of £30,000. The damages are to be calculated as follows:

Pre-trial damages:

(1) Period between fatal accident and trial: 4 years

(2) Factor for possible early death (Table D for male aged 47 and 4 years): 0.99

(3) ∴ Pre-trial damages = 4 × 0.99 × £50,000
= £198,000 (plus interest as special damages)

Post-trial pre-retirement damages:

(1) Expected period for which the deceased would have provided the dependency (Table 23 at 0 per cent for male aged 51, the age as at the date of trial): 8.80

(2) Expected period for which the dependant would have been able to receive the dependency (Table 20 at 0 per cent for female aged 50): 34.49

(3) Lesser of two periods at (1) and (2): 8.80

(4) Multiplier for term certain of 8.80 years at 3 per cent rate of return (interpolating between the values for 8 and 9 years in Table 38).
= (9 – 8.80) × 7.12 + (8.80 – 8) × 7.90
= 7.74

(5) Adjustment factor for contingencies other than mortality (in accordance with Section B). Assume medium economic activity. Factor from Table B: 0.94

(6) Adjustment factor for the risk that the deceased might have died anyway before the date of trial (Table E for male aged 47 and 4 years): 0.98

(7) Post-trial pre-retirement damages = 7.74 × 0.94 × 0.98 × £50,000
= £356,504

Post-retirement damages:

(1) Expectation of life of claimant at date of trial (Table 19 at 0 per cent for male aged 51): 29.91

(2) Expected period for which the dependant would have been able to receive the dependency (Table 20 at 0 per cent for female aged 50): 34.49

(3) Lesser of two periods at (1) and (2): 29.91

(4) Multiplier for time certain of 29.91 years at 3 per cent rate of return (interpolating between the values for 29 and 30 in Table 38)
$= (30 - 29.91) \times 19.47 + (29.91 - 29) \times 19.89 = 19.85$

(5) Deduct multiplier for post-trial pre-retirement damages before application of adjustment factors for contingencies other than mortality and for the risk that the deceased might have died anyway before the date of trial: $19.85 - 7.74 = 12.11$

(6) Adjustment factor for the risk that the deceased might have died anyway before the date of trial (Table E for male aged 47 and 4 years): 0.98

(7) Post-retirement damages = 12.11 × 0.98 × £30,000
= £356,034

Example 5

70 There are two dependants, respectively a child aged 10 and a male aged 41 at the date of the trial, which is taking place three years after the date of the fatal accident which killed the woman, at that time aged 35, on whom both were financially dependent. She worked in London for a computer company and future economic activity is deemed by the Court to be high. The Court has determined a multiplicand, up to the claimant's normal retirement age of 62, £50,000 for the male dependant and £10,000 for the child, up to the age of 21, and has decided that post-retirement damages should be payable based on a multiplier of £20,000. The damages are to be calculated as follows:

Pre-trial damages:

(1) Period between fatal accident and trial: 3 years

(2) Factor for possible early death (Table D for female aged 35 and 3 years): 1.00

(3) ∴ Pre-trial damages = 3 × 1.00 × (£50,000 + £10,000)
= £180,000 (plus interest as special damages)

Post-trial pre-retirement damages:

(1) Expected period for which the deceased would have provided the dependency should be based on female aged 38 at the date of trial with retirement age of 62. First calculate as though deceased were aged 36 and had retirement age of 60 (Table 24 at 0 per cent for female aged 36): 23.57
Then calculate as though deceased were aged 41 and had retirement age of 65 (Table 26 at 0 per cent for female aged 41): 23.34

Interpolate for age 38 with retirement age of 62
= (3 × 23.57 + 2 × 23.34)/5 = 23.48

(2) Expected period for which the male dependant would have been able to receive the dependency (Table 19 at 0 per cent for male aged 41): 39.71
Expected period for which child would have been able to receive the dependency = 11.00

(3) Lesser of two periods at (1) and (2) = 11.00 (in case of child)
23.48 (in case of man).

(4) Multiplier for term certain of 11 years at 3 per cent (Table 38): 9.39 Multiplier for term certain of 23.48 years at 3 per cent rate of return (interpolating between the values for 23 and 24 in Table 38).
= (24 – 23.48) × 16.69 + (23.48 – 23) × 17.19
= 16.93

(5) Adjustment factor for contingencies other than mortality (in accordance with Section B). Factor from Table C, allowing for occupation and geographical area: 0.96 (does not apply to child)

(6) Adjustment factor for the risk that the deceased might have died anyway before the date of trial (Table E for female aged 35 and 3 years): 1.00

(7) Pre-retirement damages = 9.39 × 1.00 × £10,000 + 16.93 × 0.96 × 1.00 × £50,000
= £93,900 + £812,640
= £906,540

Post-retirement damages:

(1) Expectation of life of deceased at date of trial (Table 20 at 0 per cent for female aged 38): 46.36

(2) Expected period for which the dependant would have been able to receive the dependency (Table 19 at 0 per cent for male aged 41): 39.71 (no post retirement dependency for child)

(3) Lesser of two periods at (1) and (2) = 39.71

(4) Multiplier for time certain of 39.71 years at 3 per cent rate of return (interpolating between the values for 39 and 40 in Table 38)
= (40 – 39.71) × 23.15 + (39.71 – 39) × 23.46 = 23.37

(5) Deduct multiplier for post trial pre-retirement damages before application of adjustment factors for contingencies other than mortality and for the

risk that the deceased might have died anyway before the date of trial: 23.37 – 16.93 = 6.44

(6) Adjustment factor for the risk that the deceased might have died anyway before the date of trial (Table E for female aged 35 and 3 years) = 1.00

(7) Post-retirement damages = 6.44 × 1.00 × £20,000
= £128,800.

Section E: Concluding remarks

71 These tables are designed to assist the courts to arrive at suitable multipliers in a range of possible situations. However, they do not cover all possibilities and in more complex situations advice should be sought from a Fellow of the Institute of Actuaries or a Fellow of the Faculty of Actuaries.

72 In cases in which the award will be large, say, about £2 million or more at current prices, or where there are significant pension rights to be taken into consideration, more accurate calculations may be necessary. In such cases advice from an actuary will be desirable.

73 In the Family Division a software program (the Duxbury Method) is used for making similar calculations in complex cases. A similar facility would be useful for more complex personal injury and fatal accident cases and it is hoped that such a programme can be made available.

Table 1: Multipliers for pecuniary loss for life (males)

Age at date of trial	Multiplier calculated with allowance for population mortality and rate of interest of											Age at date of trial
	0.0%	0.5%	1.0%	1.5%	2.0%	2.5%	3.0%	3.5%	4.0%	4.5%	5.0%	
0	73.42	61.05	51.47	43.97	38.02	33.25	29.38	26.22	23.60	21.41	19.57	0
1	73.02	60.86	51.41	43.98	38.08	33.34	29.49	26.34	23.72	21.53	19.68	1
2	72.06	60.20	50.95	43.66	37.86	33.18	29.38	26.26	23.67	21.49	19.66	2
3	71.09	59.52	50.47	43.32	37.62	33.01	29.26	26.17	23.60	21.45	19.62	3
4	70.11	58.83	49.99	42.98	37.37	32.84	29.13	26.08	23.53	21.40	19.58	4
5	69.13	58.14	49.49	42.63	37.12	32.65	29.00	25.98	23.46	21.34	19.54	5
6	68.14	57.44	48.99	42.27	36.86	32.47	28.86	25.88	23.39	21.28	19.50	6
7	67.16	56.73	48.49	41.90	36.59	32.27	28.72	25.77	23.31	21.22	19.45	7
8	66.17	56.02	47.98	41.53	36.32	32.07	28.57	25.66	23.22	21.16	19.41	8
9	65.18	55.31	47.46	41.16	36.05	31.87	28.42	25.55	23.14	21.10	19.35	9
10	64.19	54.60	46.94	40.77	35.76	31.66	28.26	25.43	23.05	21.03	19.30	10
11	63.21	53.88	46.41	40.38	35.48	31.44	28.10	25.31	22.95	20.95	19.24	11
12	62.22	53.15	45.88	39.99	35.18	31.22	27.93	25.18	22.85	20.88	19.19	12
13	61.23	52.43	45.34	39.59	34.88	30.99	27.76	25.05	22.75	20.80	19.12	13
14	60.24	51.70	44.80	39.19	34.58	30.76	27.58	24.91	22.65	20.72	19.06	14
15	59.26	50.97	44.26	38.78	34.27	30.53	27.41	24.77	22.54	20.63	18.99	15
16	58.28	50.24	43.71	38.37	33.96	30.29	27.22	24.63	22.43	20.55	18.93	16
17	57.31	49.52	43.17	37.96	33.65	30.05	27.04	24.49	22.32	20.46	18.86	17
18	56.36	48.80	42.63	37.55	33.33	29.82	26.86	24.35	22.21	20.38	18.79	18
19	55.41	48.08	42.08	37.13	33.02	29.57	26.67	24.21	22.10	20.29	18.72	19
20	54.45	47.36	41.54	36.71	32.70	29.33	26.48	24.06	21.98	20.20	18.65	20
21	53.50	46.63	40.98	36.29	32.37	29.07	26.28	23.90	21.86	20.10	18.57	21
22	52.54	45.91	40.42	35.86	32.03	28.81	26.08	23.74	21.74	20.00	18.49	22
23	51.59	45.17	39.86	35.42	31.69	28.55	25.87	23.58	21.60	19.90	18.41	23
24	50.63	44.44	39.28	34.97	31.35	28.27	25.65	23.41	21.47	19.79	18.32	24
25	49.68	43.70	38.71	34.52	30.99	27.99	25.43	23.23	21.33	19.67	18.23	25
26	48.72	42.95	38.12	34.06	30:63	27.70	25.20	23.04	21.18	19.55	18.13	26
27	47.76	42.20	37.53	33.59	30.26	27.41	24.96	22.85	21.02	19.43	18.03	27
28	46.80	41.44	36.93	33.12	29.88	27.10	24.72	22.66	20.86	19.30	17.92	28
29	45.84	40.68	36.33	32.64	29.49	26.79	24.47	22.45	20.70	19.16	17.81	29
30	44.88	39.92	35.72	32.15	29.10	26.47	24.21	22.24	20.52	19.02	17.69	30
31	43.92	39.15	35.10	31.65	28.70	26.15	23.94	22.02	20.34	18.87	17.57	31
32	42.96	38.38	34.48	31.15	28.29	25.81	23.67	21.80	20.16	18.71	17.44	32
33	42.01	37.61	33.86	30.64	27.87	25.47	23.38	21.56	19.96	18.55	17.30	33
34	41.05	36.83	33.22	30.12	27.44	25.12	23.09	21.32	19.76	18.38	17.16	34
35	40.09	36.05	32.59	29.60	27.01	24.76	22.80	21.07	19.55	18.21	17.01	35
36	39.14	35.27	31.94	29.07	26.57	24.40	22.49	20.82	19.34	18.03	16.86	36
37	38.18	34.49	31.30	28.54	26.13	24.03	22.18	20.56	19.12	17.84	16.70	37
38	37.24	33.71	30.65	28.00	25.68	23.65	21.86	20.29	18.89	17.64	16.53	38
39	36.29	32.92	30.00	27.45	25.22	23.26	21.54	20.01	18.65	17.44	16.36	39
40	35.35	32.14	29.34	26.90	24.76	22.87	21.20	19.73	18.41	17.23	16.18	40

Table 1: *continued*

Age at date of trial	Multiplier calculated with allowance for population mortality and rate of interest of											Age at date of trial
	0.0%	0.5%	1.0%	1.5%	2.0%	2.5%	3.0%	3.5%	4.0%	4.5%	5.0%	
41	34.41	31.35	28.68	26.34	24.28	22.47	20.86	19.43	18.16	17.02	15.99	41
42	33.47	30.56	28.01	25.78	23.80	22.06	20.51	19.13	17.90	16.79	15.80	42
43	32.54	29.77	27.34	25.21	23.32	21.64	20.15	18.82	17.63	16.56	15.60	43
44	31.61	28.98	26.67	24.63	22.83	21.22	19.79	18.51	17.36	16.32	15.39	44
45	30.68	28.19	26.00	24.05	22.33	20.79	19.41	18.18	17.07	16.07	15.17	45
46	29.76	27.41	25.32	23.47	21.82	20.35	19.03	17.85	16.78	15.82	14.94	46
47	28.85	26.62	24.64	22.89	21.31	19.91	18.65	17.51	16.48	15.55	14.71	47
48	27.95	25.84	23.97	22.30	20.80	19.46	18.25	17.16	16.18	15.28	14.47	48
49	27.05	25.06	23.29	21.71	20.28	19.01	17.85	16.81	15.87	15.01	14.22	49
50	26.16	24.29	22.61	21.11	19.76	18.55	17.45	16.45	15.55	14.72	13.97	50
51	25.28	23.52	21.94	20.52	19.24	18.09	17.04	16.09	15.22	14.43	13.71	51
52	24.41	22.75	21.27	19.93	18.72	17.62	16.62	15.72	14.89	14.14	13.44	52
53	23.55	21.99	20.60	19.33	18.19	17.15	16.20	15.34	14.55	13.83	13.17	53
54	22.70	21.24	19.93	18.74	17.66	16.68	15.78	14.96	14.21	13.52	12.89	54
55	21.86	20.50	19.26	18.15	17.13	16.20	15.35	14.57	13.86	13.21	12.60	55
56	21.03	19.76	18.60	17.55	16.60	15.72	14.92	14.18	13.51	12.88	12.31	56
57	20.21	19.03	17.95	16.97	16.07	15.24	14.49	13.79	13.15	12.56	12.01	57
58	19.41	18.31	17.30	16.38	15.54	14.76	14.05	13.39	12.79	12.23	11.71	58
59	18.62	17.60	16.66	15.80	15.01	14.28	13.61	13.00	12.42	11.89	11.40	59
60	17.85	16.90	16.03	15.22	14.49	13.81	13.18	12.60	12.06	11.56	11.09	60
61	17.09	16.21	15.40	14.66	13.97	13.33	12.74	12.20	11.69	11.22	10.78	61
62	16.36	15.54	14.79	14.10	13.45	12.86	12.31	11.80	11.32	10.88	10.46	62
63	15.64	14.89	14.19	13.55	12.95	12.40	11.88	11.40	10.95	10.54	10.15	63
64	14.94	14.25	13.60	13.01	12.45	11.94	11.46	11.01	10.59	10.20	9.83	64
65	14.27	13.63	13.03	12.48	11.97	11.49	11.04	10.62	10.23	9.86	9.52	65
66	13.61	13.02	12.47	11.96	11.49	11.04	10.63	10.24	9.87	9.53	9.21	66
67	12.98	12.44	11.93	11.46	11.02	10.61	10.22	9.86	9.52	9.20	8.90	67
68	12.36	11.87	11.40	10.97	10.56	10.18	9.82	9.49	9.17	8.87	8.59	68
69	11.77	11.31	10.89	10.49	10.11	9.76	9.43	9.12	8.82	8.55	8.28	69
70	11.19	10.77	10.38	10.02	9.67	9.35	9.04	8.75	8.48	8.22	7.98	70
71	10.62	10.25	9.89	9.55	9.24	8.94	8.66	8.39	8.14	7.90	7.68	71
72	10.08	9.73	9.41	9.10	8.81	8.54	8.28	8.04	7.80	7.58	7.37	72
73	9.56	9.24	8.95	8.67	8.40	8.15	7.91	7.69	7.47	7.27	7.08	73
74	9.06	8.77	8.50	8.25	8.00	7.77	7.56	7.35	7.15	6.97	6.79	74
75	8.57	8.31	8.07	7.84	7.62	7.41	7.21	7.02	6.84	6.67	6.50	75
76	8.11	7.87	7.65	7.44	7.24	7.05	6.87	6.69	6.53	6.37	6.22	76
77	7.66	7.45	7.25	7.05	6.87	6.70	6.53	6.37	6.22	6.08	5.94	77
78	7.23	7.04	6.86	6.69	6.52	6.36	6.21	6.07	5.93	5.80	5.67	78
79	6.83	6.65	6.49	6.33	6.18	6.04	5.90	5.77	5.65	5.53	5.41	79
80	6.44	6.28	6.14	5.99	5.86	5.73	5.61	5.49	5.37	5.26	5.16	80
81	6.07	5.93	5.80	5.67	5.55	5.43	5.32	5.21	5.11	5.01	4.91	81

Table 1: *contined*

Age at date of trial	Multiplier calculated with allowance for population mortality and rate of interest of											Age at date of trial
	0.0%	0.5%	1.0%	1.5%	2.0%	2.5%	3.0%	3.5%	4.0%	4.5%	5.0%	
82	5.72	5.59	5.47	5.36	5.25	5.14	5.04	4.94	4.85	4.76	4.67	82
83	5.38	5.27	5.16	5.06	4.96	4.86	4.77	4.68	4.60	4.52	4.44	83
84	5.06	4.96	4.87	4.77	4.68	4.60	4.52	4.44	4.36	4.28	4.21	84
85	4.76	4.67	4.59	4.50	4.42	4.35	4.27	4.20	4.13	4.06	4.00	85
86	4.48	4.40	4.32	4.25	4.17	4.10	4.04	3.97	3.91	3.85	3.79	86
87	4.21	4.14	4.07	4.01	3.94	3.88	3.82	3.76	3.70	3.65	3.59	87
88	3.97	3.90	3.84	3.78	3.72	3.67	3.61	3.56	3.51	3.46	3.41	88
89	3.73	3.68	3.62	3.57	3.52	3.47	3.42	3.37	3.32	3.28	3.24	89
90	3.51	3.46	3.41	3.36	3.31	3.27	3.23	3.18	3.14	3.10	3.06	90
91	3.29	3.24	3.20	3.15	3.11	3.07	3.03	3.00	2.96	2.92	2.89	91
92	3.07	3.03	2.99	2.95	2.92	2.88	2.85	2.81	2.78	2.75	2.72	92
93	2.87	2.84	2.80	2.77	2.74	2.70	2.67	2.64	2.61	2.59	2.56	93
94	2.69	2.66	2.63	2.60	2.57	2.54	2.52	2.49	2.46	2.44	2.41	94
95	2.53	2.50	2.48	2.45	2.42	2.40	2.37	2.35	2.33	2.30	2.28	95
96	2.38	2.36	2.33	2.31	2.29	2.26	2.24	2.22	2.20	2.18	2.16	96
97	2.24	2.22	2.20	2.18	2.16	2.14	2.12	2.10	2.08	2.06	2.04	97
98	2.11	2.09	2.07	2.06	2.04	2.02	2.00	1.98	1.97	1.95	1.93	98
99	1.99	1.97	1.96	1.94	1.92	1.91	1.89	1.87	1.86	1.84	1.83	99
100	1.87	1.86	1.84	1.83	1.81	1.80	1.78	1.77	1.76	1.74	1.73	100

Table 2: Multipliers for pecuniary loss for life (females)

Age at date of trial	Multiplier calculated with allowance for population mortality and rate of interest of											Age at date of trial
	0.0%	0.5%	1.0%	1.5%	2.0%	2.5%	3.0%	3.5%	4.0%	4.5%	5.0%	
0	78.96	64.89	54.15	45.85	39.35	34.21	30.08	26.73	23.99	21.70	19.79	0
1	78.46	64.62	54.03	45.82	39.38	34.27	30.16	26.83	24.08	21.80	19.88	1
2	77.50	63.98	53.59	45.52	39.18	34.13	30.07	26.76	24.04	21.77	19.86	2
3	76.53	63.31	53.14	45.21	38.97	33.99	29.97	26.69	23.99	21.73	19.84	3
4	75.55	62.64	52.68	44.89	38.75	33.83	29.86	26.61	23.93	21.69	19.81	4
5	74.56	61.96	52.21	44.57	38.52	33.67	29.74	26.53	23.87	21.65	19.78	5
6	73.57	61.28	51.73	44.24	38.28	33.51	29.63	26.45	23.81	21.61	19.75	6
7	72.58	60.59	51.25	43.90	38.05	33.34	29.51	26.36	23.75	21.56	19.71	7
8	71.59	59.90	50.77	43.56	37.80	33.16	29.38	26.27	23.68	21.51	19.68	8
9	70.60	59.21	50.28	43.21	37.55	32.98	29.25	26.17	23.61	21.46	19.64	9
10	69.61	58.51	49.78	42.86	37.30	32.80	29.12	26.08	23.54	21.41	19.60	10
11	68.62	57.81	49.28	42.50	37.04	32.61	28.98	25.97	23.47	21.35	19.56	11
12	67.63	57.10	48.78	42.13	36.78	32.42	28.84	25.87	23.39	21.29	19.51	12
13	66.64	56.39	48.27	41.76	36.51	32.22	28.69	25.76	23.31	21.23	19.46	13
14	65.65	55.68	47.75	41.39	36.23	32.02	28.54	25.65	23.22	21.17	19.42	14
15	64.66	54.97	47.23	41.01	35.95	31.81	28.39	25.54	23.14	21.10	19.37	15
16	63.67	54.25	46.71	40.63	35.67	31.60	28.23	25.42	23.05	21.03	19.31	16
17	62.69	53.53	46.18	40.24	35.38	31.39	28.07	25.30	22.95	20.96	19.26	17
18	61.71	52.81	45.66	39.85	35.09	31.17	27.91	25.17	22.86	20.89	19.20	18
19	60.73	52.09	45.12	39.45	34.80	30.95	27.74	25.04	22.76	20.82	19.15	19
20	59.75	51.37	44.58	39.05	34.49	30.72	27.57	24.91	22.66	20.74	19.08	20
21	58.77	50.64	44.04	38.64	34.18	30.48	27.39	24.77	22.55	20.65	19.02	21
22	57.79	49.90	43.49	38.22	33.87	30.24	27.20	24.63	22.44	20.57	18.95	22
23	56.80	49.17	42.93	37.80	33.55	30.00	27.01	24.48	22.33	20.48	18.88	23
24	55.82	48.43	42.37	37.37	33.22	29.74	26.82	24.33	22.21	20.38	18.81	24
25	54.84	47.68	41.80	36.94	32.88	29.49	26.61	24.17	22.09	20.29	18.73	25
26	53.86	46.93	41.23	36.50	32.54	29.22	26.41	24.01	21.96	20.18	18.65	26
27	52.88	46.18	40.65	36.05	32.20	28.95	26.19	23.84	21.82	20.08	18.56	27
28	51.90	45.43	40.07	35.59	31.84	28.67	25.97	23.67	21.68	19.97	18.47	28
29	50.92	44.67	39.48	35.13	31.48	28.39	25.75	23.49	21.54	19.85	18.38	29
30	49.94	43.91	38.88	34.67	31.11	28.09	25.52	23.30	21.39	19.73	18.28	30
31	48.96	43.14	38.28	34.20	30.74	27.80	25.28	23.11	21.23	19.60	18.18	31
32	47.98	42.38	37.68	33.72	30.36	27.49	25.03	22.91	21.07	19.47	18.07	32
33	47.01	41.61	37.07	33.23	29.97	27.18	24.78	22.71	20.91	19.34	17.96	33
34	46.03	40.84	36.46	32.74	29.58	26.86	24.53	22.50	20.74	19.20	17.84	34
35	45.06	40.06	35.84	32.25	29.18	26.54	24.26	22.28	20.56	19.05	17.72	35
36	44.09	39.29	35.22	31.75	28.77	26.21	23.99	22.06	20.38	18.90	17.59	36
37	43.12	38.51	34.59	31.24	28.36	25.87	23.71	21.83	20.19	18.74	17.46	37
38	42.16	37.73	33.96	30.73	27.94	25.53	23.43	21.60	19.99	18.58	17.32	38
39	41.20	36.95	33.33	30.21	27.51	25.18	23.14	21.36	19.79	18.41	17.18	39
40	40.24	36.17	32.69	29.68	27.08	24.82	22.84	21.11	19.58	18.23	17.03	40

Table 2: *continued*

Age at date of trial	Multiplier calculated with allowance for population mortality and rate of interest of											Age at date of trial
	0.0%	0.5%	1.0%	15%	2.0%	2.5%	3.0%	3.5%	4.0%	4.5%	5.0%	
41	39.28	35.39	32.04	29.15	26.64	24.45	22.54	20.85	19.37	18.05	16.88	41
42	38.32	34.60	31.40	28.61	26.19	24.08	22.22	20.59	19.14	17.86	16.72	42
43	37.37	33.82	30.74	28.07	25.74	23.70	21.91	20.32	18.92	17.67	16.55	43
44	36.43	33.03	30.09	27.53	25.28	23.31	21.58	20.04	18.68	17.46	16.38	44
45	35.48	32.25	29.43	26.98	24.82	22.92	21.25	19.76	18.44	17.25	16.20	45
46	34.54	31.46	28.77	26.42	24.35	22.52	20.91	19.47	18.19	17.04	16.01	46
47	33.61	30.68	28.11	25.86	23.88	22.12	20.56	19.17	17.93	16.82	15.82	47
48	32.68	29.90	27.45	25.30	23.40	21.71	20.21	18.87	17.67	16.59	15.62	48
49	31.76	29.12	26.79	24.73	22.91	21.29	19.85	18.56	17.40	16.36	15.41	49
50	30.85	28.34	26.12	24.16	22.42	20.87	19.48	18.24	17.12	16.11	15.20	50
51	29.94	27.56	25.45	23.59	21.92	20.44	19.11	17.91	16.84	15.86	14.98	51
52	29.03	26.78	24.79	23.01	21.42	20.00	18.73	17.58	16.55	15.61	14.76	52
53	28.13	26.01	24.12	22.43	20.92	19.56	18.34	17.24	16.25	15.35	14.52	53
54	27.24	25.24	23.45	21.84	20.41	19.12	17.95	16.90	15.94	15.07	14.28	54
55	26.36	24.47	22.77	21.26	19.89	18.66	17.55	16.54	15.63	14.80	14.03	55
56	25.48	23.70	22.10	20.67	19.38	18.21	17.15	16.19	15.31	14.51	13.78	56
57	24.61	22.94	21.44	20.08	18.86	17.75	16.74	15.82	14.98	14.22	13.52	57
58	23.76	22.19	20.77	19.49	18.33	17.28	16.33	15.45	14.65	13.92	13.25	58
59	22.91	21.44	20.11	18.91	17.81	16.82	15.91	15.08	14.32	13.62	12.98	59
60	22.08	20.70	19.45	18.32	17.29	16.35	15.49	14.70	13.98	13.31	12.70	60
61	21.26	19.97	18.80	17.74	16.77	15.88	15.07	14.32	13.63	13.00	12.42	61
62	20.45	19.25	18.16	17.16	16.25	15.41	14.64	13.94	13.29	12.69	12.13	62
63	19.66	18.54	17.52	16.58	15.73	14.94	14.22	13.55	12.93	12.36	11.84	63
64	18.88	17.84	16.89	16.01	15.21	14.47	13.79	13.16	12.58	12.04	11.54	64
65	18.11	17.15	16.26	15.45	14.70	14.01	13.37	12.77	12.22	11.71	11.24	65
66	17.36	16.47	15.64	14.89	14.19	13.54	12.94	12.38	11.87	11.38	10.94	66
67	16.62	15.79	15.03	14.33	13.68	13.07	12.51	11.99	11.50	11.05	10.63	67
68	15.90	15.13	14.43	13.77	13.17	12.61	12.08	11.59	11.14	10.71	10.32	68
69	15.19	14.48	13.83	13.23	12.66	12.14	11.65	11.20	10.77	10.37	10.00	69
70	14.49	13.84	13.24	12.68	12.16	11.68	11.22	10.80	10.40	10.03	9.68	70
71	13.80	13.21	12.66	12.14	11.66	11.21	10.79	10.40	10.03	9.68	9.36	71
72	13.13	12.59	12.08	11.61	11.17	10.75	10.36	10.00	9.66	9.33	9.03	72
73	12.48	11.98	11.52	11.09	10.68	10.30	9.94	9.60	9.29	8.99	8.70	73
74	11.85	11.40	10.98	10.58	10.21	9.86	9.53	9.21	8.92	8.64	8.38	74
75	11.23	10.82	10.44	10.08	9.74	9.42	9.11	8.83	8.55	8.30	8.06	75
76	10.63	10.26	9.91	9.58	9.27	8.98	8.70	8.44	8.19	7.95	7.73	76
77	10.04	9.71	9.39	9.09	8.81	8.54	8.29	8.05	7.82	7.60	7.40	77
78	9.48	9.18	8.89	8.62	8.36	8.12	7.89	7.67	7.46	7.26	7.07	78
79	8.93	8.66	8.40	8.16	7.93	7.71	7.50	7.30	7.11	6.93	6.75	79
80	8.41	8.17	7.94	7.72	7.51	7.31	7.12	6.94	6.76	6.60	6.44	80
81	7.91	7.70	7.49	7.29	7.10	6.92	6.75	6.58	6.43	6.28	6.13	81

Table 2: *continued*

Age at date of trial	Multiplier calculated with allowance for population mortality and rate of interest of											Age at date of trial
	0.0%	0.5%	1.0%	1.5%	2.0%	2.5%	3.0%	3.5%	4.0%	4.5%	5.0%	
82	7.43	7.24	7.05	6.87	6.70	6.54	6.39	6.24	6.10	5.96	5.83	82
83	6.97	6.80	6.63	6.47	6.32	6.18	6.04	5.90	5.77	5.65	5.53	83
84	6.53	6.38	6.23	6.09	5.95	5.82	5.69	5.57	5.46	5.35	5.24	84
85	6.11	5.97	5.84	5.71	5.59	5.48	5.36	5.26	5.15	5.05	4.96	85
86	5.72	5.59	5.48	5.36	5.25	5.15	5.05	4.95	4.86	4.77	4.68	86
87	5.35	5.24	5.14	5.04	4.94	4.85	4.76	4.67	4.59	4.51	4.43	87
88	5.00	4.91	4.81	4.72	4.64	4.55	4.47	4.40	4.32	4.25	4.18	88
89	4.67	4.58	4.50	4.42	4.34	4.27	4.20	4.13	4.06	4.00	3.94	89
90	4.35	4.28	4.21	4.14	4.07	4.00	3.94	3.88	3.82	3.76	3.71	90
91	4.06	4.00	3.93	3.87	3.81	3.75	3.70	3.64	3.59	3.54	3.49	91
92	3.80	3.74	3.68	3.63	3.57	3.52	3.47	3.42	3.37	3.33	3.28	92
93	3.55	3.50	3.45	3.40	3.35	3.31	3.26	3.22	3.18	3.13	3.09	93
94	3.32	3.28	3.23	3.19	3.15	3.11	3.07	3.03	2.99	2.95	2.92	94
95	3.11	3.07	3.03	2.99	2.96	2.92	2.88	2.85	2.81	2.78	2.75	95
96	2.92	2.89	2.85	2.82	2.78	2.75	2.72	2.69	2.66	2.63	2.60	96
97	2.75	2.72	2.69	2.66	2.63	2.60	2.57	2.54	2.52	2.49	2.46	97
98	2.59	2.56	2.53	2.50	2.48	2.45	2.42	2.40	2.38	2.35	2.33	98
99	2.42	2.40	2.37	2.35	2.32	2.30	2.28	2.26	2.23	2.21	2.19	99
100	2.27	2.25	2.22	2.20	2.18	2.16	2.14	2.12	2.10	2.08	2.06	100

Table 3: Multipliers for loss of earnings to pension age 55 (males)

Age at date of trial	Multiplier calculated with allowance for population mortality and rate of interest of											Age at date of trial
	0.0%	0.5%	1.0%	1.5%	2.0%	2.5%	3.0%	3.5%	4.0%	4.5%	5.0%	
16	38.10	34.66	31.65	28.99	26.65	24.58	22.75	21.12	19.66	18.36	17.19	16
17	37.12	33.85	30.97	28.44	26.19	24.20	22.43	20.85	19.44	18.17	17.04	17
18	36.15	33.04	30.30	27.88	25.72	23.81	22.10	20.58	19.21	17.98	16.88	18
19	35.18	32.24	29.63	27.31	25.25	23.41	21.77	20.30	18.98	17.78	16.71	19
20	34.21	31.42	28.94	26.73	24.77	23.00	21.43	20.01	18.73	17.58	16.53	20
21	33.24	30.60	28.25	26.15	24.27	22.59	21.07	19.71	18.48	17.36	16.35	21
22	32.27	29.78	27.55	25.56	23.77	22.16	20.71	19.40	18.21	17.13	16.16	22
23	31.30	28.95	26.85	24.96	23.25	21.72	20.33	19.08	17.94	16.90	15.95	23
24	30.32	28.12	26.13	24.35	22.73	21.27	19.95	18.74	17.65	16.65	15.74	24
25	29.35	27.28	25.41	23.72	22.20	20.81	19.55	18.40	17.35	16.39	15.52	25
26	28.37	26.44	24.68	23.09	21.65	20.33	19.14	18.04	17.04	16.12	15.28	26
27	27.40	25.59	23.95	22.45	21.09	19.85	18.71	17.67	16.72	15.84	15.04	27
28	26.42	24.74	23.20	21.80	20.52	19.35	18.27	17.29	16.38	15.55	14.78	28
29	25.44	23.88	22.45	21.14	19.94	18.84	17.82	16.89	16.03	15.24	14.50	29
30	24.47	23.02	21.69	20.47	19.34	18.31	17.36	16.48	15.67	14.91	14.22	30
31	23.49	22.15	20.92	19.78	18.74	17.77	16.88	16.05	15.29	14.58	13.92	31
32	22.51	21.28	20.14	19.09	18.12	17.22	16.39	15.61	14.89	14.22	13.60	32
33	21.53	20.40	19.36	18.39	17.49	16.66	15.88	15.16	14.48	13.85	13.27	33
34	20.55	19.52	18.57	17.68	16.85	16.08	15.36	14.68	14.06	13.47	12.92	34
35	19.57	18.64	17.77	16.95	16.19	15.48	14.82	14.20	13.61	13.07	12.55	35
36	18.60	17.75	16.96	16.22	15.52	14.87	14.27	13.69	13.15	12.65	12.17	36
37	17.62	16.86	16.14	15.47	14.84	14.25	13.70	13.17	12.68	12.21	11.77	37
38	16.64	15.96	15.32	14.72	14.15	13.62	13.11	12.63	12.18	11.76	11.35	38
39	15.67	15.06	14.49	13.95	13.45	12.96	12.51	12.08	11.67	11.28	10.91	39
40	14.69	14.16	13.66	13.18	12.73	12.30	11.89	11.50	11.13	10.78	10.45	40
41	13.71	13.25	12.81	12.39	11.99	11.61	11.25	10.91	10.58	10.27	9.97	41
42	12.74	12.34	11.96	11.59	11.24	10.91	10.59	10.29	10.00	9.72	9.46	42
43	11.76	11.42	11.09	10.78	10.48	10.19	9.92	9.65	9.40	9.16	8.93	43
44	10.79	10.50	10.22	9.96	9.70	9.46	9.22	9.00	8.78	8.57	8.37	44
45	9.81	9.57	9.34	9.12	8.91	8.70	8.51	8.31	8.13	7.95	7.78	45
46	8.84	8.64	8.46	8.28	8.10	7.93	7.77	7.61	7.46	7.31	7.16	46
47	7.86	7.71	7.56	7.42	7.28	7.14	7.01	6.88	6.76	6.64	6.52	47
48	6.89	6.77	6.65	6.54	6.43	6.33	6.23	6.13	6.03	5.93	5.84	48
49	5.91	5.82	5.74	5.66	5.58	5.50	3.42	5.34	5.27	5.20	5.13	49
50	4.93	4.87	4.81	4.76	4.70	4.64	4.59	4.53	4.48	4.43	4.38	50
51	3.95	3.92	3.88	3.84	3.80	3.77	3.73	3.70	3.66	3.63	3.59	51
52	2.97	2.95	2.93	2.91	2.89	2.87	2.85	2.82	2.80	2.79	2.77	52
53	1.99	1.98	1.97	1.96	1.95	1.94	1.93	1.92	1.91	1.90	1.89	53
54	1.00	0.99	0.99	0.99	0.99	0.98	0.98	0.98	0.98	0.97	0.97	54

Table 4: Multipliers for loss of earnings to pension age 55 (females)

Age at date of trial	Multiplier calculated with allowance for population mortality and rate of interest of											Age at date of trial
	0.0%	0.5%	1.0%	1.5%	2.0%	2.5%	3.0%	3.5%	4.0%	4.5%	5.0%	
16	38.53	35.03	31.97	29.28	26.90	24.80	22.94	21.29	19.82	18.50	17.32	16
17	37.54	34.21	31.29	28.72	26.44	24.42	22.62	21.02	19.59	18.31	17.16	17
18	36.55	33.39	30.61	28.15	25.97	24.02	22.29	20.75	19.36	18.12	17.00	18
19	35.56	32.57	29.92	27.57	25.48	23.62	21.96	20.46	19.12	17.92	16.83	19
20	34.57	31.74	29.22	26.99	24.99	23.21	21.61	20.17	18.88	17.71	16.65	20
21	33.58	30.90	28.52	26.39	24.49	22.78	21.25	19.86	18.62	17.49	16.47	21
22	32.59	30.07	27.81	25.79	23.98	22.35	20.88	19.55	18.35	17.26	16.27	22
23	31.60	29.22	27.09	25.18	23.45	21.90	20.49	19.22	18.07	17.02	16.06	23
24	30.61	28.38	26.37	24.56	22.92	21.44	20.10	18.88	17.78	16.77	15.85	24
25	29.62	27.53	25.63	23.92	22.38	20.97	19.70	18.53	17.47	16.51	15.62	25
26	28.63	26.67	24.89	23.28	21.82	20.49	19.28	18.17	17.16	16.23	15.38	26
27	27.64	25.81	24.15	22.63	21.26	20.00	18.85	17.80	16.83	15.95	15.13	27
28	26.65	24.95	23.39	21.97	20.68	19.49	18.41	17.41	16.49	15.65	14.87	28
29	25.66	24.08	22.63	21.30	20.09	18.97	17.95	17.01	16.14	15.34	14.59	29
30	24.67	23.20	21.86	20.62	19.49	18.44	17.48	16.59	15.77	15.01	14.31	30
31	23.68	22.33	21.08	19.94	18.88	17.90	17.00	16.16	15.39	14.67	14.00	31
32	22.69	21.45	20.30	19.24	18.25	17.34	16.50	15.72	14.99	14.31	13.68	32
33	21.70	20.56	19.51	18.53	17.62	16.77	15.99	15.26	14.58	13.94	13.35	33
34	20.72	19.67	18.71	17.81	16.97	16.19	15.46	14.78	14.15	13.56	13.00	34
35	19.73	18.78	17.90	17.08	16.31	15.59	14.92	14.29	13.70	13.15	12.63	35
36	18.74	17.89	17.09	16.34	15.64	14.98	14.36	13.79	13.24	12.73	12.25	36
37	17.76	16.99	16.27	15.59	14.95	14.35	13.79	13.26	12.76	12.29	11.85	37
38	16.77	16.08	15.44	14.83	14.25	13.71	13.20	12.72	12.26	11.83	11.42	38
39	15.78	15.18	14.60	14.06	13.54	13.05	12.59	12.16	11.75	11.35	10.98	39
40	14.80	14.26	13.75	13.27	12.82	12.38	11.97	11.58	11.21	10.85	10.52	40
41	13.82	13.35	12.90	12.48	12.07	11.69	11.33	10.98	10.65	10.33	10.03	41
42	12.83	12.43	12.04	11.67	11.32	10.98	10.66	10.36	10.07	9.79	9.52	42
43	11.85	11.50	11.17	10.85	10.55	10.26	9.98	9.72	9.46	9.22	8.98	43
44	10.86	10.57	10.29	10.02	9.77	9.52	9.28	9.05	8.83	8.62	8.42	44
45	9.88	9.64	9.41	9.18	8.97	8.76	8.56	8.37	8.18	8.00	7.83	45
46	8.90	8.70	8.51	8.33	8.15	7.98	7.82	7.66	7.50	7.35	7.21	46
47	7.91	7.76	7.61	7.46	7.32	7.18	7.05	6.92	6.80	6.67	6.56	47
48	6.93	6.81	6.69	6.58	6.47	6.37	6.26	6.16	6.06	5.97	5.87	48
49	5.94	5.86	5.77	5.69	5.61	5.53	5.45	5.37	5.30	5.23	5.16	49
50	4.96	4.90	4.84	4.78	4.72	4.67	4.61	4.56	4.50	4.45	4.40	50
51	3.97	3.93	3.89	3.86	3.82	3.78	3.75	3.71	3.68	3.64	3.61	51
52	2.98	2.96	2.94	2.92	2.90	2.88	2.86	2.83	2.81	2.79	2.78	52
53	1.99	1.98	1.97	1.96	1.95	1.94	1.93	1.93	1.92	1.91	1.90	53
54	1.00	1.00	0.99	0.99	0.99	0.99	0.98	0.98	0.98	0.98	0.97	54

Table 5: Multipliers for loss of earnings to pension age 60 (males)

Age at date of trial	Multiplier calculated with allowance for population mortality and rate of interest of											Age at date of trial
	0.0%	0.5%	1.0%	1.5%	2.0%	2.5%	3.0%	3.5%	4.0%	4.5%	5.0%	
16	42.62	38.33	34.63	31.43	28.64	26.20	24.07	22.20	20.55	19.09	17.79	16
17	41.64	37.54	33.99	30.91	28.22	25.86	23.79	21.97	20.36	18.93	17.66	17
18	40.67	36.76	33.35	30.39	27.79	25.51	23.51	21.74	20.17	18.78	17.54	18
19	39.70	35.97	32.71	29.86	27.36	25.16	23.22	21.50	19.98	18.62	17.40	19
20	38.74	35.17	32.06	29.33	26.92	24.80	22.92	21.26	19.77	18.45	17.26	20
21	37.77	34.38	31.40	28.78	26.47	24.43	22.61	21.00	19.56	18.27	17.12	21
22	36.80	33.58	30.74	28.23	26.01	24.05	22.30	20.74	19.34	18.09	16.96	22
23	35.83	32.77	30.07	27.67	25.55	23.66	21.97	20.46	19.11	17.90	16.80	23
24	34.87	31.96	29.39	27.11	25.07	23.26	21.64	20.18	18.87	17.69	16.63	24
25	33.90	31.15	28.70	26.53	24.59	22.85	21.29	19.89	18.62	17.48	16.45	25
26	32.92	30.33	28.01	25.94	24.09	22.43	20.93	19.58	18.37	17.26	16.26	26
27	31.95	29.50	27.31	25.34	23.58	21.99	20.56	19.27	18.10	17.03	16.07	27
28	30.98	28.67	26.60	24.74	23.06	21.55	20.18	18.94	17.82	16.79	15.86	28
29	30.00	27.84	25.88	24.12	22.53	21.09	19.79	18.60	17.52	16.54	15.64	29
30	29.03	27.00	25.16	23.50	21.99	20.63	19.39	18.25	17.22	16.28	15.41	30
31	28.06	26.15	24.43	22.87	21.44	20.15	18.97	17.89	16.91	16.00	15.17	31
32	27.08	25.31	23.69	22.22	20.88	19.66	18.54	17.52	16.58	15.72	14.92	32
33	26.11	24.45	22.95	21.57	20.31	19.16	18.10	17.13	16.24	15.42	14.66	33
34	25.13	23.60	22.19	20.91	19.73	18.64	17.65	16.73	15.88	15.10	14.38	34
35	24.16	22.74	21.43	20.24	19.13	18.12	17.18	16.32	15.52	14.78	14.09	35
36	23.19	21.88	20.67	19.55	18.53	17.58	16.70	15.89	15.14	14.44	13.79	36
37	22.22	21.01	19.90	18.87	17.91	17.03	16.21	15.45	14.74	14.08	13.47	37
38	21.25	20.14	19.12	18.17	17.28	16.47	15.70	14.99	14.33	13.71	13.14	38
39	20.28	19.27	18.33	17.46	16.65	15.89	15.18	14.52	13.91	13.33	12.79	39
40	19.31	18.39	17.54	16.74	16.00	15.30	14.65	14.04	13.46	12.93	12.42	40
41	18.34	17.51	16.74	16.01	15.33	14.70	14.10	13.53	13.01	12.51	12.04	41
42	17.38	16.63	15.93	15.27	14.66	14.08	13.53	13.02	12.53	12.07	11.64	42
43	16.41	15.74	15.12	14.53	13.97	13.44	12.95	12.48	12.04	11.62	11.22	43
44	15.44	14.85	14.30	13.77	13.27	12.80	12.35	11.93	11.53	11.15	10.78	44
45	14.48	13.96	13.47	13.00	12.56	12.14	11.74	11.36	10.99	10.65	10.32	45
46	13.52	13.06	12.63	12.22	11.83	11.46	11.10	10.77	10.44	10.14	9.84	46
47	12.56	12.16	11.79	11.43	11.09	10.77	10.45	10.16	9.87	9.60	9.34	47
48	11.60	11.26	10.94	10.63	10.34	10.06	9.79	9.53	9.28	9.04	8.81	48
49	10.64	10.36	10.08	9.82	9.57	9.33	9.10	8.88	8.67	8.46	8.26	49
50	9.68	9.45	9.22	9.00	8.79	8.59	8.40	8.21	8.03	7.85	7.68	50
51	8.72	8.53	8.35	8.17	8.00	7.83	7.67	7.52	7.37	7.22	7.08	51
52	7.77	7.61	7.47	7.33	7.19	7.05	6.93	6.80	6.68	6.56	6.44	52
53	6.81	6.69	6.58	6.47	6.36	6.26	6.16	6.06	5.96	5.87	5.78	53
54	5.85	5.76	5.68	5.60	5.52	5.44	5.36	5.29	5.22	5.15	5.08	54
55	4.89	4.83	4.77	4.71	4.65	4.60	4.55	4.49	4.44	4.39	4.34	55
56	3.92	3.88	3.85	3.81	3.77	3.74	3.70	3.67	3.63	3.60	3.57	56
57	2.95	2.93	2.91	2.89	2.87	2.85	2.83	2.81	2.79	2.77	2.75	57
58	1.98	1.97	1.96	1.95	1.94	1.93	1.92	1.91	1.90	1.89	1.88	58
59	0.99	0.99	0.99	0.99	0.98	0.98	0.98	0.98	0.97	0.97	0.97	59

Table 6: Multipliers for loss of earnings to pension age 60 (females)

Age at date of trial	Multiplier calculated with allowance for population mortality and rate of interest of											Age at date of trial
	0.0%	0.5%	1.0%	1.5%	2.0%	2.5%	3.0%	3.5%	4.0%	4.5%	5.0%	
16	43.23	38.86	35.08	31.81	28.97	26.50	24.33	22.42	20.74	19.26	17.94	16
17	42.24	38.06	34.44	31.29	28.55	26.15	24.05	22.19	20.56	19.11	17.82	17
18	41.26	37.26	33.79	30.76	28.12	25.80	23.76	21.96	20.37	18.95	17.69	18
19	40.27	36.46	33.13	30.23	27.68	25.44	23.47	21.72	20.17	18.79	17.55	19
20	39.28	35.65	32.47	29.68	27.23	25.07	23.16	21.47	19.96	18.62	17.41	20
21	38.29	34.83	31.80	29.13	26.78	24.70	22.85	21.21	19.75	18.44	17.26	21
22	37.31	34.02	31.12	28.57	26.31	24.31	22.53	20.94	19.52	18.25	17.11	22
23	36.32	33.19	30.44	28.00	25.84	23.91	22.20	20.66	19.29	18.06	16.94	23
24	35.33	32.37	29.75	27.42	25.35	23.51	21.86	20.38	19.05	17.85	16.77	24
25	34.34	31.54	29.05	26.83	24.86	23.09	21.50	20.08	18.80	17.64	16.59	25
26	33.35	30.70	28.35	26.24	24.35	22.66	21.14	19.77	18.53	17.42	16.40	26
27	32.36	29.87	27.63	25.63	23.84	22.22	20.77	19.45	18.26	17.18	16.20	27
28	31.38	29.02	26.91	25.02	23.31	21.77	20.38	19.12	17.98	16.94	15.99	28
29	30.39	28.18	26.19	24.40	22.78	21.31	19.99	18.78	17.69	16.69	15.77	29
30	29.40	27.33	25.46	23.77	22.23	20.84	19.58	18.43	17.38	16.42	15.55	30
31	28.41	26.47	24.72	23.12	21.68	20.36	19.16	18.07	17.06	16.15	15.30	31
32	27.43	25.61	23.97	22.47	21.11	19.87	18.73	17.69	16.73	15.86	15.05	32
33	26.44	24.75	23.22	21.82	20.53	19.36	18.29	17.30	16.39	15.56	14.79	33
34	25.45	23.89	22.46	21.15	19.95	18.84	17.83	16.90	16.04	15.24	14.51	34
35	24.47	23.02	21.69	20.47	19.35	18.32	17.36	16.48	15.67	14.92	14.22	35
36	23.49	22.15	20.92	19.78	18.74	17.77	16.88	16.05	15.29	14.58	13.92	36
37	22.50	21.27	20.14	19.09	18.12	17.22	16.38	15.61	14.89	14.22	13.60	37
38	21.52	20.39	19.35	18.38	17.48	16.65	15.87	15.15	14.48	13.85	13.27	38
39	20.54	19.51	18.56	17.67	16.84	16.07	15.35	14.68	14.05	13.47	12.92	39
40	19.56	18.63	17.75	16.94	16.18	15.47	14.81	14.19	13.61	13.06	12.55	40
41	18.58	17.74	16.95	16.21	15.51	14.86	14.26	13.68	13.15	12.64	12.17	41
42	17.60	16.84	16.13	15.46	14.83	14.24	13.69	13.16	12.67	12.20	11.76	42
43	16.62	15.95	15.31	14.70	414	13.60	13.10	12.62	12.17	11.75	11.34	43
44	15.65	15.04	14.48	13.94	13.43	12.95	12.49	12.06	11.66	11.27	10.90	44
45	14.67	14.14	13.64	13.16	12.71	12.28	11.87	11.49	11.12	10.77	10.44	45
46	13.70	13.23	12.79	12.37	11.98	11.60	11.24	10.89	10.56	10.25	9.95	46
47	12.72	12.32	11.94	11.58	11.23	10.90	10.58	10.28	9.99	9.71	9.45	47
48	11.75	11.41	11.08	10.77	10.47	10.18	9.91	9.64	9.39	9.15	8.91	48
49	10.78	10.49	10.21	9.95	9.69	9.45	9.21	8.99	8.77	8.56	8.36	49
50	9.80	9.56	9.33	9.11	8.90	8.69	8.50	8.31	8.12	7.94	7.77	50
51	8.83	8.64	8.45	8.27	8.09	7.92	7.76	7.60	7.45	7.30	7.16	51
52	7.86	7.70	7.56	7.41	7.27	7.14	7.00	6.88	6.75	6.63	6.51	52
53	6.88	6.77	6.65	6.54	6.43	6.33	6.22	6.12	6.03	5.93	5.84	53
54	5.91	5.82	5.74	5.65	5.57	5.49	5.42	5.34	5.27	5.20	5.13	54
55	4.93	4.87	4.81	4.75	4.70	4.64	4.59	4.53	4.48	4.43	4.38	55
56	3.95	3.91	3.88	3.84	3.80	3.77	3.73	3.69	3.66	3.63	3.59	56
57	2.97	2.95	2.93	2.91	2.89	2.86	2.84	2.82	2.80	2.78	2.77	57
58	1.99	1.98	1.97	1.96	1.95	1.94	1.93	1.92	1.91	1.90	1.89	58
59	1.00	0.99	0.99	0.99	0.99	0.98	0.98	0.98	0.98	0.97	0.97	59

Table 7: Multipliers for loss of earnings to pension age 65 (males)

Age at date of trial	Multiplier calculated with allowance for population mortality and rate of interest of											Age at date of trial
	0.0%	0.5%	1.0%	1.5%	2.0%	2.5%	3.0%	3.5%	4.0%	4.5%	5.0%	
16	46.83	41.68	37.29	33.54	30.32	27.54	25.14	23.05	21.23	19.63	18.23	16
17	45.86	40.90	36.68	33.05	29.93	27.23	24.89	22.86	21.07	19.51	18.12	17
18	44.89	40.14	36.07	32.56	29.54	26.92	24.65	22.66	20.91	19.38	18.02	18
19	43.93	39.37	35.45	32.07	29.15	26.61	24.39	22.45	20.75	19.24	17.91	19
20	42.97	38.60	34.83	31.57	28.75	26.28	24.13	22.24	20.57	19.10	17.80	20
21	42.00	37.82	34.20	31.07	28.34	25.95	23.86	22.02	20.39	18.96	17.68	21
22	41.04	37.04	33.57	30.55	27.92	25.61	23.58	21.79	20.21	18.80	17.55	22
23	40.07	36.25	32.93	30.03	27.49	25.26	23.29	21.56	20.01	18.64	17.42	23
24	39.11	35.46	32.28	29.50	27.05	24.90	23.00	21.31	19.81	18.48	17.28	24
25	38.14	34.67	31.63	28.96	26.61	24.53	22.69	21.06	19.60	18.30	17.14	25
26	37.18	33.87	30.97	28.41	26.15	24.15	22.38	20.80	19.39	18.12	16.98.	26
27	36.21	33.07	30.30	27.85	25.69	23.77	22.05	20.53	19.16	17.93	16.82	27
28	35.24	32.26	29.62	27.29	25.22	23.37	21.72	20.24	18.92	17.73	16.65	28
29	34.27	31.44	28.94	26.71	24.73	22.96	21.38	19.95	18.67	17.52	16.48	29
30	33.30	30.63	28.25	26.13	24.24	22.54	21.02	19.65	18.42	17.30	16.29	30
31	32.33	29.80	27.55	25.54	23.73	22.11	20.66	19.34	18.15	17.07	16.10	31
32	31.36	28.98	26.85	24.94	23.22	21.68	20.28	19.02	17.87	16.84	15.89	32
33	30.39	28.15	26.14	24.33	22.70	21.23	19.89	18.69	17.59	16.59	15.68	33
34	29.42	27.31	25.42	23.71	22.17	20.77	19.50	18.34	17.29	16.33	15.45	34
35	28.45	26.48	24.70	23.08	21.62	20.29	19.09	17.98	16.98	16.06	15.22	35
36	27.48	25.64	23.97	22.45	21.07	19.81	18.67	17.62	16.66	15.78	14.97	36
37	26.51	24.79	23.23	21.81	20.51	19.32	18.24	17.24	16.33	15.49	14.71	37
38	25.55	23.95	22.49	21.16	19.94	18.82	17.79	16.85	15.98	15.18	14.44	38
39	24.59	23.10	21.74	20.50	19.35	18.30	17.34	16.45	15.63	14.87	14.16	39
40	23.63	22.25	20.99	19.83	18.76	17.78	16.87	16.03	15.26	14.54	13.87	40
41	22.67	21.40	20.23	19.15	18.16	17.24	16.39	15.60	14.87	14.19	13.56	41
42	21.71	20.54	19.47	18.47	17.55	16.69	15.90	15.16	14.48	13.84	13.24	42
43	20.75	19.68	18.69	17.78	16.92	16.13	15.39	14.71	14.06	13.47	12.91	43
44	19.79	18.82	17.92	17.07	16.29	15.56	14.87	14.24	13.64	13.08	12.56	44
45	18.84	17.96	17.13	16.36	15.64	14.97	14.34	13.75	13.20	12.68	12.19	45
46	17.89	17.09	16.34	15.64	14.99	14.37	13.79	13.25	12.74	12.26	11.81	46
47	16.84	16.22	15.55	14.92	14.32	13.76	13.23	12.74	12.27	11.83	11.41	47
48	16.00	15.35	14.75	14.18	13.64	13.14	12.66	12.21	11.78	11.37	10.99	48
49	15.05	14.48	13.95	13.44	12.96	12.50	12.07	11.66	11.27	10.91	10.56	49
50	14.11	13.61	13.14	12.69	12.26	11.85	11.47	11.10	10.75	10.42	10.10	50
51	13.18	12.74	12.32	11.93	11.55	11.19	10.85	10.52	10.21	9.92	9.63	51
52	12.24	11.87	11.50	11.16	10.83	10.52	10.22	9.93	9.65	9.39	9.14	52
53	11.31	10.99	10.68	10.38	10.10	9.83	9.56	9.31	9.07	8.84	8.62	53
54	10.38	10.11	9.85	9.60	9.35	9.12	8.90	8.68	8.48	8.28	8.08	54
55	9.45	9.23	9.01	8.80	8.60	8.40	8.21	8.03	7.85	7.68	7.52	55
56	8.53	8.34	8.16	7.99	7.82	7.66	7.51	7.36	7.21	7.07	6.93	56

Table 7: *continued*

Age at date of trial	Multiplier calculated with allowance for population mortality and rate of interest of											Age at date of trial
	0.0%	0.5%	1.0%	1.5%	2.0%	2.5%	3.0%	3.5%	4.0%	4.5%	5.0%	
57	7.60	7.45	7.31	7.17	7.04	6.91	6.78	6.66	6.54	6.43	6.31	57
58	6.67	6.56	6.45	6.34	6.23	6.13	6.04	5.94	5.85	5.76	5.67	58
59	5.74	5.65	5.57	5.49	5.42	5.34	5.27	5.19	5.12	5.05	4.99	59
60	4.80	4.74	4.69	4.63	4.58	4.52	4.47	4.42	4.37	4.32	4.27	60
61	3.86	3.83	3.79	3.75	3.72	3.68	3.65	3.61	3.58	3.55	3.51	61
62	2.92	2.90	2.87	2.85	2.83	2.81	2.79	2.77	2.75	2.73	2.72	62
63	1.96	1.95	1.94	1.93	1.92	1.91	1.90	1.89	1.89	1.88	1.87	63
64	0.99	0.99	0.98	0.98	0.98	0.98	0.97	0.97	0.97	0.97	0.97	64

Table 8: Multipliers for loss of earnings to pension age 65 (females)

Age at date of trial	Multiplier calculated with allowance for population mortality and rate of interest of											Age at date of trial
	0.0%	0.5%	1.0%	1.5%	2.0%	2.5%	3.0%	3.5%	4.0%	4.5%	5.0%	
16	47.75	42.44	37.93	34.08	30.78	27.93	25.47	23.34	21.47	19.84	18.41	16
17	46.77	41.67	37.32	33.59	30.39	27.62	25.23	23.14	21.32	19.72	18.31	17
18	45.78	40.88	36.70	33.10	30.00	27.31	24.98	22.94	21.16	19.59	18.21	18
19	44.79	40.10	36.07	32.60	29.60	26.99	24.72	22.73	20.99	19.46	18.10	19
20	43.81	39.31	35.44	32.09	29.19	26.66	24.45	22.52	20.82	19.31	17.98	20
21	42.82	38.52	34.80	31.57	28.77	26.32	24.18	22.30	20.64	19.17	17.86	21
22	41.84	37.72	34.15	31.05	28.34	25.98	23.90	22.07	20.45	19.01	17.74	22
23	40.85	36.92	33.50	30.52	27.91	25.62	23.61	21.83	20.25	18.85	17.61	23
24	39.86	36.11	32.84	29.98	27.47	25.26	23.31	21.58	20.05	18.69	17.47	24
25	38.88	35.30	32.17	29.43	27.02	24.89	23.00	21.33	19.84	18.51	17.32	25
26	37.89	34.49	31.50	28.87	26.56	24.51	22.69	21.07	19.62	18.33	17.17	26
27	36.90	33.67	30.82	28.31	26.09	24.11	22.36	20.79	19.39	18.14	17.01	27
28	35.91	32.85	30.14	27.74	25.61	23.71	22.02	20.51	19.16	17.94	16.84	28
29	34.93	32.02	29.44	27.16	25.12	23.30	21.68	20.22	18.91	17.73	16.66	29
30	33.94	31.19	28.74	26.57	24.62	22.88	21.32	19.92	18.65	17.51	16.48	30
31	32.96	30.36	28.04	25.97	24.12	22.45	20.96	19.61	18.39	17.29	16.29	31
32	31.97	29.52	27.33	25.36	23.60	22.01	20.58	19.28	18.11	17.05	16.08	32
33	30.99	28.68	26.61	24.75	23.07	21.56	20.19	18.95	17.83	16.80	15.87	33
34	30.01	27.84	25.89	24.13	22.54	21.10	19.79	18.61	17.53	16.55	15.65	34
35	29.02	26.99	25.16	23.50	21.99	20.63	19.39	18.26	17.22	16.28	15.42	35
36	28.04	26.14	24.42	22.86	21.44	20.14	18.97	17.89	16.90	16.00	15.17	36
37	27.06	25.29	23.68	22.21	20.87	19.65	18.53	17.51	16.57	15.71	14.92	37
38	26.09	24.43	22.93	21.55	20.30	19.15	18.09	17.12	16.23	15.41	14.65	38
39	25.11	23.58	22.17	20.89	19.71	18.63	17.63	16.72	15.87	15.09	14.37	39
40	24.13	22.71	21.41	20.22	19.11	18.10	17.17	16.30	15.50	14.77	14.08	40
41	23.16	21.85	20.64	19.53	18.51	17.56	16.68	15.87	15.12	14.42	13.78	41
42	22.19	20.98	19.87	18.84	17.89	17.01	16.19	15.43	14.72	14.07	13.46	42
43	21.21	20.11	19.09	18.14	17.26	16.44	15.68	14.97	14.31	13.70	13.12	43
44	20.24	19.24	18.30	17.43	16.62	15.86	15.16	14.50	13.89	13.31	12.77	44
45	19.27	18.36	17.51	16.71	15.97	15.27	14.62	14.01	13.44	12.91	12.41	45
46	18.31	17.48	16.71	15.98	15.31	14.67	14.07	13.51	12.99	12.49	12.02	46
47	17.34	16.60	15.90	15.25	14.63	14.05	13.51	12.99	12.51	12.05	11.62	47
48	16.38	15.72	15.09	14.50	13.95	13.42	12.93	12.46	12.02	11.60	11.21	48
49	15.42	14.83	14.27	13.75	13.25	12.78	12.33	11.91	11.51	11.13	10.77	49
50	14.46	13.94	13.45	12.98	12.54	12.12	11.72	11.34	10.98	10.64	10.31	50
51	13.50	13.05	12.61	12.20	11.81	11.44	11.09	10.75	10.43	10.12	9.83	51
52	12.54	12.15	11.78	11.42	11.08	10.75	10.44	10.15	9.86	9.59	9.33	52
53	11.58	11.25	10.93	10.62	10.33	10.05	9.78	9.52	9.27	9.03	8.81	53
54	10.63	10.35	10.07	9.81	9.56	9.32	9.09	8.87	8.66	8.45	8.25	54
55	9.67	9.44	9.21	8.99	8.79	8.58	8.39	8.20	8.02	7.85	7.68	55
56	8.72	8.52	8.34	8.16	7.99	7.83	7.66	7.51	7.36	7.21	7.07	56

Table 8: *continued*

Age at date of trial	Multiplier calculated with allowance for population mortality and rate of interest of											Age at date of trial
	0.0%	0.5%	1.0%	1.5%	2.0%	2.5%	3.0%	3.5%	4.0%	4.5%	5.0%	
57	7.76	7.61	7.46	7.32	7.18	7.05	6.92	6.79	6.67	6.55	6.44	57
58	6.80	6.69	6.57	6.46	6.36	6.25	6.15	6.05	5.96	5.86	5.77	58
59	5.84	5.76	5.67	5.59	5.51	5.44	5.36	5.29	5.21	5.14	5.07	59
60	4.88	4.82	4.77	4.71	4.65	4.60	4.54	4.49	4.44	4.39	4.34	60
61	3.92	3.88	3.84	3.81	3.77	3.73	3.70	3.66	3.63	3.60	3.56	61
62	2.95	2.93	2.91	2.89	2.87	2.85	2.83	2.81	2.79	2.77	2.75	62
63	1.98	1.97	1.96	1.95	1.94	1.93	1.92	1.91	1.90	1.89	1.88	63
64	0.99	0.99	0.99	0.99	0.98	0.98	0.98	0.98	0.97	0.97	0.97	64

Table 9: Multipliers for loss of earnings to pension age 70 (males)

Age at date of trial	Multiplier calculated with allowance for population mortality and rate of interest of											Age at date of trial
	0.0%	0.5%	1.0%	1.5%	2.0%	2.5%	3.0%	3.5%	4.0%	4.5%	5.0%	
16	50.58	44.57	39.53	35.28	31.67	28.60	25.96	23.69	21.73	20.02	18.53	16
17	49.60	43.82	38.94	34.82	31.31	28.31	25.74	23.52	21.59	19.91	18.44	17
18	48.64	43.07	38.36	34.36	30.95	28.03	25.52	23.34	21.45	19.80	18.36	18
19	47.68	42.32	37.77	33.90	30.59	27.74	25.29	23.16	21.31	19.69	18.26	19
20	46.72	41.56	37.17	33.43	30.21	27.45	25.05	22.97	21.16	19.57	18.17	20
21	45.76	40.80	36.57	32.95	29.83	27.14	24.81	22.78	21.00	19.44	18.07	21
22	44.80	40.04	35.96	32.46	29.45	26.83	24.56	22.58	20.84	19.31	17.96	22
23	43.84	39.27	35.35	31.97	29.05	26.52	24.31	22.37	20.67	19.18	17.85	23
24	42.88	38.50	34.73	31.47	28.65	26.19	24.04	22.16	20.50	19.04	17.74	24
25	41.92	37.72	34.10	30.97	28.24	25.86	23.77	21.94	20.32	18.89	17.61	25
26	40.95	36.94	33.47	30.45	27.82	25.51	23.49	21.71	20.13	18.73	17.49	26
27	39.98	36.15	32.83	29.92	37.39	25.16	23.20	21.47	19.93	18.57	17.35	27
28	39.02	35.36	32.18	29.39	26.95	24.80	22.90	21.22	19.73	18.40	17.21	28
29	38.05	34.57	31.52	28.85	26.50	24.43	22.59	20.96	19.51	18.22	17.06	29
30	37.09	33.77	30.86	28.30	26.04	24.05	22.28	20.70	19.29	18.03	16.90	30
31	36.12	32.97	30.19	27.74	25.58	23.66	21.95	20.42	19.06	17.84	16.74	31
32	35.15	32.16	29.52	27.18	25.10	23.26	21.61	20.14	18.82	17.64	16.57	32
33	34.19	31.35	28.83	26.60	24.62	22.85	21.27	19.85	18.57	17.42	16.39	33
34	33.22	30.53	28.15	26.02	24.13	22.43	20.91	19.55	18.32	17.20	16.20	34
35	32.25	29.71	27.45	25.43	23.63	22.00	20.55	19.23	18.05	16.97	16.00	35
36	31.29	28.90	26.75	24.84	23.12	21.57	20.17	18.91	17.77	16.74	15.79	36
37	30.33	28.07	26.05	24.23	22.60	21.12	19.79	18.58	17.48	16.49	15.58	37
38	29.37	27.25	25.34	23.62	22.07	20.67	19.40	18.24	17.19	16.23	15.36	38
39	28.41	26.42	.24.63	23.00	21.54	20.20	18.99	17.89	16.88	15.96	15.12	39
40	27.46	25.60	23.91	22.38	20.99	19.73	18.58	17.53	16.57	15.69	14.88	40
41	26.51	24.76	23.18	21.75	20.44	19.24	18.15	17.15	16.24	15.40	14.62	41
42	25.55	23.93	22.45	21.10	19.87	18.75	17.71	16.77	15.90	15.10	14.36	42
43	24.61	23.10	21.72	20.46	19.30	18.24	17.27	16.37	15.55	14.78	14.08	43
44	23.66	22.26	20.98	19.80	18.72	17.72	16.81	15.96	15.18	14.46	13.79	44
45	22.71	21.42	20.23	19.14	18.13	17.20	16.34	15.54	14.81	14.12	13.49	45
46	21.77	20.58	19.48	18.47	17.53	16.66	15.86	15.11	14.42	13.77	13.17	46
47	20.84	19.74	18.73	17.79	16.92	16.11	15.36	14.67	14.02	13.41	12.85	47
48	19.90	18.90	17.97	17.11	16.30	15.56	14.86	14.21	13.61	13.04	12.51	48
49	18.98	18.06	17.21	16.42	15.68	14.99	14.35	13.74	13.18	12.65	12.16	49
50	18.05	17.22	16.45	15.73	15.05	14.42	13.82	13.27	12.74	12.25	11.79	50
51	17.14	16.39	15.68	15.03	14.41	13.83	13.29	12.77	12.29	11.84	11.41	51
52	16.22	15.55	14.92	14.32	13.76	13.23	12.74	12.27	11.83	11.41	11.02	52
53	15.31	14.71	14.14	13.61	13.11	12.63	12.18	11.75	11.35	10.97	10.61	53
54	14.41	13.87	13.37	12.89	12.44	12.01	11.61	11.22	10.86	10.51	10.18	54
55	13.51	13.04	12.59	12.17	11.77	11.39	11.02	10.68	10.35	10.04	9.74	55
56	12.61	12.20	11.81	11.44	11.08	10.75	10.42	10.12	9.82	9.54	9.28	56

Table 9: *continued*

Age at date of trial	Multiplier calculated with allowance for population mortality and rate of interest of											Age at date of trial
	0.0%	0.5%	1.0%	1.5%	2.0%	2.5%	3.0%	3.5%	4.0%	4.5%	5.0%	
57	11.72	11.37	11.03	10.70	10.39	10.10	9.81	9.54	9.28	9.04	8.80	57
58	10.83	10.53	10.24	9.96	9.69	9.44	9.19	8.95	8.73	8.51	8.30	58
59	9.95	9.69	9.45	9.21	8.98	8.76	8.55	8.35	8.15	7.97	7.78	59
60	9.07	8.86	8.65	8.45	8.26	8.08	7.90	7.73	7.56	7.40	7.25	60
61	8.19	8.02	7.85	7.68	7.53	7.37	7.23	7.08	6.95	6.81	6.68	61
62	7.31	7.17	7.04	6.91	6.78	6.66	6.54	6.42	6.31	6.20	6.10	62
63	6.43	6.33	6.22	6.12	6.02	5.92	5.83	5.74	5.65	5.56	5.48	63
64	5.55	5.47	5.39	5.32	5.24	5.17	5.10	5.03	4.96	4.90	4.83	64
65	4.67	4.61	4.55	4.50	4.45	4.40	4.35	4.30	4.25	4.20	4.15	65
66	3.77	3.73	3.70	3.66	3.63	3.59	3.56	3.53	3.49	3.46	3.43	66
67	2.86	2.84	2.82	2.80	2.78	2.76	2.74	2.72	2.70	2.68	2.66	67
68	1.93	1.92	1.91	1.91	1.90	1.89	1.88	1.87	1.86	1.85	1.84	68
69	0.98	0.98	0.98	0.97	0.97	0.97	0.97	0.97	0.96	0.96	0.96	69

Table 10: Multipliers for loss of earnings to pension age 70 (females)

Age at date of trial	Multiplier calculated with allowance for population mortality and rate of interest of											Age at date of trial
	0.0%	0.5%	1.0%	1.5%	2.0%	2.5%	3.0%	3.5%	4.0%	4.5%	5.0%	
16	51.98	45.71	40.46	36.04	32.30	29.12	26.40	24.06	22.04	20.28	18.75	16
17	50.99	44.95	39.87	35.59	31.95	28.84	26.18	23.89	21.90	20.18	18.67	17
18	50.01	44.19	39.28	35.12	31.58	28.56	25.96	23.71	21.77	20.07	18.59	18
19	49.03	43.42	38.68	34.65	31.22	28.27	25.73	23.53	21.62	19.96	18.50	19
20	48.04	42.65	38.08	34.18	30.84	27.97	25.50	23.35	21.48	19.84	18.40	20
21	47.06	41.87	37.46	33.69	30.46	27.67	25.25	23.16	21.32	19.72	18.30	21
22	46.07	41.09	36.84	33.20	30.07	27.36	25.00	22.96	21.16	19.59	18.20	22
23	45.09	40.31	36.22	32.70	29.67	27.04	24.75	22.75	21.00	19.45	18.09	23
24	44.10	39.52	35.59	32.20	29.26	26.71	24.48	22.54	20.82	19.31	17.98	24
25	43.11	38.73	34.95	31.68	28.85	26.37	24.21	22.31	20.64	19.17	17.86	25
26	42.13	37.93	34.31	31.16	28.42	26.03	23.93	22.09	20.46	19.01	17.73	26
27	41.14	37.13	33.66	30.63	27.99	25.68	23.64	21.85	20.26	18.85	17.60	27
28	40.16	36.33	33.00	30.10	27.55	25.32	23.35	21.60	20.06	18.69	17.46	28
29	39.17	35.52	32.34	29.55	27.10	24.95	23.04	21.35	19.85	18.51	17.32	29
30	38.19	34.71	31.67	29.00	26.65	24.57	22.73	21.09	19.63	18.33	17.16	30
31	37.21	33.90	31.00	28.44	26.18	24.18	22.40	20.82	19.41	18.14	17.00	31
32	36.22	33.08	30.32	27.87	25.71	23.78	22.07	20.54	19.17	17.94	16.84	32
33	35.24	32.26	29.63	27.30	25.22	23.38	21.73	20.25	18.93	17.74	16.66	33
34	34.26	31.44	28.94	26.71	24.73	22.96	21.38	19.96	18.68	17.52	16.48	34
35	33.28	30.61	28.24	26.12	24.23	22.54	21.02	19.65	18.42	17.30	16.29	35
36	32.30	29.78	27.54	25.53	23.72	22.11	20.65	19.33	18.15	17.07	16.09	36
37	31.33	28.95	26.83	24.92	23.21	21.66	20.27	19.01	17.87	16.83	15.88	37
38	30.35	28.12	26.11	24.31	22.68	21.21	19.88	18.67	17.58	16.58	15.67	38
39	29.38	27.28	25.39	23.69	22.14	20.75	19.48	18.33	17.27	16.32	15.44	39
40	28.41	26.44	24.67	23.06	21.60	20.27	19.07	17.97	16.96	16.04	15.20	40
41	27.44	25.60	23.93	22.42	21.04	19.79	18.64	17.60	16.64	15.76	14.95	41
42	26.47	24.75	23.20	21.77	20.48	19.29	18.21	17.22	16.31	15.47	14.70	42
43	25.50	23.91	22.45	21.12	19.90	18.79	17.77	16.82	15.96	15.16	14.42	43
44	24.54	23.06	21.70	20.46	19.32	18.27	17.31	16.42	15.60	14.84	14.14	44
45	23.58	22.21	20.95	19.79	18.73	17.75	16.84	16.00	15.23	14.51	13.85	45
46	22.62	21.35	20.19	19.12	18.12	17.21	16.36	15.57	14.85	14.17	13.54	46
47	21.66	20.50	19.43	18.43	17.51	16.66	15.87	15.13	14.45	13.81	13.22	47
48	20.71	19.64	18.66	17.74	16.89	16.10	15.36	14.68	14.04	13.44	12.88	48
49	19.76	18.79	17.88	17.04	16.26	15.53	14.85	14.21	13.62	13.06	12.54	49
50	18.81	17.93	17.10	16.34	15.62	14.95	14.32	13.73	13.18	12.66	12.17	50
51	17.86	17.07	16.32	15.62	14.97	14.35	13.77	13.23	12.72	12.24	11.79	51
52	16.92	16.20	15.53	14.90	14.30	13.74	13.22	12.72	12.25	11.81	11.39	52
53	15.98	15.34	14.73	14.17	13.63	13.12	12.65	12.19	11.77	11.36	10.98	53
54	15.04	14.47	13.93	13.43	12.94	12.49	12.06	11.65	11.26	10.90	10.55	54
55	14.10	13.60	13.13	12.68	12.25	11.84	11.46	11.09	10.74	10.41	10.10	55
56	13.17	12.73	12.31	11.92	11.54	11.18	10.84	10.51	10.20	9.91	9.62	56

Table 10: *continued*

Age at date of trial	Multiplier calculated with allowance for population mortality and rate of interest of											Age at date of trial
	0.0%	0.5%	1.0%	1.5%	2.0%	2.5%	3.0%	3.5%	4.0%	4.5%	5.0%	
57	12.23	11.86	11.49	11.15	10.82	10.51	10.21	9.92	9.65	9.38	9.13	57
58	11.30	10.98	10.67	10.37	10.09	9.82	9.56	9.31	9.07	8.84	8.62	58
59	10.38	10.10	9.84	9.59	9.35	9.11	8.89	8.68	8.47	8.27	8.08	59
60	9.45	9.22	9.00	8.79	8.59	8.40	8.21	8.03	7.85	7.68	7.52	60
61	8.52	8.34	8.16	7.99	7.82	7.66	7.51	7.35	7.21	7.07	6.93	61
62	7.60	7.45	7.31	7.17	7.04	6.91	6.78	6.66	6.54	6.43	6.31	62
63	6.67	6.56	6.45	6.34	6.24	6.14	6.04	5.94	5.85	5.76	5.67	63
64	5.74	5.66	5.58	5.50	5.42	5.34	5.27	5.20	5.13	5.06	4.99	64
65	4.81	4.75	4.69	4.64	4.58	4.53	4.47	4.42	4.37	4.32	4.27	65
66	3.87	3.83	3.79	3.76	3.72	3.69	3.65	3.62	3.58	3.55	3.52	66
67	2.92	2.90	2.88	2.86	2.84	2.82	2.80	2.78	2.76	2.74	2.72	67
68	1.96	1.95	1.94	1.93	1.92	1.92	1.91	1.90	1.89	1.88	1.87	68
69	0.99	0.99	0.99	0.98	0.98	0.98	0.98	0.97	0.97	0.97	0.97	69

Table 11: Multipliers for. loss of pension commencing age 55 (males)

Age at date of trial	Multiplier calculated with allowance for population mortality and rate of interest of											Age at date of trial
	0.0%	0.5%	1.0%	1.5%	2.0%	2.5%	3.0%	3.5%	4.0%	4.5%	5.0%	
0	19.94	14.21	10.17	7.30	5.26	3.80	2.76	2.00	1.46	1.07	0.79	0
1	20.10	14.40	10.35	7.47	5.41	3.93	2.86	2.09	1.53	1.13	0.83	1
2	20.11	14.48	10.46	7.59	5.52	4.03	2.95	2.17	1.60	1.18	0.87	2
3	20.12	14.56	10.57	7.70	5.63	4.13	3.04	2.24	1.66	1.23	0.92	3
4	20.13	14.63	10.68	7.82	5.74	4.23	3.13	2.32	1.73	1.29	0.96	4
5	20.13	14.71	10.79	7.94	5.86	4.34	3.23	2.40	1.80	1.35	1.01	5
6	20.14	14.79	10.90	8.06	5.98	4.45	3.32	2.49	1.87	1.41	1.06	6
7	20.14	14.87	11.01	8.18	6.10	4.56	3.42	2.58	1.94	1.47	1.12	7
8	20.14	14.94	11.12	8.31	6.22	4.68	3.53	2.67	2.02	1.54	1.17	8
9	20.15	15.02	11.24	8.43	6.35	4.80	3.63	2.76	2.10	1.61	1.23	9
10	20.15	15.10	11.35	8.56	6.48	4.92	3.74	2.86	2.19	1.68	1.29	10
11	20.15	15.18	11.47	8.69	6.61	5.04	3.86	2.96	2.28	1.76	1.36	11
12	20.16	15.25	11.58	8.82	6.74	5.17	3.97	3.06	2.37	1.84	1.43	12
13	20.16	15.33	11.70	8.96	6.88	5.30	4.09	3.17	2.46	1.92	1.50	13
14	20.17	15.41	11.82	9.09	7.02	5.43	4.22	3.28	2.56	2.00	1.57	14
15	20.17	15.50	11.94	9.23	7.16	5.57	4.34	3.40	2.66	2.10	1.65	15
16	20.18	15.58	12.07	9.37	7.31	5.71	4.48	3.52	2.77	2.19	1.74	16
17	20.19	15.67	12.19	9.52	7.46	5.86	4.61	3.64	2.88	2.29	1.82	17
18	20.21	15.76	12.32	9.67	7.61	6.01	4.75	3.77	3.00	2.40	1.92	18
19	20.22	15.85	12.46	9.82	7.77	6.16	4.90	3.91	3.13	2.51	2.01	19
20	20.24	15.94	12.59	9.98	7.93	6.32	5.05	4.05	3.25	2.62	2.12	20
21	20.26	16.03	12.73	10.14	8.10	6.49	5.21	4.19	3.39	2.74	2.22	21
22	20.27	16.13	12.87	10.30	8.27	6.65	5.37	4.34	3.52	2.87	2.34	22
23	20.29	16.22	13.01	10.46	8.44	6.83	5.54	4.50	3.67	3.00	2.46	23
24	20.31	16.32	13.15	10.63	8.62	7.00	5.71	4.66	3.82	3.14	2.58	24
25	20.33	16.41	13.29	10.80	8.80	7.18	5.88	4.83	3.98	3.28	2.71	25
26	20.35	16.51	13.44	10.97	8.98	7.37	6.06	5.00	4.14	3.43	2.85	26
27	20.36	16.61	13.58	11.14	9117	7.56	6.25	5.18	4.31	3.59	3.00	27
28	20.38	16.70	13.73	11.32	9.36	7.76	6.44	5.37	4.48	3.75	3.15	28
29	20.40	16.80	13.88	11.50	9.55	7.96	6.64	5.56	4.67	3.92	3.31	29
30	20.42	16.90	14.03	11.68	9.75	8.16	6.85	5.76	4.86	4.10	3.48	30
31	20.44	17.00	14.19	11.87	9.96	8.37	7.06	5.97	5.06	4.29	3.65	31
32	20.45	17.10	14.34	12.06	10.17	8.59	7.28	6.18	5.26	4.49	3.84	32
33	20.47	17.21	14.50	12.25	10.38	8.82	7.51	6.41	5.48	4.70	4.04	33
34	20.49	17.31	14.66	12.45	10.60	9.04	7.74	6.64	5.70	4.91	4.24	34
35	20.52	17.41	14.82	12.65	10.82	9.28	7.98	6.88	5.94	5.14	4.46	35
36	20.54	17.52	14.99	12.85	11.05	9.52	8.23	7.13	6.18	5.38	4.69	36
37	20.57	17.63	15.16	13.06	11.29	9.77	8.49	7.38	6.44	5.63	4.93	37
38	20.60	17.74	15.33	13.28	11.53	10.03	8.75	7.65	6.71	5.89	5.18	38
39	20.63	17.86	15.50	13.49	11.77	10.30	9.03	7.93	6.98	6.16	5.45	39
40	20.66	17.98	15.68	13.72	12.03	10.57	9.31	8.22	7.28	6.45	5.73	40

Table 11: *contined*

Age at date of trial	Multiplier calculated with allowance for population mortality and rate of interest of											Age at date of trial
	0.0%	0.5%	1.0%	1.5%	2.0%	2.5%	3.0%	3.5%	4.0%	4.5%	5.0%	
41	20.69	18.10	15.87	13.95	12.29	10.86	9.61	8.53	7.58	6.75	6.03	41
42	20.73	18.22	16.06	14.18	12.56	11.15	9.92	8.84	7.90	7.07	6.34	42
43	20.78	18.35	16.25	14.43	12.84	11.45	10.24	9.17	8.23	7.40	6.67	43
44	20.82	18.48	16.45	14.67	13.12	11.76	10.57	9.51	8.58	7.75	7.02	44
45	20.87	18.62	16.65	14.93	13.42	12.09	10.91	9.87	8.94	8.12	7.39	45
46	20.93	18.76	16.87	15.20	13.72	12.42	11.27	10.24	9.33	8.51	7.78	46
47	20.99	18.91	17.08	15.47	14.04	12.77	11.64	10.63	9.73	8.92	8.19	47
48	21.06	19.07	17.31	15.75	14.37	13.13	12.03	11.04	10.15	9.35	8.63	48
49	21.14	19.24	17.55	16.05	14.71	13.51	12.43	11.47	10.60	9.81	9.09	49
50	21.23	19.41	17.80	16.36	15.07	13.91	12.86	11.92	11.06	10.29	9.59	50
51	21.32	19.60	18.06	16.68	15.44	14.32	13.31	12.39	11.56	10.80	10.12	51
52	21.44	19.80	18.34	17.02	15.83	14.75	13.78	12.89	12.09	11.35	10.68	52
53	21.56	20.02	18.63	17.38	16.24	15.21	14.27	13.42	12.64	11.93	11.28	53
54	21.70	20.25	18.94	17.75	16.67	15.69	14.80	13.98	13.23	12.55	11.92	54
55	21.86	20.50	19.26	18.15	17.13	16.20	15.35	14.57	13.86	13.21	12.60	55

Table 12: Multipliers for loss of pension commencing age 55 (females)

Age at date of trial	Multiplier calculated with allowance for population mortality and rate of interest of											Age at date of trial
	0.0%	0.5%	1.0%	1.5%	2.0%	2.5%	3.0%	3.5%	4.0%	4.5%	5.0%	
0	24.92	17.58	12.46	8.86	6.33	4.54	3.26	2.36	1.71	1.24	0.91	0
1	25.07	17.78	12.66	9.05	6.50	4.68	3.38	2.46	1.79	1.31	0.96	1
2	25.09	17.88	12.79	9.19	6.63	4.80	3.49	2.54	1.86	1.37	1.01	2
3	25.10	17.97	12.93	9.33	6.76	4.92	3.59	2.63	1.94	1.43	1.06	3
4	25.10	18.07	13.06	9.47	6.90	5.05	3.70	2.73	2.01	1.49	1.11	4
5	25.11	18.16	13.19	9.62	7.04	5.17	3.81	2.82	2.09	1.56	1.17	5
6	25.11	18.25	13.32	9.76	7.18	5.30	3.93	2.92	2.18	1.63	1.22	6
7	25.11	18.35	13.46	9.91	7.33	5.44	4.05	3.02	2.27	1.70	1.29	7
8	25.12	18.44	13.60	10.06	7.47	5.57	4.17	3.13	2.36	1.78	1.35	8
9	25.12	18.54	13.73	10.21	7.62	5.71	4.29	3.24	2.45	1.86	1.42	9
10	25.12	18.63	13.87	10.37	7.78	5.86	4.42	3.35	2.55	1.95	1.49	10
11	25.13	18.73	14.01	10.53	7.94	6.00	4.56	3.47	2.65	2.03	1.56	11
12	25.13	18.82	14.16	10.69	8.09	6.15	4.69	3.59	2.76	2.13	1.64	12
13	25.13	18.92	14.30	10.85	8.26	6.31	4.84	3.72	2.87	2.22	1.72	13
14	25.14	19.02	14.44	11.01	8.42	6.47	4.98	3.85	2.99	2.32	1.81	14
15	25.14	19.12	14.59	11.18	8.59	6.63	5.13	3.99	3.11	2.43	1.90	15
16	25.15	19.22	14.74	11.35	8.77	6.80	5.29	4.13	3.23	2.54	2.00	16
17	25.15	19.32	14.89	11.52	8.95	6.97	5.45	4.27	3.36	2.65	2.10	17
18	25.16	19.42	15.05	11.70	9.13	7.15	5.61	4.42	3.50	2.77	2.20	18
19	25.17	19.52	15.20	11.88	9.31	7.33	5.78	4.58	3.64	2.90	2.31	19
20	25.18	19.63	15.36	12.06	9.50	7.51	5.96	4.74	3.78	3.03	2.43	20
21	25.19	19.73	15.52	12.24	9.70	7.70	6.14	4.91	3.94	3.17	2.55	21
22	25.19	19.84	15.68	12.43	9.89	7.90	6.33	5.08	4.09	3.31	2.68	22
23	25.20	19.94	15.84	12.62	10.09	8.10	6.52	5.26	4.26	3.46	2.82	23
24	25.21	20.05	16.00	12.82	10.30	8.30	6.72	5.45	4.43	3.62	2.96	24
25	25.22	20.16	16.17	13.01	10.51	8.51	6.92	5.64	4.61	3.78	3.11	25
26	25.23	20.26	16.33	13.21	10.72	8.73	7.13	5.84	4.80	3.95	3.26	26
27	25.24	20.37	16.50	13.42	10.94	8.95	7.35	6.05	4.99	4.13	3.43	27
28	25.25	20.48	16.67	13.62	11.16	9.18	7.57	6.26	5.19	4.32	3.60	28
29	25.26	20.59	16.85	13.83	11.39	9.41	7.80	6.48	5.40	4.51	3.78	29
30	25.27	20.70	17.02	14.04	11.62	9.65	8.04	6.71	5.62	4.72	3.97	30
31	25.28	20.82	17.20	14.26	11.86	9.90	8.28	6.95	5.85	4.93	4.17	31
32	25.29	20.93	17.38	14.48	12.10	10.15	8.53	7.20	6.08	5.16	4.38	32
33	25.30	21.05	17.56	14.71	12.35	10.41	9.79	7.45	6.33	5.39	4.61	33
34	25.32	21.16	17.75	14.94	12.61	10.67	9.06	7.72	6.59	5.64	4.84	34
35	25.33	21.28	17.94	15.17	12.87	10.95	9.34	7.99	6.86	5.90	5.08	35
36	25.35	21.40	18.13	15.41	13.13	11.23	9.63	8.28	7.13	6.17	5.34	36
37	25.37	21.53	18.33	15.65	13.41	11.52	9.92	8.57	7.43	6.45	5.61	37
38	25.39	21.65	18.52	15.90	13.69	11.82	10.23	8.88	7.73	6.74	5.90	38
39	25.41	21.78	18.73	16.15	13.97	12.12	10.55	9.20	8.05	7.05	6.20	39
40	25.44	21.91	18.93	16.41	14.27	12.44	10.87	9.53	8.38	7.38	6.52	40

Table 12: *continued*

Age at date of trial	Multiplier calculated with allowance for population mortality and rate of interest of											Age at date of trial
	0.0%	0.5%	1.0%	1.5%	2.0%	2.5%	3.0%	3.5%	4.0%	4.5%	5.0%	
41	25.46	22.04	19.14	16.67	14.57	12.76	11.21	9.87	8.72	7.72	6.85	41
42	25.49	22.18	19.36	16.94	14.87	13.10	11.56	10.23	9.08	8.08	7.20	42
43	25.53	22.32	19.57	17.22	15.19	13.44	11.92	10.60	9.45	8.45	7.57	43
44	25.56	22.46	19.80	17.50	15.52	13.80	12.30	10.99	9.85	8.84	7.96	44
45	25.60	22.61	20.03	17.79	15.85	14.16	12.69	11.39	10.26	9.25	8.37	45
46	25.65	22.76	20.26	18.09	16.20	14.54	13.09	11.81	10.69	9.69	8.80	46
47	25.70	22.92	20.51	18.40	16.56	14.94	13.51	12.25	11.14	10.14	9.26	47
48	25.76	23.09	20.76	18.72	16.92	15.34	13.95	12.71	11.61	10.62	9.75	48
49	25.82	23.26	21.02	19.04	17.30	15.76	14.40	13.18	12.10	11.13	10.26	49
50	25.89	23.44	21.28	19.38	17.70	16.20	14.87	13.68	12.62	11.66	10.80	50
51	25.96	23.62	21.56	19.73	18.10	16.66	15.36	14.20	13.16	12.22	11.37	51
52	26.05	23.82	21.85	20.09	18.53	17.13	15.87	14.75	13.73	12.81	11.98	52
53	26.14	24.03	22.14	20.47	18.96	17.62	16.41	15.32	14.33	13.44	12.63	53
54	26.24	24.24	22.45	20.85	19.42	18.13	16.97	15.92	14.96	14.10	13.31	54
55	26.36	24.47	22.77	21.26	19.89	18.66	17.55	16.54	15.63	14.80	14.03	55

Table 13: Multipliers for, loss of pension commencing age 60 (males)

Age at date of trial	Multiplier calculated with allowance for population mortality and rate of interest of											Age at date of trial
	0.0%	0.5%	1.0%	1.5%	2.0%	2.5%	3.0%	3.5%	4.0%	4.5%	5.0%	
0	15.48	10.86	7.65	5.40	3.83	2.72	1.94	1.39	0.99	0.71	0.51	0
1	15.61	11.01	7.79	5.53	3.94	2.81	2.01	1.45	1.04	0.75	0.55	1
2	15.61	11.07	7.87	5.62	4.02	2.88	2.08	1.50	1.08	0.79	0.57	2
3	15.62	11.13	7.95	5.70	4.10	2.96	2.14	1.55	1.13	0.82	0.60	3
4	15.63	11.19	8.04	5.79	4.18	3.03	2.20	1.61	1.17	0.86	0.63	4
5	15.63	11.25	8.12	5.88	4.27	3.11	2.27	1.66	1.22	0.90	0.66	5
6	15.63	11.31	8.20	5.97	4.35	3.19	2.34	1.72	1.27	0.94	0.70	6
7	15.64	11.36	8.28	6.06	4.44	3.27	2.41	1.78	1.32	0.98	0.73	7
8	15.64	11.42	8.37	6.15	4.53	3.35	2.48	1.84	1.37	1.03	0.77	8
9	15.64	11.48	8.45	6.24	4.62	3.43	2.56	1.91	1.43	1.07	0.81	9
10	15.64	11.54	8.54	6.34	4.72	3.52	2.63	1.98	1.49	1.12	0.85	10
11	15.65	11.60	8.63	6.43	4.81	3.61	2.71	2.05	1.55	1.17	0.89	11
12	15.65	11.66	8.72	6.53	4.91	3.70	2.80	2.12	1.61	1.22	0.93	12
13	15.65	11.72	8.80	6.63	5.01	3.79	2.88	2.19	1.67	1.28	0.98	13
14	15.66	11.78	8.89	6.73	5.11	3.89	2.97	2.27	1.74	1.34	1.03	14
15	15.66	11.85	8.99	6.84	5.21	3.99	3.06	2.35	1.81	1.40	1.08	15
16	15.67	11.91	9.08	6.94	5.32	4.09	3.15	2.43	1.88	1.46	1.14	16
17	15.68	11.98	9.18	7.05	5.43	4.19	3.25	2.52	1.96	1.53	1.20	17
18	15.69	12.04	9.27	7.16	5.54	4.30	3.35	2.61	2.04	1.60	1.26	18
19	15.70	12.12	9.37	7.27	5.66	4.41	3.45	2.70	2.12	1.67	1.32	19
20	15.71	12.19	9.48	7.39	5.78	4.53	3.56	2.80	2.21	1.75	1.39	20
21	15.73	12.26	9.58	7.51	5.90	4.64	3.67	2.90	2.30	1.83	1.46	21
22	15.74	12.33	9.68	7.63	6.02	4.76	3.78	3.01	2.40	1.91	1.53	22
23	15.76	12.40	9.79	7.75	6.15	4.89	3.90	3.11	2.49	2.00	1.61	23
24	15.77	12.48	9.90	7.87	6.27	5.01	4.02	3.23	2.60	2.09	1.69	24
25	15.78	12.55	10.00	7.99	6.41	5.14	4.14	3.34	2.70	2.19	1.78	25
26	15.80	12.62	10.11	8.12	6.54	5.28	4.27	3.46	2.81	2.29	1.87	26
27	15.81	12.70	10.22	8.25	6.68	5.41	4.40	3.59	2.93	2.39	1.96	27
28	15.82	12.77	10.33	8.38	6.81	5.55	4.54	3.71	3.05	2.50	2.06	28
29	15.84	12.85	10.45	8.51	6.96	5.70	4.68	3.85	3.17	2.62	2.17	29
30	15.85	12.92	10.56	8.65	7.10	5.85	4.82	3.99	3.30	2.74	2.28	30
31	15.87	13.00	10.67	8.79	7.25	6.00	4.97	4.13	3.44	2.87	2.39	31
32	15.88	13.07	10.79	8.93	7.40	6.15	5.12	4.28	3.58	3.00	2.52	32
33	15.90	13.15	10.91	9.07	7.56	6.31	5.28	4.43	3.72	3.14	2.65	33
34	15.91	13.23	11.03	9.22	7.72	6.48	5.45	4.59	3.88	3.28	2.78	34
35	15.93	13.31	11.15	9.36	7.88	6.65	5.62	4.76	4.04	3.43	2.92	35
36	15.95	13.39	11.28	9.52	8.05	6.82	5.79	4.93	4.20	3.59	3.07	36
37	15.97	13.48	11.40	9.67	8.22	7.00	5.97	5.11	4.38	3.76	3.23	37
38	15.99	13.56	11.53	9.83	8.39	7.18	6.16	5.29	4.56	3.93	3.40	38
39	16.01	13.65	11.67	9.99	8.57	7.37	6.36	5.49	4.75	4.11	3.57	39
40	16.04	13.74	11.80	10.16	8.76	7.57	6.56	5.69	4.94	4.31	3.76	40

Table 13: *continued*

Age at date of trial	Multiplier calculated with allowance for population mortality and rate of interest of											Age at date of trial
	0.0%	0.5%	1.0%	1.5%	2.0%	2.5%	3.0%	3.5%	4.0%	4.5%	5.0%	
41	16.07	13.84	11.94	10.33	8.95	7.77	6.76	5.90	5.15	4.51	3.95	41
42	16.10	13.93	12.08	10.50	9.15	7.98	6.98	6.12	5.37	4.72	4.16	42
43	16.13	14.03	12.23	10.68	9.35	8.20	7.20	6.34	5.59	4.94	4.37	43
44	16.17	14.13	12.38	10.87	9.56	8.42	7.44	6.58	5.83	5.17	4.60	44
45	16.20	14.23	12.53	11.05	9.77	8.65	7.68	6.83	6.08	5.42	4.84	45
46	16.25	14.34	12.69	11.25	9.99	8.89	7.93	7.08	6.34	5.68	5.10	46
47	16.30	14.46	12.86	11.45	10.22	9.14	8.19	7.35	6.61	5.95	5.37	47
48	16.35	14.58	13.03	11.66	10.46	9.40	8.47	7.64	6.90	6.24	5.66	48
49	16.41	14.71	13.21	11.88	10.71	9.67	8.75	7.93	7.20	6.55	5.96	49
50	16.48	14.84	13.39	12.11	10.97	9.96	9.05	8.24	7.52	6.87	6.29	50
51	16.56	14.99	13.59	12.35	11.24	10.25	9.37	8.57	7.86	7.21	6.63	51
52	16.64	15.14	13.80	12.60	11.53	10.56	9.70	8.92	8.21	7.58	7.00	52
53	16.74	15.30	14.02	12.86	11.83	10.89	10.05	9.28	8.59	7.96	7.39	53
54	16.85	15.48	14.25	13.14	12.14	11.24	10.42	9.67	8.99	8.38	7.81	54
55	16.97	15.67	14.50	13.43	12.47	11.60	10.81	10.08	9.42	8.82	8.26	55
56	17.10	15.87	14.76	13.75	12.82	11.99	11.22	10.52	9.88	9.29	8.74	56
57	17.26	16.10	15.04	14.08	13.20	12.40	11.66	10.98	10.36	9.79	9.26	57
58	17.43	16.34	15.34	14.43	13.60	12.83	12.13	11.48	10.89	10.33	9.82	58
59	17.63	16.61	15.67	14.81	14.03	13.30	12.63	12.02	11.45	10.92	10.43	59
60	17.85	16.90	16.03	15.22	14.49	13.81	13.18	12.60	12.06	11.56	11.09	60

Table 14: Multipliers for loss of pension commencing age 60 (females)

Age at date of trial	Multiplier calculated with allowance for population mortality and rate of interest of											Age at date of trial
	0.0%	0.5%	1.0%	1.5%	2.0%	2.5%	3.0%	3.5%	4.0%	4.5%	5.0%	
0	20.25	14.08	9.82	6.88	4.83	3.41	2.41	1.71	1.22	0.87	0.62	0
1	20.38	14.24	9.98	7.03	4.96	3.52	2.50	1.78	1.28	0.92	0.66	1
2	20.39	14.32	10.09	7.14	5.06	3.61	2.58	1.85	1.33	0.96	0.69	2
3	20.40	14.39	10.19	7.25	5.17	3.70	2.65	1.91	1.38	1.00	0.73	3
4	20.40	14.47	10.30	7.36	5.27	3.79	2.73	1.98	1.44	1.05	0.76	4
5	20.41	14.54	10.40	7.47	5.38	3.89	2.82	2.05	1.49	1.09	0.80	5
6	20.41	14.62	10.51	7.58	5.49	3.98	2.90	2.12	1.55	1.14	0.84	6
7	20.41	14.69	10.62	7.70	5.60	4.08	2.99	2.20	1.62	1.19	0.88	7
8	20.42	14.77	10.72	7.81	5.71	4.19	3.08	2.27	1.68	1.25	0.93	8
9	20.42	14.85	10.83	7.93	5.82	4.29	3.17	2.35	1.75	1.30	0.98	9
10	20.42	14.92	10.94	8.05	5.94	4.40	3.27	2.43	1.82	1.36	1.02	10
11	20.43	15.00	11.05	8.17	6.06	4.51	3.37	2.52	1.89	1.42	1.08	11
12	20.43	15.08	11.16	8.30	6.18	4.62	3.47	2.61	1.97	1.49	1.13	12
13	20.43	15.15	11.28	8.42	6.31	4.74	3.57	2.70	2.05	1.56	1.19	13
14	20.43	15.23	11.39	8.55	6.44	4.86	3.68	2.80	2.13	1.63	1.25	14
15	20.44	15.31	11.51	8.68	6.57	4.98	3.79	2.89	2.22	1.70	1.31	15
16	20.44	15.39	11.63	8.81	6.70	5.11	3.91	3.00	2.30	1.78	1.37	16
17	20.45	15.47	11.75	8.95	6.83	5.24	4.02	3.10	2.40	1.86	1.44	17
18	20.45	15.55	11.87	9.08	6.97	5.37	4.15	3.21	2.19	1.94	1.52	18
19	20.46	15.64	11.99	9.22	7.11	5.50	4.27	3.32	2.59	2.03	1.59	19
20	20.47	15.72	12.11	9.36	7.26	5.64	4.40	3.44	2.70	2.12	1.67	20
21	20.47	15.80	12.24	9.51	7.41	5.79	4.53	3.56	2.81	2.22	1.76	21
22	20.48	15.89	12.36	9.65	7.56	5.93	4.67	3.69	2.92	2.32	1.84	22
23	20.49	15.97	12.49	9.80	7.71	6.08	4.81	3.82	3.04	2.42	1.94	23
24	20.49	16.06	12.62	9.95	7.87	6.24	4.96	3.95	3.16	2.53	2.04	24
25	20.50	16.14	12.75	10.10	8.03	6.40	5.11	4.09	3.29	2.65	2.14	25
26	20.51	16.23	12.88	10.26	8.19	6.56	5.27	4.24	3.42	2.77	2.25	26
27	20.51	16.32	13.02	10.41	8.36	6.72	5.43	4.39	3.56	2.89	2.36	27
28	20.52	16.40	13.15	10.57	8.53	6.90	5.59	4.54	3.70	3.03	2.48	28
29	20.53	16.49	13.29	10.74	8.70	7.07	5.76	4.71	3.85	3.16	2.60	29
30	20.54	16.58	13.43	10.90	8.88	7.25	5.94	4.87	4.01	3.31	2.73	30
31	20.55	16.67	13.57	11.07	9.06	7.43	6.12	5.04	4.17	3.46	2.87	31
32	20.56	16.76	13.71	11.24	9.25	7.62	6.30	5.22	4.34	3.61	3.02	32
33	20.57	16.85	13.85	11.42	9.44	7.82	6.50	5.41	4.52	3.78	3.17	33
34	20.58	16.95	14.00	11.60	9.63	8.02	6.69	5.60	4.70	3.95	3.33	34
35	20.59	17.04	14.15	11.78	9.83	8.22	6.90	5.80	4.89	4.13	3.50	35
36	20.61	17.14	14.30	11.96	10.03	8.44	7.11	6.01	5.09	4.32	3.67	36
37	20.62	17.24	14.45	12.15	10.24	8.65	7.33	6.22	5.30	4.52	3.86	37
38	20.64	17.34	14.61	12.34	10.45	8.88	7.56	6.45	5.51	4.72	4.06	38
39	20.66	17.44	14.77	12.54	10.67	9.11	7.79	6.68	5.74	4.94	4.26	39
40	20.68	17.55	14.93	12.74	10.90	9.34	8.03	6.92	5.97	5.17	4.48	40

Table 14: *continued*

Age at date of trial	Multiplier calculated with allowance for population mortality and rate of interest of											Age at date of trial
	0.0%	0.5%	1.0%	1.5%	2.0%	2.5%	3.0%	3.5%	4.0%	4.5%	5.0%	
41	20.70	17.65	15.10	12.94	11.13	9.59	8.28	7.17	6.22	5.41	4.71	41
42	20.72	17.76	15.27	13.15	11.36	9.84	8.54	7.43	6.48	5.66	4.95	42
43	20.75	17.87	15.44	13.37	11.60	10.10	8.81	7.70	6.74	5.92	5.21	43
44	20.78	17.99	15.61	13.59	11.85	10.36	9.08	7.98	7.02	6.19	5.48	44
45	20.81	18.11	15.80	13.81	12.11	10.64	9.37	8.27	7.32	6.48	5.76	45
46	20.85	18.23	15.98	14.05	12.37	10.93	9.67	8.58	7.62	6.79	6.06	46
47	20.89	18.36	16.17	14.28	12.65	11.22	9.98	8.89	7.94	7.11	6.37	47
48	20.94	18.49	16.37	14.53	12.93	11.53	10.30	9.23	8.28	7.44	6.71	48
49	20.99	18.63	16.58	14.78	13.22	11.84	10.64	9.57	8.63	7.80	7.06	49
50	21.04	18.77	16.79	15.05	13.52	12.17	10.98	9.93	9.00	8.17	7.43	50
51	21.11	18.92	17.00	15.32	13.83	12.51	11.35	10.31	9.39	8.56	7.82	51
52	21.17	19.08	17.23	15.60	14.15	12.87	11.73	10.71	9.79	8.98	8.24	52
53	21.25	19.24	17.46	15.89	14.49	13.24	12.12	11.12	10.22	9.41	8.69	53
54	21.33	19.41	17.71	16.19	14.83	13.62	12.53	11.56	10.67	9.88	9.16	54
55	21.42	19.59	17.96	16.50	15.20	14.02	12.97	12.01	11.15	10.37	9.66	55
56	21.53	19.79	18.23	16.83	15.57	14.44	13.42	12.49	11.65	10.88	10.19	56
57	21.64	19.99	18.51	17.17	15.97	14.88	13.89	13.00	12.18	11.43	10.75	57
58	21.77	20.21	18.81	17.54	16.39	15.34	14.40	13.53	12.74	12.02	11.36	58
59	21.92	20.45	19.12	17.92	16.83	15.83	14.93	14.10	13.34	12.64	12.00	59
60	22.08	20.70	19.45	18.32	17.29	16.35	15.49	14.70	13.98	13.31	12.70	60

Table 15: Multipliers for loss of pension commencing age 65 (males)

Age at date of trial	Multiplier calculated with allowance for population mortality and rate of interest of											Age at date of trial
	0.0%	0.5%	1.0%	1.5%	2.0%	2.5%	3.0%	3.5%	4.0%	4.5%	5.0%	
0	11.31	7.81	5.41	3.76	2.62	1.83	1.28	0.90	0.63	0.45	0.32	0
1	11.41	7.92	5.51	3.85	2.69	1.89	1.33	0.94	0.66	0.47	0.34	1
2	11.41	7.96	5.57	3.91	2.75	1.94	1.37	0.97	0.69	0.49	0.35	2
3	11.42	8.00	5.63	3.97	2.81	1.99	1.41	1.01	0.72	0.52	0.37	3
4	11.42	8.05	5.69	4.03	2.86	2.04	1.46	1.04	0.75	0.54	0.39	4
5	11.42	8.09	5.74	4.09	2.92	2.09	1.50	1.08	0.78	0.56	0.41	5
6	11.43	8.13	5.80	4.15	2.98	2.14	1.55	1.12	0.81	0.59	0.43	6
7	11.43	8.17	5.86	4.22	3.04	2.20	1.59	1.16	0.84	0.62	0.45	7
8	11.43	8.22	5.92	4.28	3.10	2.25	1.64	1.20	0.88	0.64	0.47	8
9	11.43	8.26	5.98	4.34	3.16	2.31	1.69	1.24	0.91	0.67	0.50	9
10	11.43	8.30	6.04	4.41	3.23	2.37	1.74	1.28	0.95	0.70	0.52	10
11	11.44	8.34	6.10	4.48	3.29	2.43	1.79	1.33	0.99	0.73	0.55	11
12	11.44	8.39	6.17	4.55	3.36	2.49	1.85	1.38	1.03	0.77	0.57	12
13	11.44	8.43	6.23	4.61	3.43	2.55	1.90	1.42	1.07	0.80	0.60	13
14	11.44	8.48	6.29	4.68	3.50	2.62	1.96	1.47	1.11	0.84	0.63	14
15	11.45	8.52	6.36	4.76	3.57	2.68	2.02	1.53	1.15	0.88	0.67	15
16	11.45	8.57	6.42	4.83	3.64	2.75	2.08	1.58	1.20	0.92	0.70	16
17	11.46	8.61	6.49	4.90	3.71	2.82	2.15	1.64	1.25	0.96	0.73	17
18	11.47	8.66	6.56	4.98	3.79	2.89	2.21	1.69	1.30	1.00	0.77	18
19	11.48	8.71	6.63	5.06	3.87	2.97	2.28	1.76	1.35	1.05	0.81	19
20	11.49	8.76	6.70	5.14	3.95	3.04	2.35	1.82	1.41	1.10	0.85	20
21	11.50	8.82	6.78	5.22	4.03	3.12	2.42	1.88	1.47	1.15	0.90	21
22	11.51	8.87	6.85	5.31	4.12	3.20	2.50	1.95	1.53	1.20	0.94	22
23	11.52	8.92	6.93	5.39	4.20	3.29	2.57	2.02	1.59	1.25	0.99	23
24	11.53	8.97	7.00	5.48	4.29	3.37	2.65	2.09	1.66	1.31	1.04	24
25	11.54	9.03	7.08	5.56	4.38	3.46	2.74	2.17	1.72	1.37	1.09	25
26	11.55	9.08	7.15	5.65	4.47	3.55	2.82	2.25	1.79	1.43	1.15	26
27	11.56	9.13	7.23	5.74	437	3.64	2.91	2.33	1.87	1.50	1.21	27
28	11.57	9.18	7.31	5.83	4.66	3.73	3.00	2.41	1.94	1.57	1.27	28
29	11.58	9.24	7.39	5.92	4.76	3.83	3.09	2.50	2.02	1.64	1.33	29
30	11.59	9.29	7.47	6.02	4.86	3.93	3.19	2.59	2.11	1.72	1.40	30
31	11.60	9.35	7.55	6.11	4.96	4.03	3.28	2.68	2.19	1.79	1.47	31
32	11.61	9.40	7.63	6.21	5.06	4.14	3.39	2.78	2.28	1.88	1.55	32
33	11.62	9.46	7.72	6.31	5.17	4.24	3:49	2.88	2.37	1.96	1.63	33
34	11.63	9.52	7.80	6.41	5.28	4.35	3.60	2.98	2.47	2.05	1.71	34
35	11.64	9.57	7.89	6.52	5.39	4.47	3.71	3.09	2.57	2.15	1.80	35
36	11.66	9.63	7.98	6.62	5.50	4.59	3.83	3.20	2.68	2.25	1.89	36
37	11.67	9.69	8.07	6.73	5.62	4.71	3.95	3.32	2.79	2.35	1.99	37
38	11.69	9.76	8.16	6.84	5.74	4.83	4.07	3.44	2.91	2.46	2.09	38
39	11.70	9.82	8.25	6.95	5.87	4.96	4.20	3.56	3.03	2.58	2.20	39
40	11.72	9.88	8.35	7.07	5.99	5.09	4.33	3.69	3.15	2.70	2.31	40

Table 15: *continued*

Age at date of trial	Multiplier calculated with allowance for population mortality and rate of interest of											Age at date of trial
	0.0%	0.5%	1.0%	1.5%	2.0%	2.5%	3.0%	3.5%	4.0%	4.5%	5.0%	
41	11.74	9.95	8.45	7.19	6.12	5.23	4.47	3.83	3.28	2.82	2.43	41
42	11.77	10.02	8.55	7.31	6.26	5.37	4.61	3.97	3.42	2.96	2.56	42
43	11.79	10.09	8.65	7.43	6.40	5.51	4.76	4.12	3.57	3.09	2.69	43
44	11.82	10.16	8.76	7.56	6.54	5.66	4.91	4.27	3.72	3.24	2.83	44
45	11.84	10.24	8.87	7.69	6.68	5.82	5.07	4.43	3.88	3.39	2.98	45
46	11.88	10.32	8.98	7.83	6.84	5.98	5.24	4.60	4.04	3.56	3.14	46
47	11.91	10.40	9.10	7.97	6.99	6.15	5.41	4.77	4.22	3.73	3.30	47
48	11.95	10.49	9.22	8.12	7.16	6.32	5.59	4.96	4.40	3.91	3.48	48
49	11.99	10.58	9.34	8.27	7.33	6.50	5.78	5.15	4.59	4.10	3.67	49
50	12.04	10.67	9.48	8.43	7.51	6.70	5.98	5.35	4.80	4.30	3.87	50
51	12.10	10.78	9.62	8.59	7.69	6.89	6.19	5.57	5.01	4.52	4.08	51
52	12.16	10.89	9.76	8.77	7.89	7.10	6.41	5.79	5.24	4.74	4.30	52
53	12.23	11.01	9.92	8.95	8.09	7.32	6.64	6.03	5.48	4.99	4.55	53
54	12.31	11.13	10.08	9.14	8.31	7.56	6.88	6.28	5.74	5.25	4.80	54
55	12.40	11.27	10.26	9.35	8.53	7.80	7.14	6.55	6.01	5.52	5.08	55
56	12.50	11.42	10.44	9.56	8.77	8.06	7.41	6.83	6.30	5.82	5.38	56
57	12.61	11.58	10.64	9.79	9.03	8.33	7.70	7.13	6.61	6.13	5.70	57
58	12.74	11.75	10.85	10.04	9.30	8.63	8.02	7.45	6.94	6.47	6.04	58
59	12.88	11.94	11.09	10.31	9.59	8.94	8.35	7.80	7.30	6.84	6.41	59
60	13.05	12.15	11.34	10.59	9.91	9.28	8.71	8.18	7.69	7.24	6.82	60
61	13.23	12.39	11.61	10.90	10.25	9.65	9.10	8.58	8.11	7.67	7.26	61
62	13.44	12.65	11.92	11.24	10.62	10.05	9.52	9.02	8.57	8.14	7.75	62
63	13.68	12.94	12.25	11.61	11.03	10.48	9.98	9.51	9.07	8.66	8.28	63
64	13.95	13.26	12.62	12.02	11.47	10.96	10.48	10.04	9.62	9.23	8.87	64
65	14.27	13.63	13.03	12.48	11.97	11.49	11.04	10.62	10.23	9.86	9.52	65

Table 16: Multipliers for loss of pension commencing age 65 (females)

Age at date of trial	Multiplier calculated with allowance for population mortality and rate of interest of											Age at date of trial
	0.0%	0.5%	1.0%	1.5%	2.0%	2.5%	3.0%	3.5%	4.0%	4.5%	5.0%	
0	15.77	10.80	7.42	5.11	3.53	2.45	1.70	1.19	0.83	0.58	0.41	0
1	15.87	10.92	7.54	5.22	3.63	2.53	1.77	1.24	0.87	0.61	0.43	1
2	15.88	10.98	7.62	5.30	3.70	2.59	1.82	1.28	0.91	0.64	0.46	2
3	15.89	11.04	7.70	5.38	3.78	2.66	1.88	1.33	0.94	0.67	0.48	3
4	15.89	11.10	7.78	5.47	3.85	2.72	1.93	1.37	0.98	0.70	0.50	4
5	15.89	11.16	7.86	5.55	3.93	2.79	1.99	1.42	1.02	0.73	0.53	5
6	15.90	11.21	7.93	5.63	4.01	2.86	2.05	1.47	1.06	0.77	0.55	6
7	15.90	11.27	8.02	5.72	4.09	2.94	2.11	1.52	1.10	0.80	0.58	7
8	15.90	11.33	8.10	5.80	4.17	3.01	2.18	1.58	1.15	0.84	0.61	8
9	15.90	11.39	8.18	5.89	4.26	3.09	2.24	1.63	1.19	0.87	0.64	9
10	15.91	11.45	8.26	5.98	4.34	3.16	2.31	1.69	1.24	0.91	0.67	10
11	15.91	11.50	8.35	6.07	4.43	3.24	2.38	1.75	1.29	0.96	0.71	11
12	15.91	11.56	8.43	6.16	4.52	3.32	2.45	1.81	1.34	1.00	0.74	12
13	15.91	11.62	8.52	6.26	4.61	3.41	2.52	1.88	1.40	1.04	0.78	13
14	15.91	11.68	8.60	6.35	4.70	3.49	2.60	1.94	1.45	1.09	0.82	14
15	15.92	11.74	8.69	6.45	4.80	3.58	2.68	2.01	1.51	1.14	0.86	15
16	15.92	11.80	8.78	6.55	4.90	3.67	2.76	2.08	1.57	1.19	0.90	16
17	15.92	11.87	8.87	6.65	5.00	3.76	2.84	2.15	1.64	1.25	0.95	17
18	15.93	11.93	8.96	6.75	5.10	3.86	2.93	2.23	1.70	1.30	1.00	18
19	15.93	11.99	9.05	6.85	5.20	3.96	3.02	2.31	1.77	1.36	1.05	19
20	15.94	12.06	9.15	6.96	5.31	4.06	3.11	2.39	1.84	1.42	1.10	20
21	15.94	12.12	9.24	7.06	5.41	4.16	3.20	2.48	1.92	1.49	1.16	21
22	15.95	12.19	9.34	7.17	5.52	4.27	3.30	2.56	1.99	1.55	1.21	22
23	15.96	12.25	9.43	7.28	5.64	4.37	3.40	2.65	2.07	1.62	1.28	23
24	15.96	12.32	9.53	7.39	5.75	4.48	3.51	2.75	2.16	1.70	1.34	24
25	15.97	12.38	9.63	7.51	5.87	4.60	3.61	2.84	2.24	1.78	1.41	25
26	15.97	12.45	9.73	7.62	5.99	4.71	3.72	2.94	2.34	1.86	1.48	26
27	15.98	12.51	9.83	7.74	6.11	4.83	3.83	3.05	2.43	1.94	1.55	27
28	15.98	12.58	9.93	7.86	6.23	4.96	3.95	3.16	2.53	2.03	1.63	28
29	15.99	12.65	10.03	7.98	6.36	5.08	4.07	3.27	2.63	2.12	1.71	29
30	15.99	12.72	10.14	8.10	6.49	5.21	4.19	3.38	2.74	2.22	1.80	30
31	16.00	12.79	10.24	8.23	6.62	5.34	4.32	3.50	2.85	2.32	1.89	31
32	16.01	12.86	10.35	8.35	6.76	5.48	4.45	3.63	2.96	2.42	1.99	32
33	16.02	12.93	10.46	8.48	6.90	5.62	4:59	3.76	3.08	2.53	2.09	33
34	16.03	13.00	10.57	8.62	7.04	5.76	4.73	3.89	3.21	2.65	2.19	34
35	16.04	13.07	10.68	8.75	7.18	5.91	4.88	4.03	3.34	2.77	2.30	35
36	16.05	13.15	10.80	8.89	7.33	6.06	5.03	4.17	3.47	2.90	2.42	36
37	16.06	13.22	10.91	9.03	7.49	6.22	5.18	4.32	3.61	3.03	2.54	37
38	16.07	13.30	11.03	9.17	7.64	6.38	5.34	4.48	3.76	3.17	2.67	38
39	16.09	13.38	11.15	9.32	7.80	6.55	5.51	4.64	3.92	3.31	2.81	39
40	16.10	13.46	11.27	9.47	7.97	6.72	5.68	4.81	4.08	3.47	2.95	40

Table 16: *continued*

Age at date of trial	Multiplier calculated with allowance for population mortality and rate of interest of											Age at date of trial
	0.0%	0.5%	1.0%	1.5%	2.0%	2.5%	3.0%	3.5%	4.0%	4.5%	5.0%	
41	16.12	13.54	11.40	9.62	8.13	6.89	5.85	4.98	4.24	3.63	3.10	41
42	16.14	13.62	11.53	9.77	8.31	7.07	6.03	5.16	4.42	3.79	3.26	42
43	16.16	13.71	11.66	9.93	8.48	7.26	6.22	5.35	4.60	3.97	3.43	43
44	16.18	13.80	11.79	10.10	8.66	7.45	6.42	5.54	4.79	4.15	3.60	44
45	16.21	13.89	11.93	10.26	8.85	7.65	6.62	5.75	4.99	4.35	3.79	45
46	16.24	13.98	12.07	10.44	9.04	7.85	6.83	5.96	5.20	4.55	3.99	46
47	16.27	14.08	12.21	10.61	9.24	8.07	7.05	6.18	5.42	4.76	4.20	47
48	16.31	14.18	12.36	10.80	9.45	8.29	7.28	6.41	5.65	4.99	4.41	48
49	16.34	14.29	12.52	10.99	9.66	8.51	7.52	6.65	5.89	5.23	4.65	49
50	16.39	14.40	12.67	11.18	9.88	8.75	7.76	6.90	6.14	5.48	4.89	50
51	16.44	14.51	12.84	11.38	10.11	9.00	8.02	7.16	6.41	5.74	5.15	51
52	16.49	14.63	13.01	11.59	10.34	9.25	8.29	7.44	6.68	6.02	5.43	52
53	16.55	14.76	13.19	11.81	10.59	9.52	8.57	7.72	6.98	6.31	5.72	53
54	16.61	14.89	13.37	12.03	10.84	9.79	8.86	8.03	7.28	6.62	6.03	54
55	16.69	15.03	13.56	12.26	11.11	10.08	9.16	8.34	7.61	6.95	6.36	55
56	16.77	15.18	13.76	12.51	11.38	10.38	9.48	8.68	7.95	7.30	6.71	56
57	16.86	15.33	13.98	12.76	11.67	10.70	9.82	9.03	8.31	7.67	7.08	57
58	16.96	15.50	14.20	13.03	11.98	11.03	10.17	9.40	8.70	8.06	7.48	58
59	17.07	15.68	14.44	13.31	12.30	11.38	10.55	9.79	9.10	8.48	7.90	59
60	17.20	15.88	14.69	13.61	12.64	11.75	10.95	10.21	9.54	8.92	8.36	60
61	17.34	16.09	14.96	13.93	13.00	12.15	11.37	10.66	10.00	9.40	8.85	61
62	17.50	16.32	15.25	14.27	13.38	12.57	11.82	11.13	10.50	9.92	9.38	62
63	17.68	16.57	15.56	14.64	13.79	13.01	12.30	11.64	11.03	10.47	9.95	63
64	17.88	16.85	15.90	15.03	14.23	13.49	12.81	12.18	11.60	11.07	10.57	64
65	18.11	17.15	16.26	15.45	14.70	14.01	13.37	12.77	12.22	11.71	11.24	65

Table 17: Multipliers for loss of pension commencing age 70 (males)

Age at date of trial	Multiplier calculated with allowance for population mortality and rate of interest of											Age at date of trial
	0.0%	0.5%	1.0%	1.5%	2.0%	2.5%	3.0%	3.5%	4.0%	4.5%	5.0%	
0	7.61	5.17	3.52	2.40	1.65	1.13	0.78	0.54	0.37	0.26	0.18	0
1	7.68	5.24	3.59	2.46	1.69	1.17	0.81	0.56	0.39	0.27	0.19	1
2	7.68	5.27	3.62	2.50	1.73	1.20	0.83	0.58	0.40	0.28	0.20	2
3	7.68	5.30	3.66	2.54	1.76	1.23	0.86	0.60	0.42	0.30	0.21	3
4	7.69	5.32	3.70	2.58	1.80	1.26	0.88	0.62	0.44	0.31	0.22	4
5	7.69	5.35	3.74	2.61	1.83	1.29	0.91	0.64	0.46	0.32	0.23	5
6	7.69	5.38	3.77	2.65	1.87	1.32	0.94	0.67	0.47	0.34	0.24	6
7	7.69	5.41	3.81	2.70	1.91	1.36	0.97	0.69	0.49	0.35	0.25	7
8	7.69	5.44	3.85	2.74	1.95	1.39	0.99	0.71	0.51	0.37	0.27	8
9	7.69	5.46	3.89	2.78	1.99	1.43	1.02	0.74	0.53	0.39	0.28	9
10	7.70	5.49	3.93	2.82	2.03	1.46	1.06	0.76	0.55	0.40	0.29	10
11	7.70	5.52	3.97	2.86	2.07	1.50	1.09	0.79	0.58	0.42	0.31	11
12	7.70	5.55	4.01	2.91	2.11	1.54	1.12	0.82	0.60	0.44	0.32	12
13	7.70	5.58	4.05	2.95	2.15	1.57	1.15	0.85	0.62	0.46	0.34	13
14	7.70	5.61	4.09	3.00	2.20	1.61	1.19	0.88	0.65	0.48	0.36	14
15	7.70	5.64	4.14	3.04	2.24	1.66	1.23	0.91	0.68	0.50	0.38	15
16	7.71	5.67	4.18	3.09	2.29	1.70	1.26	0.94	0.70	0.53	0.39	16
17	7.71	5.70	4.22	3.14	2.33	1.74	1.30	0.97	0.73	0.55	0.41	17
18	7.72	5.73	4.27	3.19	2.38	1.79	1.34	1.01	0.76	0.58	0.44	18
19	7.72	5.77	4.31	3.24	2.43	1.83	1.38	1.05	0.79	0.60	0.46	19
20	7.73	5.80	4.36	3.29	2.48	1.88	1.42	1.08	0.82	0.63	0.48	20
21	7.74	5.83	4.41	3.34	2.53	1.93	1.47	1.12	0.86	0.66	0.51	21
22	7.74	5.87	4.46	3.39	2.59	1.98	1.51	1.16	0.89	0.69	0.53	22
23	7.75	5.90	4.51	3.45	2.64	2.03	1.56	1.20	0.93	0.72	0.56	23
24	7.76	5.94	4.55	3.50	2.70	2.08	1.61	1.25	0.97	0.75	0.59	24
25	7.76	5.97	4.60	3.56	2.75	2.14	1.66	1.29	1.01	0.79	0.62	25
26	7.77	6.01	4.65	3.61	181	2.19	1.71	1.34	1.05	0.82	0.65	26
27	7.78	6.04	4.70	3.67	2.87	2.25	1.76	1.39	1.09	0.86	0.68	27
28	7.78	6.08	4.76	3.73	2.93	2.31	1.82	1.44	1.14	0.90	0.72	28
29	7.79	6.11	4.81	3.79	2.99	2.36	1.87	1.49	1.18	0.94	0.75	29
30	7.80	6.15	4.86	3.85	3.05	2.43	1.93	1.54	1.23	0.99	0.79	30
31	7.80	6.19	4.91	3.91	3.12	2.49	1.99	1.60	1.28	1.03	0.83	31
32	7.81	6.22	4.97	3.97	3.18	2.55	2.05	1.65	1.33	1.08	0.87	32
33	7.82	6.26	5.02	4.04	3.25	2.62	2.12	1.71	1.39	1.13	0.92	33
34	7.83	6.30	5.08	4.10	3.32	2.69	2.18	1.77	1.45	1.18	0.96	34
35	7.84	6.34	5.13	4.17	3.39	2.76	2.25	1.84	1.51	1.23	1.01	35
36	7.84	6.37	5.19	4.23	3.46	2.83	2.32	1.91	1.57	1.29	1.07	36
37	7.85	6.41	5.25	4.30	3.53	2.91	2.39	1.97	1.63	1.35	1.12	37
38	7.87	6.46	5.31	4.37	3.61	2.98	2.47	2.05	1.70	1.41	1.18	38
39	7.88	6.50	5.37	4.44	3.69	3.06	2.55	2.12	1.77	1.48	1.24	39
40	7.89	6.54	5.43	4.52	3.77	3.14	2.63	2.20	1.84	1.55	1.30	40

Table 17: *continued*

Age at date of trial	Multiplier calculated with allowance for population mortality and rate of interest of											Age at date of trial
	0.0%	0.5%	1.0%	1.5%	2.0%	2.5%	3.0%	3.5%	4.0%	4.5%	5.0%	
41	7.90	6.58	5.50	4.59	3.85	3.23	2.71	2.28	1.92	1.62	1.37	41
42	7.92	6.63	5.56	4.67	3.93	3.31	2.80	2.36	2.00	1.70	1.44	42
43	7.93	6.68	5.63	4.75	4.02	3.40	2.89	2.45	2.09	1.78	1.52	43
44	7.95	6.72	5.70	4.83	4.11	3.50	2.98	2.54	2.17	1.86	1.60	44
45	7.97	6.77	5.77	4.92	4.20	3.59	3.08	2.64	2.27	1.95	1.68	45
46	7.99	6.83	5.84	5.00	4.30	3.69	3.18	2.74	2.36	2.04	1.77	46
47	8.02	6.88	5.92	5.10	4.39	3.80	3.28	2.84	2.47	2.14	1.86	47
48	8.04	6.94	6.00	5.19	4.50	3.90	3.39	2.95	2.57	2.24	1.96	48
49	8.07	7.00	6.08	5.29	4.60	4.02	3.51	3.07	2.69	2.35	2.07	49
50	8.11	7.06	6.16	5.39	4.72	4.13	3.63	3.19	2.80	2.47	2.18	50
51	8.14	7.13	6.26	5.49	4.83	4.26	3.75	3.31	2.93	2.59	2.30	51
52	8.19	7.21	6.35	5.61	4.95	4.39	3.89	3.45	3.06	2.72	2.43	52
53	8.23	7.28	6.45	5.72	5.08	4.52	4.03	3.59	3.20	2.86	2.56	53
54	8.29	7.37	6.56	5.85	5.22	4.66	4.17	3.74	3.35	3.01	2.71	54
55	8.35	7.46	6.67	5.98	5.36	4.81	4.33	3.90	3.51	3.17	2.86	55
56	8.41	7.55	6.79	6.12	5.51	4.97	4.50	4.07	3.68	3.34	3.03	56
57	8.49	7.66	6.92	6.26	5.67	5.15	4.67	4.25	3.86	3.52	3.21	57
58	8.57	7.78	7.06	6.42	5.84	5.33	4.86	4.44	4.06	3.72	3.41	58
59	8.67	7.90	7.21	6.59	6.03	5.52	5.06	4.65	4.27	3.93	3.62	59
60	8.78	8.04	7.38	6.77	6.23	5.73	5.28	4.87	4.50	4.16	3.84	60
61	8.90	8.20	7.55	6.97	6.44	5.96	5.52	5.11	4.74	4.40	4.09	61
62	9.05	8.37	7.75	7.19	6.67	6.20	5.77	5.37	5.01	4.68	4.37	62
63	9.21	8.56	7.97	7.43	6.93	6.47	6.05	5.66	5.30	4.97	4.67	63
64	9.39	8.78	8.21	7.69	7.21	6.77	6.36	5.98	5.63	5.30	5.00	64
65	9.60	9.02	8.48	7.98	7.52	7.09	6.69	6.33	5.98	5.66	5.37	65
66	9.84	9.29	8.78	8.30	7.86	7.45	7.07	6.71	6.38	6.07	5.78	66
67	10.12	9.60	9.11	8.66	8.24	7.85	7.48	7.14	6.82	6.52	6.23	67
68	10.43	9.94	9.49	9.06	8.67	8.29	7.94	7.62	7.31	7.02	6.75	68
69	10.78	10.33	9.91	9.51	9.14	8.79	8.46	8.15	7.86	7.59	7.33	69
70	11.19	10.77	10.38	10.02	9.67	9.35	9.04	8.75	8.48	8.22	7.98	70

Table 18: Multipliers for loss of pension commencing age 70 (females)

Age at date of trial	Multiplier calculated with allowance for population mortality and rate of interest of											Age at date of trial
	0.0%	0.5%	1.0%	1.5%	2.0%	2.5%	3.0%	3.5%	4.0%	4.5%	5.0%	
0	11.59	7.81	5.28	3.58	2.43	1.66	1.13	0.78	0.53	0.37	0.25	0
1	11.66	7.90	5.36	3.65	2.50	1.71	1.18	0.81	0.56	0.39	0.27	1
2	11.67	7.94	5.42	3.71	2.55	1.75	1.21	0.84	0.58	0.40	0.28	2
3	11.67	7.98	5.48	3.77	2.60	1.80	1.25	0.87	0.61	0.42	0.30	3
4	11.67	8.02	5.53	3.83	2.65	1.84	1.29	0.90	0.63	0.44	0.31	4
5	11.67	8.07	5.59	3.88	2.71	1.89	1.32	0.93	0.65	0.46	0.33	5
6	11.68	8.11	5.65	3.94	2.76	1.94	1.36	0.96	0.68	0.48	0.34	6
7	11.68	8.15	5.70	4.00	2.82	1.99	1.41	1.00	0.71	0.51	0.36	7
8	11.68	8.19	5.76	4.06	2.87	2.04	1.45	1.03	0.74	0.53	0.38	8
9	11.68	8.23	5.82	4.12	2.93	2.09	1.49	1.07	0.77	0.55	0.40	9
10	11.68	8.27	5.88	4.19	2.99	2.14	1.54	1.11	0.80	0.58	0.42	10
11	11.68	8.32	5.94	4.25	3.05	2.19	1.58	1.14	0.83	0.60	0.44	11
12	11.69	8.36	6.00	4.31	3.11	2.25	1.63	1.18	0.86	0.63	0.46	12
13	11.69	8.40	6.06	4.38	3.17	2.31	1.68	1.23	0.90	0.66	0.48	13
14	11.69	8.45	6.12	4.45	3.24	2.36	1.73	1.27	0.93	0.69	0.51	14
15	11.69	8.49	6.18	4.51	3.30	2.42	1.78	1.31	0.97	0.72	0.53	15
16	11.69	8.53	6.25	4.58	3.37	2.48	1.84	1.36	1.01	0.75	0.56	16
17	11.70	8.58	6.31	4.65	3.44	2.55	1.89	1.41	1.05	0.79	0.59	17
18	11.70	8.63	6.37	4.72	3.51	2.61	1.95	1.46	1.09	0.82	0.62	18
19	11.70	8.67	6.44	4.80	3.58	2.68	2.01	1.51	1.14	0.86	0.65	19
20	11.71	8.72	6.51	4.87	3.65	2.75	2.07	1.56	1.18	0.90	0.68	20
21	11.71	8.76	6.57	4.94	3.73	2.82	2.13	1.62	1.23	0.94	0.72	21
22	11.72	8.81	6.64	5.02	3.80	2.89	2.20	1.68	1.28	0.98	0.75	22
23	11.72	8.86	6.71	5.10	3.88	2.96	2.26	1.73	1.33	1.03	0.79	23
24	11.72	8.90	6.78	5.17	3.96	3.03	2.33	1.80	1.39	1.07	0.83	24
25	11.73	8.95	6.85	5.25	4.04	3.11	2.40	1.86	1.44	1.12	0.87	25
26	11.73	9.00	6.92	5.33	4.12	3.19	2.48	1.92	1.50	1.17	0.92	26
27	11.73	9.05	6.99	5.42	4.20	3.27	2.55	1.99	1.56	1.22	0.96	27
28	11.74	9.10	7.06	5.50	4.29	3.35	2.63	2.06	1.62	1.28	1.01	28
29	11.74	9.15	7.14	5.58	4.38	3.44	2.71	2.14	1.69	1.34	1.06	29
30	11.75	9.19	7.21	5.67	4.47	3.53	2.79	2.21	1.76	1.40	1.12	30
31	11.75	9.24	7.29	5.76	4.56	3.62	2.88	2.29	1.83	1.46	1.17	31
32	11.76	9.30	7.36	5.85	4.65	3.71	2.96	2.37	1.90	1.53	1.23	32
33	11.76	9.35	7.44	5.94	4.75	3.80	3.05	2.46	1.98	1.60	1.29	33
34	11.77	9.40	7.52	6.03	4.85	3.90	3.15	2.54	2.06	1.67	1.36	34
35	11.78	9.45	7.60	6.12	4.95	4.00	3.24	2.63	2.14	1.75	1.43	35
36	11.79	9.51	7.68	6.22	5.05	4.10	3.34	2.73	2.23	1.83	1.50	36
37	11.80	9.56	7.76	6.32	5.15	4.21	3.45	2.83	2.32	1.91	1.58	37
38	11.81	9.62	7.85	6.42	5.26	4.32	3.55	2.93	2.42	2.00	1.66	38
39	11.82	9.67	7.93	6.52	5.37	4.43	3.66	3.03	2.52	2.09	1.74	39
40	11.83	9.73	8.02	6.62	5.48	4.55	3.78	3.14	2.62	2.19	1.83	40

Table 18: *continued*

Age at date of trial	Multiplier calculated with allowance for population mortality and rate of interest of											Age at date of trial
	0.0%	0.5%	1.0%	1.5%	2.0%	2.5%	3.0%	3.5%	4.0%	4.5%	5.0%	
41	11.84	9.79	8.11	6.73	5.60	4.66	3.89	3.26	2.73	2.29	1.92	41
42	11.85	9.85	8.20	6.84	5.72	4.79	4.01	3.37	2.84	2.39	2.02	42
43	11.87	9.91	8.29	6.95	5.84	4.91	4.14	3.50	2.96	2.50	2.12	43
44	11.89	9.98	8.39	7.07	5.96	5.04	4.27	3.62	3.08	2.62	2.23	44
45	11.91	10.04	8.49	7.18	6.09	5.18	4.41	3.76	3.21	2.74	2.35	45
46	11.93	10.11	8.59	7.30	6.23	5.32	4.55	3.89	3.34	2.87	2.47	46
47	11.95	10.18	8.69	7.43	6.36	5.46	4.69	4.04	3.48	3.01	2.60	47
48	11.98	10.25	8.79	7.56	6.50	5.61	4.84	4.19	3.63	3.15	2.74	48
49	12.01	10.33	8.90	7.69	6.65	5.76	5.00	4.35	3.78	3.30	2.88	49
50	12.04	10.41	9.02	7.82	6.80	5.92	5.16	4.51	3.95	3.46	3.03	50
51	12.07	10.49	9.13	7.97	6.96	6.09	5.33	4.68	4.11	3.62	3.19	51
52	12.11	10.58	9.26	8.11	7.12	6.26	5.51	4.86	4.29	3.80	3.36	52
53	12.16	10.67	9.38	8.26	7.29	6.44	5.70	5.05	4.48	3.98	3.54	53
54	12.20	10.77	9.51	8.42	7.46	6.63	5.89	5.25	4.68	4.18	3.74	54
55	12.26	10.87	9.65	8.58	7.65	6.82	6.09	5.45	4.89	4.38	3.94	55
56	12.31	10.97	9.79	8.75	7.84	7.03	6.31	5.67	5.11	4.60	4.16	56
57	12.38	11.09	9.94	8.93	8.04	7.24	6.53	5.90	5.34	4.84	4.39	57
58	12.45	11.21	10.10	9.12	8.24	7.46	6.77	6.14	5.59	5.08	4.63	58
59	12.54	11.34	10.27	9.32	8.47	7.70	7.02	6.40	5.85	5.35	4.90	59
60	12.63	11.48	10.45	9.53	8.70	7.95	7.28	6.68	6.13	5.63	5.18	60
61	12.74	11.63	10.64	9.75	8.95	8.22	7.56	6.97	6.43	5.93	5.49	61
62	12.85	11.80	10.85	9.99	9.21	8.50	7.86	7.28	6.74	6.26	5.81	62
63	12.99	11.98	11.07	10.24	9.49	8.81	8.18	7.61	7.09	6.61	6.17	63
64	13.13	12.18	11.31	10.52	9.79	9.13	8.52	7.97	7.45	6.98	6.55	64
65	13.30	12.40	11.57	10.81	10.12	9.48	8.89	8.35	7.85	7.39	6.96	65
66	13.49	12.64	11.85	11.13	10.46	9.85	9.29	8.77	8.28	7.83	7.42	66
67	13.70	12.89	12.15	11.47	10.84	10.25	9.71	9.21	8.75	8.31	7.91	67
68	13.93	13.18	12.48	11.84	11.24	10.69	10.18	9.70	9.25	8.83	8.45	68
69	14.20	13.50	12.85	12.24	11.68	11.16	10.68	10.22	9.80	9.41	9.03	69
70	14.49	13.84	13.24	12.68	12.16	11.68	11.22	10.80	10.40	10.03	9.68	70

Table 19: Multipliers for pecuniary loss for life (males)

Age at date of trial	Multiplier calculated with allowance for projected mortality from the 1998-based population projections and rate of return of											Age at date of trial
	0.0%	0.5%	1.0%	1.5%	2.0%	2.5%	3.0%	3.5%	4.0%	4.5%	5.0%	
0	79.84	65.45	54.50	46.07	39.50	34.30	30.14	26.77	24.01	21.72	19.80	0
1	79.24	65.10	54.31	45.99	39.48	34.32	30.18	26.83	24.07	21.79	19.87	1
2	78.26	64.44	53.87	45.69	39.27	34.18	30.08	26.76	24.02	21.75	19.84	2
3	77.27	63.77	53.41	45.37	39.05	34.02	29.98	26.68	23.97	21.71	19.82	3
4	76.28	63.09	52.95	45.05	38.83	33.87	29.87	26.60	23.91	21.67	19.79	4
5	75.28	62.41	52.48	44.72	38.60	33.70	29.75	26.52	23.85	21.63	19.75	5
6	74.28	61.72	52.00	44.39	38.36	33.54	29.63	26.43	23.79	21.58	19.72	6
7	73.27	61.02	51.51	44.04	38.12	33.36	29.51	26.34	23.72	21.53	19.68	7
8	72.27	60.32	51.02	43.70	37.87	33.19	29.38	26.25	23.65	21.48	19.64	8
9	71.27	59.62	50.52	43.34	37.62	33.00	29.24	26.15	23.58	21.42	19.60	9
10	70.26	58.91	50.02	42.99	37.36	32.82	29.11	26.05	23.50	21.37	19.56	10
11	69.26	58.20	49.51	42.62	37.10	32.62	28.97	25.94	23.43	21.31	19.51	11
12	68.25	57.48	49.00	42.25	36.83	32.43	28.82	25.84	23.34	21.24	19.46	12
13	67.25	56.77	48.49	41.88	36.56	32.23	28.67	25.72	23.26	21.18	19.41	13
14	66.24	56.05	47.97	41.50	36.28	32.02	28.52	25.61	23.17	21.11	19.36	14
15	65.25	55.33	47.45	41.12	36.00	31.81	28.36	25.49	23.08	21.04	19.31	15
16	64.25	54.61	46.92	40.74	35.71	31.60	28.20	25.37	22.99	20.97	19.25	16
17	63.26	53.88	46.39	40.35	35.43	31.39	28.04	25.25	22.90	20.90	19.19	17
18	62.28	53.17	45.87	39.96	35.14	31.17	27.88	25.13	22.80	20.83	19.14	18
19	61.31	52.46	45.35	39.57	34.85	30.96	27.72	25.00	22.71	20.76	19.08	19
20	60.34	51.75	44.82	39.18	34.56	30.74	27.55	24.88	22.61	20.68	19.03	20
21	59.37	51.03	44.29	38.79	34.26	30.52	27.39	24.75	22.52	20.61	18.97	21
22	58.40	50.32	43.75	38.39	33.96	30.29	27.21	24.62	22.41	20.53	18.91	22
23	57.43	49.59	43.21	37.98	33.65	30.05	27.03	24.48	22.31	20.45	18.84	23
24	56.45	48.86	42.66	37.56	33.33	29.81	26.84	24.33	22.19	20.36	18.77	24
25	55.48	48.12	42.10	37.13	33.01	29.56	26.65	24.18	22.08	20.26	18.70	25
26	54.50	47.38	41.54	36.71	32.68	29.30	26.45	24.03	21.95	20.17	18.62	26
27	53.53	46.64	40.97	36.27	32.34	29.04	26.25	23.87	21.83	20.07	18.54	27
28	52.55.	45.89	40.40	35.83	32.00	28.77	26.04	23.70	21.70	19.96	18.46	28
29	51.57	45.14	39.82	35.38	31.65	28.50	25.82	23.53	21.56	19.86	18.37	29
30	50.59	44.39	39.23	34.92	31.29	28.22	25.60	23.35	21.42	19.74	18.28	30
31	49.61	43.62	38.63	34.45	30.92	27.92	25.37	23.17	21.27	19.62	18.18	31
32	48.62	42.86	38.03	33.98	30.55	27.63	25.13	22.98	21.12	19.50	18.08	32
33	47.64	42.08	37.42	33.49	30.16	27.32	24.88	22.78	20.95	19.36	17.97	33
34	46.65	41.30	36.81	33.00	29.77	27.00	24.63	22.57	20.78	19.23	17.86	34
35	45.66	40.52	36.18	32.50	29.37	26.68	24.36	22.36	20.61	19.08	17.74	35
36	44.66	39.72	35.55	31.99	28.95	26.34	24.09	22.13	20.42	18.93	17.61	36
37	43.67	38.93	34.90	31.47	28.53	26.00	23.81	21.90	20.23	18.77	17.48	37
38	42.67	38.13	34.26	30.95	28.11	25.65	23.52	21.66	20.03	18.60	17.34	38
39	41.68	37.33	33.61	30.42	27.67	25.29	23.22	21.42	19.83	18.43	17.19	39
40	40.70	36.52	32.95	29.88	27.23	24.93	22.92	21.17	19.62	18.25	17.04	40

Table 19: *continued*

Age at date of trial	Multiplier calculated with allowance for projected mortality from the 1998-based population projections and rate of retirn of											Age at date of trial
	0.0%	0.5%	1.0%	1.5%	2.0%	2.5%	3.0%	3.5%	4.0%	4.5%	5.0%	
41	39.71	35.72	32.30	29.34	26.79	24.56	22.62	20.91	19.40	18.07	16.89	41
42	38.73	34.92	31.64	28.80	26.33	24.18	22.30	20.64	19.18	17.88	16.73	42
43	37.75	34.11	30.97	28.25	25.87	23.80	21.98	20.37	18.95	17.69	16.56	43
44	36.77	33.30	30.30	27.69	25.41	23.41	21.65	20.09	18.71	17.49	16.39	44
45	35.80	32.49	29.62	27.12	24.93	23.00	21.31	19.80	18.47	17.27	16.21	45
46	34.82	31.68	28.94	26.54	24.44	22.59	20.96	19.50	18.21	17.05	16.02	46
47	33.84	30.85	28.25	25.96	23.95	22.17	20.59	19.19	17.94	16.82	15.82	47
48	32.86	30.02	27.54	25.36	23.44	21.74	20.22	18.87	17.66	16.58	15.61	48
49	31.87	29.19	26.83	24.76	22.92	21.29	19.84	18.54	17.38	16.33	15.39	49
50	30.89	28.35	26.12	24.14	22.39	20.83	19.44	18.19	17.07	16.07	15.15	50
51	29.91	27.51	25.40	23.52	21.85	20.37	19.03	17.84	16.76	15.79	14.91	51
52	28.93	26.67	24.67	22.90	21.31	19.89	18.62	17.48	16.45	15.51	14.66	52
53	27.96	25.84	23.95	22.27	20.76	19.41	18.20	17.11	16.12	15.22	14.41	53
54	27.00	25.01	23.23	21.64	20.21	18.93	17.78	16.73	15.79	14.93	14.14	54
55	26.06	24.18	22.51	21.01	19.66	18.44	17.34	16.35	15.45	14.62	13.87	55
56	25.12	23.36	21.79	20.37	19.10	17.95	16.91	15.96	15.10	14.31	13.59	56
57	24.20	22.55	21.08	19.75	18.54	17.46	16.47	15.57	14.75	14.00	13.31	57
58	23.30	21.76	20.38	19.13	18.00	16.97	16.03	15.18	14.40	13.68	13.03	58
59	22.42	20.99	19.69	18.52	17.45	16.48	15.60	14.79	14.05	13.37	12.74	59
60	21.56	20.23	19.01	17.91	16.91	16.00	15.16	14.40	13.69	13.05	12.45	60
61	20.72	19.47	18.34	17.31	16.37	15.51	14.72	14.00	13.34	12.72	12.16	61
62	19.88	18.72	17.67	16.71	15.83	15.02	14.28	13.60	12.97	12.39	11.85	62
63	19.05	17.98	17.00	16.10	15.28	14.53	13.83	13.19	12.60	12.05	11.54	63
64	18.22	17.23	16.33	15.49	14.73	14.02	13.37	12.77	12.21	11.70	11.22	64
65	17.40	16.49	15.65	14.88	14.17	13.51	12.91	12.34	11.82	11.34	10.89	65
66	16.58	15.74	14.97	14.26	13.60	12.99	12.43	11.91	11.42	10.97	10.54	66
67	15.76	14.99	14.28	13.63	13.02	12.46	11.94	11.45	11.00	10.58	10.18	67
b8	14.94	14.24	13.60	13.00	12.44	11.93	11.44	11.00	10.58	10.18	9.82	68
69	14.14	13.51	12.92	12.37	11.86	11.39	10.95	10.53	10.15	9.78	9.44	69
70	13.36	12.78	12.25	11.75	11.29	10.86	10.45	10.07	9.71	9.38	9.07	70
71	12.60	12.09	11.60	11.15	10.73	10.34	9.96	9.62	9.29	8.98	8.69	71
72	11.89	11.42	10.98	10.57	10.19	9.83	9.49	9.17	8.87	8.59	8.33	72
73	11.20	10.78	10.39	10.02	9.67	9.34	9.04	8.75	8.47	8.21	7.97	73
74	10.56	10.18	9.83	9.49	9.18	8.88	8.60	8.33	8.08	7.85	7.62	74
75	9.95	9.61	9.29	8.99	8.70	8.43	8.18	7.94	7.71	7.49	7.28	75
76	9.37	9.07	8.78	8.50	8.25	8.00	7.77	7.55	7.34	7.14	6.95	76
77	8.81	8.54	8.28	8.04	7.80	7.58	7.37	7.17	6.98	6.80	6.63	77
78	8.28	8.04	7.80	7.58	737	7.17	6.98	6.80	6.63	6.47	6.31	78
79	7.78	7.56	7.35	7.15	6.96	6.78	6.61	6.45	6.29	6.14	6.00	79
80	7.29	7.10	6.91	6.73	6.56	6.40	6.25	6.10	5.96	5.83	5.70	80
81	6.83	6.66	6.49	6.33	6.18	6.04	5.90	5.77	5.64	5.52	5.40	81

Table 19: *continued*

Age at date of trial	Multiplier calculated with allowance for projected mortality from the 1998-based population projections and rate of return of											Age at date of trial
	0.0%	0.5%	1.0%	1.5%	2.0%	2.5%	3.0%	3.5%	4.0%	4.5%	5.0%	
82	6.39	6.24	6.09	5.95	5.81	5.68	5.56	5.44	5.33	5.22	5.11	82
83	5.98	5.85	5.71	5.59	5.47	5.35	5.24	5.14	5.03	4.93	4.84	83
84	5.60	5.48	5.37	5.25	5.15	5.04	4.94	4.85	4.76	4.67	4.58	84
85	5.25	5.14	5.04	4.94	4.84	4.75	4.66	4.57	4.49	4.41	4.34	85
86	4.92	4.82	4.73	4.64	4.56	4.48	4.40	4.32	4.25	4.17	4.10	86
87	4.62	4.53	4.45	4.37	4.30	4.22	4.15	4.08	4.02	3.95	3.89	87
88	4.34	4.27	4.19	4.12	4.05	3.99	3.92	3.86	3.80	3.75	3.69	88
89	4.08	4.01	3.94	3.88	3.82	3.76	3.71	3.65	3.60	3.54	3.49	89
90	3.81	3.75	3.70	3.64	3.59	3.53	3.48	3.44	3.39	3.34	3.30	90
91	3.54	3.49	3.44	3.39	3.35	3.30	3.26	3.21	3.17	3.13	3.09	91
92	3.29	3.24	3.20	3.16	3.11	3.07	3.03	3.00	2.96	2.92	2.89	92
93	3.05	3.01	2.98	2.94	2.90	2.87	2.83	2.80	2.77	2.74	2.71	93
94	2.83	2.79	2.76	2.73	2.70	2.66	2.63	2.61	2.58	2.55	2.52	94
95	2.62	2.59	2.56	2.53	2.50	2.48	2.45	2.42	2.40	2.37	2.35	95
96	2.42	2.40	2.37	2.35	2.32	2.30	2.28	2.26	2.23	2.21	2.19	96
97	2.25	2.23	2.20	2.18	2.16	2.14	2.12	2.10	2.08	2.07	2.05	97
98	2.09	2.07	2.05	2.03	2.02	2.00	1.98	1.96	1.95	1.93	1.91	98
99	1.94	1.93	1.91	1.90	1.88	1.86	1.85	1.83	1.82	1.81	1.79	99
100	1.81	1.80	1.78	1.77	1.75	1.74	1.73	1.71	1.70	1.69	1.68	100

Table 20: Multipliers for pecuniary loss for life (females)

Age at date of trial	Multiplier calculated with allowance for projected mortality from the 1998-based population projections and rate of return of											Age at date of trial
	0.0%	0.5%	1.0%	1.5%	2.0%	2.5%	3.0%	3.5%	4.0%	4.5%	5.0%	
0	84.01	68.28	56.45	47.42	40.45	34.97	30.63	27.13	24.27	21.92	19.95	0
1	83.36	67.90	56.24	47.32	40.41	34.98	30.66	27.17	24.33	21.98	20.01	1
2	82.38	67.25	55.81	47.04	40.22	34.85	30.57	27.12	24.29	21.95	19.99	2
3	81.38	66.59	55.37	46.74	40.02	34.72	30.48	27.05	24.24	21.92	19.97	3
4	80.38	65.93	54.92	46.44	39.81	34.58	30.38	26.98	24.20	21.88	19.95	4
5	79.38	65.25	54.47	46.13	39.60	34.43	30.28	26.91	24.14	21.85	19.92	5
6	78.38	64.57	54.00	45.81	39.38	34.28	30.17	26.83	24.09	21.81	19.89	6
7	77.37	63.89	53.54	45.49	39.16	34.12	30.06	26.76	24.03	21.77	19.86	7
8	76.37	63.20	53.07	45.16	38.93	33.96	29.95	26.68	23.98	21.73	19.83	8
9	75.36	62.51	52.59	44.83	38.70	33.80	29.83	26.59	23.92	21.68	19.80	9
10	74.36	61.82	52.11	44.50	38.46	33.63	29.71	26.51	23.85	21.64	19.77	10
11	73.35	61.12	51.62	44.15	38.22	33.46	29.59	26.42	23.79	21.59	19.73	11
12	72.35	60.42	51.13	43.81	37.98	33.28	29.46	26.32	23.72	21.54	19.69	12
13	71.34	59.72	50.64	43.46	37.73	33.10	29.33	26.23	23.65	21.49	19.65	13
14	70.34	59.01	50.14	43.10	37.47	32.92	29.20	26.13	23.58	21.43	19.61	14
15	69.34	58.31	49.63	42.74	37.21	32.73	29.06	26.03	23.50	21.38	19.57	15
16	68.34	57.60	49.13	42.38	36.95	32.54	28.92	25.93	23.43	21.32	19.53	16
17	67.34	56.89	48.62	42.01	36.68	32.34	28.78	25.82	23.35	21.26	19.48	17
18	66.34	56.17	48.10	41.64	36.41	32.14	28.63	25.71	23.26	21.20	19.43	18
19	65.35	55.46	47.58	41.26	36.13	31.94	28.48	25.60	23.18	21.13	19.39	19
20	64.35	54.74	47.06	40.88	35.85	31.73	28.32	25.48	23.09	21.07	19.33	20
21	63.35	54.01	46.53	40.49	35.56	31.52	28.16	25.36	23.00	21.00	19.28	21
22	62.36	53.28	45.99	40.09	35.27	31.30	28.00	25.23	22.90	20.92	19.22	22
23	61.36	52.55	45.45	39.69	34.97	31.07	27.83	25.10	22.80	20.84	19.16	23
24	60.36	51.81	44.90	39.28	34.66	30.84	27.65	24.97	22.70	20.76	19.10	24
25	59.35	51.06	44.35	38.86	34.35	30.60	27.47	24.83	22.59	20.68	19.03	25
26	58.35	50.32	43.79	38.44	34.02	30.35	27.28	24.68	22.48	20.59	18.97	26
27	57.35	49.57	43.22	38.01	33.70	30.10	27.09	24.54	22.36	20.50	18.89	27
28	56.35	48.81	42.65	37.58	33.37	29.85	26.89	24.38	22.24	20.40	18.82	28
29	55.35	48.06	42.08	37.14	33.03	29.59	26.69	24.22	22.12	20.31	18.74	29
30	54.35	47.30	41.49	36.69	32.68	29.32	26.48	24.06	21.99	20.20	18.66	30
31	53.35	46.53	40.91	36.24	32.33	29.05	26.26	23.89	21.85	20.09	18.57	31
32	52.35	45.76	40.32	35.78	31.97	28.76	26.04	23.71	21.71	19.98	18.48	32
33	51.35	44.99	39.72	35.31	31.61	28.48	25.81	23.53	21.57	19.87	18.38	33
34	50.35	44.22	39.11	34.84	31.24	28.18	25.58	23.34	21.42	19.74	18.28	34
35	49.35	43.44	38.50	34.36	30.86	27.88	25.34	23.15	21.26	19.62	18.18	35
36	48.35	42.66	37.89	33.87	30.47	27.57	25.09	22.95	21.10	19.49	18.07	36
37	47.36	41.87	37.27	33.38	30.08	27.26	24.84	22.75	20.93	19.35	17.96	37
38	46.36	41.09	36.64	32.88	29.68	26.94	24.58	22.53	20.76	19.21	17.84	38
39	45.36	40.29	36.01	32.38	29.27	26.61	24.31	22.32	20.58	19.06	17.72	39
40	44.37	39.50	35.38	31.86	28.86	26.27	24.03	22.09	20.39	18.90	17.59	40

Table 20: *continued*

Age at date of trial	Multiplier calculated with allowance for projected mortality from the 1998-based population projections and rate of return of											Age at date of trial
	0.0%	0.5%	1.0%	1.5%	2.0%	2.5%	3.0%	3.5%	4.0%	4.5%	5.0%	
41	43.37	38.70	34.73	31.34	28.44	25.93	23.75	21.86	20.20	18.74	17.46	41
42	42.38	37.90	34.09	30.82	28.01	25.57	23.46	21.62	20.00	18.58	17.32	42
43	41.39	37.10	33.43	30.29	27.57	25.21	23.16	21.37	19.80	18.40	17.17	43
44	40.40	36.29	32.78	29.75	27.13	24.85	22.86	21.12	19.58	18.23	17.02	44
45	39.41	35.49	32.11	29.20	26.67	24.47	22.55	20.85	19.36	18.04	16.86	45
46	38.42	34.67	31.44	28.65	26.21	24.09	22.23	20.58	19.13	17.85	16.70	46
47	37.43	33.86	30.77	28.09	25.75	23.70	21.90	20.31	18.90	17.64	16.53	47
48	36.45	33.05	30.09	27.52	25.27	23.30	21.56	20.02	18.65	17.44	16.35	48
49	35.47	32.23	29.41	26.95	24.79	22.89	21.21	19.73	18.40	17.22	16.16	49
50	34.49	31.41	28.72	26.37	24.30	22.48	20.86	19.42	18.14	17.00	15.97	50
51	33.52	30.59	28.03	25.79	23.81	22.05	20.50	19.11	17.88	16.77	15.77	51
52	32.55	29.78	27.34	25.20	23.30	21.62	20.13	18.80	17.60	16.53	15.56	52
53	31.59	28.96	26.65	24.61	22.80	21.19	19.75	18.47	17.32	16.28	15.35	53
54	30.63	28.14	25.95	24.01	22.28	20.74	19.37	18.14	17.03	16.03	15.12	54
55	29.68	27.33	25.25	23.41	21.76	20.29	18.98	17.80	16.73	15.77	14.89	55
56	28.73	26.51	24.55	22.80	21.24	19.84	18.58	17.45	16.42	15.50	14.66	56
57	27.79	25.70	23.85	22.19	20.71	19.38	18.18	17.09	16.11	15.22	14.41	57
58	26.86	24.90	23.15	21.58	20.18	18.91	17.77	16.73	15.79	14.94	14.16	58
59	25.95	24.11	22.46	20.98	19.65	18.44	17.36	16.37	15.47	14.65	13.91	59
60	25.05	23.32	21.77	20.38	19.12	17.98	16.94	16.00	15.14	14.36	13.64	60
61	24.16	22.54	21.09	19.77	18.58	17.50	16.52	15.63	14.81	14.06	13.38	61
62	23.27	21.76	20.39	19.16	18.04	17.02	16.09	15.24	14.46	13.75	13.10	62
63	22.38	20.97	19.69	18.53	17.48	16.52	15.64	14.84	14.10	13.43	12.80	63
64	21.47	20.17	18.98	17.90	16.91	16.01	15.18	14.43	13.73	13.09	12.50	64
65	20.56	19.35	18.25	17.24	16.32	15.48	14.70	13.99	13.34	12.73	12.17	65
66	19.64	18.53	17.51	16.57	15.72	14.93	14.21	13.54	12.93	12.36	11.83	66
67	18.72	17.69	16.76	15.89	15.10	14.37	13.70	13.08	12.50	11.97	11.47	67
68	17.80	16.86	16.00	15.21	14.48	13.80	13.18	12.60	12.07	11.57	11.10	68
69	16.89	16.04	15.25	14.52	13.85	13.23	12.65	12.12	11.62	11.16	10.73	69
70	16.01	15.23	14.51	13.85	13.23	12.66	12.13	11.64	11.17	10.74	10.34	70
71	15.20	14.44	13.79	13.20	12.62	12.10	11.61	11.16	10.73	10.33	9.96	71
72	14.30	13.69	13.10	12.50	12.03	11.55	11.11	10.69	10.30	9.93	9.58	72
73	13.60	12.98	12.44	11.90	11.46	11.03	10.62	10.23	9.87	9.53	9.21	73
74	12.80	12.29	11.80	11.30	10.91	10.51	10.14	9.79	9.45	9.14	8.85	74
75	12.10	11.63	11.19	10.80	10.38	10.02	9.67	9.35	9.04	8.76	8.49	75
76	11.40	11.00	10.59	10.20	9.86	9.53	9.22	8.92	8.64	8.38	8.13	76
77	10.80	10.38	10.02	9.70	9.36	9.06	8.77	8.50	8.25	8.00	7.77	77
78	10.10	9.79	9.46	9.20	8.86	8.59	8.33	8.08	7.85	7.63	7.42	78
79	9.50	9.21	8.92	8.60	8.38	8.13	7.90	7.67	7.46	7.26	7.07	79
80	8.90	8.65	8.39	8.10	7.91	7.68	7.47	7.27	7.08	6.90	6.72	80
81	8.40	8.12	7.88	7.70	7.45	7.25	7.06	6.88	6.70	6.54	6.38	81

Table 20: *continued*

Age at date of trial	Multiplier calculated with allowance for projected mortality from the 1998-based population projections and rate of return of											Age at date of trial
	0.0%	0.5%	1.0%	1.5%	2.0%	2.5%	3.0%	3.5%	4.0%	4.5%	5.0%	
82	7.80	7.61	7.40	7.20	7.01	6.83	6.66	6.49	6.34	6.19	6.04	82
83	7.30	7.12	6.94	6.80	6.59	6.43	6.27	6.13	5.99	5.85	5.72	83
84	6.90	6.68	6.51	6.40	6.20	6.06	5.92	5.78	5.66	5.54	5.42	84
85	6.40	6.27	6.12	6.00	5.84	5.71	5.59	5.47	5.35	5.24	5.14	85
86	6.00	5.90	5.77	5.60	5.52	5.40	5.29	5.18	5.07	4.97	4.88	86
87	5.70	5.57	5.45	5.30	5.23	5.12	5.02	4.92	4.83	4.73	4.65	87
88	5.40	5.29	5.18	5.10	4.97	4.88	4.78	4.69	4.61	4.52	4.44	88
89	5.10	5.03	4.93	4.80	4.74	4.66	4.57	4.49	4.41	4.33	4.26	89
90	4.90	4.78	4.69	4.60	4.52	4.44	4.36	4.29	4.21	4.14	4.08	90
91	4.60	4.52	4.44	4.40	4.28	4.21	4.14	4.07	4.01	3.94	3.88	91
92	4.30	4.24	4.17	4.10	4.03	3.96	3.90	3.84	3.78	3.72	3.67	92
93	4.00	3.95	3.89	3.80	3.77	3.71	3.65	3.60	3.55	3.50	3.45	93
94	3.70	3.67	3.61	3.60	3.51	3.46	3.41	3.36	3.31	3.27	3.22	94
95	3.40	3.40	3.35	3.30	3.26	3.21	3.17	3.13	3.09	3.05	3.01	95
96	3.20	3.14	3.10	3.10	3.02	2.98	2.94	2.91	2.87	2.84	2.80	96
97	2.90	2.90	2.86	2.80	2.79	2.76	2.73	2.69	2.66	2.63	2.60	97
98	2.70	2.68	2.64	2.60	2.58	2.56	2.53	2.50	2.47	2.45	2.42	98
99	2.50	2.48	2.45	2.40	2.40	2.38	2.35	2.33	2.30	2.28	2.26	99
100	2.30	2.31	2.29	2.30	2.24	2.22	2.20	2.18	2.16	2.14	2.12	100

Table 21: Multipliers for loss of earnings to pension age 55 (males)

Age at date of trial	Multiplier calculated with allowance for projected mortality from the 1998-based population projections and rate of return of											Age at date of trial
	0.0%	0.5%	1.0%	1.5%	2.0%	2.5%	3.0%	3.5%	4.0%	4.5%	5.0%	
16	38.25	34.79	31.75	29.08	26.73	24.65	22.81	21.17	19.70	18.40	17.22	16
17	37.26	33.97	31.07	28.52	26.26	24.26	22.48	20.90	19.48	18.21	17.07	17
18	36.28	33.15	30.39	27.96	25.79	23.87	22.15	20.62	19.25	18.01	16.90	18
19	35.30	32.34	29.71	27.39	25.32	23.47	21.82	20.34	19.01	17.82	16.74	19
20	34.33	31.52	29.03	26.81	24.83	23.06	21.47	20.05	18.77	17.61	16.56	20
21	33.35	30.70	28.34	26.23	24.34	22.64	21.12	19.75	18.51	17.39	16.38	21
22	32.38	29.88	27.64	25.63	23.83	22.22	20.76	19.44	18.25	17.17	16.19	22
23	31.40	29.04	26.93	25.03	23.32	21.77	20.38	19.12	17.97	16.93	15.98	23
24	30.43	28.21	26.21	24.41	22.79	21.32	19.99	18.78	17.69	16.68	15.77	24
25	29.45	27.37	25.49	23.79	22.25	20.86	19.59	18.44	17.39	16.43	15.55	25
26	28.47	26.52	24.76	23.16	21.71	20.39	19.18	18.08	17.08	16.16	15.31	26
27	27.49	25.68	24.02	22.52	21.15	19.90	18.76	17.71	16.76	15.88	15.07	27
28	26.52	24.82	23.28	21.87	20.58	19.40	18.32	17.33	16.42	15.58	14.81	28
29	25.54	23.96	22.52	21.21	20.00	18.89	17.87	16.94	16.07	15.27	14.54	29
30	24.56	23.10	21.76	20.54	19.41	18.37	17.41	16.53	15.71	14.95	14.25	30
31	23.58	22.23	21.00	19.85	18.80	17.83	16.93	16.10	15.33	14.62	13.95	31
32	22.60	21.36	20.22	19.16	18.18	17.28	16.44	15.66	14.94	14.26	13.64	32
33	21.62	20.48	19.43	18.46	17.55	16.71	15.93	15.21	14.53	13.90	13.31	33
34	20.64	19.60	18.64	17.74	16.91	16.13	15.41	14.73	14.10	13.51	12.96	34
35	19.66	18.71	17.84	17.02	16.25	15.54	14.87	14.25	13.66	13.11	12.59	35
36	18.67	17.82	17.02	16.28	15.58	14.93	14.32	13.74	13.20	12.69	12.21	36
37	17.69	16.92	16.21	15.53	14.90	14.30	13.74	13.22	12.72	12.25	11.81	37
38	16.71	16.02	15.38	14.77	14.20	13.66	13.15	12.67	12.22	11.79	11.39	38
39	15.72	15.12	14.54	14.00	13.49	13.01	12.55	12.11	11.70	11.31	10.94	39
40	14.74	14.21	13.70	13.22	12.77	12.34	11.93	11.54	11.17	10.82	10.48	40
41	13.77	13.30	12.86	12.43	12.03	11.65	11.29	10.94	10.61	10.30	10.00	41
42	12.79	12.39	12.00	11.63	U.28	10.95	10.63	10.33	10.03	9.75	9.49	42
43	11.81	11.47	11.14	10.82	10.52	10.23	9.95	9.69	9.43	9.19	8.96	43
44	10.83	10.54	10.27	10.00	9.74	9.49	9.26	9.03	8.81	8.60	8.40	44
45	9.86	9.62	9.38	9.16	8.95	8.74	8.54	8.35	8.16	7.98	7.81	45
46	8.88	8.68	8.49	8.31	8.14	7.97	7.80	7.64	7.49	7.34	7.19	46
47	7.90	7.74	7.59	7.45	7.31	7.17	7.04	6.91	6.79	6.66	6.55	47
48	6.92	6.80	6.68	6.57	6.46	6.36	6.25	6.15	6.05	5.96	5.86	48
49	5.94	5.85	5.76	5.68	5.60	5.52	5.44	5.37	5.29	5.22	5.15	49
50	4.95	4.89	4.83	4.77	4.72	4.66	4.60	4.55	4.50	4.45	4.40	50
51	3.97	3.93	3.89	3.85	3.81	3.78	3.74	3.71	3.67	3.64	3.60	51
52	2.98	2.96	2.94	2.91	2.89	2.87	2.85	2.83	2.81	2.79	2.77	52
53	1.99	1.98	1.97	1.96	1.95	1.94	1.93	1.92	1.91	1.90	1.90	53
54	1.00	0.99	0.99	0.99	0.99	0.99	0.98	0.98	0.98	0.98	0.97	54

Table 22: Multipliers for loss of earnings to pension age 55 (females)

Age at date of trial	Multiplier calculated with allowance for projected mortality from the 1998-based population projections and rate of return of											Age at date of trial
	0.0%	0.5%	1.0%	1.5%	2.0%	2.5%	3.0%	3.5%	4.0%	4.5%	5.0%	
16	38.60	35.09	32.02	29.32	26.94	24.84	22.97	21.32	19.84	18.52	17.33	16
17	37.61	34.27	31.34	28.76	26.48	24.45	22.65	21.05	19.62	18.33	17.18	17
18	36.61	33.45	30.66	28.19	26.00	24.06	22.32	20.77	19.39	18.14	17.02	18
19	35.62	32.62	29.97	27.61	25.52	23.65	21.98	20.49	19.15	17.94	16.85	19
20	34.63	31.79	29.27	27.03	25.03	23.24	21.63	20.19	18.90	17.73	16.67	20
21	33.64	30.95	28.56	26.43	24.52	22.81	21.27	19.89	18.64	17.51	16.48	21
22	32.65	30.11	27.85	25.83	24.01	22.37	20.90	19.57	18.37	17.28	16.29	22
23	31.65	29.27	27.13	25.21	23.48	21.93	20.52	19.24	18.09	17.04	16.08	23
24	30.66	28.42	26.40	24.59	22.95	21.47	20.12	18.90	17.79	16.78	15.86	24
25	29.67	27.57	25.67	23.95	22.40	21.00	19.72	18.55	17.49	16.52	15.63	25
26	28.67	26.71	24.93	23.31	21.85	20.51	19.30	18.19	17.18	16.25	15.40	26
27	27.68	25.85	24.18	22.66	21.28	20.02	18.87	17.81	16.85	15.96	15.15	27
28	26.69	24.98	23.42	22.00	20.70	19.51	18.42	17.43	16.51	15.66	14.88	28
29	25.70	24.11	22.66	21.33	20.11	19.00	17.97	17.02	16.15	15.35	14.61	29
30	24.71	23.24	21.89	20.65	19.51	18.47	17.50	16.61	15.79	15.02	14.32	30
31	23.72	22.36	21.11	19.96	18.90	17.92	17.02	16.18	15.40	14.68	14.02	31
32	22.73	21.48	20.33	19.26	18.28	17.37	16.52	15.74	15.01	14.33	13.70	32
33	21.74	20.59	19.54	18.55	17.64	16.80	16.01	15.28	14.60	13.96	13.36	33
34	20.75	19.71	18.74	17.83	16.99	16.21	15.48	14.80	14.17	13.57	13.02	34
35	19.76	18.81	17.93	17.10	16.33	15.61	14.94	14.31	13.72	13.17	12.65	35
36	18.77	17.92	17.11	16.36	15.66	15.00	14.38	13.80	13.26	12.75	12.26	36
37	17.79	17.01’	16.29	15.61	14.97	14.37	13.81	13.28	12.78	12.31	11.86	37
38	16.80	16.11	15.46	14.85	14.27	13.73	13.22	12.74	12.28	11.85	11.44	38
39	15.81	15.20	14.62	14.08	13.56	13.07	12.61	12.18	11.76	11.37	11.00	39
40	14.82	14.29	13.78	13.29	12.83	12.40	11.99	11.59	11.22	10.87	10.53	40
41	13.84	13.37	12.92	12.50	12.09	11.71	11.34	10.99	10.66	10.35	10.04	41
42	12.85	12.45	12.06	11.69	11.34	11.00	10.68	10.37	10.08	9.80	9.53	42
43	11.87	11.52	11.19	10.87	10.57	10.28	10.00	9.73	9.48	9.23	8.99	43
44	10.88	10.59	10.31	10.04	9.78	9.53	9.30	9.07	8.85	8.63	8.43	44
45	9.90	9.66	9.42	9.20	8.98	8.77	8.57	8.38	8.19	8.01	7.84	45
46	8.91	8.72	8.53	8.34	8.17	7.99	7.83	7.67	7.51	7.36	7.22	46
47	7.93	7.77	7.62	7.47	7.33	7.19	7.06	6.93	6.81	6.68	6.57	47
48	6.94	6.82	6.70	6.59	6.48	6.37	6.27	6.17	6.07	5.97	5.88	48
49	5.95	5.86	5.78	5.69	5.61	5.53	5.46	5.38	5.31	5.23	5.16	49
50	4.96	4.90	4.84	4.78	4.73	4.67	4.62	4.56	4.51	4.46	4.41	50
51	3.98	3.94	3.90	3.86	3.82	3.79	3.75	3.71	3.68	3.65	3.61	51
52	2.99	2.96	2.94	2.92	2.90	2.88	2.86	2.84	2.82	2.80	2.78	52
53	1.99	1.98	1.97	1.96	1.95	1.94	1.94	1.93	1.92	1.91	1.90	53
54	1.00	1.00	0.99	0.99	0.99	0.99	0.98	0.98	0.98	0.98	0.97	54

Table 23: Multipliers for loss of earnings to pension age 60 (males)

Age at date of trial	Multiplier calculated with allowance for projected mortality from the 1998-based population projections and rate of return of											Age at date of trial
	0.0%	0.5%	1.0%	1.5%	2.0%	2.5%	3.0%	3.5%	4.0%	4.5%	5.0%	
16	42.93	38.59	34.85	31.60	28.79	26.33	24.18	22.29	20.62	19.15	17.84	16
17	41.94	37.79	34.20	31.08	28.36	25.98	23.90	22.06	20.43	19.00	17.72	17
18	40.96	36.99	33.55	30.55	27.93	25.63	23.61	21.82	20.24	18.84	17.59	18
19	39.98	36.20	32.91	30.03	27.50	25.28	23.32	21.59	20.05	18.68	17.45	19
20	39.01	35.40	32.25	29.49	27.06	24.92	23.02	21.34	19.84	18.51	17.32	20
21	38.04	34.61	31.60	28.95	26.61	24.55	22.72	21.09	19.63	18.34	17.17	21
22	37.07	33.80	30.93	28.40	26.16	24.17	22.40	20.83	19.42	18.15	17.02	22
23	36.09	32.99	30.26	27.84	25.69	23.78	22.07	20.55	19.19	17.96	16.86	23
24	35.12	32.18	29.58	27.27	25.21	23.38	21.74	20.27	18.95	17.76	16.69	24
25	34.14	31.36	28.89	26.69	24.72	22.97	21.39	19.98	18.70	17.55	16.51	25
26	33.17	30.54	28.19	26.10	24.23	22.55	21.04	19.67	18.45	17.33	16.33	26
27	32.20	29.71	27.49	25.51	23.72	22.12	20.67	19.36	18.18	17.11	16.13	27
28	31.22	28.88	26.79	24.90	23.20	21.67	20.29	19.04	17.90	16.87	15.93	28
29	30.25	28.05	26.07	24.29	22.68	21.22	19.90	18.70	17.61	16.62	15.71	29
30	29.27	27.21	25.35	23.66	22.14	20.76	19.50	18.36	17.31	16.36	15.49	30
31	28.29	26.36	24.62	23.03	21.59	20.28	19.09	18.00	17.00	16.09	15.25	31
32	27.32	25.51	23.88	22.39	21.03	19.79	18.66	17.63	16.68	15.80	15.00	32
33	26.34	24.66	23.13	21.73	20.46	19.29	18.22	17.24	16.34	15.51	14.74	33
34	25.36	23.80	22.38	21.07	19.88	18.78	17.77	16.84	15.98	15.19	14.46	34
35	24.38	22.94	21.61	20.40	19.28	18.25	17.30	16.43	15.62	14.87	14.17	35
36	23.40	22.07	20.84	19.71	18.67	17.71	16.82	16.00	15.24	14.53	13.87	36
37	22.42	21.19	20.06	19.02	18.05	17.15	16.32	15.55	14.84	14.17	13.55	37
38	21.44	20.31	19.27	18.31	17.42	16.59	15.82	15.10	14.43	13.80	13.22	38
39	20.46	19.43	18.48	17.60	16.77	16.01	15.29	14.62	14.00	13.42	12.87	39
40	19.48	18.55	17.69	16.88	16.12	15.42	14.75	14.14	13.56	13.01	12.50	40
41	18.51	17.67	16.88	16.15	15.46	14.81	14.20	13.63	13.10	12.60	12.12	41
42	17.54	16.78	16.07	15.41	14.78	14.19	13.64	13.12	12.62	12.16	11.72	42
43	16.57	15.89	15.25	14.66	14.09	13.56	13.06	12.58	12.13	11.71	11.31	43
44	15.60	15.00	14.43	13.90	13.39	12.91	12.46	12.03	11.62	11.24	10.87	44
45	14.63	14.10	13.60	13.12	12.67	12.25	11.84	11.46	11.09	10.74	10.41	45
46	13.66	13.20	12.76	12.34	11.94	11.57	11.21	10.86	10.54	10.23	9.93	46
47	12.69	12.29	11.91	11.55	11.20	10.87	10.55	10.25	9.96	9.69	9.42	47
48	11.72	11.38	11.05	10.74	10.44	10.15	9.88	9.62	9.37	9.12	8.89	48
49	10.74	10.46	10.18	9.92	9.66	9.42	9.19	8.96	8.74	8.54	8.33	49
50	9.77	9.53	9.30	9.08	8.87	8.67	8.47	8.28	8.10	7.92	7.75	50
51	8.80	8.61	8.42	8.24	8.07	7.90	7.73	7.58	7.42	7.28	7.13	51
52	7.83	7.67	7.53	7.38	7.24	7.11	6.98	6.85	6.73	6.61	6.49	52
53	6.86	6.74	6.62	6.51	6.41	6.30	6.20	6.10	6.00	5.91	5.82	53
54	5.88	5.80	5.71	5.63	5.55	5.47	5.40	5.32	5.25	5.18	5.11	54
55	4.91	4.85	4.79	4.74	4.68	4.62	4.57	4.52	4.46	4.41	4.36	55
56	3.94	3.90	3.86	3.82	3.79	3.75	3.72	3.68	3.65	3.61	3.58	56
57	2.96	2.94	2.92	2.90	2.88	2.86	2.84	2.82	2.80	2.78	2.76	57
58	1.98	1.97	1.96	1.95	1.94	1.93	1.92	1.92	1.91	1.90	1.89	58
59	1.00	0.99	0.99	0.99	0.99	0.98	0.98	0.98	0.98	0.97	0.97	59

Table 24: Multipilers for loss of earnings to pension age 60 (females)

Age at date of trial	Multiplier calculated with allowance for projected mortality from the 1998-based population projections and rate of return of											Age at date of trial
	0.0%	0.5%	1.0%	1.5%	2.0%	2.5%	3.0%	3.5%	4.0%	4.5%	5.0%	
16	43.38	38.99	35.19	31.90	29.05	26.56	24.38	22.47	20.78	19.29	17.97	16
17	42.39	38.18	34.54	31.38	28.62	26.21	24.10	22.24	20.60	19.14	17.84	17
18	41.40	37.38	33.89	30.85	28.19	25.86	23.81	22.00	20.40	18.98	17.72	18
19	40.41	36.57	33.23	30.31	27.75	25.50	23.52	21.76	20.21	18.82	17.58	19
20	39.42	35.76	32.57	29.77	27.30	25.13	23.21	21.51	20.00	18.65	17.44	20
21	38.43	34.95	31.89	29.21	26.85	24.76	22.90	21.25	19.78	18.47	17.29	21
22	37.43	34.12	31.21	28.65	26.38	24.37	22.58	20.98	19.56	18.28	17.14	22
23	36.44	33.30	30.53	28.08	25.90	23.97	22.25	20.71	19.33	18.09	16.97	23
24	35.45	32.47	29.84	27.50	25.42	23.56	21.90	20.42	19.08	17.88	16.80	24
25	34.46	31.64	29.13	26.91	24.92	23.14	21.55	20.12	18.83	17.67	16.62	25
26	33.46	30.80	28.43	26.31	24.41	22.72	21.19	19.81	18.57	17.45	16.43	26
27	32.47	29.96	27.71	25.70	23.90	22.28	20.81	19.49	18.30	17.21	16.23	27
28	31.48	29.11	26.99	25.09	23.37	21.83	20.43	19.16	18.02	16.97	16.02	28
29	30.49	28.27	26.27	24.47	22.84	21.37	20.03	18.82	17.72	16.72	15.80	29
30	29.50	27.41	25.53	23.83	22.29	20.90	19.63	18.47	17.42	16.46	15.57	30
31	28.51	26.56	24.79	23.19	21.74	20.42	19.21	18.11	17.10	16.18	15.33	31
32	27.52	25.70	24.05	22.54	21.17	19.92	18.78	17.73	16.77	15.89	15.08	32
33	26.53	24.84	23.29	21.88	20.60	19.42	18.34	17.34	16.43	15.59	14.82	33
34	25.55	23.97	22.53	21.21	20.01	18.90	17.88	16.94	16.08	15.28	14.54	34
35	24.56	23.10	21.76	20.54	19.41	18.37	17.41	16.53	15.71	14.95	14.25	35
36	23.57	22.23	20.99	19.85	18.80	17.83	16.93	16.10	15.33	14.61	13.95	36
37	22.59	21.35'	20.21	19.15	18.18	17.27	16.43	15.65	14.93	14.26	13.63	37
38	21.60	20.47	19.42	18.44	17.54	16.70	15.92	15.20	14.52	13.89	13.30	38
39	20.62	19.58	18.62	17.73	16.90	16.12	15.40	14.72	14.09	13.50	12.95	39
40	19.63	18.69	17.82	17.00	16.24	15.52	14.86	14.23	13.65	13.10	12.58	40
41	18.65	17.80	17.01	16.26	15.57	14.91	14.30	13.73	13.19	12.68	12.20	41
42	17.67	16.91	16.19	15.52	14.88	14.29	13.73	13.20	12.71	12.24	11.80	42
43	16.69	16.01	15.36	14.76	14.19	13.65	13.14	12.66	12.21	11.78	11.38	43
44	15.71	15.10	14.53	13.99	13.48	13.00	12.54	12.11	11.69	11.31	10.94	44
45	14.73	14.20	13.69	13.21	12.76	12.33	11.92	11.53	11.16	10.81	10.47	45
46	13.75	13.28	12.84	12.42	12.02	11.64	11.28	10.93	120.60	10.29	9.99	46
47	12.77	12.37	11.98	11.62	11.27	10.94	10.62	10.31	10.02	9.74	9.48	47
48	11.79	11.45	11.12	10.81	10.50	10.22	9.94	9.67	9.42	9.18	8.94	48
49	10.81	10.52	10.25	9.98	9.72	9.48	9.24	9.01	8.80	8.59	8.38	49
50	9.84	9.60	9.37	9.14	8.93	8.72	8.52	8.33	8.15	7.97	7.80	50
51	8.86	8.66	8.48	8.29	8.12	7.95	7.78	7.63	7.47	7.32	7.18	51
52	7.88	7.73	7.58	7.43	7.29	7.15	7.02	6.89	6.77	6.65	6.53	52
53	6.90	6.78	6.67	6.56	6.45	6.34	6.24	6.14	6.04	5.94	5.85	53
54	5.92	5.84	5.75	5.67	5.59	5.51	5.43	5.35	5.28	5.21	5.14	54
55	4.94	4.88	4.82	4.76	4.71	4.65	4.60	4.54	4.49	4.44	4.39	55
56	3.96	3.92	3.88	3.85	3.81	3.77	3.74	3.70	3.67	3.63	3.60	56
57	2.98	2.95	2.93	2.91	2.89	2.87	2.85	2.83	2.81	2.79	2.77	57
58	1.99	1.98	1.97	1.96	1.95	1.94	1.93	1.92	1.91	1.90	1.90	58
59	1.00	0.99	0.99	0.99	0.99	0.98	0.98	0.98	0.98	0.98	0.97	59

Table 25: Multipliers for loss of earnings to pension age 65 (males)

Age at date of trial	Multiplier calculated with allowance for projected mortality from the 1998-based population projections and rate of return of											Age at date of trial
	0.0%	0.5%	1.0%	1.5%	2.0%	2.5%	3.0%	3.5%	4.0%	4.5%	5.0%	
16	47.44	42.17	37.69	33.87	30.59	27.76	25.32	23.20	21.35	19.74	18.31	16
17	46.45	41.39	37.07	33.38	30.20	27.45	25.07	23.00	21.20	19.61	18.21	17
18	45.48	40.62	36.46	32.89	29.81	27.14	24.83	22.80	21.03	19.48	18.10	18
19	44.51	39.84	35.84	32.39	29.41	26.83	24.57	22.60	20.87	19.35	18.00	19
20	43.53	39.07	35.22	31.89	29.01	26.50	24.31	22.39	20.70	19.21	17.89	20
21	42.57	38.29	34.59	31.39	28.60	26.17	24.05	22.17	20.53	19.07	17.77	21
22	41.60	37.50	33.96	30.88	28.19	25.84	23.77	21.95	20.34	18.92	17.65	22
23	40.62	36.71	33.32	30.35	27.76	25.49	23.49	21.72	20.15	18.76	17.52	23
24	39.65	35.92	32.67	29.82	27.33	25.13	23.19	21.48	19.95	18.60	17.38	24
25	38.68	35.12	32.01	29.28	26.88	24.76	22.89	21.23	19.75	18.42	17.24	25
26	37.71	34.32	31.35	28.74	26.43	24.39	22.58	20.97	19.53	18.25	17.09	26
27	36.73	33.51	30.68	28.18	25.97	24.01	22.26	20.70	19.31	18.06	16.94	27
28	35.76	32.70	30.01	27.62	25.50	23.61	21.93	20.43	19.08	17.86	16.77	28
29	34.79	31.89	29.32	27.05	25.02	23.21	21.59	20.14	18.84	17.66	16.60	29
30	33.81	31.07	28.64	26.47	24.53	22.80	21.24	19.85	18.59	17.45	16.42	30
31	32.84	30.25	27.94	25.88	24.03	22.37	20.88	19.54	18.32	17.23	16.23	31
32	31.86	29.42	27.23	25.28	23.52	21.94	20.51	19.22	18.05	16.99	16.03	32
33	30.89	28.59	26.52	24.67	23.00	21.49	20.13	18.89	17.77	16.75	15.82	33
34	29.91	27.75	25.80	24.05	22.47	21.03	19.73	18.55	17.48	16.50	15.60	34
35	28.93	26.90	25.07	23.42	21.92	20.56	19.32	18.20	17.17	16.23	15.37	35
36	27.95	26.05	24.34	22.78	21.37	20.08	18.90	17.83	16.85	15.95	15.12	36
37	26.97	25.20	23.60	22.13	20.80	19.58	18.47	17.45	16.52	15.66	14.87	37
38	25.99	24.35	22.85	21.48	20.22	19.08	18.03	17.06	16.17	15.36	14.60	38
39	25.01	23.49	22.09	20.81	19.64	18.56	17.57	16.66	15.82	15.04	14.32	39
40	24.04	22.63	21.33	20.14	19.04	18.03	17.10	16.24	15.45	14.71	14.03	40
41	23.07	21.77	20.57	19.46	18.44	17.50	16.62	15.82	15.07	14.37	13.73	41
42	22.10	20.91	19.80	18.77	17.83	16.95	16.13	15.38	14.67	14.02	13.41	42
43	21.14	20.04	19.02	18.08	17.20	16.39	15.63	14.92	14.27	13.65	13.08	43
44	20.17	19.17	18.24	17.37	16.56	15.81	15.11	14.45	13.84	13.27	12.73	44
45	19.21	18.30	17.45	16.66	15.92	15.22	14.58	13.97	13.40	12.87	12.37	45
46	18.25	17.42	16.65	15.93	15.26	14.62	14.03	13.47	12.95	12.45	11.99	46
47	17.28	16.54	15.85	15.20	14.58	14.01	13.46	12.95	12.47	12.02	11.59	47
48	16.32	15.66	15.03	14.45	13.90	13.37	12.88	12.42	11.98	11.56	11.17	48
49	15.35	14.77	14.21	13.69	13.19	12.73	12.28	11.86	11.46	11.09	10.73	49
50	14.39	13.87	13.38	12.92	12.48	12.06	11.67	11.29	10.93	10.59	10.27	50
51	13.42	12.97	12.54	12.14	11.75	11.38	11.03	10.70	10.38	10.07	9.78	51
52	12.46	12.07	11.70	11.35	11.01	10.69	10.38	10.09	9.80	9.54	9.28	52
53	11.50	11.17	10.85	10.55	10.26	9.98	9.71	9.46	9.21	8.98	8.75	53
54	10.55	10.27	10.00	9.74	9.50	9.26	9.03	8.81	8.60	8.40	8.20	54
55	9.60	9.37	9.14	8.93	8.72	8.52	8.33	8.14	7.96	7.79	7.62	55
56	8.65	8.46	8.28	8.10	7.93	7.77	7.61	7.45	7.31	7.16	7.02	56

Table 25: *continued*

Age at date of trial	Multiplier calculated with allowance for projected mortality from the 1998-based population projections and rate of return of											Age at date of trial
	0.0%	0.5%	1.0%	1.5%	2.0%	2.5%	3.0%	3.5%	4.0%	4.5%	5.0%	
57	7.70	7.55	7.40	7.26	7.13	7.00	6.87	6.74	6.62	6.51	6.39	57
58	6.75	6.64	6.53	6.42	6.31	6.21	6.11	6.01	5.92	5.82	5.73	58
59	5.80	5.72	5.64	5.56	5.48	5.40	5.32	5.25	5.18	5.11	5.04	59
60	4.85	4.79	4.74	4.68	4.62	4.57	4.52	4.46	4.41	4.36	4.31	60
61	3.90	3.86	3.82	3.79	3.75	3.72	3.68	3.65	3.61	3.58	3.55	61
62	2.94	2.92	2.90	2.88	2.85	2.83	2.81	2.79	2.77	2.76	2.74	62
63	1.97	1.96	1.95	1.94	1.93	1.92	1.91	1.91	1.90	1.89	1.88	63
64	0.99	0.99	0.99	0.98	0.98	0.98	0.98	0.98	0.97	0.97	0.97	64

Table 26: Multipliers for loss of earnings to pension age 65 (females)

Age at date of trial	Multiplier calculated with allowance for projected mortality from the 1998-based population projections and rate of return of											Age at date of trial
	0.0%	0.5%	1.0%	1.5%	2.0%	2.5%	3.0%	3.5%	4.0%	4.5%	5.0%	
16	48.06	42.69	38.13	34.24	30.91	28.04	25.56	23.41	21.54	19.89	18.45	16
17	47.07	41.91	37.52	33.76	30.52	27.74	25.32	23.22	21.38	19.77	18.35	17
18	46.08	41.13	36.89	33.26	30.13	27.42	25.07	23.02	21.22	19.64	18.25	18
19	45.08	40.34	36.27	32.76	29.73	27.10	24.81	22.81	21.06	19.51	18.14	19
20	44.09	39.54	35.63	32.25	29.32	26.77	24.55	22.60	20.88	19.37	18.03	20
21	43.10	38.75	34.99	31.73	28.90	26.44	24.27	22.38	20.70	19.22	17.91	21
22	42.11	37.95	34.34	31.21	28.48	26.09	23.99	22.15	20.52	19.07	17.79	22
23	41.12	37.14	33.69	30.68	28.04	25.73	23.70	21.91	20.32	18.91	17.65	23
24	40.12	36.33	33.02	30.13	27.60	25.37	23.40	21.66	20.12	18.74	17.52	24
25	39.13	35.52	32.36	29.58	27.15	25.00	23.10	21.41	19.91	18.57	17.37	25
26	38.14	34.70	31.68	29.03	26.69	24.62	22.78	21.15	19.69	18.39	17.22	26
27	37.15	33.88	31.00	28.46	26.22	24.22	22.45	20.87	19.46	18.20	17.06	27
28	36.16	33.05	30.31	27.89	25.74	23.82	22.12	20.59	19.23	18.00	16.89	28
29	35.17	32.22	29.62	27.31	25.25	23.41	21.77	20.30	18.98	17.79	16.72	29
30	34.18	31.39	28.92	26.72	24.75	23.00	21.42	20.00	18.73	17.58	16.54	30
31	33.19	30.56	28.21	26.12	24.25	22.57	21.05	19.69	18.46	17.35	16.34	31
32	32.20	29.72	27.50	25.51	23.73	22.13	20.68	19.37	18.19	17.12	16.14	32
33	31.21	28.88	26.78	24.90	23.21	21.68	20.29	19.04	17.91	16.87	15.93	33
34	30.22	28.03	26.06	24.28	22.67	21.22	19.90	18.70	17.61	16.62	15.71	34
35	29.24	27.18	25.32	23.64	22.12	20.74	19.49	18.35	17.31	16.35	15.48	35
36	28.25	26.33	24.59	23.00	21.57	20.26	19.07	17.98	16.99	16.08	15.24	36
37	27.27	25.47	23.84	22.36	21.00	19.77	18.64	17.61	16.66	15.79	14.99	37
38	26.28	24.61	23.09	21.70	20.43	19.26	18.20	17.22	16.31	15.49	14.72	38
39	25.30	23.75	22.33	21.03	19.84	18.74	17.74	16.81	15.96	15.17	14.44	39
40	24.32	22.88	21.57	20.35	19.24	18.22	17.27	16.40	15.59	14.84	14.15	40
41	23.34	22.01	20.79	19.67	18.63	17.67	16.79	15.97	15.21	14.50	13.85	41
42	22.36	21.14	20.02	18.98	18.01	17.12	16.29	15.53	14.81	14.15	13.53	42
43	21.38	20.27	19.23	18.27	17.38	16.55	15.78	15.07	14.40	13.78	13.20	43
44	20.41	19.39	18.44	17.56	16.74	15.97	15.26	14.60	13.97	13.39	12.85	44
45	19.43	18.51	17.64	16.84	16.08	15.38	14.72	14.11	13.53	12.99	12.48	45
46	18.46	17.62	16.84	16.10	15.42	14.77	14.17	13.60	13.07	12.57	12.10	46
47	17.48	16.73	16.02	15.36	14.74	14.15	13.60	13.08	12.59	12.13	11.70	47
48	16.51	15.84	15.21	14.61	14.05	13.52	13.02	12.55	12.10	11.68	11.28	48
49	15.54	14.94	14.38	13.85	13.34	12.87	12.42	11.99	11.58	11.20	10.84	49
50	14.57	14.04	13.55	13.07	12.63	12.20	11.80	11.42	11.05	10.71	10.38	50
51	13.60	13.14	12.71	12.29	11.90	11.52	11.16	10.82	10.50	10.19	9.89	51
52	12.63	12.24	11.86	11.50	11.16	10.83	10.51	10.21	9.93	9.65	9.39	52
53	11.67	11.33	11.01	10.70	10.40	10.11	9.84	9.58	9.33	9.09	8.86	53
54	10.70	10.42	10.14	9.88	9.63	9.39	9.15	8.93	8.71	8.51	8.31	54
55	9.74	9.50	9.27	9.05	8.84	8.64	8.44	8.25	8.07	7.90	7.72	55
56	8.77	8.58	8.40	8.22	8.04	7.88	7.71	7.56	7.40	7.26	7.12	56

Table 26: *continued*

Age at date of trial	Multiplier calculated with allowance for projected mortality from the 1998-based population projections and rate of return of											Age at date of trial
	0.0%	0.5%	1.0%	1.5%	2.0%	2.5%	3.0%	3.5%	4.0%	4.5%	5.0%	
57	7.81	7.66	7.51	7.37	7.23	7.09	6.96	6.84	6.71	6.59	6.48	57
58	6.84	6.73	6.61	6.50	6.39	6.29	6.19	6.09	5.99	5.90	5.81	58
59	5.88	5.79	5.71	5.63	5.55	5.47	5.39	5.32	5.24	5.17	5.10	59
60	4.91	4.85	4.79	4.73	4.68	4.62	4.57	4.51	4.46	4.41	4.36	60
61	3.94	3.90	3.86	3.82	3.79	3.75	3.72	3.68	3.65	3.61	3.58	61
62	2.96	2.94	2.92	2.90	2.88	2.86	2.84	2.82	2.80	2.78	2.76	62
63	1.98	1.97	1.96	1.95	1.94	1.93	1.93	1.92	1.91	1.90	1.89	63
64	1.00	0.99	0.99	0.99	0.99	0.98	0.98	0.98	0.98	0.97	0.97	64

Table 27: Multipliers for loss of earnings to pension age 70 (males)

Age at date of trial	Multiplier calculated with allowance for projected mortality from the 1998-based population projections and rate of return of											Age at date of trial
	0.0%	0.5%	1.0%	1.5%	2.0%	2.5%	3.0%	3.5%	4.0%	4.5%	5.0%	
16	51.72	45.48	40.25	35.85	32.13	28.96	26.26	23.93	21.92	20.18	18.66	16
17	50.73	44.71	39.66	35.39	31.77	28.68	26.04	23.76	21.79	20.07	18.57	17
18	49.75	43.95	39.07	34.93	31.41	28.40	25.82	23.58	21.65	19.96	18.49	18
19	48.78	43.20	38.48	34.47	31.05	28.12	25.59	23.41	21.51	19.85	18.40	19
20	47.81	42.44	37.88	34.00	30.68	27.83	25.36	23.23	21.37	19.74	18.31	20
21	46.84	41.68	37.28	33.53	30.31	27.53	25.13	23.04	21.22	19.62	18.21	21
22	45.87	40.91	36.68	33.05	29.93	27.23	24.89	22.85	21.06	19.50	18.11	22
23	44.90	40.14	36.06	32.56	29.54	26.92	24.64	22.65	20.90	19.37	18.01	23
24	43.93	39.36	35.44	32.06	29.14	26.59	24.38	22.44	20.73	19.23	17.90	24
25	42.96	38.59	34.82	31.56	28.73	26.27	24.11	22.22	20.56	19.09	17.78	25
26	41.99	37.80	34.18	31.05	28.31	25.93	23.84	22.00	20.38	18.94	17.66	26
27	41.02	37.01	33.55	30.53	27.89	25.58	23.56	21.77	20.19	18.78	17.53	27
28	40.04	36.22	32.90	30.00	27.46	25.23	23.27	21.53	19.99	18.62	17.40	28
29	39.07	35.43	32.25	29.46	27.02	24.87	22.97	21.28	19.79	18.45	17.26	29
30	38.10	34.63	31.59	28.92	26.57	24.50	22.66	21.03	19.57	18.27	17.11	30
31	37.12	33.82	30.92	28.37	26.11	24.11	22.34	20.76	19.35	18.09	16.96	31
32	36.15	33.01	30.25	27.81	25.64	23.72	22.01	20.49	19.12	17.90	16.79	32
33	35.17	32.20	29.57	27.23	25.16	23.32	21.68	20.20	18.88	17.69	16.62	33
34	34.20	31.38	28.88	26.65	24.68	22.91	21.33	19.91	18.63	17.48	16.44	34
35	33.22	30.55	28.18	26.07	24.18	22.49	20.97	19.60	18.37	17.26	16.25	35
36	32.24	29.72	27.47	25.47	23.67	22.05	20.60	19.29	18.10	17.03	16.05	36
37	31.26	28.88	26.76	24.86	23.15	21.61	20.21	18.96	17.82	16.78	15.84	37
38	30.28	28.05	26.04	24.24	22.62	21.15	19.82	18.62	17.52	16.53	15.62	38
39	29.30	27.21	25.32	23.62	22.08	20.69	19.42	18.27	17.22	16.27	15.39	39
40	28.33	26.37	24.59	22.99	21.53	20.21	19.01	17.91	16.91	16.00	15.16	40
41	27.36	25.53	23.86	22.35	20.98	19.73	18.59	17.54	16.59	15.71	14.91	41
42	26.40	24.69	23.13	21.71	20.42	19.24	18.16	17.17	16.26	15.42	14.65	42
43	25.43	23.84	22.39	21.06	19.85	18.73	17.71	16.78	15.91	15.12	14.38	43
44	24.47	22.99	21.64	20.40	19.27	18.22	17.26	16.37	15.56	14.80	14.10	44
45	23.51	22.14	20.89	19.74	18.67	17.70	16.79	15.96	15.19	14.47	13.81	45
46	22.55	21.29	20.13	19.06	18.07	17.16	16.31	15.53	14.80	14.13	13.50	46
47	21.59	20.43	19.36	18.37	17.46	16.61	15.82	15.09	14.40	13.77	13.18	47
48	20.63	19.57	18.58	17.67	16.83	16.04	15.31	14.63	13.99	13.39	12.84	48
49	19.66	18.70	17.80	16.96	16.19	15.46	14.78	14.15	13.56	13.00	12.48	49
50	18.70	17.83	17.01	16.25	15.53	14.87	14.24	13.66	13.11	12.59	12.11	50
51	17.74	16.95	16.21	15.52	14.87	14.26	13.69	13.15	12.65	12.17	11.72	51
52	16.79	16.08	15.41	14.79	14.20	13.64	13.12	12.63	12.17	11.73	11.32	52
53	15.84	15.21	14.61	14.05	13.52	13.02	12.54	12.10	11.67	11.27	10.90	53
54	14.89	14.33	13.80	13.30	12.83	12.38	11.95	11.55	11.17	10.80	10.46	54
55	13.96	13.46	12.99	12.55	12.13	11.73	11.35	10.98	10.64	10.31	10.00	55
56	13.02	12.59	12.18	11.79	11.42	11.06	10.73	10.41	10.10	9.81	9.53	56

Table 27: *continued*

Age at date of trial	Multiplier calculated with allowance for projected mortality from the 1998-based population projections and rate of return of											Age at date of trial
	0.0%	0.5%	1.0%	1.5%	2.0%	2.5%	3.0%	3.5%	4.0%	4.5%	5.0%	
57	12.09	11.72	11.37	11.03	10.70	10.39	10.10	9.81	9.54	9.29	9.04	57
58	11.17	10.86	10.55	10.26	9.98	9.71	9.45	9.21	8.97	8.74	8.53	58
59	10.26	9.99	9.73	9.48	9.25	9.02	8.80	8.58	8.38	8.18	8.00	59
60	9.35	9.12	8.91	8.70	8.50	8.31	8.12	7.94	7.77	7.60	7.44	60
61	8.43	8.25	8.08	7.91	7.74	7.58	7.43	7.28	7.14	7.00	6.86	61
62	7.52	7.38	7.24	7.10	6.97	6.84	6.72	6.60	6.48	6.37	6.26	62
63	6.61	6.50	6.39	6.28	6.18	6.08	5.98	5.89	5.80	5.71	5.62	63
64	5.69	5.61	5.53	5.45	5.37	5.30	5.22	5.15	5.08	5.01	4.95	64
65	4.77	4.71	4.65	4.60	4.54	4.49	4.44	4.39	4.34	4.29	4.24	65
66	3.84	3.80	3.76	3.73	3.69	3.66	3.62	3.59	3.56	3.52	3.49	66
67	2.90	2.88	2.86	2.84	2.82	2.80	2.78	2.76	2.74	2.72	2.70	67
68	1.95	1.94	1.93	1.92	1.91	1.90	1.90	1.89	1.88	1.87	1.86	68
69	0.99	0.98	0.98	0.98	0.98	0.97	0.97	0.97	0.97	0.97	0.96	69

Table 28: Multipliers for loss of earnings to pension age 70 (females)

Age at date of trial	Multiplier calculated with allowance for projected mortality from the 1998-based population projections and rate of return of											Age at date of trial
	0.0%	0.5%	1.0%	1.5%	2.0%	2.5%	3.0%	3.5%	4.0%	4.5%	5.0%	
16	52.57	46.18	40.84	36.34	32.54	29.31	26.55	24.18	22.14	20.36	18.82	16
17	51.58	45.42	40.25	35.88	32.18	29.03	26.33	24.01	22.01	20.26	18.74	17
18	50.58	44.65	39.65	35.42	31.82	28.75	26.11	23.84	21.87	20.15	18.65	18
19	49.59	43.88	39.05	34.95	31.46	28.46	25.89	23.66	21.73	20.04	18.57	19
20	48.60	43.10	38.44	34.47	31.08	28.17	25.66	23.48	21.58	19.93	18.48	20
21	47.61	42.32	37.83	33.99	30.70	27.87	25.42	23.29	21.43	19.81	18.38	21
22	46.62	41.54	37.21	33.50	30.31	27.56	25.17	23.09	21.28	19.68	18.28	22
23	45.63	40.75	36.58	33.00	29.91	27.24	24.91	22.89	21.11	19.55	18.17	23
24	44.63	39.96	35.95	32.49	29.51	26.91	24.65	22.68	20.94	19.41	18.06	24
25	43.64	39.16	35.31	31.98	29.09	26.58	24.38	22.46	20.76	19.27	17.94	25
26	42.65	38.36	34.66	31.46	28.67	26.23	24.10	22.23	20.58	19.11	17.82	26
27	41.65	37.56	34.01	30.93	28.24	25.88	23.82	22.00	20.39	18.96	17.69	27
28	40.66	36.75	33.35	30.39	27.80	25.52	23.52	21.75	20.19	18.79	17.55	28
29	39.67	35.94	32.69	29.85	27.35	25.16	23.22	21.50	19.98	18.62	17.41	29
30	38.68	35.13	32.02	29.30	26.90	24.78	22.91	21.25	19.77	18.44	17.26	30
31	37.69	34.31	31.35	28.74	26.43	24.40	22.59	20.98	19.54	18.26	17.11	31
32	36.70	33.49	30.67	28.17	25.96	24.00	22.26	20.70	19.31	18.06	16.94	32
33	35.71	32.67	29.98	27.60	25.48	23.60	21.92	20.42	19.07	17.86	16.77	33
34	34.73	31.84	29.28	27.01	24.99	23.19	21.57	20.13	18.82	17.65	16.59	34
35	33.74	31.01	28.58	26.42	24.49	22.76	21.22	19.82	18.57	17.43	16.41	35
36	32.76	30.18	27.88	25.82	23.98	22.33	20.85	19.51	18.30	17.20	16.21	36
37	31.77	29.34	27.17	25.22	23.47	21.89	20.47	19.19	18.02	16.97	16.01	37
38	30.79	28.50	26.45	24.60	22.94	21.44	20.08	18.85	17.73	16.72	15.79	38
39	29.81	27.66	25.72	23.98	22.40	20.98	19.68	18.51	17.44	16.46	15.57	39
40	28.83	26.81	24.99	23.35	21.86	20.50	19.27	18.15	17.13	16.19	15.33	40
41	27.85	25.96	24.26	22.71	21.30	20.02	18.85	17.78	16.81	15.91	15.09	41
42	26.87	25.11	23.51	22.06	20.74	19.52	18.42	17.40	16.47	15.62	14.83	42
43	25.89	24.26	22.77	21.40	20.16	19.02	17.97	17.01	16.13	15.32	14.57	43
44	24.92	23.40	22.01	20.74	19.57	18.50	17.52	16.61	15.77	15.00	14.29	44
45	23.95	22.54	21.25	20.07	18.98	17.97	17.05	16.19	15.40	14.67	13.99	45
46	22.97	21.68	20.48	19.39	18.37	17.43	16.57	15.76	15.02	14.33	13.69	46
47	22.00	20.81	19.71	18.69	17.75	16.88	16.07	15.32	14.62	13.97	13.37	47
48	21.04	19.94	18.93	18.00	17.13	16.32	15.56	14.86	14.21	13.60	13.03	48
49	20.07	19.07	18.15	17.29	16.49	15.74	15.04	14.39	13.78	13.21	12.68	49
50	19.10	18.20	17.36	16.57	15.84	15.15	14.51	13.91	13.34	12.81	12.31	50
51	18.14	17.33	16.56	15.85	15.18	14.55	13.96	13.40	12.88	12.39	11.93	51
52	17.18	16.45	15.76	15.11	14.51	13.93	13.39	12.89	12.41	11.96	11.53	52
53	16.23	15.57	14.95	14.37	13.82	13.31	12.82	12.36	11.92	11.51	11.12	53
54	15.27	14.69	14.14	13.62	13.13	12.66	12.22	11.81	11.41	11.04	10.68	54
55	14.32	13.81	13.32	12.86	12.42	12.01	11.62	11.24	10.89	10.55	10.22	55
56	13.37	12.92	12.50	12.09	11.71	11.34	10.99	10.66	10.34	10.04	9.75	56

Table 28: *continued*

Age at date of trial	Multiplier calculated with allowance for projected mortality from the 1998-based population projections and rate of return of											Age at date of trial
	0.0%	0.5%	1.0%	1.5%	2.0%	2.5%	3.0%	3.5%	4.0%	4.5%	5.0%	
57	12.42	12.04	11.67	11.32	10.98	10.66	10.35	10.06	9.78	9.51	9.25	57
58	11.48	11.15	10.83	10.53	10.24	9.96	9.69	9.44	9.19	8.96	8.73	58
59	10.54	10.26	9.99	9.73	9.48	9.25	9.02	8.80	8.59	8.38	8.19	59
60	9.59	9.36	9.14	8.92	8.72	8.52	8.33	8.14	7.96	7.79	7.62	60
61	8.65	8.46	8.28	8.10	7.93	7.77	7.61	7.46	7.31	7.16	7.02	61
62	7.71	7.56	7.41	7.27	7.14	7.00	6.87	6.75	6.63	6.51	6.40	62
63	6.76	6.65	6.53	6.42	6.32	6.22	6.12	6.02	5.92	5.83	5.74	63
64	5.81	5.73	5.64	5.56	5.48	5.41	5.33	5.26	5.19	5.12	5.05	64
65	4.86	4.80	4.74	4.68	4.63	4.57	4.52	4.47	4.42	4.37	4.32	65
66	3.90	3.86	3.83	3.79	3.75	3.72	3.68	3.65	3.61	3.58	3.55	66
67	2.94	2.92	2.90	2.88	2.85	2.83	2.81	2.79	2.77	2.76	2.74	67
68	1.97	1.96	1.95	1.94	1.93	1.92	1.91	1.90	1.90	1.89	1.88	68
69	0.99	0.99	0.99	0.98	0.98	0.98	0.98	0.98	0.97	0.97	0.97	69

Table 29: Multipliers for toss of pension commencing age 55 (males)

Age at date of trial	Multiplier calculated with allowance for projected mortality from the 1998-based population projections and rate of return of											Age at date of trial
	0.0%	0.5%	1.0%	1.5%	2.0%	2.5%	3.0%	3.5%	4.0%	4.5%	5.0%	
0	25.94	18.26	12.90	9.16	6.53	4.67	3.35	2.42	1.75	1.27	0.93	0
1	26.07	18.44	13.10	9.34	6.69	4.81	3.47	2.52	1.83	1.33	0.98	1
2	26.07	18.53	13.23	9.48	6.83	4.93	3.58	2.60	1.90	1.39	1.03	2
3	26.07	18.63	13.36	9.63	6.96	5.06	3.68	2.70	1.98	1.46	1.08	3
4	26.07	18.72	13.50	9.77	7.10	5.18	3.80	2.79	2.06	1.52	1.13	4
5	26.07	18.81	13.63	9.92	7.24	5.31	3.91	2.89	2.14	1.59	1.19	5
6	26.06	18.90	13.76	10.06	7.39	5.44	4.03	2.99	2.23	1.66	1.25	6
7	26.06	18.99	13.90	10.21	7.53	5.58	4.15	3.09	2.31	1.74	1.31	7
8	26.05	19.08	14.03	10.36	7.68	5.72	4.27	3.20	2.41	1.82	1.37	8
9	26.05	19.17	14.17	10.52	7.83	5.86	4.40	3.31	2.50	1.90	1.44	9
10	26.04	19.26	14.31	10.67	7.99	6.00	4.53	3.43	2.60	1.98	1.51	10
11	26.03	19.35	14.45	10.83	8.15	6.15	4.66	3.54	2.70	2.07	1.59	11
12	26.03	19.45	14.59	10.99	8.31	6.30	4.80	3.67	2.81	2.16	1.67	12
13	26.02	19.54	14.73	11.15	8.47	6.46	4.94	3.80	2.92	2.26	1.75	13
14	26.01	19.63	14.88	11.31	8.64	6.62	5.09	3.93	3.04	2.36	1.84	14
15	26.01	19.73	15.02	11.48	8.81	6.78	5.24	4.06	3.16	2.47	1.93	15
16	26.00	19.82	15.17	11.65	8.98	6.95	5.40	4.21	3.29	2.58	2.03	16
17	26.00	19.92	15.32	11.83	9.16	7.13	5.56	4.35	3.42	2.69	2.13	17
18	26.00	20.02	15.47	12.00	9.35	7.30	5.73	4.51	3.56	2.81	2.23	18
19	26.00	20.12	15.63	12.19	9.54	7.49	5.90	4.66	3.70	2.94	2.35	19
20	26.01	20.23	15.79	12.37	9.73	7.68	6.08	4.83	3.85	3.08	2.47	20
21	26.01	20.33	15.95	12.56	9.93	7.87	6.26	5.00	4.00	3.22	2.59	21
22	26.02	20.44	16.12	12.75	10.13	8.07	6.45	5.18	4.17	3.36	2.72	22
23	26.02	20.54	16.28	12.95	10.33	8.28	6.65	5.36	4.33	3.51	2.86	23
24	26.03	20.65	16.44	13.14	10.54	8.48	6.85	5.55	4.51	3.67	3.00	24
25	26.03	20.75	16.61	13.34	10.75	8.70	7.06	5.74	4.69	3.84	3.15	25
26	26.03	20.86	16.78	13.54	10.97	8.92	7.27	5.95	4.88	4.01	3.31	26
27	26.03	20.97	16.95	13.75	11.19	9.14	7.49	6.16	5.07	4.19	3.48	27
28	26.03	21.07	17.12	13.96	11.42	9.37	7.72	6.37	5.28	4.38	3.65	28
29	26.03	21.18	17.29	14.17	11.65	9.61	7.95	6.60	5.49	4.58	3.83	29
30	26.03	21.28	17.46	14.38	11.88	9.85	8.19	6.83	5.71	4.79	4.03	30
31	26.03	21.39	17.64	14.60	12.12	10.09	8.43	7.07	5.94	5.00	4.23	31
32	26.02	21.49	17.81	14.81	12.36	10.35	8.69	7.32	6.18	5.23	4.44	32
33	26.02	21.60	17.99	15.04	12.61	10.60	8.95	7.57	6.42	5.47	4.66	33
34	26.01	21.70	18.17	15.26	12.86	10.87	9.22	7.84	6.68	5.71	4.90	34
35	26.00	21.80	18.34	15.48	13.11	11.14	9.49	8.11	6.95	5.97	5.14	35
36	25.99	21.90	18.52	15.71	13.37	11.42	9.77	8.39	7.23	6.24	5.40	36
37	25.98	22.00	18.70	15.94	13.64	11.70	10.07	8.68	7.51	6.52	5.67	37
38	25.97	22.11	18.88	16.18	13.90	11.99	10.37	8.99	7.81	6.81	5.95	38
39	25.96	22.21	19.06	16.42	14.18	12.29	10.68	9.30	8.13	7.12	6.25	39
40	25.95	22.31	19.25	16.66	14.46	12.59	11.00	9.63	8.45	7.44	6.56	40

Table 29: *continued*

Age at date of trial	Multiplier calculated with allowance for projected mortality from the 1998-based population projections and rate of return of											Age at date of trial
	0.0%	0.5%	1.0%	1.5%	2.0%	2.5%	3.0%	3.5%	4.0%	4.5%	5.0%	
41	25.95	22.42	19.44	16.91	14.75	12.91	11.33	9.97	8.79	7.78	6.89	41
42	25.94	22.53	19.64	17.16	15.05	13.23	11.67	10.32	9.15	8.13	7.24	42
43	25.94	22.65	19.83	17.42	15.35	13.57	12.02	10.68	9.52	8.50	7.61	43
44	25.94	22.76	20.03	17.69	15.66	13.91	12.39	11.06	9.90	8.89	7.99	44
45	25.94	22.88	20.24	17.96	15.98	14.26	12.77	11.46	10.30	9.29	8.40	45
46	25.94	22.99	20.44	18.23	16.31	14.63	13.16	11.86	10.72	9.72	8.82	46
47	25.94	23.11	20.65	18.51	16.64	15.00	13.56	12.28	11.16	10.16	9.27	47
48	25.94	23.22	20.86	18.79	16.98	15.38	13.97	12.72	11.61	10.62	9.74	48
49	25.94	23.34	21.07	19.08	17.32	15.77	14.40	13.17	12.08	11.11	10.24	49
50	25.93	23.46	21.29	19.37	17.68	16.17	14.84	13.64	12.58	11.62	10.76	50
51	25.94	23.58	21.51	19.67	18.04	16.59	15.29	14.13	13.09	12.16	11.31	51
52	25.95	23.72	21.74	19.98	18.42	17.02	15.77	14.65	13.63	12.72	11.89	52
53	25.97	23.86	21.98	20.31	18.81	17.47	16.27	15.19	14.21	13.32	12.51	53
54	26.01	24.01	22.24	20.65	19.22	17.95	16.79	15.75	14.81	13.95	13.17	54
55	26.06	24.18	22.51	21.01	19.66	18.44	17.34	16.35	15.45	14.62	13.87	55

Table 30: Multipliers for loss of pension commencing age 55 (females)

Age at date of trial	Multiplier calculated with allowance for projected mortality from the 1998-based population projections and rate of return of											Age at date of trial
	0.0%	0.5%	1.0%	1.5%	2.0%	2.5%	3.0%	3.5%	4.0%	4.5%	5.0%	
0	29.68	20.74	14.56	10.27	7.27	5.17	3.70	2.65	1.91	1.38	1.00	0
1	29.80	20.93	14.76	10.46	7.45	5.33	3.82	2.76	1.99	1.45	1.06	1
2	29.81	21.03	14.91	10.62	7.60	5.46	3.94	2.85	2.07	1.51	1.11	2
3	29.81	21.14	15.06	10.78	7.75	5.60	4.06	2.95	2.16	1.58	1.17	3
4	29.80	21.24	15.21	10.94	7.90	5.74	4.18	3.06	2.24	1.65	1.22	4
5	29.80	21.35	15.36	11.10	8.06	5.88	4.30	3.16	2.33	1.73	1.28	5
6	29.80	21.45	15.51	11.27	8.22	6.02	4.43	3.27	2.43	1.81	1.35	6
7	29.79	21.55	15.66	11.44	8.38	6.17	4.56	3.39	2.52	1.89	1.42	7
8	29.79	21.66	15.82	11.61	8.55	6.33	4.70	3.51	2.62	1.97	1.49	8
9	29.78	21.76	15.97	11.78	8.72	6.48	4.84	3.63	2.73	2.06	1.56	9
10	29.77	21.86	16.13	11.95	8.89	6.64	4.98	3.75	2.84	2.15	1.64	10
11	29.77	21.97	16.29	12.13	9.07	6.81	5.13	3.88	2.95	2.25	1.72	11
12	29.76	22.07	16.45	12.31	9.25	6.98	5.29	4.02	3.07	2.35	1.81	12
13	29.75	22.18	16.61	12.49	9.43	7.15	5.44	4.16	3.19	2.45	1.90	13
14	29.75	22.29	16.77	12.68	9.62	7.33	5.61	4.30	3.32	2.56	1.99	14
15	29.74	22.39	16.94	12.86	9.81	7.51	5.77	4.45	3.45	2.68	2.09	15
16	29.74	22.50	17.10	13.05	10.00	7.70	5.95	4.61	3.59	2.80	2.19	16
17	29.73	22.61	17.27	13.25	10.20	7.89	6.12	4.77	3.73	2.93	2.30	17
18	29.73	22.72	17.44	13.45	10.41	8.09	6.31	4.94	3.88	3.06	2.42	18
19	29.73	22.83	17.62	13.65	10.61	8.29	6.50	5.11	4.03	3.19	2.54	19
20	29.72	22.94	17.79	13.85	10.83	8.49	6.69	5.29	4.19	3.34	2.67	20
21	29.72	23.06	17.96	14.06	11.04	8.71	6.89	5.47	4.36	3.49	2.80	21
22	29.71	23.17	18.14	14.26	11.26	8.92	7.10	5.66	4.54	3.65	2.94	22
23	29.70	23.28	18.32	14.48	11.48	9.14	7.31	5.86	4.72	3.81	3.08	23
24	29.70	23.39	18.50	14.69	11.71	9.37	7.53	6.07	4.91	3.98	3.24	24
25	29.69	23.50	18.68	14.91	11.94	9.60	7.75	6.28	5.10	4.16	3.40	25
26	29.68	23.61	18.86	15.13	12.18	9.84	7.98	6.50	5.30	4.34	3.57	26
27	29.67	23.72	19.04	15.35	12.42	10.09	8.22	6.72	5.51	4.54	3.75	27
28	29.66	23.83	19.23	15.58	12.66	10.34	8.46	6.96	5.73	4.74	3.93	28
29	29.65	23.95	19.42	15.81	12.91	10.59	8.72	7.20	5.96	4.96	4.13	29
30	29.64	24.06	19.61	16.04	13.17	10.85	8.98	7.45	6.20	5.18	4.34	30
31	29.63	24.17	19.80	16.28	13.43	11.12	9.24	7.71	6.45	5.41	4.55	31
32	29.62	24.29	19.99	16.52	13.70	11.40	9.52	7.98	6.70	5.65	4.78	32
33	29.61	24.40	20.18	16.76	13.97	11.68	9:80	8.25	6.97	5.91	5.02	33
34	29.60	24.51	20.38	17.01	14.24	11.97	10.10	8.54	7.25	6.17	5.27	34
35	29.59	24.63	20.58	17.26	14.52	12.27	10.40	8.84	7.54	6.45	5.53	35
36	29.58	24.74	20.78	17.51	14.81	12.57	10.71	9.15	7.84	6.74	5.81	36
37	29.57	24.86	20.98	17.77	15.11	12.88	11.03	9.47	8.15	7.04	6.10	37
38	29.56	24.98	21.18	18.03	15.40	13.21	11.36	9.80	8.48	7.36	6.40	38
39	29.55	25.09	21.39	18.30	15.71	13.53	11.70	10.14	8.82	7.69	6.72	39
40	29.54	25.21	21.60	18.57	16.02	13.87	12.05	10.50	9.17	8.04	7.06	40

Table 30: *continued*

Age at date of trial	Multiplier calculated with allowance for projected mortality from the 1998-based population projections and rate of return of											Age at date of trial
	0.0%	0.5%	1.0%	1.5%	2.0%	2.5%	3.0%	3.5%	4.0%	4.5%	5.0%	
41	29.53	25.33	21.81	18.85	16.34	14.22	12.41	10.86	9.54	8.40	7.42	41
42	29.53	25.45	22.03	19.13	16.67	14.57	12.78	11.24	9.92	8.78	7.79	42
43	29.52	25.58	22.24	19.41	17.00	14.94	13.17	11.64	10.32	9.18	8.18	43
44	29.52	25.70	22.47	19.71	17.34	15.31	13.56	12.05	10.74	9.59	8.59	44
45	29.51	25.83	22.69	20.00	17.69	15.70	13.97	12.47	11.17	10.03	9.02	45
46	29.51	25.96	22.92	20.30	18.05	16.10	14.40	12.92	11.62	10.48	9.48	46
47	29.51	26.09	23.15	20.61	18.42	16.50	14.83	13.37	12.09	10.96	9.96	47
48	29.51	26.23	23.39	20.93	18.79	16.92	15.29	13.85	12.58	11.46	10.47	48
49	29.52	26.37	23.63	21.25	19.18	17.36	15.76	14.35	13.10	11.99	11.00	49
50	29.53	26.51	23.88	21.59	19.57	17.80	16.24	14.86	13.63	12.54	11.56	50
51	29.54	26.66	24.14	21.93	19.98	18.27	16.75	15.40	14.20	13.12	12.16	51
52	29.57	26.81	24.40	22.28	20.41	18.75	17.27	15.96	14.78	13.73	12.78	52
53	29.59	26.98	24.67	22.64	20.84	19.24	17.82	16.54	15.40	14.37	13.45	53
54	29.63	27.15	24.96	23.02	21.29	19.76	18.39	17.16	16.05	15.05	14.15	54
55	29.68	27.33	25.25	23.41	21.76	20.29	18.98	17.80	16.73	15.77	14.89	55

Table 31: Multipliers for loss of pension commencing age 60 (males)

Age at date of trial	Multiplier calculated with allowance for projected mortality from the 1998-based population projections and rate of return of											Age at date of trial
	0.0%	0.5%	1.0%	1.5%	2.0%	2.5%	3.0%	3.5%	4.0%	4.5%	5.0%	
0	21.29	14.76	10.28	7.18	5.04	3.54	2.50	1.77	1.26	0.90	0.64	0
1	21.39	14.91	10.43	7.32	5.16	3.65	2.59	1.84	1.32	0.94	0.68	1
2	21.39	14.99	10.54	7.44	5.27	3.74	2.67	1.91	1.37	0.99	0.71	2
3	21.39	15.06	10.64	7.55	5.37	3.84	2.75	1.98	1.43	1.03	0.75	3
4	21.39	15.13	10.75	7.66	5.48	3.93	2.83	2.05	1.48	1.08	0.79	4
5	21.39	15.21	10.85	7.77	5.59	4.03	2.92	2.12	1.54	1.13	0.83	5
6	21.38	15.28	10.96	7.89	5.70	4.13	3.00	2.19	1.60	1.18	0.87	6
7	21.38	15.35	11.07	8.00	5.81	4.23	3.09	2.27	1.67	1.23	0.91	7
8	21.37	15.43	11.17	8.12	5.93	4.34	3.18	2.35	1.73	1.28	0.95	8
9	21.37	15.50	11.28	8.24	6.04	4.44	3.28	2.43	1.80	1.34	1.00	9
10	21.36	15.57	11.39	8.36	6.16	4.55	3.38	2.51	1.87	1.40	1.05	10
11	21.36	15.65	11.50	8.49	6.28	4.67	3.48	2.60	1.95	1.46	1.10	11
12	21.35	15.72	11.61	8.61	6.41	4.78	3.58	2.69	2.03	1.53	1.16	12
13	21.34	15.79	11.73	8.74	6.53	4.90	3.69	2.78	2.11	1.60	1.22	13
14	21.34	15.87	11.84	8.87	6.66	5.02	3.80	2.88	2.19	1.67	1.28	14
15	21.33	15.94	11.96	9.00	6.79	5.15	3.91	2.98	2.28	1.74	1.34	15
16	21.32	16.02	12.07	9.13	6.93	5.27	4.03	3.08	2.37	1.82	1.41	16
17	21.32	16.09	12.19	9.27	7.06	5.40	4.15	3.19	2.46	1.90	1.48	17
18	21.32	16.18	12.31	9.41	7.21	5.54	4.27	3.30	2.56	1.99	1.55	18
19	21.32	16.26	12.44	9.55	7.35	5.68	4.40	3.42	2.66	2.08	1.63	19
20	21.33	16.34	12.57	9.69	7.50	5.82	4.53	3.54	2.77	2.17	1.71	20
21	21.33	16.43	12.69	9.84	7.65	5.97	4.67	3.66	2.88	2.27	1.80	21
22	21.33	16.51	12.82	9.99	7.81	6.12	4.81	3.79	3.00	2.38	1.89	22
23	21.33	16.59	12.95	10.14	7.96	6.27	4.96	3.93	3.12	2.48	1.98	23
24	21.33	16.68	13.08	10.29	8.12	6.43	5.10	4.06	3.24	2.60	2.08	24
25	21.33	16.76	13.21	10.45	8.29	6.59	5.26	4.21	3.37	2.71	2.19	25
26	21.33	16.84	13.34	10.60	8.45	6.76	5.42	4.35	3.51	2.84	2.30	26
27	21.33	16.93	13.48	10.76	8.62	6.93	5.58	4.51	3.65	2.96	2.41	27
28	21.33	17.01	13.61	10.92	8.79	7.10	5.75	4.66	3.80	3.10	2.53	28
29	21.32	17.09	13.75	11.09	8.97	7.28	5.92	4.83	3.95	3.24	2.66	29
30	21.32	17.18	13.88	11.25	9.15	7.46	6.10	5.00	4.11	3.38	2.79	30
31	21.32	17.26	14.02	11.42	9.33	7.64	6.28	5.17	4.27	3.53	2.93	31
32	21.31	17.34	14.16	11.59	9.51	7.83	6.47	5.35	4.44	3.69	3.08	32
33	21.30	17.42	14.29	11.76	9.70	8.03	6.66	5.54	4.62	3.86	3.23	33
34	21.29	17.50	14.43	11.93	9.89	8.22	6.86	5.73	4.80	4.03	3.39	34
35	21.28	17.58	14.57	12.10	10.09	8.43	7.06	5.93	4.99	4.21	3.56	35
36	21.27	17.66	14.70	12.28	10.28	8.63	7.27	6.13	5.19	4.40	3.74	36
37	21.25	17.74	14.84	12.46	10.48	8.85	7.48	6.35	5.39	4.60	3.92	37
38	21.24	17.81	14.98	12.64	10.69	9.06	7.70	6.57	5.61	4.80	4.12	38
39	21.23	17.89	15.12	12.82	10.90	9.29	7.93	6.79	5.83	5.02	4.32	39
40	21.21	17.97	15.27	13.01	11.11	9.51	8.17	7.03	6.06	5.24	4.54	40

Table 31: *continued*

Age at date of trial	Multiplier calculated with allowance for projected mortality from the 1998-based population projections and rate of return of											Age at date of trial
	0.0%	0.5%	1.0%	1.5%	2.0%	2.5%	3.0%	3.5%	4.0%	4.5%	5.0%	
41	21.20	18.05	15.42	13.20	11.33	9.75	8.41	7.27	6.30	5.48	4.77	41
42	21.19	18.14	15.57	13.39	11.55	9.99	8.66	7.53	6.56	5.72	5.01	42
43	21.19	18.22	15.72	13.59	11.78	10.24	8.92	7.79	6.82	5.98	5.26	43
44	21.18	18.31	15.87	13.79	12.02	10.50	9.19	8.06	7.09	6.25	5.52	44
45	21.17	18.39	16.02	14.00	12.26	10.76	9.47	8.35	7.38	6.53	5.80	45
46	21.16	18.48	16.18	14.20	12.50	11.03	9.75	8.64	7.67	6.83	6.09	46
47	21.15	18.56	16.34	14.41	12.75	11.30	10.04	8.94	7.98	7.14	6.39	47
48	21.14	18.65	16.49	14.62	13.00	11.58	10.34	9.25	8.30	7.46	6.71	48
49	21.13	18.73	16.65	14.84	13.26	11.87	10.65	9.58	8.63	7.79	7.05	49
50	21.12	18.82	16.81	15.06	13.52	12.16	10.97	9.91	8.98	8.15	7.41	50
51	21.11	18.91	16.98	15.28	13.79	12.47	11.30	10.26	9.34	8.52	7.78	51
52	21.10	19.00	17.15	15.51	14.07	12.79	11.64	10.63	9.72	8.90	8.17	52
53	21.11	19.10	17.33	15.75	14.36	13.11	12.00	11.01	10.12	9.32	8.59	53
54	21.12	19.21	17.51	16.01	14.66	13.46	12.38	11.41	10.54	9.75	9.04	54
55	21.14	19.33	17.71	16.27	14.98	13.82	12.77	11.83	10.98	10.21	9.51	55
56	21.18	19.46	17.92	16.55	15.31	14.20	13.19	12.28	11.45	10.70	10.01	56
57	21.23	19.61	18.16	16.85	15.67	14.60	13.63	12.75	11.95	11.22	10.56	57
58	21.32	19.79	18.42	17.18	16.05	15.03	14.11	13.26	12.49	11.79	11.14	58
59	21.43	20.00	18.70	17.53	16.47	15.50	14.62	13.81	13.07	12.39	11.77	59
60	21.56	20.23	19.01	17.91	16.91	16.00	15.16	14.40	13.69	13.05	12.45	60

Table 32: Multipliers for loss of pension commencing age 60 (females)

Age at date of trial	Multiplier calculated with allowance for projected mortality from the 1998-based population projections and rate of return of											Age at date of trial
	0.0%	0.5%	1.0%	1.5%	2.0%	2.5%	3.0%	3.5%	4.0%	4.5%	5.0%	
0	24.92	17.16	11.87	8.24	5.74	4.02	2.82	1.99	1.41	1.00	0.71	0
1	25.02	17.31	12.03	8.40	5.88	4.14	2.92	2.07	1.47	1.05	0.75	1
2	25.02	17.40	12.15	8.52	6.00	4.24	3.01	2.14	1.53	1.10	0.79	2
3	25.02	17.49	12.28	8.65	6.12	4.35	3.10	2.22	1.59	1.15	0.83	3
4	25.02	17.57	12.40	8.78	6.24	4.46	3.19	2.29	1.66	1.20	0.87	4
5	25.01	17.66	12.52	8.91	6.37	4.57	3.29	2.38	1.72	1.25	0.91	5
6	25.01	17.74	12.64	9.04	6.49	4.68	3.39	2.46	1.79	1.31	0.96	6
7	25.00	17.83	12.77	9.18	6.62	4.80	3.49	2.54	1.86	1.37	1.01	7
8	25.00	17.92	12.89	9.31	6.75	4.92	3.59	2.63	1.94	1.43	1.06	8
9	24.99	18.00	13.02	9.45	6.89	5.04	3.70	2.72	2.01	1.49	1.11	9
10	24.99	18.09	13.15	9.59	7.02	5.16	3.81	2.82	2.09	1.56	1.17	10
11	24.98	18.17	13.27	9.73	7.16	5.29	3.92	2.92	2.18	1.63	1.22	11
12	24.97	18.26	13.40	9.88	7.30	5.42	4.04	3.02	2.26	1.70	1.28	12
13	24.97	18.35	13.53	10.02	7.45	5.56	4.16	3.12	2.35	1.78	1.35	13
14	24.96	18.43	13.67	10.17	7.60	5.69	4.28	3.23	2.45	1.86	1.42	14
15	24.96	18.52	13.80	10.32	7.75	5.83	4.41	3.34	2.54	1.94	1.49	15
16	24.95	18.61	13.94	10.47	7.90	5.98	4.54	3.46	2.65	2.03	1.56	16
17	24.95	18.70	14.07	10.63	8.06	6.13	4.68	3.58	2.75	2.12	1.64	17
18	24.94	18.79	14.21	10.79	8.22	6.28	4.82	3.71	2.86	2.21	1.72	18
19	24.94	18.88	14.35	10.95	8.38	6.44	4.96	3.84	2.97	2.31	1.81	19
20	24.93	18.97	14.49	11.11	8.55	6.60	5.11	3.97	3.09	2.42	1.90	20
21	24.93	19.06	14.63	11.27	8.72	6.76	5.26	4.11	3.22	2.53	1.99	21
22	24.92	19.16	14.78	11.44	8.89	6.93	5.42	4.25	3.34	2.64	2.09	22
23	24.92	19.25	14.92	11.61	9.06	7.10	5.58	4.40	3.48	2.76	2.19	23
24	24.91	19.34	15.07	11.78	9.24	7.28	5.75	4.55	3.62	2.88	2.30	24
25	24.90	19.43	15.21	11.95	9.42	7.46	5.92	4.71	3.76	3.01	2.42	25
26	24.89	19.52	15.36	12.13	9.61	7.64	6.09	4.87	3.91	3.14	2.54	26
27	24.88	19.61	15.51	12.31	9.80	7.83	6.27	5.04	4.06	3.29	2.66	27
28	24.87	19.70	15.66	12.49	9.99	8.02	6.46	5.22	4.23	3.43	2.80	28
29	24.86	19.79	15.81	12.67	10.19	8.22	6.65	5.40	4.39	3.59	2.93	29
30	24.85	19.88	15.96	12.86	10.39	8.42	6.85	5.59	4.57	3.75	3.08	30
31	24.84	19.97	16.11	13.04	10.59	8.63	7.05	5.78	4.75	3.91	3.23	31
32	24.83	20.06	16.27	13.24	10.80	8.84	7.26	5.98	4.94	4.09	3.39	32
33	24.82	20.16	16.42	13.43	11.01	9.06	7.48	6.19	5.13	4.27	3.56	33
34	24.81	20.25	16.58	13.62	11.23	9.28	7.70	6.40	5.34	4.46	3.74	34
35	24.79	20.34	16.74	13.82	11.45	9.51	7.93	6.62	5.55	4.66	3.93	35
36	24.78	20.43	16.90	14.03	11.68	9.75	8.16	6.85	5.77	4.87	4.12	36
37	24.77	20.52	17.06	14.23	11.90	9.99	8.40	7.09	6.00	5.09	4.33	37
38	24.76	20.62	17.23	14.44	12.14	10.23	8.65	7.34	6.24	5.32	4.54	38
39	24.74	20.71	17.39	14.65	12.38	10.49	8.91	7.59	6.49	5.56	4.77	39
40	24.73	20.80	17.56	14.86	12.62	10.75	9.18	7.86	6.74	5.80	5.01	40

Table 32: *continued*

Age at date of trial	Multiplier calculated with allowance for projected mortality from the 1998-based population projections and rate of return of											Age at date of trial
	0.0%	0.5%	1.0%	1.5%	2.0%	2.5%	3.0%	3.5%	4.0%	4.5%	5.0%	
41	24.72	20.90	17.73	15.08	12.87	11.01	9.45	8.13	7.01	6.06	5.26	41
42	24.71	21.00	17.90	15.30	13.12	11.28	9.73	8.41	7.29	6.34	5.52	42
43	24.70	21.09	18.07	15.53	13.38	11.56	10.02	8.71	7.58	6.62	5.80	43
44	24.69	21.19	18.24	15.76	13.65	11.85	10.32	9.01	7.89	6.92	6.09	44
45	24.68	21.29	18.42	15.99	13.92	12.15	10.63	9.33	8.20	7.23	6.39	45
46	24.67	21.39	18.60	16.23	14.19	12.45	10.95	9.65	8.53	7.56	6.71	46
47	24.66	21.49	18.79	16.47	14.48	12.76	11.28	9.99	8.88	7.90	7.05	47
48	24.66	21.60	18.97	16.72	14.77	13.08	11.62	10.34	9.23	8.26	7.40	48
49	24.66	21.70	19.16	16.97	15.07	13.41	11.97	10.71	9.61	8.64	7.78	49
50	24.66	21.82	19.36	17.23	15.37	13.75	12.34	11.09	10.00	9.03	8.17	50
51	24.66	21.93	19.56	17.49	15.69	14.11	12.71	11.49	10.40	9.44	8.59	51
52	24.67	22.05	19.77	17.77	16.01	14.47	13.11	11.90	10.83	9.88	9.03	52
53	24.68	22.18	19.98	18.05	16.35	14.85	13.52	12.33	11.28	10.34	9.49	53
54	24.71	22.31	20.20	18.34	16.70	15.24	13.94	12.78	11.75	10.82	9.99	54
55	24.73	22.45	20.43	18.64	17.06	15.64	14.38	13.25	12.24	11.33	10.51	55
56	24.77	22.59	20.67	18.95	17.43	16.07	14.84	13.75	12.76	11.86	11.06	56
57	24.81	22.75	20.92	19.28	17.82	16.51	15.33	14.26	13.30	12.43	11.64	57
58	24.87	22.92	21.18	19.62	18.23	16.97	15.84	14.81	13.88	13.04	12.27	58
59	24.95	23.11	21.47	19.99	18.66	17.46	16.37	15.39	14.49	13.68	12.93	59
60	25.05	23.32	21.77	20.38	19.12	17.98	16.94	16.00	15.14	14.36	13.64	60

Table 33: Multipliers for loss of pension commencing age 65 (males)

Age at date of trial	Multiplier calculated with allowance for projected mortality from the 1998-based population projections and rate of return of											Age at date of trial
	0.0%	0.5%	1.0%	1.5%	2.0%	2.5%	3.0%	3.5%	4.0%	4.5%	5.0%	
0	16.79	11.47	7.86	5.41	3.73	2.58	1.79	1.25	0.87	0.61	0.43	0
1	16.87	11.58	7.98	5.51	3.82	2.66	1.86	1.30	0.91	0.64	0.45	1
2	16.87	11.64	8.06	5.60	3.90	2.73	1.91	1.34	0.95	0.67	0.48	2
3	16.87	11.70	8.14	5.68	3.98	2.79	1.97	1.39	0.99	0.70	0.50	3
4	16.87	11.75	8.22	5.76	4.06	2.86	2.03	1.44	1.03	0.73	0.52	4
5	16.86	11.81	8.30	5.85	4.14	2.93	2.09	1.49	1.07	0.76	0.55	5
6	16.86	11.87	8.38	5.94	4.22	3.01	2.15	1.54	1.11	0.80	0.58	6
7	16.86	11.92	8.46	6.02	4.30	3.08	2.21	1.60	1.15	0.84	0.61	7
8	16.85	11.98	8.54	6.11	4.39	3.16	2.28	1.65	1.20	0.87	0.64	8
9	16.85	12.04	8.63	6.20	4.47	3.24	2.35	1.71	1.25	0.91	0.67	9
10	16.84	12.09	8.71	6.29	4.56	3.32	2.42	1.77	1.30	0.95	0.70	10
11	16.83	12.15	8.79	6.39	4.65	3.40	2.49	1.83	1.35	0.99	0.74	11
12	16.83	12.20	8.88	6.48	4.74	3.48	2.56	1.89	1.40	1.04	0.77	12
13	16.82	12.26	8.96	6.57	4.84	3.57	2.64	1.96	1.46	1.09	0.81	13
14	16.82	12.32	9.05	6.67	4.93	3.65	2.72	2.03	1.51	1.13	0.85	14
15	16.81	12.38	9.14	6.77	5.03	3.75	2.80	2.10	1.57	1.18	0.89	15
16	16.81	12.43	9.23	6.87	5.13	3.84	2.88	2.17	1.64	1.24	0.94	16
17	16.80	12.49	9.32	6.97	5.23	3.93	2.97	2.24	1.70	1.29	0.99	17
18	16.80	12.55	9.41	7.07	5.33	4.03	3.06	2.32	1.77	1.35	1.03	18
19	16.80	12.62	9.50	7.18	5.44	4.13	3.15	2.40	1.84	1.41	1.09	19
20	16.80	12.68	9.60	7.29	5.55	4.24	3.24	2.49	1.91	1.48	1.14	20
21	16.80	12.75	9.70	7.40	5.66	4.34	3.34	2.58	1.99	1.54	1.20	21
22	16.80	12.81	9.80	7.51	5.77	4.45	3.44	2.67	2.07	1.61	1.26	22
23	16.80	12.87	9.89	7.62	5.89	4.56	3.54	2.76	2.15	1.69	1.32	23
24	16.80	12.94	9.99	7.74	6.01	4.68	3.65	2.86	2.24	1.76	1.39	24
25	16.80	13.00	10.09	7.85	6.13	4.79	3.76	2.96	2.33	1.84	1.46	25
26	16.80	13.06	10.19	7.97	6.25	4.91	3.87	3.06	2.42	1.92	1.53	26
27	16.79	13.13	10.29	8.09	6.37	5.03	3.99	3.17	2.52	2.01	1.61	27
28	16.79	13.19	10.39	8.21	6.50	5.16	4.11	3.28	2.62	2.10	1.69	28
29	16.78	13.25	10.49	8.33	6.63	5.29	4.23	3.39	2.72	2.19	1.77	29
30	16.78	13.31	10.59	8.45	6.76	5.42	4.36	3.51	2.83	2.29	1.86	30
31	16.77	13.38	10.70	8.57	6.89	5.55	4.48	3.63	2.95	2.39	1.95	31
32	16.76	13.44	10.80	8.70	7.03	5.69	4.62	3.76	3.06	2.50	2.05	32
33	16.75	13.50	10.90	8.83	7.16	5.83	4.75	3.89	3.18	2.61	2.15	33
34	16.74	13.55	11.00	8.95	7.30	5.97	4.89	4.02	3.31	2.73	2.26	34
35	16.73	13.61	11.10	9.08	7.44	6.12	5.04	4.16	3.44	2.85	2.37	35
36	16.71	13.67	11.21	9.21	7.59	6.27	5.19	4.30	3.57	2.98	2.48	36
37	16.70	13.73	11.31	9.34	7.73	6.42	5.34	4.45	3.72	3.11	2.61	37
38	16.68	13.78	11.41	9.47	7.88	6.57	5.49	4.60	3.86	3.25	2.74	38
39	16.67	13.84	11.52	9.61	8.03	6.73	5.65	4.76	4.01	3.39	2.87	39
40	16.65	13.90	11.62	9.74	8.19	6.90	5.82	4.92	4.17	3.54	3.01	40

Table 33: *continued*

Age at date of trial	Multiplier calculated with allowance for projected mortality from the 1998-based population projections and rate of return of											Age at date of trial
	0.0%	0.5%	1.0%	1.5%	2.0%	2.5%	3.0%	3.5%	4.0%	4.5%	5.0%	
41	16.64	13.95	11.73	9.88	8.35	7.06	5.99	5.09	4.34	3.70	3.16	41
42	16.63	14.01	11.84	10.03	8.51	7.24	6.17	5.27	4.51	3.86	3.32	42
43	16.61	14.07	11.95	10.17	8.67	7.41	6.35	5.45	4.69	4.04	3.48	43
44	16.60	14.13	12.06	10.31	8.84	7.59	6.54	5.64	4.87	4.22	3.66	44
45	16.59	14.19	12.17	10.46	9.01	7.78	6.73	5.83	5.06	4.40	3.84	45
46	16.57	14.25	12.28	10.61	9.19	7.97	6.93	6.03	5.26	4.60	4.03	46
47	16.56	14.31	12.40	10.76	9.36	8.16	7.13	6.24	5.47	4.81	4.23	47
48	16.54	14.37	12.51	10.92	9.54	8.36	7.34	6.45	5.69	5.02	4.44	48
49	16.52	14.42	12.62	11.07	9.73	8.56	7.55	6.68	5.91	5.24	4.66	49
50	16.50	14.48	12.74	11.22	9.91	8.77	7.78	6.91	6.14	5.48	4.89	50
51	16.48	14.54	12.85	11.38	10.10	8.98	8.00	7.14	6.39	5.72	5.13	51
52	16.47	14.60	12.97	11.55	10.30	9.20	8.24	7.39	6.64	5.98	5.39	52
53	16.46	14.67	13.10	11.72	10.50	9.43	8.49	7.65	6.91	6.25	5.66	53
54	16.45	14.74	13.23	11.89	10.72	9.67	8.75	7.92	7.19	6.53	5.94	54
55	16.46	14.82	13.36	12.08	10.94	9.92	9.01	8.21	7.48	6.83	6.25	55
56	16.47	14.90	13.51	12.27	11.17	10.18	9.30	8.51	7.79	7.15	6.57	56
57	16.50	15.00	13.67	12.48	11.42	10.46	9.60	8.83	8.13	7.49	6.92	57
58	16.55	15.13	13.85	12.71	11.69	10.76	9.92	9.17	8.48	7.86	7.30	58
59	16.62	15.27	14.06	12.96	11.98	11.08	10.27	9.54	8.87	8.26	7.70	59
60	16.71	15.43	14.28	13.23	12.29	11.43	10.65	9.93	9.28	8.68	8.14	60
61	16.82	15.61	14.52	13.52	12.62	11.80	11.04	10.35	9.72	9.14	8.61	61
62	16.94	15.81	14.77	13.83	12.97	12.19	11.47	10.81	10.20	9.64	9.12	62
63	17.08	16.02	15.05	14.16	13.35	12.60	11.92	11.28	10.70	10.16	9.66	63
64	17.23	16.24	15.34	14.51	13.75	13.04	12.39	11.80	11.24	10.73	10.25	64
65	17.40	16.49	15.65	14.88	14.17	13.51	12.91	12.34	11.82	11.34	10.89	65

Table 34: Multipliers for loss of pension commencing age 65 (females)

Age at date of trial	Multiplier calculated with allowance for projected mortality from the 1998-based population projections and rate of return of											Age at date of trial
	0.0%	0.5%	1.0%	1.5%	2.0%	2.5%	3.0%	3.5%	4.0%	4.5%	5.0%	
0	20.26	13.75	9.36	6.40	4.39	3.02	2.09	1.45	1.01	0.70	0.49	0
1	20.34	13.87	9.49	6.52	4.50	3.11	2.16	1.50	1.05	0.74	0.52	1
2	20.34	13.94	9.59	6.62	4.59	3.19	2.23	1.56	1.09	0.77	0.54	2
3	20.34	14.01	9.69	6.72	4.68	3.27	2.29	1.61	1.14	0.80	0.57	3
4	20.33	14.08	9.78	6.82	4.77	3.35	2.36	1.67	1.18	0.84	0.60	4
5	20.33	14.15	9.88	6.92	4.87	3.43	2.43	1.73	1.23	0.88	0.63	5
6	20.33	14.21	9.97	7.02	4.96	3.52	2.50	1.79	1.28	0.92	0.66	6
7	20.32	14.28	10.07	7.13	5.06	3.61	2.58	1.85	1.33	0.96	0.69	7
8	20.32	14.35	10.17	7.23	5.16	3.70	2.66	1.91	1.38	1.00	0.73	8
9	20.31	14.42	10.27	7.34	5.26	3.79	2.73	1.98	1.44	1.05	0.76	9
10	20.31	14.49	10.37	7.45	5.37	3.88	2.82	2.05	1.49	1.09	0.80	10
11	20.30	14.56	10.47	7.56	5.47	3.98	2.90	2.12	1.55	1.14	0.84	11
12	20.30	14.62	10.57	7.67	5.58	4.08	2.99	2.19	1.62	1.19	0.88	12
13	20.29	14.69	10.68	7.78	5.69	4.18	3.07	2.27	1.68	1.25	0.93	13
14	20.29	14.76	10.78	7.90	5.81	4.28	3.17	2.35	1.75	1.30	0.98	14
15	20.28	14.83	10.89	8.01	5.92	4.39	3.26	2.43	1.82	1.36	1.02	15
16	20.28	14.90	10.99	8.13	6.04	4.50	3.36	2.51	1.89	1.42	1.07	16
17	20.27	14.97	11.10	8.25	6.16	4.61	3.46	2.60	1.96	1.49	1.13	17
18	20.27	15.05	11.21	8.38	6.28	4.72	3.56	2.69	2.04	1.55	1.18	18
19	20.26	15.12	11.32	8.50	6.40	4.84	3.67	2.79	2.12	1.62	1.24	19
20	20.26	15.19	11.43	8.63	6.53	4.96	3.78	2.88	2.21	1.70	1.31	20
21	20.25	15.26	11.54	8.75	6.66	5.08	3.89	2.98	2.30	1.77	1.37	21
22	20.25	15.33	11.65	8.88	6.79	5.21	4.00	3.09	2.39	1.85	1.44	22
23	20.24	15.41	11.76	9.01	6.92	5.33	4.12	3.19	2.48	1.93	1.51	23
24	20.23	15.48	11.88	9.14	7.06	5.47	4.24	3.31	2.58	2.02	1.59	24
25	20.22	15.55	11.99	9.28	7.20	5.60	4.37	3.42	2.68	2.11	1.66	25
26	20.21	15.62	12.11	9.41	7.34	5.74	4.50	3.54	2.79	2.20	1.75	26
27	20.20	15.69	12.22	9.55	7.48	5.88	4.63	3.66	2.90	2.30	1.83	27
28	20.19	15.76	12.34	9.69	7.63	6.02	4.77	3.79	3.01	2.41	1.92	28
29	20.18	15.83	12.46	9.83	7.78	6.17	4.91	3.92	3.13	2.51	2.02	29
30	20.17	15.90	12.58	9.97	7.93	6.32	5.06	4.05	3.26	2.63	2.12	30
31	20.16	15.98	12.69	10.12	8.09	6.48	5.21	4.19	3.39	2.74	2.23	31
32	20.15	16.05	12.81	10.26	8.24	6.64	5.36	4.34	3.52	2.86	2.34	32
33	20.14	16.12	12.94	10.41	8.40	6.80	5.52	4.49	3.66	2.99	2.45	33
34	20.13	16.19	13.06	10.56	8.57	6.97	5.68	4.64	3.81	3.13	2.57	34
35	20.12	16.26	13.18	10.72	8.73	7.14	5.85	4.80	3.96	3.26	2.70	35
36	20.10	16.33	13.30	10.87	8.90	7.31	6.02	4.97	4.11	3.41	2.83	36
37	20.09	16.40	13.43	11.03	9.08	7.49	6.20	5.14	4.27	3.56	2.97	37
38	20.07	16.47	13.56	11.18	9.25	7.67	6.38	5.32	4.44	3.72	3.12	38
39	20.06	16.54	13.68	11.35	9.43	7.86	6.57	5.50	4.62	3.89	3.28	39
40	20.05	16.62	13.81	11.51	9.62	8.05	6.76	5.69	4.80	4.06	3.44	40

Table 34: *continued*

Age at date of trial	Multiplier calculated with allowance for projected mortality from the 1998-based population projections and rate of return of											Age at date of trial
	0.0%	0.5%	1.0%	1.5%	2.0%	2.5%	3.0%	3.5%	4.0%	4.5%	5.0%	
41	20.03	16.69	13.94	11.67	9.80	8.25	6.96	5.89	4.99	4.24	3.61	41
42	20.02	16.76	14.07	11.84	9.99	8.45	7.17	6.09	5.19	4.43	3.79	42
43	20.00	16.83	14.20	12.01	10.19	8.66	7.38	6.30	5.39	4.63	3.98	43
44	19.99	16.91	14.34	12.19	10.39	8.87	7.60	6.52	5.61	4.83	4.17	44
45	19.98	16.98	14.47	12.36	10.59	9.09	7.82	6.75	5.83	5.05	4.38	45
46	19.96	17.05	14.61	12.54	10.80	9.31	8.05	6.98	6.06	5.28	4.60	46
47	19.95	17.13	14.75	12.73	11.01	9.54	8.29	7.22	6.30	5.51	4.83	47
48	19.94	17.21	14.89	12.91	11.22	9.78	8.54	7.47	6.56	5.76	5.07	48
49	19.93	17.29	15.03	13.10	11.45	10.02	8.80	7.74	6.82	6.02	5.33	49
50	19.92	17.37	15.18	13.30	11.67	10.27	9.06	8.01	7.09	6.29	5.59	50
51	19.92	17.45	15.33	13.49	11.91	10.53	9.33	8.29	7.38	6.58	5.88	51
52	19.92	17.54	15.48	13.70	12.15	10.80	9.62	8.58	7.68	6.88	6.17	52
53	19.92	17.63	15.64	13.91	12.40	11.07	9.91	8.89	7.99	7.19	6.49	53
54	19.93	17.73	15.81	14.13	12.65	11.36	10.22	9.21	8.32	7.52	6.82	54
55	19.94	17.83	15.98	14.35	12.92	11.65	10.54	9.54	8.66	7.87	7.17	55
56	19.95	17.93	16.15	14.58	13.19	11.96	10.87	9.89	9.02	8.24	7.54	56
57	19.98	18.05	16.34	14.83	13.48	12.28	11.21	10.26	9.40	8.63	7.93	57
58	20.02	18.17	16.54	15.08	13.78	12.62	11.58	10.64	9.80	9.04	8.35	58
59	20.07	18.32	16.75	15.35	14.10	12.98	11.97	11.05	10.23	9.48	8.80	59
60	20.14	18.47	16.98	15.64	14.44	13.35	12.37	11.49	10.68	9.95	9.28	60
61	20.22	18.64	17.22	15.95	14.79	13.75	12.80	11.94	11.16	10.45	9.80	61
62	20.31	18.82	17.47	16.26	15.16	14.16	13.25	12.42	11.67	10.97	10.34	62
63	20.39	19.00	17.73	16.58	15.54	14.59	13.72	12.92	12.20	11.53	10.91	63
64	20.48	19.17	17.99	16.91	15.92	15.03	14.20	13.45	12.75	12.11	11.52	64
65	20.56	19.35	18.25	17.24	16.32	15.48	14.70	13.99	13.34	12.73	12.17	65

Table 35: Multipliers for loss of pension commencing age 70 (males)

Age at date of trial	Multiplier calculated with allowance for projected mortality from the 1998-based population projections and rate of return of											Age at date of trial
	0.0%	0.5%	1.0%	1.5%	2.0%	2.5%	3.0%	3.5%	4.0%	4.5%	5.0%	
0	12.53	8.43	5.68	3.85	2.61	1.78	1.21	0.83	0.57	0.39	0.27	0
1	12.59	8.51	5.77	3.92	2.67	1.83	1.25	0.86	0.60	0.41	0.29	1
2	12.59	8.55	5.83	3.98	2.73	1.88	1.29	0.89	0.62	0.43	0.30	2
3	12.59	8.59	5.88	4.04	2.78	1.92	1.33	0.92	0.64	0.45	0.31	3
4	12.59	8.64	5.94	4.10	2.84	1.97	1.37	0.96	0.67	0.47	0.33	4
5	12.59	8.68	6.00	4.16	2.89	2.02	1.41	0.99	0.70	0.49	0.35	5
6	12.58	8.72	6.06	4.22	2.95	2.07	1.45	1.02	0.72	0.51	0.36	6
7	12.58	8.76	6.12	4.28	3.01	2.12	1.50	1.06	0.75	0.54	0.38	7
8	12.57	8.80	6.18	4.35	3.07	2.17	1.54	1.10	0.78	0.56	0.40	8
9	12.57	8.84	6.24	4.41	3.13	2.23	1.59	1.13	0.81	0.58	0.42	9
10	12.56	8.88	6.30	4.48	3.19	2.28	1.63	1.17	0.85	0.61	0.44	10
11	12.56	8.92	6.36	4.54	3.25	2.34	1.68	1.21	0.88	0.64	0.46	11
12	12.55	8.96	6.42	4.61	3.32	2.39	1.73	1.26	0.91	0.67	0.49	12
13	12.55	9.00	6.48	4.67	3.38	2.45	1.78	1.30	0.95	0.70	0.51	13
14	12.54	9.05	6.54	4.74	3.45	2.51	1.84	1.35	0.99	0.73	0.54	14
15	12.54	9.09	6.60	4.81	3.52	2.58	1.89	1.39	1.03	0.76	0.56	15
16	12.53	9.13	6.67	4.88	3.59	2.64	1.95	1.44	1.07	0.79	0.59	16
17	12.53	9.17	6.73	4.95	3.66	2.70	2.00	1.49	1.11	0.83	0.62	17
18	12.53	9.22	6.80	5.03	3.73	2.77	2.06	1.54	1.15	0.87	0.65	18
19	12.53	9.26	6.87	5.10	3.80	2.84	2.13	1.60	1.20	0.91	0.68	19
20	12.53	9.31	6.94	5.18	3.88	2.91	2.19	1.65	1.25	0.95	0.72	20
21	12.53	9.36	7.00	5.26	3.96	2.98	2.26	1.71	1.30	0.99	0.75	21
22	12.53	9.40	7.07	5.34	4.04	3.06	2.32	1.77	1.35	1.03	0.79	22
23	12.52	9.45	7.14	5.42	4.12	3.14	2.39	1.83	1.40	1.08	0.83	23
24	12.52	9.49	7.21	5.50	4.20	3.21	2.47	1.90	1.46	1.13	0.87	24
25	12.52	9.54	7.28	5.58	4.28	3.29	2.54	1.96	1.52	1.18	0.92	25
26	12.51	9.58	7.36	5.66	4.36	3.37	2.61	2.03	1.58	1.23	0.96	26
27	12.51	9.63	7.43	5.74	4.45	3.46	2.69	2.10	1.64	1.29	1.01	27
28	12.51	9.67	7.50	5.83	4.54	3.54	2.77	2.17	1.71	1.34	1.06	28
29	12.50	9.72	7.57	5.91	4.63	3.63	2.85	2.25	1.77	1.40	1.11	29
30	12.49	9.76	7.64	6.00	4.72	3.72	2.94	2.33	1.85	1.47	1.17	30
31	12.48	9.80	7.71	6.08	4.81	3.81	3.02	2.41	1.92	1.53	1.23	31
32	12.48	9.84	7.79	6.17	4.90	3.90	3.11	2.49	1.99	1.60	1.29	32
33	12.47	9.89	7.86	6.26	5.00	4.00	120	2.57	2.07	1.67	1.35	33
34	12.45	9.93	7.93	6.35	5.09	4.09	3.30	2.66	2.15	1.74	1.42	34
35	12.44	9.97	8.00	6.44	5.19	4.19	3.39	2.75	2.24	1.82	1.49	35
36	12.43	10.00	8.07	6.53	5.29	4.29	3.49	2.85	2.32	1.90	1.56	36
37	12.41	10.04	8.14	6.62	5.39	4.40	3.59	2.94	2.42	1.99	1.64	37
38	12.40	10.08	8.21	6.71	5.49	4.50	3.70	3.04	2.51	2.07	1.72	38
39	12.38	10.12	8.29	6.80	5.59	4.61	3.80	3.15	2.61	2.16	1.80	39
40	12.37	10.16	8.36	6.89	5.70	4.72	3.91	3.25	2.71	2.26	1.89	40

Table 35: *continued*

Age at date of trial	Multiplier calculated with allowance for projected mortality from the 1998-based population projections and rate of return of											Age at date of trial
	0.0%	0.5%	1.0%	1.5%	2.0%	2.5%	3.0%	3.5%	4.0%	4.5%	5.0%	
41	12.35	10.19	8.43	6.99	5.81	4.83	4.03	3.36	2.81	2.36	1.98	41
42	12.34	10.23	8.51	7.09	5.92	4.95	4.14	3.48	2.92	2.46	2.08	42
43	12.32	10.27	8.58	7.19	6.03	5.06	4.26	3.60	3.04	2.57	2.18	43
44	12.30	10.31	8.66	7.28	6.14	5.19	4.39	3.72	3.16	2.68	2.29	44
45	12.29	10.35	8.73	7.38	6.26	5.31	4.51	3.84	3.28	2.80	2.40	45
46	12.27	10.39	8.81	7.49	6.37	5.44	4.64	3.97	3.41	2.93	2.52	46
47	12.25	10.42	8.88	7.59	6.49	5.56	4.78	4.11	3.54	3.05	2.64	47
48	12.23	10.46	8.96	7.69	6.61	5.70	4.91	4.25	3.68	3.19	2.77	48
49	12.21	10.49	9.03	7.79	6.73	5.83	5.05	4.39	3.82	3.33	2.90	49
50	12.18	10.52	9.11	7.90	6.86	5.97	5.20	4.54	3.96	3.47	3.04	50
51	12.16	10.56	9.18	8.00	6.98	6.10	5.35	4.69	4.12	3.62	3.19	51
52	12.14	10.59	9.26	8.11	7.11	6.25	5.50	4.85	4.28	3.78	3.35	52
53	12.12	10.63	9.34	8.22	7.25	6.40	5.66	5.01	4.45	3.95	3.51	53
54	12.11	10.67	9.43	8.34	7.39	6.55	5.82	5.18	4.62	4.12	3.69	54
55	12.10	10.72	9.51	8.46	7.53	6.71	6.00	5.36	4.80	4.31	3.87	55
56	12.09	10.77	9.61	8.58	7.68	6.88	6.18	5.55	5.00	4.50	4.07	56
57	12.10	10.83	9.71	8.72	7.84	7.06	6.37	5.75	5.20	4.71	4.28	57
58	12.13	10.91	9.83	8.87	8.02	7.26	6.58	5.97	5.43	4.94	4.50	58
59	12.17	11.00	9.96	9.03	8.21	7.47	6.80	6.20	5.67	5.18	4.75	59
60	12.22	11.10	10.11	9.21	8.41	7.69	7.04	6.45	5.92	5.44	5.01	60
61	12.28	11.22	10.26	9.40	8.63	7.93	7.29	6.72	6.20	5.72	5.29	61
62	12.36	11.35	10.43	9.61	8.86	8.18	7.56	7.00	6.49	6.02	5.60	62
63	12.44	11.48	10.61	9.82	9.10	8.45	7.85	7.30	6.80	6.34	5.92	63
64	12.53	11.62	10.80	10.04	9.36	8.73	8.15	7.62	7.13	6.68	6.27	64
65	12.63	11.78	11.00	10.28	9.62	9.02	8.47	7.96	7.49	7.05	6.65	65
66	12.74	11.94	11.20	10.53	9.91	9.33	8.80	8.31	7.86	7.44	7.05	66
67	12.86	12.11	11.43	10.79	10.21	9.67	9.16	8.70	8.26	7.86	7.48	67
68	12.99	12.30	11.67	11.08	10.53	10.02	9.55	9.11	8.70	8.32	7.96	68
69	13.15	12.52	11.94	11.39	10.89	10.41	9.97	9.56	9.18	8.82	8.48	69
70	13.36	12.78	12.25	11.75	11.29	10.86	10.45	10.07	9.71	9.38	9.07	70

Table 36: Multipliers for loss of pension commencing age 70 (females)

Age at date of trial	Multiplier calculated with allowance for projected mortality from the 1998-based population projections and rate of return of											Age at date of trial
	0.0%	0.5%	1.0%	1.5%	2.0%	2.5%	3.0%	3.5%	4.0%	4.5%	5.0%	
0	15.76	10.53	7.06	4.75	3.21	2.17	1.48	1.01	0.69	0.47	0.32	0
1	15.82	10.63	7.16	4.84	3.29	2.24	1.53	1.05	0.72	0.49	0.34	1
2	15.82	10.68	7.24	4.92	3.35	2.29	1.57	1.08	0.75	0.52	0.36	2
3	15.82	10.73	7.31	4.99	3.42	2.35	1.62	1.12	0.78	0.54	0.38	3
4	15.82	10.79	7.38	5.07	3.49	2.41	1.67	1.16	0.81	0.56	0.40	4
5	15.82	10.84	7.45	5.14	3.56	2.47	1.72	1.20	0.84	0.59	0.42	5
6	15.81	10.89	7.53	5.22	3.63	2.53	1.77	1.24	0.87	0.62	0.44	6
7	15.81	10.94	7.60	5.29	3.70	2.59	1.82	1.28	0.91	0.64	0.46	7
8	15.80	10.99	7.67	5.37	3.77	2.66	1.88	1.33	0.94	0.67	0.48	8
9	15.80	11.05	7.75	5.45	3.85	2.72	1.93	1.38	0.98	0.70	0.50	9
10	15.80	11.10	7.82	5.53	3.92	2.79	1.99	1.42	1.02	0.73	0.53	10
11	15.79	11.15	7.90	5.61	4.00	2.86	2.05	1.47	1.06	0.77	0.56	11
12	15.79	11.20	7.98	5.69	4.08	2.93	2.11	1.52	1.10	0.80	0.58	12
13	15.78	11.26	8.05	5.78	4.16	3.00	2.17	1.58	1.15	0.84	0.61	13
14	15.78	11.31	8.13	5.86	4.24	3.08	2.24	1.63	1.19	0.87	0.64	14
15	15.77	11.36	8.21	5.95	4.32	3.15	2.30	1.69	1.24	0.91	0.67	15
16	15.77	11.42	8.29	6.04	4.41	3.23	2.37	1.75	1.29	0.95	0.71	16
17	15.76	11.47	8.37	6.13	4.50	3.31	2.44	1.81	1.34	1.00	0.74	17
18	15.76	11.52	8.45	6.22	4.59	3.39	2.51	1.87	1.39	1.04	0.78	18
19	15.75	11.58	8.53	6.31	4.68	3.48	2.59	1.93	1.45	1.09	0.82	19
20	15.75	11.63	8.62	6.40	4.77	3.56	2.67	2.00	1.51	1.14	0.86	20
21	15.74	11.69	8.70	6.49	4.86	3.65	2.75	2.07	1.57	1.19	0.90	21
22	15.74	11.74	8.78	6.59	4.96	3.74	2.83	2.14	1.63	1.24	0.95	22
23	15.73	11.79	8.87	6.69	5.05	3.83	2.91	2.22	1.69	1.30	0.99	23
24	15.72	11.85	8.95	6.78	5.15	3.93	3.00	2.29	1.76	1.35	1.04	24
25	15.72	11.90	9.04	6.88	5.25	4.02	3.09	2.37	1.83	1.41	1.10	25
26	15.71	11.95	9.12	6.98	5.36	4.12	3.18	2.46	1.90	1.48	1.15	26
27	15.70	12.01	9.21	7.08	5.46	4.22	3.27	2.54	1.98	1.54	1.21	27
28	15.69	12.06	9.30	7.19	5.57	4.32	3.37	2.63	2.06	1.61	1.27	28
29	15.68	12.11	9.38	7.29	5.68	4.43	3.47	2.72	2.14	1.68	1.33	29
30	15.67	12.17	9.47	7.39	5.79	4.54	3.57	2.81	2.22	1.76	1.39	30
31	15.66	12.22	9.56	7.50	5.90	4.65	3.67	2.91	2.31	1.84	1.46	31
32	15.65	12.27	9.65	7.61	6.01	4.76	3.78	3.01	2.40	1.92	1.54	32
33	15.64	12.33	9.74	7.72	6.13	4.88	3:89	3.11	2.49	2.00	1.61	33
34	15.62	12.38	9.83	7.83	6.25	5.00	4.01	3.22	2.59	2.09	1.69	34
35	15.61	12.43	9.92	7.94	6.37	5.12	4.12	3.33	2.69	2.18	1.77	35
36	15.60	12.48	10.01	8.05	6.49	5.24	4.24	3.44	2.80	2.28	1.86	36
37	15.59	12.53	10.10	8.16	6.61	5.37	4.37	3.56	2.91	2.38	1.95	37
38	15.57	12.58	10.20	8.28	6.74	5.50	4.50	3.68	3.02	2.49	2.05	38
39	15.56	12.64	10.29	8.40	6.87	5.63	4.63	3.81	3.14	2.60	2.15	39
40	15.54	12.69	10.38	8.52	7.00	5.77	4.76	3.94	3.27	2.71	2.26	40

Table 36: *continued*

Age at date of trial	Multiplier calculated with allowance for projected mortality from the 1998-based population projections and rate of return of											Age at date of trial
	0.0%	0.5%	1.0%	1.5%	2.0%	2.5%	3.0%	3.5%	4.0%	4.5%	5.0%	
41	15.53	12.74	10.48	8.64	7.13	5.91	4.90	4.07	3.39	2.83	2.37	41
42	15.51	12.79	10.57	8.76	7.27	6.05	5.04	4.21	3.53	2.96	2.49	42
43	15.49	12.84	10.67	8.88	7.41	6.20	5.19	4.36	3.67	3.09	2.61	43
44	15.48	12.89	10.76	9.01	7.55	6.35	5.34	4.51	3.81	3.23	2.74	44
45	15.46	12.94	10.86	9.13	7.70	6.50	5.50	4.66	3.96	3.37	2.87	45
46	15.45	13.00	10.96	9.26	7.84	6.66	5.66	4.82	4.11	3.52	3.01	46
47	15.43	13.05	11.06	9.39	7.99	6.82	5.82	4.99	4.28	3.67	3.16	47
48	15.42	13.10	11.16	9.53	8.15	6.98	5.99	5.16	4.44	3.84	3.32	48
49	15.40	13.16	11.26	9.66	8.30	7.15	6.17	5.33	4.62	4.01	3.48	49
50	15.39	13.21	11.37	9.80	8.46	7.33	6.35	5.52	4.80	4.19	3.66	50
51	15.38	13.27	11.47	9.94	8.63	7.51	6.54	5.71	4.99	4.37	3.84	51
52	15.37	13.33	11.58	10.08	8.80	7.69	6.73	5.91	5.19	4.57	4.03	52
53	15.36	13.39	11.69	10.23	8.97	7.88	6.94	6.11	5.40	4.78	4.23	53
54	15.36	13.45	11.81	10.39	9.15	8.08	7.15	6.33	5.62	4.99	4.44	54
55	15.35	13.52	11.93	10.54	9.34	8.28	7.36	6.55	5.85	5.22	4.67	55
56	15.36	13.59	12.05	10.71	9.53	8.50	7.59	6.79	6.08	5.46	4.91	56
57	15.37	13.67	12.18	10.88	9.73	8.72	7.82	7.03	6.33	5.71	5.16	57
58	15.38	13.75	12.32	11.06	9.94	8.95	8.07	7.29	6.60	5.98	5.43	58
59	15.42	13.85	12.47	11.25	10.16	9.20	8.34	7.57	6.88	6.27	5.72	59
60	15.46	13.96	12.63	11.45	10.40	9.46	8.62	7.86	7.18	6.57	6.02	60
61	15.51	14.08	12.81	11.67	10.65	9.73	8.91	8.17	7.50	6.90	6.35	61
62	15.56	14.20	12.98	11.89	10.90	10.01	9.21	8.49	7.83	7.24	6.70	62
63	15.62	14.32	13.16	12.11	11.16	10.31	9.53	8.82	8.18	7.60	7.06	63
64	15.66	14.44	13.33	12.33	11.43	10.60	9.85	9.17	8.54	7.97	7.45	64
65	15.70	14.55	13.51	12.56	11.69	10.90	10.18	9.52	8.92	8.36	7.85	65
66	15.74	14.66	13.68	12.78	11.96	11.21	10.53	9.90	9.31	8.78	8.28	66
67	15.78	14.78	13.86	13.02	12.25	11.54	10.89	10.28	9.73	9.21	8.74	67
68	15.83	14.90	14.05	13.27	12.55	11.88	11.27	10.70	10.17	9.68	9.23	68
69	15.90	15.05	14.26	13.54	12.87	12.25	11.68	11.14	10.65	10.19	9.76	69
70	16.01	15.23	14.51	13.85	13.23	12.66	12.13	11.64	11.17	10.74	10.34	70

Table 37: Discounting factors for term certain

Term	Factor to discount value of multiplier for a period of deferment 1.5%	2.0%	2.5%	3.0%	3.5%	4.0%	4.5%	5.0%	Term
1	0.9852	0.9804	0.9756	0.9709	0.9662	0.9615	0.9569	0.9524	1
2	0.9707	0.9612	0.9518	0.9426	0.9335	0.9246	0.9157	0.9070	2
3	0.9563	0.9423	0.9286	0.9151	0.9019	0.8890	0.8763	0.8638	3
4	0.9422	0.9238	0.9060	0.8885	0.8714	0.8548	0.8386	0.8227	4
5	0.9283	0.9057	0.8839	0.8626	0.8420	0.8219	0.8025	0.7835	5
6	0.9145	0.8880	0.8623	0.8375	0.8135	0.7903	0.7679	0.7462	6
7	0.9010	0.8706	0.8413	0.8131	0.7860	0.7599	0.7348	0.7107	7
8	0.8877	0.8535	0.8207	0.7894	0.7594	0.7307	0.7032	0.6768	8
9	0.8746	0.8368	0.8007	0.7664	0.7337	0.7026	0.6729	0.6446	9
10	0.8617	0.8203	0.7812	0.7441	0.7089	0.6756	0.6439	0.6139	10
11	0.8489	0.8043	0.7621	0.7224	0.6849	0.6496	0.6162	0.5847	11
12	0.8364	0.7885	0.7436	0.7014	0.6618	0.6246	0.5897	0.5568	12
13	0.8240	0.7730	0.7254	0.6810	0.6394	0.6006	0.5643	0.5303	13
14	0.8118	0.7579	0.7077	0.6611	0.6178	0.5775	0.5400	0.5051	14
15	0.7999	0.7430	0.6905	0.6419	0.5969	0.5553	0.5167	0.4810	15
16	0.7880	0.7284	0.6736	0.6232	0.5767	0.5339	0.4945	0.4581	16
17	0.7764	0.7142	0.6572	0.6050	0.5572	0.5134	0.4732	0.4363	17
18	0.7649	0.7002	0.6412	0.5874	0.5384	0.4936	0.4528	0.4155	18
19	0.7536	0.6864	0.6255	0.5703	0.5202	0.4746	0.4333	0.3957	19
20	0.7425	0.6730	0.6103	0.5537	0.5026	0.4564	0.4146	0.3769	20
21	0.7315	0.6598	0.5954	0.5375	0.4856	0.4388	0.3968	0.3589	21
22	0.7207	0.6468	0.5809	0.5219	0.4692	0.4220	0.3797	0.3418	22
23	0.7100	0.6342	0.5667	0.5067	0.4533	0.4057	0.3634	0.3256	23
24	0.6995	0.6217	0.5529	0.4919	0.4380	0.3901	0.3477	0.3101	24
25	0.6892	0.6095	0.5394	0.4776	0.4231	0.3751	0.3327	0.2953	25
26	0.6790	0.5976	0.5262	0.4637	0.4088	0.3607	0.3184	0.2812	26
27	0.6690	0.5859	0.5134	0.4502	0.3950	0.3468	0.3047	0.2678	27
28	0.6591	0.5744	0.5009	0.4371	0.3817	0.3335	0.2916	0.2551	28
29	0.6494	0.5631	0.4887	0.4243	0.3687	0.3207	0.2790	0.2429	29
30	0.6398	0.5521	0.4767	0.4120	0.3563	0.3083	0.2670	0.2314	30
31	0.6303	0.5412	0.4651	0.4000	0.3442	0.2965	0.2555	0.2204	31
32	0.6210	0.5306	0.4538	0.3883	0.3326	0.2851	0.2445	0.2099	32
33	0.6118	0.5202	0.4427	0.3770	0.3213	0.2741	0.2340	0.1999	33
34	0.6028	0.5100	0.4319	0.3660	0.3105	0.2636	0.2239	0.1904	34
35	0.5939	0.5000	0.4214	0.3554	0.3000	0.2534	0.2143	0.1813	35
36	0.5851	0.4902	0.4111	0.3450	0.2898	0.2437	0.2050	0.1727	36
37	0.5764	0.4806	0.4011	0.3350	0.2800	0.2343	0.1962	0.1644	37
38	0.5679	0.4712	0.3913	0.3252	0.2706	0.2253	0.1878	0.1566	38
39	0.5595	0.4619	0.3817	0.3158	0.2614	0.2166	0.1797	0.1491	39
40	0.5513	0.4529	0.3724	0.3066	0.2526	0.2083	0.1719	0.1420	40
41	0.5431	0.4440	0.3633	0.2976	0.2440	0.2003	0.1645	0.1353	41
42	0.5351	0.4353	0.3545	0.2890	0.2358	0.1926	0.1574	0.1288	42
43	0.5272	0.4268	0.3458	0.2805	0.2278	0.1852	0.1507	0.1227	43
44	0.5194	0.4184	0.3374	0.2724	0.2201	0.1780	0.1442	0.1169	44

Table 37: *continued*

	Factor to discount value of multiplier for a period of deferment							
Term	1.5%	2.0%	2.5%	3.0%	3.5%	4.0%	4.5%	5.0%	Term
45	0.5117	0.4102	0.3292	0.2644	0.2127	0.1712	0.1380	0.1113	45
46	0.5042	0.4022	0.3211	0.2567	0.2055	0.1646	0.1320	0.1060	46
47	0.4967	0.3943	0.3133	0.2493	0.1985	0.1583	0.1263	0.1009	47
48	0.4894	0.3865	0.3057	0.2420	0.1918	0.1522	0.1209	0.0961	48
49	0.4821	0.3790	0.2982	0.2350	0.1853	0.1463	0.1157	0.0916	49
50	0.4750	0.3715	0.2909	0.2281	0.1791	0.1407	0.1107	0.0872	50
51	0.4680	0.3642	0.2838	0.2215	0.1730	0.1353	0.1059	0.0831	51
52	0.4611	0.3571	0.2769	0.2150	0.1671	0.1301	0.1014	0.0791	52
53	0.4543	0.3501	0.2702	0.2088	0.1615	0.1251	0,0970	0.0753	53
54	0.4475	0.3432	0.2636	0.2027	0.1560	0.1203	0.0928	0.0717	54
55	0.4409	0.3365	0.2572	0.1968	0.1508	0.1157	0.0888	0.0683	55
56	0.4344	0.3299	0.2509	0.1910	0.1457	0.1112	0.0850	0.0651	56
57	0.4280	0.3234	0.2448	0.1855	0.1407	0.1069	0.0814	0.0620	57
58	0.4217	0.3171	0.2388	0.1801	0.1360	0.1028	0.0778	0.0590	58
59	0.4154	0.3109	0.2330	0.1748	0.1314	0.0989	0.0745	0.0562	59
60	0.4093	0.3048	0.2273	0.1697	0.1269	0.0951	0.0713	0.0535	60
61	0.4032	0.2988	0.2217	0.1648	0.1226	0.0914	0.0682	0.0510	61
62	0.3973	0.2929	0.2163	0.1600	0.1185	0.0879	0.0653	0.0486	62
63	0.3914	0.2872	0.2111	0.1553	0.1145	0.0845	0.0625	0.0462	63
64	0.3856	0.2816	0.2059	0.1508	0.1106	0.0813	0.0598	0.0440	64
65	0.3799	0.2761	0.2009	0.1464	0.1069	0.0781	0.0572	0.0419	65
66	0.3743	0.2706	0.1960	0.1421	0.1033	0.0751	0.0547	0.0399	66
67	0.3688	0.2653	0.1912	0.1380	0.0998	0.0722	0.0524	0.0380	67
68	0.3633	0.2601	0.1865	0.1340	0.0964	0.0695	0.0501	0.0362	68
69	0.3580	0.2550	0.1820	0.1301	0.0931	0.0668	0.0480	0.0345	69
70	0.3527	0.2500	0.1776	0.1263	0.0900	0.0642	0.0459	0.0329	70
71	0.3475	0.2451	0.1732	0.1226	0.0869	0.0617	0.0439	0.0313	71
72	0.3423	0.2403	0.1690	0.1190	0.0840	0.0594	0.0420	0.0298	72
73	0.3373	0.2356	0.1649	0.1156	0.0812	0.0571	0.0402	0.0284	73
74	0.3323	0.2310	0.1609	0.1122	0.0784	0.0549	0.0385	0.0270	74
75	0.3274	0.2265	0.1569	0.1089	0.0758	0.0528	0.0368	0.0258	75
76	0.3225	0.2220	0.1531	0.1058	0.0732	0.0508	0.0353	0.0245	76
77	0.3178	0.2177	0.1494	0.1027	0.0707	0.0488	0.0337	0.0234	77
78	0.3131	0.2134	0.1457	0.0997	0.0683	0.0469	0.0323	0.0222	78
79	0.3084	0.2092	0.1422	0.0968	0.0660	0.0451	0.0309	0.0212	79
80	0.3039	0.2051	0.1387	0.0940	0.0638	0.0434	0.0296	0.0202	80

Table 38: Multipliers for pecuniary loss for term certain

	Multiplier for regular frequent payments for a term certain at rate of return of								
Term	1.5%	2.0%	2.5%	3.0%	3.5%	4.0%	4.5%	5.0%	Term
1	0.99	0.99	0.99	0.99	0.98	0.98	0.98	0.98	1
2	1.97	1.96	1.95	1.94	1.93	1.92	1.91	1.91	2
3	2.93	2.91	2.89	2.87	2.85	2.83	2.81	2.79	3
4	3.88	3.85	3.81	3.77	3.74	3.70	3.67	3.63	4
5	4.82	4.76	4.70	4.65	4.59	4.54	4.49	4.44	5
6	5.74	5.66	5.58	5.50	5.42	5.35	5.27	5.20	6
7	6.65	6.54	6.43	6.32	6.22	6.12	6.02	5.93	7
8	7.54	7.40	7.26	7.12	6.99	6.87	6.74	6.62	8
9	8.42	8.24	8.07	7.90	7.74	7.58	7.43	7.28	9
10	9.29	9.07	8.86	8.66	8.46	8.27	8.09	7.91	10
11	10.15	9.88	9.63	9.39	9.16	8.93	8.72	8.51	11
12	10.99	10.68	10.39	10.10	9.83	9.57	9.32	9.08	12
13	11.82	11.46	11.12	10.79	10.48	10.18	9.90	9.63	13
14	12.64	12.23	11.84	11.46	11.11	10.77	10.45	10.14	14
15	13.44	12.98	12.54	12.12	11.72	11.34	10.98	10.64	15
16	14.24	13.71	13.22	12.75	12.30	11.88	11.48	11.11	16
17	15.02	14.43	13.88	13.36	12.87	12.41	11.97	11.55	17
18	15.79	15.14	14.53	13.96	13.42	12.91	12.43	11.98	18
19	16.55	15.83	15.17	14.54	13.95	13.39	12.87	12.38	19
20	17.30	16.51	15.78	15.10	14.46	13.86	13.30	12.77	20
21	18.03	17.18	16.39	15.65	14.95	14.31	13.70	13.14	21
22	18.76	17.83	16.97	16.17	15.43	14.74	14.09	13.49	22
23	19.48	18.47	17.55	16.69	15.89	15.15	14.46	13.82	23
24	20.18	19.10	18.11	17.19	16.34	15.55	14.82	14.14	24
25	20.87	19.72	18.65	17.67	16.77	15.93	15.16	14.44	25
26	21.56	20.32	19.19	18.14	17.18	16.30	15.48	14.73	26
27	22.23	20.91	19.71	18.60	17.59	16.65	15.80	15.01	27
28	22.90	21.49	20.21	19.04	17.97	16.99	16.09	15.27	28
29	23.55	22.06	20.71	19.47	18.35	17.32	16.38	15.52	29
30	24.20	22.62	21.19	19.89	18.71	17.64	16.65	15.75	30
31	24.83	23.17	21.66	20.30	19.06	17.94	16.91	15.98	31
32	25.46	23.70	22.12	20.69	19.40	18.23	17.16	16.19	32
33	26.07	24.23	22.57	21.08	19.73	18.51	17.40	16.40	33
34	26.68	24.74	23.01	21.45	20.04	18.78	17.63	16.59	34
35	27.28	25.25	23.43	21.81	20.35	19.04	17.85	16.78	35
36	27.87	25.74	23.85	22.16	20.64	19.28	18.06	16.96	36
37	28.45	26.23	24.26	22.50	20.93	19.52	18.26	17.13	37
38	29.02	26.70	24.65	22.83	21.20	19.75	18.45	17.29	38
39	29.58	27.17	25.04	23.15	21.47	19.97	18.64	17.44	39
40	30.14	27.63	25.42	23.46	21.73	20.19	18.81	17.58	40
41	30.69	28.08	25.78	23.76	21.97	20.39	18.98	17.72	41
42	31.23	28.52	26.14	24.06	22.21	20.59	19.14	17.86	42
43	31.76	28.95	26.49	24.34	22.45	20.78	19.30	17.98	43
44	32.28	29.37	26.83	24.62	22.67	20.96	19.44	18.10	44

Table 38: *continued*

Term	Multiplier for regular frequent payments for a term certain at rate of return of 1.5%	2.0%	2.5%	3.0%	3.5%	4.0%	4.5%	5.0%	Term
45	32.80	29.78	27.17	24.88	22.89	21.13	19.58	18.21	45
46	33.30	30.19	27.49	25.15	23.10	21.30	19.72	18.32	46
47	33.80	30.59	27.81	25.40	23.30	21.46	19.85	18.43	47
48	34.30	30.98	28.12	25.64	23.49	21.62	19.97	18.53	48
49	34.78	31.36	28.42	25.88	23.68	21.77	20.09	18.62	49
50	35.26	31.74	28.72	26.11	23.86	21.91	20.20	18.71	50
51	35.73	32.10	29.00	26.34	24.04	22.05	20.31	18.79	51
52	36.20	32.47	29.28	26.56	24.21	22.18	20.42	18.87	52
53	36.66	32.82	29.56	26.77	24.37	22.31	20.51	18.95	53
54	37.11	33.17	29.82	26.97	24.53	22.43	20.61	19.03	54
55	37.55	33.51	30.08	27.17	24.69	22.55	20.70	19.10	55
56	37.99	33.84	30.34	27.37	24.83	22.66	20.79	19.16	56
57	38.42	34.17	30.59	27.56	24.98	22.77	20.87	19.23	57
58	38.84	34.49	30.83	27.74	25.12	22.88	20.95	19.29	58
59	39.26	34.80	31.06	27.92	25.25	22.98	21.03	19.34	59
60	39.67	35.11	31.29	28.09	25.38	23.07	21.10	19.40	60
61	40.08	35.41	31.52	28.26	25.50	23.17	21.17	19.45	61
62	40.48	35.70	31.74	28.42	25.62	23.26	21.24	19.50	62
63	40.88	36.00	31.95	28.58	25.74	23.34	21.30	19.55	63
64	41.26	36.28	32.16	28.73	25.85	23.42	21.36	19.59	64
65	41.65	36.56	32.36	28.88	25.96	23.50	21.42	19.64	65
66	42.02	36.83	32.56	29.02	26.07	23.58	21.47	19.68	66
67	42.40	37.10	32.75	29.16	26.17	23.65	21.53	19.72	67
68	42.76	37.36	32.94	29.30	26.27	23.73	21.58	19.75	68
69	43.12	37.62	33.13	29.43	26.36	23.79	21.63	19.79	69
70	43.48	37.87	33.31	29.56	26.45	23.86	21.68	19.82	70
71	43.83	38.12	33.48	29.68	26.54	23.92	21.72	19.85	71
72	44.17	38.36	33.65	29.80	26.63	23.98	21.76	19.88	72
73	44.51	38.60	33.82	29.92	26.71	24.04	21.80	19.91	73
74	44.85	38.83	33.98	30.03	26.79	24.10	21.84	19.94	74
75	45.18	39.06	34.14	30.15	26.87	24.15	21.88	19.97	75
76	45.50	39.29	34.30	30.25	26.94	24.20	21.92	19.99	76
77	45.82	39.51	34.45	30.36	27.01	24.25	21.95	20.02	77
78	46.14	39.72	34.60	30.46	27.08	24.30	21.99	20.04	78
79	46.45	39.93	34.74	30.56	27.15	24.35	22.02	20.06	79
80	46.75	40.14	34.88	30.65	27.21	24.39	22.05	20.08	80

Acturial formulae and basis

The functions tabulated are:

Tables 1, 2, 19, and 20	$\bar{a}_x$
Tables 3, 4, 21 and 22	$\bar{a}_{x:\overline{55-x}\rceil}$
Tables 5, 6, 23 and 24	$\bar{a}_{x:\overline{60-x}\rceil}$
Tables 7, 8, 25 and 26	$\bar{a}_{x:\overline{65-x}\rceil}$
Tables 9, 10, 27 and 28	$\bar{a}_{x:\overline{70-x}\rceil}$
Tables 11, 12 , 29 and 30	$_{(55-x)|}\bar{a}_{55}$
Tables 13, 14, 31 and 32	$_{(60-x)|}\bar{a}_{60}$
Tables 15, 16, 33 and 34	$_{(65-x)|}\bar{a}_{65}$
Tables 17, 18, 35 and 36	$_{(70-x)|}\bar{a}_{70}$
Table 37:	$1/(1+i)^n$
Tables 38:	$\bar{a}_{\overline{n}\rceil}$

- Mortality: English Life Tables No. 15 (Tables 1 to 18)
- Mortality assumptions for 1998-based official population projections for England and Wales (Tables 19 to 36)
- Loadings: None
- Rate of return: As stated in the Tables

APPENDIX IA

NIL DISCOUNT OGDEN TABLES

Nil discount columns are set out below under their respective Ogden Table number.

Age*	Table 11	Table 12	Table 13	Table 14	Table 15	Table 16	Table 17	Table 18
18	61.40	66.08	45.42	46.02	40.92	41.36	15.98	20.06
19	60.42	65.08	44.45	45.03	39.95	40.37	15.98	20.05
20	59.45	64.08	43.47	44.04	38.97	39.37	15.98	20.04
21	58.48	63.08	42.51	43.04	38.00	38.38	15.98	20.04
22	57.51	62.08	41.54	42.05	37.03	37.39	15.97	20.03
23	56.54	61.08	40.57	41.06	36.06	36.39	15.97	20.02
24	55.56	60.08	39.59	40.07	35.08	35.40	15.97	20.01
25	54.58	59.08	38.62	39.07	34.11	34.41	15.96	20.00
26	53.61	58.08	37.65	38.08	33.14	33.42	15.96	19.99
27	52.63	57.08	36.68	37.10	32.17	32.43	15.95	19.98
28	51.65	56.08	35.71	36.11	31.19	31.44	15.95	19.97
29	50.67	55.08	34.74	35.12	30.22	30.45	15.94	19.96
30	49.69	54.08	33.76	34.13	29.24	29.46	15.93	19.95
31	48.70	53.08	32.79	33.14	28.27	28.47	15.92	19.94
32	47.72	52.08	31.81	32.15	27.29	27.49	15.91	19.92
33	46.73	51.07	30.84	31.16	26.31	26.50	15.89	19.91
34	45.74	50.07	29.86	30.18	25.34	25.51	15.88	19.89
35	44.75	49.07	28.89	29.19	29.36	24.52	15.87	19.88
36	43.76	48.06	27.91	28.20	23.38	23.54	15.85	19.86
37	42.76	47.06	26.93	27.22	22.40	22.55	15.83	19.84
38	41.77	46.05	25.96	26.24	21.43	21.57	15.81	19.82
39	40.77	45.05	24.98	25.25	20.45	20.58	15.79	19.80
40	39.78	44.05	24.01	24.27	19.47	19.60	15.77	19.77
41	38.79	43.05	23.04	23.30	18.50	18.62	15.75	19.75
42	37.81	42.05	22.07	22.32	17.53	17.64	15.73	19.73
43	36.82	41.05	21.11	21.34	16.56	16.66	15.71	19.71
44	35.83	40.06	20.14	20.37	15.59	15.68	15.69	19.69
45	34.84	39.06	19.17	19.39	14.61	14.70	15.67	19.67
46	33.85	38.07	18.20	18.42	13.64	13.73	15.65	19.64
47	32.85	37.07	17.23	17.45	12.67	12.75	15.62	19.62
48	31.86	36.08	16.26	16.48	11.69	11.77	15.60	19.60
49	30.87	35.09	15.30	15.51	10.72	10.80	15.58	19.58
50	29.89	34.11	14.34	14.54	9.75	9.82	15.56	19.56
51	28.92	33.12	13.38	13.58	8.78	8.85	15.54	19.55
52	27.96	32.15	12.43	12.61	7.81	7.87	15.54	19.54
53	27.00	31.20	11.47	11.65	6.85	6.90	15.53	19.55
54	26.05	30.27	10.52	10.69	5.88	5.92	15.53	19.58
55	25.12	29.37	9.58	9.73	4.91	4.94	15.54	19.63
56	24.19	28.46	8.63	8.77	3.94	3.96	15.56	19.69
57	23.28	27.56	7.69	7.81	2.96	2.98	15.59	19.75
58	22.38	26.66	6.74	6.85	1.98	1.99	15.64	19.81
59	21.49	25.74	5.80	5.88	1.00	1.00	15.70	19.86
60	20.61	24.81	4.85	4.91	0.00	0.00	15.77	19.90
61	19.74	23.86	3.89	3.94			15.85	19.92
62	18.88	22.90	2.94	2.96			15.95	19.93
63	18.03	21.92	1.97	1.98			16.06	19.94
64	17.19	20.95	0.99	1.00			16.20	19.95
65	16.36	19.98	0.00	0.00			16.36	19.98

*We have confined these extracted figures to ages between 18 and 65, being ages at which a deceased could have continued to provide a dependency.

APPENDIX I

MULTIPLIER APPROPRIATE TO FIXED PERIOD

Years	Multiplier calculated with allowance for rate of interest of:								Years
	1.5%	2%	2.5%	3%	3.5%	4%	4.5%	5%	
1	1.0	1.0	1.0	1.0	1.0	1.0	1.0	1.0	1
2	2.0	2.0	2.0	1.9	1.9	1.9	1.9	1.9	2
3	2.9	2.9	2.9	2.9	2.9	2.8	2.8	2.8	3
4	3.9	3.8	3.8	3.8	3.7	3.7	3.7	3.6	4
5	4.8	4.8	4.7	4.6	4.6	4.5	4.5	4.4	5
6	5.7	5.7	5.6	5.5	5.4	5.3	5.3	5.2	6
7	6.6	6.5	6.4	6.3	6.2	6.1	6.0	5.9	7
8	7.5	7.4	7.3	7.1	7.0	6.9	6.7	6.6	8
9	8.4	8.2	8.1	7.9	7.7	7.4	7.6	7.3	9
10	9.3	9.1	8.9	8.7	8.5	8.3	8.1	7.9	10
11	10.1	9.9	9.6	9.4	9.2	8.9	8.7	8.5	11
12	11.0	10.7	10.4	10.1	9.8	9.6	9.3	9.1	12
13	11.8	11.5	11.1	10.8	10.5	10.2	9.9	9.6	13
14	12.6	12.2	11.8	11.5	11.1	10.8	10.5	10.1	14
15	13.4	13.0	12.5	12.1	11.7	11.3	11.0	10.6	15
16	14.2	13.7	13.2	12.7	12.3	11.9	11.5	11.1	16
17	15.0	14.4	13.9	13.4	12.9	12.4	12.0	11.6	17
18	15.8	15.1	14.5	14.0	13.4	12.9	12.4	12.0	18
19	16.5	15.8	15.2	14.5	13.9	13.4	12.9	12.4	19
20	17.3	16.5	15.8	15.1	14.5	13.9	13.3	12.8	20
21	18.0	17.2	16.4	15.6	15.0	14.3	13.7	13.1	21
22	18.8	17.8	17.0	16.2	15.4	14.7	14.1	13.5	22
23	19.5	18.5	17.5	16.7	15.9	15.2	14.5	13.8	23
24	20.2	19.1	18.1	17.2	16.3	15.5	14.8	14.1	24
25	20.9	19.7	18.7	17.7	16.8	15.9	15.2	14.4	25
26	21.6	20.3	19.2	18.1	17.2	16.3	15.5	14.7	26
27	22.2	20.9	19.7	18.6	17.6	16.7	15.8	15.0	27
28	22.9	21.5	20.2	19.0	18.0	17.0	16.1	15.3	28
29	23.6	22.1	20.7	19.5	18.3	17.3	16.4	15.5	29
30	24.2	22.6	21.2	19.9	18.7	17.6	16.7	15.8	30
31	24.8	23.2	21.7	20.3	19.1	17.9	16.9	16.0	31
32	25.5	23.7	22.1	20.7	19.4	18.2	17.2	16.2	32
33	26.1	24.2	22.6	21.1	19.7	18.5	17.4	16.4	33
34	26.7	24.7	23.0	21.4	20.0	18.8	17.6	16.6	34
35	27.3	25.2	23.4	21.8	20.3	19.0	17.9	16.8	35
36	27.9	25.7	23.8	22.2	20.6	19.3	18.1	17.0	36
37	28.4	26.2	24.3	22.5	20.9	19.5	18.3	17.1	37
38	29.0	26.7	24.7	22.8	21.2	19.8	18.5	17.3	38

APPENDIX I *continued*

Years	Multiplier calculated with allowance for rate of interest of								Years
	1.5%	2%	2.5%	3%	3.5%	4%	4.5%	5%	
39	29.6	27.2	25.0	23.1	21.5	20.0	18.6	17.4	39
40	30.1	27.6	25.4	23.5	21.7	20.2	18.8	17.6	40
41	30.7	28.1	25.8	23.8	22.0	20.4	19.0	17.7	41
42	31.2	28.5	26.1	24.1	22.2	20.6	19.1	17.9	42
43	31.8	28.9	26.5	24.3	22.4	20.8	19.3	18.0	43
44	32.3	29.4	26.8	24.6	22.7	21.0	19.4	18.1	44
45	32.8	29.8	27.2	24.9	22.9	21.1	19.6	18.2	45
46	33.3	30.2	27.5	25.1	23.1	21.3	19.7	18.3	46
47	33.8	30.6	27.8	25.4	23.3	21.5	19.8	18.4	47
48	34.3	31.0	28.1	25.6	23.5	21.6	20.0	18.5	48
49	34.8	31.4	28.4	25.9	23.7	21.8	20.1	18.6	49
50	35.3	31.7	28.7	26.1	23.9	21.9	20.2	18.7	50

NOTE: This Table should be used in conjunction with the Actuarial Tables. It has been kindly prepared by Mr J. Prevett, O.B.E., F.I.A.

APPENDIX II
GROSS RETURN ON INDEX-LINKED GOVERNMENT SECURITIES

Date	Gross Return (%)	After Deduction of Tax at 10%	After Deduction of Tax at 15%	After Deduction of Tax at 25%	After Deduction of Tax at 40%
1999					
Jan.	1.88	1.69	1.60	1.41	1.13
Feb.	1.88	1.69	1.60	1.41	1.13
Mar.	1.76	1.59	1.50	1.32	1.06
Apr.	1.85	1.67	1.57	1.39	1.11
May	1.86	1.67	1.58	1.40	1.12
June	1.90	1.71	1.62	1.43	1.14
July	1.95	1.76	1.66	1.46	1.17
Aug.	2.15	1.94	1.83	1.61	1.29
Sept.	2.13	1.92	1.81	1.60	1.28
Oct.	2.01	1.81	1.71	1.51	1.21
Nov.	1.84	1.66	1.56	1.38	1.10
Dec.	1.80	1.62	1.53	1.35	1.08
1998					
Jan.	3.06	2.75	2.60	2.30	1.84
Feb.	2.98	2.68	2.53	2.24	1.79
Mar.	2.85	2.57	2.42	2.14	1.71
Apr.	2.82	2.54	2.40	2.12	1.69
May	2.68.	2.41	2.28	2.01	1.61
June	2.65	2.39	2.25	1.99	1.59
July	2.57	2.31	2.18	1.93	1.54
Aug.	2.40	2.16	2.04	1.80	1.44
Sept.	2.47	2.22	2.10	1.85	1.48
Oct.	2.43	2.19	2.07	1.82	1.46
Nov.	2.22	2.00	1.89	1.67	1.33
Dec.	1.94	1.75	1.65	1.46	1.16
1997					
Jan.	3.55	3.20	3.02	2.66	2.13
Feb.	3.43	3.09	2.92	2.57	2.06
Mar.	3.60	3.24	3.06	2.70	2.16
Apr.	3.58	3.22	3.04	2.68	2.15
May	3.68	3.31	3.13-.	2.76	2.21
June	3.63	3.27	3.09	2.72	2.18
July	3.53	3.18	3.00	2.65	2.12
Aug.	3.56	3.20	3.00	2.67	2.14
Sept.	3.32	2.99	2.82	2.49	1.99
Oct.	3.10	2.79	2.64	2.32	1.86
Nov.	3.08	2.77	2.62	2.31	1.85
Dec.	3.02	2.72	2.87	2.26	1.81

APPENDIX II *continued*

Date	Gross Return (%)	After Deduction of Tax at 10%	After Deduction of Tax at 15%	After Deduction of Tax at 25%	After Deduction of Tax at 40%
1996					
Jan.	3.58	3.22	3.04	2.69	2.15
Feb.	3.77	3.39	3.20	2.83	2.26
Mar.	3.77	3.39	3.20	2.83	2.26
Apr.	3.71	3.34	3.15	2.78	2.23
May	3.87	3.48	3.29	2.90	2.32
June	3.82	3.44	3.25	2.87	2.29
July	3.79	3.41	3.22	2.84	2.27
Aug.	3.72	3.35	3.16	2.79	2.23
Sept.	3.62	3.26	3.08	2.72	2.17
Oct.	3.60	3.24	3.06	2.70	2.16
Nov.	3.46	3.11	2.94	2.60	2.08
Dec.	3.53	3.18	3.00	2.65	2.12
1995					
Jan.	3.89	3.50	3.31	2.92	2.33
Feb.	3.89	3.50	3.31	2.92	2.33
Mar.	3.87	3.48	3.29	2.90	2.32
Apr.	3.79	3.41	3.22	2.84	2.27
May	3.56	3.20	3.00	2.67	2.14
June	3.78	3.40	3.21	2.84	2.27
July	3.65	3.29	3.10	2.74	2.19
Aug.	3.56	3.20	3.00	2.67	2.14
Sept.	3.69	3.32	3.14	2.77	2.21
Oct.	3.68	3.31	3.13	2.76	2.21
Nov.	3.53	3.18	3.00	2.65	2.12
Dec.	3.52	3.17	2.99	2.64	2.11
1994					
Jan.	2.93	2.64	2.49	2.20	1.76
Feb.	3.26	2.93	2.77	2.45	1.96
Mar.	3.41	3.07	2.90	2.56	2.05
Apr.	3.50	3.15	2.98	2.63	2.10
May	3.90	3.51	3.32	2.93	2.34
June	3.95	3.56	3.36	2.96	2.37
July	3.98	3.58	3.38	2.99	2.39
Aug.	3.76	3.38	3.20	2.82	2.26
Sept.	3.86	3.47	3.28	2.90	2.32
Oct.	3.89	3.50	3.31	2.92	2.33
Nov.	3.86	3.47	3.28	2.90	2.32
Dec.	3.88	3.49	3.30	2.91	2.33

APPENDIX II *continued*

Date	Gross Return (%)	After Deduction of Tax at 10%	After Deduction of Tax at 15%	After Deduction of Tax at 25%	After Deduction of Tax at 40%
1993					
Jan.	3.71	3.34	3.15	2.78	2.23
Feb.	3.47	3.12	2.95	2.60	2.08
Mar.	3.41	3.07	2.90	2.56	2.05
Apr.	3.57	3.21	3.03	2.68	2.14
May	3.56	3.20	3.00	2.67	2.14
June	3.52	3.17	2.99	2.64	2.11
July	3.38	3.04	2.87	2.54	2.03
Aug.	3.24	2.92	2.75	2.43	1.94
Sept.	3.18	2.86	2.70	2.39	1.91
Oct.	3.14	2.83	2.67	2.36	1.88
Nov.	3.08	2.77	2.62	2.31	1.85
Dec.	2.86	2.57	2.43	2.15	1.72
1992					
Jan.	4.29	3.86	3.65	3.22	2.57
Feb.	4.29	3.86	3.65	3.22	2.57
Mar.	4.57	4.11	3.88	3.43	2.74
Apr.	4.49	4.04	3.82	3.37	2.69
May	4.31	3.88	3.66	3.23	2.59
June	4.35	3.92	3.70	3.26	2.61
July	4.58	4.12	3.89	3.44	2.75
Aug.	4.72	4.25	4.01	3.54	2.83
Sept.	4.11	3.70	3.49	3.08	2.47
Oct.	3.67	3.30	3.12	2.75	2.20
Nov.	3.88	3.49	3.30	2.91	2.33
Dec.	3.83	3.45	3.26	2.87	2.30
1991					
Jan.	4.14	3.73	3.52	3.11	2.48
Feb.	4.16	3.74	3.54	3.12	2.50
Mar.	4.14	3.73	3.52	3.11	2.48
Apr.	4.14	3.73	3.52	3.11	2.48
May	4.22	3.80	3.59	3.17	2.53
June	4.36	3.92	3.71	3.27	2.62
July	4.39	3.95	3.73	3.29	2.63
Aug.	4.31	3.88	3.66	3.23	2.59
Sept.	4.22	3.80	3.59	3.17	2.53
Oct.	4.23	3.81	3.60	3.17	2.54
Nov.	4.30	3.87	3.66	3.23	2.58
Dec.	4.45	4.01	3.78	3.34	2.67

APPENDIX II *continued*

Date	Gross Return (%)	After Deduction of Tax at 10%	After Deduction of Tax at 15%	After Deduction of Tax at 25%	After Deduction of Tax at 40%
1990					
June	4.21	3.79	3.58	3.16	2.53
July	4.30	3.87	3.66	3.23	2.58
Aug.	4.32	3.89	3.67	3.24	2.59
Sept.	4.35	3.92	3.70	3.26	2.61
Oct.	4.34	3.91	3.69	3.26	2.60
Nov.	4.17	3.75	3.54	3.13	2.50
Dec.	4.18	3.76	3.55	3.14	2.51

Appendix G

The Motor Insurers' Bureau Agreements

Contents

* * *

1 Compensation of victims of uninsured drivers

THIS AGREEMENT is made the thirteenth day of August 1999 between the Secretary of State for the Environment, Transport and the Regions (hereinafter referred to as "the Secretary of State") and the MOTOR INSURERS' BUREAU, whose registered office is at 152 Silbury Boulevard, Milton Keynes MK9 1NB (hereinafter referred to as "MIB") and is supplemental to an Agreement (hereinafter called "the Principal Agreement") made the 31st Day of December 1945 between the Minister of War Transport and the insurers transacting compulsory motor insurance business in Great Britain by or on behalf of whom the said Agreement was signed and in pursuance of paragraph 1 of which MIB was incorporated.

IT IS HEREBY AGREED AS FOLLOWS

INTERPRETATION

1. General definitions

In this Agreement, unless the context otherwise requires, the following expressions have the following meanings—

"1988 Act" means the Road Traffic Act 1988;

"1988 Agreement" means the Agreement made on 21 December 1988 between the Secretary of State for Transport and MIB;

"bank holiday" means a day which is, or is to be observed as, a bank holiday under the Banking and Financial Dealings Act 1971;

"claimant" means a person who has commenced or who proposes to commence relevant proceedings and has made an application under this Agreement in respect thereof;

"contract of insurance" means a policy of insurance or a security covering a relevant liability;

"insurer" includes the giver of a security;

"MIB's obligation" means the obligation contained in clause 5;

"property" means any property whether real, heritable or personal;

"relevant liability" means a liability in respect of which a contract of insurance must be in force to comply with Part VI of the 1988 Act;

"relevant proceedings" means proceedings in respect of a relevant liability (and "commencement", in relation to such proceedings means, in England and Wales, the date on which a Claim Form or other originating process is issued by a Court or, in Scotland, the date on which the originating process is served on the Defender);

"relevant sum" means a sum payable or remaining payable under an unsatisfied judgment, including—

(a) an amount payable or remaining payable in respect of interest on that sum, and

(b) either the whole of the costs (whether taxed or not) awarded by the Court as part of that judgment or, where the judgment includes an award in respect of a liability which is not a relevant liability, such proportion of those costs as the relevant liability bears to the total sum awarded under the judgment:

"specified excess" means £300 or such other sum as may from time to time be agreed in writing between the Secretary of State and MIB;

"unsatisfied judgment" means a judgment or order (by whatever name called) in respect of a relevant liability which has not been satisfied in full within seven days from the date upon which the claimant became entitled to enforce it.

2 Meaning of references

(1) Save as otherwise herein provided, the Interpretation Act 1978 shall apply for the interpretation of this Agreement as it applies for the interpretation of an Act of Parliament.

(2) Where, under this Agreement, something is required to be done—

(a) within a specified period after or from the happening of a particular event, the period begins on the day after the happening of that event;

(b) within or not less than a specified period before a particular event, the period ends on the day immediately before the happening of that event.

(3) Where, apart from this paragraph, the period in question, being a period of seven days or less, would include a Saturday, Sunday or bank holiday or Christmas Day or Good Friday, that day shall be excluded.

(4) Save where expressly otherwise provided, a reference in this Agreement to a numbered clause is a reference to the clause bearing that number in this Agreement and a reference to a numbered paragraph is a reference to a paragraph bearing that number in the clause in which the reference occurs.

(5) In this Agreement—

(a) a reference (however framed) to the doing of any act or thing by or the happening of any event in relation to the claimant includes a reference to the doing of that act or thing by or the happening of that event in relation to a Solicitor or other person acting on his behalf, and

(b) a requirement to give notice to, or to serve documents upon, MIB or an insurer mentioned in clause 9(1)(a) shall be satisfied by the giving of the notice to, or the service of the documents upon, a Solicitor acting on its behalf in the manner provided for.

3. Claimants not of full age or capacity

Where, under and in accordance with this Agreement—

(a) any act or thing is done to or by a Solicitor or other person acting on behalf of a claimant,

(b) any decision is made by or in respect of a Solicitor or other person acting on behalf of a claimant, or

(c) any sum is paid to a Solicitor or other person acting on behalf of a claimant,

then, whatever may be the age or other circumstances affecting the capacity of the claimant, that act, thing, decision or sum shall be treated as if it had been done to or by, or made in respect of or paid to a claimant of full age and capacity.

PRINCIPAL TERMS

4. Duration of Agreement

(1) This Agreement shall come into force on 1st October 1999 in relation to accidents occurring on or after that date and, save as provided by clause 23, the 1988 Agreements shall cease and determine immediately before that date.

(2) This Agreement may be determined by the Secretary of State or by MIB giving to the other not less than twelve months' notice in writing but without prejudice to its continued operation in respect of accidents occurring before the date of termination.

5. MIB's obligation to satisfy compensation claims

(1) Subject to clauses 6 to 17, if a claimant has obtained against any person in a Court in Great Britain a judgment which is an unsatisfied judgment then MIB will pay the relevant sum to, or to the satisfaction of, the claimant or will cause the same to be so paid.

(2) Paragraph (1) applies whether or not the person liable to satisfy the judgment is in fact covered by a contract of insurance and whatever may be the cause of his failure to satisfy the judgment.

EXCEPTIONS TO AGREEMENT

6. (1) Clause 5 does not apply in the case of an application made in respect of a claim of any of the following descriptions (and, where part only of a claim satisfies such a description, clause 5 does not apply to that part)

(a) a claim arising out of a relevant liability incurred by the user of a vehicle owned by or in the possession of the Crown, unless—

   (i) responsibility for the existence of a contract of insurance under Part VI of the 1988 Act in relation to that vehicle had been undertaken by some other person (whether or not the person liable was in fact covered by a contract of insurance), or
   (ii) the relevant liability was in fact covered by a contract of insurance;

(b) a claim arising out of the use of a vehicle which is not required to be covered by a contract of insurance by virtue of section 144 of the 1988 Act, unless the use is in fact covered by such a contract;

(c) a claim by, or for the benefit of, a person ("the beneficiary") other than the person suffering death, injury or other damage which is made either—

   (i) in respect of a cause of action or a judgment which has been assigned to the beneficiary, or

(ii) pursuant to a right of subrogation or contractual or other right belonging to the beneficiary;

(d) a claim in respect of damage to a motor vehicle or losses arising therefrom where, at the time when the damage to it was sustained—

(i) there was not in force in relation to the use of that vehicle such a contract of insurance as is required by Part VI of the 1988 Act, and
(ii) the claimant either knew or ought to have known that that was the case;

(e) a claim which is made in respect of a relevant liability described in paragraph (2) by a claimant who, at the time of the use giving rise to the relevant liability was voluntarily allowing himself to be carried in the vehicle and, either before the commencement of his journey in the vehicle or after such commencement if he could reasonably be expected to have alighted from it, knew or ought to have known that—

(i) the vehicle had been stolen or unlawfully taken,
(ii) the vehicle was being used without there being in force in relation to its use such a contract of insurance as would comply with Part VI of the 1988 Act,
(iii) the vehicle was being used in the course of furtherance of a crime, or
(iv) the vehicle was being used as means of escape from, or avoidance of, lawful apprehension.

(2) The relevant liability referred to in paragraph (1)(e) is a liability incurred by the owner or registered keeper or a person using the vehicle in which the claimant was being carried.

(3) The burden of proving that the claimant knew or ought to have known of any matter set out in paragraph (1)(e) shall be on MIB but, in the absence of evidence to the contrary, proof by MIB of any of the following matters shall be taken as proof of the claimant's knowledge of the matter set out in paragraph (1)(e)(ii)—

(a) that the claimant was the owner or registered keeper of the vehicle or had caused or permitted its use;

(b) that the claimant knew the vehicle was being used by a person who was below the minimum age at which he could be granted a licence authorising the driving of a vehicle of that class;

(c) that the claimant knew that the person driving the vehicle was disqualified for holding or obtaining a driving licence;

(d) that the claimant knew that the user of the vehicle was neither its owner nor registered keeper nor an employee of the owner or registered keeper nor the owner or registered keeper of any other vehicle.

(4) Knowledge which the claimant has or ought to have for the purposes of paragraph (1)(e) includes knowledge of matters which he could reasonably be expected to have been aware of had he not been under the self-induced influence of drink or drugs.

(5) For the purposes of this clause-

(a) a vehicle which has been unlawfully removed from the possession of the Crown shall be taken to continue in that possession whilst it is kept so removed,

(b) references to a person being carried in a vehicle include references to his being carried upon, entering, getting on to and alighting from the vehicle, and

(c) "owner", in relation to a vehicle which is the subject of a hiring agreement or a hire-purchase agreement, means the person in possession of the vehicle under that agreement.

CONDITIONS PRECEDENT TO MIB'S OBLIGATION

7. Form of application

(1) MIB shall incur no liability under MIB's obligation unless an application is made to the person specified in clause 9(1)—

(a) in such form,

(b) giving such information about the relevant proceedings and other matters relevant to this Agreement, and

(c) accompanied by such documents a MIB may reasonably require.

(2) Where an application is signed by a person who is neither the claimant nor a Solicitor acting on his behalf MIB may refuse to accept the application (and shall incur no liability under MIB's obligation) until it is reasonably satisfied that, having regard to the status of the signatory and his relationship to the claimant, the claimant is fully aware of the contents and effect of the application but subject thereto MIB shall not refuse to accept such an application by reason only that it is signed by a person other than the claimant or his Solicitor.

8. Service of notices, etc.

Any notice required to be given or documents to be supplied to MIB pursuant to clauses 9 to 12 of this Agreement shall be sufficiently given or supplied only if sent by facsimile transmission or by Registered or Recorded Delivery post to MIB's registered office for the time being and delivery shall be proved by the production of a facsimile transmission report produced by the sender's facsimile machine or an appropriate postal receipt.

9. Notice of relevant proceedings

(1) MIB shall incur no liability under MIB's obligation unless proper notice of the bringing of the relevant proceedings has been given by the claimant not later than fourteen days after the commencement of those proceedings—

(a) in the case of proceedings in respect of a relevant liability which is covered by a contract of insurance with an insurer whose identity can be ascertained, to that insurer;

(b) in any other case, to MIB.

(2) In this clause "proper notice" means, except in so far as any part of such information or any copy document or other thing has already been supplied under clause 7—

(a) notice in writing that proceedings have been commenced by Claim Form, Writ, or other means,

(b) a copy of the sealed Claim Form, Writ or other official document providing evidence of the commencement of the proceedings and, in Scotland, a statement of the means of service,

(c) a copy or details of any insurance policy providing benefits in the case of the death, bodily injury or damage to property to which the proceedings relate where the claimant is the Insured party and the benefits are available to him,

(d) copies of all correspondence in the possession of the claimant or (as the case may be) his Solicitor or agent to or from the Defendant or the Defender or (as the case may be) his Solicitor, insurers or agent which is relevant to—

(i) the death, bodily injury or damage for which the Defendant or Defender is alleged to be responsible, or
(ii) any contract of insurance which covers, or which may or has been alleged to cover, liability for such death, injury or damage the benefit of which is, or is claimed to be, available to Defendant or Defender,

(e) subject to paragraph (3), a copy of the Particulars of Claim whether or not indorsed on the Claim Form, Writ or other originating process, and whether or not served (in England and Wales) on any Defendant or (in Scotland) on any Defender, and

(f) a copy of all other documents which are required under the appropriate rules of procedure to be served on a Defendant or Defender with the Claim Form, Writ or other originating process or with the Particulars of Claim,

(g) such other information about the relevant proceedings as MIB may reasonably specify.

(3) If, in the case of proceedings commenced in England or Wales, the Particulars of Claim (including any document required to be served therewith) has not yet been served with the Claim Form or other originating process paragraph (2)(e) shall be sufficiently complied with if a copy there of is served on MIB not later than seven days after it is served on the Defendant.

10. Notice of service of proceedings

(1) This clause applies where the relevant proceedings are commenced in England or Wales.

(2) MIB shall incur no liability under MIB's obligation unless the claimant has, not later than the appropriate date, given notice in writing to the person specified in clause 9(1) of the date of service of the Claim Form or other originating process in the relevant proceedings.

(3) In this clause, "the appropriate date" means the day falling—

(a) seven days after—

- (i) the date when the claimant receives notification from the Court that service of the Claim Form or other originating process has occurred,
- (ii) the date when the claimant receives notification from the Defendant that service of the Claim Form or other originating process has occurred, or
- (iii) the date of personal service, or

(b) fourteen days after the date when service is deemed to have occurred in accordance with the Civil Procedure Rules,

whichever of those days occurs first.

11. Further information

(1) MIB shall incur no liability under MIB's obligation unless the claimant has, not later than seven days after the occurrence of any of the following events, namely—

(a) the filing of a defence in the relevant proceedings,

(b) any amendment to the Particulars of Claim or any amendment of or addition to any schedule or other document required to be served therewith, and

(c) either—

(i) the setting down of the case for trial, or
(ii) where the court gives notice to the claimant of the trial date, the date when that notice is received, given notice in writing of the date of that event to the person specified in clause 9(1) and has, in the case of the filing of a defence or an amendment of the Particulars of Claim or any amendment of or addition to any schedule or other document required to be served therewith, supplied a copy thereof to that person.

(2) MIB shall incur no liability under MIB's obligation unless the claimant furnishes to the person specified in clause 9(1) within a reasonable time after being required to do so such further information and documents in support of his claim as MIB may reasonably require notwithstanding that the claimant may have complied with clause 7(1).

12. Notice of intention to apply for judgment

(1) MIB shall incur no liability under MIB's obligation unless the claimant has, after commencement of the relevant proceedings and not less than thirty-five days before the appropriate date, given notice in writing to the person specified in clause 9(1) of his intention to apply for or to sign judgment in the relevant proceedings.

(2) In this clause, "the appropriate date" means the date when the application for judgment is made or, as the case may be, the signing of judgment occurs.

13. Section 154 of the 1988 Act

MIB shall incur no liability under MIB's obligation unless the claimant has as soon as reasonably practicable—

(a) demanded the information and, where appropriate, the particulars specified in section 154(1) of the 1988 Act, and

(b) if the person of whom the demand is made fails to comply with the provisions of that subsection—

(i) made a formal complaint to a police officer in respect of such failure, and
(ii) used all reasonable endeavours to obtain the name and address of the registered keeper of the vehicle or, if so required by MIB, has authorised MIB to take such steps on his behalf.

14. Prosecution of proceedings

MIB shall incur no liability under MIB's obligation—

(a) unless the claimant has, if so required by MIB and having been granted a full indemnity by MIB as to costs, taken all reasonable steps to obtain judgment against every person who may be liable (including any person who may be vicariously liable) in respect of the injury or death or damage to property, or

(b) if the claimant, upon being requested to do so by MIB, refuses to consent to MIB being joined as a party to the relevant proceedings.

15. Assignment of judgment and undertakings

MIB shall incur no liability under MIB's obligation unless the claimant has—

(a) assigned to MIB or its nominee the unsatisfied judgment, whether or not that judgment includes an amount in respect of a liability other than a relevant liability, and any order for costs made in the relevant proceedings, and

(b) undertaken to repay to MIB any sum paid to him—

(i) by MIB in discharge of MIB's obligation if the judgment is subsequently set aside either as a whole or in respect of the part of the relevant liability to which that sum relates;
(ii) by any other person by way of compensation or benefit for the death, bodily injury or other damage to which the relevant proceedings relate, including a sum which would have been deductible under the provisions of clause 17 if it had been received before MIB was obliged to satisfy MIB's obligation.

LIMITATIONS ON MIB'S LIABILITY

16. Compensation for damage to property

(1) Where a claim under this Agreement includes a claim in respect of damage to property, MIB's obligation in respect of that part of the relevant sum which is awarded for such damage and any losses arising there from (referred to in this clause as "the property damage compensation") is limited in accordance with the following paragraphs.

(2) Where the property damage compensation does not exceed the specified excess, MIB shall incur no liability.

(3) Where the property damage compensation in respect of any one accident exceeds the specified excess but does not exceed £250,000, MIB shall incur liability only in respect of the property damage compensation less the specified excess.

(4) Where the property damage compensation in respect of any one accident exceeds £250,000, MIB shall incur liability only in respect of the sum of £250,000 less the specified excess.

17. Compensation received from other sources

Where a claimant has received compensation from—

(a) the Policyholders Protection Board under the Policyholders Protection Act 1975, or

(b) an insurer under an insurance agreement or arrangement, or

(c) any other source,

in respect of the death, bodily injury or other damage to which the relevant proceedings relate and such compensation has not been taken into account in the calculation of the relevant sum MIB may deduct from the relevant sum, in addition to any sum deductible under clause 16, an amount equal to that compensation.

MISCELLANEOUS

18. Notifications of decisions by MIB

Where a claimant—

(a) has made an application in accordance with clause 7, and

(b) has given to the person specified in clause 9(1) proper notice of the relevant proceedings in accordance with clause 9(2),

MIB shall—

(i) give a reasoned reply to any request made by the claimant relating to the payment of compensation in pursuance of MIB's obligation, and
(ii) as soon as reasonably practicable notify the claimant in writing of its decision regarding the payment of the relevant sum, together with the reasons for that decision.

19. Reference of disputes to the Secretary of State

(1) In the event of any dispute as to the reasonableness of a requirement made by MIB for the supply of information or documentation or for the taking of any step by the claimant, it may be referred by the claimant or MIB to the Secretary of State whose decision shall be final.
(2) Where a dispute is referred to the Secretary of State—

(a) MIB shall supply the Secretary of State and, if it has not already done so, the claimant with notice in writing of the requirement from which the dispute arises, together with the reasons for that requirement and such further information as MIB considers relevant, and

(b) where the dispute is referred by the claimant, the claimant shall supply the Secretary of State and, if he has not already done so, MIB with notice in writing of the grounds on which he disputes the reasonableness of the requirement.

20. Recoveries

Nothing in this Agreement shall prevent an insurer from providing by conditions in a contract of insurance that all sums paid by the insurer or by MIB by virtue of the Principal Agreement or this Agreement in or towards the discharge of the liability of the insured shall be recoverable by them or by MIB from the insured or from any other person.

21. Apportionment of damage, etc.

(1) Where an unsatisfied judgment which includes an amount in respect of a liability other than a relevant liability has been assigned to MIB or its nominee in pursuance of clause 15 MIB shall—

(a) apportion any sum it receives in satisfaction or partial satisfaction of the judgment according to the proportion which the damages awarded in respect of the relevant liability bear to the damages awarded in respect of the other liability, and

(b) account to the claimant in respect of the moneys received properly apportionable to the other liability.

(2) Where the sum received includes an amount in respect of interest or an amount awarded under an order for costs, the interest or the amount received in pursuance of the order shall be dealt with in the manner provided in paragraph (1).

22. Agents

MIB may perform any of its obligations under this Agreement by agents.

23. Transitional provisions

(1) The 1988 Agreement shall continue in force in relation to claims arising out of accidents occurring before 1st October 1999 with the modifications contained in paragraph (2).

(2) In relation to any claim made under the 1988 Agreement after this Agreement has come into force, the 1988 Agreement shall apply as if there were inserted after clause 6 thereof—

"6A. Where any person in whose favour a judgment in respect of a relevant liability has been made has—

(a) made a claim under this Agreement, and

(b) satisfied the requirements specified in clause 5 hereof,

MIB shall, if requested to do so, give him a reasoned reply regarding the satisfaction of that claim.".
IN WITNESS where of the Secretary of State has caused his Corporate Seal to be hereunto affixed and the Motor Insurers' Bureau has caused its Common Seal to be hereunto affixed the day and year first above written.

Notes

The following notes are for the guidance of anyone who may have a claim on the Motor Insurers' Bureau under this Agreement and their legal advisers. They are not part of the Agreement, their purpose being to deal in ordinary language with the situations which most readily occur. They are not in any way a substitute for reading and applying the terms of this or any other relevant Agreement, nor are they intended to control or influence the legal interpretation of the Agreement. Any enquiries, requests for application forms and general correspondence in connection with the Agreement should be addressed to: Motor Insurers Bureau, 152 Silbury Boulevard, Central Milton Keynes, Milton Keynes, MK9 1NB. Tel: 01908 830001, Fax: 01918 671681, DX: 84753 Milton Keynes 3

1. Introduction—MIB's role and application of the Agreement

1.1 The role of MIB under this Agreement is to provide a safety net for innocent victims of drivers who have been identified but are uninsured. MIB's funds for this purpose are obtained from levies charged upon insurers and so come from the premiums which are charged by those insurers to members of the public.

1.2 MIB has entered into a series of Agreements with the Secretary of State and his predecessors in office. Under each Agreement MIB undertakes obligations to pay defined compensation in specific circumstances. There are two sets of Agreements, one relating to victims of uninsured drivers (the "Uninsured Drivers" Agreements) and the other concerned with victims of hit and run or otherwise untraceable drivers (the "Untraced Drivers" Agreements). These Notes are addressed specifically to the procedures required to take advantage of the rights granted by the Uninsured Drivers Agreements. However, it is not always certain which of the Agreements applies. For guidance in such cases please see the note on **Untraced Drivers** at paragraph 11 below.

1.3 In order to determine which of the Uninsured Drivers Agreements is applicable to a particular victim's claim, regard must be had to the date of the relevant accident. This Agreement only applies in respect of claims arising on or after

1st October 1999. Claims arising earlier than that are covered by the following Agreements:—

1.3.1 Claims arising in respect of an incident occurring between 1st July 1946 and 28th February 1971 are governed by the Agreement between the Minister of Transport and the Bureau dated 17th June 1946.

1.3.2 Claims arising in respect of an incident occurring between 1st March 1971 and 30th November 1972 are governed by the Agreement between the Secretary of State for the Environment and the Bureau dated 1st February 1971.

1.3.3 Claims arising in respect of an incident occurring between 1st December 1972 and 30th December 1988 are governed by the Agreement between the Secretary of State and the Bureau dated 22nd November 1972.

1.3.4 Claims arising in respect of an incident occurring between 31st December 1988 and 30th September 1999 are governed by the Agreement between the Secretary of State and the Bureau dated 21st December 1988.

2. MIB's obligation

2.1 MIB's basic obligation (see clause 5) is to satisfy judgments which fall within the terms of this Agreement and which, because the Defendant to the proceedings is not insured, are not satisfied.

2.2 This obligation is, however, not absolute. It is subject to certain exceptions where MIB has no liability (see clause 6), there are a number of pre-conditions which the claimant must comply with (see clauses 7 to 15) and there are some limitations on MIB's liability (see clauses 16 and 17).

2.3 MIB does not have to wait for a judgment to be given; it can become party to the proceedings or negotiate and settle the claim if it wishes to do so.

3. Claims which MIB is not obliged to satisfy

MIB is not liable under the Agreement in the case of the following types of claim.

3.1 A claim made in respect of an unsatisfied judgment which does not concern a liability against which Part VI of the Road Traffic Act 1988 requires a vehicle user to insure (see section 145 of the Act). An example would be a case where the accident did not occur in a place specified in the Act. See the definitions of "unsatisfied judgment" and "relevant liability" in clause 1.

3.2 A claim in respect of loss or damage caused by the use of a vehicle owned by or in the possession of the Crown (that is the Civil Service, the armed forces and so on) to which Part VI does not apply. If the responsibility for motor insurance has been undertaken by someone else or the vehicle is in fact insured, this exception does not apply. See clause 6(1)(a).

3.3 A claim made against any person who is not required to insure by virtue of section 144 of the Road Traffic Act 1988. See clause 6(1)(b).

3.4 A claim (commonly called subrogated) made in the name of a person suffering damage or injury but which is in fact wholly or partly for the benefit or another who has indemnified, or is liable to indemnify, that person. See clause 6(1)(c).

3.5 A claim in respect of damage to a motor vehicle or losses arising from such damage where the use of the damaged vehicle was itself not covered by a contract of insurance as required by law. See clause 6(1)(d).

3.6 A claim made by a passenger in a vehicle where the loss or damage has been caused by the user of that vehicle if:—

3.6.1 the use of the vehicle was not covered by a contract of insurance; and

3.6.2 the claimant knew or could be taken to have known that the vehicle was being used without insurance, had been stolen or unlawfully taken or was being used in connection with crime.

See clause 6(1)(e), (2), (3) and (4).

3.7 A claim in respect of property damage amounting to £300 or less, £300 being the "specified excess". See clause 16(2).

3.8 Where the claim is for property damage, the first £300 of the loss and so much of it as exceeds £250,000. See clause 16(3) and (4).

4. Procedure after the accident and before proceedings

4.1 The claimant must take reasonable steps to establish whether there is in fact any insurance covering the use of the vehicle which caused the injury or damage. First, a claimant has statutory rights under section 154 of the Road Traffic Act 1988 to obtain relevant particulars which he must take steps to exercise even if that involves incurring expense and MIB will insist that he does so. See clause 13(a).

4.2 Other steps will include the following:—

4.2.1 The exchange of names, addresses and insurance particulars between those involved either at the scene of the accident or afterwards.

4.2.2 Corresponding with the owner or driver of the vehicle or his representatives. He will be obliged under the terms of his motor policy to inform his insurers and a letter of claim addressed to him will commonly be passed to the insurers who may reply on his behalf. See clause 9(2)(d).

4.2.3 Where only the vehicle's number is known, enquiry of the Driver and Vehicle Licensing Agency at Swansea SA99 1BP as to the registered keeper of the vehicle is desirable so that through him the identity of the owner or driver can be established or confirmed.

4.2.4 Enquiries of the police (see clause 13(b)).

4.3 If enquiries show that there is an insurer who is obliged to accept and does accept the obligation to handle the claim against the user of the vehicle concerned, even though the relevant liability may not be covered by the policy in question, then the claim should be pursued with such insurer.

4.4 If, however, enquiries disclose that there is no insurance covering the use of the vehicle concerned or if the insurer cannot be identified or the insurer asserts that it is under no obligation to handle the claim or if for any other reason it is clear that the insurer will not satisfy any judgment, the claim should be directed to MIB itself.

5. When proceedings are commenced or contemplated

5.1 As explained above, MIB does not have to wait for a judgment to be obtained before intervening. Claimants may apply to MIB before the commencement of proceedings. MIB will respond to any claim which complies with clause 7 and must give a reasoned reply to any request for compensation in respect of the claim (see clause 18) although normally a request for compensation will not be met until MIB is satisfied that it is properly based. Interim compensation payments are dealt with at paragraph 8 below.

5.2 It is important that wherever possible claims should be made using MIB's application form, fully completed and accompanied by documents supporting the claim, as soon as possible to avoid unnecessary delays. See clause 7(1). Copies of the form can be obtained on request made by post, telephone, fax or the DX or on personal application to MIB's offices.

5.3 The claimant must give MIB notice *in writing* that he has commenced legal proceedings. The notice, the completed application form (if appropriate) and all necessary documents must be received by MIB no later than 14 days after the date of commencement of proceedings. See clause 9(1) and (2)(a). The date of commencement is determined in accordance with the definitions of "relevant proceedings" and "commencement" given in clause 1.
This notice *must* have with it the following:—

5.4.1 a copy of the document originating the proceedings, usually in England and Wales a Claim Form and in Scotland a Sheriff Court Writ or Court of Session Summons (see clause 9(2)(b));

5.4.2 normally the Particulars of Claim endorsed on or served with the Claim Form or Writ (see clause 9(2)(e), although this document may be served later in accordance with clause 9(3) if that applies);

5.4.3 in any case the documents required by the relevant rules of procedure (see clause 9(2)(f).

5.5 In addition, other items as mentioned in clause 9(2), *e.g.* correspondence with the Defendant (or Defender) or his representatives, need to be supplied where appropriate.

5.6 It is for the claimant to satisfy himself that the notice has in fact been received by MIB. Clause 8 applies to service of documents by post and fax. MIB prefer service by fax as it is almost instantaneous and can be confirmed quickly. Claimants should note that service of documents by DX is not permitted under the Agreement since delivery cannot be proved.

5.7 It should be noted that when MIB has been given notice of a claim, it may elect to require the claimant to bring proceedings and attempt to secure a judgment against the party whom MIB alleges to be wholly or partly responsible for the loss or damage or who may be contracted to indemnify the claimant. In such a case MIB must indemnify the claimant against the costs of such proceedings. Subject to that, however, MIB's obligation to satisfy the judgment in the action will only arise if the claimant commences the proceedings and takes all reasonable steps to obtain a judgment. See clause 14(a).

6. Service of proceedings

6.1 If proceedings are commenced in England or Wales the claimant *must* inform MIB of the date of service (see clause 10(1) and (2)).

6.2 If service of the Claim Form is effected by the Court, notice must be given within 7 days from the earliest of the dates listed in clause 10(3)(a)(*i*) *or* (*ii*) or within 14 days from the date mentioned in clause 10(3)(b) (the date of deemed service under the court's rules of procedure). Claimants are advised to take steps to ensure that the court or the defendant's legal representatives inform them of the date of service as soon as possible. Although a longer period is allowed than in other cases, service may be deemed to have occurred without a Claimant knowing of it until some time afterwards.

6.3 Where proceedings are served personally, notice must be given 7 days from the date of personal service (see clause 10(3)(a)(iii)).

6.4 In Scotland, proceedings are commenced at the date of service (see clause 1) so notice should already have been given under clause 9 and clause 10 does not apply there.

7. After service and before judgment

7.1 Notice of the filing of a defence, of an amendment to the Statement or Particulars of Claim, and the setting down of the case for trial must be given not later than 7 days after the occurrence of such events and a copy of the document must be supplied (see clause 11(1)).

7.2 MIB may request further information and documents to support the claim where it is not satisfied that the documents supplied with the application form are sufficient to enable it to assess its liability under the Agreement (see clause 11(2)).

7.3 If the claimant intends to sign or apply for judgment he must give MIB notice of the fact before doing so. This notice must be given at least 35 days before the application is to be made or the date when judgment is to be signed (see clause 12).

7.4 At no time must the claimant oppose MIB if it wishes to be joined as a party to proceedings and he must if requested consent to any application by MIB to be joined. Conflicts may arise between a Defendant and MIB which require MIB to become a Defendant or, in Scotland, a party Minuter if a defence is to be filed on its behalf (see clause 14(b)).

8. Interim payments

In substantial cases, the claimant may wish to apply for an interim payment. MIB will consider such applications on a voluntary basis but otherwise the claimant has the right to apply to the court for an interim payment order which, if granted, will be met by MIB.

9. After judgment

9.1 MIB's basic obligation normally arises if a judgment is not satisfied within 7 days after the claimant has become entitled to enforce it (see clause 1). However, that judgment may in certain circumstances be set aside and with it MIB's obligation to satisfy it. Sometimes MIB wishes to apply to set aside a judgment either wholly or partially. If MIB decides not to satisfy a judgment it will notify the claimant as soon as possible. Where a judgment is subsequently set aside, MIB will require the claimant to repay any sum previously paid by MIB to discharge its obligation under the Agreement (see clause 15(b)).

9.2 MIB is not obliged to satisfy a judgment unless the claimant has in return assigned the benefit to MIB or its nominee (see clause 15(a)). If such assignment is effected and if the subject matter of the judgment includes claims in respect of which MIB is not obliged to meet any judgment and if MIB effects any recovery on the judgment, the sum recovered will be divided between MIB and the claimant in proportion to the liabilities which were and which were not covered by MIB's obligation (see clause 21).

10. Permissible deductions from payments by MIB

10.1 Claims for loss and damage for which the claimant has been compensated or indemnified, *e.g.* under a contract of insurance or under the Policyholders Protection Act 1975, and which has not been taken into account in the judgment, may be deducted from the sum paid in settlement of MIB's obligation (see clause 17).

10.2 If there is a likelihood that the claimant will receive payment from such a source after the judgment has been satisfied by MIB, MIB will require him to undertake to repay any sum which duplicates the compensation assessed by the court (see clause 15(b)).

11. Untraced drivers

11.1 Where the owners or driver of a vehicle cannot be identified application may be made to MIB under the relevant Untraced Drivers Agreement. This provides, subject to specified conditions, for the payment of compensation for personal injury. It *does not* provide for compensation in respect of damage to property.

11.2 In those cases where it is unclear whether the owner or driver of a vehicle has been correctly identified it is sensible for the claimant to register a claim under both this Agreement and the Untraced Drivers Agreement following which MIB will advise which Agreement will, in its view, apply to the circumstances of the particular case.

2 Compensation of victims of untraced drivers

THE AGREEMENT RECITALS

(1) On 21 April 1969 the Minister of Transport and Motor Insurer's Bureau entered into an Agreement ("the First Agreement") to secure compensation for third party victims of road accidents when the driver responsible for the accident could not be traced.

(2) The First Agreement was replaced by a new Agreement ("the Second Agreement") which operated in respect of accidents occuring on or after 1 December 1972.

(3) The Second Agreement was added to by a Supplemental Agreement dated 7 December, 1977 ("the Third Agreement") which operated in respect of accidents occuring on or after 3 January 1978.

(4) The Second Agreement and the Third Agreement have now been replaced by a new Agreement ("this Agreement") which operates in respect of accidents occuring on or after 1 July 1996.

(5) The text of this Agreement is as follows:

TEXT OF THE AGREEMENT:

AN AGREEMENT made the Fourteenth day of June 1996 between the Secretary of State for Transport ("the Secretary of State") and the Motor Insurers' Bureau whose registered office is at 152 Silbury Boulevard, Central Milton Keynes, MK9 1NB (the MIB.).

IT IS HEREBY AGREED as follows:

1 (1) Subject to paragraph (2) of this Clause, this Agreement applies to any case in which an application is made to MIB for a payment in respect of the death of or bodily injury to any person caused by or arising out of the use of a motor vehicle on a road in Great Britain and the case is one in which following conditions are fulfilled, that is to say:

(*a*) the event giving rise to the death or injury occurred on or after 1 July 1996;

(*b*) the applicant for the payment either;

(i) is unable to trace any person responsible for the death or injury, or
(ii) in a case which Clause 5 applies where more than one person was

responsible, is unable to trace one of those persons. (Any person so untraced is referred to as "the untraced person");

(*c*) the death or injury was caused in such circumstances that on the balance of probabilities the untraced person would be liable to pay damages to the applicant in respect of the death or injury;

(*d*) the liability of the untraced person to pay damages to the applicant is one which is required to be covered by insurance or security under Part VI of the Road Traffic Act 1988 "the 1988 Act", it being assumed for this purpose, in the absence of evidence to the contrary, that the vehicle was being used in circumstances in which the user was required by the 1988 Act to be insured or secured against third party risks;

(*e*) the death or injury was not caused by the use of the vehicle by the untraced person in any deliberate attempt to cause the death or injury of the person in respect of which an application is made;

(*f*) the application is made in writing within three years from the date of the event giving rise to the death or injury; and

(*g*) the incident was reported to the police within fourteen days or as soon as the applicant reasonably could and the applicant co-operated with the police.

(2) This Agreement does not apply to a case in which:

(*a*) the death or bodily injury in respect of which any such application is made was caused by or arose out of the use of a motor vehicle which at the time of the event giving rise to the death or bodily injury was owned by or in the possession of the Crown, unless the case is one in which some other person has undertaken responsibility for the existence of a contract of insurance under the 1988 Act;

(*b*) at the time of the accident the person suffering death or bodily injury in respect of which the application is made was allowing himself to be carried in a vehicle and either before or after the commencement of his journey in the vehicle, if he could reasonably be expected to have alighted from the vehicle, he knew or had reason to believe that the vehicle:

(i) had been stolen or unlawfully taken, or
(ii) was being used without there being in force in relation to its use a contract of insurance which complied with the 1988 Act; or
(iii) was being used in the course or furtherance of crime; or
(iv) was being used as a means of escape from or avoidance of lawful apprehension.

(3) For the purpose of paragraph (2) of this Clause:

(*a*) a vehicle which has been unlawfully removed from the possession of the Crown shall be taken to continue in that possession whilst it is kept so removed;

(*b*) references to a person being carried in a vehicle include references to his being carried in or upon, or entering or getting onto or alighting from the vehicle;

(*c*) "owner" in relation to a vehicle which is the subject of a hiring agreement or a hire purchase agreement means the person in possession of the vehicle under that agreement.

2 (1) An application to the MIB for a payment in respect of the death or bodily injury to any person may be made:

(*a*) by the person for whose benefit that payment is to be made ("the applicant"); or

(*b*) by any solicitor acting for the applicant; or

(*c*) by any other person whom MIB may be prepared to accept as acting for the applicant.

(2) Any decision made, or award or payment given or other thing done in accordance with this Agreement to or by a person acting under paragraph 1(*b*) and (1)(*c*) of this Clause on behalf of the applicant, or in relation to an application made by such person, shall whatever may be the age, or the circumstances affecting the capacity, of the applicant, be treated as having the same effect as if it had been done to or by, or in relation to an application made by, an applicant of full age and capacity.

3 Subject to the following provisions of this Agreement, the MIB shall, on any application made to it in a case to which this Agreement applies, award to the applicant in respect of the death or injury for which the application is made a payment of an amount which shall be assessed in like manner as a court applying English law in a case where the event giving rise to the death or injury occurred in England or Wales or applying the law of Scotland in a case where that event occurred in Scotland, would assess the damages which the applicant would have been entitled to recover from the untraced person in respect of that death or injury if the applicant had brought successful proceedings to enforce a claim for such damages against the untraced person.

4 In assessing the level of an award in accordance with Clause 3, the MIB shall be under no obligation to include any sum in respect of loss of earnings suffered by the applicant where and in so far as the applicant has in fact been paid wages or salary or any sum in lieu of the same, whether or not such payments were made subject to an undertaking on the part of the applicant to repay the same in the event of the applicant recovering damages.

5 (1) This Clause applies to any case:

(*a*) to which this Agreement applies; and

(*b*) the death or bodily injury in respect of which an application has been made to the MIB under this Agreement ("the relevant death or injury") was caused:

(i) partly by the untraced person and partly by an identified person or by identified persons, or
(ii) partly by the untraced person and partly by some other untraced person or persons whose master or principal can be identified; and

(*c*) in circumstances making the identified person or persons or any master or principal ("the identified person") liable to the applicant in respect of the relevant death or injury.

(2) If in a case to which this Clause applies one of the conditions in paragraph (3) of this Clause is satisfied, the amount of the award to be paid by the MIB to the applicant in respect of the relevant death or injury shall be determined in accordance with paragraph (4) of this Clause and its liability to the applicant shall be subject to paragraph (7) of this Clause and Clause 6 of this Agreement.

(3) The conditions referred to in paragraph (2) of this Clause are:

(*a*) that the applicant has obtained a judgment in respect of the relevant death or injury against the identified person ("the original judgment") which has not been satisfied in full within three months from the date on which the applicant became entitled to enforce it ("the three month period"); or

(*b*) that the applicant:

(i) has not obtained and has not been required by the MIB to obtain a judgment in respect of the relevant death or injury against the identified person; and
(ii) has not received any payment by way of compensation from the identified person or persons.

(4) The amount to be awarded by the MIB to the applicant in a case to which this Clause applies shall be determined as follows:

(*a*) if the condition in paragraph (3)(*a*) of this Clause is satisfied and the original judgment is wholly unsatisfied within the three month period, the amount to be awarded shall be an amount equal to the proportion of a full award attributable to the untraced person;

(*b*) if the condition in paragraph (3)(*a*) of this Clause is satisfied and the original judgment is satisfied in part only within the three month period, the amount to be awarded:

(i) if the unsatisfied part of the original judgment is less than the proportion of a full award attributable to the untraced person, shall be an amount equal to that unsatisfied part; or

(ii) if the unsatisfied part of the original judgment is equal to or greater than the proportion of a full award attributable to the untraced person, shall be an amount equal to the untraced person's proportion;

(*c*) if the condition in paragraph (3)(*b*) of this Clause is satisfied the amount to be awarded shall be an amount equal to the proportion of a full award attributable to the untraced person.

(5) The following provisions of this paragraph shall have effect in any case in which an appeal from or any proceeding to set aside the original judgment is commenced within a period of three months beginning on the date on which the applicant became entitled to enforce the original judgment:

(*a*) until the appeal or proceeding is disposed of the provisions of this Clause shall have effect as if for the three month period there were substituted a period expiring on the date when the appeal or proceeding is disposed of;

(*b*) if as a result of the appeal or proceeding the applicant ceases to be entitled to receive any payment in respect of the relevant death or injury from any of the person or persons against whom he has obtained the original judgment, the provisions of this Clause shall have effect as if he had neither obtained nor been required by the MIB to obtain a judgment against any person or persons;

(*c*) if as a result of the appeal or proceeding, the applicant becomes entitled to recover an amount which differs from that which he was entitled to recover under the original judgment the provisions of this Clause shall have effect as if for the reference in paragraph (3)(*a*) to the original judgment there were substituted a reference to the judgment under which the applicant became entitled to the different amount;

(*d*) if as a result of the appeal or proceeding the applicant remains entitled to enforce the original judgment the provisions of this Clause shall have effect as if for the three month period there were substituted a period of three months beginning on the date on which the appeal or other proceeding was disposed of.

The provisions of this paragraph shall apply also in any case where any judgment given upon any appeal or proceeding is itself the subject of a further appeal or similar proceeding and shall apply in such a case in relation to that further appeal or proceeding in the same manner as they apply in relation to the first mentioned appeal or proceeding.

(6) In this Clause:

(*a*) "full award" means the amount which would have fallen to be awarded to the applicant under Clause 3 in respect of the relevant death or injury if the untraced person had been adjudged by a court to be wholly responsible for that death or injury; and

(*b*) "the proportion of a full award attributable to the untraced person" means that proportion of a full award which on the balance of probabilities would have been apportioned by a court in proceedings between the untraced person and any other person liable in respect of the same event as the share to be borne by the untraced person in the responsibility for the event giving rise to the relevant death or injury.

(7) The MIB shall not be under any liability in respect of the relevant death or injury if the applicant is entitled to receive compensation from the MIB in respect of that death or injury under any agreement providing for the compensation of victims of uninsured drivers entered into between the Secretary of State and the MIB.

6 (1) Any liability falling upon the MIB upon an application made to it under this Agreement, in respect of any death or injury, shall be subject to the following conditions:

(*a*) the applicant shall give all assistance as may reasonably be required by or on behalf of the MIB to enable any investigation to be carried out under this Agreement, including, in particular the provision of statements and information either in writing, or, if required, orally at an interview or interviews between the applicant and any person acting on behalf of MIB;

(*b*) at any time before the MIB has communicated its decision upon the application to the applicant, the applicant shall, subject to the following provisions of this Clause, take all steps as in the circumstances it is reasonable for the MIB to require him to take to obtain judgment against any person or persons in respect of their liability to the applicant for the death or injury as having caused or contributed to that death or as being the master or principal of any person who has caused or contributed to that death or injury; and

(*c*) if required by the MIB the applicant shall assign to the MIB or to its nominee any judgment obtained by him (whether or not obtained in accordance with a requirement under subparagraph (*b*) of this paragraph) in respect of the death or injury to which his application to the MIB relates upon terms as will secure that the MIB or its nominee shall be accountable to the applicant for any amount by which the aggregate of all sums recovered by the MIB or its nominee under the judgment (after deducting all reasonable expenses incurred in effecting recovery) exceeds the amount payable by the MIB to the applicant under this Agreement in respect of that death or injury.

(2) If the MIB requires the applicant to bring proceedings against any specified person or persons:

(*a*) the MIB shall indemnify the applicant against all costs reasonably incurred by him in complying with that requirement unless the result of those proceedings materially contributes to establishing that the untraced person did not cause or contribute to the relevant death or injury; and

(*b*) the applicant shall, if required by the MIB and at its expense, provide the MIB with a transcript of any official shorthand note taken in those proceedings of any evidence given or judgment delivered therein.

(3) In the event of a dispute arising between the applicant and the MIB as to the reasonableness of any requirement by the MIB under paragraph (1)(*b*) of this Clause or as to whether any costs as referred to in paragraph (2)(*a*) of this Clause were reasonably incurred, that dispute shall be referred to the Secretary of State whose decision shall be final. Provided that any dispute arising between the applicant and the MIB as to whether the MIB is required to indemnify him under paragraph (2)(*a*) of this Clause shall, in so far as it depends on the question whether the result of any proceedings which the MIB has required the applicant to bring against any specified person or persons has or has not materially contributed to establish that the untraced person did not cause or contribute to the relevant death or injury, be referred to the arbitrator in accordance with the following provisions of this Agreement, whose decision on that question shall be final.

7 The MIB shall cause any application made to it for a payment under this Agreement to be investigated and, unless it decides that the application should be rejected because a preliminary investigation has disclosed that the case is not one to which this Agreement applies, it shall cause a report to be made on the application and on the basis of that report it shall decide whether to make an award and, if so, the amount of the award which shall be calculated in accordance with the provisions of this Agreement.

8 The MIB may before coming to a decision on any application made to it under this Agreement request the applicant to provide it with a statutory declaration to be made by the applicant, setting out to the best of his knowledge, information and belief the facts and circumstances upon which his claim to an award under this Agreement are based, or facts and circumstances as may be specified by it.

9 (1) The MIB shall notify its decision to the applicant and when so doing shall:

(*a*) if the application is rejected because a preliminary investigation has disclosed that it is not one made in a case to which this Agreement applies, give its reasons for the rejection; or

(*b*) if the application has been fully investigated provide him with a statement setting out:

(i) the circumstances in which the death or injury occurred and the relevant evidence;
(ii) the circumstances relevant to the assessment of the amount to be awarded to the applicant under this Agreement and the relevant evidence; and
(iii) if it refuses to make an award, its reasons for that refusal; and

(*c*) in a case to which Clause 5 of this Agreement applies specify the way in which the amount of that award has been computed and its relation to those provisions of Clause 5 which are relevant to its computation.

(2) Where the MIB has decided that it will not indemnify the applicant against the costs of any proceedings which it has under Clause 6(1)(*b*) required him to bring against any specified person or persons on the ground that those proceedings have materially contributed to establish that the untraced person did not cause or contribute to the relevant death or injury, it shall give notice to the applicant of that decision, together with its reasons for it and shall provide the applicant with a copy of any transcript of any evidence given or judgment delivered in those proceedings as is mentioned in Clause 6(2)(*b*) which it regards as relevant to that decision.

10 (1) Subject to the provisions of this Agreement, where the MIB has decided to make an award to the applicant, it shall pay the applicant the amount of that award if:

(*a*) it has been notified by the applicant that the award is accepted; or

(*b*) at the expiration of the period during which the applicant may give notice of an appeal under Clause 11 the applicant has not given the MIB either any notification of acceptance of its award or a notice of an appeal under Clause 11.

(2) Such payment as is made under paragraph (1) of this Clause shall discharge the MIB from all liability under this Agreement in respect of the death or injury for which that award has been made.

11(1) The applicant shall have a right of appeal to an arbitrator against any decision notified to him by the MIB under Clause 9 if:

(*a*) he gives notice to the MIB, that he wishes to appeal against its decision ("the notice of appeal");

(*b*) he gives the MIB the notice of appeal within 6 weeks from the date when he was given notice of the decision against which he wishes to appeal; and

(*c*) he has not previously notified the MIB that he has accepted its decision.

(2) The grounds of appeal are as follows:

(*a*) where the application has not been the subject of a full investigation:

(i) that the case is one to which this Agreement applies; and
(ii) that the application should be fully investigated by the MIB with a view to its deciding whether or not to make an award to him and, if so the amount of that award; or

(*b*) where the application has been fully investigated:
(i) that the MIB was wrong in refusing to make an award; or
(ii) that the amount it has awarded to the applicant is insufficient; or

(*c*) in a case where a decision not to indemnify the applicant against the costs of any proceedings has been notified to the applicant by the MIB under Clause 9(2), that that decision was wrong.

12 A notice of appeal under Clause 11 hereof shall state the grounds of the appeal and shall be accompanied by an undertaking given by the applicant or by the person acting on his behalf under Clause 2(1)(*b*) and 2(1)(*c*), that:

(*a*) the applicant will accept the decision of the arbitrator; and

(*b*) the arbitrator's fee shall be paid to the MIB by the applicant or by the person who has given the undertaking in any case where the MIB is entitled to reimbursement of that fee under the provisions of Clause 22.

13 (1) When giving notice of his appeal or at any time before doing so, the applicant may:

(*a*) make comments to the MIB on its decision; and

(*b*) supply it with such particulars he thinks fit of any further evidence not contained in the written statement supplied to him by the MIB which he considers is relevant to the application.

(2) The MIB may, before submitting the applicant's appeal to the arbitrator:

(*a*) cause an investigation to be made into the further evidence supplied by the applicant under paragraph (1)(*b*) of this Clause; and

(*b*) report to the applicant the result of that investigation and of any change in its decision which may result from it.

(3) The applicant may, within six weeks from the date on which the report referred to in paragraph (2)(*b*) of this Clause was sent to him, unless he withdraws his appeal, make such comments on the report as he may desire to have submitted to the arbitrator.

14 (1) In a case where the MIB receives from the applicant a notice of appeal in which the only ground of appeal which is stated is that the amount awarded

to the applicant is insufficient, before submitting that appeal to the arbitrator, MIB may:

(*a*) give notice to the applicant that if the appeal proceeds it will request the arbitrator to decide whether the case is one in which the MIB should make an award at all; and

(*b*) at the same time as complying with paragraph (1)(*a*) of this Clause provide the applicant with a statement setting out such comments as it may consider relevant to the decision which the arbitrator should come to on that question.

(2) Where the MIB gives the applicant notice under paragraph (1)(*a*) of this Clause, the applicant may, within six weeks from the date on which that notice is given:

(*a*) make comments to the MIB and supply it with particulars of other evidence not contained in any written statement provided to him by the MIB as he may consider relevant to the question which the arbitrator is by that notice requested to decide; and

(*b*) Clause 13 shall apply in relation to any comments made or particulars supplied by the applicant under paragraph (2)(*a*) of this Clause.

15 (1) Subject to paragraph (2) of this Clause, where the MIB receives a notice of appeal from the applicant under the provisions of this Agreement, unless the appeal is previously withdrawn, it shall:

(*a*) submit that appeal to an arbitrator for a decision; and

(*b*) send to the arbitrator for the purpose of obtaining his decision:

(i) the application made by the applicant;
(ii) a copy of its decision as notified to the applicant; and
(iii) copies of all statements, declarations, notices, undertakings, comments, transcripts, particulars of reports provided, given or sent to the MIB under this Agreement either by the applicant or any person acting for him under Clause 2(1)(*b*) or 2(1)(*c*) or given or sent to the applicant or a person acting for him under Clause 2(1)(*b*) or 2(1)(*c*) by the MIB.

(2) In a case where the MIB causes an investigation to be made under Clause 13, the MIB shall not comply with paragraph (1) of this Clause until:

(*a*) the expiration of six weeks from the date on which it sent the applicant a report as to the result of that investigation; or (*b*) the expiration of six weeks from the date on which it gave the applicant notice under Clause 14(1); or

(*c*) the expiration of six weeks from the date on which it sent the applicant a report as to the result of that investigation, if it has caused an investigation to be made into any evidence supplied under Clause 14(2).

16 On an appeal made by the applicant in accordance with this Agreement:

(*a*) if the appeal is against a decision by the MIB rejecting an application because a preliminary investigation has disclosed that the case is not one to which this Agreement applies, the arbitrator shall decide whether the case is or is not one to which this Agreement applies and, if he decides that it is such a case, shall remit the application to the MIB for full investigation and a decision in accordance with the provisions of this Agreement;

(*b*) if the appeal is against a decision by the MIB given after an application has been fully investigated by it (whether before the appeal or in consequence of its being remitted for such investigation under paragraph (*a*) of this Clause) the arbitrator shall decide, as may be appropriate, having regard to the grounds stated in the notice of appeal and to any notice given by the MIB to the applicant under Clause 14, whether the MIB should make an award under this Agreement to the applicant and, if so, the amount which it should award to him under the provisions of this Agreement;

(*c*) if the appeal relates to a dispute which has arisen between the applicant and the MIB which is required by the proviso to Clause 6(3) to be referred to the arbitrator, the arbitrator shall also give his decision on that dispute. Provided that where the arbitrator has allowed an appeal under paragraph (*a*) of this Clause all the provisions of this Agreement shall apply as if the case were an application to which this Agreement applies upon which the MIB had not communicated a decision.

17 (1) Subject to paragraph (2) of this Clause, the arbitrator shall decide the appeal on the documents submitted to him under Clause 15(1)(*b*) and no further evidence shall be produced to him.

(2) The following shall apply where documents have been submitted to the arbitrator under Clause 15(1)(*b*):

(*a*) the arbitrator shall be entitled to ask the MIB to make any further investigation which he considers desirable and to submit a written report of its findings to him for his consideration; and

(*b*) the MIB shall send a copy of that report to the applicant who shall be entitled to submit written comments on it to the MIB within four weeks of the date on which that copy is sent to him; and (*c*) the MIB shall transmit those comments to the arbitrator for his consideration.

18 The arbitrator by whom an appeal made by an applicant in accordance with the provisions of this Agreement shall be considered shall be an arbitrator to be selected by the Secretary of State from two panels of Queen's Counsel appointed respectively by the Lord Chancellor and the Lord Advocate for the purpose of determining appeals under this Agreement, the arbitrator to be selected from the panel appointed by the Lord Chancellor in cases where the event giving rise to the death or injury occurred in England or Wales and from the panel appointed by the Lord Advocate where that event occurred in Scotland.

19 The arbitrator shall notify his decision on any appeal under this Agreement to the MIB and the MIB shall forthwith send a copy of the arbitrator's decision to the applicant.

20 Subject to the provisions of this Agreement, the MIB shall pay the applicant any amount which the arbitrator has decided shall be awarded to him, and that payment shall discharge the MIB from all liability under this Agreement in respect of the death or injury in respect of which that decision has been given.

21 Each party to the appeal will bear their own costs.

22 The MIB shall pay the arbitrator a fee approved by the Lord Chancellor or the Lord Advocate, as the case may be, after consultation with the MIB. Provided that, in any case where it appears to the arbitrator, that there were no reasonable grounds for the appeal, the arbitrator may in his discretion decide:

(*a*) that his fee ought to be paid by the applicant; and

(*b*) that the person giving the undertaking required by Clause 12 shall be liable to reimburse the MIB the amount of the fee paid by it to the arbitrator, except in so far as that amount is deducted by the MIB from any amount which it is liable to pay to the applicant in consequence of the decision of the arbitrator.

23 If in any case it appears to the MIB that by reason of the applicant being under the age of majority or of any other circumstances affecting his capacity to manage his affairs it would be in the applicant's interest that all or some part of the amount which would otherwise be payable to him under an award made under this Agreement should be administered for him by the Family Welfare Association or by some other body or person under a trust or by the Court of Protection (or in Scotland by the appointment of a Judicial Factor) the MIB may establish for that purpose a trust of the whole or part of the amount to take effect for a period and under provisions as may appear to it to be appropriate in the circumstances of the case or may initiate or cause any other person to initiate process in that Court and otherwise cause any amount payable under the award to be paid to and administered thereby.

24 In any case in which an application has been made to the MIB under Clause 2(1) and in which a preliminary investigation under Clause 7 has disclosed that the case is one to which the Agreement, save for Clause 5, applies, the MIB may,

instead of causing a report to be made on the application as provided by Clause 7, make, or cause to be made, to the applicant an offer to settle his application in a specified sum, assessed in accordance with Clause 3.

25 Where an offer is made under Clause 24, there shall be provided to the applicant (at the same time) in writing particulars of:

(*a*) the circumstances in which the death or injury occurred and the relevant evidence; and

(*b*) the circumstances relevant to the assessment of the amount to be awarded to the applicant and the relevant evidence.

26 (1) On receipt by the MIB or its agent of an acceptance of the offer referred to in Clause 24:

(*a*) this acceptance shall have effect in relation to the application as if in Clause 7 the words "and, unless the MIB decides" to the end of that Clause, and Clauses 9 to 22 inclusive were omitted; and

(*b*) the MIB shall pay to the applicant the amount specified in the offer.

(2) The payment made by the MIB under paragraph (1)(*b*) of this Clause shall discharge it from all liability under this Agreement in respect of the death or injury for which the payment has been made.

27 This Agreement may be determined at any time by the Secretary of State or by the MIB by either of them giving to the other no less than twelve months previous notice in writing. Provided that this Agreement shall continue to have effect in any case where the event giving rise to the death or injury occurred before the date on which this Agreement terminates in accordance with any notice so given.

28 From 14 June 1996 the following periods of operation shall apply:

(*a*) this Agreement shall come into operation on 1 July 1996 in relation to accidents occurring on or after that date;

(*b*) the Second Agreement shall cease and determine except in relation to applications arising out of accidents which occurred on or after 1st December 1972 and before 1 July 1996; and

(*c*) the Third Agreement shall cease and determine except in relation to accidents occurring on or after 3 January 1978 and before 1 July 1996.

IN WITNESS whereof the Secretary of State for Transport has caused his Corporate Seal to be hereto affixed and the Motor Insurers' Bureau has caused its Common Seal to be hereto affixed the day and year first above written.

(LS) THE CORPORATE SEAL of THE SECRETARY OF STATE FOR TRANSPORT hereunto affixed is authenticated by:
Steven Norris
Parliamentary Under Secretary of State
Department of Transport

(LS) THE COMMON SEAL of THE MOTOR INSURERS' BUREAU was hereunto affixed in the presence of:
James A Read
Leslie Howell
Directors of the Board of Management

Anthony Dand
Secretary

NOTES

The following Notes are for the guidance of those who may wish to make application to the Motor Insurers' Bureau for payment under the Agreement, and for the guidance of their legal advisers, but they must not be taken as making unnecessary a careful study of the Agreement itself. Communications connected with the Agreement should be addressed to the Motor Insurers' Bureau ("the MIB"), whose address in 152 Silbury Boulevard, Central Milton Keynes, MK9 1NB.

1 This Agreement replaces a previous one dated 22 November 1972 and a Supplemental Agreement dated 7 December 1977 and continues the arrangements which have existed since 1946 under which the MIB has made ex gratia payments in respect of death or personal injuries resulting from the use on the road of a motor vehicle the owner or driver of which cannot be traced. Provision is made for an appeal against the MIB's decision in such cases.

2 The Agreement dated 22 November 1972 applies to a death or bodily injury arising out of an accident occurring on a road in Great Britain on or after 1 December 1972 and before 3 January 1978. The Agreement dated 22 November 1972 as supplemented by the Supplemental Agreement dated 7 December 1977 applies in relation to accidents occurring on or after 3 January 1978 and before 1 July 1996. This Agreement applies in relation to accidents occurring on or after 1 July 1996.

3 Subject to the terms of the Agreement, the MIB will accept applications for a payment in respect of the death of, or bodily injury to any person resulting from the use of a motor vehicle on a road in Great Britain in any cases in which:

(*a*) the applicant for the payment cannot trace any person responsible for the death or injury (or, in certain circumstances, a person partly responsible) (Clause 1(1)(*b*)); and

(*b*) the death or injury was caused in such circumstances that the untraced person would be liable to pay damages to the applicant in respect of the death or injury (Clause 1(1)(*c*)); and

(c) the untraced person's liability to the applicant is one which at the time the accident occurred, was required to be covered by insurance or security (Clause 1(1)(*d*)).

The MIB will not deal with the following:

(*a*) deliberate "running down" cases (Clause 1(1)(*e*));

(*b*) certain other cases relating to Crown vehicles; and

(*c*) certain categories of "voluntary" passenger (Clause 1(2)–(4)).

4 Applications for a payment under the Agreement must be made in writing to the MIB within 3 years of the date of the accident giving rise to the death or injury (Clause 1(1)(*f*)).

5 Under Clause 3, the amount which the MIB will award will (except for the exclusion of those elements of damages mentioned in Clause 4 be assessed in the same way as a court would have assessed the amount of damages payable by the untraced person had the applicant been able to bring a successful claim for damages against him.

6 Clause 5 relates to cases where an untraced person, and identified person are partly responsible for a death or injury, and defines the conditions under which the MIB will in such cases make a contribution in respect of the responsibility of the untraced person.

7 Under Clause 6(1)(*b*), the MIB may require the applicant to bring proceedings against any identified person who may be responsible for the death or injury, subject to indemnifying the applicant as to his costs as provided in Clause 6(2) and (3).

8 On receipt of an application, the MIB will, if satisfied that the application comes within the terms of the Agreement, investigate the circumstances and, when this has been done, decide whether to make a payment and, if so, how much (Clause 7).

9 The MIB may request the applicant to make a statutory declaration setting out all, or some, of the facts on which his application is based (Clause 8).

10 The MIB may notify the applicant of its decision, setting out the circumstances of the case and the evidence on which it bases its decision, and, if it refuses to make a payment, the reasons for the refusal (Clause 9).

11 If the applicant wishes to appeal against the decision on the grounds specified in Clause 11(2), he must notify the MIB within six weeks of being notified of the decision, and he or any person acting on his behalf shall give the undertakings set out in Clause 12.

12 The MIB may, as a result of the comments made and further evidence submitted by the applicant on its decision, investigate the further evidence, and if so it will communicate with the applicant again. In such a case the applicant

will have six weeks from the date of that further communication in which to decide whether or not to go on with the appeal (Clause 13).

13 Where the applicant appeals only on the ground that the amount awarded to him is too low, the MIB may give him notice that if the matter proceeds to appeal, it will ask the arbitrator to decide also the issue of the MIB's liability to make any payment. The applicant will have six weeks from the date of any such notice in which to comment to the MIB on this intention (Clause 14).

14 Appeals will be decided by an arbitrator who will be a Queen's Counsel selected by the Secretary of State for Transport from one of two panels to be appointed by the Lord Chancellor and the Lord Advocate respectively (Clause 18).

15 All appeals will be decided by the arbitrator on the basis of the relevant documents (as set out in Clause 15) which will be sent to him by the MIB. If the arbitrator asks the MIB to make a further investigation, the applicant will have an opportunity to comment on the result of that investigation (Clause 17).

16 The arbitrator may, at his discretion, award the cost of his fee against the applicant if he considers the appeal unreasonable; otherwise, each party to the appeal will bear their own costs, the MIB paying the arbitrator's fee (Clause 21 and 22).

17 In certain circumstances, the MIB may establish a trust for the benefit of an applicant of the whole or part of any award (Clause 23).

Appendix H

The Human Body: Bones and Muscles

Contents

* * *

1 Anterior View of Skeleton

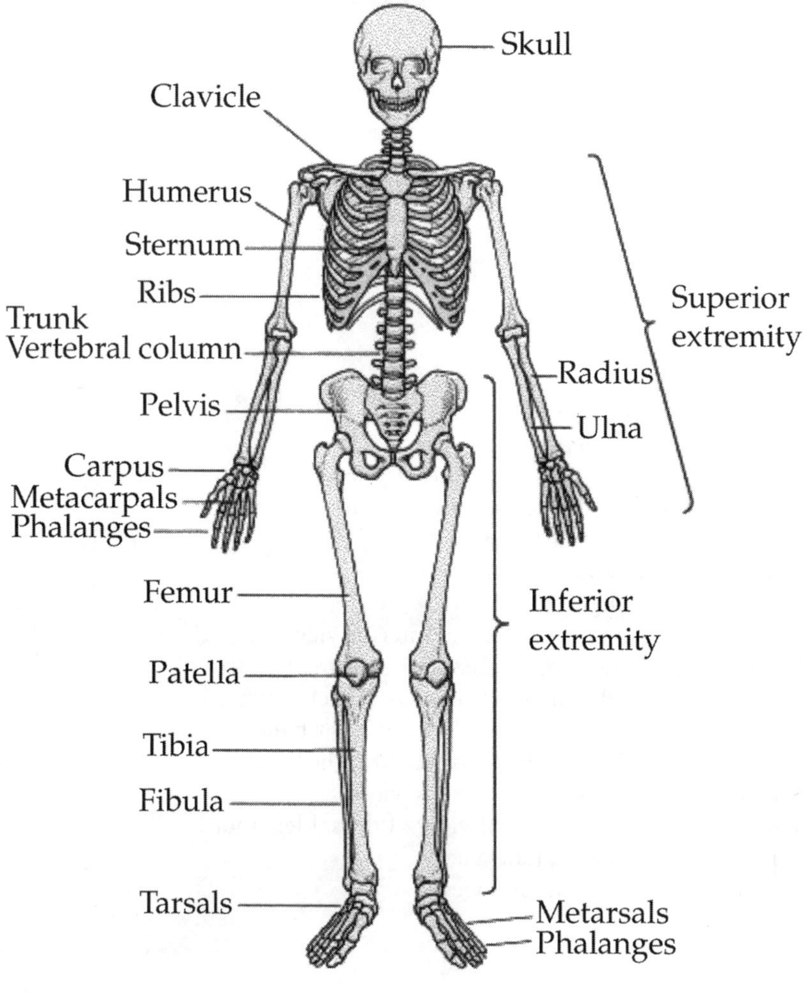

2 Lateral View of Skeleton

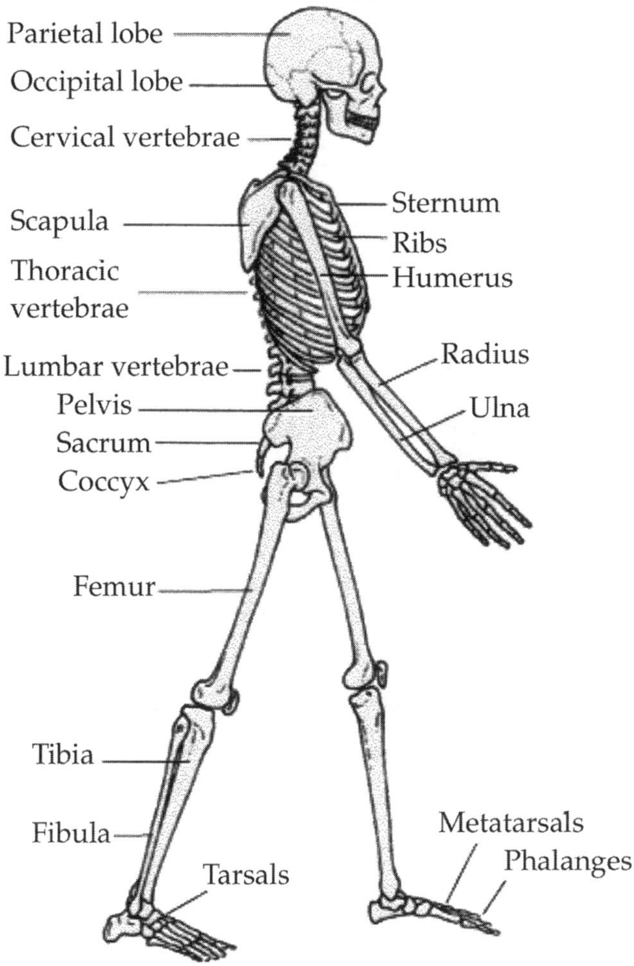

3 Superficial Layer of Muscles
Anterior view

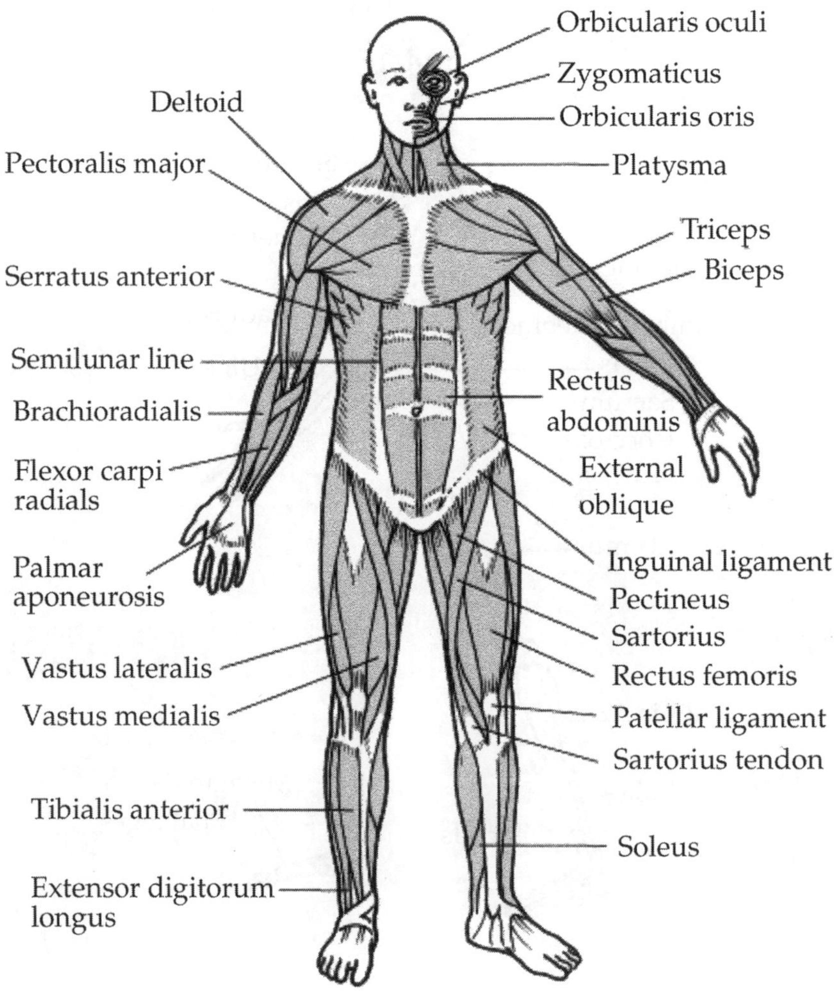

4 Superficial Layer of Muscles
Posterior view

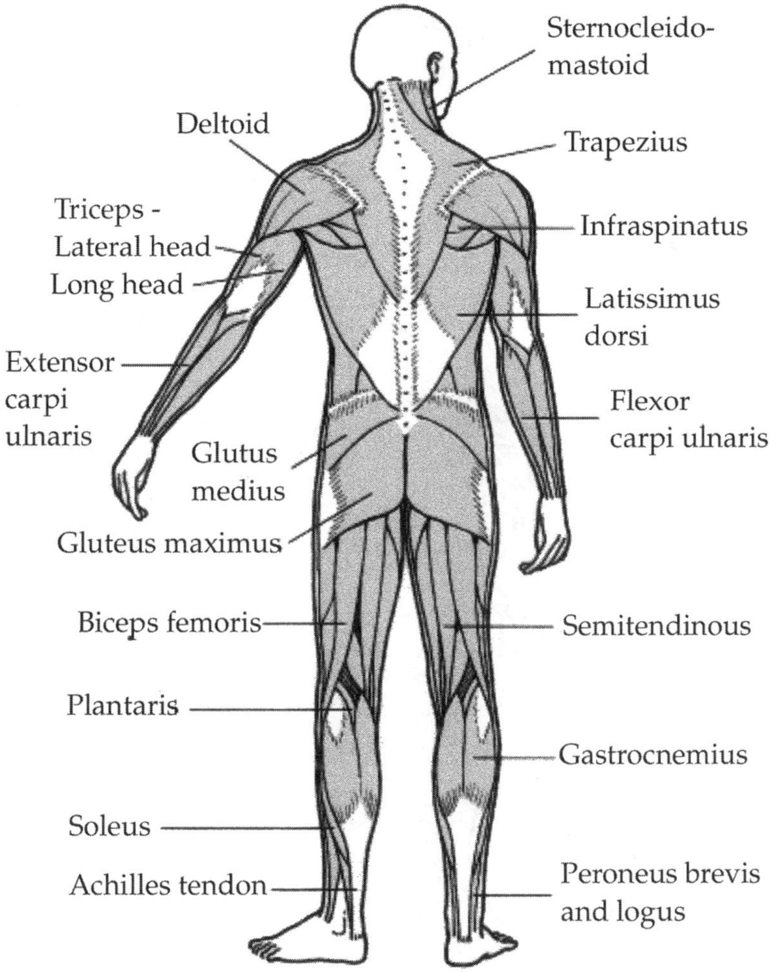

5 Spinal Column
Lateral view

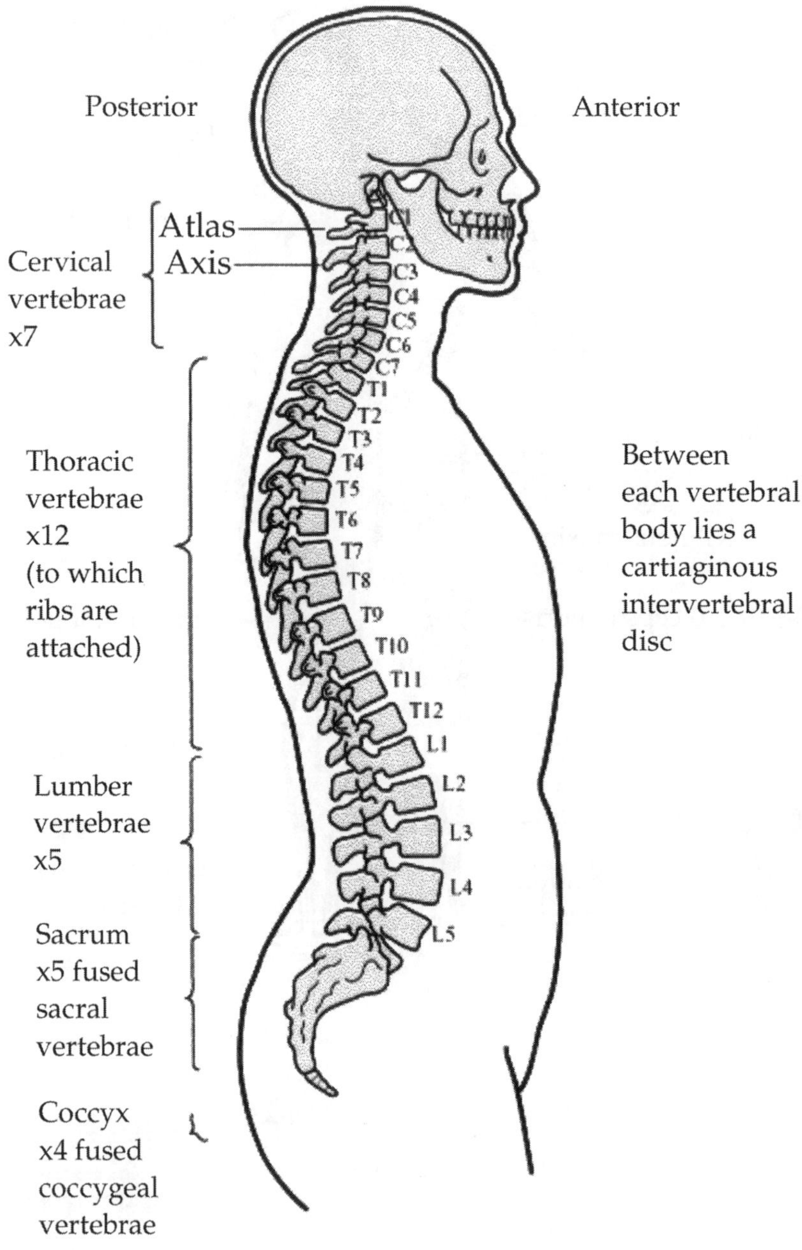

6 Lateral View of Skull

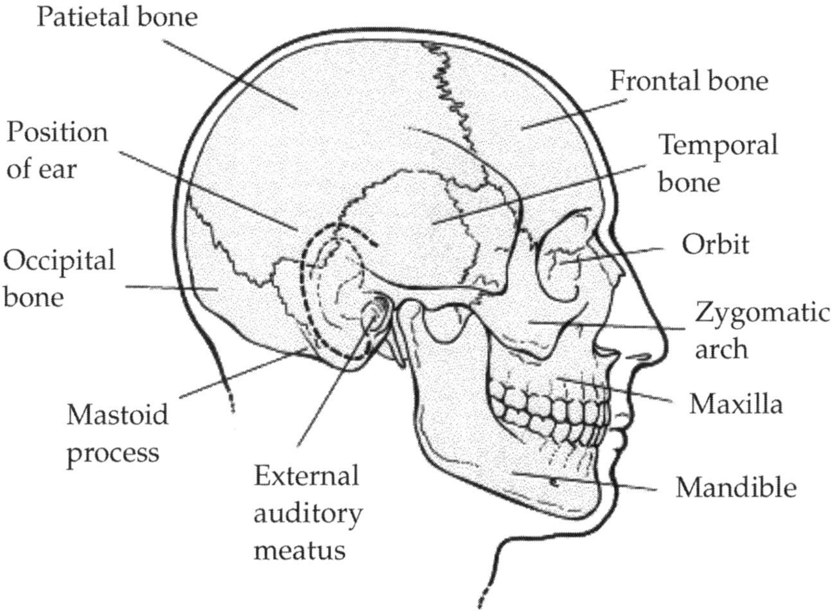

7 Upper Set of Adult Teeth

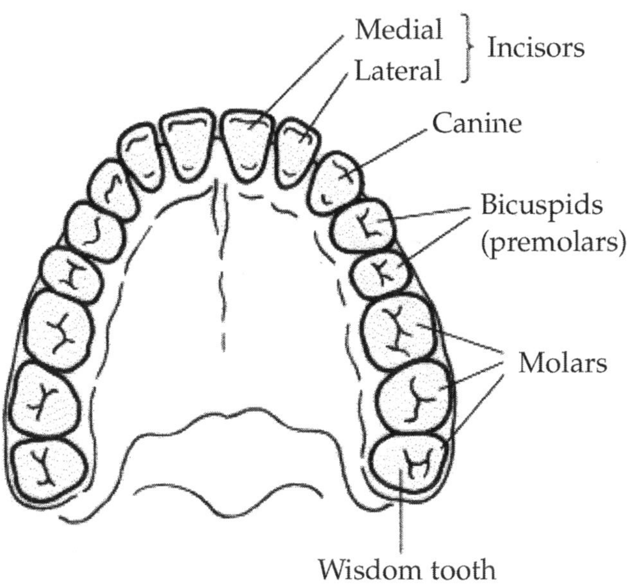

8 Bones of the Arm and Shoulder
Anterior view

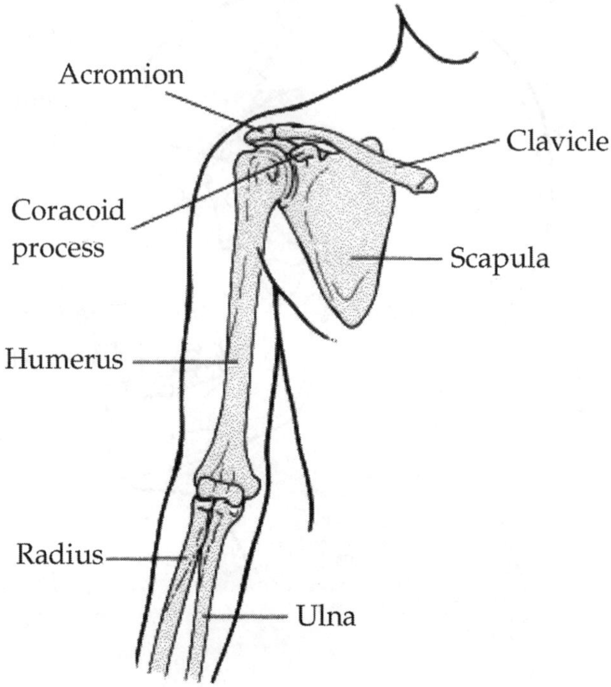

9 Bones of the Elbow Joint
Lateral view of the left arm

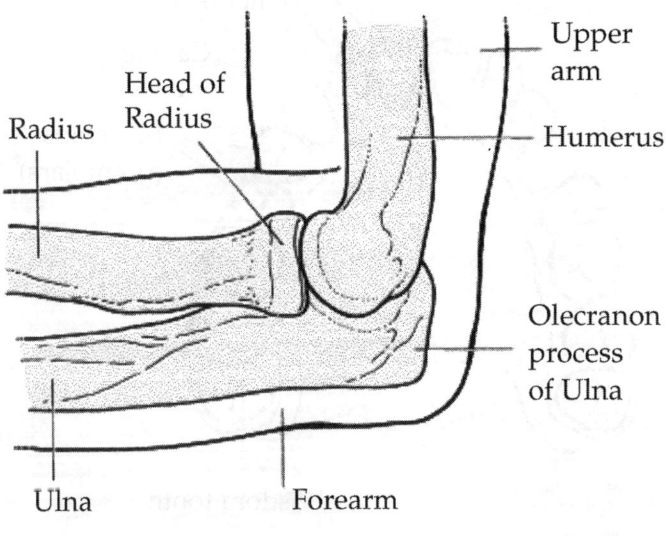

10 Bones of the Hand and Wrist
Palmar aspect of right hand

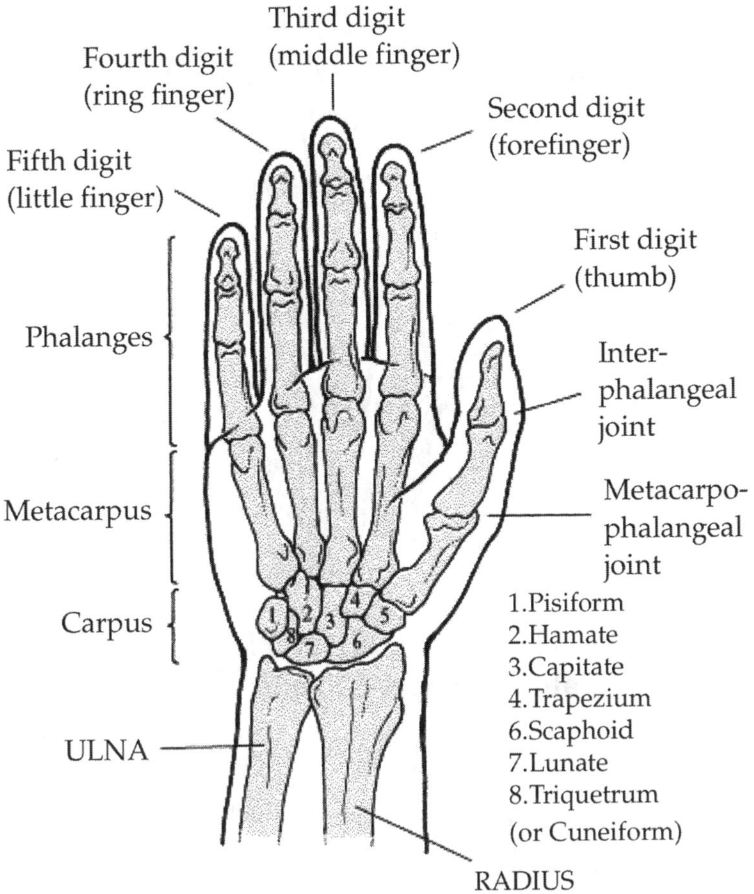

11 Muscles of the Hand
Dorsal aspect of right hand

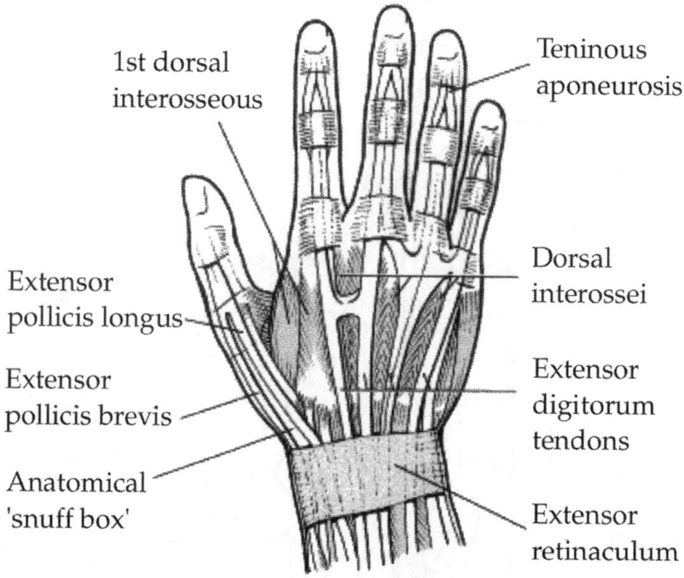

12 Muscles of the Hand
Palmar aspect of right hand

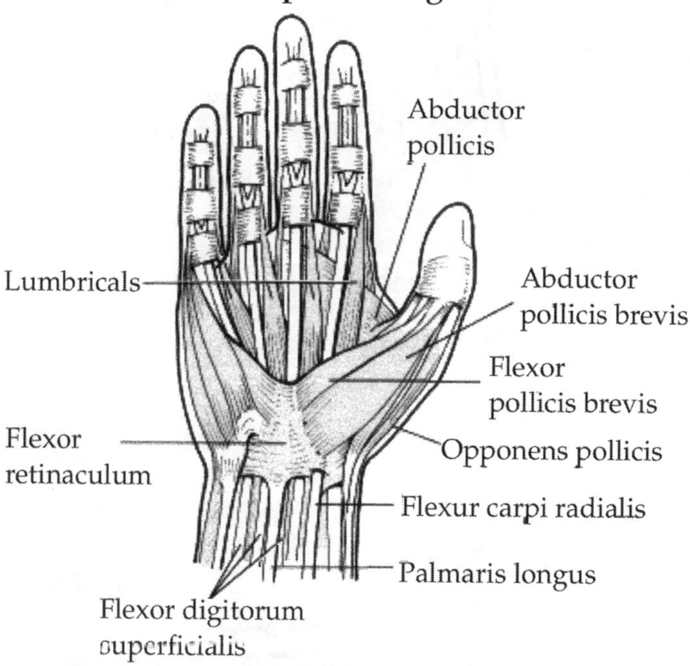

13 Bones of the Hip and Leg
Anterior view

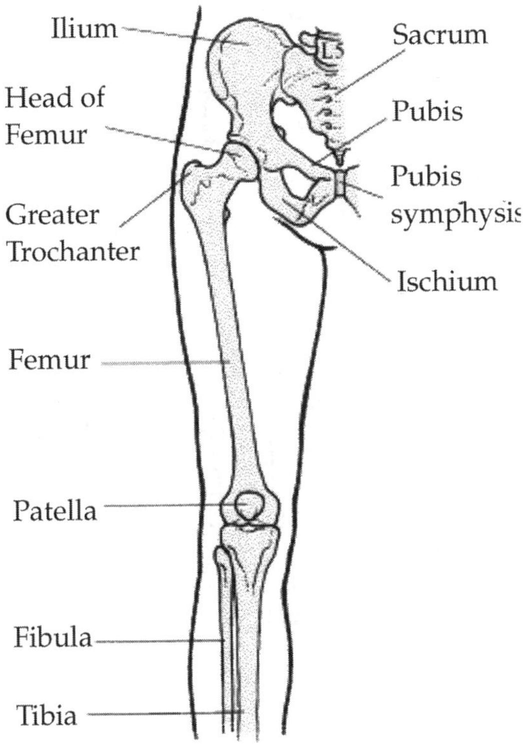

14 Bones of the Foot
Superficial view of dorsal left foot

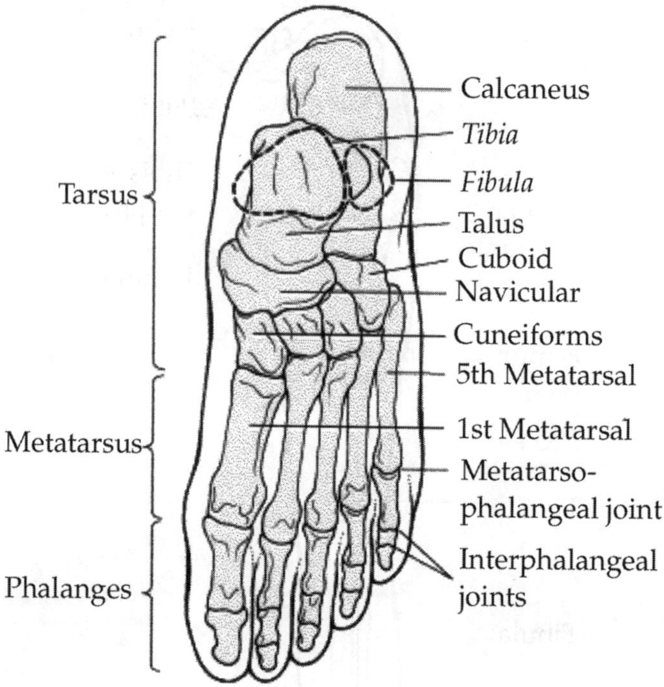

15 Muscles of the Foot
Lateral view

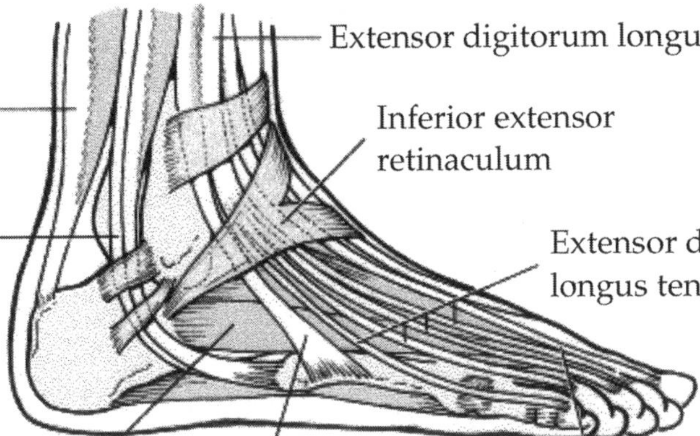

16 Muscles of the Foot
Medial view

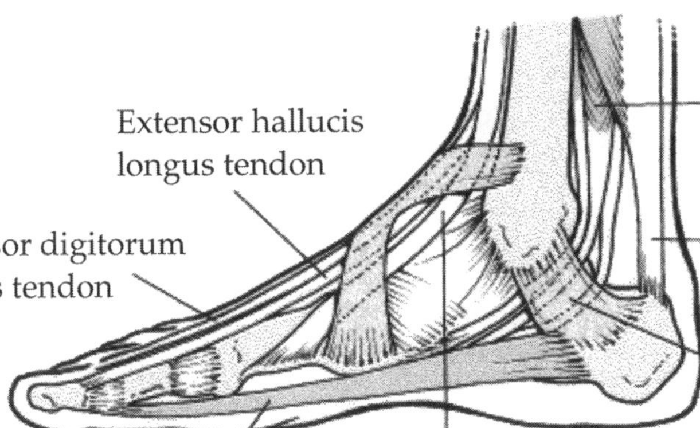

Appendix I

Pre-Action Protocol for Personal Injury Claims

Contents

* * *

1 Introduction

1.1 Lord Woolf in his final Access to Justice Report of July 1996 recommended the development of pre-action protocols: "To build on and increase the benefits of early but well informed settlement which genuinely satisfy both parties to dispute."

1.2 The aims of pre-action protocols are:

- more pre-action contact between the parties
- better and earlier exchange of information
- better pre-action investigation by both sides
- to put the parties in a position where they may be able to settle cases fairly and early without litigation
- to enable proceedings to run to the court's timetable and efficiently, if litigation does become necessary.

1.3 The concept of protocols is relevant to a range of initiatives for good litigation and pre-litigation practice, especially:

- predictability in the time needed for steps pre-proceedings
- standardisation of relevant information, including documents to be disclosed.

1.4 The Courts will be able to treat the standards set in protocols as the normal reasonable approach to pre-action conduct. If proceedings are issued, it will be for the court to decide whether non-compliance with a protocol should merit adverse consequences. Guidance on the court's likely approach will be given from time to time in practice directions.

1.5 If the court has to consider the question of compliance after proceedings have begun, it will not be concerned with minor infringements, *e.g.* failure by a short period to provide relevant information. One minor breach will not exempt the 'innocent' party from following the protocol. The court will look at the effect of non-compliance on the other party when deciding whether to impose sanctions.

2 Notes of Guidance

2.1 The protocol has been kept deliberately simple to promote case of use and general acceptability. The notes of guidance which follow relate particularly to issues which arose during the piloting of the protocol.

Scope of The Protocol

2.2 This protocol is intended to apply to all claims which include a claim for personal injury (except industrial disease claims) and to the entirety of those claims: not only to the personal injury element of a claim which also includes, for instance, property damage.

2.3 This protocol is primarily designed for those road traffic, tripping and slipping and accident at work cases which include an element of personal injury with a value of less than £15,000 which are likely to be allocated to the fast track. This is because time will be of the essence, after proceedings are issued, especially for the defendant, if a case is to be ready for trial within 30 weeks of allocation. Also, proportionality of work and costs to the value of what is in dispute is particularly important in lower value claims. For some claims within the value "scope" of the fast track some flexibility in the timescale of the protocol may be necessary, see also paragraph 3.8.

2.4 However, the "cards on the table" approach advocated by the protocol is equally appropriate to some higher value claims. The spirit, if not the letter of the protocol, should still be followed for multi-track type claims. In accordance with the sense of the civil justice reforms, the court will expect to see the spirit of reasonable pre-action behaviour applied in all cases, regardless of the existence of a specific protocol. In particular with regard to personal injury cases worth more than £15,000, with a view to avoiding the necessity of proceedings parties are expected to comply with the protocol as far as possible, *e.g.* in respect of letters before action, exchanging information and documents and agreeing experts.

2.5 The timetable and the arrangements for disclosing documents and obtaining expert evidence may need to be varied to suit the circumstances of the case. Where one or both parties consider the detail of the protocol is not appropriate to the case, and proceedings are subsequently issued, the court will expect an explanation as to why the protocol has not been followed, or has been varied.

Early Notification

2.6 The claimant's legal representative may wish to notify the defendant and/or his insurer as soon as they know a claim is likely to be made, but before they are able to send a detailed letter of claim, particularly for instance, when the defendant has no or limited knowledge of the incident giving rise to the claim or where the claimant is incurring significant expenditure as a result of the accident which he hopes the defendant might pay for, in whole or in part. If the claimant's representative chooses to do this, it will not start the timetable for responding.

The Letter of Claim

2.7 The specimen letter of claim at Annex A will usually be sent to the individual defendant. In practice, he/she may have no personal financial interest in the financial outcome of the claim/dispute because he/she is insured. Court imposed sanctions for non-compliance with the protocol may be ineffective against an insured. This is why the protocol emphasises the importance of passing the letter of claim to the insurer and the possibility that the insurance cover might be affected. If an insurer receives the letter of claim only after some delay by the insured, it would not be unreasonable for the insurer to ask the claimant for additional time to respond.

Reasons for Early Issue

2.8 The protocol recommends that a defendant be given three months to investigate and respond to a claim before proceedings are issued. This may not always be possible, particularly where a claimant only consults a solicitor close to the end of any relevant limitation period. In these circumstances, the claimant's solicitor should give as much notice of the intention to issue proceedings as is practicable and the parties should consider whether the court might be invited to extend time for service of the claimant's supporting documents and for service of any defence, or alternatively, to stay the proceedings while the recommended steps in the protocol are followed.

Status of Letters of Claim and Response

2.9 Letters of claim and response are not intended to have the same status as a statement of case in proceedings. Matters may come to light as a result of investigation after the letter of claim has been sent, or after the defendant has responded, particularly if disclosure of documents takes place outside the recommended three-month period. These circumstances could mean that the 'pleaded' case of one or both parties is presented slightly differently than in the letter of claim and response. It would not be consistent with the spirit of the protocol for a party to "take a point" on this in the proceedings, provided that there was no obvious intention by the party who changed their position to mislead the other party.

Disclosure of Documents

2.10 The aim of the early disclosure of documents by the defendant is not to encourage "fishing expeditions" by the claimant, but to promote an early exchange of relevant information to help in clarifying or resolving issues in dispute. The claimant's solicitor can assist by identifying in the letter of claim or in a subsequent letter the particular categories of documents which they consider are relevant.

Experts

2.11 The protocol encourages joint selection of, and access to, experts. Most frequently this will apply to the medical expert, but on occasions also to liability experts, *e.g.* engineers. The protocol promotes the practice of the claimant obtaining a medical report, disclosing it to the defendant who then asks questions and/or agrees it and does not obtain his own report. The Protocol provides for nomination of the expert by the claimant in personal injury claims because of the early stage of the proceedings and the particular nature of such claims. If proceedings have to be issued, a medical report must be attached to these proceedings. However, if necessary after proceedings have commenced and with the permission of the court, the parties may obtain further expert reports. It would be for the court to decide whether the costs of more than one expert's report should be recoverable.

2.12 Some solicitors choose to obtain medical reports through medical agencies, rather than directly from a specific doctor or hospital. The defendant's prior consent to the action should be sought and, if the defendant so requests, the agency should be asked to provide in advance the names of the doctor(s) whom they are considering instructing.

Negotiations/Settlement

2.13 Parties and their legal representatives are encouraged to enter into discussions and/or negotiations prior to starting proceedings. The protocol does not specify when or how this might be done but parties should bear in mind that the courts increasingly take the view that litigation should be a last resort, and that claims should not be issued prematurely when a settlement is in reasonable prospect.

Stocktake

2.14 Where a claim is not resolved when the protocol has been followed, the parties might wish to carry out a "stocktake" of the issues in dispute, and the evidence that the court is likely to need to decide those issues, before proceedings are started. Where the defendant is insured and the pre-action steps have been conducted by the insurer, the insurer would normally be expected to nominate solicitors to act in the proceedings and the claimant's solicitor is recommended to invite the insurer to nominate solicitors to act in the proceedings and do so 7–14 days before the intended issue date.

3 The Protocol

Letter of Claim

3.1 The claimant shall send to the proposed defendant two copies of a letter of claim, immediately sufficient information is available to substantiate a realistic claim and before issues of quantum are addressed in detail. One copy of the letter is for the defendants, the second for passing on to his insurers.

3.2 The letter shall contain **a clear summary of the facts** on which the claim is based together with an indication of the **nature of any injuries** suffered and of **any financial loss incurred.** In cases of road traffic accidents, the letter should provide the name and address of the hospital where treatment has been obtained and the claimant's hospital reference number.

3.3 Solicitors are recommended to use a **standard format** for such a letter—an example is at Annex A: this can be amended to suit the particular case.

3.4 The letter should ask for **details of the insurer** and that a copy should be sent by the proposed defendant to the insurer where appropriate. If the insurer is known, a copy shall be sent directly to the insurer. Details of the claimant's National Insurance number and date of birth should be supplied to the defendant's insurer once the Defendant has responded to the letter of claim and confirmed the identity of the insurer. This information should not be supplied in the letter of claim.

3.5 **Sufficient information** should be given in order to enable the defendant's insurer/solicitor to commence investigations and at least put a broad valuation on the 'risk'.

3.6 The **defendant should reply within 21 calendar days** of the date of posting of the letter identifying the insurer (if any). If there has been no reply by the defendant or insurer within 21 days, the claimant will be entitled to issue proceedings.

3.7 The **defendant**('s insurers) will have a **maximum of three months** from the date of acknowledgment of the claim **to investigate.** No later than the end of that period the defendant (insurer) shall reply, stating whether liability is denied and, if so, giving reasons for their denial of liability.

3.8 Where the accident occurred outside England and Wales and/or where the defendant is outside the jurisdiction, the time periods of 21 days and three months should normally be extended up to 42 days and six months.

3.9 Where **liability is admitted,** the presumption is that the defendant will be bound by this admission for all claims with a total value of up to £15,000.

Documents

3.10 If the **defendant denies liability,** he should enclose with the letter of reply, **documents** in his possession which are **material to the issues** between the parties, and which would be likely to be ordered to be disclosed by the court, either on an application for pre-action disclosure, or on disclosure during proceedings.

3.11 Attached at Annex B are **specimen,** but non-exhaustive, **lists** of documents likely to be material in different types of claim. Where the claimant's investigation of the case is well advanced, the letter of claim could indicate which classes of documents are considered relevant for early disclosure. Alternatively these could be identified at a later stage.

3.12 Where the defendant admits primary liability, but alleges contributory negligence by the claimant, the defendant should give reasons supporting those allegations and disclose those documents from Annex B which are relevant to the issues in dispute. The claimant should respond to the allegations of contributory negligence before proceedings are issued.

Special Damages

3.13 The claimant will send to the defendant as soon as practicable a Schedule of Special Damages with supporting documents, particularly where the defendant has admitted liability.

Experts

3.14 Before any party instructs an expert he should give the other party a list of the **name**(s) of **one or more experts** in the relevant speciality whom he considers are suitable to instruct.

3.15 Where a medical expert is to be instructed the claimant's solicitor will organise access to relevant medical records—see specimen letter of instruction at Annex C.

3.16 **Within 14 days** the other party may indicate **an objection** to one or more of the named experts. The first party should then instruct a mutually acceptable expert. It must be emphasised that if the Claimant nominates an expert in the original letter of claim, the Defendant has 14 days to object to one or more of the named experts after expiration of the period of 21 days within which he has to reply to the letter of claim, as set out in paragraph 3.6.

3.17 If the second party objects to all the listed experts, the parties may then instruct **experts of their own choice.** It would be for the court to decide subsequently, if proceedings are issued, whether either party had acted unreasonably.

3.18 If the **second party does not object to an expert nominated,** he shall not be entitled to rely on his own expert evidence within that particular speciality unless:

(a) the first party agrees,

(b) the court so directs, or

(c) the first party's expert report has been amended and the first party is not prepared to disclose the original report.

3.19 **Either party may send to an agreed expert written questions** on the report, relevant to the issues, via the first party's solicitors. The expert should send answers to the questions separately and directly to each party.

3.20 The cost of a report from an agreed expert will usually be paid by the instructing first party: the costs of the expert replying to questions will usually be borne by the party which asks the questions.

3.21 Where the defendant admits liability in whole or in part, before proceedings are issued, any medical report obtained by agreement under this protocol should be disclosed to the other party. The claimant should delay issuing proceedings for 21 days from disclosure of the report, to enable the parties to consider whether the claim is capable of settlement. The Civil Procedure Rules Part 36 permit claimants and defendants to make offers to settle pre-proceedings. Parties should always consider before issuing if it is appropriate to make Part 36 Offer. If such an offer is made, the party making the offer must always supply sufficient evidence and/or information to enable the offer to be properly considered.

Annex A
Letter of Claim

To
Defendant
Dear Sirs
Re: Claimant's full name
Claimant's full address
Claimant's Clock or Works Number
Claimant's Employer (name and address)

We are instructed by the above named to claim damages in connection with an ***accident at work/road traffic accident/tripping accident* on** day **of** (*year*) at (***place of accident which must be sufficiently detailed to establish location***)

Please confirm the identity of your insurers. Please note that the insurers will need to see this letter as soon as possible and it may affect your insurance cover and/or the conduct of any subsequent legal proceedings if you do not send this letter to them.

The circumstances of the accident are:-
(***brief outline***)

The reason why we are alleging fault is:
(***simple explanation e.g. defective machine, broken ground***)

A description of our clients' injuries is as follows:-
(***brief outline***)
(***In cases of road traffic accidents***)
Our client (state hospital reference number) received treatment for the injuries at name and address of hospital).
He is employed as (***occupation***) and has had the following time off work (***dates of absence***). His approximate weekly income is (insert if known).
If you are our client's employers, please provide us with the usual earnings details which will enable us to calculate his financial loss.
We are obtaining a police report and will let you have a copy of the same upon your undertaking to meet half the fee.
We have also sent a letter of claim to (***name and address***) and a copy of that letter is attached. We understand their insurers are (***name, address and claims number if known***).
At this stage of our enquiries we would expect the documents contained in parts (***insert appropriate parts of standard disclosure list***) to be relevant to this action.
A copy of this letter is attached for you to send to your insurers. Finally we expect an acknowledgment of this letter within 21 days by yourselves or your insurers.
Yours faithfully

ANNEX B
PRE-ACTION PERSONAL INJURY PROTOCOL
STANDARD DISCLOSURE LISTS
FAST TRACK DISCLOSURE

RTA Cases

Section A

In all cases where liability is at issue —

(i) Documents identifying nature, extent and location of damage to defendant's vehicle where there is any dispute about point of impact.

(ii) MOT certificate where relevant.

(iii) Maintenance records where vehicle defect is alleged or it is alleged by defendant that there was an unforeseen defect which caused or contributed to the accident.

Section B

Accident involving commercial vehicle as potential defendan —

(i) Tachograph charts or entry from individual control book.

(ii) Maintenance and repair records required for operators' licence where vehicle defect is alleged or it is alleged by defendants that there was an unforeseen defect which caused or contributed to the accident.

Section C

Cases against local authorities where highway design defect is alleged.

(i) Documents produced to comply with Section 39 of the Road Traffic Act 1988 in respect of the duty designed to promote road safety to include studies into road accidents in the relevant area and documents relating to measures recommended to prevent accidents in the relevant area.

Highway Tripping Claims

Documents from Highway Authority for a period of 12 months prior to the accident —

(i) Records of inspection for the relevant stretch of highway.

(ii) Maintenance records including records of independent contractors working in relevant area.

(iii) Records of the minutes of Highway Authority meetings where maintenance or repair policy has been discussed or decided.

(iv) Records of complaints about the state of highways.

(v) Records of other accidents which have occurred on the relevant stretch of highway.

Workplace Claims

(i) Accident book entry.

(ii) First aider report.

(iii) Surgery record.

(iv) Foreman/supervisor accident report.

(v) Safety representatives accident report.

(vi) RIDDOR report to HSE.

(vii) Other communications between defendants and HSE.

(viii) Minutes of Health and Safety Committee meeting(s) where accident/matter considered.

(ix) Report to DSS.

(x) Documents listed above relative to any previous accident/matter identified by the claimant and relied upon as proof of negligence.

(xi) Earnings information where defendant is employer.

Documents produced to comply with requirements of the Management of Health and Safety at Work Regulations 1992—

(i) Pre-accident Risk Assessment required by Regulation 3.

(ii) Post-accident Re-Assessment required by Regulation 3.

(iii) Accident Investigation Report prepared in implementing the requirements of Regulations 4,6 and 9.

(iv) Health Surveillance Records in appropriate cases required by Regulation 5.

(v) Information provided to employees under Regulation 8.

(vi) Documents relating to the employees health and safety training required by Regulation 11.

Workplace Claims—Disclosure where Specific Regulations Apply

Section A—Workplace (Health Safety and Welfare) Regulations 1992

(i) Repair and maintenance records required by Regulation 5.

(ii) Housekeeping records to comply with the requirements of Regulation 9.

(iii) Hazard warning signs or notices to comply with Regulation 17 (Traffic Routes).

Section B—Provision and Use of Work Equipment Regulations 1992

(i) Manufacturers' specifications and instructions in respect of relevant work equipment establishing its suitability to comply with Regulation 5.

(ii) Maintenance log/maintenance records required to comply with Regulation 6.

(iii) Documents providing information and instructions to employees to comply with Regulation 8.

(iv) Documents provided to the employee in respect of training for use to comply with Regulation 9.

(v) Any notice, sign or document relied upon as a defence to alleged breaches of Regulations 14 to 18 dealing with controls and control systems.

(vi) Instruction/training documents issued to comply with the requirements of Regulation 22 insofar as it deals with maintenance operations where the machinery is not shut down.

(vii) Copies of markings required to comply with Regulation 23.

(viii) Copies of warnings required to comply with Regulation 24.

Section C—Personal Protective Equipment at Work Regulations 1992

(i) Documents relating to the assessment of the Personal Protective Equipment to comply with Regulation 6.

(ii) Documents relating to the maintenance and replacement of Personal Protective Equipment to comply with Regulation 7.

(iii) Record of maintenance procedures for Personal Protective Equipment to comply with Regulation 7.

(iv) Records of tests and examinations of Personal Protective Equipment to comply with Regulation 7.

(v) Documents providing information, instruction and training in relation to the Personal Protective Equipment to comply with Regulation 9.

(vi) Instructions for use of Personal Protective Equipment to include the manufacturers' instructions to comply with Regulation 10.

Section D—Manual Handling Operations Regulations 1992

(i) Manual Handling Risk Assessment carried out to comply with the requirements of Regulation 4(1)(b)(i).

(ii) Re-assessment carried out post-accident to comply with requirements of Regulation 4(1)(b)(i).

(iii) Documents showing the information provided to the employee to give general indications related to the load and precise indications on the weight of the load and the heaviest side of the load if the centre of gravity was not positioned centrally to comply with Regulation 4(1)(b)(iii).

(iv) Documents relating to training in respect of manual handling operations and training records.

Section E—Health and Safety (Display Screen Equipment) Regulations 1992

(i) Analysis of work stations to assess and reduce risks carried out to comply with the requirements of Regulation 2.

(ii) Re-assessment of analysis of work stations to assess and reduce risks following development of symptoms by the claimant.

(iii) Documents detailing the provision of training including training records to comply with the requirements of Regulation 6.

(iv) Documents providing information to employees to comply with the requirements of Regulation 7.

Section F—Control of Substances Hazardous to Health Regulations 1988

(i) Risk assessment carried out to comply with the requirements of Regulation 6.

(ii) Reviewed risk assessment carried out to comply with the requirements of Regulation 6.

(iii) Copy labels from containers used for storage handling and disposal of carcinogenics to comply with the requirements of Regulation 7(2A)(h).

(iv) Warning signs identifying designation of areas and installations which may be contaminated by carcinogenics to comply with the requirements of Regulation 7(2A)(h).

(v) Documents relating to the assessment of the Personal Protective Equipment to comply with Regulation 7(3A).

(vi) Documents relating to the maintenance and replacement of Personal Protective Equipment to comply with Regulation 7(3A).

(vii) Record of maintenance procedures for Personal Protective Equipment to comply with Regulation 7(3A).

(viii) Records of tests and examinations of Personal Protective Equipment to comply with Regulation 7(3A).

(ix) Documents providing information, instruction and training in relation to the Personal Protective Equipment to comply with Regulation 7(3A).

(x) Instructions for use of Personal Protective Equipment to include the manufacturers' instructions to comply with Regulation 7(3A).

(xi) Air monitoring records for substances assigned a maximum exposure limit or occupational exposure standard to comply with the requirements of Regulation 7.

(xii) Maintenance examination and test of control measures records to comply with Regulation 9.

(xiii) Monitoring records to comply with the requirements of Regulation 10.

(xiv) Health surveillance records to comply with the requirements of Regulation 11.

(xv) Documents detailing information, instruction and training including training records for employees to comply with the requirements of Regulation 12.

(xvi) Labels and Health and Safety data sheets supplied to the employers to comply with the CHIP Regulations.

Section G—Construction (Design and Management) Regulations 1994

(i) Notification of a project form (HSE F10) to comply with the requirements of Regulation 7.

(ii) Health and Safety Plan to comply with requirements of Regulation 15.

(iii) Health and Safety file to comply with the requirements of Regulations 12 and 14.

(iv) Information and training records provided to comply with the requirements of Regulation 17.

(v) Records of advice from and views of persons at work to comply with the requirements of Regulation 18.

Section H—Pressure Systems and Transportable Gas Containers Regulations 1989

(i) Information and specimen markings provided to comply with the requirements of Regulation 5.

(ii) Written statements specifying the safe operating limits of a system to comply with the requirements of Regulation 7.

(iii) Copy of the written scheme of examination required to comply with the requirements of Regulation 8.

(iv) Examination records required to comply with the requirements of Regulation 9.

(v) Instructions provided for the use of operator to comply with Regulation 11.

(vi) Records kept to comply with the requirements of Regulation 13.

(vii) Records kept to comply with the requirements of Regulation 22.

Section I—Lifting Plant and Equipment (Records of Test and Examination Etc.) Regulations 1992

(i) Record kept to comply with the requirements of Regulation 6.

Section J—The Noise at Work Regulations 1989

(i) Any risk assessment records required to comply with the requirements of Regulations 4 and 5.

(ii) Manufacturers' literature in respect of all ear protection made available to claimant to comply with the requirements of Regulation 8.

(iii) All documents provided to the employee for the provision of information to comply with Regulation 11.

Section K—Construction (Head Protection) Regulations 1989

(i) Pre-accident assessment of head protection required to comply with Regulation 3(4).

(ii) Post-accident re-assessment required to comply with Regulation 3(5).

Section L—The Construction (General Provisions) Regulations 1961

(i) Report prepared following inspections and examinations of excavations etc. to comply with the requirements of Regulation 9.

(ii) Report prepared following inspections and examinations of work in cofferdams and caissons to comply with the requirements of Regulations 17 and 18.

N.B. Further Standard Discovery lists will be required prior to full implementation.

Annex C
Letter of Instruction to Medical Expert

Dear Sir,

Re: (***Name and Address***)
D.O.B. —
Telephone No. —
Date of Accident —

We are acting for the above named in connection with injuries received in an accident which occurred on the above date. The main injuries appear to have been (**main injuries**).

We should be obliged if you would examine our Client and let us have a full and detailed report dealing with any relevant pre-accident medical history, the injuries sustained, treatment received and present condition, dealing in particular with the capacity for work and giving a prognosis.

It is central to our assessment of the extent of our Client's injuries to establish the extent and duration of any continuing disability. Accordingly, in the prognosis section we would ask you to specifically comment on any areas of continuing complaint or disability or impact on daily living. If there is such continuing disability you should comment upon the level of suffering or inconvenience caused and, if you are able, give your view as to when or if the complaint or disability is likely to resolve.

Please send our Client an appointment direct for this purpose. Should you be able to offer a cancellation appointment please contact our Client direct. We confirm we will be responsible for your reasonable fees.

We are obtaining the notes and records from our Client's GP and Hospitals attended and will forward them to you when they are to hand/or please request the GP and Hospital records direct and advise that any invoice for the provision of these records should be forwarded to us.

In order to comply with Court Rules we would be grateful if you would insert above your signature a statement that the contents are true to the best of your knowledge and belief.

In order to avoid further correspondence we can confirm that on the evidence we have there is no reason to suspect we may be pursuing a claim against the hospital or its staff.

We look forward to receiving your report within [   ] weeks. If you will not be able to prepare your report within this period please telephone us upon receipt of these instructions.

When acknowledging these instructions it would assist if you could give an estimate as to the likely time scale for the provision of your report and also an indication as to your fee.

Yours faithfully

Pre-Action Protocol for the Resolution of Clinical Disputes

Clinical Disputes Forum

Contents

Executive Summary

1 The Clinical Disputes Forum is a multi-disciplinary body which was formed in 1997, as a result of Lord Woolf's 'Access to Justice' inquiry. One of the aims of the Forum is to find less adversarial and more cost-effective ways of resolving disputes about healthcare and medical treatment. The names and addresses of the Chairman and Secretary of the Forum can be found at Annex E.

2 This protocol is the Forum's first major initiative. It has been drawn up

carefully, including extensive consultations with most of the key stakeholders in the medico-legal system.

3 The protocol—

- encourages a climate of openness when something has 'gone wrong' with a patient's treatment or the patient is dissatisfied with that treat-ment and/ or the outcome. This reflects the new and developing requirements for clinical governance within healthcare;
- provides general guidance on how this more open culture might be achieved when disputes arise;
- recommends a timed sequence of steps for patients and healthcare providers, and their advisers, to follow when a dispute arises. This should facilitate and speed up exchanging relevant information and increase the prospects that disputes can be resolved without resort to legal action.

4 This protocol has been prepared by a working party of the Clinical Disputes Forum. It has the support of the Lord Chancellor's Department, the Department of Health and NHS Executive, the Law Society, the Legal Aid Board and many other key organisations.

1 Why this Protocol?

Mistrust in Healthcare Disputes

1.1 The number of complaints and claims against hospitals, G.P.s, dentists and private healthcare providers is growing as patients become more prepared to question the treatment they are given, to seek explanations of what happened, and to seek appropriate redress. Patients may require further treatment, an apology, assurances about future action, or compensation. These trends are unlikely to change. The Patients' Charter encourages patients to have high expectations, and a revised NHS Complaints Procedure was implemented in 1996. The civil justice reforms and new Rules of Court should make litigation quicker, more user friendly and less expensive.

1.2 It is clearly in the interests of patients, healthcare professionals and providers that patients' concerns, complaints and claims arising from their treatment are resolved as quickly, efficiently and professionally as possible. A climate of mistrust and lack of openness can seriously damage the patient/clinician relationship, unnecessarily prolong disputes (especially litigation), and reduce the resources available for treating patients. It may also cause additional work for, and lower the morale of, healthcare professionals.

1.3 At present there is often mistrust by both sides. This can mean that patients fail to raise their concerns with the healthcare provider as early as possible. Sometimes patients may pursue a complaint or claim which has little merit, due to a lack of sufficient information and understanding. It can also mean that patients become reluctant, once advice has been taken on a potential claim, to disclose sufficient information to enable the provider to investigate that claim efficiently and, where appropriate, resolve it.

1.4 On the side of the healthcare provider this mistrust can be shown in a reluctance to be honest with patients, a failure to provide prompt clear explanations, especially of adverse outcomes (whether or not there may have been negligence) and a tendency to "close ranks" once a claim is made.

What Needs to Change

1.5 If that mistrust is to be removed, and a more co-operative culture is to develop—

- healthcare professionals and providers need to adopt a constructive approach to complaints and claims. They should accept that concerned patients are entitled to an explanation and an apology, if warranted, and to appropriate redress in the event of negligence. An overly defensive approach is not in the long-term interest of their main goal: patient care;
- patients should recognise that unintended and/or unfortunate consequences of medical treatment can only be rectified if they are brought to the attention of the healthcare provider as soon as possible.

1.6 A protocol which sets out "ground rules" for the handling of disputes at their early stages should, if it is to be subscribed to, and followed —

- encourage greater openness between the parties;
- encourage parties to find the most appropriate way of resolving the particular dispute;
- reduce delay and costs;
- reduce the need for litigation.

Why this Protocol now?

1.7 Lord Woolf in his Access to Justice Report in July 1996, concluded that major causes of costs and delay in medical negligence litigation occur at the pre-action stage. He recommended that patients and their advisers, and healthcare providers, should work more closely together to try to resolve disputes co-operatively, rather than proceed to litigation. He specifically recommended a pre-action protocol for medical negligence cases.

1.8 A fuller summary of Lord Woolf's recommendations is at Annex D.

Where the Protocol Fits in

1.9 Protocols serve the needs of litigation and pre-litigation practice, especially —

- predictability in the time needed for steps pre-proceedings;

- standardisation of relevant information, including records and documents to be disclosed.

1.10 Building upon Lord Woolf's recommendations, the Lord Chancellor's Department is now promoting the adoption of protocols in specific areas, including medical negligence.

1.11 It is recognised that contexts differ significantly. For example: patients tend to have an ongoing relationship with a G.P. more so than with a hospital; clinical staff in the National Health Service are often employees, while those in the private sector may be contractors; providing records quickly may be relatively easy for G.P.s and dentists, but can be a complicated procedure in a large multi-department hospital. The protocol which follows is intended to be sufficiently broadly based, and flexible, to apply to all aspects of the health service: primary and secondary; public and private sectors.

Enforcement of the Protocol and Sanctions

1.12 The civil justice reforms will be implemented in April 1999. One new set of Court Rules and procedures is replacing the existing rules for both the High Court and county courts. This and the personal injury protocol are being published with the Rules, practice directions and key court forms. The courts will be able to treat the standards set in protocols as the normal reasonable approach to pre-action conduct.

1.13 If proceedings are issued it will be for the court to decide whether non-compliance with a protocol should merit sanctions. Guidance on the court's likely approach will be given from time to time in practice directions.

1.14 If the court has to consider the question of compliance after proceedings have begun it will not be concerned with minor infringements, *e.g.* failure by a short period to provide relevant information. One minor breach will not entitle the 'innocent' party to abandon following the protocol. The court will look at the effect of non-compliance on the other party when deciding whether to impose sanctions.

2 The Aims of the protocol

2.1 The ***general*** aims of the protocol are—

- to maintain/restore the patient/healthcare provider relationship;
- to resolve as many disputes as possible without litigation.

2.2 The ***specific*** objectives are—

Openness

- to encourage early communication of the perceived problem between patients and healthcare providers;

- to encourage patients to voice any concerns or dissatisfaction with their treatment as soon as practicable;
- to encourage healthcare providers to develop systems of early reporting and investigation for serious adverse treatment outcomes and to provide full and prompt explanations to dissatisfied patients;
- to ensure that sufficient information is disclosed by both parties to enable each to understand the other's perspective and case, and to encourage early resolution;

Timeliness

- to provide an early opportunity for healthcare providers to identify cases where an investigation is required and to carry out that investigation promptly;
- to encourage primary and private healthcare providers to involve their defence organisations or insurers at an early stage;
- to ensure that all relevant medical records are provided to patients or their appointed representatives on request, to a realistic timetable by any healthcare provider;
- to ensure that relevant records which are not in healthcare providers' possession are made available to them by patients and their advisers at an appropriate stage;
- where a resolution is not achievable to lay the ground to enable litigation to proceed on a reasonable timetable, at a reasonable and proportionate cost and to limit the matters in contention;
- to discourage the prolonged pursuit of unmeritorious claims and the prolonged defence of meritorious claims.

Awareness of Options

- to ensure that patients and healthcare providers are made aware of the available options to pursue and resolve disputes and what each might involve.

2.3 This protocol does not attempt to be prescriptive about a number of related clinical governance issues which will have a bearing on healthcare providers' ability to meet the standards within the protocol. Good clinical governance requires the following to be considered—

(a) **Clinical risk management:** the protocol does not provide any detailed guidance to healthcare providers on clinical risk management or the adoption of risk management systems and procedures. This must be a matter for the NHS Executive, the National Health Service Litigation Authority, individual trusts and providers, including GPs, dentists and the private sector. However, effective co-ordinated, focused clinical risk management strategies and procedures can help in managing risk and in the early identification and investigation of adverse outcomes.

(b) **Adverse outcome reporting:** the protocol does not provide any detailed guidance on which adverse outcomes should trigger an investigation. However, healthcare providers should have in place procedures for such investigations, including recording of statements of key witnesses. These procedures should also cover when and how to inform patients that an adverse outcome has occurred.

(c) **The professional's duty to report:** the protocol does not recommend changes to the codes of conduct of professionals in healthcare, or attempt to impose a specific duty on those professionals to report known adverse outcomes or untoward incidents. Lord Woolf in his final report suggested that the professional bodies might consider this. The General Medical Council is preparing guidance to doctors about their duty to report adverse incidents and to co-operate with inquiries.

3 The Protocol

3.1 This protocol is not a comprehensive code governing all the steps in clinical disputes. Rather it attempts to set out **a code of good practice** which parties should follow when litigation might be a possibility.

3.2 The **commitments** section of the protocol summarises the guiding principles which healthcare providers and patients and their advisers are invited to endorse when dealing with patient dissatisfaction with treatment and its outcome, and with potential complaints and claims.

3.3 The **steps** section sets out in a more prescriptive form, a recommended sequence of actions to be followed if litigation is a prospect.

(a) Good Practice Commitments

3.4 **Healthcare providers** should —

(i) ensure that **key staff,** including claims and litigation managers, are appropriately trained and have some knowledge of healthcare law, and of complaints procedures and civil litigation practice and procedure;

(ii) develop an approach to **clinical governance** that ensures that clinical practice is delivered to commonly accepted standards and that this is routinely monitored through a system of clinical audit and clinical risk management (particularly adverse outcome investigation);

(iii) set up **adverse outcome reporting systems** in all specialties to record and investigate unexpected serious adverse outcomes as soon as possible. Such systems can enable evidence to be gathered quickly, which makes it easier to provide an accurate explanation of what happened and to defend or settle any subsequent claims;

(iv) use the results of **adverse incidents and complaints positively** as a guide to how to improve services to patients in the future;

(v) ensure **that patients receive clear and comprehensible information** in an accessible form about how to raise their concerns or complaints;

(vi) establish **efficient and effective systems of recording and storing patient records,** notes, diagnostic reports and X-rays, and to retain these in accordance with Department of Health guidance (currently for a minimum of eight years in the case of adults, and all obstetric and paediatric notes for children until they reach the age of 25);

(vii) **advise patients** of a serious adverse outcome and provide on request to the patient or the patient's representative an oral or written explanation of what happened, information on further steps open to the patient, including where appropriate an offer of future treatment to rectify the problem, an apology, changes in procedure which will benefit patients and/or compensation.

3.5 **Patients and their advisers** should—

(i) **report any concerns and dissatisfaction** to the healthcare provider as soon as is reasonable to enable that provider to offer clinical advice where possible, to advise the patient if anything has gone wrong and take appropriate action;

(ii) consider the **full range of options** available following an adverse outcome with which a patient is dissatisfied, including a request for an explanation, a meeting, a complaint, and other appropriate dispute resolution methods (including mediation) and negotiation, not only litigation;

(iii) **inform the healthcare provider when the patient is satisfied** that the matter has been concluded: legal advisers should notify the provider when they are no longer acting for the patient, particularly if proceedings have not started.

(b) Protocol Steps

3.6 The steps of this protocol which follow have been kept deliberately simple. An illustration of the likely sequence of events in a number of healthcare situations is at Annex A.

Obtaining the Health Records

3.7 Any request for records by the **patient** or their adviser should —

- **provide sufficient information** to alert the healthcare provider where an adverse outcome has been serious or had serious consequences;

- be as **specific as possible** about the records which are required.

3.8 Requests for copies of the patient's clinical records should be made using the Law Society and Department of Health approved **standard forms** (enclosed at Annex B), adapted as necessary.

3.9 The copy records should be provided **within 40 days** of the request and for a cost not exceeding the charges permissible under the Access to Health Records Act 1990 (currently a maximum of £10 plus photocopying and postage).

3.10 In the rare circumstances that the healthcare provider is in difficulty in complying with the request within 40 days, the **problem should be explained** quickly and details given of what is being done to resolve it.

3.11 It will not be practicable for healthcare providers to investigate in detail each case when records are requested. But healthcare providers should **adopt a policy on which cases will be investigated** (see paragraph 3.5 on clinical governance and adverse outcome reporting).

3.12 If the healthcare provider fails to provide the health records within 40 days, the patient or their adviser can then apply to the court for an **order for pre-action disclosure.** The new Civil Procedure Rules should make pre-action applications to the court easier. The court will also have the power to impose costs sanctions for unreasonable delay in providing records.

3.13 If either the patient or the healthcare provider considers **additional health records are required from a third party,** in the first instance these should be requested by or through the patient. Third party healthcare providers are expected to co-operate. The Civil Procedure Rules will enable patients and healthcare providers to apply to the court for pre-action disclosure by third parties.

Letter of Claim

3.14 Annex C1 to this protocol provides **a template for the recommended contents of a letter of claim:** the level of detail will need to be varied to suit the particular circumstances.

3.15 If, following the receipt and analysis of the records, and the receipt of any further advice (including from experts if necessary—see Section 4), the patient/adviser decides that there are grounds for a claim, they should then send, as soon as practicable, to the healthcare provider/potential defendant, a **letter of claim.**

3.16 This letter should contain a **clear summary of the facts** on which the claim is based, including the alleged adverse outcome, and the **main allegations of negligence.** It should also describe the **patient's injuries,** and present condition and prognosis. The **financial loss** incurred by the plaintiff should be outlined with an indication of the heads of damage to be claimed and the scale of the loss, unless this is impracticable.

3.17 In more complex cases a **chronology** of the relevant events should be provided, particularly if the patient has been treated by a number of different healthcare providers.

3.18 The letter of claim **should refer to any relevant documents,** including health records, and if possible enclose copies of any of those which will not already be in the potential defendant's possession, e.g. any relevant general practitioner records if the plaintiff's claim is against a hospital.

3.19 **Sufficient information** must be given to enable the healthcare provider defendant to **commence investigations** and to put an initial valuation on the claim.

3.20 Letters of claim are **not** intended to have the same formal status as a **pleading,** nor should any sanctions necessarily apply if the letter of claim and any subsequent statement of claim in the proceedings differ.

3.21 **Proceedings should not be issued until after three months from the letter of claim,** unless there is a limitation problem and/or the patient's position needs to be protected by early issue.

3.22 The patient or their adviser may want to make an **offer to settle** the claim at this early stage by putting forward an amount of compensation which would be satisfactory (possibly including any costs incurred to date). If an offer to settle is made, generally this should be supported by a medical report which deals with the injuries, condition and prognosis, and by a schedule of loss and supporting documentation. The level of detail necessary will depend on the value of the claim. Medical reports may not be necessary where there is no significant continuing injury, and a detailed schedule may not be necessary in a low value case. The Civil Procedure Rules are expected to set out the legal and procedural requirements for making offers to settle.

The Response

3.23 Attached at Annex C2 is a template for the suggested contents of the **letter of response.**

3.24 The healthcare provider should **acknowledge** the letter of claim **within 14 days of receipt** and should identify who will be dealing with the matter.

3.25 The healthcare provider should, **within three months** of the letter of claim, provide a **reasoned answer**—

- if the **claim is admitted** the healthcare provider should say so in clear terms;
- if only **part of the claim is admitted** the healthcare provider should make clear which issues of breach of duty and/or causation are admitted and which are denied and why;
- if it is intended that any **admissions will be binding;**
- if the claim is denied, this should include specific comments on the allegations of negligence, and if a synopsis or chronology of relevant events has been provided and is disputed, the healthcare provider's version of those events;
- where additional documents are relied upon, e.g. an internal protocol, copies should be provided.

3.26 If the patient has made an offer to settle, the healthcare provider should **respond to that offer** in the response letter, preferably with reasons. The provider may make its own offer to settle at this stage, either as a counter offer to the patient's, or of its own accord, but should accompany any offer by any supporting medical evidence, and/or by any other evidence in relation to the value of the claim which is in the healthcare provider's possession.

3.27 If the parties reach agreement on liability, but time is needed to resolve the value of the claim, they should aim to agree a reasonable period.

4 Experts

4.1 In clinical negligence disputes expert opinions may be needed —

- on breach of duty and causation;
- on the patient's condition and prognosis;
- to assist in valuing aspects of the claim.

4.2 The civil justice reforms and the new Civil Procedure Rules will encourage economy in the use of experts and a less adversarial expert culture. It is recognised that in clinical negligence disputes, the parties and their advisers will require flexibility in their approach to expert evidence. Decisions on whether experts might be instructed jointly, and on whether reports might be disclosed sequentially or by exchange, should rest with the parties and their advisers. Sharing expert evidence may be appropriate on issues relating to the value of the claim. However, this protocol does not attempt to be prescriptive on issues in relation to expert evidence.

4.3 Obtaining expert evidence will often be an expensive step and may take time, especially in specialised areas of medicine where there are limited numbers of suitable experts. Patients and healthcare providers, and their advisers, will therefore need to consider carefully how best to obtain any necessary expert help quickly and cost-effectively. Assistance with locating a suitable expert is available from a number of sources.

5 Alternative Approaches to Settling Disputes

5.1 It would not be practicable for this protocol to address in any detail how a patient or their adviser, or healthcare provider, might decide which method to adopt to resolve the particular problem. But, the courts increasingly expect parties to try to settle their differences by agreement before issuing proceedings.

5.2 Most disputes are resolved by discussion and negotiation. Parties should bear in mind that carefully planned face-to-face meetings may be particularly helpful in exploring further treatment for the patient, in reaching understandings about what happened, and on both parties' positions, in narrowing the issues in dispute and, if the timing is right, in helping to settle the whole matter.

5.3 Summarised below are some other alternatives for resolving disputes —

- The revised NHS Complaints Procedure, which was implemented in April 1996, is designed to provide patients with an explanation of what happened and an apology if appropriate. It is not designed to provide compensation for cases of negligence. However, patients might choose to use the procedure if their only, or main, goal is to obtain an explanation, or to obtain more information to help them decide what other action might be appropriate.

- Mediation may be appropriate in some cases: this is a form of facilitated negotiation assisted by an independent neutral party. It is expected that the new Civil Procedure Rules will give the court the power to stay proceedings for one month for settlement discussions or mediation.
- Other methods of resolving disputes include arbitration, determination by an expert, and early neutral evaluation by a medical or legal expert. The Lord Chancellor's Department has produced a booklet on "Resolving Disputes Without Going to Court", LCD 1995, which lists a number of organisations that provide alternative dispute resolution services.

Annex A
Illustrative Flowchart

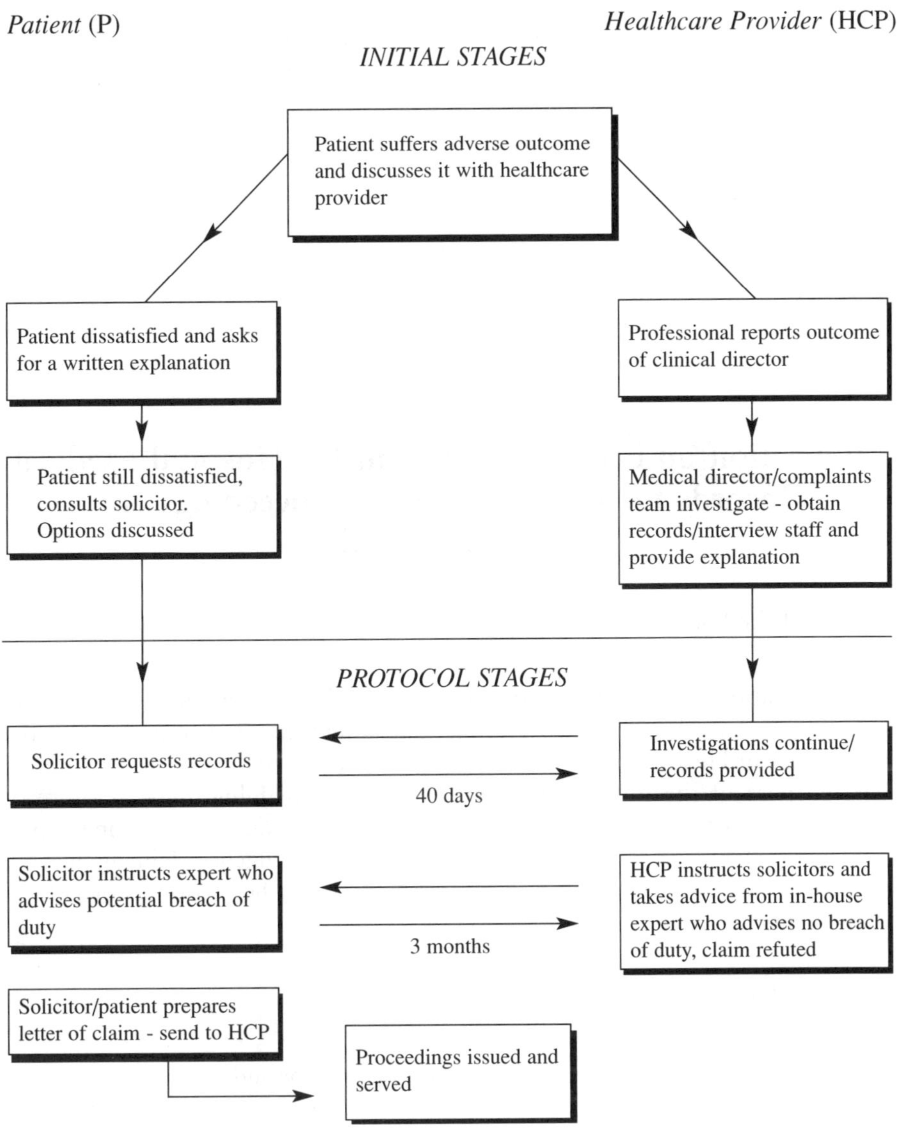

ANNEX B
MEDICAL NEGLIGENCE AND PERSONAL INJURY CLAIMS

A PROTOCOL FOR OBTAINING
HOSPITAL MEDICAL RECORDS

CIVIL LITIGATION COMMITTEE

Revised Edition
June 1998

THE LAW SOCIETY

Application on behalf of a Patient for Hospital Medical Records for use when Court Proceedings are Contemplated

Purpose of the Forms

This application form and response forms have been prepared by a working party of the Law Society's Civil Litigation Committee and approved by the Department of Health for use in NHS and Trust hospitals.

The purpose of the forms is to standardise and streamline the disclosure of medical records to a patient's solicitors, who are investigating pursuing a personal injury claim against a third party, or a medical negligence claim against the hospital to which the application is addressed and/or other hospitals or general practitioners.

Use of the Forms

Use of the forms is entirely voluntary and does not prejudice any party's right under the Access to Health Records Act 1990, the Data Protection Act 1984, or ss. 33 and 34 of the Supreme Court Act 1981. However, it is Department of Health policy that patients be permitted to see what has been written about them, and that healthcare providers should make arrangements to allow patients to see all their records, not only those covered by the Access to Health Records Act 1990. The aim of the forms is to save time and costs for all concerned for the benefit of the patient and the hospital and in the interests of justice. Use of the forms should make it unnecessary in most cases for there to be exchanges of letters or other enquiries. If there is any unusual matter not covered by the form, the patient's solicitor may write a separate letter at the outset.

Charges for Records

The Access to Health Records Act 1990 prescribes a maximum fee of £10. Photocopying and postage costs can be charged in addition. No other charges may be made.

The NHS Executive guidance makes it clear to healthcare providers that 'it is a perfectly proper use' of the 1990 Act to request records in that framework for the purpose of potential or actual litigation, whether against a third party or against the hospital or trust.

The 1990 Act does not permit differential rates of charges to be levied if the application is made by the patient, or by a solicitor on his or her behalf, or whether the response to the application is made by the healthcare provider directly (the medical records manager or a claims manager) or by a solicitor.

The NHS Executive guidance recommends that the same practice should be followed with regard to charges when the records are provided under a voluntary agreement as under the 1990 Act, except that in those circumstances the £10 access fee will not be appropriate.

The NHS Executive also advises—

- that the cost of photocopying may include 'the cost of staff time in making copies' and the costs of running the copier (but not costs of locating and sifting records);
- that the common practice of setting a standard rate for an application or charging an administration fee is not acceptable because there will be cases when this fails to comply with the 1990 Act.

Records: what might be included

X-rays and test results form part of the patient's records. Additional charges for copying X-rays are permissible. If there are large numbers of X-rays, the records officer should check with the patient/solicitor before arranging copying.

Reports on an "adverse incident" and reports on the patient made for risk management and audit purposes may form part of the records and be disclosable: the exception will be any specific record or report made solely or mainly in connection with an actual or potential claim.

Records: quality standards

When copying records healthcare providers should ensure —

1. All documents are legible, and complete, if necessary by photocopying at less than 100 per cent size.

2. Documents larger than A4 in the original, *e.g.* ITU charts, should be reproduced in A3, or reduced to A4 where this retains readability.

3. Documents are only copied on one side of paper, unless the original is two sided.

4. Documents should not be unnecessarily shuffled or bound and holes should not be made in the copied papers.

Enquiries/further information

Any enquiries about the forms should be made initially to the solicitors making the request. Comments on the use and content of the forms should be made to the Secretary, Civil Litigation Committee, The Law Society, 113 Chancery Lane, London WC2A 1PL, telephone 0171 320 5739, or to the NHS Management Executive, Quarry House, Quarry Hill, Leeds LS2 7UE.
The Law Society
May 1998

Application on behalf of a patient for hospital medical records for use when court proceedings are contemplated

This should be completed as fully as possible

Insert Hospital Name and Address — **TO: Medical Records Officer** — **Hospital**

1a)	Full name of patient (including previous surnames)	
b)	Address now	
c)	Address at start of treatment	
d)	Date of birth (and death, if applicable)	
e)	Hospital ref. no if available	
f)	N.I. number, if available	
2.	This application is made because the patient is considering	
a)	a claim against your hospital as detailed in para 7 overleaf	YES/NO
b)	pursuing an action against someone else	YES/NO
3	Department(s) where treatment was received	

4	Name(s) of consultant(s) at your hospital in charge of the treatment	
5	Whether treatment at your hospital was private or NHS, wholly or in part	
6	A description of the treatment received, with approximate dates	
7	If the answer to Q2(a) is 'Yes' details of	
	a) the likely nature of the claim	
	b) grounds for the claim	
	c) approximate dates of the events involved	
8	If the answer to Q2(b) is 'Yes' insert	
	a) the names of the proposed defendants	
	b) whether legal proceedings yet begun	YES/NO
	c) if appropriate, details of the claim and action number	
9	We confirm we will pay reasonable copying charges	
10	We request prior details of	
	a) photocopying and administration charges for medical records YES/NO	
	b) number of and cost of copying x-ray and scan films YES/NO	
11	Any other relevant information, particular requirements, or any particular documents not required (e.g. copies of computerised records)	
	Signature of Solicitor	
	Name	
	Address	
	Ref.	
	Telephone Number	
	Fax number	

	Please print name beneath each signature. Signature by child over 12 but under 18 years also requires signature by parent
Signature of patient Signature of parent or next friend if appropriate	
Signature of personal representative where patient has died	

First response to application for hospital records

NAME OF PATIENT Our ref Your ref		
1	Date of receipt of patient's application	
2	We intend that copy medical records will be dispatched within 6 weeks of that date	YES/NO
3	We require pre-payment of photocopying charges	YES/NO
4	If estimate of photocopying charges requested or pre-payment required the amount will be	£ /notified to you
5	The cost of x-ray and scan films will be	£ /notified to you
6	If there is any problem, we shall write to you within those 6 weeks	YES/NO
7	Any other information Please address further correspondence to	
	Signed	
	Direct telephone number	
	Direct fax number	
	Dated	

Second response enclosing patient's hospital medical records

Address

Our Ref.
Your Ref.

1	NAME OF PATIENT We confirm that the enclosed copy medical records are all those within the control of the hospital, relevant to the application which you have made to the best of our knowledge and belief, subject to paras 2–5 below	YES/NO
2	Details of any other documents which have not yet been located	
3	Date by when it is expected that these will be supplied	
4	Details of any records which we are not producing	
5	The reasons for not doing so	
6	An invoice for copying and administration charges is attached	YES/NO
	Signed	
	Date	

Annex C
Templates for Letters of Claim and Response

C1 Letter of Claim

Essential Contents

1. Client's name, address, date of birth, etc.

2. Dates of allegedly negligent treatment

3. Events giving rise to the claim:
   - an outline of what happened, including details of other relevant treatments to the client by other healthcare providers.

4. Allegation of negligence and causal link with injuries:

- an outline of the allegations or a more detailed list in a complex case;
- an outline of the causal link between allegations and the injuries complained of.

5. The Client's injuries, condition and future prognosis

6. Request for clinical records (if not previously provided)
   - use the Law Society form if appropriate or adapt;
   - specify the records require;
   - if other records are held by other providers, and may be relevant, say so;
   - state what investigations have been carried out to date, *e.g.* information from client and witnesses, any complaint and the outcome, if any clinical records have been seen or experts advice obtained.

7. The likely value of the claim
   - an outline of the main heads of damage, or, in straightforward cases, the details of loss. Optional information

What investigations have been carried out

An offer to settle without supporting evidence
Suggestions for obtaining expert evidence
Suggestions for meetings, negotiations, discussion or mediation

Possible enclosures

Chronology
Clinical records request form and client's authorisation
Expert report(s)
Schedules of loss and supporting evidence

C2 Letter of response

Essential Contents

1. Provide **requested records** and invoice for copying:
   - explain if records are incomplete or extensive records are held and ask for further instructions;
   - request additional records from third parties.

2. **Comments on events and/or chronology:**
   - if events are disputed or the healthcare provider has further information or documents on which they wish to rely, these should be provided, *e.g.* internal protocol;
   - details of any further information needed from the patient or a third party should be provided.

3. **If breach of duty and causation are accepted:**
   - suggestions might be made for resolving the claim and/or requests for further information;
   - a response should be made to any offer to settle.

4. **If breach of duty and/or causation are denied:**
   - a bare denial will not be sufficient. If the healthcare provider has other explanations for what happened, these should be given at least in outline;
   - suggestions might be made for the next steps, *e.g.* further investigations, obtaining expert evidence, meetings/ negotiations or mediation, or an invitation to issue proceedings.

Optional Matters

An offer to settle if the patient has not made one, or a counter offer to the patient's with supporting evidence

Possible enclosures:

Clinical records
Annotated chronology
Expert reports

Annex D
Lord Woolf's Recommendations

1. Lord Woolf in his Access to Justice Report in July 1996, following a detailed review of the problems of medical negligence claims, identified that one of the major sources of **costs and delay** is **at the pre-litigation stage** because—

(a) Inadequate incident reporting and record keeping in hospitals, and mobility of staff, make it difficult to establish facts, often several years after the event.

(b) Claimants must incur the cost of an expert in order to establish whether they have a viable claim.

(c) There is often a long delay before a claim is made.

(d) Defendants do not have sufficient resources to carry out a full investigation of every incident, and do not consider it worthwhile to start an investigation as soon as they receive a request for records, because many cases do not proceed beyond that stage.

(e) Patients often give the defendant little or no notice of a firm intention to pursue a claim. Consequently, many incidents are not investigated by the defendants until after proceedings have started.

(f) Doctors and other clinical staff are traditionally reluctant to admit negligence or apologise to, or negotiate with, claimants for fear of damage to their professional reputations or career prospects.

2. Lord Woolf acknowledged that under the present arrangements **healthcare providers,** faced with possible medical negligence claims, have a number of **practical problems** to contend with—

(a) Difficulties of finding patients' records and tracing former staff, which can be exacerbated by late notification and by the health care provider's own failure to identify adverse incidents.

(b) The healthcare provider may have only treated the patient for a limited time or for a specific complaint: the patient's previous history may be relevant but the records may be in the possession of one of several other healthcare providers.

(c) The large number of potential claims which do not proceed beyond the stage of a request for medical records, or an explanation; and that it is difficult for healthcare providers to investigate fully every case whenever a patient asks to see the records.

Annex E
How to Contact the Forum

The Clinical Disputes Forum
Chairman
Dr Alastair Scotland
Medical Director and Chief Officer
National Clinical Assessment Authority
9th Floor, Market Towers
London
SW8 5NQ Telephone: 020 7273 0850

Secretary
Sarah Leigh
c/o Margaret Dangoor
3 Clydesdale Gardens
Richmond
Surrey
TW10 5EG Telephone: 0181 408 1012

Index